Women and Gender
Making a Difference

Fourth Edition

Women and Gender
Making a Difference
Fourth Edition

Janice D. Yoder
University of Akron

2013
Sloan Publishing
Cornwall-on-Hudson, NY 12520

Library of Congress Cataloging-in-Publication Data

Library of Congress Cataloging-in-Publication Data

Yoder, Janice D.
Women and gender : making a difference / Jan Yoder. -- 4th ed.
p. cm.
ISBN 978-1-59738-040-9
1. Feminist psychology. I. Title.
BF201.4.Y63 2013
155.3'33--dc23
2012003290

Cover art: "Graceful Moves" by Margarete Warfield, www.margaretwarfield.com
Cover design by Amy Rosen, K&M Design

Sloan Publishing, LLC
220 Maple Road
Cornwall-on-Hudson, NY 12520

Printed in the United States of America

10 9 8 7 6 5 4 3 2 1

ISBN 13: 978-1-59738-040-9
ISBN 10: 1-59738-040-7

For John, Kate, and Dan...
of course.

Contents

Preface

As I write this introduction, it has been six years since the last edition of this text was published in 2006.[1] I admit that I have ridden a roller coaster of thinking about whether or not to even attempt this fourth edition. In 2007, I thought I had reached a crossroads so that if I headed down the path toward being editor of *Psychology of Women Quarterly* (*PWQ*), I would forego undertaking any future editions of this text. As I captured in my reflections about textbook writing for the anniversary celebration of the journal *Sex Roles* (Yoder, 2010), I chose the journal because I thought, somewhat ironically, that being editor of an openly feminist journal gave me more latitude to (a) connect the personal to the political and (b) put women, and the service of women, front-and-center.

Obviously, even though I remain editor, something changed my mind—as evidenced by the very existence of this fourth edition. This opportunity began with a shift in the textbook market sensed by Bill Webber, this text's unfailingly intuitive publisher. Interest in a social justice approach to thinking specifically about women and women's lives appears to be on the rise again. I too saw this shift reflected in data from my own research on teaching and about feminist self-labeling and beliefs, and well as in publications in PWQ.

In research on teaching, my colleagues Ann Fischer and Arnie Kahn along with honors student Jessica Groden and I surveyed five different Psychology of Women classes taught by the three of us instructors across three different campuses and using different textbooks (Yoder et al., 2007). Across these classes a consistent picture emerged about the importance of having students grasp the ideas of social constructionism and the role social context plays in understanding sex and gender (see Yoder & Kahn, 2003). These data thus provided empirical evidence to support a major approach I had taken across the opening six chapters of the third edition and that continues in this fourth edition—an approach that links gender with status and power.

Simultaneously in my research with colleague Andrea Snell and honors student Ann Tobias, we teased apart the roles played by women students' feminist self-labeling and endorsement of feminist beliefs. We concluded that labeling alone was related to reported feminist activism (Yoder et al., 2011) and that beliefs, most notably established feminist beliefs, were most strongly linked to positive personal well-being with liberation, that is,

---

[1] For reviews of previous editions see Bernice Lott (2000) in *Contemporary Psychology, 45*(2), pp. 177-178; Lisa Bowleg (2000) in *Psychology of Women Quarterly, 24*(3); Patricia Connor-Greene (2001) in *Sex Roles, 44*(7/8), 485-487; and Virginia Norris (2003) in *Psychology of Women Quarterly, 27*, 276-277.

well-being combined with a social justice orientation (Yoder et al., in press). Both studies highlighted the role that social justice plays not only within feminism as a social activist movement but also in individual women's personal wellness. More recent research by Bonnie Moradi, Annelise Martin, and Melanie Brewster (in press) associates students' feminist self-labeling with having positive contact with self-identified feminists and provides a tested classroom intervention to achieve this connection.

Additionally in *PWQ*, I am watching a growing body of research debunk the presumed personal empowerment that women allegedly wield by engaging in self-sexualizing behavior, as well as identify ways for women to promote their own true empowerment. Regarding the former, for example, women exposed to presumably empowering yet still sexualized media messages (in comparison to typical passive variations) were similarly negatively affected—feeling objectified and dissatisfied with their weight (Halliwell et al., 2011). As for genuine empowerment, understanding the conditions and connections that both promote and inhibit women from confronting sexism directed at both one's self and others opens doors for the development of more effective interventions aimed at truly empowering women on behalf of themselves (the personal) and women overall (the political; Good et al., in press).

All of these threads combined to suggest that the themes of the third edition continued to be valuable and hold sway over students' thinking. Gender *is* linked to social power so that the personal continues to not only connect to the political—but also to be compromised without this connection. Furthermore, although understanding gender, men, and masculinity certainly contributes to our understanding of women and women's lives and thus cannot be ignored, putting women at the center of one's focus in order to better serve women remains a worthy venture that lies at the heart of adopting an overarching feminist orientation. This understanding makes this book not just for women, or psychologists, or scholars interested in women and gender; it is a book for *anyone interested in social justice*. Re-invigorated, I thus built on the groundwork laid in the third edition to update this fourth edition.

As previously, I worked hard in this edition to strike a balance between being academically rigorous and engaging to readers. As in the third edition, I cite over 2,000 resources, mostly in peer-reviewed academic journals; of these references over 640 (28%) have been published in 2006 or afterwards. On the other hand, I avoided jargon yet used and defined academic terms in the glossary; adopted a writing style that is informal yet well documented; and illustrated key points with personal stories as well as boxes, tables, and figures that help clarify, enrich, or expand a point and make it more resonant to the reader. Building on my tradition of "field testing" an edition with my own class while I write, students in my Fall 2011 Psychology of Women class at the University of Akron report that they read a chapter in a single sitting because the "story" flows.

Although the chapters of the text can stand alone and be re-ordered by an instructor, my overall organization lays out Chapters 1 through 6 as foundational chapters that develop key issues and understandings that enrich the remaining more applied and topical chapters. Themes related to essential and constructionist thinking, connecting gender to stereotyping and power, intersectionality with gender as one element in understanding human diversity, and the importance of social context are recalled throughout Chapters 7 through 14 to better explicate each topic area. I find in my own classes that carefully laying this groundwork pays off because students then have the tools to dig into these later topical chapters and see connections they might otherwise have missed.

I encourage readers to work interactively with this book; interspersed throughout it are brief exercises to get you thinking about the points being discussed and each chapter opens with a tickler meant to be thought-provoking and engaging. Continually think about what you are reading within the context of your own life—does it resonate; spur you to see the world differently; etc? I have drawn on the most up-to-date materials; this is one area where critical readers readily reject a piece of research because "it's too old." "Dated" research that shows linkages among factors is still very useful and I do draw on these integrative materials, but most specific studies and research findings reported here are contemporary.

I think you'll find that you want to talk about these materials with others, both in class and outside. As we will see in the last chapter, most readers of these kinds of texts and students in these classes come away from these experiences seeing the world through different lenses.[2] This book should engender feelings, challenge opinions, and change behaviors. A common mistake for an author is to fail to acknowledge these effects and to leave readers groping for something to do with them. I sincerely hope that you'll find the last chapter of this book helpful in this regard so that it won't decay on your bookshelf or go into a used-book pile without making a difference in you and how you think. To fail in this way would be the most disappointing indictment of my feminist approach.

What's Different about This Edition?

The fundamental themes, topical coverage, and organization of the fourth edition parallel those of the third. Across the full book, ideas are updated with recent references, and fascinating recent studies are discussed in detail. With well over 600 references to scholarship published within the past six years, the fourth edition should leave readers with the sense that they are at the cutting edge of what is happening within the field of the Psychology of Women.

The broadest revamp is across the second half of Chapter 12 on Mental Health, which now frames the discussion of feminist therapy theory using the updated principles for doing feminist psychotherapy developed for the American Psychological Association's Practice Directorate (American Psychological Association, 2007). My treatment of intersexuality in Chapter 3 was refined and expanded with thanks to Rebecca Jordan-Young's (2010) book, *Brain Storm: The Flaws in the Science of Sex Differences*. Additionally, booming research focused on ambivalent sexism (in Chapter 7) and on body image and objectification (in Chapter 10) encouraged me to do some basic re-structuring in those chapters in order to best highlight recent theoretical developments and findings.

A NOTE FOR INSTRUCTORS

Every time I participate in a workshop for teachers of Psychology of Women or Gender classes, a question soon arises about the title and focus of the course: Women OR Gender. Putting "women" front and center makes clear the instructor's valuing of women and

---

[2]For a fascinating typology of how students may bring different orientations to challenging classes such as ones focused on women and gender, see Barlow & Becker-Blease (in press). Their matrix laying out four types of students resonated with my experiences as an instructor and deepen my own understandings of in-class processes.

women's experiences but seems to exclude men. Opting for "gender" implies inclusion but opens up the greater likelihood of judgmental comparisons of (oftentimes deficient) women with (typically normative) men. A duality of women OR gender is established suggesting different course content, core values, and, fundamentally, politics, with "gender" regarded as less radically charged.

The most satisfying resolution would be to acknowledge openly that the course is feminist but this pushes the political line even farther. Pragmatically I'd settle for a course label of either Women or Gender knowing that there really is no duality here. Both can be addressed productively with the contents of this book because I adopt a women-centered perspective that values diverse women and women's experiences and that is rooted in *gendered* understandings of power.

An example may clarify. Consider women's leadership. We can describe women's styles of leadership as precisely these--*women's* styles (without judgmental comparisons with men's). We can learn even more about women's leadership by understanding the role gender plays (Yoder, 2001). If we envision leaders as cool, calm, collected, rational, and powerful decision-makers, then cultural taboos against public displays of emotion by men makes men suitable candidates for these leadership roles. At the same time, culturally based liberties allowing women's public expressiveness work to undermine women's perceived suitability in these power-based contexts. By doing both, women's leadership can be described as women's and can be understood better within a gendered context that relates to issues of power and empowerment.

In this example and throughout this book, descriptions of women and gendered understandings converge to provide one central feminist focus. Given this convergence, this book is equally appropriate for a course focused on women, gender, or feminism, and it readily can be combined with a compatible text on men and masculinity. In addition, an instructor's manual is available for adopters; contact Sloan Publishing to request a copy (www.sloanpublishing.com).

ACKNOWLEDGMENTS

I am indebted to so many people who helped challenge, refine, and expand my thinking for the editions of this book, although in all fairness to them, I ultimately am responsible for what appears in these pages. I owe much to my colleague Ann Fischer who turned me on to Allan Johnson's work and who generously shares her ideas, materials, inspiration, and support. Similarly, Arnie Kahn and Bonnie Moradi continually offer their advice, materials, expertise, and support. My thinking always is challenged and expanded by my extensive network of feminist friends and scholars both on the Executive Committee of the Society of the Psychology of Women (Div. 35) and in Akron (especially Jan Bean, Carolyn Behrman, T.J. Boisseau, Julie Drew, Elizabeth Reilly, Kathy Feltey, Sharon Kruse, Diane Moran, Andee Snell, and Sheryl Stevenson). Bill Webber and Sloan Publishing have given me an unfettered opportunity to take this book to its next level in what continues to be a labor of love. My family (John, Kate, and Dan Zipp as well as my animal companions, Meg and Emma) came through once again, largely seeing my back at a computer and dealing with my angst and frequent sleeplessness. Finally, this text builds on the contributions of those who helped with earlier editions, and I continue to be grateful for their input.

About the Author

Jan Yoder earned her doctorate in psychology in 1979 from the State University of New York at Buffalo. Her interests in women, gender, and feminism developed professionally through her observations of the first women cadets at West Point and personally through her own struggles with sexual harassment, dual-career challenges, work-family juggling, and women's universal exposure to sexism. Her job paths traveled a circuitous but enlightening route through West Point, where she stood out as one of the first two civilian women to teach there; through a small student-centered college in St. Louis, Webster University; through an exhilarating foray into the world of advertising and marketing research in Chicago at DDB Needham Worldwide; to large research-oriented universities in Milwaukee and finally Akron. The wealth of these diverse experiences comes through in this book as she blends a strong research base with her sensitivity to women's and men's everyday lives and with an engaging style that comes from teaching for over 30 years in a variety of college and university settings.

Her teaching has been recognized with the Heritage Award for Distinguished, Long-standing, and Substantial Contributions to Feminist Teaching from the Society for the Psychology of Women (SPW; APA, Division 35) in 2006, with the Teacher-Scholar Award from the University of Akron in 2008, and with both university (1994) and college (1996) distinguished teaching awards at the University of Wisconsin-Milwaukee. Her involvement in research culminated in 2010 when she became Editor of *Psychology of Women Quarterly*, the official journal of SPW published by Sage, which put her at the cutting edge of reviewing feminist research—an ideal vantage from which to write this text. Her service to SPW, spanning over two decades, was recognized in 2010 with the Sue Rosenberg Zalk Award for Distinguished Service—service that includes being President of SPW in 2000-2001 as well as secretary, program chair, newsletter editor, and other assorted positions. She continues to live in Akron, Ohio with her soul-mate, sociologist John Zipp, and is deeply proud of her children as they work toward finishing graduate school (Kate) and college (Dan). With an increasingly empty nest, she is re-discovering hobbies of gardening , reading, and hiking and appreciates the unfailing companionship of her stay-at-home cat (Emma) and dog (Meg).

Chapter 1

The Power of Difference
The Need to Forge Human Connections

Think about playing the game "20 Questions." One person thinks of a specific item, and the goal of the other players is to name that item by asking up to 20 questions with "yes" or "no" answers. The guesser wants to identify the item with the fewest questions; the questioner wants to stump the guesser.

This common game keeps impatient kids (and even adults) occupied while they wait in lines, take long drives, etc. It draws on a natural human tendency to categorize. By working our way through a hierarchy of categories, often starting with a very global question like "Is it alive?," we try to win this game by funneling down to the specific item. According to cognitive psychologists, this human propensity to categorize gives us the building blocks for thinking (Markman, 1999; Woll, 2002).

Box 1.1   Imagine playing "20 Questions" to identify a single individual.

If your initial questions established that the target is human, your obvious next step would be to ask questions that categorize people. This round of the game would turn toward a process social psychologists call **social categorization**[1] (Hampson, 1988). Look at the picture in Box 1.1. To identify the specific person being considered in the game, how might you start?

You are likely to ask about one of the three primary categories for humans based on *sex*, *age*, and *race/ethnicity* (Schneider, 2004). Categorizing people on the basis of these three social markers is done so frequently that it readily becomes unconscious and effortless (Ito & Urland, 2003). Of these three primary categories, sex may be the most efficient (about 50:50) and most accurate. Although we may look at a person and not know for sure how old they are and what their racial/ethnic background is, we rarely misidentify people's sex. Think how disconcerting it is to encounter a person whose sex is not readily apparent. A whole comedic act on the television show *Saturday Night Live* centered on trying to the guess the sex of the character "Pat."

This fundamental categorization of people into the sex categories of female and male is what this book is all about. Sometimes girls/women and boys/men are different, and often-times large variations exist among individual women and among individual men. Some-times women and men are deeply similar, and at other times, they just appear different because of the gendered social contexts in which they live. Differences can be enriching on the one hand and can lead to disconnection, stereotyping, and even violence on the other hand. Ultimately, differences are linked to power, inequality, and social injustice. My goals for this book are to expose these linkages and seek ways to break them.

GENDER AS A SOCIAL CATEGORY

Although gender is a primary social category, it is part of a broader array of social catego-ries captured in the Diversity Wheel created by Marilyn Loden and Judy Rosener (1991) (see Figure. 1.2). To best understand the wheel, walk yourself around it by identifying each aspect of yourself. Using myself as an example, in the inner wheel, I'm 58 years old, White, Swiss/Polish/Austrian, female, nondisabled,[2] and heterosexual. In the outer ring,

---

[1] Definitions for words in bold print can be found in the Glossary.

[2] Following the lead of Johnson (2006), I use the term "nondisabled" to capture the reality that we are all vulnerable to changing our place in this category involuntarily and at any time.

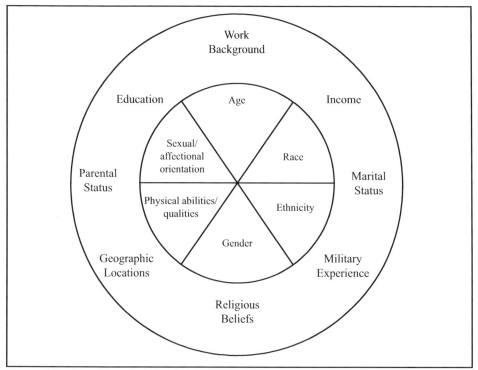

Figure 1.2.   The Diversity Wheel: Primary and Secondary Dimensions of Diversity
Source: Loden & Rosener (1991). Reproduced with permission from McGraw-Hill companies.

I'm a college professor, affluent, married, with no true military experience (although I taught as a civilian at West Point), was raised Catholic in Pennsylvania, live now in Ohio, have two kids, and earned my Ph.D. in psychology.

Think about your list around the wheel. Does it capture who you are? In all likelihood, you'll think that it says very little about who you are—about your hopes, dreams, and feelings—that is, those qualities that are at the center of your own essence (Johnson, 2006). However, if you think about these social categories more, they do represent how *others* often see you and can affect how they think, feel, and act toward you. This is a fundamental point about social categories. They aren't about you at all, but rather are **social representations** of you. Furthermore, the characteristics that form the inner ring are more difficult, if not impossible, for you to change.

There are two important points about the social categories represented in the Diversity Wheel that I want to explore more fully. First, every social category evokes differences: older/younger, Black/Latina, (dis)abled, etc. For almost every individual, these designations sort into groups to which I do (**in-group**) and do not (**out-group**) identify and belong (Deaux et al., 1995).[3] More importantly, these differences are not value-free. Rather, our culture assigns power to these differences such that one designation is dominant or powerful compared to the subordinated other(s) within each category. But before we get into these points, let's first examine gender as a social category.

---

[3]Note that this is a rather simplistic overview of social identity. For example, some multiracial individuals struggle to establish their identity without fitting easily into any single category designation (see Root, 1996).

Why Gender?

Are you: ☐ male ☐ female (check one)

Almost every time you complete a survey, you encounter an item like the one above. In all likelihood, you check a box without even thinking. Humor me with what seems like a crazy request: Stop and think about how you know which box to check. Make the most objective case you can to support your choice of boxes.

Now, consider the possibility that tomorrow morning you woke up as the other sex. How might your life be changed? What would happen if you dressed the same way you did the day before? Would your name seem out of place? What would change about your daily activities? What would be better and what would be worse? In all likelihood, at least some things would change. Gender matters. Indeed, it fundamentally affects both our experiences and our identity.

To really shift social categories in our example above, you would need to do more than dress and act differently. For the transformation to be complete, you would need to undergo some serious physical changes. If you go back to the inner circle of the Diversity Wheel, each entry has a different interplay of physical and psychosocial factors. For example, biologists generally agree that there are no clear biological markers to distinguish the races, yet physical characteristics, such as skin color, have been socially designated to demarcate race (Johnson, 2006).[4] Although researchers continue to look for the "gay gene," genetics does not distinguish the categories associated with sexual orientation as clearly as it does for sex.

The category of gender then serves as a complex case for exploring this basis for difference. I argued above that it's the social meaning that we give to differences that can link social categories to power. For example, being White would carry no privilege in a society where everyone was White. However, when we turn our thoughts to gender, **patriarchy**, which privileges men and boys, is almost universal. The pervasiveness of patriarchy suggests that there's something more fundamental than culturally supplied social meanings that maintain distinctions between female and male.

This fundamental "something" oftentimes refers to biology (genes, hormones, brains, reproduction) where some clear markers seem to establish undeniable differences between girls/women and boys/men. I bet that if you return to your defense of which box you checked (female or male), your most convincing evidence had something to do with biological markers of sex (e.g., having a vagina or penis). This thinking about sex is captured more broadly by a perspective called **essentialism**, which claims that differences reflect the very natures (essences) of women and men. In other words, this approach tends to root differences *inside* women and men by emphasizing the way they are "naturally."

Essentialist thinking extends beyond biology to any explanation for differences between women and men that focuses on women and men themselves as the cause of the difference. Consider the common adage referring to children: "Boys will be boys." This statement first sets up an assumption of difference (in that boys are *not* girls), and then goes on to ground that difference *within* boys themselves (biology and/or personality). Such "essentializing" of differences makes them seem stable, unchangeable (Unger, 1979), and universal (Craw-

---

[4]This point is captured well with the concept of "sociorace," which highlights how race is socially constructed (Helms & Cook, 1999).

ford, 1989). Thus, what is implied in this statement really is: *all* boys *always* will be boys. Examining folk wisdom about sex differences, the more students believed that sex differences were caused by biological factors, the more difficult they thought it would be to eliminate those differences (Martin & Parker, 1995). Furthermore, essentializing gender differences appears to be strongest in contexts where change is threatening the status quo and by the people most threatened by that change (Morton et al., 2009).

Before reading on, turn your attention to the person pictured in Box 1.3. Is this person female or male? How certain are you? Again humor me and articulate your strongest defense for your choice.

Genitals aren't an option here so you might try to discern some secondary sex characteristics (looking for breasts or facial hair). If those "certainties" don't work out (stay tuned for Chapter 3), you might turn to clothing, hair styles, jewelry, etc. Sometimes you don't even need these visual markers—a name or a disembodied voice over the telephone will suffice.

Now let's return to what would change in your life if you awoke tomorrow as the other sex: your name, your clothes, your hair, your voice. You could enact these changes without having to transform your body and probably pass as the other sex. This sense of what makes up gender is captured by **social constructionists** who view gender as something we do, create, or construct with the consensus of others (Gergen, 1985; West & Zimmerman, 1987). In contrast to essentialist thinking, which frames sex as something we ARE, social constructionists regard gender as something we DO. You don't simply have a gender; you work at creating one, often unconsciously, by actively "**doing gender**." How specifically we enact our gender is dictated by our culture, reflecting the general consensus of others about what is and is not appropriate for girls/women and boys/men. You understand this social constructionist alternative if you can make sense of the statement "All gender is drag" (Butler, 1990).

The question that opened this section focused on why gender forms a social category, that is, why we readily divide people into girls/women and boys/men. Essentialists would

---

Box 1.3 *Not* doing gender

One way to get a clearer sense of how we all "do" gender in our everyday lives is to imagine how we might NOT do gender. In other words, consider what you might do every day to minimize differences between girls/women and boys/men. Next, expand your focus outward, and think about how you might minimize gender differences in your relationships (with intimates, friends, and coworkers) and in various organizations (schools, stores, and your workplace). Finally, what might we as a society do to de-emphasize gender differences. Consider, for example, language and the media.

I think this exercise shows how widespread doing gender is as well as how "natural" it appears. Is this naturalness because these differences truly reflect our differences (essentialism) or because everything that is so widely accepted and pervasive comes to feel natural (social constructionism)? How might history affect your answer to this last question?

say because it's a universal biological/physical fact. Social constructionists would argue that there are social meanings attached to this major division that might, for example, work to fill different social roles (e.g., mother and breadwinner) (Eagly, 1987). Indeed, the origins for this division of humans into female and male raises all sorts of interesting arguments (Sanday, 1981a), but many of these are beyond our interests here.

The key point I want to make is that only social constructionism opens up the possibility that differences can be modified, leading us next to ask how far we want to go with these modifications and for what purpose. Might there be ways to assign individuals to roles, for example, that draw on individual abilities and preferences rather than on assumptions about social categories? If we are simply what our bodies or personalities determine us to be (essentialism), questions such as this one make no sense.

Sex, Gender, and Difference

We need to digress for a moment and reflect upon the language we have been using. I have switched back and forth from the terms *sex* and *gender* above in a way that may make them look synonymous. They aren't—and like most psychologists, I find distinguishing between these constructs useful (Muehlenhard & Peterson, 2011). **Sex** implies biological bases (such as chromosomes, hormones, genitals, etc.) (Unger, 1979). (Sex is not to be confused with **sexuality**, which deals with sexual activities and reproduction.) **Gender**, in contrast, implies psychologically, socially, and culturally based differences between women and men. On the face of it, sex seems more determined and unchangeable; gender, more malleable.

If we dig deeper, though, biological sex isn't as immutable as we might have thought at first. There is growing evidence that not only does biology affect behavior, but experiences affect biology as well, reflecting what has been called a **principle of reciprocal determinism** (Cacioppo & Berntson, 1992). For example, the brains of adults exposed to long-term childhood sexual abuse may differ from those without these experiences (Mukerjee, 1995); women in close contact may synchronize their menstrual cycles (McClintock, 1971); and men's testosterone levels may vary with changes in their social rank within a confined group (Jeffcoate et al., 1986). Even chromosomes may change what activates and slows them (their epigenome) with exposure to the environment so that the more identical twins live apart, the less genetically similar they become (Heine-Suner et al., 2005). The relationship is reciprocal and circular: biology influences behavior *and* behavior changes biology.

If we view biology as a prime directive that shapes everything subsequent to it, then it is easy to see that biology isn't a very promising possibility for reducing inequities between women and men. A perspective of biological determinism would argue that differences are natural (hence good?) and trying to change them might even prove harmful to individuals. This line of reasoning then is inconsistent with a social justice agenda. Ignoring biological explorations would be logical—arguing instead for an exclusive emphasis on gender.

However, I believe that as the flexibility of biology becomes more and more acknowledged, social scientists will find it useful to let go of the presumed distinction between sex and gender, nature and nurture (see Riger, 2000a, Chapters 2 and 3). This opens the door to regarding *sex and gender as inseparable and intertwined* so that a holistic understanding of women and men, girls and boys, will include biology (sex) and what our culture makes of our biological sex (gender). This argument will be pursued more fully in Chapter 3.

FEMINIST VALUES

You may have noticed that a rather serious assumption runs through the above discussion of sex, gender, and how we explain differences between girls/women and boys/men (essentialist or social constructionist). That assumption rests on valuing change to an unfair system that perpetuates inequities. Although this book is grounded in research and scholarship, here is one place where scientific data do little to set our course. Now I'm talking about **values**.

Our values lie at the very core of what we do both personally and professionally. Whenever we as researchers choose to pursue one research project, we necessarily disregard a whole array of potential other questions. Similarly, whenever we as instructors elect to cover one topic and to focus on certain theory and research related to that topic, we give less consideration to other possible topics and approaches (Kinsler & Zalk, 1996). These choices may reflect funding opportunities (some research attracts grants more readily than others), whether or not results are likely to be published in highly ranked journals, researchers' particular interests, what our colleagues hold in high esteem, what is and is not covered in textbooks, and so on. Underlying all of these choices, whether apparent or not, whether explored or not, are values.

Let me come forward then with my values. With no apologies for using the f-word, I identify as a feminist. This raises an obvious question: What is a feminist? Ideologically, there is a wide array of feminisms (Henley et al., 1998), but they all converge, along with young women's lay definitions (Rudolfsdottir & Jolliffe, 2008), on the notion of social justice—ensuring "a society based on fairness and equality for its members regardless of social status" (Tuleya, 2007). Research, theory, teaching, and practice in feminist psychology all contribute to the feminist goal of social change to end sexism in our own thinking, in our relationships with others, and in larger organizations and social institutions. *Feminism is fundamentally about a social justice agenda.*

Social justice doesn't seem to be such a radical goal to pursue, yet negative stereotyping about feminists continues to undermine women's self-identification as feminists (Roy et al., 2007); to implicitly associate feminist with bad, not good, words (Jenen, 2009); and to link feminists with romantic incompatibility (Rudman & Fairchild, 2007) and being lesbian (Wilkinson, 2008). In contrast to these stereotypes, I happen to be married (over 30 years!); have two awesome kids, a loveable dog, and an endearing cat; live in a medium-sized city; and drive a Hyundai (if I had a van I'd look like a soccer mom). Much of what I study as a feminist psychologist seeps into my personal life (and vice versa), so you'll come to know my family in some of the examples I use. My partner, John Zipp, also is an academic (sociology); my daughter Kate was born in 1986 and Dan in 1991. As I write this, Kate is 25 and Dan, 20.

I am open about my feminist values. It's important for you to be forthcoming with your own. You may find that much of the research described throughout this book resonates with your own experiences or helps you to understand those experiences. What is more challenging to explore is those times when scholarship diverges from your experiences or from widely held folk wisdom or makes you feel uncomfortable or defensive.

These are times to engage in active self-reflection. Ask new questions that may reconcile your experiences with the general patterns supported by the research. Recognize that "bandwagon concepts" supported by folk wisdom may be intuitively obvious, simple, and basically satisfying, but may be rooted in unquestioned myth rather than researched evidence (Mednick, 1989). Also, consider how the research itself may be narrow or flawed. It is in this way that we move beyond the limits of what we know so far. To me this is the excitement of our exploration—the challenge of asking questions, thinking, and going beyond one's own narrow view of the world. Our journey will be frustrating at times, but it will be compelling and well worth your investment.

GENDER DIFFERENCES AND POWER

I have made the case so far that sex and gender intertwine to form a social category through which we divide girls/women from boys/men. Whatever the origins of this distinction, it clearly is long-standing and almost fully, if not completely, universal. Consistent with a social constructionist view, this social category rests on the social meanings we give to sex, basing this social category truly on "gender." Following this social constructionist logic even farther, we actively work to maintain this gendered divide—by "doing gender" in our everyday lives, we make it clear that we are either female OR male.

Stepping back for a moment and looking at the big picture of the arguments I am developing, it's important to remind ourselves that there is nothing inherently wrong with differences. In fact, seeking novelty may be a fundamental human preference (Milewski & Siqueland, 1975). Just think how boring the world would be if everyone was a clone of the same one person. The trouble with difference then is not difference per se but rather the linkages we socially construct between social category differences (that is, group differences) and power (Johnson, 2006). This linkage brings in comparisons of groups as dominant (privileged) and subordinate (oppressed).

Privilege exists when a group gets something of value, denied to others, simply by being a member of the dominant group, not because of something deserving an individual did (McIntosh, 1995). For example, as a married heterosexual I qualify for family health insurance; as a White person, I won't wonder if I was pulled over for "driving while White"; as a Christian, I get my major holidays off from work; as nondisabled, I can hear a movie in a theatre; etc. It is rare to find someone in our culture who isn't privileged in some ways by a dominant category to which they belong. In fact, one of the biggest benefits of privilege is the luxury of being oblivious to the benefits it brings our way (Johnson, 2006).

The corollary of privilege for dominant category designations is **oppression** of the subordinated category or categories (Johnson, 2006). Oppression refers to the social forces that make it more difficult to reach one's goals (Fyre, 1983). Privilege and oppression exist within a **system of inequality**. Both exist as a consequence of social categorization, so that members of a dominant social category benefit from privilege and members of a subordinated social category are disadvantaged by oppression. Both are *group* processes, so that being privileged doesn't guarantee any single individual happiness or success, nor does oppression cause all members of a group to fail miserably. Neither, though, serves to level the playing field.

The next step in our reasoning takes us to the relationship between gender and power, or more specifically, between being male and privileged and being female and oppressed within a system of inequality. Thus, we explore male privilege, female oppression, and systems of inequality in the following pages.

Male Privilege

Privilege based on group membership comes in two forms: unearned entitlements and conferred dominance (McIntosh cited in Johnson, 2006). **Unearned entitlements** are fundamental valuables everyone should have, such as feelings of safety and esteem. For example, we'll see in Chapter 13 that women's general sense of safety is compromised by the very threat of sexual harassment and rape so that men have the privilege of thinking much less about their vulnerabilities in these areas. **Conferred dominance** takes privilege a step farther by granting men power over women and thus less inhibited access to resources and rewards than allotted women. There is solid research evidence linking men to resources (Ridgeway, 1991); greater power in interpersonal relationships (Felmlee, 1994), families, sexuality, the workplace, and politics (Lips, 1991); and male privilege itself (Ridgeway & Smith-Lovin, 1999). Indeed, one goal of diversity classes is to raise awareness of male privilege (Case, 2007).

Male dominance may be one of those intuitively obvious concepts that is hard to document. A concrete example of research illustrating both its power and its subtlety may help (Dovidio et al., 1988). Dominance in this research was measured by how much two people looked at each other while speaking and listening.[5] **Visual dominance** is established whenever one looks at one's partner more when speaking than when listening (saying, in combination, "Look at me I'm talking to you!" and "I don't need to pay attention to you"). In contrast, being visually submissive occurs when one looks at one's partner more when listening than when speaking (saying together, "See, I'm paying attention to you" and "You don't need to pay attention to me"). Notice that this measure taps patterns of *nonverbal* dominance largely outside the awareness of both parties in an interaction.

Dovidio and his colleagues conducted two studies, both with pairs of women and men (mixed sex dyads) talking together in 3-minute discussion sessions. In the first study, they measured each person's **expert power** by asking participants to identify areas in which they felt especially knowledgeable. They then formed dyads in which one party had more expert power than their partner on the assigned discussion topic. In the second study, the researchers randomly assigned **reward power** to one over the other partner by telling one participant in each pair that they could judge their partner's work and award extra research credits to them. In both studies there were control conditions in which power was not measured or manipulated. In these control conditions then, the only power differences between women and men that might exist would be based on differences associated with their gender. The design of this series of two studies is diagrammed in Figure 1.4.

When power differences between partners were based on expert or reward power, women and men behaved similarly. Women and men high in expert or reward power exhibited more visual dominance during their interaction with their partner, and women and men low in these forms of power engaged in patterns of eye contact indicative of submissiveness. This pattern makes it clear in these studies that visual dominance is connected to power and that when power is clearly established, women act similarly to men. Most interestingly in the control conditions, men displayed visual patterns similar to those exhibited by high power women and men. Additionally, control women showed visual submissiveness similar to both women and men with low power. Not knowing

---

[5]I should note that there are racial/ethnic differences in eye contact, with Dovidio and his colleagues' work largely drawing on Whites' propensities (Sue & Sue, 2003, pp. 129-130).

Groups	Outcome
Study 1(a): woman has expert power	woman is visually dominant/ man is submissive
Study 1(b): man has expert power	man is visually dominant/ woman is submissive
Study 2(a): woman gives rewards	woman is visually dominant /man is submissive
Study 2(b): man gives rewards	man is visually dominant/ woman is submissive
Control: no power manipulation	man is visually dominant/ woman is submissive

Figure 1.4
Dyads comprising one woman and one man were randomly assigned to one of the five groups designated above. The partners then engaged in a discussion between themselves that was video-taped and later coded for eye contact as an indicator of visual dominance and submissiveness.

Source: Adapted from Dovido et al. (1988). The relationship of social power to visual displays of dominance between women and men. *Journal of Personality and Social Psychology 54*, 233–242.

anything more than the sex of one's partner, visual dominance was expressed by men, not women.

Female Oppression

Just as boys' and men's unawareness of male dominance doesn't mean it doesn't exist, the same can be said for the oppression of women and girls (Johnson, 2006). As we'll see in Chapter 14, some women accept without question their subordinated place in the Diversity Wheel (Downing & Roush, 1985). One purpose of this book is to critically examine evidence about when and how women, as a social category, are regarded, and when disadvantages are documented, to challenge them. (Remember our social justice agenda.) The validity of claims of both privilege and oppression cannot be based on feelings or opinions, but rather they must be grounded in scholarly evidence. This is the ultimate challenge for this text. To start, we need to explore the relationship between privilege and oppression within systems of inequality.

Systems of Inequality

There are four points that I'd like to make here (Johnson, 2006). First, one must be a member of an oppressed group to be affected by that form of oppression. Second, few people are universally oppressed. Third, being privileged is not the same as being oppressive. Fourth, being oppressed does not free one from the possibility of being oppressive. In other words, men cannot be directly oppressed by sexism; few men are completely privileged; being male doesn't necessary make one sexist; and being female does not automatically make girls and women nonsexist. All of these outcomes occur because sexism resides in a system of inequity that encompasses all of us.

Sexism and men. A growing body of research evidence points to the negative health consequences of strong beliefs in traditional masculinity by men (Addis & Mahalik, 2003; Good & Sherrod, 2001). For example, men are more likely than women to engage in risky behaviors (like reckless driving) and are less likely to take preventive and remedial health measures (like regularly seeing a physician and seeking care for psychological distress). Men not only perpetrate violence much more than women, but men also are the more likely victims of violence. Men who associate being masculine with toughness have more difficulties in their intimate relationships and experience more psychological stress.

Although it is clear that demands of **hypermasculinity** can be painful for boys and men, is this sexism? The answer, Allan Johnson (2006, p. 39) says, rests in the *balance* between costs and benefits. For example, not being able to openly express some emotions like being hurt and crying may be painful. However, as Jack Sattel (1976) points out, expressing hurt ultimately makes one vulnerable by showcasing one's deepest emotions, and researchers find that men are most likely to fall back into rigid gender stereotypic thinking when they feel emotionally vulnerable (Vogel et al., 2003). In contrast, refusal to express what one is feeling can be empowering—it not only avoids exposure but also keeps outsiders at bay (see Sprecher & Felmlee, 1997). On balance, boys and men as a group, unlike girls and women, gain much more from their social category than they lose. Peter Blood and his colleagues (1995, p. 159) sum up this point: "However much men are hurt by sex roles in this country, the fact remains that they are not systematically denied power simply because of being born a certain sex, as women are."

This doesn't mean that men and masculinity should be ignored; in fact, these topics can merit a course in and of themselves. However, this book purposively is a psychology of women text. By this I mean that I put women front and center in my analyses, and the value of my work is determined by how well it serves a social justice agenda (Kahn & Yoder, 1989). The key, I think, is to adopt a women-centered perspective that values diverse women and women's experiences and that is rooted in gendered understandings.

An example may clarify. Consider women's leadership (Yoder, 2001). We can describe women's styles of leadership as precisely that: *women's* styles (recognizing that they are diverse and without judgmental comparisons with men's). We can learn even more about women's leadership by understanding the role gender plays. If we envision leaders as cool, calm, collected, rational, and powerful decision-makers, then cultural taboos against public displays of emotion by men make men suitable candidates for these leadership roles. At the same time, culturally based liberties allowing women's public expressiveness work to undermine women's perceived suitability in these power-based contexts. Following this logic, not only do men generally make good leaders in these power-based contexts, but women also make bad leaders. By focusing on women (women-centered) and the gendered context (gender-sensitive), women's leadership can be described as women's (without being seen as deviant from men's) and contexts can be examined that both exaggerate and minimize the importance of power (versus cooperation, for example). In leadership, and throughout this book, descriptions of women and gendered understandings converge to provide one central feminist focus.

Interlocking oppressions. Take another walk around the Diversity Wheel, identifying the areas now where you are a member of an oppressed social category. Very few people can avoid being oppressed by some characteristic perceived by others. Sometimes this makes it difficult to sort out what the basis for an oppression is. For example, is the need for "big boys" not to cry a matter of their gender category or pressure to avoid being labeled gay (homophobia)? Oppressions support each other (Pharr, 1988).

Nowhere was this point of interlocking oppressions clearer to me than in raising my daughter. As parents, John and I talked openly about wanting Kate to be free from restrictions in clothing, staying clean, washing long hair, etc. We soon developed a reputation among our family members as being opposed to anything feminine for Kate, so some relatives took it upon themselves to offer her dresses, hair ribbons, and other feminine accoutrements. Kate would come back from family visits with all kinds of new items that quickly fell into disuse at home. When she got older, we'd talk about how she felt about these things and the assumption that we forbade them because they were "sexist." Kate is the one who eventually pinpointed the true fear among her relatives. They weren't really worried about her identity as a girl (Kate had a strong sense of being female), but rather feared that she would grow up to be a lesbian. We'll see in Chapter 4 that there are strong ties to how we do gender in how we raise girls and boys that are intermeshed with homophobia.

Another important point here is that by grouping people into social categories, we gloss over individual and subgroup diversity among them. Stop for a moment and think of a woman. Feel free to stereotype!

This is the typical procedure of **stereotyping** studies; give raters (commonly, mostly White college students) a stimulus and ask them to describe that person. Usually, "a woman" is described, among other things, as being neat, talkative, vain, gentle, passive, dependent, and tender (Broverman et al., 1970). But, who is this woman? Is she an African American woman? Hope Landrine found that these women were rated as dirty, hostile, and superstitious; as strong and domineering in a more recent study (Donovan, 2011). Is she a working class woman? Landrine (1985) found that these women were evaluated negatively as confused, dirty, hostile, illogical, impulsive, incoherent, inconsiderate, irresponsible, and superstitious. Furthermore, Landrine's data showed that stereotypes of the "typical" woman overlapped with those of White, middle class women. In other words, the "typical" woman we likely described at the start of this section is not typical at all. Rather, she is a specific kind of woman, a woman who is White and middle class (and probably a lot of other things we assumed, like heterosexual, young, and physically able). A women-centered psychology must be inclusive of *all* women—recognizing both commonalties and diversity (Yoder & Kahn, 1993).

Divisions among women have been fostered by the assumption that sex and gender can be studied in isolation of other ascribed social statuses (Cole, 2009). Although the Diversity Wheel does an excellent job of facilitating our understandings of various social categories, it does draw clear lines around each entry, implying that these are separate and distinct categories. In reality, each of us is a jumbled mix of categories such that no one stands without the others—an understanding that is captured by an approach called **intersectionality**. To get a clearer sense of how this point fits in with some of the ideas we have discussed so far, take a look at Figure 1.5.

To capture this idea of the intersection of multiple social categories, Candace West and Sarah Fenstermaker (1995) describe how to "**do difference**" from the perspective of social constructionism. Every one of our social category memberships is constructed, day-in and day-out, through interactions with other people. Each defines us within our society, and all are constructed in unison, affecting each other in intersecting ways.

An example from my own research with women firefighters may help bring home this last point (Yoder & Aniakudo, 1997; Yoder & Berendsen, 2001). Very few professional firefighters (less than 5%) are women. They stand out as different from "normal" firefighters (men) and are frequently considered deficient. They often are excluded, are marginal-

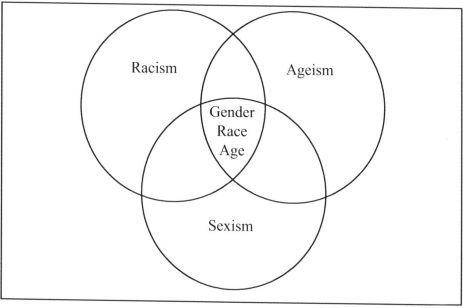

Figure 1.5

If we consider only the three social categories that people register first (gender, race, age), we each have social representations (how others see us) as well as our own individual identities and experiences at the intersection of all three (the center area). Considered within a system of inequality, on the other hand, few of us are oppressed by sexism, racism, and ageism; rather, we spread across all areas of the chart, oppressed by some and privileged by others.

ized as outsiders, and are harassed (Yoder & Aniakudo, 1996). One part of how others deal with their difference is to rely on gender stereotypes about women. This process of being stereotyped happens for both Black and White women firefighters, with both groups reporting stereotyping in equal measure.

However, there are key differences in how this stereotyping qualitatively plays out for women in each racial/ethnic category. The stereotype that Black women cope with marks them as self-sufficient and independent so that even when they need help, others typically don't think it's necessary. In contrast, the stereotype for White women often includes imagine of being fragile and needing care, so that these women commonly feel overprotected by their male counterparts. In both cases, women are stereotyped and these stereotypes limit how effectively they can do their jobs. Moreover, the specific ways these processes occur differ, in that Black women report feeling overburdened; White women, underburdened. A fuller understanding of the intersectionality of each woman's experience must reach beyond just understanding her gender to seeing how it is shaped by other social categories as well.

A *womEn*-centered exploration must stress the plurality of "women." Women are diverse; no singular, generic woman exists—although we may be misled to think so by conjuring up our culture's mainstream assumptions for women (White, middle class, heterosexual, Christian, physically able, young, mother…). One core goal for this book is that we not lose track of this **diversity** as we review research and that we don't stereotypically include some groups of women only when the topic "fits." Watch for this throughout the book, and keep it in the back of your mind as you think about each topic we cover.

Privileged ≠ oppressive. Powerful words like privilege, oppression, and injustice are uncomfortable. They can readily imply meanness by an individual and arouse guilt in that person. Some of these reactions come from the **individualism** of Western culture, which stresses individual over group needs (Oyserman & Lee, 2008). When we think individuals control much of what they do, it's easy to blame individual men for women's oppression.

Think of a time when you didn't like what you saw yourself doing. Allan Johnson (2006) does this quite effectively by describing himself when he plays the board game *Monopoly*. He becomes cut-throat competitive with his own kids, driving them out of the game by greedily gobbling up their properties. Is this part of his nature? Cleary, he can be induced to behave this way, but usually only in the context of this game of unchecked capitalism. Certainly, we all incur personal responsibility for what we do, but as social psychologists have long shown, the worst (and the best) in people can be drawn out by the social context in which we operate.

This understanding takes us to men and the role men play in a psychology of women. One potential role is as the "bad guy." Understanding that sexism is part of a larger system of inequalities should help us understand why being privileged by the system isn't the same as being oppressive as an individual. Lots of good people, like Johnson playing *Monopoly*, get caught up in bad situations without being "bad guys."

A frequent claim leveled against women feminists is that we engage in **male bashing** (the derogation of men and boys for being male). Remember that our goal is to end sexism, not hate men. Sue Cataldi (1995) writes a thoughtful analysis of the discourse used to talk about "male bashing" and how charges of man hating serve to undermine women's solidarity as feminists and silence their voices. She concludes: "One can be against sexism without hating men, just as one can be against racism without hating Whites or against homophobia without hating heterosexuals" (p. 77).

I think a better approach is to draw men into being pro-feminist in support of a social movement to end sexist oppression. An understandable barrier against drawing men into the women's movement rests in *ignoring* male privilege. Why would men work to change a status quo that benefits them? Putting this question out there bluntly is a first step toward working through it successfully.

It's somewhat idealistic to conclude that it's simply "the right thing to do." Johnson (2006) calls this the "tin-can" approach, which does capture well the underlying message of begging and the disempowerment that implies for members of the oppressed group. More effectively, men need to recognize that they can benefit themselves by supporting the feminist agenda we outlined here. Because, as we have seen, oppressions sustain each other, men who are devalued because of their race/ethnicity, age, sexual orientation, etc. are indirectly oppressed by sexism as well (Blood et al., 1995). For example, an all-too-common practice in both the military and sports is to challenge men's masculinity and heterosexuality by demeaning them as "girls." The effectiveness of this epithet in controlling men's behavior is rooted in homophobia that in turn maintains gendered divisions.

I think there's another reason if we look beyond ourselves to the other significant people in our lives. What about mothers, daughters, partners, sisters, friends, and coworkers? We will learn that one consequence of seeing differences, instead of similarities, is disrupted connection. Each and every one of these relationships with women in men's lives suffers when sources of connection, understanding, and empathy are broken. Feminism isn't about male bashing; it's about **social justice**—something we all have a stake in pursuing.

Oppressed ≠ non-oppressive. The same reasoning that led us to the conclusion above that men can support a feminist agenda explains why all women don't necessarily openly and without reservations embrace feminism. Indeed, at a more personal level, it helps us understand why even feminists can be sexist sometimes. We all are part of larger systems of inequality that force us to work actively and continuously at breaking free of just going along the easily sexist "path of least resistance" (Johnson, 2006).

If Johnson can't play Monopoly without turning into someone he doesn't want to be and I can't look through a fashion magazine without feeling inadequate about my body, why should any of us do these things? We need to recognize how these systemic forces are affecting us, and then take charge of them, rather than let them take charge of us. Paradoxically, personal empowerment may depend on how much we understand when we do, and especially when we don't, control our own lives.

CONSEQUENCES OF GENDER DIFFERENCES

We have seen that it's the linkage of difference to power that makes difference troublesome. Here I want to examine exactly what troubles gender difference may produce. The *American Heritage Dictionary* (2006) identifies three primary definitions of different: (1) not alike in character or quality (dissimilar); (2) distinct or separate ("other"); and (3) differing from all others (unusual). These definitions give us clues about what these negative consequences of difference may be. We shall see that dissimilarity can result in designations of normal for the privileged group and deficiency for the subordinated; regarding other people as "other" can produce stereotyping and disrupt contact between groups; and unusualness can lead to loss of connection between individuals (see Table 1.6).

Dissimilarity: Normal versus Deficient

Consider the following results from a large study of a nationally representative sample of lesbian and heterosexual women. The authors (Hegarty & Pratto, 2004, p. 448) concluded:

> Interview studies show that straight and lesbian women recall very different childhood experiences. In one study, 90% of the lesbians interviewed recalled

TABLE 1.6
Aspects and Consequences of Difference

Definitions of Difference	Consequences
(1) Unlike in form, quality, amount, or nature DISSIMILAR	Normal versus deficient
(2) Distinct or separate "OTHER"	Stereotyping
(3) Differing from all others UNUSUAL	Disrupted connection between individuals

enjoying extremely "female-typed" activities from childhood (e.g., dolls, hop-scotch). 65% of the straight women interviewed recalled enjoying such activities.

Social group	Percent who enjoyed activities
Lesbians	90%
Straight women	65%

Take a minute and in your own words, please explain this difference.

It doesn't take a rocket scientist to notice that the results appear counterintuitive; that is, they run against common stereotyping of lesbians as unfeminine. Indeed, the data above were fabricated as part of a larger study by Peter Hegarty and Felicia Pratto (2004). In their study, some undergraduates read the version above, whereas for others, the percentages were switched so that their "results" were consistent with folk wisdom about lesbians and heterosexual women. Three pieces of data were collected from the students who read one version. Trained coders, unaware of which version the student read, judged the explanations that students wrote for: (1) how many times lesbians and heterosexual women were mentioned, (2) references to how accurate they believed these reports of childhood experiences were; and (3) students also guessed what the two percentages might be if a second study was conducted.

Notice that we are looking inside one subcategory (women) of the broader social category of gender (women and men). Within this subcategory of women, heterosexual women represent the dominant, privileged group, in contrast to lesbians as a subordinated, oppressed group, at least in terms of their sexual orientation. Turning to the results of Hegarty and Pratto's study, regardless of which version students read, they made significantly more references to lesbians than to heterosexual women. In other words, lesbians' memories took center stage in their explanations. What heterosexual women purportedly did was taken for granted (normalized) and what lesbians reportedly did needed explaining. Thus, the dominant group, heterosexual women, was set up as the standard against which lesbians needed to be understood. This pattern illustrates the first part, **normality**, of the normal-deficient consequence of difference.

The second part of this consequence, **deficiency**, is a bit more subtle. When students predicted the likely outcomes in a follow-up study, they estimated that the results would be closer to those in the first study for heterosexual women than for lesbians. In other words, the data from heterosexual women would hold up better over repeated testings presumably because heterosexual women are providing more valid data. In contrast, there's something relatively deficient about the data coming from lesbian interviewees.

What's most fascinating about Hegarty and Pratto's study is that it demonstrates the process through which difference produces both a normalized, baseline group (heterosexual women) and a deficient "other" group (lesbians). We see in these data firsthand how women and men college students construct meaning from the differences they see in research findings.

Hegarty and Pratto's experiment demonstrates the process of how normalizing the dominant group and questioning the oppressed group happens. Turning to the social category of gender, the process of normalizing men as the dominant group and regarding women as the subordinated group as comparatively deficient is not uncommon in the social sciences. **Androcentric bias** refers to this male-centeredness, such that what men do is regarded as normative (that is, what should be done) and what women do is considered relatively deficient.[6]

Take a look at the incomplete bar chart in Figure 1.7 and take a minute to finish it. Peter Hegarty and his colleagues (2010) ran a series of six experiments to explore the subtle biases we take for granted in seemingly objective charts and graphs. They found that people expected the first (left) bar to represent men and, in separate studies and independent of gender, to represent the more powerful party, even when not rating power. In fact, these parallels serve to link being male to being powerful, a point we'll explore later. For now, these two findings collude to make it likely that you labeled the left bar "men" and drew it taller.

If, on the other hand, you wanted to illustrate that women were more powerful, you would have had to break one of these unspoken rules by putting women first or by drawing the taller bar to the right. Whatever you did, one point that emerges from these studies is that androcentric bias typically continues in subtle ways. When we put men "first" (to the left) on a chart, they automatically become the comparison point, that is, the group against which the bars to the right are compared, thus conforming to an androcentric bias. The good news though is that we need not succumb to this bias; when we think about it, we are capable of flipping our perspective to make women the default gender (Hegarty, 2006), giving us two ways to think about the same phenomenon and thus expanding our perspective.

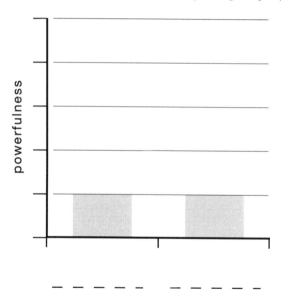

Figure 1.7
Assume that there is a gender difference in powerfulness and illustrate that difference in the above chart by: (1) labeling each bar (fill in the two blank lines on the x-axis to label each bar so one is for women; the other, for men), and (2) extend each bar vertically to illustrate the difference.

---

[6]Ironically, the equation of maleness with generic humanness misses the essential nature of masculinity—of what men are like as *men*. A corrective to this oversight is offered by profeminist approaches to men's studies (in APA's Division 51 on Men and Masculinity).

"Other": Stereotyping and Disrupted Contact

Thinking about women as a group as "other" compared to men as a group is a concept that has been part of feminist thinking for a long time (De Beauvoir, 1952). As with androcentric bias described above, we continue to talk here about women and men as groups, in this case distinct and separate groups. The cognitive process of thinking about women and men as different is referred to as **gender polarization** (Bem, 1993). Such thinking is based on two critical assumptions: first, that women and men are represented by two mutually exclusive groups with no overlap, and second, that each group is homogeneous (that is, all women are alike as women and all men are alike as men).

This point may seem as obvious as my earlier request to check the box that describes you: male or female. Surely, we all know which box to check so that all women, and only women, check female and all men, and only men, check male. Even the language we commonly use to relate women and men as the "opposite" sex captures this distinction and separateness. Pictorially, this comparison would look like the figures below.

Girls and Women	Boys and Men

Try to think of a characteristic that would sort all girls and women into the first square and all boys and men into the second. If you think having a penis or not works, check out Chapter 3. If you think reproductive differences sort effectively, consider women who have had a hysterectomy or men with insufficient sperm counts. Obviously, no personality trait (aggressiveness, sociability, etc.) would do it. Try self-identification, but then what would we do with transgender folks (Diamond & Butterworth, 2008)? Boxing everyone in isn't as easy as it might look on first blush.

However, we squeeze people into these two boxes every day. As we saw at the opening of this chapter, sex (or, as we now know, our perceptions of others' sex) is one of the three primary indicators by which we sort people into social categories. What are the costs associated with this distinction and separation, and who do they affect? Conversely, does anyone benefit?

The **out-group homogeneity** effect (that is, regarding members of the "other" group as all alike) (Judd & Park, 1988) sets up **sexist stereotyping**. As we'll see in Chapter 7, stereotypes move from being simple descriptors of what women and men as groups are like, to proscribing what they *should* be like and, in taking this leap, work to limit the possibilities open to girls and women (Glick & Fiske, 1999a). By confining us to the square above designated by our gender, they literally box us into what's expected of us as members of our gender category. This process has real implications for how far each of us can and cannot develop our own individual propensities and abilities. For example, in Chapter 5 we'll see that expectations regarding the gender appropriateness of occupations can subtly channel women and men away from certain college majors and career paths toward others.

Outside our homes in the public sphere of our lives, such as in our schools and our workplaces, contact between women as a group and men as a group is surprisingly limited. Just think back to your schools before college and picture your lunchrooms and playgrounds. As we'll see in Chapter 4, these likely were gender segregated (Maccoby, 1990). Much to my chagrin, my son's middle school actually instituted separate girls' and boys' lunchtimes to be able to ascertain easily if kids were where they were supposed to be during lunch and recess. The principal defended this policy, even though we know that everyday, casual relationships between girls and boys are central to breaking down stereotyping and discomfort between two groups (Pipher, 1994). However, as we'll discover in Chapter 9, we largely segregate occupations by gender, so maybe schools are simply preparing us well for what lies ahead.

Stereotyping and limited contact occur between groups. They work together to reinforce each other in a cycle of less contact and greater stereotyping. Mere contact alone cannot bridge in-groups with out-groups, but rather this contact must be equal-status, involve intergroup cooperation, be sustained over time, take place within a social climate that favors equality, and allow for potential friendships to develop (Pettigrew, 1998). Individual women and men interact with each other every day, but is that enough to break down stereotyping? Read on...

Unusualness: Disrupted Connection

In our private lives many women and men live in intimate interdependence, unlike most of the social groups around the Diversity Wheel (Lee et al., 2010). Yet these close interactions between women and men don't appear to guarantee connection because they co-exist within systems of inequality. All kinds of popular debates ask "What do women want?," "Why can't women and men get along?," and so on.

The ultimate popularized example of this difference thinking is captured in the very title of a bestseller on this topic: *Men Are from Mars, Women Are from Venus: The Classic Guide for Understanding the Opposite Sex* (Gray, 2004). In fact, this book (first published in 1992) has garnered so much popular attention that a noted gender psychologist, Rosalind Barnett, co-authored a book for a general audience tackling the gender myths perpetuated by Gray's book and showing how these misconceptions about differences hurt women's relationships, children, and jobs (Barnett & Rivers, 2004).

Take, for example, intimate relationships. A survey for the National Marriage Project at Rutgers University of over 1,000 Americans, age 20 to 29, concluded that most are looking for a "soul mate for life" (Whitehead & Popenoe, 2001). There's a "two cultures" model of intimate, heterosexual relationships, played up in the popular media by books like Gray's, that claims that women and men want different things from their relationships and communicate differently so that they never can connect fully with each other (Dion & Dion, 2001). Indeed, the very definition of "manhood," at least in the abstract, assumes disconnected autonomy from others (Parent & Moradi, 2011).

We'll see in Chapter 8 that this differences model resides more in popular folk wisdom than in scholarly evidence. Ironically, folk wisdom about the "war" between the sexes may undermine not only people's expectations about the likelihood of finding the soul mate they seek, but also the very interactions that are part of being connected to one's soul mate when they are found. We'll see that intimate relationships based on equal sharing don't just happen; rather, they take considerable, never-ending work (Blaisure & Allen, 1995; Knudson-Martin & Mahoney, 2005)

At its most extreme, the disconnection that results from seeing another individual as unusual (and not like me) is a critical first step psychologists have identified toward violence. Social psychologist Erwin Staub (1989) looked at various national cases of genocide and identified a slow progression of difference thinking as one important step toward committing otherwise unthinkable acts. As people begin to think about others as less and less like themselves, and thus less and less human, pathways toward unspeakable violence are forged.

As we'll see in Chapter 13, a similar pattern of objectifying women combines with motivations of entitlement and for dominance to underlie acceptance of rape myths and propensities for men to sexually abuse women (Hill & Fischer, 2001). I certainly do *not* mean to exaggerate the role of difference thinking by implying that it alone inevitably leads to rape. However, it is clear that people who are respectful of others cannot take these steps. Nowhere is it clearer to me that enlisting men in such efforts is important.

My general point here is that we need to think more deeply about difference thinking (gender polarization) and whether what it does for us outweighs some potentially significant costs. This is why I am starting this book with this very fundamental exploration of social categorization and difference, and why the next few chapters will explore these ideas more fully. I think that by taking a closer look at the power of difference, we'll be well prepared to think more critically and thoughtfully about the applied chapters that compose the second half of this text.

CHAPTER SUMMARY

Because the overall focus on this text is on sex as a major marker for social categorization, we started by exploring how social representations in general can lead to difference thinking. Difference is linked with power in systems of inequality that promote both privilege for members of dominant groups and oppression of subordinated group members. Seeing people as members of in-groups, to which I belong, and out-groups takes a step toward three consequences. First, differences set up one group to be normative in contrast to deficient others. Second, differences can encourage stereotyping, and third, differences can disrupt connection between individuals.

Gender is just one of many ways in which we categorize people around the Diversity Wheel. However, even among the core characteristics that define similarities and differences among people, gender is primary. The frequency with which gender is used to sort individuals into groups of female and male can be understood to result from either the fundamental essentialism of this difference or our vigilant social construction of gender through hard, yet often unconscious, work throughout our everyday lives.

This understanding puts gender differences and power at center stage in this text. By thinking of women and men as different (gender polarization), we can readily slide down a slippery slope toward androcentric bias, that is, seeing men as the normal standard and women as relatively deficient, toward sexist stereotyping and disrupted contact, and toward disrupted connected. The system of gender inequality this reinforces confers dominance and unearned entitlements on privileged men and disadvantages women.

Ironically, even most men ultimately are not benefited by this system of interlocking oppressions that work to sustain each other. Rather, an overall social justice agenda is needed to dismantle these systems of inequality, including the feminist agenda we have seen helps give meaning to the body of theory and research we construct as social scientists. Indeed, what lies ahead for us in this book is an exploration of this theory and research, especially focused on the power of gender differences.

WHAT LIES AHEAD

This first chapter sets up the four themes that run across this book. First, we are striving to construct a psychology that is guided by a social justice agenda and given meaning by our feminist values. To do this, we need to understand difference and how it relates to power, privilege, oppression, and systems of inequality. In short, we need to transform psychology.

Second, we need to understand that transformation is an ongoing process of continual change and critical thinking, not a static endpoint. In the next chapter, we'll look at how far we have come in this transformation by looking back at our history and critically examining the tools (our methods) that got us where we are today. We'll raise questions about the very questions we ask (and don't ask), about how we frame our questions, and about how we collect data and interpret our findings.

Third, we began to explore the need to take a holistic approach to understanding women and gender by bringing together nature (biology), nurture (socialization), and social context (environment). Within this way of thinking, sex (biology) and gender (how culture makes meaning of sex) are inseparable and intertwined.

Finally, there is no singular woman's experience, but rather a wide diversity of women and men and their experiences must be brought together. It is clear that psychology has been transformed by feminists and feminist theories, research, and practice, and that this process continues.

Throughout our odyssey through this feminist approach to psychology, there undoubtedly will be times when we become frustrated, overwhelmed, and angry. This course hits too close to home to be approached dispassionately. It is not uncommon for folks to approach this course with feelings of apprehension, wariness, and suspicion. You may find yourself disturbed by what you'll read, motivating you to dismiss some conclusions or argue vehemently against them. You also may be disturbed by events and people in your everyday life that you hadn't noticed or cared about before reading this text. These are critical moments. Try not to let them pass without exploring what you're feeling and why. You may seek out additional readings or others to talk with at these points. Remember through these times that being aware of this work is better than ignoring it, for awareness is a first step toward realizing the social justice we all deserve (see Greenwood & Christian, 2008).

SUGGESTED READINGS

Johnson. A. G. (2006). *Privilege, power, and difference* (2ⁿᵈ ed). New York: McGraw Hill.

This very reader friendly book brings together much of the logic and research that links difference to power, privilege, oppression, and systems of inequality. Allan Johnson helps put gender within this paradigm as well as connects gender to other markers of social identity around the Diversity Wheel. I recommend this book highly as a supplement to this chapter.

Muehlenhard, C. L., & Peterson, Z. D. (2011). Distinguishing between *sex* and *gender*: History, current conceptualizations, and implications. *Sex Roles*. doi: 10.1007/s11199-011-9932-5.

Without offering any easy answers, this insightful article explores the history, current thinking, and unresolved issues in defining sex and gender, leaving the reader with a more nuanced and complex understanding of these seemingly simple terms.

Zucker, A.N. (2004). Disavowing social identities: What it means when women say "I'm not a feminist but…" *Psychology of Women Quarterly, 28*, 423-435.

Alyssa Zucker explores what it means to be an "egalitarian," that is, a woman who adopts feminist values but eschews the label of "feminist." Her data argue that there's more in a name than we might think, sparking discussion of what feminism is and means.

Bem, S. L. (1993). *The lenses of gender: Transforming the debate on sexual inequality.* New Haven, CT: Yale University Press.

Sandra Bem takes a careful look at how three schemas (lenses through which we perceive our social worlds), androcentrism, gender polarization, and biological essentialism, work together to perpetuate systems of gender inequality.

Gergen, K. J., & Gergen, M. (2004). *Social construction: Entering the dialogue.* Chagrin Falls, OH: Taos Institute Publications.

Kenneth and Mary Gergen provide an up-to-date introduction to the ideas of social construction.

Chapter 2

Transforming Psychology
There's No Turning Back

History: Rewinding the Videotape
   Psychology and Women
   The Psychology of Women: Historical Trends and Patterns
Psychology of Women Today: Pressing Pause
   Contemporary Perspectives and Trends
   Within the Discipline of Psychology
Feminist Research: Playing Forward
   Decisions, Decisions
   Innovations in Research
   Feminist Approaches to Doing Research
   Intersectionality: Diversity in Feminist Research
   What We Know about Gender Differences
   Where We Look for Differences
   Overlooking Similarity
   Declaring Difference
   Summarizing Data
Chapter Summary

Dora, at age 18, finds herself caught in a web of family affairs that sound like they came straight out of a soap opera. Her father appears to be having an extramarital affair with his friend's wife. Dora's problems are with her father's friend, Mr. K.

Mr. K always seemed attracted to Dora. Starting when she was 7, Mr. K grabbed every opportunity he could to take her on long, unchaperoned walks and buy her expensive gifts. As Dora got older, she became more and more uncomfortable with his attentions, but she didn't fully understand why until she was 14. Mr. K invited her to watch a festival from his office window, and when she arrived, she was surprised to find him alone. He kissed her deeply, and as he pulled her close to himself, she felt his erection.

It was at this point in time that Dora started to develop what her family referred to as "symptoms." These symptoms worsened over time as Mr. K's pursuit of her intensified. Dora's father insisted that Dora see the therapist he chose. He tells the therapist that Dora is defiant and willful and beseeches the therapist to "bring her to reason."

Slowly Dora's side of the story unfolds in therapy. She concludes that her father and Mr. K have reached an unspoken agreement through which her father ignores Mr. K's interest in Dora and Mr. K. ignores his wife's relationship with Dora's father.

The therapist keeps detailed notes about this case and makes it clear in his log that he believes Dora's story and her conclusions. However, he withholds telling her this for fear that it will encourage her disruptive behavior. He labels her behavior "neurotic." After only 3 months, Dora ends her therapy. In his follow-up notes, the therapist concludes that Dora terminated her sessions because she was offended when her sexual attraction to the therapist himself was not reciprocated.

What's happening here?

With our twenty-first century sensibilities, it's hard for us not to see Dora as the unfortunate victim of a seriously messed up situation. She is caught up in a dysfunctional family in which her childhood sexual abuse is secreted away and allowed to continue by her father's betrayal of her. When she tries to break out of the cycle by being defiant, she is drawn back into the drama by being cast as "neurotic." Therapy, which should focus on helping her, serves to maintain the charade and even adds to it when Dora is sexualized by the therapist himself. My guess is that most of us cheered for Dora and her defiance when she terminated her therapy, and I doubt that any of us would recommend this therapist to our friends.

Yet that therapist, Sigmund Freud, came highly recommended, and Dora's case as Freud reports it is among the cornerstones for psychoanalytic thinking (Hare-Mustin, 1983; Lakoff, 1990). In it we recognize Freud's developing ideas of fantasies of childhood sexuality and client-therapist transference. Although this case helped develop contemporary therapy as we know it today, we'd be hard pressed to represent this case as an example of "good" therapy.

This case, and our reaction to it, capture the transformation of psychology across its over 100 years as an academic and applied discipline. The androcentric perspective that victimized Dora twice (first, by sexually abusing her, and second, by invalidating that abuse by dismissing it as fantasy) would likely be replaced by an understanding that affirms her experiences and reactions and that would work toward empowering her. Psychology today has been transformed to its very core by the questions, probing, analyses, and alternatives offered by a feminist perspective. Whether we openly acknowledge the role feminism has played in this transformation or not, it is clear that there is no turning back. Psychology and the way we approach women and gender have been altered irrevocably.

The purposes of this chapter are to introduce the field of the Psychology of Women and research findings comparing women and men. I draw on Stephanie Riger's (2000b) metaphor of a videotape to explore the field: (1) rewinding to examine our history; (2) pausing to look at a present snapshot; and (3) playing forward using feminist research methodologies which hold the key to developing future research.

Keep in mind what Dora's story taught us: what may seem so obvious to us in retrospect didn't appear all that unusual while it was happening. Recognizing this point serves as a good reminder that what may seem normal now may, years from now in retrospect, look so obviously wrong. Of course, I will use current theory, research, and practice to ground my points, knowing full well though that they are dynamic and evolving. *Psychology has been transformed and is continually transforming.*

Finally, in this chapter I want to follow up on the ideas about difference that we started in Chapter 1. I'll review how we determine gender differences and what today's data tell us. This review will lay the groundwork for the next five chapters, where we'll explore *why* these differences occur and when they may not really underscore differences—serving instead to obscure fundamental similarities among all people (Hyde, 2005).

HISTORY: REWINDING THE VIDEOTAPE

Our interest in the history of psychology begins in two areas: looking at the roles women played as psychologists and looking at the way psychologists thought about women. The first of these areas makes women the subjects of doing psychology; the second, the objects of that psychology. Finally, we'll look at the Psychology of Women as a specialty area within the overall discipline of psychology to briefly describe its history.

Psychology and Women

On the face of it, histories look like simple recordings of past events. However, if we think more deeply about history, we can readily see that histories tell their stories through the perspective of the "winners." For example, think about how the "American Revolution" would be portrayed if the British won and George Washington was hung as a traitor.

Women as psychologists.   Pick up most beginning psychology texts, and even many history texts, and simply glance through the pictures. Who are the notables deemed worthy of photographs? Do they represent all areas of psychology that were ever explored? Certainly not! But even some dead ends like phrenology (reading bumps on people's head to decipher their personalities) appear in their pages. What's *not* likely to appear, or to appear only as a special example, are women and psychologists of color.

To make psychologists who were women and their work visible in the history of psychology, our thinking progresses through three different, but not necessarily smooth and clear-cut phases (Crawford & Marecek, 1989; Lerner, 1992). In the early phase, questions are raised about *androcentric bias* by pointing out how women are left out of psychology's history.

In the next *compensatory phase*, women are "discovered," both as doers and objects of study. Biographers "discover" women and their work and contribute their once-invisible biographies to psychology's history.[1] At the next level, an ongoing process of *transformation* begins that irrevocably alters the field and how its work is approached. Women and their work are not just add-ons, but their ideas and lives are integrated into the mainstream of psychology's history, changing its flow. It is this last integrative step that re-writes, and thus transforms, the way we look at our history in psychology.

A brief look at the history of psychology suggests that **androcentric bias** has appeared throughout it and may even persist to some degree today. Although women did not have opportunities equal to those of men at the time (Furumoto & Scarborough, 1986), there were indeed some very influential women. How many of the following psychologists can you identify? (You'll want to read footnote 2 and review Box 2.1.)

Christine Ladd Franklin	Diane Halpern
Mary Whiton Calkins	Sharon Stephens Brehm
Margaret Floy Washburn	Carol D. Goodheart
Leona Tyler	Melba J. T. Vasquez
Florence Denmark	Suzanne Bennett Johnson
Janet Taylor Spence	Leta Stetter Hollingworth
Bonnie Strickland	Ruth Howard (Beckham)
Dorothy Cantor	Martha Bernal
Norine Johnson	Maime Phipps Clark[2]

Women as research subjects. Not only were women psychologists and their work overlooked, but women often were excluded as research participants. Kathleen Grady (1981) counted twice as many men as women in psychological studies. In addition, having studied only men, researchers all-too-often generalized their results to women (Reardon & Prescott, 1977). This exclusive concentration of researchers and theorists on being male-centered is part of what we have seen defines androcentric bias.

Even the inclusion of men in research was not inclusive of all men; psychologists uncritically relied on readily available White, educated, upper class, heterosexual, male college students (Lykes & Stewart, 1986), a pattern that persists into the twenty-first century (Whorley & Addis, 2006). Beyond exclusion of people as research participants was the marginalizing of diverse ideas and perspectives. Robert Guthrie (1976) made this more insidious form of exclusion clear in his seminal book, *Even the Rat Was White*. There certainly is a place for

---

[1]The Society for the Psychology of Women's quarterly newsletter, *The Feminist Psychologist*, routinely contains a heritage column devoted to a woman who figured in psychology's history.

[2]Ladd-Franklin, Calkins, and Washburn were the only three women among 50 psychologists listed by James McKeen Cattell in 1903 as the most famous psychologists in the United States. Ladd-Franklin developed an influential theory of color vision; Calkins invented the paired associate technique (not Freud); and Washburn, the first woman to earn her Ph.D. in psychology, wrote "The Animal Mind" which has been cited as a precursor and impetus to behaviorism. Fourteen women are the only women APA presidents from 1892-2012: Calkins (1905), Washburn (1921), Anastasi (1972), Tyler (1973), Denmark (1980), Spence (1984), Strickland (1989), Cantor (1996), N. Johnson (2001), Halpern (2004), Brehm (2007), Goodheart (2010), Vasquez (2011; the first Latina), and S. B. Johnson (2012). Hollingworth, often declared the "mother" of the psychology of women, debunked myths that menstruation adversely affects women's performance and that women are intellectually inferior to men. Howard and Bernal were the first African American and Chicana women, respectively, to earn PhDs in psychology. Clark's work with her often-cited partner, Kenneth Clark, was critical to the U.S. Supreme Court's desegregation decision in *Brown v. the Board of Education* (Russo & Denmark, 1987). For more about women in psychology, also see Furumoto and Scarborough (1986), O'Connell & Russo (1990), Paludi (1992), Denmark et al. (2008), and http://psychology.okstate.edu/museum/women/cover2.html (retrieved June 2011).

Box 2.1

Carolyn Wood Sherif (1922–1982) was an early president of the Society for the Psychology of Women (1979) and is remembered through the society's most prestigious research award. Her presidential address, published in 1982, urged psychologists to conceptualize gender much like we are doing here; that is, as a social category that is integrated into each individual's identity and that is linked to social power and inequities. Her paper Bias in Psychology, reprinted as a tribute in 1998, makes many of the points still pertinent to our discussion of research in this chapter. Like many others, I personally pay tribute to her as a mentor and an inspiration.

Source: Photo from the Archives of the History of American Psychology at The University of Akron.

single-gender research and for research that describes the perspective of a specified group of people. The mistake is not in doing it, but in letting those excluded groups go understudied and in overgeneralizing conclusions beyond the restrictive group actually studied.

When psychologists did study women, it often was in stereotyped areas, such as motherhood (critiqued by Eyer, 1992), self-disclosure (Dindia & Allen, 1992), and neurosis and depression (Lerman, 1986), and excluded men. Both patterns served to limit what we know about women—such as ignoring critical areas like women's physical health and male violence against women—and about men—such as overlooking some men's emotional connections with others (Hurtado & Sinha, 2008).

Granted, the history of psychology was unrepresentative, but have we learned from it? Although it is clear that substantial progress has been made throughout psychology (Adler & Johnson, 1994), there remain resistant pockets of journals (e.g., in behavioral psychology) where the sex of participants is not even listed in articles, yet alone systemically explored (Sigmon et al., 2007). An informal review of 31 social psychology articles in which gender differences were tested and confirmed revealed that 18 (58%) of these articles offered no speculation about why this gender difference occurred, suggesting that the difference itself was enough of an (essentializing) explanation (Yoder & Kahn, 2003). It looks like we still have room for improvement.

The Psychology of Women: Historical Perspectives and Trends

Marianne LaFrance and her colleagues (2004) outline the perspectives and trends that characterized the historical development of the Psychology of Women we are studying today. The earliest attempts to include women in psychological research typically did so by comparing women to men. Given what we know about **androcentric bias**, it's not surprising that this approach too often concluded that women are a problem by documenting their deficiencies (for example, see Boring, 1951). In a reversal of this theme, some more recent comparative work exalted the specialness of women, for example, by glorifying women's caring (Gilligan, 1982).

A second major thread of theory and research emerged in the 1970s with Sandra Bem's (1974) introduction of the concept of **androgyny**. Before this, masculine and feminine identity were conceptualized as endpoints of the same scale so that people high in **masculinity** were, by definition, low in **femininity**. Androgyny, the blending of both high feminine with high masculine traits, was based on an understanding that these were two independent clusters of characteristics. Furthermore, these psychological clusters of traits did not map onto the sex of respondents or their sexual orientation (Dancey, 1992; Spence & Helmreich, 1978). Although stereotypes of masculine heterosexual men and feminine heterosexual women continued to define what we culturally think is appropriate for each gender, self-descriptions defied the simple categorizations culturally prescribed. Thus, the hope of androgyny rested in individual differences, not gender prescriptions, such that androgynous women and men might blend the best of both gender configurations and be flexible enough to do both feminine-typed and masculine-typed tasks (Bem, 1975). Although androgyny itself has largely fallen into disuse, the research that this concept sparked that focuses on individual rather than group differences remains vibrant (Spence, 2011).

The next phase of thinking about sex was to see it as a **stimulus variable**; that is, as a source of stereotyping and social categorization (Deaux, 1984; Sherif, 1982). Terminology in the area shifted from talking about sex to gender (Muehlenhard & Peterson, 2011) as theorists and researchers began to look at how others treated people based on their perceived membership in the social categories of female and male.

The most recent addition to thinking about sex, gender, and sexuality emerged in **social constructionism** (Marecek et al., 2004). We have seen that the central understanding of social construction is captured in the notion of **doing gender**. Gender involves concepts and categories we work at projecting. We use these categories to think about people and what people do. Most important, social constructionists focus on power and hierarchy, looking at how status, entitlement, efficacy, and self-respect play out in our social exchanges with others and are internalized into our own thinking.

PSYCHOLOGY OF WOMEN TODAY: PRESSING PAUSE

Contemporary Perspectives and Trends

If you read across the current literature on the psychology of women (and gender), you will see examples of each of these four historic perspectives and trends. Rather than replacing each other in a neat progression of ideas, each perspective continues to contribute in some form to a richer understanding of sex, gender, and sexuality. Let's fast forward our videotape then pause it on a still image of where the Psychology of Women is today.

Gender comparisons. Over the first 10 years of the 21st century, over 21,000 journal articles and over 2,300 dissertations were catalogued by PsycINFO under the keyword "human sex differences."[3] Clearly research comparing women and men is still happening.

---

[3] PsycINFO is an online abstracting service for research published in psychology. I started this search using the Thesaurus term "human sex differences" as a keyword, and then I limited entries to peer-reviewed journal articles with humans and written in English.

Especially informative contemporary comparative studies have moved beyond simply documenting and compiling gender similarities and differences. Rather, these studies focus on how characteristics of individuals and of social settings can serve as **moderators** that can exaggerate or wipe out gender differences. They also explore the processes through which individual qualities, that is, **mediators**, can link gender with given outcomes. In sum, this area has grown much more complicated than saying women do this and men do that. Instead, the current study of gender comparisons builds models that designate *when* women and men are similar and different and *how* these similarities and differences come about.

To illustrate both types of models, let's focus on gender differences in job pay which, we'll see in Chapter 9, continue to disadvantage women. A well-established gender difference concerns self-pay: even when women contribute the same quantity and quality of work as men, women tend to pay themselves less—a phenomenon called **depressed entitlement** (Jost, 1997).

Mary Hogue and I (2003) recreated this gender difference for a control group of women and men and then added two experimental conditions to our model: one in which women and men were told that women were generally more skilled at the task they would be doing (raising women's, but not men's, task status) and a second in which women and men were told that high school students usually did the upcoming task, thus lending educational status to these college students' task performance. We found that status *moderated* (interacted with) gender such that status-enhanced women in both our added conditions paid themselves similarly to men and more than control women. Thus, when women's status was enhanced, the gender difference in self-pay failed to emerge, suggesting that it is women's generally lower status that is driving depressed entitlement—not being a woman per se (see Figure 2.2). In this way, our moderator (status) qualified when gender affected self-pay, limiting the effect to when the playing field was tilted by status differences between women and men.

My second example illustrates a *mediated* model and focuses on college students' expected pay for their first post-college job in their chosen career field. Again, gender played a role such that women anticipated lower pay. However, when Mary Hogue and her co-authors (2010) took into account how female-typed each student's job intention was, gender no longer predicted entry-level pay (see Figure. 2.b). Rather, job intentions explained expected pay such that the more female-typed an individual's job intention was, the lower her or his projected pay was. Although it certainly was true that women's job intentions were, overall, more female-typed than men's, the degree to which both women *and* men pursued female-typed jobs, the lower their expected pay. Knowing this, we could

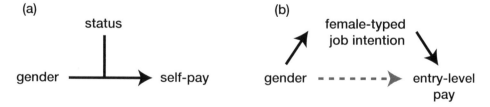

(a)

status

gender ⟶ self-pay

(b)

female-typed job intention

gender ------▶ entry-level pay

Figure 2.2
(a) Diagrams social status as a moderator of the relationship between gender and self-pay (Hogue & Yoder, 2003); (b) Diagrams job intention as fully mediating the (apparent) relationship between gender and expected entry-level pay (Hogue et al., 2010).

work to equalize expected pay by equalizing job intentions (or by reducing the pay gap between female- and male-typed jobs!), instead of assuming that there's just something essentially wrong with women's pay expectancies.

Androgyny and individual differences. The concept of androgyny still merits some attention, although we'll see in Chapter 6 that problems with measuring femininity and masculinity have muted the promise of this once-vaulted concept. The residual of androgyny that remains active in contemporary research on the Psychology of Women is a broader exploration of **individual differences**, both within and across genders. Personality traits and attitudes oftentimes distinguish individuals more than clustering people into two groups (female and male).

A strong, current example can be found in the Ambivalent Sexism Inventory, which measures **sexist prejudice** (Glick & Fiske, 2001a). As we'll see in Chapter 7, sexist prejudice refers to attitudes that serve to oppress girls and women. Although American women as a group generally score as less sexist than men as a group, there are wide individual differences among both women and men. For example, individual women and men who held hostile attitudes about women negatively evaluated women in nontraditional career roles (Glick & Fiske, 1996). What the individual difference of **ambivalent sexism** shows us here is that it predicts attitudes about career women better than the social categories of women and men.

Gender as a stimulus variable. This approach in the Psychology of Women opened the door we stepped through in Chapter 1 to thinking about gender as a social category through which others perceive and act toward us. A research example from this approach helps to demonstrate what I mean by a **stimulus variable**.

Hilary Takiff and her colleagues (2001) examined the status implications involved in how college students address their professors. Not so surprisingly, 243 students who recorded how they referred to their current instructors were significantly more likely to address their professor by title (Dr. Yoder) when that professor was male. A second study with different students explored the impact of both title and professors' sex as interacting stimulus variables. Each student read one transcript of a presumed class session. The transcripts were varied in how the female or male professor was addressed, using either title or first name. Reading the title ascribed more status to the instructor, regardless of gender, and women instructors addressed by title were regarded as less accessible than similar men.

This pattern of findings across the two studies suggests that men are addressed more commonly by title because they are perceived as higher status without affecting their accessibility. Women need to work harder to get the title they deserve and suffer a setback in doing so. Notice that whatever respect each individual professor might command by their preparation, talents, etc., as well as however accessible each is, are overshadowed to some extent by something instructors cannot control—how students perceive them because of their sex category.

Gender as socially constructed. **Social constructionism** has expanded not only our thinking about what gender is but also our approaches to studying gender. When we talked about social construction in Chapter 1, we saw that we needed to think more deeply about things we do almost reflexively (for example, check a box indicating that we are female or male).[4] The dominant way in which social constructionists explore gender issues, then, is through subtle means like **discursive analysis**, which looks for recurrent themes (interpretative repertoires) in the everyday language people use.

For example, Brendan Gough (1998) brought together working and middle class, second-year university psychology students in Britain, aged 20 to 50, to participate in three all-male discussion groups focused on masculinity in the 1990s. He recorded their open and free discussions in response to a series of general questions he threw out to them, such as, "What do you *not* like about feminist women?" Common throughout the discussion that ensued across multiple topics was an unspoken need to appear egalitarian and not openly hostile toward women. Yet also repeated in many statements were contradictions that backed off from truly nonsexist beliefs (consistent with some of the ambivalence we touched on above with the Ambivalent Sexism Inventory).

Take, for instance, one response to the question about feminists. One man said that feminists "…inflame things, so many things I disagree with, like about 'em, quite a lot of it is fair enough but at the same time they take it too far…" (p. 39). Generally, this characterization of feminists is negative, in that the speaker disagrees with them and, most importantly, diminishes their cause by saying that they inflame things and take them too far. On the other hand, he recognizes that they have legitimate claims regarding injustice and even likes them, defusing charges that he is sexist. The discussion that follows this opening statement in response to the interviewer's question continued the theme of not supporting the goals of the women's movement while still claiming to be pro-feminist.

Integrating themes and perspectives.   The case that I will make in this book is that much, although clearly not all, of the work being done in psychology overall and within the Psychology of Women makes comparisons of women with men. However, pointing out differences is just the start. A more meaningful understanding comes from exploring *why* these differences do (and do not) occur. I think this can happen by weaving together the four areas above, and I believe that the thread that can do this integration is an understanding of how difference is linked to power, privilege, oppression, and systems of inequality. The following chapters will review what we know using each of the four perspectives above and will seek to tie them together by taking a look at how the topic considered deals with issues of power.

Within the Discipline of Psychology

One strong indicator of how mainstream a specialty area is comes from examining how that area fits into the organization of the overall discipline. There is no doubt but that the Psychology of Women has become entrenched as a legitimate area of study within the discipline of psychology. There are college courses like the one you're taking: 85 (56%) of the 152 doctoral programs responding to a survey conducted by APA offered at least one undergraduate course on women (Women's Programs Office, 1998).[5] In 2008, 70% (2,362

---

[4]Another example is the order in which we commonly say things, like "male and female." I make a conscious effort to flip this wording so that subordinated groups come first. My bet is that, try as I might, I goof this up sometimes.

[5]More information about the Women's Programs Office, which is part of the Public Interest Directorate of the American Psychological Association, can be found at *http://www.apa.org/pi/women/* (retrieved June 2011).

of 3,361) of all new doctorates in psychology in the United States were earned by women (National Science Foundation, 2009), and in 2010, 57% of the members of the American Psychological Association were women (2010 APA Member Profile).[6] In 2009, women were fully 71% of undergraduate psychology majors (Carnevale, Strohl, & Melton, 2009).

There are recognized organizations within psychology: the Society for the Psychology of Women (Division 35; established in 1973)[7]; the Association for Women in Psychology (established 1969)[8]; the Women's Program Office (established 1977); and Office of Lesbian and Gay Concerns[9] (both in the Public Interest Directorate of APA). There are journals devoted exclusively to research and theory in the field: *Sex Roles* (published since 1975), *Psychology of Women Quarterly* (1976), *Women & Therapy* (1982), and *Feminism & Psychology* (1991). Sociologists for Women in Society (SWS) in the American Sociological Association (ASA) publishes *Gender & Society* (1987), which includes research of interest to feminist psychologists. In sum, the area has all the trappings of other specialty areas within the discipline.

Unlike many of these other areas, the Psychology of Women cuts across the field, emerging in everything from experimental and cognitive to developmental, clinical, counseling, social, history, testing, and health psychologies (O'Connell & Russo, 1991). The core focus that ties this all together is women; *women*, women's lives, and gender are put at the center of what we do in order to create a psychology *for* women.

Additionally, the Psychology of Women, with its gender-sensitive understanding, helped spawn a Psychology of Men and Masculinity (Lisak, 2000) as a field of study and as a recognized organization in psychology (APA Division 51–The Society for the Psychological Study of Men and Masculinity[SPSMM], established in 1977 and inaugurating its journal, *Psychology of Men and Masculinity*, in 2000). The key point that distinguishes this field and gives it a complementary pro-feminist flavor is its focus on "men the particular, not man the generic" (Lisak, 2000, p. 3).

FEMINIST RESEARCH: PLAYING FORWARD

As we look to the future of the Psychology of Women, as well as think critically about its present and past, we need to consider our research methods. Like all of psychology, we are talking about an art and a science here—a body of knowledge based on scholarship, not opinion. Yet I made an argument in Chapter 1 for the legitimate role of values in giving meaning to the psychology we do (construct). It is this somewhat paradoxical blend that

---

[6]For more information about the gender composition of psychology, request a free copy of the October 1995 report on "the Changing Gender Composition of Psychology" from the Women's Program Office of the American Psychological Association. Interestingly, the honorary title of APA "fellow" has been bestowed on about 5% of all APA members, and only 29% of these select fellows are women.

[7]To become a student member in the Society for the Psychology of Women, Division 35 of APA, visit our website at *http://www.apadivisions.org/division-35/* (retrieved June 2011).

[8]To learn more about AWP, including how to join as a student, explore our website at *http://awpsych.org/* (retrieved June 2011).

[9]APA offices can be reached by contacting the American Psychological Association at 750 First St., NE, Washington, DC 20002-4242, (202) 336-5500; or visit APA's home page at *http://www.apa.org*. To e-mail APA's Practice Directorate: *publicinterest@apa.org*.

feminist methodologists grapple with, and indeed some of this thinking is helping to transform research across the discipline.

Put into perspective for readers of this text, I am asking you to base your thinking on systematic evidence about which you think critically. There's a balance to be struck here between the extremes of unexamined acceptance of data, on the one hand, and dismissal of anything and everything that might be less than perfect, on the other hand. *I am asking you to think.*

I will not cover the fundamentals of doing psychological research here. Instead, I want to highlight some of the innovations to research that adopting the feminist value of working toward social justice entails.

Decisions, Decisions

Every study begins with a research question so that oftentimes we don't think about the major value judgment that is made by deciding to invest time, energy, and resources in this project instead of another. Furthermore, how this question itself is framed can have a significant impact on how the project proceeds. An example from developmental psychology that explored "maternal separation anxiety" will help.

The implied question underlying much of this research was: Is day care bad for children? As we'll see in Chapter 8, researchers studied aggressive displays by children in day care, defiance, sociability, intellectual achievement, and so on. Even when positive outcomes were found, they often were presented as inadequate compensations for the "obvious" drawbacks of other-than-mother care.

Louise Silverstein (1991) approached this same area of study with a differently framed question. She argues that given trends in the employment of mothers, it is unlikely that day care will disappear as an option. She then suggests that we explore how to make day care *more effective* for children and their families. What makes day care work not only for children but also for their families? This new question inspires a very different, proactive, and expansive approach to doing research. In sum, the questions we ask (and don't ask), and how they are framed, matter.

Beyond questions, designing an actual study is filled with other critical decisions. Again, considering maternal attachment, who will participate? What about paternal separation? What will be measured? Why separation *anxiety*? Why not relief after a weekend of sibling fights, facing stacks of work to do on the job, with the security that providers are caring and well trained, and with kids happy to see their friends? Where will we study them? In high-quality day-care centers, in laboratories...? Who will study them? Government agents pushing workfare, graduate student novices...? What if problems are found? How do we interpret these? Bad kids, bad moms, bad providers, inadequate provisions? Where can we disseminate these findings? Magazines, political pamphlets, newspapers, scholarly journals? Each and every one of these decisions matters, so we need to think critically about them.

Innovations in Research

The traditional experimental approach in psychology drew on the philosophy of **positivism**, the belief that there is an objective truth out there and the job of scientists is to dis-

Box 2.3
The more politically controversial a research topic is, the more every research decision can make a difference in the outcome, and the more clear, systematic research we need over unexamined folk wisdom. Many of these topics deal with issues involving mothers, from blending family with work to abortion and child care.

cover it (Kuhn, 1970). When we recognize all the decisions that go into doing research, the very foundation of research's objectivity seems shaky. Returning to our day care example, no doubt there are Moms who are anxious about dropping off their kids, and some days are worse than others. Was the child coughing through the night; are there family members who disapprove; does the woman like her job and find it rewarding; is the childcare arrangement stable and enriched; is there a broad public outcry that discourages separation before kindergarten but lauds it afterwards? ... These are questions about culture, history, and context that have been raised by feminist scholars (Peplau & Conrad, 1989; Sherif, 1979; Unger, 1983).

Furthermore, comparing women with men violates the keystone of true experiments (random assignment), making these comparisons **quasi-experimental** and open to all the questions about causality that come with correlational designs. Involving outside observers, and even the experimenters themselves, can raise **experimenter effects**; that is, expectations about gender roles that become self-fulfilling.

Overall, all research should be suspect, but that doesn't mean that it cannot be useful. Most of what is published in academic journals has been carefully and thoughtfully reviewed by experts (and online searches like PsycINFO can limit entries to peer-reviewed journals). Still, we have seen that publication is no replacement for thinking....

...and searching more. The best approach is not to rely on any one study or any one methodology. There are surveys, interviews, case histories, archival records, biographies, experiments done in labs as well as in real-life field settings, observations, focus groups, and ethnographies. Furthermore, there are more social and physical scientists than just psychologists addressing a question; there are historians, sociologists, anthropologists, political scientists, biologists, economists, etc. A feminist psychology of women and gender offers us an approach to doing and understanding research that is problem-centered, multi-methodological, and multidisciplinary. No one study in any one discipline stands alone to answer a question. Rather, it is the **triangulation**, the bringing together, of the pieces that helps us formulate an answer.

This is my immodest goal for this book: to integrate masses of well-done and up-to-date research to give us an evolving picture of a feminist psychology of women and gender that is more like a videotape than a stagnant snapshot (Riger, 2000b). As we discussed previously, our movie will be a work-in-progress rather than a finished product. This is both the frustration and the challenge of *doing* (constructing) psychology.

Feminist Approaches to Doing Research

Sue Wilkinson (2001) describes three theoretical perspectives for *doing* (constructing) feminist research that capture what we have been discussing here. **Feminist positivist empiricism**, the mainstream approach of American psychology, uses conventional scientific methods to observe and measure behavior. The hallmark of this approach is quantitative, statistical data analyses. **Feminist experiential research** emphasizes individual experiences and seeks to give women opportunities to express themselves on their own terms and with their own "voice." These qualitative analyses of people's experiences as they describe them in their own words often provide a richer, deeper understanding of a social process.

Looking back to Chapter 1 where I described my own work with women firefighters (Yoder & Berendsen, 2001), a quantitative data analysis approach to survey data found that both Black and White women reported being stereotyped by their colleagues. This finding was probed more fully in subsequent interviews in which the form this stereotyping took was different for the two groups. In contrast to Black women who felt overburdened as a consequence of their stereotype of self-reliance, White women felt underburdened as the result of their stereotype of fragility. Both feminist approaches to research have been used to make gender comparisons, study individual differences, and explore gender as a stimulus variable.

Feminist social constructionists claim that all that we observe, measure, and experience is mediated through language; that is, we give meaning to what we think, feel, and do by naming it. We saw this approach being used by Gough (1998) in his **discursive analysis** of men's discussions in all-male groups about feminists. This relatively new addition to the arsenal of research strategies available to psychologists not only is inspiring innovative research, but also is forcing feminist psychologists to look more closely at how we ourselves talk about things. For example, we saw that the very term "depressed entitlement" made assumptions about whose self-pay was normative (men's) and who was harming themselves (women).

Intersectionality: Diversity in Feminist Research

Feminist research overall must be inclusive of *all* women by capturing their commonalities and the richness of their diversity, both as individuals and as members of various subgroups represented around the Diversity Wheel we explored in Chapter 1. This last point about subgroups returns to us to thinking about **intersectionality**, the understanding that gender is constructed in combination with a full range of **social representations**. Feminist research necessarily must be ever vigilant about this point (Bowen et al., 2010; Chisholm & Greene, 2008).

Elizabeth Cole (2009) identifies three questions that feminist researchers need to ask across every stage of the research process (see Table 2.4). Asking "Who is included in this category?" is intended to highlight the diversity we have seen represented within social categories; within the category of women, we need to consider race/ethnicity, social class, age, etc. This question directs us to consider what groups may, and may not, be covered by our hypotheses, in our sampling, by the measures we select, through our analyses, and in how we generalize our findings. Across each of these phases of doing research, we also need to ask "What role does inequality play?" and "Where are the similarities?"

Irma Corral and Hope Landrine (2010) provide many thought-provoking examples of issues regarding intersectionality raised by asking these types of questions. Regarding Cole's second question about inequality for example, we all probably think that a dollar is a dollar, so that when we report the income of an individual, we believe it is an objective measure of socioeconomic status (SES). However, when we consider differences in what a dollar will buy, equal incomes can have unequal uses. Women and people of color pay more for goods and services (for example, cars and haircuts), food costs more in poor neighborhoods, and individual income goes a lot farther in a dual-earning than in a single-

TABLE 2.4
Three Questions that Encourage Thinking about Intersectionality in Research

Research Stage	Question		
	Who is included within this category?	What role does inequality play?	Where are the similarities?
Generation of hypotheses	Is attuned to diversity within categories	Literature review attends to social and historical context of inequality	May be exploratory rather than hypothesis-testing to discover similarities
Sampling	Focuses on neglected groups	Category of memberships marks groups with unequal access to power	Includes diverse groups connected by common relationships to social and institutional power
Operational-ization	Develops measures from the perspective of the group being studied	If comparative, differences are conceptualized as stemming from structural inequality (upstream) rather than as primarily individual-level differences	Views social categories in terms of individual and institutional practices, rather than primarily as characteristics of individuals
Analysis	Attends to diversity within a group and may be conducted separately for each group studied	Tests for both similarities and differences	Interest is not limited to differences
Interpretation of findings	No group's findings are interpreted to represent a universal or normative experience	Differences are interpreted in light of groups' structural positions	Sensitivity to nuanced variations across groups is maintained, even when similarities are identified

Source: Taken from Cole, E. R. (2009). Intersectionality and research in psychology. American Psychologist, 64, 170–180, p. 172.

earning household. Corral and Landrine conclude that when we take a better informed looked at SES, we find that it underlies a wide range of health outcomes that often are misleadingly attributed to ethnic and/or gender groups.

What We Know About Gender Differences

Over the next five chapters, we explore explanations for why gender differences exist as well as how these differences fit into a system of inequality. We examined the connection between difference with privilege, oppression, power, and systems of inequality in general in Chapter 1. In these next chapters, we build on that foundation to make these linkages specific to sex, gender, and sexuality. Because difference lies at the start of our work, we need to lay some groundwork about what we know about gender differences themselves.

Before we begin this next section on understanding gender differences, I want to urge to you in hang in there with me through some possibly challenging, but not indecipherable, considerations involving statistics. Some readers may see these references to stat concepts and tune out. Please don't. There is nothing here that goes beyond some very basic stats, and the outcome will be worth it. You'll be able to read and make meaning of a very complex tool (**meta analysis**) for reporting information about group differences (a tool that can extend to relationships—correlations—between variables as well).

Where We Look for Differences

 *Fingerprints*—what in the world could fingerprints have to do with comparisons of women and men? As incredible as it may sound, scientists actually have thought to study the "dermatoglyphic asymmetry" of women's and men's fingerprints. Dermatoglyphic asymmetry reflects one's "ridge-count asymmetry"; that is, the difference between the number of ridges on the digits of one's left and right hands. Ridges on fingerprints are fixed by about the 4th month of fetal life and appear to have a genetic link. This reasoning set the stage for comparing women and men, and lo and behold, somewhat different patterns emerged (Kimura & Carson, 1995). It didn't take long to relate these patterns to cognitive tests, suggesting that the pattern more common among women was associated with superior verbal abilities.

There are lots of questionable methodological procedures and leaps of logic here so please don't jump to the conclusion that fingerprints matter. Rather, the point I do want to make, echoing Michael Carroll (1998), is that *work that compares women and men gets attention whenever it supports prevailing gender ideologies.* If these fingerprint patterns didn't already fit with our folk wisdom about women's verbal abilities, would we be more skeptical about these data?

Remember Hegarty and Pratto's (2004) study that we talked about in Chapter 1. Students read data about lesbians' and heterosexual women's memories of their childhood play. When the data purportedly showed that lesbians engaged in more female-typed play than heterosexuals, students questioned that finding more than when the contrived data fit with stereotyping about sexual orientation. In contrast, we know better: the data should have been questioned in *both* versions because memories often are inaccurate. So, stay alert to when you do, and when you don't, automatically take a closer look.

Overlooking Similarity

Having made a value-laden choice about where to even begin comparing women and men, a second common problem rests on our very human propensity to find differences more intriguing than similarities (Hyde, 2005). Which finding is more exciting and likely to make newspaper headlines: "Women and Men Read Maps Similarly" or "Men Are Better at Reading Maps than Women"? Gender differences are more appealing to read about and to study than gender similarities, and they oftentimes fit with our folk wisdom about women and men.

But even researchers with the most unbiased intentions find themselves limited by the way we typically do research in psychology. Think back to your first statistics class or most of the journal articles you've read in psychology. The name of the game is finding statistical significance, that is, difference. We want to reject the null hypothesis of no difference, no effect, and accept the alternative. It is simplest then to compare women with men, looking for a difference between the two groups. If we don't find a difference, we are left to wonder if there really isn't one or if what we measured wasn't sensitive enough to detect a difference that really exists. Given how we go about doing research, finding a statistically defensible difference then is just more satisfying. All of this conspires to fill psychology journals with studies touting gender differences rather than similarities, and these differences then make their way into the popular press.

We can see evidence of this process in gender "differences" that seem to diminish over time. In 1974, Eleanor Maccoby and Carol Nagy Jacklin published a book, *The Psychology of Sex Differences*, which summarized an extensive body of research evidence that they read. Among other things, they concluded that women's verbal abilities were superior to men's. Thus when Janet Hyde and Marcia Linn (1988) examined gender differences in verbal abilities, they statistically compared findings published prior to Maccoby and Jacklin's book with those published subsequently. Hyde and Linn found a significant difference between these two time periods such that gender differences appeared larger before the book was published than afterwards ($d = -0.23$ before 1974; -0.10 after 1974). This pattern suggests that once the book established this difference, findings of similarity, which before would have gone unnoticed, became publishable.

I open this section with these two points because I believe they are important to keep in mind as we turn to evidence about where sex and gender differences do exist. Both points speak to the big picture here, a picture in which we may, or may not, want to think about women and men as different overall. Given the whole universe of possible comparisons we might make to completely look for similarities and differences, it's probably more accurate to say that more similarities (both in number and meaningfulness) connect all people than differentiate us.

Declaring Difference

To test for differences between women and men, researchers generally create tests to measure one or more psychological functions, directly observe women and men in action, or ask individuals to rate how they think about themselves using a variety of adjectives (self-report measures). They then compare the responses of groups of women with groups of men, statistically analyze the data, and declare that women and men are different whenever their mean scores fall far enough apart to meet our statistical criterion. This seems objective enough.

However, there are at least two serious problems with this **comparative approach**. I find it easiest to think about these problems if I visualize gender comparisons graphically. If we graph the scores from a large group of women in a frequency distribution and do the same with the scores from a large group of men, we can compare the two distributions according to (1) the mean (arithmetic average) or median (50th percentile) scores, (2) how dispersed or spread out the scores are (the **standard deviation**), and (3) how much the two distributions overlap each other. Some possible configurations appear in Figure 2.5.

Although mean (or median) differences between two groups, such as women and men, do indicate that the groups, on average, differ, they do not automatically mean that all members of one group outscore the other. In other words, two groups' scores can overlap substantially even when their averages differ significantly (Lott, 1997). Expressed graphically, the distributions in Figure 2.5(a) illustrate an average difference and no overlap (psychologists never have found a difference between women and men such that all members of one group outscored all members of the other group). Yet when we assert that women and men are the "opposite" sexes, we imply that there is no overlap between their distributions of scores. (Referring to the "other" sex or gender reduces this misleading connotation.)

Contrast the graph in Figure 2.5(a) with the way even relatively huge, real average differences overlap in Figure 2.5(b). By far, one of the largest differences between girls and boys across childhood and adolescence found to date involves simple throwing velocity—how fast each can throw a ball. Assuming that both distributions are normal and equally spread, graphs of these distributions and their overlap appear as Figure 2.5(b). Although about 98% of all girls throw slower than the average boy at the mean, there still is some overlap between their speeds, as indicated by the shaded area. Furthermore, a few fast-throwing girls outperform some boys. In sum, when one compares an individual girl with an individual boy, it is likely that he will throw a ball faster than she, but there will be notable exceptions to this rule. As we'll see, no psychological differences, nor most motor differences for that matter, come even close to the size of this difference in throwing speed. The overlap between girls' and boys', men's and women's, cognitive and social scores will

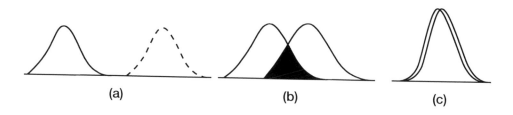

$$(a) \qquad\qquad (b) \qquad\qquad (c)$$

Figure 2.5

Line graphs of three combinations: (a) two frequency distributions with no overlap; (b) two distributions showing that 98% of girls throw a ball slower than the average boy; and (c) overlapping curves illustrating women's and men's math abilities (Hyde, 1994).

be more like Figure 2.5(c), which shows the gender distributions for women's and men's math abilities (Hyde, 1994). Here, there is much more overlap.

Our analysis so far assumes that the distribution of scores for women is similar in shape to the distribution for men. Often we think of this shape in terms of a "normal" bell curve and of distributions that are similarly dispersed or spread out (as indicated by the standard deviation). However, distributions can vary in both their shape and dispersion. For example, there could be a handful of exceptionally high scorers in one group who pull up the group's mean score, although most women and men score similarly.

In sum, the first problem with how psychologists study gender differences involves how we define difference—is it an average difference, a difference in dispersion, or a notable degree of nonoverlap? All three pieces of the puzzle are important to consider.

One final point about declaring difference before we move on is that we are focusing on **intergroup differences**. There probably is no measure on which the difference between girls/women and boys/men isn't dwarfed by the variability among women and among men (**intragroup differences**). For example, if you think about throwing speed, which shows a relatively huge difference between groups of girls and boys, recall individual girls and boys you have seen throw a ball. The variability within each sex is likely very large. Extend your thinking to areas where intergroup differences are much smaller, such as math abilities. You know intuitively that there are very skilled to very poor individual girls and boys; that is, lots of intragroup variability.

Summarizing Data

Traditionally, psychologists summarized research data by writing a **narrative review** (Hyde & Grabe, 2008). Quite simply, the author(s) read all the relevant research on a topic and reported their impressions and conclusions. More recently, computerized abstracts (such as PsycINFO) have helped to identify the work that's been done in an area, including references to some unpublished works that are too often lost to readers. A second approach takes the review process a step further and provides a list of publications and their conclusions so that studies showing (1) no differences, (2) differences favoring women, and (3) differences favoring men can be counted or tallied. In **counting reviews**, a difference is declared when the scales tip toward one of these three patterns. This is the procedure that Maccoby and Jacklin (1974) used in their seminal and very comprehensive review.

The most recent development in the area of literature reviews is a statistical technique called **meta analysis**. Essentially, meta analysis pools data from a large number of studies (sometimes 100 or more). In a typical research study, a researcher combines data from a sizable sample of individual research participants. In meta analysis, the units of analysis are not individual research participants, but rather are individual studies, each weighted for the number of participants involved in it. When large numbers of women and men are compared in a typical study, a z-score may be calculated to capture the dispersion of scores around the mean of zero. When studies involving women and men are compared in a meta analysis, a d **statistic** (also referred to as an **effect size**) is computed that tells us the degree of difference between the two groups. The d statistic tells us how far apart the means for women and men are in **standard deviation** units.

If you think about this, a $d = 0$ would indicate that two groups scored identically. When can we conclude that the difference between two groups is greater than zero? Remember that a large number of studies, each involving a substantial number of research participants, is summarized in these calculations so that it doesn't take much for a *d* to be statistically significant. But what is *meaningful?* The general convention in psychology is to consider a *d* around ±0.20 as small; around ±0.50 as moderate; and around ±0.80 as large (Cohen, 1977). Moderate effect sizes (around ±0.50) correspond to group differences that people would normally notice in their day-to-day lives and large differences (around ±0.80) are "grossly perceptible" (Cohen, 1977, p. 27). Thus, if we find *d* = +0.50 for aggression, we should notice in our everyday interactions that one gender (in this case men) is more aggressive, on average, than the other.

The numeric size of a *d* also tells us about the degree of overlap in the distributions of the scores for the two groups being compared. For a small effect size of about ±0.20, the distributions will overlap by 85% (Eagly, 1995). As we have seen earlier, overlap means not only that some people have similar scores, but also that some members of the group that generally scores lower actually outscore some members of the other group. For example, although adolescent and adult women exhibit more democratic leadership as a group than do men as a group (*d* = –0.22) (Eagly & Johnson, 1990), about 85% share comparable degrees of democratic leadership, and a few men are more democratic than many women. Even with larger *d*s, there are substantial degrees of overlap: 67% for moderate *d*s of about ±0.50; 53% overlap for large differences of about ±0.80 (Eagly, 1995).

Note that *d*s can be positive or negative depending on which mean arbitrarily is entered first. Although I would have chosen to do the opposite (consistent with my preference to put subordinated groups first), a convention seems to be popular in the literature in which a positive effect (+*d*) indicates that men typically outscore women on the variable tested and a negative *d* (–*d*) indicates that women's scores averaged higher than men's. To make it easier to go from here to others' work, I reluctantly have accepted that convention.

All of this information about *d*s is captured in Table 2.6; if you understand this table, this is most of what you'll need to know about meta analysis. A *d* score tells us three things: (1) its size and how detectable a difference is in everyday life; (2) the degree of overlap of the two distributions; and (3) which group's mean outscored the other's, as indicated by the sign (+ or –) of the score.

An overview of meta-analytic findings.   Now that we understand the fundamentals of meta analysis, let's take a look at how the technique has been used to explore gender differences. Remember that multiple studies exploring the same measured (dependent) variable must exist for the meta-analyst to do her or his work. There are all kinds of singular studies in the literature that compare women and men so where meta analysis is done, and not done, tells us something about where researchers have concentrated their efforts.

The list in Table 2.7 is not an exhaustive list of meta analyses comparing women and men. Rather, I made choices about what to include based on prior catalogues of findings

TABLE 2.6
Interpreting Effect Sizes

$d = \pm 0.20$	small	overlap=85%	not detectable, but potentially important
$d = \pm 0.50$	moderate	overlap=67%	detectable
$d = \pm 0.80$	large	overlap=53%	grossly perceptible

TABLE 2.7
Sample Meta-Analytic Differences

	d	Larger for	Size[a]
PHYSICAL AND MOTOR COMPARISONS			
Height[b]	+2.60	men	very large
Throwing velocity	+2.18	boys & young men	very large
Flexibility	−.29	girls	small
Activity level	+.49	boys & men	moderate
COGNITIVE ABILITIES			
Memory[c]	−.20 to −.56	women	small to mod.
Verbal abilities	−0.2 to −.40	girls & women	small to mod.
Math abilities	−.14 to −.16	depends on task	small
Spatial abilities	+.13 to +.73	boys & men	small to large
SOCIAL VARIABLES			
Aggression (all types)	+.50	boys & men	moderate
Helping (public)	+.74	men	large
Anxiety[d]	−.30	girls and women	small to mod.
Empathy (self-report)[e]	−.91	girls and women	large
Leader emergence[f]	+.49	men	moderate
Smiling	−.40	young & adult women	moderate
Gazing during conversations[e]	−.68	women	large
Risk-taking (observed driving)[g]	+.17	men	small
Attitudes about casual sexuality	+.81	men	large
Sexual satisfaction	−.06	equal in adults	
Moral reasoning: Care	−.28	girls and women	small
Moral reasoning: Justice	+.19	boys & men	large
SELF-REPORTED PERSONALITY TRAITS			
Neuroticism (anxiety)	−.32	young & adult women	small
Agreeableness (tenderminded)	−.91	young & adult women	large
PSYCHOLOGICAL WELL-BEING			
Life satisfaction	−.03	equal in adults, inc the elderly (+.08)	
Well-being	−.07	equal in adults, inc the elderly (−.06)	
Self-Esteem	+.21	boys & men	small

Note. Unless otherwise noted, data taken from Hyde (2005).
[a] Size categories follow the convention used by Hyde (2005) for absolute values of |d| where small = .11 < |d| < .35; moderate = .36 < |d| < .65; large |d| = .66 – 1.00; and very large |d| > 1.00. [b] Thomas & French, 1985.
[c] Single studies reported by Halpern, 2000, pp. 92-93. [d] Feingold, 1995. [e] Reported in Hyde & Frost (1993).
[f] Eagly & Karau, 1991. [g] Byrnes et al., 1999.

(Hyde, 2005) and on differences that we will explore in the next chapters of this text. I have grouped these findings into studies of (1) physical and motor differences, (2) cognitive abilities, (3) social variables, (4) personality traits, and (5) psychological well-being. At first glance, this table may appear intimidating, but if you hone in on a specific variable and think about what you know about d values and their meaning, tables like this one here and in published papers should be quick and valuable reservoirs of information.

I admittedly cherrypicked the variables I included in this table, selecting entries that have been the center of controversies (math abilities) and that we'll refer to later in this text. Given that over the next few chapters I often want to explore gender differences in depth, this abridged table gives the impression that there are more differences than similarities between women and men. Stepping back from this table to look at a fuller array of 128 effect sizes across 46 studies catalogued by Janet Hyde (2005), she notes that fully 30% of these effects are close to zero ($|d| < .10$) and an additional 48% are small (between .11 and .35). Beyond this general point, there are a few more specific points I'd like you to notice about Table 2.7.

First, nothing comes close in size to some very large physical differences like height (d $\approx +2.0$) and throwing velocity (+2.18). The difference between my partner and me (over a foot—he's 6'6") is far greater than the average height difference between the sexes (about 5 inches), yet even with a difference this relatively huge, we manage to live in much the same physical environment (although I hate when he moves my driver's seat in my car).

Second, there's no category in which all the effects favor one sex over the other. Third, we'll see that some of these (mostly physical and cognitive abilities) vary with age and with the measure used to define the targeted variable.

Fourth, the skills captured by each entry range from the simple (smiling) to the much more complex (math abilities). For example, math abilities can range from computational skills (adding numbers, which interestingly favor girls and women with $d = -0.14$) to general math performance (+.16, although a newer study [Lindberg et al., 2008] clocks in with a virtually negligible difference of $d = +.05$). We really can't say that men are better than women at all types of math, if at all.

Finally, the way we categorized the items in Table 2.7 is not the only, nor necessarily the best, way. Diane Halpern (2000) raises this question in relation to cognitive abilities, following up on the point I just made about math. Instead of using the usual divisions of verbal, math, and visual-spatial abilities, Halpern (p. 123) groups together the tasks on which women as a group, then men as a group, excel. For women, these tasks include language production; synonym generation; word fluency; memory for words, objects, and locations; anagrams; and computation. Men show superiority in mathematical problem solving, verbal analogies, mental rotation, spatial perception, and tasks that generate and use information in visual displays. Notice how some skills for both women and men cut across the standard verbal, math, and spatial categories.

Rather, Halpern suggests that we might look at the cognitive *processes* that underlie these two sets of abilities. The tasks at which women excel require rapid access to and retrieval of information stored in memory. The tasks at which men excel draw on the ability to maintain and manipulate mental representations. Still, much of how we think about these skills is divided along the lines used in our table, so we will need to keep to this typology in our later explorations. However, Halpern's insight may open up possibilities for the future of work in this area.

Interpreting meta analyses. Finding effect sizes and tabulating them are starting points from which we might begin to understand women and men. The size of each effect tells us whether or not that difference will be detectable in our everyday lives. In fact, Janet Swim (1994) compared meta-analytic findings with college students' judgments about the size of gender differences. She concluded that students in introductory psychology classes were pretty accurate in their assessments; in other words, their judgments of gender differences often paralleled the findings of meta-analysts. (If anything, students underestimated differences.)

However, the full story is never this simple. Even seemingly small differences can have meaningful impacts on the lives of girls/women and boys/men (Rosenthal, 1991). For example, a study at the University of California at Berkeley concluded that if SAT scores projected women's college grades without bias, fully 5% more women would have been admitted to their university (that's 200–300 students) (Leonard & Jiang, 1995).

Small differences also can lead to big consequences because they can compound over time. Richard Martell and his colleagues (1996) used a computer simulation to look at how small gender differences repeated over the course of 20 promotion cycles can significantly change the gender composition of an organization. They started with a hypothetical organization with eight tiers ranging from 10 top jobs to 500 lowest level jobs. The distribution of women and men at each level at the outset was equal, and the different people within each tier were given different performance scores, so that the average and dispersion for women and men at each level was equal to start, making women and men as groups equally qualified. In sum, they started with a completely equal structure with regard to gender.

Then Martell and his collaborators ran 20 promotion cycles in which the computer program fairly promoted the individuals at each level of the organization with the highest performance scores. However, before making its selections, the men were allotted a bias point advantaging them by a mere 5% of the variability in scores. This small benefit compounded over cycles produced a final organization in which only 29% of the top positions were held by women and fully 58% of the lowest jobs were allocated to women. In a second simulation, even a seemingly minute 1% advantage at each promotion created an imbalanced organization with 35% women top executives and 53% women low level workers. Small differences can have large impacts over time.

CHAPTER SUMMARY

In this chapter, we ran an imaginary videotape through time, rewinding back to view psychology's general history as well as trends in the Psychology of Women. Psychology's history was not always inclusive of women as both psychologists and as research participants. Looking back to re-place women in this history, we need to do more than simply rediscover forgotten pieces, but rather transform our understandings of history. Such a transformed view of psychology is captured in a brief history of the Psychology of Women that (1) made gender comparisons, (2) explored androgyny, (3) recast gender as a stimulus variable, and (4) looked at power through the lens of social construction.

Pausing our video on the present, these four trends in the Psychology of Women continue today. Greater care is taken not to repeat androcentric bias in our gender comparisons and to expand the promise of androgyny to a much broader range of individual difference variables such as ambivalent sexism. No longer a peripheral specialty area, Psychology of Women has developed into a mainstream field within psychology with its own college courses, textbooks, journals, and professional organizations.

Our research methods help us look back to how we got here as well as forward to where they can take us. Given the questions about traditional positivism raised by feminists and other critics, we have a multimethodological, multidisciplinary, problem-centered body of scholarship from which we can triangulate findings and draw systematic conclusions. Certainly we have come a long way—and there's no turning back.

Finally, we examined the best evidence about where gender differences appear to reside, identifying mainly cognitive abilities (memory, verbal, math, and spatial) as well as a wide array of social variables. In the next four chapters, we'll seek to explain why these differences emerge by exploring biology, socialization in childhood and across the life span, and present social context. Within each of these areas, we'll see how our understandings of sex and gender differences relate to issues of power, privilege, oppression, and systems of inequality.

SUGGESTED READINGS

Rutherford, A., Vaughn-Blount, K., & Ball, L. C. (2010). Responsible opposition, disruptive voices: Science, social change, and the history of feminist psychology. *Psychology of Women Quarterly, 34*, 460–474.

Alexandra Rutherford, Kelli Vaughn-Blount, and Laura Ball trace where feminist psychology has succeeded and been challenged since the 1980s to realize its social change agenda, giving us a vision of where we might go into the future.

Furumoto, L., & Scarborough, E. (1986). Placing women in the history of psychology: The first American women psychologists. *American Psychologist, 41*, 35–42.

This is an excellent article on history because Laurel Furumoto and Elizabeth Scarborough look at trends in women's participation as psychologists in the field that connect individual women's stories.

LaFrance, M., Paluck, E. L., & Brescoll, V. (2004). Sex changes: A current perspective on the psychology of gender. In A. H. Eagly, A. E. Beall, & R. J. Sternberg (Eds)., *The psychology of gender*, 2nd ed., pp. 328–344. New York: Guilford.

This is my original resource for the perspectives and trends in the Psychology of Women. Marianne LaFrance, Elizabeth Levy Paluck, and Victoria Brescoll provide a more in-depth look at this history and its continuing residuals.

Sherif, C. W. (1998). Bias in psychology. *Feminism & Psychology, 8*, 58–75.

I find this classic article by Carolyn Wood Sherif (first published in 1979) timeless in raising important questions about how we do research in psychology and our too common failure to put our findings into their social and historical context.

Hyde, J. S., & Grabe, S. (2008). Meta-analysis in the psychology of women. In F. L. Denmark & M. A. Paludi (Eds.), *Psychology of women: A handbook of issues and theories*, 2nd ed., pp. 142–173. Westport, CT: Praeger.

Janet Hyde and Shelly Grabe provide an accessible and comprehensive overview of meta analysis and its meaning.

Chapter 3

Sex&Gender&Sexuality
Intersecting Continua

Sex, Gender, and Intersexuality
    Typical Reproductive Development
    Intersexed Development
Biological Bases for Difference
Hormones
    Childhood Behaviors
    Core Gender Identity
    Sexual Orientation
    Social Variables
    Cognitive Abilities
    Section Summary
Sexed Brains
    Brain Size
    Brain Structures and Functions
Evolutionary Psychology
    Mate Selection
    Relational Jealousy
    Male Dominance
    Feminism and Evolutionary Psychology
Biology, Difference, and Power
    Folk Wisdom about Causality, Determinism, and Control
    Behavior Affects Biology
    Language: The Power to Name
Chapter Summary

Special Delivery

It's a baby!

Baby Jan

Born: December 31, 1952
6 lbs. 13 ozs. 19"
Helen and Dan Yoder

I happened upon the birth announcement my parents sent out when I was born. It looked a lot like the one above, but one prominent bit of information from the original is missing in my re-creation. The original was adorned with a pink ribbon and announced "It's a girl!" Check out the announcements and congratulatory cards you'll find in almost any store and most, if not all, will highlight the sex of the baby (Bridges, 1993), and they most commonly will express pride in the birth of a son and happiness in the birth of a daughter (Gonzalez & Koestner, 2005). Interestingly, daughters whose mothers more frequently told them the story of their birth exhibited higher self-esteem and stronger attachment to their mother than daughters who heard this story less often (Hayden et al., 2006).

What would parents do if they weren't sure about the sex of their baby? Usually knowing whether it's a girl or a boy is one of the first pieces of information parents get about their newborn. Although we usually take the accuracy of a doctor's immediate pronouncement for granted, how does that doctor know?

Easy answer: genitals. As you may have guessed from the fact that I asked this question, nature is not always this accommodating. We will start this chapter by looking at **intersexuality**, physically falling somewhere between completely biologically female or male. My first point is that even biological sex isn't as clear-cut as we may have thought.

Understanding how fetuses develop into girls and boys leads us to my second point in this chapter about the impact of biology on gender differences. Experiments with animals that would be unethical with humans allow researchers to manipulate biology and then note the impact of these changes on subsequent behavior. However, there are leaps of faith to be made when generalizing from one species of animal to another, yet alone from animals to humans (Weinstein, 1993). When nature deviates from the typical, it gives researchers an opportunity to look for correlational patterns in human biological development and subsequent behavior. We'll explore some of what we know about links between prenatal development and later behavioral expression in girls/women and boys/men that may contribute to group differences. We'll also review some normal biological changes within individuals that predict task performance.

Finally, we'll explore the meaning of biological causes as explanations for gender differences. We'll see that some of our folk wisdom about biology is a far cry from the more sophisticated understandings by biopsychologists themselves. I suspect that you'll come away from this chapter with a very different idea about what it means to be a woman or a man than when you began.

SEX, GENDER, AND INTERSEXUALITY

When medical personnel in the delivery room quickly look at the visible genitals of a new-born in order to declare its sex, they are informed by only part of the complete picture. The **external genitalia** of a clitoris, labia minora and majora, and vaginal orifice (a girl) are typically accompanied by XX **chromosomes**, ovaries (**gonads**), a balance of more estrogens and less androgens (**gonadal hormones**), and fallopian tubes and a uterus (**internal accessory organs**). Similarly, a boy's penis and scrotum are usually packaged with XY chromosomes, testes, more androgens and less estrogens, plus vas deferens and seminal vesicles.

Notice that by announcing the birth of a girl or boy, two assumptions are made. First, there are two, and only two, possibilities: girl *or* boy (**dimorphism**). Second, there is an internally consistent set of five components (external genitalia, chromosomes, gonads, gonadal hormones, and internal accessory organs) that sort into just these two possibilities. However, the interplay among these components is much more complex than this dimorphism suggests. A look at how the external genitals develop will help make this point clearer.

Typical Reproductive Development

Eventual female and male fetuses start out with similar sex organs (the gonadal ridges, internal ducts, and external genitalia) (see Figure 3.1). At 6 to 7 weeks gestation, every fetus has the potential (called a **bipotential**) to develop its **indifferent gonad** into either a female or male configuration.

This is where the chromosomes come in, determining whether the gonadal ridge develops into either an ovary (female) or a testis (male). If a Y chromosome is present, the tissue of the indifferent gonad organizes into an embryonic testis. This testis then synthesizes one hormone to block female development and a second set of hormones (**androgens**) to masculinize the external genitalia. The genital tubercle grows into the penis, and the genital swellings fuse to form a scrotum.

Without the Y chromosome, the ultimately female embryo develops ovaries. In a less well-understood process, the genital tubercle becoming the clitoris; the genital swellings, the labia majora; and the genital folds, the labia minora. The key points for our upcoming discussion are that a fetus has the potential to develop either way and that **chromosomes** and **hormones** play central roles during a limited critical period in fetal development toward channeling that development along feminized or masculinized paths.

Intersexed Development

Each of the five categories of reproductive parts (chromosomes, gonads, gonadal hormones, internal reproductive structures, and external genitalia) may better be thought of as a continuum, not as a discrete category that represents an either-or, all-or-nothing duality.[1] *Healthy* children are born with all sorts of combinations and variations of these parts. The old term for these people was "hermaphrodites," capturing the idea that these people are

---

[1]The following discussion of intersexuality draws on four main sources: the Johns Hopkins Children's Center website (*http://www.hopkinschildrens.org/intersex/*); Anne Fausto-Sterling's (2000) book, *Sexing the Body*; Suzanne Kessler's (1998) book, *Lessons from the Intersexed*; and Rebecca Jordan-Young's (2010) book, *Brain Storm: The Flaws in the Science of Sex Differences*.

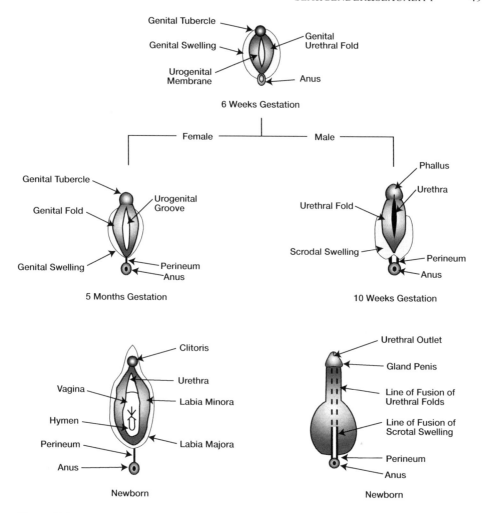

Figure 3.1

Typical sex differentiation. Development of female and male external genitalia begins with the indifferent gonad but takes a different route after 6 weeks gestation depending on the chromosomes present.

blends of female and male. However, this terminology retains the notion that there is a discrete combination that is female and another that is male, with hermaphrodites simply being parts of each (or both). A better approach is to think of continua whereby each and every one of us falls somewhere between two extreme possibilities for each of the five parts. Some of us define all the endpoints; others fall somewhere in between. To capture this conceptualization, more modern terminology has moved to **intersexed**.

Wait, you may insist. These are rare conditions, hardly meriting mention let alone such an extended discussion. You may be surprised by the scholarly estimates. No one knows an exact figure, but a reasonable ballpark is 1.7% of all live births, many of which are not obviously detectable (Fausto-Sterling, 2000, p. 51). If this still seems miniscule, consider this: at this rate, a medium-sized city of 300,000 people would likely have 5,100 people with some form of intersexed development. Being intersexed is not spread uniformly around the world; there are pockets where genetic contributions to some forms of intersexuality make them more prevalent.

Chromosomes, gonads, and hormones.   Let's play out this idea of continua of sexual development more concretely starting with sex **chromosomes**. There are an array of variations in chromosomes other than XX and XY, with the most common being Turner and Klinefelter Syndromes. Females with **Turner Syndrome** are missing a second X chromosome (XO); their ovaries do not develop, their stature is short, and they lack secondary sex characteristics. Treatment usually involves estrogen and growth hormones. Males with **Klinefelter Syndrome** receive an extra X chromosome (XXY) causing breast enlargement at puberty and infertility. Treatment typically includes **testosterone** therapy.

The middle ground for the gonads (ovaries and testes) includes all sorts of combinations involving both functional and nonfunctional ovary(ies) and testis(es) as well as fully functional pairs of each (called ovo-testes). As for the gonadal hormones, we *all* have some concentrations of **estrogens** and **androgens** in our bodies. Estrogen is secreted by the ovaries, which also produce progesterone so that we misleadingly think of estrogen as a "female" hormone. Androgens are the general name for the "male" sex hormones secreted by the testes, which include several types of testosterone.

The tendency to label these hormones as "female" and "male" ignores the fact that the adrenal cortex produces androgens in women (as do the ovaries in small amounts) and estrogens in men (as do the testes in small amounts) (Becker & Breedlove, 1992). All are involved in tissue growth beyond the reproductive system, so discussing them primarily within the framework of sexuality belies their true general growth function. We would be better served to think of these hormones as general *growth hormones* (Fausto-Sterling, 2000, p. 28). Androgens can even be converted to estrogens in a woman's body, further blurring this distinction between these two types of hormones.

What does differentiate women and men, girls and boys, is the *concentrations* of each of these hormones. But even this blurs at times. Across prenatal development, XY fetuses have higher levels of testosterone than XX fetuses between 8 to 24 weeks gestation; then after that, gondadal hormone levels are low in both sexes (Hines, 2004a). Even during the prenatal period of peak difference, an examination of the amniotic fluid surrounding the embryo reveals that 25% of the males and 9% of the females had overlapping levels of testosterone (Finegan et al., 1989). A second surge in testosterone occurs in boys from their first to sixth month of infancy (Hines, 2004a); however, only at puberty is there no overlap between girls' and boys' testosterone levels (Hoyenga & Hoyenga, 1993). In sum, both women and men possess both estrogen and testosterone; women generally have more of the former and men more of the latter. Again, a continuum better characterizes them than the dimorphism with which we began.

Genitals: Size matters.   We all probably think we know the difference between a clitoris and a penis, but they really are just socially constructed designations for different ranges along a continuum measuring the size of the *same tissue*. Of all the possible ways to assign gender to a baby, phallus size seems to take primacy in today's medical community. (Interestingly, gonads were primary in the 19th century.)

The medical community has established size standards for identifying clitorises and penises (see Figure 3.2). These are based more on psychological adequacy or appear-

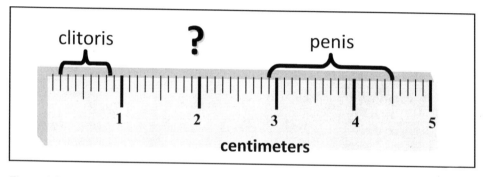

Figure 3.2
Phallus size matters. Although nature typically groups the same genital tissue into two clusters between 0.2 to .85 (a clitoris) and 2.9 to 4.5 (a penis) centimeters, a few ambiguous phalluses fall in between. Did nature make a mistake or is that what nature intended? Is tissue measuring 2.0 centimeters an enlarged clitoris or a "micropenis"? Interestingly, undergraduates estimate newborns' clitorises as bigger than they typically are (.9 to 1.9 centimeters) and newborn penises as smaller (2.1 to 3.6 cm) (Kessler, 1998, p. 100). In addition to phallus size, genitals can be ambiguous because they include a structure that resembles partially fused labia or a split scrotum, or the urethral (urinary) opening may not be at the tip of the penis.

ance than on physical health or utility. A clitoris needs to be ascetically acceptable to a future sexual partner (not too big). A penis needs to do three things: allow its holder to urinate standing, measure up to public scrutiny, and in its adult form, penetrate a vagina. To accomplish the first task, it needs to have its urethral opening at the tip. A study of 500 men hospitalized for an aliment other than **hypospadius** found that only 55% fit the standard for "normality"; most of the deviations were mild, unknown, and accommodated by their holders (cited in Fausto-Sterling, 2000, p. 57). As for sexual utility, phallus size at birth appears unrelated to size and function at puberty (Fausto-Sterling, 2000, p. 58).

Genitals and intersexuality.   *Intersex* babies come with one of three natural configurations of external genitalia: female, ambiguous, or male but with a small "micropenis," making phallus size an inadequate indicator of intersexuality. For example, XY ("male") intersex babies can have genitals that look female. In these cases, the genital tubercle developed into a clitoris, the genital swellings into the labia majora, and the genital folds into the labia minora. These babies are likely to be assigned as girls at birth despite their genetic "maleness."

XY ("male") babies also can have "under-masculinized" ambiguous genitals if they are exposed to less-than-normal amounts of androgens. For example, when there is a genetically inherited change in the fetus's receptor cells for testosterone, called **Complete Androgen Insensitivity Syndrome** (CAIS), cells cannot capture and use testosterone to shape development in a masculine direction. Given this under-masculinization of the baby's genitals, CAIS babies are raised as girls, often without any awareness that something is unusual. This syndrome is usually first detected at puberty when adolescents with CAIS develop breasts and a feminine body shape but fail to menstruate. Interestingly, it is rare for people with either complete or partial AIS to initiate sex re-assignment and to express serious discontent with their initially assigned sex (Mazur, 2005). This syndrome is relatively rare, estimated to occur in 1 to 5 of every 100,000 live births (Cohen-Bendahan et al., 2005).

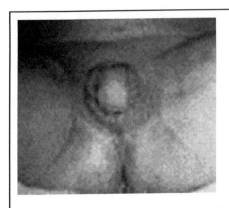

Figure 3.3
A CAH infant with XX chromosomes and fully masculinized external genitalia.

XX ("female") babies can be exposed prenatally to greater-than-normal amounts of androgens (produced by their own adrenal glands) causing their developing genitals to masculinize, even though their internal reproductive organs are those of a potentially fertile woman. These babies are diagnosed with **Congenital Adrenal Hyperplasia** (CAH). Their genitals can appear fully masculine (see Figure 3.3) or ambiguous, and they commonly are raised as girls, although some are designated as boys. The incidence of CAH is estimated at about 1 in 14,000 live births (Hines, 2004a, p. 16).

When a newborn's phallus is ambiguous, sex assignment is typically determined by a team of physicians who move quickly, often citing parents' impatience, to decipher nature's "intention" and fix the "mistake." Given that technology in reconstructive/ cosmetic surgery is more advanced for feminizing than masculinizing ambiguous phalluses, various degrees of clitoral reduction or elimination often are attempted, setting the child up for likely future operations, hormone therapies, etc. Both Suzanne Kessler (1998) and Anne Fausto-Sterling (2000) decry the lack of empirical support for the efficacy of surgical intervention, and Kessler especially documents the pain and scarring that often accompany these multiple interventions.

Some people who are intersexed are becoming more militant about medical approaches to children with ambiguous genitals. For example, the Intersex Society of North America "is devoted to systemic change to end shame, secrecy, and unwanted genital surgeries for people born with an anatomy that someone decided is not standard for male or female" [ISNA, 2011]. This organization recommends a model of care that is patient-centered, rather than surgery-centered.

BIOLOGICAL BASES FOR DIFFERENCE

Our rather detailed overview of reproductive development leads to two important conclusions. First, even biology does not cleanly sort women and men into two groups. Second, although we talk about feminizing and masculinizing development as though they are endpoints on the same one continuum, they really exist as multiple continua that are sometimes separate (estrogens/androgens) and other times, the same (clitoris/penis).

The above discussion also lays the groundwork for us to explore biology as an explanation for some of the gender differences we saw in Chapter 2. As we have seen, a fetus's reproductive structures develop in response to both chromosomes and hormones. These typically sort us into female or male categories, which are formalized at birth, usually based on genitals, with our sex assignment (see Figure 3.4). From birth on, environment comes into play so that ongoing behaviors throughout childhood and adulthood reflect an interchange between nature (biology) and nurture (environment).

A relatively new and fascinating area of study draws on a **neuroendrocrine approach** by examining the relationship between reproductive hormones in the brain and gender differences in human behavior (Hampson & Moffat, 2004). There are two major strands of research in this area of **brain organization research**, with the first looking at how prenatal exposure to hormones during *fetal* brain development may affect later behavior (**organizational effects**), and the second focusing on concentrations of hormones and their impact on specific activities of the *adult* brain (**activational effects**). In contrast to organizational effects, which are relatively permanent, activational effects can come and go within the same individual.

As you can see in Figure 3.4, the causal pathways considered by a neuroendrocrine approach are complex. Hormones, both prenatally and throughout life, are expected to affect human brains and work with them to impact behavior. We'll start by looking at research that connects both prenatal and ongoing hormones to childhood and adult behavior, specifically behaviors that distinguish girls/women and boys/men as groups. Because organizational effects presumably shape female and male brains prenatally, we'll then look at evidence for the existence of different female and male brains.

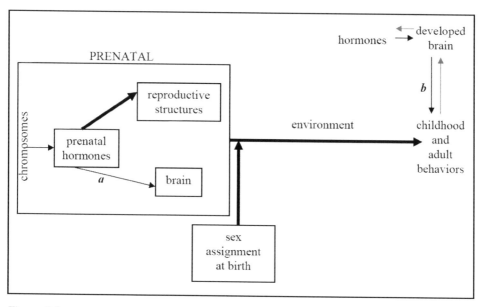

Figure 3.4

A general schematic of a neuroendrocrine approach, which predicts organizational and activational effects of hormones on the prenatal and developed brain, respectively, and ultimately on childhood and adult behaviors. A time line representing individual development runs from left to right, with boxed entries representing discrete events and open items ongoing events across the life course.

[a]Organizational effects
[b]Activational effects

HORMONES

We have seen that the reproductive hormones, estrogen and the androgens including testosterone, play a major role in how human reproductive structures, like the clitoris and penis, develop. Nature provides researchers with a **naturalistic study** of the impact of hormones with the birth of CAH (**Congenital Adrenal Hyperplasia**) and CAIS (**Complete Androgen Insensitivity Syndrome**) babies. Keep in mind though that these studies are necessarily not true experiments; rather, they either compare people with and without CAH and/or CAIS (quasi-experiments) or rely on retrospective accounts (Jordan-Young, 2010).

Because CAH babies, with XX chromosomes, were exposed to an unusually large amount of androgens prenatally, their external genitals are masculinized to various degrees. If their external genitals are ambiguous, they usually undergo genetic testing and, based on their chromosomes, are reared as girls—often after surgically feminizing their genitals and being treated with hormones (Hines, 2004b). A small subset of CAH babies go undetected because their genitals fit the standards for a penis, and thus begin life as boys. Oftentimes these boys are reassigned to be girls when other signs of CAH are noticed early in their childhood. However, a few CAH children continue as boys, providing researchers with a convenient, albeit small, comparison sample of CAH children for whom sex assignment is male. In contrast, because CAIS typically is not detected until puberty, these chromosomal XY babies who did not respond to their prenatal exposure to androgens commonly are reared as girls and remain so (Mazur, 2005).

These trends give researchers three groups with unusual hormonal backgrounds to study: (1) CAH girls with high androgen exposure, (2) CAH boys with XX chromosomes and high androgen exposure, and (3) CAIS girls who were unaffected by the androgens to which they were exposed (see Table 3.5). If androgen (which typically affects male development) is involved in differences between women and men, we would expect CAH girls to behave more like unaffected[2] boys than unaffected girls and CAIS insensitive girls to be more like unaffected girls than unaffected boys (see Figure 3.6). If CAH boys behave more like unaffected boys, this too would be consistent with an explanation involving hormones (because both share androgen exposure and utilization) and that trumps genes (because they have XX and XY chromosomes, respectively). *Thus what we learn about hormones comes from consistent patterns of comparisons.*

To control to some degree for socialization experiences, the unaffected siblings of these children without these syndromes become good comparisons. However, like all naturalistic studies, our findings remain correlational with lots of possible alternative explanations (Cohen-Bendahan et al., 2005). For example, the parents of CAH girls know that their daughters were born with a more penis-like clitoris, and the girls themselves often come to know about their histories. This could impact how they are treated and think about themselves (Bem, 1993; Jordan-Young, 2010). Although parents generally report that they treat their CAH daughter like any other girl (Berenbaum & Hines, 1992), they are often told to expect tomboyism and impaired fertility—raising the possibility that their expectations set up a developmental context that is unique to CAH girls (Jordan-Young, 2010).

---

[2]Notice the care I took in NOT using the term "normal." Clearly unaffected girls and boys are statistically *normative* because most humans develop as either XX girls not exposed to masculinizing androgens prenatally or XY boys exposed to and sensitive to this wash of androgens in the womb. "Normal" though also can connote *natural*, and both CAH and CAIS children are born naturally without intervention. How we think and talk about these issues can affect how we feel about medical interventions to change atypical genitals as well as sex assignment.

TABLE 3.5
The Relationships Among Chromosomes, Prenatal Androgens,
Sex Assignment, and Phallus Development

		Androgen Exposure or Sensitivity	
		High	Low/None
Chromosomes	XX	CAH girls CAH boys -------------- ambiguous phallus or penis	unaffected girls -------------- clitoris
	XY	unaffected boys -------------- penis	CAIS girls -------------- ambiguous phallus or clitoris

Note: The designation as girl or boy reflects the assigned sex, usually determined by phallus size and its label.

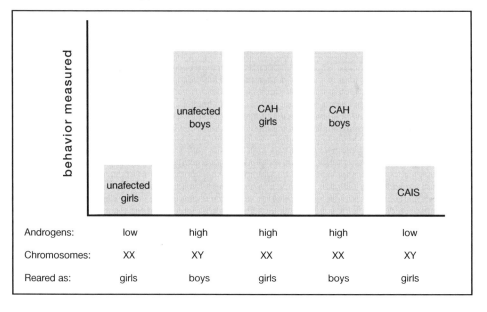

Figure. 3.6

The pattern of comparisons we'd expect in order to show that hormones affect the behavior being measured. The behavior selected to measure originally must show a significant difference between unaffected girls and boys (the two left bars). Think about what these patterns would need to look like to suggest that chromosomes or rearing are largely responsible for the difference between unaffected girls and boys.

Much of this work on the *organizational effects* of prenatal hormones so far has concentrated on explaining known gender differences in childhood play behavior, core gender identity, sexual orientation, social variables (e.g., aggression and nurturing), and cognitive abilities (Hines, 2004a, 2004b; Jordan-Young, 2010). The one area where extensive work on the *activational effects* of adult hormones has been studied is with cognitive skills. We'll explore each of these in turn.

Childhood Behaviors

Earlier studies had linked CAH girls with elevated levels of tomboyism, yet other research showed that describing one's self as a tomboy in childhood is common among women, rising to almost 80% in **cohorts** of women under 25 years-old (Morgan, 1998). The addition of comparison groups in more recent studies with CAH children, although still necessarily correlational, makes patterns of findings with CAH children more compelling (reported in Hines, 2004a), although far from conclusive (Jordan-Young, 2010).

Looking at childhood play (Hines, 2004a), CAH girls across various countries reported increased preferences for male-typed toys (trucks) and reduced interests in female-typed toys (dolls). Observers confirm these toy preferences, and they hold up in contrast to unaffected sisters who made more traditional toy choices. Playmate preferences for CAH girls ran about 50:50 for girl and boy peers, in contrast to their unaffected relatives who, like children in general, favored playmates of their own sex, typically 80 to 90% of the time.

On a more global measure of preschool activities, which catalogues a wide range of activities in 2 to 7 year-olds from wearing gender-typed clothing and rough-and-tumble play, CAH girls as a group showed more male-typical behavior than unaffected girls (Hines, 2004b). However, CAH girls' behaviors fell short of those of unaffected boys so that they scored in the middle between typical girls and boys. CAH boys did not differ from unaffected boys.

Furthermore, although we know that the linkage between human and animal data is tenuous, the findings above do fit with some evidence from animal research. For example, female rhesus monkeys purposively exposed to androgens prenatally engaged in higher levels of rough-and-tumble play than control monkeys (reported in Hines, 2004b, p. 112). These findings are consistent with a model hypothesizing that prenatal hormones permanently affect the developing human brain (have organizational effects). Yet these effects overall are relatively small, represent a narrow subset of all behaviors that could be studied, and cannot be disentangled from the developmental context in which they occur (Jordan-Young, 2010).

Core Gender Identity

Core gender identity (in which girls and women regard their fundamental self as female; boys and men, male) is probably one of the largest psychological gender differences (Collaer & Hines, 1995). Very few people report dissatisfaction with their sex assignment, and even fewer are diagnosed with **gender identity disorder** (GID),[3] which includes persistent discomfort with one's assigned sex and its gender role as well as by desires to be the other sex. There is no solid evidence to link GID with genetic or hormonal abnormalities (Hines, 2004a). However, flipping the way we look at core gender identity, there is some evidence that GID is more common in CAH girls than would be expected by the scarcity of both CAH and GID in the general population. Furthermore, some CAH girls, despite their XX chromosomes, are somewhat less satisfied with their sex assignment than control women. Interestingly, XY CAIS adults without ovaries and reared as women appear just as content to be women as women in general. Obviously, there's a lot of complexity here.

---

[3]Using population estimates from other sources, Collaer & Hines (1995, p. 62) report incidences of GID for only one in every 50,000 to 100,000 genetic females and one in 20,000 to 30,000 genetic males.

These waters are muddied even further by another form of intersexuality in which enzyme deficiencies cause genitalia to be ambiguous or feminine at birth, yet at puberty the body masculinizes (with male patterns of hair, genitals, and muscle development). These European and North American children typically have their gonads removed so that they remain as girls, in contrast to other cultures where genital variability is part of their conceptualizations of femininity and masculinity (see Fausto-Sterling, 1993). Indeed, there are cultures where more than two sexes are considered normal (Imperato-McGinley et al., 1979; Herdt & Davidson, 1988) so that core gender identity can be much more fluid. What seems to be most clear from these patterns is that the context in which these children are raised matters (Jordan-Young, 2010).

Sexual Orientation

There is some evidence to support the possibility that prenatal hormones may affect, but not totally determine, sexual orientation. CAH women are more likely to be lesbian or bisexual than their unaffected relatives and perhaps exhibit some reduced sexual interest (Hines, 2004a). However, remember that many of these women experienced multiple genital surgeries that may not have been completely satisfactory so that these experiences may contribute to the dissatisfaction these women report (Karkazis, 2008).

There is another group of women whose experiences shed further light on organizational effects regarding sexual orientation. From 1947 until 1971, a half to four million American pregnant women were given a synthetic estrogen, **diethylstilbestrol** (DES), in hopes of preventing miscarriage (Collaer & Hines, 1995). Although later shown to be ineffective, these DES-exposed girls and boys become part of our story here because DES has been shown to masculinize brain development and behaviors of animals without masculinizing their genitals. Thus DES girls parallel CAH girls in that both have XX chromosomes and were exposed prenatally to masculinizing hormones. Melissa Hines (2004a) described three samples across which 40% of 90 DES-exposed women were bisexual or lesbian, compared to only 5% of their unexposed sisters. These findings are consistent with those for CAH women without the alternative possibilities introduced by masculinized genitals and surgeries.

CAIS women are as likely as other women to pursue sexual relationships with men and to marry (Hines, 2004a). If you think about it, this raises some provocative questions about the relationship between biological sex and sexuality. Genetically, CAIS women are XY, making their relationships with men homosexual. However, according to both sex assignment and hormone sensitivity, these women are heterosexual. The conceptually distinct line between sex and sexuality starts to blur here, raising fascinating questions about our definition of sexual orientation. Maybe checking a box on a survey indicating either lesbian/gay or heterosexual is just as ambiguous as we have discovered checking either female or male can be.

Social Variables

As we saw in Chapter 2, although a huge number of social variables exist on which no gender differences have been found or have not been thoroughly studied, quite a few gender differences have been rather clearly established. One of these is aggression, which in popular lure is associated with **testosterone** (an androgen). However, the linkage between prenatal exposure to androgens and later aggressive behavior is inconsistent. On the one hand, there is no evidence of more fighting by CAH girls compared to female controls. On the other hand, CAH girls scored higher than unaffected female relatives on an aggression subscale of a paper-and-pencil inventory (Hines, 2004b, p. 138-9), possibly highlighting the impact of self-expectancies.

Melissa Hines (2004a) reviews several studies with CAH girls that suggest that nurturing interests, such as in babysitting and having children of one's own, are lower in CAH girls than in their unaffected female relatives, yet again this outcome could be influenced by these girls' expected infertility (Jordan-Young, 2010). The one study completed to date with CAIS girls found no differences between them and female controls. Showing the opposite pattern than CAS girls, CAH boys (with XX chromosomes) reported *more* nurturing than unaffected boys. The first two of these findings suggest that hormones may have organizational effects on later nurturing, and the last finding begins to implicate genes, although (as always) intertwined with context.

Cognitive Abilities

Organizational effects. Early research on prenatal exposure to androgens suggested a link between androgens and IQ, but later analyses showed that this correlation was really the result of **selection bias**. People who received hormone treatments and others who became involved in research studies tended to come from more educated backgrounds (Collaer & Hines, 1995). This is a good example of how we can be less skeptical about, and thus fooled by, data that fit with our expectations.

Better controlled research on the organizational effects of hormones and specific cognitive abilities (verbal, math, and spatial skills) finds little consistent evidence of a clear relationship (Hines, 2004a). For example, there are studies that show enhanced, equal, and impaired spatial abilities among CAH women. Studies of math abilities among both women and men diagnosed as CAH suggest *reduced* skills, rather than the elevated ones general male superiority in math would predict. However, cognitive abilities do appear to show some *activational effects* associated with adult hormones. Read on…

Activational effects: Estrogen. Again, nature sets up some interesting comparisons for researchers, involving both young and midlife women (generally with higher concentrations of estrogen than men) and young and midlife men (generally with higher concentrations of androgens than women). Starting with adult women, estrogen levels vary across young women's menstrual cycles then decline and stabilize with menopause. During **menses** (when a woman is menstruating), the amount of estrogen secreted into her bloodstream (**estradiol**) is low, not differing much from postmenopausal women. In menstruating women, estradiol levels peak by 5 to 12 times during the three days preceding **ovulation** (when the woman releases the egg from her ovary) and in the second half of her menstrual cycle after ovulation occurs. As techniques for pinpointing where women are in their cycle grew more accurate, researchers were able to compare women's performance on cognitive tests at higher and lower estrogen periods. The idea is to look for changes in scores from the same individual and see if these changes map onto her pattern of fluctuations in estrogen levels across her menstrual cycle.

In addition to the natural cycles of changing estrogen levels that women experience, there are three groups for whom estrogen levels have been manipulated deliberately. The first involves women taking oral contraceptives, which themselves vary in their levels of estrogen (and progestrin); the second capitalizes on the use of high doses of ethinyl estradiol to induce the development of secondary sex characteristics in transsexual men; and the third includes hormone replacement therapy for postmenopausal women as well as women whose ovaries were removed surgically (Hampson & Moffat, 2004). A lot of uncertainty is reduced if findings triangulate across both naturally occurring and manipulated (but obviously select) samples.

Such **triangulation** is possible with a relatively large number of studies using spatial tasks on which men outscore women with moderate to large effect sizes. The general pattern is consistent with predictions that elevated estrogens are related to disrupted performance (reviewed by Hampson & Moffat, 2004). Individual women's performance was better on spatial tests during the lowest estrogen phases of their menstrual cycles and worsened when estrogen levels rose.[4] As a group, women on the higher dosage oral contraceptives performed worst on spatial tasks, and estrogen use by a small group of transsexual men was associated with declines in their scores on a mental rotation task.

The corollary of *disruptive* effects of estrogen on tasks on which men in general show superiority is *facilitative* effects of estrogen on tasks on which women typically show an advantage. Although less studied than the deficient findings reported above (androcentric bias?), there is some convergent evidence that estrogen is related to better performance on some verbal tasks. Verbal fluency (word production) was improved at higher estrogen levels for healthy young women, and estrogen use by transsexual men was linked to improvement of their verbal fluency.

In older women, much of researchers' focus on cognitive abilities has concentrated specifically on memory. As Diane Halpern (2000, p. 92-3) points out, memory is a complex skill with no one way to measure it globally. Memories can be **episodic** (about one's own life) or **semantic** (involving facts, historical events not experienced personally, and word knowledge). They can involve grocery lists, name-face associations, short-term memories only 1 to 2 minutes old, etc. Although no one simple test of memory exists, there is a pattern across some studies to suggest that women's memories are better than men's.

This female advantage may be related to estrogen levels. In a series of studies (reported by Hampson and Moffat, 2004), women's memories for factual details of short stories and word pairs were tested both before and after removal of their ovaries (which results in immediate menopause brought on by estrogen reduction). Insuring that both the experimenters and the women themselves did not know which condition they were in, half the women received estrogen immediately after surgery and the other half did not. Women who received immediate estrogen saw no changes in their performance on memory tasks in contrast to the untreated women (taking a **placebo**) whose scores fell after surgery. Taking this study to its next step, the untreated women's sugar pills were replaced with real estrogen pills, and their memory scores improved.

Subsequent studies extended these findings to memory tasks involving nonverbal materials (geometric designs) and to women who completed menopause naturally. Additional research comparing matched sets of postmenopausal women taking and not taking estro-

---

[4]As a control, these women's performance remained stable across their menstrual cycle on other tasks for which no gender differences exist.

gen replacement found that women *not* taking estrogen committed fully 40% more errors than the other women on verbal and spatial tests of working memory. Younger women scored worse on this same measure of working memory when they were in the phase of their menstrual cycle where estrogen levels were low.

Activation effects: Testosterone. Although we are accustomed to hearing about estrogen changes in women, we seem to hear less about daily, seasonal, and age-related changes in testosterone levels in men and to forget that women have variable levels of testosterone themselves. For both women and men, testosterone levels peak in the early morning then bottom out 12 hours later (see Figure 3.7) (Hampson & Moffat, 2004). For men, testosterone concentrations are higher in autumn than spring (possibly to make births more likely in the spring). From ages 30 to 80, men's testosterone declines by as much as 50%, suggesting *male andropause*. Testosterone levels even vary by culture (possibly reflecting both dietary and lifestyle differences), such that these levels are notably high in men living in Western, industrialized countries.

Again, these naturally occurring variations set up predictions about patterns relating hormones to performance on some cognitive tasks. On both spatial and math (but not verbal) tasks, *moderate* levels of testosterone appear to promote best performance. Looking at groups of men and women, men with lower (more moderate) testosterone levels scored better than men high in testosterone, and women with higher (more moderate) testosterone concentrations outperformed women with lower levels.

Turning to changes across the day within individuals, men's repeated spatial performance peaked later in the day when their testosterone levels were lower (more moderate) in contrast to women, whose scores were best in the early morning when their testosterone levels were highest (more moderate). This pattern is diagrammed in Figure 3.7. Exploring seasonal changes, men's spatial performances were strongest in the spring when their testosterone concentrations were lower (more moderate). Finally, transsexual women who were treated with androgens in the course of becoming male showed increases in their spatial abilities.

At older ages, interest in cognitive abilities again shifts to memory. In a 10-year **longitudinal study** of men aged 50 to 91, higher testosterone levels were associated with higher scores on visual and verbal memory tasks and with less decline in visual memory with

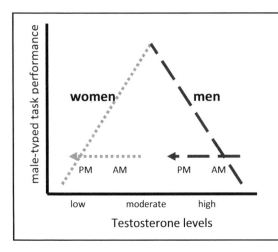

Figure 3.7

Individual women's and men's testosterone levels fall through the day, so that they typically perform best at moderate testosterone levels; that is, morning for women and later in the day for men.

age. Comparisons of older men taking testosterone supplements with men taking **placebos** showed fewer errors in working memory, improved verbal memory, and better recall of traveled routes in treated men.

Section Summary

Across all the studies we have examined here, a consistent pattern emerges that does suggest that reproductive hormones have an impact (Hines, 2010). These patterns appear both across some studies exploring prenatal hormone exposure yielding permanent organizational predispositions, as well as across some studies with adults whose concentrations of both female-associated (estrogens) and male-associated (androgens including testosterone) hormones are related to cognitive performance. The clearest conclusion is that brain organization research is likely to continue.

However, we must continually put these findings in context, including what isn't found (given the vast array of possible outcomes that could be studied), the environment in which these necessarily "post-natal" studies take place; the limitations of not being able to randomly assign people to experimental manipulations, as well as of extrapolating from animals to humans; and methodological inconsistencies (Jordan-Young, 2010). For example, Rebecca Jordan-Young (2010, p. 214) identifies "five main research models where there are data bearing on early hormone exposures and sex-typed interests." Ideally, evidence from each method would converge; however, Jordan-Young concludes that "there is no specific kind of sex-typed interest that is consistently linked to prenatal hormone exposures by more than one research model" (p. 228). Additionally, if hormones are used to explain differences between the sexes, researchers also need to more routinely demonstrate how they affect variations within the sexes (as we have seen with some cognitive differences).

Thus my goal in lending such extensive coverage to brain organization research is not so much about the specific findings about hormones, but rather about giving you the background to read this complex literature and to ask critical questions along the way. Indeed, this last point extends to the notion of "sexed" brains, which, like our reproductive structures, are affected as they develop by chromosomes and hormones. (Take another look at Figure 3.4 here.) So, let's now move from hormones to brains.

SEXED BRAINS

We already have seen that something as clearly "sexed" as our reproductive structures isn't dimorphic. Thus it should be equally clear that something as complex and still unknown as the brain should *not* be dimorphic (Bishop & Wahlsten, 1997). Rather, women's and men's brains are more similar than they are different, exhibiting no gross structural differences (Halpern, 2000, p. 194). Although the brain is involved in sexual behavior and clearly sex-typed functions, like menstruation, there is no reason to generalize without some skepticism from these functions to others, like the cognitive abilities and social variables that make up much of our list of declared gender differences.

Research in this area is still in its infancy, yet hints about subtle sex differences in human brains are intriguing. Researchers seeking brain differences have focused on size, structures, and functionality.

Brain Size

The most enduring pseudo-claim about brain size is that bigger brains signal higher intelligence favoring men (Lynn, 1994). Diane Halpern (2000, p. 196) lays this bogus claim to rest by seriously pointing to no evidence of gender differences in overall intelligence and by humorously pointing out that there's no relationship between hat size and intelligence within sexes. In fact, she cites evolutionary evidence that brains have been shrinking over the past 25,000 years, yet one would be hard pressed to make the case that our currently smaller brains are less intelligent!

Brain Structures and Functions

Three brain structures have captured much of the attention of researchers in this area. The hippocampus and the hypothalamus became likely suspects because each is linked to reproductive hormones. Interest in the **corpus callosum** followed a more circuitous route.

Hippocampus. The **hippocampus** is involved in estrogen feedback loops in adult women and is affected by concentrations of testosterone (reported in Halpern, 2000, pp.197-198). Although animal studies point to associations between sex differences and the hippocampus, studies with humans are rare. However, one provocative study found that after surgical removal of the right hippocampus, women, but not men, experienced declines in their visual-spatial memory.

The hypothalamus, genes, gender, and sexuality. The **hypothalamus** becomes a likely suspect in our search for gender differences in the brain because it plays a role in regulating the amounts of hormones, including the reproductive hormones, circulating in our bodies. In women, estrogen from the ovaries activates the hypothalamus, which stimulates the pituitary gland to release a LH-surge (luteinizing hormone), triggering ovulation. In contrast to this LH-surge, men's hypothalamus produces a steady flow of LH (necessary for sperm formation). The involvement of the hypothalamus in reproductive activities is clear and different for women and men.[5]

One area of the hypothalamus (INAH-3) can be about 2.5 times larger in volume for male than female humans (Allen et al., 1989). However, Anne Fausto-Sterling (1992) points out that there is a ten-fold variation in volumes within each sex that dwarfs the between-sexes difference and that there is a large amount of overlap such that many women are similar to many men. However, INAH-3 retook center stage when Simon LeVay (1991) reported that this cell group was smaller in gay men (suggesting questionable parallels with women) than in heterosexual men.

The next major chapter in this developing story came from research with twins. **Monozygotic** (identical) twins share identical genes because they come from one divided sperm-fertilized egg. In contrast, **dizygotic** (fraternal) twins share the same prenatal environment, but no more genes than any pair of siblings, because they developed from two independently fertilized eggs. If genes are involved, we would expect those who share more genes

---

[5]Although earlier research focused on a cluster of cells in the hypothalamus called the sexually dimorphic nucleus (SDN) in rats, there is no solid evidence for the existence of SDN in humans (Fausto-Sterling, 1992, pp. 244–247).

to be more likely to share their sexual orientation; in other words, we'd expect **concordance** between these two variables.

Pursuing this logic, researchers found that fully 52% of 56 monozygotic gay men had a gay twin brother, compared to only 22% of 54 dizygotic twin gay men and 11% of 57 non-genetically related adopted brothers (Bailey & Pillard, 1991). A similar pattern emerged for lesbians: 48% of monozygotic twins were both lesbian, 16% of dizygotic twins, and only 6% of adoptive sisters (J.M. Bailey et al., 1993). Although not all genetically identical women and men shared their sexual orientation (leaving plenty of room for environmental influences), the pattern is consistent with a genetic *component*: the stronger the genetic link, the more concordance there is with sexual orientation.

More recent, larger studies frame their data in terms of heritability. Using statistical procedures to compare twin correlations using the same logic about concordance that we just developed, **heritability** refers to the percentage of variability in a trait within a population that is due to genetic effects (ranging from zero, none, to 100%, i.e., totally genetically controlled). Kendler et al. (2000) reported a heritability estimate for sexual orientation of 62% for American men and women. Although a common pattern is to find that heritability in sexual orientation is stronger for men than for women (Mustanski & Bailey, 2003), a large population-based Australian study using an expanded definition of homosexuality found the reverse: 50 to 60% heritability for women and about 30% for men (Kirk et al., 2000).

Note that our interest has shifted here from a brain structure (the hypothalamus) to biological linkages in families, that is, to genes. The search for the "gay gene" is unlikely to come up with any single gene, but rather a *chromosomal region* (Mustanski & Bailey, 2003). Because some evidence points to transmission of sexual orientation through maternal lines, researchers have tended to focus on the X chromosome of men contributed by their mother. One particular *region*, X_q28, has proved somewhat promising for molecular biologists, although it has been ruled out as a potential site for lesbian development. In sum, the search for a "gay gene" is far from conclusive.

A second area where genes and heritability have attracted research attention concerns cognitive abilities. Here again concordance rates of monozygotic with dizygotic twins suggest some impact of genetic inheritance. Estimates of heritability in a recent study were 62% for general cognitive ability, 55% for verbal ability, 32% for spatial ability, 62% for speed of cognitive processing, and 52% for memory (McClearn & Johansson, 1997). However, there is a large leap from overall heritability to sex-linked heritability. For example, the search for a link between the X chromosome and visual-spatial ability turned up more disconfirming than supportive evidence (Halpern, 2000, pp. 144–148; Turkheimer & Halpern, 2009). Again, it seems likely that any search for genetic linkages with complex human behaviors will have to focus more broadly than on any single gene.

The corpus callosum and laterality. The human brain is divided into two structurally similar halves (**hemispheres**), popularly referred to as the left and right brains. Each hemisphere controls the opposite side of the body so that what we do with our left hand is controlled by our right hemisphere; with our right hand, by our left hemisphere. The two cerebral hemispheres are connected by the **corpus callosum**, a huge mass of nerve fibers. Anne Fausto-Sterling (1992, p. 228) draws an analogy between the corpus callosum and a phone cable connecting all of the United States with Europe. Thousands of connections run through this cable; we might cut a few to see what happens, but we'd be lucky to link a general region in one country with another vague location in another.

Although speculation that great men have large corpus collosa dates back as far as 1908 (and E.A. Spitzka), recent interest took off with Roger Sperry's work with split-brain patients whose corpus callosa were severed (through damage or purposively to relieve severe symptoms of epilepsy) (taken from Halpern, 2000). Almost every beginning psychology textbook tells about split-brain patients whose verbal and spatial skills were disrupted when their hemispheres lost the ability to communicate. These studies suggest that the two hemispheres of the brain, although structurally parallel, may *process* information differently. **Hemispheric dominance** (lateralization) refers to the relatively *greater* importance of one hemisphere over the other in processing information, not the exclusive processing of information by one hemisphere.

Generally, researchers studying laterality propose *functional* differences in how women and men use their left and right hemispheres. It is argued that typically men show greater **specialization**, with the left side more active in handling verbal processes and the right side, visuospatial processing. In contrast, it is hypothesized that women use both hemispheres more equally to engage in both forms of cognitive processing, referred to as **bilateralization**.

Research evidence for this gender difference comes from triangulating evidence from a variety of sources (see Halpern, 2000, pp. 198-218). For example, if women indeed communicate more across hemispheres, we might expect to find evidence of larger corpus callosa in women than in men. Although highly controversial, a review comes to this conclusion (Bigler et al., 1997, cited in Halpern, 2000, p. 200). Furthermore, there are some animal studies that link the size of the adult corpus callosum to prenatal exposure to reproductive hormones.

Other studies uncover some gender differences in how strokes affect women and men; how brain activity while doing tasks differs for women and men; how interfering in a hemisphere's functioning (for example, by tapping one's hand) disrupts cognitive task performance; and how divided visual fields can present information to only one hemisphere. Overall reviews of these vast bodies of research are mixed, with some reviews confirming gender differences in laterality (Voyer, 1996) and others rejecting them (Sommer et al., 2004). The best conclusion at this time is that some small differences may exist on some specific tasks (some visual, auditory, and language tasks) (Halpern, 2000; Hines, 2004a; Hiscock et al., 2001; Voyer, 1996).

The best supported hypothesis to date about *why* gender differences in laterality may exist is the **cognitive crowding hypothesis** forwarded by Jerre Levy (1969). Levy proposes that spatial performance with its required precision is strengthened if one hemisphere is drawn on more heavily to process information with less interference from competing demands (e.g., specialized is better for spatial processing). In contrast, verbal processing, which is a more global skill, is hypothesized to be enhanced if more cortical space is given over to it, suggesting better verbal performance using bilateralization (favoring women). Thus, gender differences in cognitive skills (wherein spatial scores favor men; verbal, women) and lateralization (wherein specialization used by men favors spatial abilities; bilateralization used by women favors verbal abilities) map onto each other.

Overall, the picture remains murky. Handedness plays a role in lateralization (remember that the hemispheres control opposite sides of the body and hence the opposite hand).

More men than women are left-handed—although the vast majority of people throughout the world are right handed and different cultures and historic periods have different norms about enforcing right-handedness (Papadatou-Pastou et al., 2008). Even the menstrual cycle has been implicated, such that during menstruation right-hemisphere superiority has been found for women's face perception (Heister et al., 1989). Anne Fausto-Sterling (1992) points to wider variations within groups of women and within groups of men (**intragroup differences**) than exist between women and men (**intergroup differences**). In other words, an individual woman is just as likely to differ from another woman as from a man, and there are women and men who are alike. All this argues for some skepticism concerning presumed differences in both structure and functions of the brain, and the need for much more gender-sensitive research.

EVOLUTIONARY PSYCHOLOGY

Darwin's ideas about evolution by natural and sexual selection have made their way into psychology in the form of **evolutionary psychology** (Confer et al., 2010; Gowaty, 2001). For evolutionary psychologists, gender differences and similarities exist today because they proved to be *adaptive* solutions to problems of *survival* and *reproduction* faced by our ancestors (Kenrick et al., 2004). Like the hormonal and brain ideas we just explored, it is the presumed linkage between reproduction with childhood and adult behaviors that connects our interests in sex, gender, and sexuality with evolutionary thinking.

The evolutionary emphasis on reproduction as a fundamental drive readily leads us to consider sexual selection and parental investment; that is, the pressures women and men face regarding their own *genetic* continuation through reproduction. From an evolutionary perspective, differences between women and men are rooted in their differing amounts of **parental investment**. Because women bear the responsibilities of pregnancy and lactation (often overextended to all of childrearing), for women to successfully produce the next generation, they need to invest heavily in a limited number of offspring. Men can opt for a strategy of spreading their genes widely across multiple partners, or can choose to invest heavily (like women) in a select few (for whom they want to be assured of their own paternity). Interestingly, when modern men make a more selective choice, their offspring have a greater chance of survival and differences between women and men tend to be narrower (Geary, 1998).[6]

These differences in parental investment underlie differences in **sexual selection**; that is, how individuals choose a mate (or at least, someone to mate with). Two important parts of sexual selection are **intrasexual selection** (competition among members of the same sex for *prized* mates) and **epigamic selection** (choosing partners with features associated with likely reproductive success) (Kenrick et al., 2004). Three gendered implications of these evolutionary ideas that have received strong research attention involve (1) men's preferences for fertile women and women's preferences for successful breadwinners (mate selection), (2) relational jealousy, and (3) men's aggression and dominance as means to best other men in their competition for prized (fertile) women.

---

[6]Indeed, some fascinating research begins to connect the two strands of research we have been exploring (hormones and evolution). Men who were most affected by exposure to auditory, visual, and olfactory cues from newborn babies during prenatal classes experienced hormonal changes around the birth of their baby that may facilitate paternal behavior (Storey et al., 2000).

Mate Selection

Studies of mate selection draw on surveys in which respondents rate their preferences for characteristics of mates and/or rank their preferences, as well as on content analyses of personal ads. These studies converge on a consistent pattern wherein women value status and resources, and men look for attractiveness and health (Feingold, 1992; Shackelford et al., 2005).

The most famous data come from the International Mate Selection Project, which sampled about 5,000 women and 5,000 men from 37 cultures globally about their mate preferences (Buss, 1989). This survey identified four continua on which people base their preferences, each of which involves a tradeoff between two endpoints: Love *vs* Status/ Resources; Dependable/Stable *vs* Good Looks/Health; Education/Intelligence *vs* Desire for Home/Children; and Sociability *vs* Similar Religion (Shackelford et al., 2005). Women and men differed on the first three of these, paralleling what evolutionary psychologists would predict. Women valued status/resources, dependability/stability, and education/intelligence in a long-term mate more than men. Conversely, men wanted good looks/health and desire for home and family more in a potential mate than did women.

A meta analysis of the data above confirmed the general universality of these patterns across cultures. Interestingly, although ambitiousness was more valued by women than men globally, North American women especially looked for this quality in their mates (Feingold, 1992). Using additional studies, this meta-analysis also showed large (socioeconomic status [SES] and ambitiousness, each with $d \approx -.70$) and small (character and intelligence ds $\approx -.30$) gender differences on selection ratings preferred by women and predicted by evolutionary psychology, but no gender differences on characteristics unrelated to parental investment's predictions (e.g., humor and personality ds $\approx -.10$). Additionally, these gender differences appeared in personal ads where women sought socioeconomic status ($d = -.57$) and character ($d = -.39$) more than men. These patterns held across generations from the 1940s through the end of the 1980s.

Relational Jealousy

Given evolutionary psychologists' speculation about sexual selection and parental investment, one might expect heterosexual men to be more concerned about sexual infidelity (sexuality without attachment) by a female partner (Is her child mine?), and heterosexual women about emotional infidelity (an intense emotional attachment) by a male partner (Will he stick around?). However, a recent meta-analysis concluded that when forced to choose which type of cheating is worse, both women and men picked emotional infidelity (Carpenter, 2012).

Furthermore, Christopher Carpenter (2012) found that ratings by gay men and lesbians paralleled those for heterosexuals—based on shared stereotyping of their partner. When one's partner is male (for gay men and heterosexual women), emotional infidelity is expected to lead to sexual infidelity, whereas sexual infidelity may occur without emotional attachment. In contrast, when one's partner is female (for lesbians and heterosexual men), a platonic, nonsexual emotional attachment is considered feasible, whereas a sexual, nonemotional attachment is not. Pulling all these patterns together, social explanations focused on social-cognitive appraisals of how threatening each type of infidelity is (Is it *just* sex?)

and on stereotyping of gender-expected involvement by one's partner seem to explain these findings better than an evolutionary perspective.

Male Dominance

One of the biggest differences in children's socialization has to do with the segregation of girls with girls and boys with boys. The social relationships that generally develop among girls and among boys are markedly different, in that dominance hierarchies involving a number of status-ranked boys, often engaged in open competition, are more common among boys than girls, who typically form friendship pairs (reviewed in Geary et al., 2003).

These dominance hierarchies stress the importance of physical size, skill, musculature, and social and cognitive competencies (leadership and mastery skills) that facilitate group performance (so my team can beat yours). The emotional needs of this arrangement demand aggression and fearlessness. Thus, big, tough individual boys are most prized. Coalition building among boys provides protection from other boys as well as within the group of friends. David Geary and his colleagues (2003) argue that these childhood lessons set the stage for adult behaviors that contribute to survival and reproductive success.

Notice how this thinking goes beyond the overly simplified equation of physically better men beat out other men and are chosen by fertile women. I use this example here because it highlights the growing complexity of evolutionary theories beyond individual choices into complex systems whereby what individuals do combines into patterns of behavior at a group level. It's this kind of thinking that begins to integrate evolution with culture (Kenrick et al., 2004).

Feminism and Evolutionary Psychology

The relationship between feminist and evolutionary psychologists historically has been an uneasy one (Bem, 1993; Bleier, 1984; Fausto-Sterling, 1992; Sayers, 1982). However, contemporary versions of evolutionary psychology have moved beyond claims of cross-cultural universality and beyond searches for single genes (now focused on polygenic explanations that include environmental input) to forward testable hypotheses and to integrate the importance of learning and socialization into explanations that include evolutionary components (Confer et al., 2010). Probably the best way to think about evolutionary psychology may be to see it as offering a potentially useful piece to a much bigger puzzle, especially when we want to ask not only how a mechanism works (the proximate explanation) but also *why* it exists (the ultimate explanation).

BIOLOGY, DIFFERENCE, AND POWER

I share many feminists' concerns about biological explanations for gender differences. I resent the disproportionate media attention they attract (Choi, 2001) and the objectivity they are almost automatically granted as "hard" science (Schiebinger, 1992). Most troubling, I worry about how rooting differences between women and men in **biological essentialism** can undermine progress toward gender and sexual equity (Bem, 1993).

Some very troubling ideas have come from these research areas. For example, exaggerated claims in the news media early in the 1980s about genetic determinants of math abilities misinformed some parents, who excused or even discouraged their daughters from succeeding at math because it just isn't in their natures (Eccles & Jacobs, 1986). Thornhill and Palmer's (2000) conclusion that men with few prospects for being chosen as mates (because of poverty and lack of education) are driven to rape to satisfy evolutionary urges is chilling. I cringe when I hear evolutionists talk about teenage boys whose unreciprocated dating preferences are said to focus on women in their twenties because they are fertile (Kenrick et al., 1996).

At these times, I need to remind myself that bad research occurs everywhere. We need to think about other ways to explain research and then test the alternatives. For example, Thornhill and Palmer's imprisoned rapists may come disproportionately from lower socioeconomic classes because they are more likely to be reported, caught, and convicted than men with more status and resources. I asked my then 14-year-old son about dating, and although he volunteered that a date with Halle Berry sounded awfully good, he thought it had more to do with who is sexualized in movies and on TV than mating (which then got too gross to talk about with his Mom!).

Good researchers are very clear about how their work showing heritability or permanent brain organization affected by prenatal hormones are NOT determinants of behavior, but rather establish predispositions or ranges of possibilities (Choi, 2001; Jordan-Young, 2010). No gene makes it impossible for girls to learn math! When we stop and think about it, this point seems obvious. But there's research to suggest that we all don't think about this point as deeply as we should. With hope, after reading this chapter you have a more informed base from which to think critically about these issues in all their complexity.

Folk Wisdom about Causality, Determinism, and Control

For example, consider how you feel when you see TV ads saying that your cholesterol levels come from diet and family (genes) and then going on to promote a pill. These ads are capitalizing on a common misperception that risks for illnesses with a genetic component cannot be controlled without taking a pill (Marteau & Senior, 1997). Although the biological representation of the causes of cholesterol levels is fundamentally true, some problems arise with how these facts are used and interpreted.

Turning to gender differences, Celeste Condit and her colleagues (2003) formed 17 focus groups where people came together to discuss several questions, including "Do males and females have the same genes?" Generally, people were savvy about knowing that the answer is more complex than "yes" or "no" given the reality that of the 23 **chromosomes** we all inherited, only one (typically XX or XY) is related to sex. The subsequent interpretation of what this means though divided participants into two camps: one that stressed "essential differences" and the other that emphasized "mostly similarity."

Folk theories about gender differences also vary across individuals in how much weight is given to biological causes. Most revealing is that people who stress biology are also likely to assume that gender differences will be difficult to eliminate (Martin & Parker, 1995; Yoder et al., 2007). As for attitudes about homosexuality, attributing homosexuality to biological causes only persuades people who were accepting in the first place (Boysen & Vogel, 2007).

Additionally, popular attitudes can confuse **heritability** with **innateness** (Mustanski & Bailey, 2003). For example, an attitude survey conducted with Americans in 1983 found that only 16% believed that "homosexuality is something people are born with" (innateness'). By 2000, when there had been more publicity about the presumed "gay gene," that percentage more than doubled to 35% (reported in Bem, 2000, p. 532). Innate traits are possessed at birth (green eyes); heritability refers to a predisposition or a tendency that *may* or *may not* develop. Thus, if sexual orientation was innate, its heritability score would be 100% (which it never is). My point is that by emphasizing biology as the cause of essentialized differences and by confusing heritability with innateness, lay people's interpretations of biological information about hormones, brain structures and functions, and genes can head down a path toward biological determinism (Bem, 1993), coming to accept the dictum that "anatomy is destiny."

Beyond popular attitudes, even the scientific community can be affected by folk wisdom about gender differences. In hindsight, the political biases of the scientific community are obvious in previously held, then rejected beliefs. For example, leading scientists once maintained that educating women would have the side effect of drying up their uteruses, leading to "race suicide" among exactly the people "best suited" to breed the next generation (see Gould, 1981). Today, feminist critics like Anne Fausto-Sterling (2000) caution that our assumptions about passive female development, that is, that without a Y chromosome a fetus will develop into a female by default (a conclusion slowly being challenged: see Hughes, 2004; Yao, 2005), is based more on biologists' expectations about women's passivity than on full explorations of other possibilities.[7] Where we do and don't look for biological and evolutionary evidence can reflect highly politicized choices.

Behavior Affects Biology

If you turn back to Figure 3.4, there's a vague gray line going back from behaviors to the brain and hormones. When we think of biology as a determinant of behavior, we often ignore the possibility of reverse influence. Some new strands of research are waking up to this "backwards" path, and some fascinating findings are beginning to emerge about the *reciprocal causality* between brains and behavior (Cacioppo & Berntson, 1992). I made these arrows shaded, not because they are less important, but rather to remind us how they often are understudied.

For example, we have seen that hormones may have organizational effects on the brain that are permanent by birth. However, brain development does not stop at birth. Although the total number of nerve cells may be established during the first half of gestation, glial cells (which are involved in making myelin, the electrical insulation for nerve fibers) and neural pathways continue to multiply across about the first 4 years of life (Fausto-Sterling, 1992, pp. 73–74). Even the shape and size of structures, like the corpus callosum (Burke & Yeo, 1994), change with age (Driesen & Raz, 1995; Murphy et al., 1996) and disease (Fausto-Sterling, 1992, p. 239).

We also tend to think of brain growth as something that happens through addition, and indeed this is true prenatally. The brain starts as a hollow tube, gradually adding new

---

[7]Another possibility suggests that estrogen (or other hormones produced by the ovaries) plays an active role in feminization and demasculinizing (see Collaer & Hines, 1995, for an overview).

nerve cells (estimated at a mind-boggling rate of a quarter of a million neurons per minute) that migrate out to their proper locations, until the brain assumes the adult shape we are accustomed to seeing (Kolb, 1989). At this point, the brain "overproduces" neurons and synaptic connections, both by as much as a factor of two. Much of brain development after birth involves the chiseling away of unused, excess cells and connections—something of a "use-it-or-lose-it" process. Such cell death and synaptic loss can continue at a slowed rate throughout adulthood, although most occurs throughout childhood. Brain development after birth, then, is more a *subtraction* of cells and connections, paradoxically at the same time that functions are expanding.

We might expect then that if the brain is damaged, some cells and connections that otherwise might have decayed may be retained and thus recover at least some of the functionality lost to the damage, especially for young children (Kolb, 1989). This ability to pick up lost functionality refers to the brain's **plasticity**. Furthermore, drawing on results that are far from conclusive, Mukerjee (1995) proposes that "sexual and other abuses may alter a brain region," specifically the hippocampus. Across all this evidence, the pattern is clear: *brains are not immutable and unreceptive to experiences.*

Environment can affect more of our bodies than just our brains. For example, a fascinating study of the menstrual cycles of college women living in dormitories found the cycles of roommates and close friends (defined as women who mutually reported spending lots of time together) converged across the first 4 months of dorm life (McClintock, 1971). Similar **menstrual synchrony** has been documented among lesbian couples (Weller & Weller, 1992). Thus, close social interaction among women may alter their menstrual cycles, suggesting that environment can change biology. Pursuing this reasoning further, even if biological sex differences in human brains are established, we still will be left with the proverbial chicken-or-egg question. Do brain differences cause variability in the behaviors of women and men, or do the variable experiences of women and men produce different brains?

Language: The Power to Name

We saw that feminist social constructionists look closely at language as a way to unobtrusively gauge how we think about various concepts and as shaping how we think about things. We defined sex in Chapter 1 as assuming a biological base and gender as connoting more social and cultural underpinnings. This chapter did a lot to blur the lines between sex and gender by showing that human hormones, brain structures and functions, and genes work inside a social environment. For example, even if estrogen levels do affect memory, there's training, memory aids, and individual variations that make the biological part (sex) only a piece of a complete explanation for gender differences in memory. It's impossible to completely separate out what causes intergroup memory differences between women and men. Rather sex and gender are so intertwined in working together throughout the lives of all individuals that they become inseparable. We really should talk about "sex&gender" combined in a **psychobiosocial model** (Halpern, 1997).

The same can be said for sexuality. Even if sexual orientation begins with a "gay gene," it certainly doesn't end there. Rather, it gets caught up in how we are raised ("Be feminine, wear a skirt and sit like a lady!"; "Big boys don't cry!") and what we feel is appropriate for women (dating men) and men (dating women). The lines dividing sex, gender, and sexuality blur and likewise become inseparable in their influence on each of us so that we really should talk about "sex&gender&sexuality"—inseparably combined in ways paralleling what we explored previously about **intersectionality** (Diamond & Butterworth, 2008).

Rebecca Jordan-Young (2010, p. 15) captures this point by thinking about sex&gender&sexuality as three-ply yarn. Three-ply yarn is made up of three distinguishable yet intertwined strands that are fuzzy around the edges and that would be useless if separated. Additionally, this yarn has the potential to be woven into a theoretically infinite number of patterns and products, illustrating what scientists call the **norm of reaction**. A classic example from botanists (Hiesey et al., 1942 cited in Jordan-Young, 2010, p. 273) demonstrates how genetically identical clones of plants grow to look remarkably different in different climates. Thus *genetic expression* is a dynamic, environmentally contingent process that is responsive to developmental conditions and random events.

Furthermore, we saw that even the division of biological sex into two separate and inclusive categories, female and male, is not the way it really is. Everything from clitorises to penises, estrogen to androgens, bilateral to specialized lie along continua. Additionally, there is no one definitive characteristic that alone determines one's sex.

Now think how much more complex these continua become when we talk about markers of gender like femininity and masculinity and of sexuality like gay, bisexual, and heterosexual. Is there a defining feature that makes a person "feminine" or heterosexual? In fact, try to define sexuality.[8] Is it always about reproduction? What constitutes sexual behavior? Is it behavior alone that defines one's sexual orientation, or might it involve a complex array of behaviors, attitudes, identity, fantasies and desires, and feelings? And exactly when it is that a person crosses the line from being heterosexual to gay? For example, researchers have identified a "mostly straight" sexual identity among women that is separate from those of mostly straight, bisexual, and lesbian identities (Thompson & Morgan, 2008). With hope, none of these three basic notions about sex, gender, and sexuality are as simple now as they may have been when you started reading this chapter.

This last point raises some questions about how we should talk about the differences between girls/women and boys/men that we explored here. Are they "sex" differences or "gender" differences? Some authors make note of this dilemma and then fall back on the term "sex" because their focus is largely biological (Halpern, 2000). Although I applaud that they make this point, I think that the use of "sex" to denote anything other than clear biological markers (e.g., hormones) misses the point we are making about biology being not only just one piece of the puzzle but also inseparable from gender. Given the folk wisdom that readily can link biology to determinism, I have elected here to use the terminology of "gender" differences when referring to childhood and adult behaviors (cognitive abilities, etc.). With hope, this purposive use of language will help remind us that sex&gender cannot be studied in isolation.

CHAPTER SUMMARY

This chapter may raise more questions than it answers, but I find the ways it expands my thinking fascinating. Simple things like female or male, clitoris or penis, and gay or hetero-

---

[8] See the classroom exercise developed by medical anthropologist Carole Vance and described by Jordan-Young (2010, pp. 14-15).

sexual all become murkier. Despite this complexity, there are some simple and consistent messages to take away from this review.

First, continua rather than dimorphism better capture what sex, gender, and sexuality are. Second, none of these operates independently of the others. Some behaviors in which children and adults engage, from play though cognitive tasks, appear to rely, at least in part, on hormones, brain structures and functions, and genes (including the evolution of them). Although we separate our thinking about biology from environment and about nature from nurture, understanding gender differences really is a big puzzle with many interlocking pieces. These pieces represent biology and evolution, socialization (Chapter 4) and development across the life course (Chapter 5), individual differences, and current gender roles, expectations, and statues (Chapter 6). Furthermore, the picture these puzzle pieces make tells us about power, privilege, oppression, and systems of inequality (Chapter 7).

Ruth Hubbard (1990) brings this **dialectical model** to life most clearly with the following example, which also takes us into the next chapter on socialization.

If a society puts half its children in dresses and skirts but warns them not to move in ways that reveal their underpants, while putting the other half in jeans and overalls and encouraging them to climb trees and play ball and other active outdoor games; if later, during adolescence, the half that has worn trousers is exhorted to "eat like a growing boy," while the half in skirts is warned to watch its weight and not get fat; if the half in jeans trots around in sneakers or boots, while the half in skirts totters about on spike heels, then these two groups of people will be biologically as well as socially different. Their muscles will be different, as will their reflexes, posture, arms, legs and feet, hand-eye coordination, spatial perception, and so on. They will also be biologically different if, as adults, they spend eight hours a day sitting in front of a visual display terminal or work on a construction job or in a mine…There is no way to sort out the biological and social components that produce these differences, therefore no way to sort nature from nurture, when we confront sex differences or other group differences in societies in which people, as groups, do not have equal access to resources and power and hence live in different environments (pp. 115–116).

SUGGESTED READINGS

Intersex Society of North America. *http://www.isna.org*
    This website of the Intersex Society of North America is an excellent resource for current information translated into useful language for everyday readers as well as political action on issues of intersexuality.

Hines, M. (2004a). Androgen, estrogen, and gender: Contributions of the early hormone environment to gender-related behavior (pp. 9–37).

Hampson, E., & Moffat, S. D. (2004). The psychobiology of gender: Cognitive effects of reproductive hormones in the adult nervous system (pp. 38–64), in A. H. Eagly, A. E. Beall, & R. J. Sternberg (Eds.), *The psychology of gender (*2nd ed.). New York: Guilford.
    Both chapters from the same graduate-level text give excellent, although densely packed, overviews of research on human hormones.

Halpern, D. F. (2000). *Sex differences in cognitive abilities* (3rd ed.). Mahwah, NJ: Erlbaum. (A 4th edition was released by Psychology Press in Sept. 2011.)

This clear and approachable book is probably the most authoritative resource for information about gender differences in cognitive abilities, including laterality.

Jordan-Young, R. (2010). Chapter 9: Taking context seriously. *Brain storm: The flaws in the science of sex differences* (pp. 236-268). Cambridge, MA: Harvard University Press.

This chapter explores how we need to take context into account when we draw conclusions from brain organization research, especially studies with CAH girls.

Mustanski, B. S., & Bailey, M. (2003). A therapist's guide to the genetics of human sexual orientation. *Sexual and Relationship Therapy, 18*, 429-436.

This brief article is sensitive and friendly to a lay reader interested in better understanding the "gay gene" and its implications for people's lives.

Gowaty, P. A. (2001). Women, psychology, and evolution. In R. K. Unger (Ed.), *Handbook of the psychology of women and gender* (pp. 53-65). New York: Wiley.

Patricia Gowaty writes most comprehensively about evolutionary psychology from a feminist perspective and in a style that is friendly for readers not well versed in evolutionary terminology.

Chapter 4

Growing Up
Learning to Be Ourselves in a Gender-Polarized World

Difference: Girls Will Be Girls
    Beliefs About Gender
    Gender Identity
    Preferences
    Behavioral Enactment
Explaining Differences
Children's Relationships: Psychoanalysis
Children's Learning: Socialization Theories
Social Cognitive Theory
    Building One's Gender Schema
    Self-Regulation and Efficacy
    Gendered Culture
Differential Treatment by Socializing Agents
    Parents and Families
    Schools and Teachers
    Peers
    Media
Dynamic Learning
An Integrated Understanding
Breaking the Cycle
Chapter Summary

Jot down a few words to describe each 9-month-old child. How strong, cute, sturdy, cuddly, confident, and fragile is each baby?

You just participated in a "Baby X" study. You know nothing about the babies pictured, but you have a first impression similar to any initial reaction when you first meet someone. Commonly it's hard to tell the sex of babies, so we look for clues in their dress and surroundings to make these judgments. The girl on the left is clothed in her holiday finery and is sitting in one of her presents, a sled, with her new Cabbage Patch doll. Pretty cute and cuddly. The boy on the right is dressed for some serious play in overalls and Nikes and is about to throw that ball. He looks sturdy and ready for action. Do your descriptions capture these gender-related differences? How did they come about?

As you may have guessed, the two baby pictures are of my daughter, Kate. In a series of 23 "Baby X" studies similar to this one,[1] people repeatedly described the "girl" as more feminine and the "boy" as more masculine (Stern & Karraker, 1989). The central point I want to make here is not that you can be fooled into giving different descriptions, but rather that it's impossible to tell which came first: Kate's true essence ("girls will be girls…") or how she is socially constructed through her interactions with others ("people expect girls to be girls…").

Two major foci organize this chapter. First, we'll need to establish that girls as a group and boys as a group differ in key ways. Our focus here is not so much on whether or not differences exist (popular wisdom assumes that they do), but rather on identifying where systematic differences do and do not exist. We need to keep in mind throughout this overview that we are talking about groups, not individuals. Individual girls and boys do all kinds of different things, but we'll concentrate on consistent **intergroup differences** across girls as one group and boys as another as well as on developmental trends over time as girls and boys grow up.

---

[1] Only two of these 23 studies used photographs; the remainder used either videotapes of or direct interaction with "Baby X." In addition, in the real studies, people interacted with only one dressed-up version of the same child.

The second, more interesting focus questions why intergroup differences in girls and boys occur. In this chapter, we'll explore the experiences of girls and boys throughout childhood. **Psychoanalysis** (with its roots in Freud's thinking) may help us understand the dynamics of parenting. **Socialization theorists** will expose gendered treatment by socializing agents (parents, schools, peers, and the media) as well as the cognitive development of children themselves. Most important, we'll examine how children's experiences help maintain a system of inequality that privileges and empowers boys over girls.

DIFFERENCE: GIRLS WILL BE GIRLS...

Diane Ruble, Carol Lynn Martin, and Sheri Berenbaum (2006)[2] pulled together much of the empirical work comparing girls and boys and offered a helpful framework to organize their summary. They clustered findings into four global content areas: (1) general concepts or beliefs about gender, (2) gender identity or self-perception, (3) preferences, and (4) behavioral enactment and adoption. The following overview captures the general developmental trends that run across these four content areas, recognizing that our concentration on differences overlooks many shared similarities between girls and boys (Hyde, 2005).

Beliefs about Gender

Infants as young as 3 to 4 months can distinguish between male and female faces, and by 6 months can do so without hair or clothing cues. By around 2 years, children can match pictured faces to the labels of female and male, and they begin to use these labels—which, in turn, predicts increases in gender-typed play (Zosuls et al., 2009). Beyond simple labeling, a key developmental step in children's understanding of sex and gender is to grasp **gender constancy**; that is, to realize that girls will be female throughout their lives and never will be male, and vice versa for boys

For example, my son, Dan, at age 3 declared that he wanted to be a mom when he grew up. When we challenged him on this declaration, he thought for a moment and conceded that if he couldn't be a mother, he'd settle for being a lion. It was clear that Dan, like most 3-year-olds, hadn't achieved a stable understanding of his sex. A few theorists believe that gender constancy is achieved around age 3 to 4, with most agreeing that Dan will have accomplished this understanding by age 6 to 7. Achieving an understanding of gender constancy lays the groundwork for doing gender-typing (Arthur et al., 2009).

As early as 2-years old, children start to understand some concrete gender stereotypes, such as matching a gender-typed toy with the face of a child (a doll with a girl). Stereotype knowledge of both child and adult activities expands greatly from ages 3 to 5, topping out around kindergarten or first grade. Stereotype knowledge about less concrete social and personal qualities (aggressiveness and politeness) emerge a bit later (around age 5) increase steadily across elementary school, and are more rigidly applied by children to children than to adults. Preschoolers' gender-typing extends to styles (colors and clothing) and symbols (butterflies for girls and grizzlies for boys). For example, I clearly

---

[2]Unless otherwise indicated, the findings reported in this major section are based on research reviewed by Ruble, Martin, and Berenbaum (2006; also see Halim & Ruble, 2010). Please see Ruble et al. for specific citations, although updates to their review are cited throughout this section.

remember Kate painstakingly using "girl" and "boy" colors for the thank-you notes she was drawing.

Generally, girls are more knowledgeable about gender stereotypes and also are more flexible in their personal acceptance of them. Through adolescence, increasing cognitive flexibility competes with increasing pressures to conform to adult stereotypes, leading to fluctuations in the flexibility of adolescents' gender-typing.

As for girls' and boys' relationships, young children regard these similarly, but increasingly different perceptions begin from 4 to 6 years-old. By preschool children realize that boys prefer to play in groups and are more competitive (Weinberger & Stein, 2008), and preschoolers will use gender as a reason to exclude others from their play. By ages 9 to 11, children's conceptions of friendships differ, with girls stressing intimacy and boys, power and control. By age 10, children will acknowledge that girls and women are less valued than boys and men.

Throughout the above review, there are few differences between what girls and boys as *subjects* think. Differences are much more common in perceptions of and expectations for females and males as *objects* of thought (stereotyping). Girls and boys hold consistent beliefs about expected differences between girls and boys, reflecting folk wisdom that girls will be girls....

Gender Identity

Gender identity refers to how we perceive ourselves as female and male. At the most basic level, this is anatomic, but it also includes how we present ourselves as female or male. Thus, our gender identity includes how we label ourselves (woman or man), how we view our activities and interests (being a mother and liking football), how we perceive our own personality characteristics (caring and being assertive), and how we regard our social relationships, including our friendships and sexual orientation (Halim & Ruble, 2010).

Most children can accurately label themselves as a girl or boy by around 18 to 24 months, and by 27 to 30 months they can sort a photo of themselves into a pile of same-sex children. By 8 to 9 years most girls and boys rate themselves consistent with gender-typed patterns of traits. Identifying oneself retrospectively as a "tomboy" is normative for women, especially in younger cohorts (Morgan, 1998), is typically socially acceptable, is unrelated to adult sexual orientation (Peplau et al., 1998), and predicts greater **agency** (feeling in control) in adulthood (Volkom, 2003).

Preferences

Satisfaction with one's *assigned sex* is almost universal, although around age 13 a gender difference does emerge, such that more girls than boys wish to switch. High school girls in the 1980s were more content than those growing up in the 1950s.

Trends for *toy and activity* preferences parallel patterns for stereotype awareness. More rigid gender-appropriate preferences develop during the preschool years, peaking around kindergarten. Even in relatively egalitarian countries like Sweden, children's toy boxes reflect stereotyping (Nelson, 2005). Gender-consistent play activities reach over 80% by age 4 and then become almost universal by age 7. Girls show less investment in being congruent than boys, becoming less rigidly gender-typed than boys during the middle grades.

Children's reported and observed preferences for *same-sex peers* are solidly documented, and they appear universal across non-Western and Western cultures. Children are more drawn to their own sex than actively avoidant of the other sex. There are several reasons why girls may prefer girls; and boys, boys. First, girls tend to share a belief that similarity of feelings is important, in contrast to boys, who generally report similarity in activities and interests. Second, the sexes vary in their interactional styles. Play for girls is marked by cooperation, politeness, and interaction with others, in contrast to boys' play, which is more rough-and-tumble, aimed at attaining dominance, and restrictive of interaction. Third, children (especially those who view gender as important; Susskind & Hodges, 2007) show patterns of **in-group** evaluative bias, such that girls assign more positive qualities to girls and boys to boys (Robnett & Susskind, 2010). Fourth, boys value gender equality less than girls, becoming especially negative in 6th to 8th grades, in contrast to girls, for whom valuation of gender equality increases. Finally, children themselves like peers better when they play stereotypically with same-sex friends (Colwell & Lindsey, 2005). All these combine to make being with girls more appealing for girls, and being with boys more attractive to boys.

Finally, *appearance* is more sanctioned for boys and *play style* for girls. Children are intolerant of boys who wear feminine hairstyles and clothes as well as girls who play like boys (Blakemore, 2003). Not surprisingly, when my son at age 2 borrowed his big sister's barrettes to "look pretty" for a parade, he was immediately pressured by his peers to remove them.

Behavioral Enactment

This final content category deals with the activities girls and boys do day to day, especially toy and activity choices. Overall, gender-congruent play becomes quite stable as early as 2 to 3 years. Boys more actively avoid gender-incongruent *play* than girls. From ages 5 to 13, how boys generally spend their leisure time becomes more masculine, whereas for girls, their television viewing becomes more feminine while their toy preferences, computer games, and sports become less feminine (Cherney & London, 2006). Girls' leisure time is more often spent shopping and socializing; boys' time is spent in less structured activities and sports. Girls spend more time doing indoor tasks; boys, outdoor chores.[3] These differences don't mean that girls always do girl-congruent activities, and boys, boys', but the overall pattern lead Martin and her colleagues (2006, p. 869) to conclude that, at least during preschool, "the two sexes engage in such different activities, they are almost like two separate cultures."

Extensive research on *cognitive skills* turns up some gender differences in children, although there are no gender differences in overall intellectual ability. The largest area of difference involves spatial skills (see Chapter 6 for more on cognitive skills). Turning to *physical performance*, boys are more active (Campbell & Eaton, 1999) and better at physical activities, in contrast to girls, who perform better on fine eye-motor and flexibility tasks.

---

[3]How children and adolescents spend their time varies widely globally yet remains gendered. For example, youth in nonindustrial societies spend most of their time doing work, with girls doing unpaid household labor, and boys being paid and drawn away from home (Larson & Verma, 1999).

Box 4.1
Over 90% of Halloween costumes are gender-typed and often depict heroes (Nelson, 2000). Girls' costumes depict beauty queens and princesses, as well as traditional roles, animals, and foodstuffs. For boys, warriors and villains dominate.

In the area of *social skills*, differences in aggressiveness are most pronounced in childhood, with boys being more aggressive. Storytelling by boys has more aggressive content, in contrast to prosocial content by girls (Strough & Diriwaechter, 2000). Self-report measures show girls to be more empathetic than boys, but physiological and unobtrusive measures yield no differences. Early similarities in the expression of emotions diverge in elementary school, when girls begin to express less anger (Cox et al., 2000) and emotions that might hurt others' feelings, and boys start to hide negative emotions like sadness (Oliver & Green, 2001). Girls understand complex emotions better than boys (Bosacki & Moore, 2004).

Regarding *social relationships*, we already have seen that gender segregation among peers is common. In fact, 4-year-old children interact with same-sex peers 3 times more often than with other-sex peers. By age 6, this difference expands to 11 times more often with same- than other-sex playmates. Even though both girls and boys acquire more other-sex friends from grades 6 through 10, young women's and men's friendship networks in Grade 10 remain 75% same-sex (Poulin & Pedersen, 2007). Thus, children's and young adults' worlds outside the home are likely to be gender-segregated as measured by both actual behaviors and preferences, thus reinforcing a self-perpetuating cycle whereby preferences shape choices, and the experiences resulting from these choices affect preferences.

EXPLAINING DIFFERENCES

Although certainly not completely polarized, a strong case can be made for two different patterns for growing up: one for girls and another for boys. Throughout the above descriptions I tried to keep my narrative just that—*descriptive*. We have reviewed evidence that girls and boys share similar concepts of differences between what's female and male; may develop identities that encompass different gender **scripts**; and exhibit different preferences for assigned sex, toys and activities, peers, appearance, and play style. Furthermore, children engage in different behavioral patterns of play; cognitive, physical, and social behavior; and social interaction. Our next step will be to be to explain these differences. We'll concentrate on two dominant approaches: psychoanalytic and socialization.

CHILDREN'S RELATIONSHIPS: PSYCHOANALYSIS

Classic Freudian psychoanalysis describes women's and girls' development as a deviation from a male model (**androcentrism**) and is rooted in the assumption that anatomy is destiny (**biological essentialism**). Many of Freud's successors in psychoanalysis digressed from the original theory by rejecting both. Instead, they posited a variety of social influences to explain, among other things, how gender identity is learned. The common threads linking these Neo-Freudian theories to psychoanalysis are fundamental beliefs in the primacy of childhood relationships with parents (mostly mothers) for personality development (Jacklin & McBride-Chang, 1991), the stages of psychosexual development (including the critical phallic stage), the power of unconscious motives, and the importance of childhood experiences in affecting stable personality and later relationship formation (Westen, 1998).

One contemporary, feminist, psychoanalytic reformulation of the **phallic stage** of development is offered by Nancy Chodorow in her widely acclaimed book, *The Reproduction of Mothering* (1978). Chodorow begins her analysis with the Western cultural norm for families composed of an employed father, nonemployed mother, and children. (Chodorow realizes that this does not describe the majority of families today, but it is what we think of as the "ideal" family.) She agrees with Freud that prior to entering the phallic stage, girls and boys are privy to an ideal emotional relationship with their mother (at least from the child's perspective) that is exclusive, intense, and characterized by boundary confusion such that the child does not feel separate from the mother. In other words, the mother is there to meet the child's every need—and selflessly does so.

With the onset of the phallic stage, mothers come to treat their sons as sexual objects (psychologically, not physically) because: (1) the father is distant and less affectionate (he's off at his job a lot), and (2) she, like the rest of society, overvalues males. This sets up the classic Freudian **Oedipal complex**, such that the boy, who also sexually desires his mother, wants to be rid of his father. This stage is successfully resolved when the boy shifts his identification from his mother to his father, thus developing his own heterosexuality and masculinity. An essential part of his masculinity involves his rejection of the mother, symbolically generalizing to all that is feminine. In addition, because his father is away a lot, the masculinity that the boy develops does not come from direct contact with his father, but rather is culled from the culture as a whole. Thus the boy's masculinity is more stereotyped than directly modeled. In addition, as part of masculine stereotyping, the boy adopts a logical, rational orientation so that he thinks as a detached, analytic problem solver. This orientation encourages him to strive for autonomy and to be anxious about forming emotional ties with others.

A girl also enters the phallic stage having been in an ideal pre-Oedipal relationship with her mother. Freud believes that the **Electra complex** is triggered for a girl when she realizes that she has no penis. However, Chodorow points out that Freud never explains why a girl suddenly comes to "miss" her "lost" organ. Chodorow argues that what a girl does come to realize at this stage is not that her mother castrated her, but that boys are preferred by mothers (and society as a whole) and that boys are granted greater independence than girls. This creates ambivalence for the girl in her relationship with her mother: on the one hand, she wants to retain her warm, fuzzy attachment to her mother; on the other hand, she'd like to be both independent and loved like a son.

All is achieved to some degree by identifying with her mother so that the girl develops her own heterosexuality and femininity. In contrast to the boy's masculinity, the girl's femininity is learned in direct interaction with her mother so that she develops a hands-on gender identity (that is not undermined by the girl's resentment that her mother castrated her, as Freud believed). In fact, there is research evidence finding that daughters at age 4 to 5 show signs of more intense closeness to their mother than sons (Benenson et al., 1998). As part of her femininity and in relations with her mother, the girl develops a strong relational, nurturing orientation (for empirical support, see Finlay & Love, 1998).

Chodorow then plays out the maturation of these children. Both have become heterosexual so they form adult relationships with the other sex. If they pursue the norm of the "ideal" family, the rational man will be employed, the relational woman will turn to her sons to fill the emotional gap left by the distant, logical/rational father, and the whole cycle will reproduce itself.

Chodorow calls for dual-parenting to break this cycle. If fathers, as well as mothers, participate in the raising of their children, then boys will develop a version of masculinity that is hands-on and that includes the care and nurturing of children. (It seems logical to extend this reasoning to dual-employment so that girls internalize the independent, rational aspects of their employed mothers into their directly acquired version of femininity—but this goes beyond Chodorow's speculation.) A potential Catch-22 of this argument is that the work of parenting may not be compatible with men's rational, nonrelational orientation. Despite this limitation, the main point for us is that Chodorow offers a version of psychoanalytic reasoning that is true to the major underpinnings of psychosexual development without relying on biological determinants of personality development, and instead drawing on feminist understandings of male dominance, compulsory heterosexuality, and sexist stereotyping.

Nancy Chodorow's theory lacks the extensive empirical grounding we'll see underlying the socialization theories we consider next, and her model is rooted in a European-American framework, although other authors have expanded its reach (for example, see Segura & Pierce, 1993). However, Chodorow makes at least three important points. First and foremost, change is possible; personality development is not slavishly attached to whether or not an individual possesses a penis. Second, she links intrapsychic development to broad social structures; it is society's framing of families as employed men with dependent wives and children that underlies and maintains the cycle of mothering. And third, Chodorow's analysis strikes a resonant chord with feminist activists who advocate equal sharing of childrearing responsibilities.

CHILDREN'S LEARNING: SOCIALIZATION THEORIES

Socialization theories stress that culture is passed on to children through active learning. Because girls and boys are treated differently, they actively learn different aspects of the culture through a process of **gender differentiation** (or gender-typing). Thus, *socialization takes place within a gendered social context.*

Kay Bussey and Albert Bandura (1999; 2004) proposed **social cognitive theory** as a comprehensive model of socialized learning and then applied this model specifically to

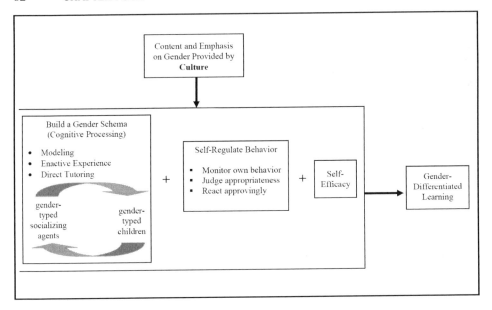

Figure 4.2

Social cognitive theory's model of gender-differentiated learning draws on three principles fundamental to general socialization theories: (1) socializing agents treat girls and boys differently; (2) children dynamically interact with socializing agents to build their own gender schema, which they self-regulate; and (3) these processes are shaped by culture.

gender differentiation. This model, diagrammed in Figure 4.2, brings together three important pieces of former socialization theories: (1) socializing agents, (2) the dynamics of a child's active learning, and (3) culture. We first lay out this model then go on to explore research evidence supporting it.

SOCIAL COGNITIVE THEORY

An important part of learning about gender involves building a **gender schema**; that is, an internal cognitive framework that helps the child organize and understand the meaning of female and male (Bem, 1981; Martin & Halverson, 1983; Markus et al., 1982). This gender schema is developed through two general learning processes whereby new information is **assimilated** into existing schema, and the schema themselves are adjusted to **accommodate** new, discordant information.

Building One's Gender Schema

Constructing one's gender schema depends on the interaction of the child with **socializing agents** including parents, schools, peers, and the media. These socializing agents serve as sources of information for children: they enact behaviors that children can observe so as to uncover the underlying rules and structures of one's culture (**modeling**); they reward and punish the behaviors tried out by children and thus teach them what works to get children

Box 4.3

Sociocognitive theorists emphasize that children actively build their own gender schema so that we'd expect the stereotypes they hold about gender to bias their memories. Joshua Susskind (2003) showed second and fourth graders a series of pictures depicting women and men engaged in stereotypic, neutral, or counterstereotypic (like the one here) activities, repeating different pictures for different children. Children then rated how many times they saw each picture. Children's frequency estimates were greater for stereotyped than other pictures, suggesting that they remembered (assimilated) pictures better if they fit into their gender schema.

what they value and what doesn't work (**enactive experience**); and they directly tell children what they expect of them and others as girls and boys, women and men (**direct tutoring**). Sometimes there are consistent patterns across these experiences, but oftentimes, there are contradictions, even from a particular socializing agent. For example, it's not uncommon for parents to preach egalitarianism, yet most domestic work and responsibilities are shouldered by a woman.

Socializing agents don't simply impose their gender-typing onto unsuspecting children. Rather, children build their gender schema through active engagement with socializing agents. Socialization theorists have moved toward recognizing that not only do socializing agents treat girls and boys differently, but also girls and boys can become gender-typed themselves so that they encourage gender-typed treatment (Crouter & Booth, 2003).

Self-Regulation and Efficacy

So far, we've explained how a child builds her or his own gender schema. We now need to explain how these cognitive understandings of sex and gender translate into behavior that is different for girls and for boys. A key in this process is to shift regulation of one's behavior from external socializing agents to *self-regulating* ones. To make this shift, children need to monitor their own gender-linked conduct, make judgments about the appropriateness of what they are doing, and react in either self-approving or disapproving ways. In sum, children need to match what they are doing against what they are thinking.

Central to making "good" matches between cognition and behaviors is personal **agency,** or self-efficacy. **Self-efficacy** is the belief that one has the capabilities to produce positive outcomes for one's self. Thus, cognitive understandings of gender identity, gender constancy, and knowledge of gender stereotyping become linked to gender-differentiated behavior by this matching process.

To bring this model to life, consider one of the most central gender differences found by researchers and one that is especially promising for integrating the theories—sex-segregated play and preferences (Ruble et al., 2006). One of the strongest models of children's sex-segregated play is adults' sex-segregated employment: children typically see women working with women and men with men. They also observe adult women interacting more, and more closely, with women friends and men with men friends. In terms of enactive experience, children who attempt to cross gender boundaries may experience negative outcomes (derision). Girls who seriously and aggressively play sports and boys who head for the doll corner are likely to encounter some negative reactions. Finally, parents may directly instruct girls to play with girls and invite all girls to play; peers may openly redirect cross-gender behavior; schools may have girls line up in one place and boys in another; and the media may openly mock children who attempt to play with the "wrong" group. Thus, girls learn to be with girls and boys with boys because of what they see (modeling), what they try out (enactive experience), and what they are told (direct tutoring).

Consistent with this gender schema, then, an individual girl begins to monitor her own behavior, playing more and more with only girls and avoiding boys and masculine activities. We end up with a girl who lives mostly in a world of girls. In sum, we produce a gender-differentiated behavior that continues on its own accord and is repeated across the child's life course.

Gendered Culture

Why do children build a gender schema rather than schema based on other features (e.g., eye color)? Sandra Bem (1993) answers that it is because gender is so salient and pervasive in our gender-polarized culture. Just look at our previous review of developmental trends and notice how young children are when they start recognizing and using gender categories. The primacy of gender as a social category encourages children to attend to and process gender-relevant information. Indeed, children's actions have been shown to vary according to the salience of gender in specific contexts (Messner, 2000).

Thus gender differentiation takes place within a specific cultural context so that **femininity** and **masculinity** are expressed in ways unique to that context (see Leaper, 2000). This approach is also useful for bringing multicultural elements beyond gender (such as the impact of race and ethnicity, class, religion, etc.) into our understanding of socialization processes (Reid et al., 1995). For example, the degree of acculturation of six ethnic groups of women is associated with gender differentiation such that those more in tune with American culture display more Americanized gender stereotyping (Sassler, 2000).

Socialization theorists (as well as others) induce their ideas from a large body of research concluding that growing up female is different from growing up male. I summarize this research in the next section. But before we get caught up in this specific research, I want to point out two patterns that others (Sandra Bem and Hilary Lips) have gleaned from their reviews. Both draw on our understanding that there's more to difference thinking than simple, value-free difference. Rather, there's power and oppression in differences that extend beyond individuals to construct a more pervasive, and often self-sustaining, system of inequality.

Sandra Bem (1993) points to the consistent pattern of greater rigidity of gender role socialization for boys than girls. Our sanctions for deviant boys ("sissy," "gay") are much stronger than for girls ("tomboy"). This pattern speaks volumes about the overall tendency in our society to prize masculine and devalue feminine activities. When girls seek out masculine activities, they understandably are going for what our society values. When boys participate in the feminine sphere, they are both rejecting their valuable birthright and settling for less (Bem, 1993, pp. 149–151). Given this reasoning, boys' deviations commit a much bigger mistake than girls'.

Homophobic fears also help to sustain this pattern, with socializing agents anxious that feminine leanings in boys may be early signs of adult homosexuality (Sandnabba & Ahlberg, 1999). Indeed, the **sexual orientation hypothesis** proposes that men and boys acting in feminine ways are more likely to be perceived as gay than girls and women with masculine leanings (McCreary, 1994). This presumed linkage between "feminine" males and homosexuality is consistent with the combination of findings that more fathers insist that sons do not violate gender-role dictates for play (Turner & Gervai, 1995), that boys are more likely to believe that their father will disapprove of cross-gender behavior (Raag & Rackliff, 1998) and that men hold more negative attitudes about homosexuality (Whitley & Kite, 2010). In general, parental homophobia and traditional gender-role attitudes go hand-in-hand (Holtzen & Agresti, 1990).

Hilary Lips (2002) highlights patterns in research findings whereby girls learn a habit of silence, self-doubt, and acquiescence (powerlessness). In contrast, boys consistently appear to be encouraged to achieve mastery over tasks and influence over people (power). Although both girls and boys arguably start with the same potential to develop wings and take flight, Lips asserts that a fundamental, pervasive **meta-message** that comes through for girls serves to clip their wings and hold them back. She sums up the socialization of girls as conveying a **cultural preparedness for powerlessness**.

As we now turn to research findings, consider who has the most to gain from adhering to these practices. Would I benefit my son as much as my daughter by following rigid gendered dictates in American culture? Given our valuation of those traits and behaviors that accompany the agentic masculine role, clearly my son has more to gain by sticking to them. When we factor in other forms of oppression, it becomes more and more understandable that women and girls, as well as those subordinated based on other statuses (such as race and sexual orientation), would have even less to gain by promoting gender polarization.

DIFFERENTIAL TREATMENT BY SOCIALIZING AGENTS

Research by socialization theorists typically clusters socializing agents into four categories: parents and families, schools and teachers, peers, and the media. Our focus here is on how these sources treat girls and boys differently, thereby setting up different contexts in which girls and boys grow up. Please note that I have worked hard to use only up-to-date research to describe contemporary socialization practices, although I will draw on older research to underscore process effects (how certain practices relate to specific outcomes).

Parents and Families

Across many different cultures, parents typically want at least one child of each sex (Hank, 2007). Parents *believe* that they treat girls and boys comparably, and indeed on many dimensions they do (Raley & Bianchi, 2006). Furthermore, the individual characteristics of children affect how parents treat them (Karraker & Coleman, 2005), and parents seem to rely less on gender as their children get older (van Wel et al., 2002). However, patterns that do consistently identify differences are quite telling. For example, from the very start, parents of

Box 4.4
What message about the gender-typing of driving does what's happening in the front seat send to those watching, day in and day out, in the back seat?

newborn girls described their daughters as finer featured, less strong, more delicate, and more feminine than the parents of newborn boys rated their sons (Karraker, Vogel, & Lake, 1995).

Not surprisingly, parents prefer gender-appropriate *toys* for their children, more often honoring both girls' and boys' requests for gender-congruent toys (Etaugh & Liss, 1992) and redirecting children's cross-gender toy choices (Leaper et al., 1995). However, when parents choose toys to actually play with, they (like their children) gravitate toward male-typed toys (Idle et al., 1993), allowing greater flexibility with girls than boys (Wood et al., 2002). Nowhere is this clearer than with electronic and computer games where the interests (Cassell & Jenkins, 1998) and efficacy (Whitley, 1997) of boys dominate. This makes life simple for sons: parents prefer and actually play with masculine toys. For daughters, the message is mixed: many "boys'" toys are more engaging, but parents don't desire them for their daughters.

There is some evidence that parents *communicate* differently with daughters and sons. For example, parents allowed greater risk-taking by boys (Morrongiello & Hogg, 2004), and they reacted to boys' risk-taking with discipline and to girls' with safety rules (Morrongiello et al., 2010). Parents also generally use more affiliative, friendly speech with boys and more assertive speech with girls (Shinn & O'Brien, 2008). Fathers especially were more likely to tell their son family stories with autonomy themes (Fiese & Skillman, 2000). Daughters' stories more commonly included emotional references (Flannagan & Perese, 1998), and they talked about frustrations in conversations with mothers (Aldrich & Tenenbaum, 2006). Mothers engage in more conversations with their young daughters and give more instructions to their sons (Clearfield & Nelson, 2006).

What parents themselves *do and say* every day sends different messages to girls and boys. Children are astute observers of how parents interact with each other, picking up gendered stereotypes (Meyer et al., 1991). For example, when my son was 4 years old, he declared that he would only do "boy" jobs. I was stunned. Deciding to play this out, I asked him just what "boy" jobs he intended to do. Defiantly he retorted: "Laundry—just like Dad!" I just smiled... Also, family dynamics are different when parents together are involved with their child instead of just one; for example, mothers become less involved and more negative in these triadic interactions (Lindsey & Caldera, 2006).

Obviously, families themselves are *diverse*, varying according to composition, living arrangements, race, ethnicity, class, geography, and parental sexual orientation (Davenport & Yurich, 1991). For example, across families, children with other-sex older siblings were most gender-typed (Golombok et al., 2000). Thus, it is important to remember that there is a lot of **intersectionality** going on here so that what we know about one contributor (such as gender) likely varies across diverse families.

Reviewing patterns across race/ethnicity (Reid et al., 2008), generally African American families are low in gender polarization. In contrast, Asian and Latino families are commonly more traditional and less flexible in their expectancies for gender-typed behaviors. However, these comparisons would surely be better informed if they also took into account factors like social class and mothers' employment status.

Across a wide range of measures of self-esteem and psychological well-being there are few differences between children reared by homosexual versus heterosexual parents (Biblarz & Stacey, 2010). Children raised in lesbian families are no more likely than other children to be homosexual, although the former may more readily explore same-sex relationships (Golombok & Tasker, 1996), show more empathy for social diversity, and are less confined by gender stereotypes (Biblarz & Stacey, 2010). A dated but exemplary intersectional study of African American lesbian mothers suggests that they treat their children with even less gender polarization than other mothers (Hill, 1987).

Schools and Teachers

The lessons children learn at school about their gender identities and roles come from how teachers treat them, from how schools are structured, from counselors and other specialists, and from the materials to which they are exposed. All come together to produce an educational climate that two long-time researchers, in their review of research spanning over 20 years, summarized as "shortchanging girls" (Sadker & Sadker, 1994)—and that a more recent review finds largely unchanged (Meece & Scantlebury, 2006).

Myra and David Sadker (1994) describe the *gendered lessons* taught at school: girls learn to speak quietly, to defer to boys, to avoid math and science, to value neatness over innovation, and to stress appearance over intelligence. Girls also experience an erosion of their achievements so that their tendency to outperform boys when they first start school degenerates to a point where they lag behind boys by high school graduation. Other studies add that girls learn to present themselves as modest, self-deprecating, passive, and obedient compared to boys, who learn to be self-assertive and self-promoting (Ellis, 1993). A clever observational study of preschool practices involving children's body movements, comportment, and use of physical space records some subtle ways in which girls and boys are shaped to conform to gender expectations (Martin, 1998).

Although teachers generally espoused nontraditional gender beliefs for both adults and children, they tended to be more accepting of cross-gender behavior from girls than boys (Cahill & Adams, 1997). Researchers observing preschool teachers concluded that they pay less attention to girls, express more emotion toward girls, comment on girls' appearance, and use gender-typed toys and classroom activities (Chick et al., 2003). Teachers continue to expect girls to excel in verbal abilities; boys, in math (Herbert & Stipek, 2005). Some of these teachers' attitudes may be facilitated by the stereotyped textbooks that are used to train them (Yanowitz & Weathers, 2004).

A clever study of gender bias reported by 350 fourth, sixth, and eighth graders in interviews and daily diaries found that fully 76% of these students noted awareness of, witnessing, or being targeted by some forms of gender bias across sports, school, and home life (C. S. Brown et al., 2011). The most common complaints centered on preferential treatment by teachers and discrimination in sports participation. Can you guess which of these complaints came from boys and which from girls? To be sure, check out the footnote below.[4]

One might expect gender-segregated education to avoid some of these pitfalls, especially for girls; however, the data are, at best, mixed. On the one hand, there is some evidence of less gender stereotyping (Campbell & Evans, 1993; Lawrie & Brown, 1992) and higher career aspirations (Watson et al., 2002) in all-girl schools. On the other hand, few differences between the career pursuits of thousands of alumnae from coed and all-girl high schools were found (Duncan et al., 2002). Home background appears to be a better predictor of girls' achievement in physics than the gender composition of girls' schools (Young & Fraser, 1992). Neither predominately Black nor White colleges seem to offer African American women an ideal setting from which to develop academically, personally, and in relationships with men (Gillem, 1996).

Other educators focus on making changes within existing *school systems*. Simply adding male teachers is not sufficient (Sargent, 2005). The Sadkers (1994) recommend over 250 books with strong female characters. Others recommend teacher-training reform that makes teachers aware of subtle, and often unintended, gender-biased practices (Vandell & Dempsey, 1991), as well as policy development to encourage diversity (Maras & Archer, 1997). Two leading organizations pursuing such reforms are the American Association of University Women (AAUW) and the Association of American Colleges and Universities. For example, the AAUW published a report and video exploring such schoolwide reforms as team teaching and cooperative learning and their impact on girls in middle schools (AAUW, 1996) and another focused on Latina girls (Ginorio & Huston, 2000). Another strong resource is "The Girls Report" commissioned by the National Council for Research on Women (Phillips, 1998).

Peers

Relatively little is published about the patrolling of children's gender-role conformity by peers, and their influence seems more subtle than overt. More children in an ethnically diverse group of third-to-sixth graders wanted to be friends with a fictitious child who behaved in gender-traditional ways than with a "deviant" child (Zucker et al., 1995). Even playing gender-inconsistent musical instruments is disliked (Harrison & O'Neill, 2002). Middle class, mostly White girls and boys, ages 7 to 12, positively evaluated the performance of a videotaped fifth-grade girl exhibiting masculine stereotyped behavior, but demeaned her personality (McAninch et al., 1996).

The clearest link between playing with same-sex peers and sex-differentiated behavior has been provided by Carol Martin and Richard Fabes (2001). The more both girls and boys play with same-sex peers, the more their behavior conforms to gender stereotypes. Not too surprisingly, boys who play largely with other boys belittle feminine stereotyped traits (Robnett & Susskind, 2010). This pattern carries over into adolescence where gender segregation and gender-typing are related (Mehta & Strough, 2010). Indeed, Eleanor

---

[4]Boys are more likely to say things like: "Some teachers automatically think girls are smarter than boys and are more mature," whereas girls will complain about sports: "When girls want to play basketball no one wants to pick them because they are girls" (p. 466).

Maccoby (1998) roots the development of gender-differentiated behavior squarely in the gender-segregated peer groups of children.

The relative paucity of research in this area is inconsistent with a recent debate in developmental psychology on the impact of peers. Group socialization theory, forwarded by Judith Rice Harris (1998), posits that children's interactions with groups of peers are the critical determinants of socialization, outweighing even the influence of parents. A more balanced argument is offered by Deborah Vandell (2000), who regards socialization as resulting from the complex interplay of parenting, the child's preferences and capabilities, multiple social relationships (among which peers are only one), and multiple contexts (including home, schools, and neighborhoods). Given this renewed interest in the field as a whole, the role of peers in gender socialization may attract more research attention in the future.

Media

A rich and extensive body of research considers everything from birth announcements to educational materials, storybooks and comics, children's magazines, videogames, television programs, cartoons, and advertisements. Girls/women generally are underrepresented and /or stereotyped; for example, in preschool education software (Sheldon, 2004), in comics (Glascock & Preston-Schreck, 2004), on the television shows (Luecke et al., 1995) and cartoons (Swan, 1995) children watch, in coloring books (Fitzpatrick & McPherson, 2010), and in popular children's picture books (Hamilton et al, 2006). Video games especially have garnered a lot of recent attention. These games, their covers, and their magazines typically highlight male characters (Burgess et al., 2007), sexualize female characters (Jansz & Martis, 2007) and portray them as helpless (Ogletree & Drake, 2007), and link male protagonists with aggressiveness (Dill & Thill, 2007) and power (Miller & Summers, 2007).

Over time, there have been some positive changes. On television, women's occupations shifted from traditional to gender-neutral through the 1990s (Signorielli & Bacue, 1999). In picture books, although girls' roles remain largely confined to the home, boys have moved in, although somewhat stereotypically and with few positive models of fatherhood (Anderson & Hamilton, 2005).

Still, there hasn't been the consistent forward progress we might expect. Girls in storybooks remain consistently passive and dependent across 50 years (Kortenhaus & Demar-

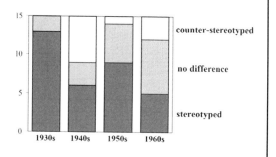

Figure 4.5
Roger Clark and his colleagues (2003) rated 15 different personal qualities (e.g., aggressive and submissive) exhibited by characters portrayed in Caldecott award-winning and runner-up children's books across four decades. Comparing these ratings for female and male characters, they classified each portrayal as gender-stereotyped, not different, or counter-stereotyped. Notice that stereotyping does not decline in a neat, progressively more egalitarian pattern, but rather fluctuates according to the sociopolitical climate of each time period.

est, 1993), and the gender-typed marketing of toys hasn't changed in 25 years (and across five continents) (Furnham & Twiggy, 1999). Toys targeting girls remain focused on feminine qualities, like attractiveness and nurturance, whereas boys' toys continue to promote masculine-typed characteristics, such as violence and competitiveness (Blakemore & Centers, 2005). Even books touted as "nonsexist" because they portrayed female characters in male-stereotypic roles continue to rely on feminine stereotypes to describe personality, domestic chores, and leisure activities (Diekman & Murnen, 2004).

If we relied on these sources to teach us about the roles and activities of girls and boys, we'd learn that girls and women need to be rescued, are less adventurous, engage in fewer occupations, and play less powerful and more passive roles (Brabant & Mooney, 1997; Tepper & Cassidy, 1999). We'd discover that masculinity is linked to violence (Palmerton & Judas, 1994) and that boys and men are aggressive, argumentative, and competitive (Evans & Davies, 2000). We'd see that one way to make cartoon characters "bad" is to have them deviate from gender stereotypes (Ogletree et al., 2004). We'd find that the fantasy play promoted for girls involves nurturance, grooming, mothering, and theatrics, in contrast to boys engaging in working, building, managing, and battling (Kline, 1993). At the very start of children's lives, we'd see that birth announcements herald pride in the birth of a son and happiness in the birth of a daughter (Gonzalez & Koestner, 2005).

DYNAMIC LEARNING

Does all this differential treatment have an impact on girls and boys? Because we ethically and practically can't randomly assign children to different forms of socialization, the critical experimental test of this linkage cannot be conducted. However, two types of studies can inform our understanding: (1) short-term experiments exposing participants to stereotyped images and measuring their impact and (2) correlational studies exploring the amount of exposure a child has to gender-differentiating socializing agents. The latter approach predicts that the more experience a child has with gender-typing agents, the more she or he will exhibit gender-congruent behavior. Across both types of studies, *exposure* is the key element.

A few short-term experiments do find a link between exposure to sexist displays and responses from adult audiences. Many of these types of exposure experiments have focused on the impact of media on women's body image concerns. For example, Emma Halliwell and her colleagues (2011) randomly assigned British women to view control, sexually passive, or sexually agentic (presumably empowering) print images of women. *Both* types of sexualized images produced heightened weight dissatisfaction in women viewers.

In direct tests of children's responsiveness to external pressure, Donna Fisher-Thompson and Theresa Burke (1998) actively encouraged or discouraged third and fourth graders to engage in cross-gender activities. On a subsequent task, discouraged children avoided gender-incongruent activities, but encouraged children did not differ from a control group that was neither encouraged nor discouraged. Jennifer Pike and Nancy Jennings (2005) exposed first and second graders to non-toy commercials or either traditional or nontraditional toy ads targeting a boys' toy. Children, especially boys, in the traditional condition felt most strongly that the targeted toy was for boys.

Turning to correlational studies, age should be indicative of greater exposure. Arguably, older children have had more chances to be influenced by gender-typed agents than younger ones. The general pattern through the early school years is that gender-typing increases as children age (Ruble et al., 2006). Similarly, a meta analysis concluded that as exposure to gender stereotyping in media increased, so did gender-typed behavior and endorsement of traditional gender attitudes, especially among children (Oppliger, 2007).

Another indicator of exposure is amount of television viewing as well as book and magazine selections. Surprisingly, television exposure appears less powerful in more recent studies of both stereotyping (Ward et al., 2005) and body image concerns (Tiggemann, 2006), yet fashion magazines continue to be linked with issues regarding thinness (Tiggemann, 2006). Among children, greater exposure to sexist cartoons is associated with more traditional job expectations (Thompson & Zerbinos, 1997), and conversely, reading about strong same-sex characters is linked to higher self-esteem (Ochman, 1996).

Tarja Raag (1999) related 4 to 5 year-olds' perceptions of significant others' proscriptions with children's toy choice. Both girls and boys who thought one or more familiar people disapproved of cross-gender play were more likely to make gender-congruent toy choices, and boys (but not girls) actually played less with gender-inappropriate toys. Similarly, children whose parents held traditional attitudes showed more gender-typed behavior toward babies, such that girls displayed more interest in, nurturance toward, and interaction with babies than boys (Blakemore, 1998).

Finally, researchers have examined parental attitudes arguing that children (especially girls) exposed to nontraditional parents will be less gender-typed. Indeed, although children generally tend to be less traditional than their parents (Cichy et al., 2007), children's gender-role attitudes are linked to those of their parents (Sutfin et al., 2008). A more complex study of family patterns identified three clusters of families (Marks et al., 2009). In two of these clusters, patterns were as we'd expect: egalitarian parents had egalitarian children, and when both parents were traditional and the mother was more so, these children endorsed traditional views. However, in a third cluster when both parents were traditional but the father was more so than the mother, the two siblings studied (the first- and second-born) were both *egalitarian*. In fact, across all 358 families, siblings always shared similar attitudes. Notice, though, that there is no consistent pattern here for one parent with one child: traditional mothers and fathers can have traditional *or* egalitarian children depending on which one is more traditional than the other. In sum, family dynamics appear quite complicated, sometimes showing transmission (similarity) and other times revealing a "rebellion" effect.

What families *do* may be more consistently related to children's gender-role attitudes than parental attitudes. Parents with unequal divisions of household labor and employment had children who held more traditional occupational aspirations (Fulcher et al., 2008) and who grew up to allocate household chores more traditionally (Cunningham, 2001). Children whose mothers modeled nontraditional activities in the home (mow the lawn) were less likely to show gender-typed preferences for themselves (Serbin et al., 1993). Analyzing daily phone interviews with 9- to 11-year-olds, fathers in single-earner families spent more time with their sons, in contrast to fathers in dual-earner couples who spent equal amounts of time with their daughters and sons (Crouter & Crowley, 1990), and college students raised by single mothers were more nontraditional than those reared in two-parent families (Slavkin & Stright, 2000).

The bottom line is that the *causal link between what we know socializing agents do and what children think and do is tenuous*. There is ample evidence that socializing agents do not treat girls and boys similarly, and also evidence that girls and boys are differentiated, at least in some important ways. It seems logical that the former causes the latter, but other possibilities exist. Maybe children themselves act differently (because of their biologies or how they think), and socializing agents are simply picking up on those differences. Maybe there are outside factors that simultaneously affect both children and these socializing agents. The safest conclusion proposes a circular pattern: socializing agents influence what children think, feel, and do, and these children, in turn, affect how socializing agents respond to them.

AN INTEGRATED UNDERSTANDING

We have seen that biology, evolution, family dynamics (Chodorow, 1978), and socialization practices all contribute a piece to a complex puzzle for understanding how gender differences come about. Each tells part of the story of gender differentiation. Together these theories create a holistic human psychology that helps us understand all three core aspects of who we are: how we think, feel, and act—all within the context of our culture.

At least four common perspectives are shared by each component. First, each combines essentialist elements with constructionist ones. Each says something about who we ARE (via our genes, anatomy, or the cognitive schema we develop) and what we DO (via our interactions with our physical, interpersonal, social, and cultural environments). Second, learning occurs through human interaction. Third, each assumes that how we think, feel, and act occurs within a specific cultural context. Childhood socialization does not take place in a vacuum; rather, it takes place in relation to others. Furthermore, social institutions or contexts shape our relationships with others. Fourth, each emphasizes the importance of childhood as a formative stage in personality development.

BREAKING THE CYCLE

How, then, do we break the cycle of sexist socialization? Both Chodorow and social cognitive theorists describe self-perpetuating cycles that serve to maintain the gender differentiation of generation after generation of children. Chodorow argues that we can break this cycle by engaging in dual-parenting so that children have both female and male models of nurturing (be they parents or other significant people). Social cognitive theorists call for

Box 4.6

When children imagined a man doing something counterstereotypic like sewing, they went on to expect another man to be more stereotyped (Hughes & Seto, 2003). Such compensatory expectancies say a lot about the resistance of stereotypes to change.

changing gender schema and socializing agents. But for those of us who are parents, we know that we control an ever-shrinking portion of our children's socialization. There are powerful forces out there (schools, friends, and the media) that seem to effortlessly derail even our most dedicated efforts.

If socialization is confined to childhood, then activists might question why we should forsake generations of adults, whose socialization is complete, in hopes that the next generation will transcend our culture. Indeed, this is the Catch-22 of turning to socialization for broad social changes toward nonsexism: How do we socialize children to be nonsexist within a sexist context? Isn't socialization the passing on of one's culture to the next generation? How do we do that within a sexist culture? And, even if we are successful with a few children, aren't we condemning them to being regarded as social deviates? How do these children cope with being out of synchrony with the majority in their culture?

Sandra Bem (1983) helps us tackle at least some of these questions by allowing for individual differences in **gender schematicity**; that is, how rigidly gender differentiating the cognitive lenses (**schema**) are through which an individual views the world. Every child is exposed to different degrees of gender-polarized socializing agents and thus will develop individualized degrees of gender schema formation.

My daughter, Kate, encountered a most amazing example of gender-schematic thinking when she was in kindergarten. Every week a different "letter person" visited her classroom. When Mr. T came, they learned that Mr. T liked lots of things starting with the letter "t": tomatoes, turquoise, turtles, etc. Kate excitedly reported on the interests of each character: Mr. T, Mr. B., Mr. M, etc., becoming increasingly agitated that no "girl" characters had shown up. Needless to say, she was ecstatic when "Miss A" appeared, soon followed by "Miss E." Unbelievably, someone had gendered the alphabet: consonants were boys and vowels were girls! (The school told me that this was part of a nationwide program, not the machination of some clueless teacher.) No matter how important we claimed vowels to be ("You can't make a word without one"), Kate was crushed that there were fully 21 boy letters and only 5 girls. (I can't help but wonder if the school would have been as tolerant of this system if racial or class dualities had been used. It's easy and instructive to consider these kinds of absurd statements here, especially regarding the letter Y [intersexed?]).

Taking this thinking about gender schematicity one step farther, Bem (1983) gives us some pointers on how to "raise gender-aschematic children in a gender-schematic society." First, Bem suggests that we teach our children that the only differences between women and men, girls and boys are anatomical and reproductive and that these differences have very little real bearing on our opportunities, our identities, and so on. This second point is critical to avoid regressing to **biological essentialism** and the reassertion that "anatomy is destiny" (Lott, 1997), or that genes dictate group differences like making girls more nurturing than boys (Cole et al., 2007).

Teaching anatomical difference as the defining, *but not constraining*, feature of sex counters the pervasive tendency for most children to learn to distinguish the sexes by relying on external indicators such as clothing, interests, and hairstyles. Bem (1989) illustrated how persistently some children over-rely on exterior signs of gender. She showed children pictures of a nude toddler, followed by pictures of the same toddler outfitted to look like a boy or a girl. Gender-schematic children misidentified the anatomically known boy as a girl when he wore a cheap wig with ponytails.

Teaching children to rely on external cues to determine gender can lead to some humorous, but telling declarations by children. Bem (1993, p. 149) relates the story of her son, who wore barrettes in his hair to nursery school where he was hounded by another boy to a point where her son exposed his genitals to "prove" his maleness. Undeterred by what should have been the definitive proof, the other boy persisted: "Everybody has a penis; only girls wear barrettes."

Furthermore, relying on external, changeable cues to determine another's sex conveys a message that "being male or female is something to work at, to accomplish, and to be sure not to lose, rather than something one is biologically" (Bem, 1993, p. 148). Bem argues that such fear of gender bending (confusing one's gender) contributes to adults' attempts to prove that they are "real" women and men by limiting their choices to those deemed gender-appropriate, thus reinforcing rather than challenging stereotypes.

In contrast, children who define sex by anatomical differences avoid relying on restrictive stereotyping to define another's gender (Bem, 1989). Only about half the 3- through early 5-year-olds tested could correctly identify the sex of toddlers who were nude from the waist down. But of the children who made correct identifications, fully 74% showed gender constancy as they accurately named the sex of a child they had seen nude, even when that child was dressed or coifed to look like the other sex.

A second positive strategy caregivers can adopt is to provide children with alternative schemas to a gender schema. One such alternative is an **individual-differences schema**. This schema is constructed around the idea that individuals are unique so that what defines them is their own interests, preferences, and activities, not necessarily those dictated by their gender. Accordingly, Billy likes football because Billy likes football, not because he is a boy. Similarly, Billy likes cooking because Billy likes cooking, not because Billy is a sissy. (My kids have even discovered advantages from adopting this perspective. They tell me that they don't like zucchini because it doesn't taste good to them; just because I like it, doesn't mean they should like it too!)

A **cultural-relativism schema** helps children understand that people in different cultures and different historical times held different beliefs about what was appropriate for women and men, girls and boys. My daughter is stunned by videos like "Anne of Green Gables," which shows orphaned Anne being shunted from family to family to help with the housework, and "League of Their Own," where women baseball players are trivialized with makeup and skirted uniforms that offer no protection against severe bruises from sliding into base (Randle, 1992). The lesson such exposure to variety teaches is that no one point of view is sacrosanct.

A third alternative schema helps children deal with their difference from more strongly gender-typed peers, teachers, and others: a **sexism schema**. Having a sexism schema—a way to label unfair treatment as sexist—discourages children from internalizing sexist ideas. For example, a substitute gym teacher told my fourth-grade daughter's class that boys were good at many sports because they had more experience playing them; in contrast, girls' expertise was limited to jumping rope. Combine this with the fact that much more attention is afforded male than female athletes, and my daughter eventually could believe this to be true. This stereotype would be reinforced by her not participating in sports, thus becoming incompetent at them.

Instead, Kate's fine-tuned sexism antenna went up. She discussed the situation with us at home that night, and the next day she complained to her teacher. Having a wonderfully sensitive teacher, her teacher soon discovered that other girls were disturbed by the comment and invited the gym teacher to talk to the class. This, of course, opened up a whole discussion about women and sports. Similarly, Sandra Bem's son didn't discard his barrettes just because another boy was being sexist about it.

Lindsay Lamb and her colleagues (2009) tested an intervention with elementary school children in which they practiced challenging sexist remarks. Participants did notice and confront more remarks than before the intervention and in comparison to a storytelling-only control group. Participation also produced less gender-typing in girls—but it failed to influence boys. In a different study, college students kept daily diaries recording sexist events, which in itself made women's beliefs less sexist (Becker & Swim, 2011). However, to have a similar impact on men, men needed to both acknowledge sexist daily hassles in their diaries and express empathy for the women more commonly targeted by these events. Looking across both studies, having a well developed sexism schema itself may keep my daughter from assimilating sexism into her self schema, but for my son, he may also need some empathy training.

CHAPTER SUMMARY

We reviewed a lot of compelling evidence in this chapter that writes two different **scripts** for growing up female and male in North American culture. Chodorow's psychoanalytic approach describes two different personality configurations resulting from parent-child socialization practices: a girls' version that stresses nurturance and relational thinking and a boys' version that emphasizes autonomy, detachment, and rational thinking. Social cognitive theorists highlight the roles socialization agents (including parents, schools, peers, and the media) and children themselves actively play to again write different scripts for girls and boys.

Across both approaches, gender becomes a focal point for socialization processes because our society polarizes people along gendered lines. An integrated approach to understanding the role of socialization in shaping gender identity and roles draws on both theories and their data as well as on the biological and evolutionary contributions we reviewed in the previous chapter.

Two general patterns emerged from our review of research that highlighted the greater rigidity of boys' socialization and girls' preparation for powerlessness. Both patterns fit with our understanding that difference is not value-free, but rather leads down a slippery slope involving power, oppression, and systems of inequality. Indeed, it is this understanding that lies at the heart of challenges to feminists interested in changing socialization practices. How does one eliminate sexist socialization when socialization itself is reflective of and surrounded by a sexist culture? The answer lies beyond any individual, although individual parents can find some help by confining difference to anatomical and reproductive distinctions that are not constraining and by encouraging their child to develop alternative schemas, such as a sexism schema.

On a personal note, people often smile at me knowingly and assert: "Now that you have a boy and a girl, you must realize that there's something about girls that makes them different from boys," implying a presumably undeniable and immutable essential difference. Recognizing that my own children are temperamentally quite different and that essentialism must have played some role in this, I always smile back and conclude: "Yes, Kate is

Kate and Dan is Dan." Gendering children to me is like gendering the alphabet—why do it? Rather, let each child be whatever she or he becomes, neither restricted nor promoted by their sex and gender. We all need to learn to be ourselves in a gender-polarized world.

SUGGESTED READINGS

Chodorow, N. (2002). The cycle completed: Mothers and children. *Feminism & Psychology, 12*, 11–17.

The basic introduction to *The Reproduction of Mothering* in this chapter should make this excerpt from this generally obtuse book understandable and meaningful to readers. From the very outset,f this excerpt hits the nail on its head: "Families create children gendered, heterosexual, and ready to marry" (p. 11).

Lips, H. M. (2002). Female powerlessness: Still a case of "cultural preparedness"? In A. E. Hunter & C. Forden (Eds.), *Readings in the psychology of gender* (pp. 19–37). Boston, MA: Allyn and Bacon.

Hilary Lips does an outstanding job of stepping back from the overwhelming detail of the huge body of socialization research to see the global patterns of power and powerlessness in everyday socialization practices.

Maccoby, E. E. (2003). The gender of child and parent as factors in family dynamics. In A. C. Crouter & A. Booth (Eds.), *Children's influence on family dynamics* (pp. 191–206). Mahwah, NJ: Erlbaum.

Eleanor Maccoby makes a strong case for the reciprocal relationship between socializing agents (in this case, parents) and active children.

Leaper, C. (2000). The social construction and socialization of gender during development. In P. H. Miller & E. K. Scholnick (Eds.), *Toward a feminist developmental psychology* (pp. 127–152). Florence, KY: Taylor & Francis/Routledge.

Campbell Leaper further develops the concepts of feminism, social construction, and socialization that we have explored in this text to propose the pursuit of a feminist developmental psychology.

Chapter 5

Changes Across the Life Course
Women's Lives from Adolescence through Old Age

In this chapter, we explore issues of gender and aging. Just as we have seen that gender is socially constructed, there is a socially constructed, normative pattern expected for aging. This is captured in the concept of the **life course**, a cultural ideal of an age-related progression or sequence of roles and group memberships that an individual is expected to follow

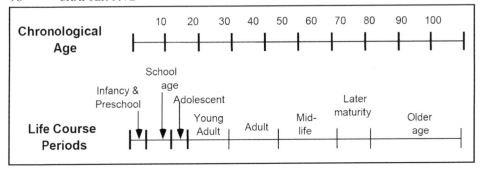

Box 5.1   A time line of an expected life course, with thinner vertical lines indicating discretionary time frames. Some time periods are legally mandated, like when to start school, be employed, and drink alcohol. Others are more subjective, such as at what age are you an adult? Reach midlife? Where do your own education, employment, and relationships fit into this time line? Do they unfold in nice, neat, linear progressions? Think both about what you have already done as well as your projections for your future.

as she or he matures (Atchley, 1994). Before you read on, take a look at Box 5.1 and think about your own life course.

My goals for this chapter are twofold: (1) to examine how gender identity changes across women's and men's lives and (2) to explore the life work women do across the course of their lives. A lifespan perspective regards aging as an active and individualized process. Each of us will work out our own life paths in response to our own interests and desires, to the opportunities that present themselves, and to our broader culture (George, 1996). We'll make choices that will move us along certain trajectories and away from others, sometimes in patterns that are neither linear nor progressive. Understanding how others have worked through their own aging may give us a fuller picture of where our present choices may lead and what our future options may be.

AGING ACROSS THE LIFE COURSE

Two conceptually distinct influences are intermeshed in discussions of age-related change. How people grapple with their life's work may be affected by their chronological age (the effects of age itself) and by their experiences because they matured during a specific time period (the effects of a specific **cohort** or generation with its own unique history). For example, Alyssa Zucker and Abigail Stewart (2007) explored the relationships three cohorts of women, who graduated from the University of Michigan in 1951/52, 1972, and 1992, had with feminism. Each identified social and historical events that occurred during their own identity-forming adolescence as most important, such as identifying different influential figures (Eleanor Roosevelt for the oldest, Gloria Steinem for the middle group, and Hillary Clinton for the youngest). Notice that although the process and timing of feminist development was largely shared, the events that shaped each cohort's views both unified that cohort and distinguished it from the others.

Emphasizing age or cohort may lead to very different expectations. For example, if a change is indeed related to age, then we would expect most people around a certain age to experience similar changes. Thus, on our time line we'd all do the same things at age 60. If, in contrast, change is bound to cohort, we would expect the change being studied to result only for those with shared historical experiences.

For example, women in their late 60s who were born in the 1920s recorded retrospective accounts of their work lives. None of the married women studied described uninterrupted, continuous career paths, compared to fully 55% of the never married women (Keating & Jeffrey, 1983). These women's work lives spanned a world war and the baby boom of the late 1940s through 1960s. Do you think their work patterns will parallel those of current high-school girls who expect to combine career and family (Davey, 1998) or currently employed women, the majority of whom are employed even when they have preschoolers? Probably not. To extrapolate from this cohort of women to successive cohorts of women would likely lead to faulty overgeneralizations about the continuity of women's work-force participation.

Is aging, then, an unpredictable, individualistic process that defies generalizations? Clearly, we each forge our own unique path through life. Following a national sample of high-school graduates across 8 years, researchers found that it took fully 1,827 different sequences to capture the experiences of 7,095 women (Rindfuss et al., 1987). Longitudinal data from 592 African American and 3,001 White women begun after the birth of their first child identified 105 and 255 role sequences across 10 years, respectively, using only two classifications of employed or not (Vandenheuvel, 1997). In fact, continuous employment was enacted by only 11% of the Black and 13% of the White women. These mothers followed all kinds of unique employment paths by dropping in and out of the labor force across a 10-year period. Thus, the common expectations we hold about the various stages on our timeline in Box 5.1 may not play out so neatly in our own lived experiences.

In addition, even these expectations about how a "normal" life course should play out can change across cohorts. For example, there are normative beliefs about "developmental deadlines"—that is, when a developmental marker should be completed, such as finishing college or having a baby (Wrosch & Heckhausen, 2005). Reviewing these changing patterns for having a child, Claire Etaugh (2008) points out that rates of being childfree have gone up (in 1976, only 10% of U.S. women age 40 to 44 had no children; in 2004, this figure rose to 19%), and U.S. women are having babies at later ages (reaching record highs in 2003 when 100,000 women between 40 to 44 years-old and 6,000 between 45 and 49 had a baby). Thus, this highly salient developmental marker for women, having a baby, is shifting overall—and even dropping off the life course timeline for a growing number of women.

Still, the life course remains an important part of understanding "lifespan development" in stages. Together with an understanding of aging as a process (Fuller-Iglesias et al., 2008), it becomes a good starting point from which to explore women's lives. Although many concepts have been studied across the life course, gender role attitudes (our expectations about being female and male) and behaviors are especially central to feminist psychology, so we start here. We then examine selected issues likely to involve women at the expected periods of the life course diagrammed in Figure 5.1.

GENDER IDENTITY ACROSS THE LIFE COURSE

A generally accepted truism about gender-role attitudes and behaviors is that they pass through phases (James et al., 1995). In early childhood, they are thought to be vague and unorganized, becoming more rigid throughout childhood and slowly gaining in flexibility through adolescence and into adulthood, until an androgynous conceptualization that

Box 5.2
My father may display more feminine traits and roles in retirement than he did when I was growing up, not simply because he aged, but because times have changed across his lifetime. Thus what look like age-related cross-over effects may actually be cohort effects.

blends femininity with masculinity emerges in old age. To reach this eventual **androgyny**, a cross-over occurs for women and men, such that women gain in masculinity as they age in contrast to men who add feminine traits (Gutmann, 1987).

Folk wisdom tends to accept the **cross-over model**. Undergraduates asked to project ratings of femininity and masculinity for themselves into the future, and retirees asked to complete these scales retrospectively, described their older selves as both more feminine-typed *and* more masculine-typed than their younger selves (McCreary, 1990). However, is this move toward similar gender identities the result of simple aging? Maybe not. Few studies have followed people longitudinally as they age so that changes in societal attitudes across cohorts may play a role in such apparent cross-over. A longitudinal study finds that: (1) a majority (54%) of older people remained in the same gender-identity category over the past 10 years and (2) the largest proportion of men labeled feminine/expressive appear in the *youngest* age group (Hyde et al., 1991).

The first finding suggests limited change across the age span, contrary to the predictions of cross-over theory for this age period. The second finding is consistent with our speculation about changing times—in the 1990s, young men's descriptions are more likely to include "feminine" terms. Another study with older participants finds limited evidence of cross-over, and much of what little is found is restricted to women and men who have lived traditional lives (James et al., 1995).

Additionally, the attitudes and behaviors of different cohorts appear to be more complex than our likely simple belief that young adults are the most flexible. For example, more recent comparisons of six age groups ranging from 12 to 17 years old to over 80 documented that the oldest women were *less* likely than the youngest and midlife women to endorsed masculine and androgynous traits, whereas men in their 70s *more* strongly endorsed androgynous traits than younger men aged 12 to 29 (Strough et al., 2007). The overall message here, then, is that gender-role attitudes and behaviors appear to depend largely on cohorts, with no clear patterns of simple changes as people age.

GOALS FOR A LIFE COURSE ANALYSIS

The most obvious life course changes for women are those readily identified by biological changes such as menarche (the onset of menstruation), child bearing, and menopause (the end of menstruation). Overemphasis on biological events in women's lives readily can lead to **biological essentialism** (an over-reliance on biological explanations). When women's life course centers on attractiveness, fertility, and youth, aging becomes the loss of these defining womanly functions.

Furthermore, **androcentric bias** has fostered the assumption that understanding men's life course will inform us equally about women's (Wine, 1985). When we studied men's retirement patterns, for example, women were expected to either follow the same trends or be irrelevant because they didn't participate in the workforce. Mary Gergen (1990) concludes that by moving beyond biology and andocentric bias, we can construct women's lives in richer and more diverse ways. Indeed, our goals here are: (1) to debunk simple biologizing myths about women's life course and (2) to sketch a richer picture of developmental issues central to women's lives.

Through the remainder of this chapter, I will describe a sampling of challenges that are typically confronted by women at certain periods of their life course. The list is by no means exhaustive. Some issues are exclusive to women (e.g., menarche); most are not. However, all may be approached somewhat differently by girls and women compared to boys and men.

Furthermore, I'll try to avoid thinking in terms of "development," which assumes a linear progression such that decisions made at earlier stages limit later choices. Life is not that restrictive. For example, women who forego college during early adulthood certainly can assume the role of student, but with a different orientation, later in life. Not having children in one's twenties does not preclude having children in one's forties. (I had mine when I was 33 and 38.) Indeed, recent research shows that among college-educated women who expressed regrets about either traditional or nontraditional family role choices, those who made desired changes in response to those regrets achieved favorable midlife well-being (Stewart & Vandewater, 1999).

However, our culture dictates normative periods for making life course decisions, and these will be vaguely followed here, with the understanding that each individual's life cycle is flexible. The following discussion is framed using each of these normative periods: adolescence, young adulthood, midlife, and old age. (Note that I skip much on adulthood, and only look at the choice to be a mother in young adulthood, because these two periods are assumed by much of the subsequent research in this book.)

ADOLESCENCE

A clear biological marker of adolescence is the onset of puberty; but a more social indicator of adolescence tied to progression through the school system is simple chronological age, typically the second decade of life (Petersen, 1988). Folk wisdom alleges that this developmental period is stormy (the "terrible teens") because adolescents struggle to control their "raging hormones" (Offer & Schonert-Reichl, 1992). This assessment is believed to be especially true for adolescent girls,[1] whose progression through adolescence is unmistakably distinguished by the onset of menstruation (**menarche**), on average at age 12 in the United States.[2]

---

[1]As we have seen, language influences how we think, so the terms we use to designate different ages become important. I will follow the guidelines of APA's *Publication Manual* (2010) by referring to girls (12 and younger), young women or adolescents (13 to 17), and women (18 and older).

[2]For good information about menstruation provided by the U.S. Department of Health and Human Services,

Christy Buchanan and her colleagues (1992) conclude that when we compare adolescents to both younger children and adults, teenagers do indeed experience more mood swings, more intense moods, lower or more variable energy levels, more restlessness, higher anxiety, and heightened self-consciousness. But there's a lot of variability across individuals and within genders. Little evidence exists to support the myths that adolescence is stormier for girls and that changes in mood are linked to hormonal fluctuations. The myth of the "terrible teens" is generally just that—a socially constructed exaggeration reflective of overly simplified "biologizing."

What is the major life work for girls during this phase of their life course? Adolescence itself presents a variety of challenges for girls, including maintenance of self-esteem, identity formation, social development, and future planning (Petersen, 1988).

Self-Esteem

Self-esteem is a complex construct for psychologists who have developed a variety of standardized and well-researched measures to assess it.[3] A meta-analysis of this well-grounded scholarship was done by Kristen Kling and her associates (1999). Defining self-esteem as global positive or negative feelings one has about oneself, they confirmed a difference between girls'/women's and boys'/men's self-esteem that was small ($d = +0.21$) and favored males. The gender gap widened as girls and boys aged, reaching its peak at age 15 to 18 years old and closing through adulthood.[4]

A consistent finding across these studies is that children's self-esteem changes across their school years. In addition, women's self-esteem is negatively affected by lower socioeconomic status (Twenge & Campbell, 2002) and immediately by poor grades, especially in nontraditional classes such as engineering (Crocker et al., 2003). Girls' team sports achievements in early adolescence predict positive self-esteem in middle adolescence (Pedersen & Seidman, 2004), but this relationship between sports participation and bolstered self-esteem can be threatened by disapproving peers (Daniels & Leaper, 2006). Thus, self-esteem changes in different contexts across girls' and women's lives.

Additionally, there are individual variations in self-esteem among women. The more important college women believe it is to be like their ideal woman, the more these women tie their self-worth to their appearance, academic competence, approval from others, and winning a competition (Sanchez & Crocker, 2005). In turn, the more contingent these women feel their self-worth is, the lower their self-esteem.

Both these individual differences and the impact of contexts make it clear that girls can be inoculated against potential drops in their self-esteem. Girls who take a variety of math and science courses throughout middle and high school typically maintain higher levels of self-esteem (AAUW, 1992), and advanced-level course-taking is associated positively

---

visit The National Women's Health Information Center at http://www.womenshealth.gov (retrieved June 2011).

[3]A common assumption, rooted in the classic doll studies of racial preference used to argue for the desegregation of public schools, is that African Americans struggle with deficits in self-esteem. Distinguishing between Blacks' perceptions of what others may think of them (as tapped by the doll studies) and what Blacks think of themselves (self-esteem), a recent meta-analysis of 261 comparisons found no differences in standard measures of the self-esteem of Black and White children, adolescents, and adults (Gray-Little & Hafdahl, 2000).

[4]Grouping by age, the effect sizes were $+0.16$ at ages 7 to 10; $+0.23$ at ages 11 to 14; $+0.33$ at ages 15 to 18; $+0.18$ at ages 19 to 22; $+0.10$ at ages 23 to 59; and -0.03 after 60 years.

with sports participation (Pearson et al., 2009). Physically active young women have a more positive self-image than inactive peers (Covey & Feltz, 1991), and college women athletes exhibit favorable levels of instrumentality and internal locus of control (Parsons & Betz, 2001). Precollege participation in sports by girls is related to positive self-esteem (Bowker et al., 2003; Richman & Shaffer, 2000). Supportive parenting practices, which foster pride in female identity, point out sexist barriers, and encourage nontraditional conduct, are linked to daughters' positive esteem (Michaelieu, 1997).

Since Title IX[5] was passed in the United States in 1972, girls' participation in interscholastic sports has shown an eightfold increase, and the number of intercollegiate women athletes has shot up 300% (Sklover, 1997). Although NCAA coverage of women's college sports has improved (Cunningham et al., 2004), women's inclusion in athletic administration has lagged behind women's participation as athletes (Whisenant, 2003; Whisenant et al., 2002), especially at schools with sexist nicknames (Ward, 2004). Male college athletes benefit from $179 million more in athletic scholarships than female students (Sklover, 1997). It seems that sports affects not only self-image, but opportunities as well.

Although a key issue for girls throughout their middle and high school years is to maintain self-esteem, the gender gap in self-esteem disappears in adulthood (Kling et al., 1999). April Chatham-Carpenter and Victoria DeFrancisco (1998) took an informative look at the meaning of self-esteem to adult women. A diverse group of 59 women, ages 21 to 94, participated in 1 to 2 hour interviews that explored their definition of self-esteem and the characteristics of people with high and low levels. Their lay definition of self-esteem conformed to that of psychologists (i.e, an evaluation of self) and included awareness that self-esteem changes across contexts and requires attention and tending to be maintained. African American women especially noted the importance of family and churches in childhood as protections against racism. White women were more likely to mention struggles for approval and with dependency as threats to their developing self-esteem. Across all women, three themes emerged as central to maintaining positive esteem: voice (speaking out, confidence, self-reliance, willingness to take risks, and living life fully); the importance of one's inner self or self-perspective; and concern for others.

Identity Formation

Erik Erikson (1959) regards identity development as the primary life work of adolescence. The type of identity Erikson envisions is one of autonomy and individualism—learning to be one's self, independent of others. According to Carol Gilligan and other researchers associated with the Harvard Project on Women's Psychology and Girls' Development, Erickson's views conflict with girls' desires for intimacy and connection with other people as well as cultural stereotypes about girls' relational values (see Tolman & Brown, 2001). For **self-in-relation theorists**, the main developmental challenge for adolescent girls is to connect in relation with others *and* form an autonomous identity (Lytle et al., 1997).

Finding voice. An individual woman's identity development is disrupted to the extent that she engages in four processes, each of which trades away individual independence in

---

[5]Title IX of the U.S. Education Amendments of 1972 states: "No person in the United States shall, on the basis of sex, be excluded from participation in, be denied the benefits of, or be subjected to discrimination under any educational program or activity receiving federal financial assistance."

exchange for connection with others (Jack & Dill, 1992; Remen et al., 2002; Smolak & Munstertieger, 2002). Women scoring high in *Externalized Self-Perception* tend to judge themselves using external standards. A high degree of *Care as Self-Sacrifice* subverts one's own needs in favor of those of other people. *Silencing the Self* involves inhibiting self-statements and actions in order to avoid conflict and the potential loss of relationship. *Divided Self* complies with feminine role demands as the inner self grows angry and hostile with these accommodations.

Drawing on intensive interviews with 100 educationally privileged young women across 5 years, L. M. Brown and Carol Gilligan (1993) describe how these adolescents struggle to stay true to their own thoughts, feelings, and experiences as they increasingly come into conflict with White, middle-class cultural expectations for girls/women and ideals of femininity, captured in a "tyranny of nice and kind" (p. 53). In Gilligan's words, they struggled to find their "voice"; that is, their essence as human beings.

Brown and Gilligan found that some young women bury their feelings underground, leading double lives. Others work so hard to conform to conventional feminine ideals that they lose touch with their suppressed feelings and begin to show signs of psychological disturbance. Still others resist and come into open conflict with other people. Most commonly, these resistors are working-class or young women of color (e.g., Latinas; Denner & Dunbar, 2004) who were already marginalized at the exclusive private school they attended.

Self-silencing is not confined to young women's adolescence. For example, women care-providers for their intimate partner with cancer often self-silenced in order to fulfill their perceived feminine role of putting another person first (in contrast to self-silencing masculine stoicism for men; Ussher & Perz, 2010). For both women and men caregivers, self-silencing was linked to depression and anxiety, with women reporting higher levels than men of each. Among college women, high degrees of self-silencing combined with high levels of awareness of one's emotional states make women more vulnerable to disordered eating (Shouse & Nilsson, 2011).

Returning to adolescence, subsequent studies with obvious resistors (specifically, culturally diverse and economically disadvantaged young women) make resisting a less appealing strategy than it may appear at first blush. For example, a study with 26 "at-risk" young women confirmed a pattern of resistance complete with loud expressions of voice (J. M. Taylor et al., 1995). Still, these adolescents reported losses or betrayals in relationships as well as some disconnection from their own feelings and desires. For example, African American young women frequently commented on how their opposition to conventional standards of femininity brought them into conflict with powerful institutions such as schools. Often these adolescents were not effective in resisting oppression, both individually and collectively, and struggled to maintain their self-esteem (Way, 1998).

Helping young women find their voice may be as simple as listening and validating, yet many girls do not find these opportunities often with parents or in their schools (AAUW, 1999). An effective intervention brought young women together to talk about their experiences and the harm they felt as part of their school (Piran, 2001). Finding one teacher was enough to let girls express themselves and verified their experiences (L.M. Brown, 1998). An approach to helping girls and young women that has achieved popularity both within and outside of professional psychology is offered by Mary Pipher (1994) in her book *Reviving Ophelia*.

Moral development. Like Erickson's singular focus on independent identity formation, Lawrence Kolhberg (1981) based his ideas about moral development solely on a **justice orientation**, which sought to balance rights and responsibilities. According to Kohlberg, at the most rudimentary level, *preconventional* reasoning is egocentric so that what's regarded as just is what gets rewarded and/or avoids punishment. At the next, *conventional* level, societal conventions about fairness become important so that approval and disapproval of others influence moral reasoning. At the most advanced, *postconventional* stage, abstract principles about justice are considered that move beyond the individual and what others regard as moral.

Analyzing women's decision making about abortion, Carol Gilligan (1982) concluded that women constructed their moral reasoning using a "different voice" that reflected a **caring orientation** (weighing concerns about hurt and caring). Paralleling Kohlberg's levels, Gilligan argued that this caring orientation could range from simple egocentrism through complex, abstract thinking. Furthermore, she concluded that this "different voice" was largely women's. Meta analysis shows that in some ways Gilligan was right, although gender differences in both a justice ($d = +0.19$) and caring ($d = -.28$) orientation are small (Jaffee & Hyde, 2000). A recent large-scale study further challenges this gender difference by showing that women outscored men in both caring and justice, wanting to *both* connect with others and take action in response to media coverage of crisis events with moral implications (Mainiero et al., 2008).

Although Gilligan's addition of a caring orientation does fill in a gap left by Kohlberg's exclusive focus on justice, there are individual and context variations that undermine the ideas that women's morality is different, inferior, or superior to men's. Gender differences in both caring and justice reasoning change with age,[6] and gender discrepancies in caring reasoning increase with higher socioeconomic status (Jaffee & Hyde, 2000).

The gap between women and men can be narrowed by using moral dilemmas specifically designed to elicit either caring or justice reasoning, and care-based approaches are more likely to be used by both women and men when interacting with friends than with strangers (Ryan et al., 2004). Furthermore, stereotyping about women being caring may contribute to this apparent gender difference. Gender differences in caring rationales are bigger when respondents generate their own dilemmas, as opposed to using standardized content (Jaffee & Hyde, 2000 and when gender is made salient to respondents (Ryan et al., 2004). Overall, these findings confirm that a caring orientation is not exclusive to women's thinking, just as a justice perspective is not exclusive to men's (Crandall et al., 1999).

Lesbian identity formation. Heterosexual identity development in our culture is relatively easy—it's what's expected of us. But, how does a girl or woman develop a lesbian or bisexual identity?[7] There are at least two approaches to this question (Kitzinger & Wilkinson, 1995). The **essentialist** position assumes that homosexuality is part of one's true nature so that "coming out" is simply a series of stages through which one must pass in

---

[6]Gender differences in caring orientation: $d = -0.08$ (children under 12); $d = -0.53$ (12 to 19 years old); $d = -0.18$ (college students); and $d = -0.33$ (20 to 49 year old). Justice orientation: $d = +0.35$ (children under 12); $d = +0.22$ (12 to 19 years old); $d = +0.04$ (college students); and $d = +0.40$ (20 to 49 years old).

[7]For information about transgender identity development, see Gagne et al., 1997.

order to accept the inevitable. Indeed, this often is how gays describe their identity development (Epstein, 1987). On the other hand, there is evidence that the development of our sexual identities does not follow a progressive, stage-wise pattern (Rust, 1993).

A **social constructionist** position, in contrast, argues that lesbian and bisexual identity is pieced together from scraps of evidence interpreted as indicative of one's own sexual identity. Celia Kitzinger and Sue Wilkinson (1995) describe many barriers that illustrate lesbians' resistance to claiming a lesbian identity. For example, although most lesbians report having heterosexual experiences, the myth that lesbians feel no heterosexual attraction keeps some women from interpreting even direct sexual experience as lesbianism: "It's just sex—I was only experimenting, and anyway I'm sexually attracted to men, too" (Kitzinger & Wilkinson, 1995, p. 99).[8] These authors go on to detail how women make the transition to a lesbian identity and how, even after claiming this identity, lesbians continue to work at constructing it, often by becoming involved in lesbian communities.

Social Development

Jane Loevinger (1976) defines social maturity as a progression through stages of increasingly complex perceptions of ourselves and others. (This argument parallels the logic of moral development we just reviewed.) As people mature, we become increasingly aware of our own motivations, moving from concrete to abstract thinking and from an orientation rooted in the immediate present to considerations for the future. For all adolescents, dramatic personality advances occur between seventh and twelfth grades, with young women forging ahead at a faster rate of development. Pulling together data from 65 studies, Lawrence Cohn (1991) finds that, by adolescence, moderately large differences between young women and men appear. Through beginning adulthood, this difference is slight, then disappears in the thirties. Thus gender differences in social maturity at one phase of the life course (adolescence) fade at later periods (young adulthood).

Another expression of adolescents' social development revolves around how prestige is achieved. Research with high-school graduates of the early 1980s (1979 to 1982) and late 1980s (1988 to 1989) shows that gender norms defining social status for women and men remain different and basically constant across the decade (Suitor & Reavis, 1995). Young women acquire prestige mainly through physical appearance, sociability, and school achievement. Young men achieve status through sports, grades, and intelligence. There were a few changes for young women that reflect less traditionalism across the decade: young women's acquisition of prestige through both sports and sexual activity increased, whereas the importance of cheerleading declined. This is a pattern we'll see often in gender research: things change a bit, but basically remain the same.

Future Planning

Future planning is a central issue for adolescents because choices made here mark the beginnings of some trajectories and the rejection of others. Jari-Erik Nurmi (1991, p. 34) concludes that "studies show unexpected similarity in adolescents' interests across cul-

---

[8]Paula Rust (2000) reports data collected for the National Health and Social Life Survey finding that 3.3% of women had both female and male sexual partners since puberty, whereas only 0.2% of women had only women partners.

tures: they all seem to be most interested in two main domains of their future life, work and education."

Look around any college or university, and you'll surely find the gender composition of classes, majors, and even departmental faculty varies widely from largely female to balanced to largely male domains. How these divisions come about depends on the choices individuals make, as well as gendered social forces that simultaneously push women and men away from some possibilities and pull them toward others. The language we use to talk about research in this area, occupational "choice," adequately captures the role played by the individual but misses the often subtle *channeling* that gendered socialization and contexts exert to ultimately limit the full range of educational and occupational possibilities that ideally should be open to everyone.

As we continue to see, contexts matter. For example, sociologist Chardie Baird (2008) concluded that young women living in U.S. counties where the divorce rate and percentage of employed women were low and most people were employed in the wholesale and retail industrial sector were *less* likely to aspire to paid employment, after controlling for obvious influences like socioeconomic status and education. Of course, there are individual variations within these communities that speak to the importance of individual choices and pursuits, but such broader influences (like the community in which one lives) should not be overlooked.

Furthermore, if this process is culturally gendered, we would expect **intergroup differences** in the interests, goals, and actions of women and men. A meta analysis of gender differences in vocational interests did find some large and consistent differences between women and men as groups (Su et al., 2009). Men generally prefer working with things; women, with people ($d = +.93$). Specifically, women show stronger interests in artistic (creative expression, including writing; –35), social (helping people; –.68), and conventional (structured environments like business; –.33) areas and less in realistic (working with gadgets or outdoors; +.84) and investigative/science (+.26) domains. Not surprisingly, men favor engineering (+1.11), science (+.36), and math (+.34).

Women are more likely than men to strategize about combining work and family (Konrad, 2003) and to consider the timing of childbearing (Mahaffy & Ward, 2002). Throughout middle and high school, girls and boys share similar ideal and real aspirations for prestigious careers (Watson et al., 2002), although college women pull back from powerful masculine-stereotyped careers more than high school women, possibly showing signs that reality is setting in (Lips, 2004). A large-scale meta analysis concluded that gender similarities in preferences for job attributes are more prevalent than differences (Konrad et al., 2000).

The model diagrammed in Figure 5.3 describes two paths leading to group differences in interests, goals, and actions (actual pursuits) involving both socialization and proximal (immediate) contexts. In the previous chapter, we examined socialization practices and how these occur within a gendered culture. Taking this socio-cognitive model and extending it to occupational pursuits, these socialization practices affect both individual girls' and boys' expectations about success and subjective task values.

Expectancies and values. Expectations for success in any college major or occupation are shaped by beliefs in the congeniality of the area itself, as well as one's own competence. For example, women in male-dominated academic areas (math, science, and engineering)

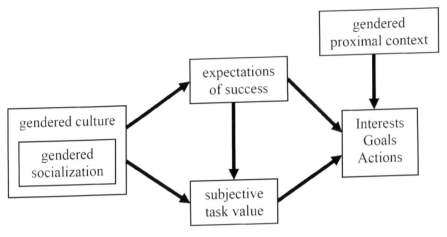

Figure 5.3   A simplified model of educational and occupational decision making. It synthesizes elements of Lent, Brown, and Hackett's (1994) Social Cognitive Career Theory with Eccles' (1994) Model of Achievement-Related Choices, showing how gender affects both the individual and her or his social context.

reported higher levels of **sexist discrimination** and **stereotype threat** and thought more about changing their major than did women in traditional majors (Steele et al., 2002). Girls starting high school were more likely to enroll in math classes if they held favorable beliefs about their math competence (whereas for boys, grades predicted enrollment; Crombie et al., 2005). There's some evidence that although gifted girls' math confidence may match boys', girls' confidence in other areas, such as reading, outstripped their own math confidence so that their movement away from math was less of a push than a pull toward reading (Eccles & Harold, 1992). Obviously, what shapes expectancies is very complex.

The values of girls and boys also can differ, possibly reflecting different family/work mandates for women (mother) and men (breadwinner) (Eccles, 1994; Riggs, 1997). If indeed men fulfill their family role through successful employment, then their values will lead them to perceive utility in job training (perceived utility values), to be interested in pay and status reward (intrinsic interest values), to regard employment as central to self-image (attainment values), and to perceive costs mainly in relation to failed employment, not jeopardized parenting (perceived costs). For women, work and family are separate, and sometimes conflicting, spheres. Consistent with this reasoning, men are more likely than women to report single-minded devotion to one specific goal (employment). In contrast, women seem to value competence in a wider range of activities (including work and family).

Proximal contexts.   Our interests, goals, and "choices" also are affected by the immediate (proximal) gender-typing of college majors and occupations within our culture. Such gender-typing rests largely on who we see doing and not doing different jobs, the language we use to talk about jobs, and how jobs are presented.

Potential explanations for the gender-typing of occupations have considered job content, occupational demands, and gender ratios. The arguments centered on job content suggest that women and men bring different personality characteristics with them to employment; in other words, they are cut out for different occupations. Reasoning regarding occupa-

Box 5.4

Is this who we picture when we think of a fireman? Both the language we use ("fireman") and who we likely see do this job (over 95% of firefighters are men) converge to shape our thinking about firefighting as a masculine occupation.

tional demands reverses this logic: the work demands of the occupations themselves necessitate differential hiring. Finally, the logic of *gender ratios* simply suggests that who does a job predicts future candidates. Research teasing apart these three possibilities is consistent with the gender ratios explanation (Krefting et al., 1978). In sum, who we see engaged in a specific occupation cues us as to the appropriateness of that occupation for ourselves.

How jobs are presented and language also play a role in this process. Danielle Gaucher and her colleagues (2011) conducted a clever series of five studies that first looked at how over 4,000 real-world job advertisements described the jobs for which they were recruiting applicants. Ads for jobs in male-dominated occupations and in male-dominated academic fields used more masculine-stereotyped wording (e.g., leader, competitive, dominant) than did ads in female-dominated areas. In contrast, there were no differences across ads in their use of feminine-stereotyped words (support, understanding, interpersonal). As we will see later when we talk about stereotyping in Chapter 7, these differences are quite subtle, but as Gaucher and her co-authors go on to show, they are not without consequences.

Across their next three experimental studies, these authors documented that college students perceived occupations as employing more men than women (the gender ratios we just discussed) when ads for jobs used masculine- over feminine-typed wording. Furthermore, college women considered these subtlely masculine-typed jobs to be less appealing and did so because they felt a weaker sense of belongingness (but did not feel underqualified) toward these jobs. In sum, there is strong evidence that gendered wording in job advertisements persists (also see Pedriana, 2004) and subtlely works to shape how adults and children (Liben et al., 2002) think about the gender-appropriateness of various occupations and academic fields.

Gender ratios, language, and recruiting strategies all conspire to limit the field of viable occupational options considered by girls and boys. In fact, in my own studies with women firefighters, we began our interviews by asking women how they decided to be firefighters. Most said that they never even contemplated firefighting—it was not one of the options they considered viable. Then, someone in firefighting (typically a husband, relative, or friend) told them of openings for women, or they saw a woman firefighter, or they chanced upon some recruitment campaign specifically aimed at women. In other words, a person or event had to challenge their long-held perception of firefighting as closed to women. Similar stereotyping of occupations has been shown to limit the set of viable options considered by lesbians (Morrow et al., 1996), and 6 to 8 year-old girls continue to prefer occupations regarded as feminine over masculine ones (Teig & Susskind, 2008).

In sum, we have seen that the vocational and educational choices of adolescent girls and boys differ and that this **intergroup difference** arises from their expectations for success, their values, and the options they consider viable. These factors have been shown to affect career development patterns of White women, African American women (Hackett & Byars, 1996), and Latinas (Gomez & Fassinger, 1994). Although we each exercise some choice in what future plans we elect to pursue, there are many external forces channeling us away from some options and encouraging others. To focus exclusively on "choices" tends to root differences within girls and boys, women and men, and can support the **essentializing** conclusion that girls and women, because of deficiencies within (e.g., lack of confidence), make less lucrative choices. The model we explored blends influences both within and outside individuals, leading up to vocational interests, goals, and pursuits.

YOUNG ADULTHOOD: CHOOSING MOTHERHOOD?

One critical decision often encountered in women's young adulthood concerns mothering. As we have seen, an overwhelming majority of women have or will have a baby sometime during their lives, and college women implicitly identify strongly with the concept of motherhood (as strongly as they identify with their college education; Devos et al., 2008). Biologizing arguments evoke evolutionary maternal instincts, penis envy, and "biological clocks" (Schwartz, 1989), ignoring the social pressures that both encourage motherhood and discourage being childfree—pressures that are so forceful that Nancy Russo and Kim Vaz (2001) refer to a "motherhood mandate." Women who struggle to conceive blend these reasons for having children into their own thinking, referring to motherhood as a "natural instinct," as "a stage in the development of a relationship," and as a "social expectation" (Ulrich & Weatherall, 2000).

Some interesting exceptions to the motherhood mandate speak volumes about how we think about mothering (also see Chapter 8). First, single motherhood is devalued in both the popular press and within psychology (Smith, 1997). Interviews with 26 women who chose single motherhood reveal that they legitimate their choice with their age, responsibility, social maturity, and fiscal soundness (Bock, 2000). Second, lesbian mothers combine a marginalized identity (being lesbian) with a mainstream one (being a mother) (Hequembourg & Farrell, 1999) to challenge heterosexual norms that underlie our thinking about parenting (Dalton & Bielby, 2000; Dunne, 2000). Third, physically disabled women oftentimes face opposition to, or even restriction of, their reproductive freedom (Lonsdale, 1992).

One of the clearest ways to see a norm like the motherhood mandate in action is to watch what happens when it is violated. If there is a mandate dictating motherhood for women, then remaining *voluntarily* childfree should be regarded as deviant, and as such, should be demeaned. A study using hypothetical vignettes describing heterosexual childless couples found that college students rated neither infertility nor childlessness very negatively—although being temporarily, rather than permanently, childfree was considered more acceptable (Koropeckyj-Cox et al., 2007). In sum, there may be some signs of change regarding the continuing acceptance of the motherhood mandate.

Rosemary Gillespie (2003) interviewed 25 White women aged 21 to 50 about their desire/decision to be childfree. Their comments illustrated two patterns. The first centered on the attractions (or "pulls" toward childlessness), such as increased freedom and autonomy, a closer relationship with a partner, and a wider range of opportunities. The second theme centered on disincentives (or "pushes") away from motherhood, like loss of other opportunities and disinterest in the activities associated with mothering.

Deciding whether or not to become a mother is intimately intertwined today with decisions about employment—with tradeoffs between career and family more commonly contemplated by women (Brown & Diekman, 2010). Statistically, the normative woman is employed, even if she has preschool children (*Statistical Abstracts of the United States*, 2011, p. 385, Table 598). About 62% of mothers with children under 6 were in the workforce in 2009, a figure that reached a plateau across the 1990s and 2000s after increasing from 30% in 1970 to 45% in 1980. Furthermore, many college students aspire to combine both employment and motherhood in their lives (Erchull et al., 2010).

Kathleen Gerson (1985) interviewed three groups of heterosexual women (homemakers, childfree career women, and combiners) about how they made their decisions. Surprisingly, she found that homemakers and careerists were the most attitudinally similar: they shared the assumption that motherhood and careers are incompatible—they simply took opposite paths. The attitudinal gulf now between employed and at-home mothers may be even more intense than when Gerson did her research, with at-home mothers especially vulnerable to devaluation of the mother role (Johnston & Swanson, 2004).

Gerson also found that what these adult women thought they would do when they themselves were children (their aspirations) were only somewhat related to what they did as adults. Fully 67% of those who aspired to be homemakers when they grew up veered toward employment as adults; 60% of those who expected employment ended up as homemakers. What were more closely related to adult pursuits were largely unanticipated *pulls* and *pushes*. For example, some women were pushed out of the workforce by deadend, unstimulating jobs and pulled into the domestic sphere by a spouse who looked askance at employed mothers. Others were pulled into the workforce by financial pressures resulting from a divorce or fulfilling work successes and pushed away from domestic activities by the isolation of homemaking. A more recent study found similar patterns highlighting that early gender-role attitudes do predict marriage, children, and employment, but with interference from various situational factors (pulls and pushes) (Corrigall & Konrad, 2007).

All women in Gerson's study described costs and benefits associated with their decisions, but careerists, homemakers, and combiners weighed them differently. All thought that having children would be fulfilling, but *careerists* oftentimes dismissed this and/or found themselves in positions where their spouses either didn't want children or made it clear that they would not participate sufficiently in their care. They highlighted the costs children would exact on their careers. Some *homemakers* described deadend jobs that pushed them from the workforce and spousal attitudes and comfortable finances that pulled them toward home. *Combiners* reported failed marriages or egalitarian fathers who shared in domestic responsibilities as well as enthusiasm for their employment.

Strategies for combining career and family include limiting family size and interrupting employment. (The possibility of sharing child rearing with a partner is explored in Chapter 8.) Indeed, the more college students expected work-family conflict, the more they endorsed delaying marriage and restricting the number of children they will have (or for men, having none) (Weer et al., 2006).

As for interruptions, research exploring the combination of employment and motherhood has found that continuously employed mothers are belittled, as compared to those who interrupted their careers (Bridges & Etaugh, 1995). Also, employed mothers are regarded

Box 5.5
Combining Career and Family

Consider your post-college plans for a career, an intimate relationship, and parenting. In the circle, make a pie chart graphing how much of your life you expect to devote to each of these three areas. For example, you would divide the circle into three equal slices if you expect to give each equal weight.

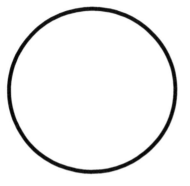

This is what Jennifer Kerpelman and Paul Schvaneveldt (1999) asked of 969 never married, childless women and men between the ages of 18 to 25 years. They sorted each response into one of four categories: balanced (equal thirds), family-oriented (both relationship and parental roles exceeded one-third of the pie), career-oriented (the career slice was greater than one-third, with both the other two less than one-third), and career/relationship-oriented (both career and relationship exceed one-third each). A family-oriented pattern emerged as the most popular configuration for both women and men, but even stronger for women. A similar pattern was found among married women and men in computer and law firms (Cinamon & Rich, 2002)

	Women	*Men*
Balanced	22%	24%
Family oriented	57%	45%
Career oriented	9%	15%
Career/Relationship oriented	12%	16%

as less well-adjusted (Etaugh & Poertner, 1991), more stressed (Etaugh & Moss, 2001), and less dedicated to their families (Etaugh & Nekolny, 1990) than nonemployed mothers, as well as less effective than fathers (Bridges et al., 2002). Mothers employed full-time are seen as less nurturing than mothers who reduced their work hours (Etaugh & Folger, 1998).

A study of 194 college women reported that nearly all expected new mothers to quit their jobs or reduce their hours of employment temporarily (Weinshenker, 2006). Although the interrupted career may represent the ideal of many college women, the realities of employment with limited maternity leave (current U.S. law mandates only 12 weeks of *unpaid* leave and does not cover all workers) may constrain the realization of such an ideal. (We'll explore this point further in Chapters 8 and 9.)

A key to successfully blending marriage with career may be, somewhat paradoxically, to anticipate and plan for conflict. Survey data from 117 women who were college seniors in 1967 and who were surveyed again in 1981 revealed that those women who as seniors anticipated conflict combined work and family more often than women who also wanted careers as seniors but unrealistically expected no conflict (Tangri & Jenkins, 1997). Those women who expected conflict asserted their career intentions with their spouse, postponed childbearing, and had fewer children (just like Gerson's combiners). Ironically, the women who as seniors did not anticipate conflict ended up experiencing more actual conflict in their marriage than those who had anticipated it. In sum, the decision about whether or not to have children and combine this with employment is complex, and the burden and consequences of this decision fall disproportionately on the shoulders of women.

MIDLIFE: UPS AND DOWNS

A student working with a team of undergraduates doing some research for the first edition of this book approached her charge to find studies about "what it's like to be an older woman" with a very simple question: "What's old?" (She suggested 40, which immediately struck me, then 44, as way too low!) Going back to the life course diagrammed in Box 5.1 at the start of this chapter, my question here has to do with the subjective merger of chronological age with life course (e.g., when does adulthood start?).

When researchers ask people to designate ages for different life events and stages, a general consensus does emerge. For example, 462 women and men aged 16 to 70 generally agreed that women are middle aged at about 42 (45 for men); old at about 65 (70 for men); best looking at approximately 25 (30 for men); and in their prime around 35 (38 for men) (Zepplin et al., 1987). The pattern of consistently younger ages for women than men is statistically significant, suggesting that women "age" earlier and differently than men (Canetto et al., 1995).

There's an old adage that you're as old as you feel. Not surprisingly, even elderly women and men think of themselves as younger than they are (averaging 13 years) (Kleinspehn-Ammerlahn et al., 2008). Seven related markers remind us of our age: body signals (more frequent aches and pains); time markers (birthdays and anniversaries); generational reminders (being a senior member of one's work group and watching parents age); contextual reminders (as not being fully welcomed in certain places and with people of different ages); mortality reminders (the death of friends and others one's age); human development reminders (being aware of the wisdom of one's judgment); and life-course reminders (becoming a grandparent). We all encounter reminders in our day-to-day lives that make us stop and become increasingly sensitive to our own aging.

Biological Decline?

Evolutionary psychologists and psychoanalysts, who link women's psychology to reproduction, regard menopause (the end of menstruation and hence fertility) as the defining time marker of midlife (Gergen, 1990).[9] For American women, early signs of menopause typically begin about 7 years prior to reaching full **menopause** (defined as 1 full year without menstruating) at age 50 (see Chrisler, 2008). The most consistently reported sign[10]

---

[9]For information about menopause decisions, such as the decision to use hormone replacement therapy, visit the website for the Boston Women's Health Book Collective at *http://www.ourbodiesourselves.org* (Retrieved June 2011). Other good resources are *Menopause: Me and You* (Voda, 1997) and *Mind over Menopause* (Kagan, Kessel, & Benson, 2004).

[10]Typically, the term "symptom" is used to designate a sign or indicator of menopause, implying that menopause is a disease rather than a normal stage of female physiological development (Cole & Rothblum, 1990). This perception of menopause as related to disease is promoted by discussions of menopause that use terms to

of menopause is the hot flash, a sensation of heat, typically restricted to the face and upper torso, which lasts for a few minutes. Estimates of the prevalence of hot flashes range from 43% to 93% of menopausal American women, but anywhere between 16% to 80% of women report experiencing no menopausal indicators. Previously dismissed as figments of women's imaginations, hot flashes may be linked to reductions in estrogen. Cross-cultural variations emerge in women's attitudes about and experiences with menopause, suggesting that at least some menopausal symptoms are socially constructed (Etaugh, 2008) For example, Japanese women are less likely than U.S. and Canadian women to report having hot flashes.

In popular lore, menopause is associated with depression, irritability, and mood swings. There is no solid evidence that these or other psychological indicators are more prevalent in menopausal women than other women (Avis, 2003). Even if individual women seem to experience elevated levels of psychological distress during menopause, there are a host of other nonbiological factors that could play a role. For many women, menopause coincides with other life events such as children leaving home, changes in identity and body image, possible divorce or widowhood, career changes, illness of parents or partners, and so on. Indeed, among many women themselves, menopause just isn't regarded as that big a deal (Stewart & Newton, 2010). Focusing on menopause as the single or most critical contributor to psychological distress in the midst of such a long list of social possibilities and disregarding many women's subjective experiences is simply another example of misplaced **biological essentialism** (Rostosky & Travis, 1996). In fact, middle-aged women themselves generally report positive as well as negative attitudes toward menopause (Huffman et al., 2005). (I personally regarded every hot flash as a step toward greater liberation.)

Related to women's waning fertility is the life-course reminder of the passage of children from their parental home, presumably leaving women with an "empty nest." Folklore links "empty nest syndrome" to a variety of maladies for midlife women like depression. Studies of marital satisfaction indeed do record changes associated with the presence and ages of children (Etaugh & Bridges, 2006), such that satisfaction peaks before the birth of the first child and hits lows when children are preschoolers and teenagers. However, satisfaction levels *grow* with the passage of children from the home, almost returning to the peak of the "honeymoon" years. Clearly, this pattern is inconsistent with the gloomy prospects portended by "empty nest" speculation. A new trend throughout the 1990s in which fully 25% of adult children returned to live at home needs to spark new research in this area (Whitbourne & Skultely, 2006). In addition, by age 47, half of American women have a grandchild and will spend half their lives as grandmothers (Etaugh & Bridges, 2006).

The biologizing of women's aging has challenged their sexuality as well by using some frightful and fatalistic terminology, such as "vaginal atrophy" (Cole & Rothblum, 1990), which contributes to women's misperceptions of menopause as a "deficiency disease" (Shore, 1999). Although clitoral response does not seem to change with age, less muscle tension can develop during sexual arousal, vaginal secretions can decrease, and orgasmic contractions can decline in number and intensity (Etaugh, 2008). Yet other women point out that increased satisfaction with their partner at this age and freedom from fears of pregnancy contribute to heightened sexual desire and pleasure. An ongoing survey of 280

---

pathologize it (Tavris, 1992) and is shared by many adult women whose primary sources of information are friends and popular books and magazines (Mansfield & Voda, 1993).

women averaging 51 years old, taking part in the Midlife Women's Health Survey found that a majority experienced no changes in their sexual responses across the past year (Mansfield & Koch, 1998). Ellen Cole and Esther Rothblum (1990) report that lesbian sexuality at midlife can be "as good or better than ever."

This overemphasis on a biomedical model of menopause paints an overall picture of decline and degeneration that is not consistent with the fuller consideration of women's midlife we are examining here (Rostosky & Travis, 2000). One area that attracts much attention about women's aging (possibly because it is linked with sexuality and fertility?) is physical attractiveness. Indeed, there are a variety of body signals associated with aging for women (Etaugh, 2008). Typically, hair becomes thinner and grayer; weight increases until about age 50 and redistributes to the abdomen, buttocks, and upper arms; wrinkles and age spots may appear; and even height may shrink an inch or two. Personally, I don't find it coincidental that as my generation of baby boomers ages, there's a newfound interest in tight "abs" (abdominal muscles)—our surest sign of aging. Mary Gergen (1990) sums up this forecast of decline with the title of her rejoinder to it: "Finished at 40."

The aging human body and mind are both believed to decline with age (Stewart & Newton, 2010). Men's feelings about physical decrements tend to focus on losing capabilities and functionality; women, on losing attractiveness—although not to the extreme that some media sources claim. There even may be an fsupside to liberation from demands for women's attractiveness, including greater independence (Niemela & Lento, 1993) and self-confidence (Helson & Wink, 1992). However, women also describe how lowered demands for attractiveness seem to be accompanied by reduced social visibility and loss of power (Halliwell & Dittmar, 2003).

We have been exploring the **intersection** of both ageism and sexism in women's lives. **Ageism** refers to prejudicial attitudes and discriminatory practices directed toward the aged and the process of aging (Schaie, 1988). If we move beyond visions of women rooted in their reproductive capacities, then images of older women become more balanced. When we view women as *more* than physically attractive mechanisms for reproduction, even physical aging need not be regarded as declining.

Not Finished at 40

This fuller view of midlife and older women encourages us to take another look at life beyond age 40. Valory Mitchell and Ravenna Helson (1990) reviewed data from a sample of 700 college alumnae aged 26 to 80, and concluded that many women in their fifties seemed to be in the "prime of life." Fully half of the 51-year-old women in their longitudinal study evaluated their lives as "first-rate," the most favorable endorsement of any age group tested. These women portrayed themselves as financially comfortable, as healthier than women in their forties, as less concerned about loneliness, as engaged in politics and social issues, as valuing friendships, as autonomous, and as having high levels of life satisfaction (also see Helson et al., 2002). Life for these affluent, college-educated women was far from finished!

These positive patterns of aging ring true for many lesbians as well. A study of 110 midlife lesbians found that the majority reported feeling fulfilled, self-confident, self-accepting, and self-directed (Sang, 1993). They described heightened desires to have fun and lowered achievement orientation.

In a second analysis with the college alumnae described above who are now in their fifties, Ravenna Helson (1992) reviewed 88 written accounts in which they recounted a "time of personal difficulty" during different periods of their adult lives. A majority was in stable heterosexual relationships, and most were employed at least part-time. Different themes dominated their stories at different ages. Although these themes were not restricted to any one age, they did tend to cluster in certain age periods.

When these midlife women looked back over their lives, stories attributed to ages 21 to 26 oftentimes described themselves as lonely, isolated, unattractive, and inferior. A second theme focused on a bad partner—someone who possessed an unknown and undesirable characteristic (e.g., being alcoholic), or who developed a serious weakness (e.g., being suicidal), or who was a neglectful workaholic. Around both age 30 and 40, their most common struggle centered on a search for independent identity, typically separate from that of a spouse. The sequel of this search for independence appeared in the stories describing events around ages 36 to 46. These critical periods generally took one of two forms: grappling with discrimination at work or dealing with a partner's abandonment. Finally, two themes dominated the years from 47 to 53 focusing on destructive relationships with partner, parents, or children or overload, pressure from work, parental care, and so on. Although themes changed with age, nothing in these women's stories suggests that life at 50 is any more or less difficult than at any other time period.

In fact, life for many women in their 50s is best described as a time of *review*; that is, a time to step back and evaluate the different aspects of their lives (Etaugh, 2008; Etaugh & Bridges, 2006). Oftentimes, the dominant theme of this review centers on developing or strengthening an independent identity; that is, on affirming one's own well-being. Women who express regrets with their choices when younger experience heightened well-being if they make modifications to their current life course in response to those regrets (e.g., switching jobs and going back to school). The success of this assessment focuses not so much on the path one has taken (careerist, homemaker, combiner), but rather on how well one has fulfilled her chosen role. Women who have attained their occupational goals, who continue to build their career, or who have fulfilled their goals as homemakers exhibit strong levels of psychological and physical health.

Many of our misconceptions about aging come from misleading media representations and our own ignorance; researchers find that both younger and older people are largely uninformed about the normal changes that accompany aging (Bailey, 1991). Until recently, social scientists have provided little to fill in the gaps, but this is changing. Balanced views of a full range of changes across this point in women's life cycles are appearing (for example, see Etaugh & Bridges, 2006).

LATER MATURITY AND OLDER WOMEN: UPS AND DOWNS

If life isn't over at 40, it's certainly not over when women reach 60 and beyond. With life expectancies creeping upward, more and more women and men will be grappling with the issues associated with being elderly. Women tend to face different retirement and financial circumstances than men and a greater likelihood of widowhood, both of which (along with health issues) can affect women's well-being.

Retirement and Financial Security

We tend to think of retirement as the cessation of employment—pretty simple. However, for many people retirement is not such an all-or-nothing proposition. Some older people "retire" from a long-term job and then go on to accept "bridge" employment that is part- or even full-time (Feldman, 1994). This is especially true for working-class women who have had less opportunity to save for a financially secure retirement (Perkins, 1993). Consequently, researchers define retirement in a variety of ways, including self-attributed (the person reports that she or he is retired), pension (receiving Social Security and/or other pension arrangements), and degree of retirement (measured by reported number of hours employed per week) (Talaga & Beehr, 1995).

Exploring the factors that influence women's and men's decisions to retire, interesting similarities and differences were found (Talaga & Beehr, 1995). Folk wisdom contends that women retire when their spouses do, but when we look at degree of retirement, women actually worked for pay for more hours each week when their spouses were retired than when they were employed. Women described themselves as retired more often when their spouse reported ill health (self-report), but they worked as many hours as women with a healthy spouse (degree of retirement). The former may be in keeping with gender-role expectations that women should retire when their husband needs them, but the latter speaks to the reality of these women's working lives. Again, as we'd predict given women's expected caretaker role, women were more likely to report retirement and actually worked for pay less often when they had dependents in the home. When couples were both employed during childrearing, they tended to retire together; in couples where the woman reentered the workforce after childrearing, women retired more slowly (Henretta, et al., 1993). Thus, the decision to retire for a woman is complexly linked to her work history and familial obligations and expectations.

One of the clearest obstacles differentially impacting women and men retirees is *financial*. In 1980, women's chances to retire with a private pension were less than men's, and when women did have such resources, their income averaged only 59% of men's (Arber & Ginn, 1994). Financial insecurity tends to be even more severe for African American women (Logue, 1991). Not surprisingly, older women report experiencing more psychological distress related to finances than men (Keith, 1993). The average woman over 65 in 2005 lived on an annual income of $15,615, compared to an average of $29,171 for men (Older Women's League, 2005). These gender differences have been attributed to women's typically shorter employment histories, greater likelihood of interruptions, and lower wages. A link between poverty and gender among the elderly holds across African American, Latina, and White women (Hardy & Hazelrigg, 1995).

Widowhood

Because women tend to marry older men and because women's average life expectancy is longer, widowhood is a more likely prospect for women than men. In 2009 in the United States, there were 2.8 million widowers and 11.4 million widows (*Statistical Abstracts of the United States*, 2011, p. 52, Table 56). Additionally, widowers are more likely than widows to remarry so that elderly women are 3 times as likely to live alone as elderly men (Etaugh, 2008).

Being widowed is one of life's most stressful events, affecting women's mental and physical health during the first year and generally extending to 2 to 4 years (Etaugh, 2008). However, studies comparing the physical and mental health of widows with married women of the same age generally find no differences between the two groups. Two critical factors in how well a woman adjusts to widowhood may be her financial security and the expectedness of her husband's death. Loss of the husband's income can be exacerbated by medical costs incurred by his illness. Younger widows typically experience more distress than older women, possibly because they did not anticipate the death of their spouse. Additionally, younger widows are less likely to be financially secure, to be free of childrearing responsibilities, and to have friends in similar circumstances.

Loneliness is thought to be one of the most pressing difficulties of widowhood. Researchers find that older women tend to expand their social support networks more so than older men. These friendships and community ties serve as buffers against loneliness (Patrick et al., 2001) and even bolster physical health (Hessler et al., 1995; Shye et al., 1995). With years of experience as the social planners for their families, women report less loneliness and more connection to an active social network. Religious participation provides strong social supports for African American (Nye, 1993) and White (Neill & Kahn, 1999) women, as does involvement in the gay community for older lesbians (Quam & Whitford, 1992). Although living alone is related to depression among both elderly women and men, women report less depressive symptomology than men (Dean et al., 1992). More active day-to-day socializing may be a key to women's positive adjustment (Barer, 1994).

Children perceived by their parents as supportive also play an important role. However, children are more likely to regard a widowed mother as self-sufficient than a widowed father, and thus may offer fewer supports to their mother. Similarly, older women report more positive beliefs about their own self-efficacy than do men (Bosscher et al., 1995). These attitudes often combine to leave women to face more caretaking responsibilities than similarly situated men.

Health and Well-Being

Physical and psychological well-being are obviously connected, especially so for the elderly. Although women, on average, live longer than men, elderly women are prone to chronic illnesses (Etaugh, 2008). These patterns leave more surviving women in need of physical caretaking.

Although a meta analysis of subjective well-being shows that the gap between women and men favors men, especially at older ages, gender explains little of this difference, especially when widowhood, health, and socioeconomic status are factored in (Pinquart & Sorensen, 2001). Indeed, one survey of 60 to 65-year-old Australians concluded that well-being is enhanced by reductions in previous life stressors (Burns & Leonard, 2005). Unlike men, women's feelings of positive well-being are not compromised by reliance on others for personal assistance (Penning & Strain, 1994). In fact, women are more likely than men to increase their feelings of personal control by entering into reciprocal helping relationships where they both give and receive assistance (Silverstein & Waite, 1993).

Not surprisingly, the major concerns of older women focus on health maintenance, household management, budgeting, and limitations of their own activities (Heidrich &

Warning

When I am an old woman I shall wear purple
With a red hat which doesn't go, and doesn't suit me.
And I shall spend my pension on brandy and summer gloves
And satin sandals, and say we've no money for butter.
I shall sit down on the pavement when I'm tired
And gobble up samples in shops and press alarm bells
And run my stick along the public railings
And make up for the sobriety of my youth.
I shall go out in my slippers in the rain
And pick the flowers in other people's gardens
And learn to spit.

You can wear terrible shirts and grow more fat
And eat three pounds of sausages at a go
Or only bread and pickle for a week
And hoard pens and pencils and beermats and things in boxes.

But now we must have clothes that keep us dry
And pay our rent and not swear in the street
And set a good example for the children.
We must have friends to dinner and read the papers.

But maybe I ought to practise a little now?
So people who know me are not too shocked and surprised
When suddenly I am old, and start to wear purple.

Source. "Warning" by Jenny Joseph, from *Selected Poems*, Bloodaxe/Dufour, 1992. Reprinted with permission of John Johnson Ltd.

Ryff, 1992). Because men generally remain more physically capable, men's daily routines include higher activity levels, more involvement in hobbies and household maintenance, more participation in organizational activities, and consequently greater independence (Barer, 1994). In contrast, more women describe a more passive approach to their daily schedules. A 90-year-old woman reports: "What used to take me three hours to do, now takes me three days. And then I need a two-hour nap in the middle of the day, so I lose those hours" (Barer, 1994, p. 35). Other women cope successfully by focusing on social comparisons with those less well-off than themselves (Heidrich, 1993), by engaging in physical activity such as walking or gymnastics (Ruuskanen & Ruoppila, 1994), and by maintaining a future orientation (Whitbourne & Powers, 1994).

POSITIVE AGING

When younger people read the literature describing late maturity and older ages, it is easy to be discouraged about their own prospects. Some of these feelings reasonably come from how we as a culture and within psychology have socially constructed aging as "…decline, deficits, disasters, and death" (Gergen & Gergen, 2010, p. 340). Kenneth and Mary Gergen (2010, p. 354) have cleverly drawn on the concepts we have already explored surrounding **social constructionism** to put the common adage "…aging is what we make it" into practice. They launched a free, bimonthly newsletter to share ideas about "positive aging"(*www.positiveaging.net*).

They argue that aging involves a continually changing and unpredictable context that can successfully be negotiated through improvisation: "To sustain a condition of positive aging in a constantly changing ocean of contingencies requires imagination and innovation" (p. 347). In their workshops with older participants, they simply ask: "Are there ways in which these conditions may be reconstructed in such a way that a sense of well-being may be restored?" (p. 348). They find that even impending death can be "reconstructed" in ways that are acceptable and even adventuresome. Given that aging is inevitable for each of us, knowing about the "downs" we discussed here may help prepare us, as well as give us some insights about how to see the "up" side to growing older.

Live long and prosper.

CHAPTER SUMMARY

We explored two approaches to studying aging. First, we followed gender identity across the life course, noting that cohort, rather than age, may be the source of greater androgyny at older ages. Second, we described the issues that typically confront girls and women at different periods in their life course. Past attempts to restrict our understanding of women's life courses to unique biological markers, like menarche and menopause, have been replaced by feminist reconceptualizations of these biological markers as well as by a broadening of our focus to encompass psychological and sociological indicators of how women generally live their lives. This transformed view of human development moves beyond childhood to explore change across the life course and to describe women's lives independent from the patterns of men's lives.

In adolescence, key issues for girls and young women focus on maintaining high levels of self-esteem, forming an identity, developing socially, and planning for the future, including educational and vocational interests, goals, and pursuits. For example, we saw that occupational plans are affected by both individuals' choices as well as subtle channeling effects from both socialization practices and proximal contexts, including who does certain jobs (gender ratios), the language that is used to describe workers, and how jobs are presented. In young adulthood, one decision demand often focuses attention on the decision to be a mother as well as the pushes and pulls involved in the decision about combining employment with mothering.

A balanced view of women at midlife includes prejudicial attitudes and discriminatory practices (ageism) that diminish women's power, as well as close friendships and feelings of autonomy that enhance women's well-being. A similar balance of minuses and pluses emerges from the life stories of older women. On the one hand, these women are especially vulnerable to financial shortfalls and chronic, nonfatal illnesses. On the other hand, many older women nurture rich networks of social and physical supports as well as the freedoms to deviate from social dictates and to explore new opportunities. Growing research evidence suggests that we need not be finished at 40, or 60, or beyond, and that, through the art of improvisation, we can age positively.

SUGGESTED READINGS

Miller, J. B. (1986). All this, but not enough. Chapter 10 in *Toward a new psychology of women* (2nd ed.). (pp. 115-124). Boston, MA: Beacon.

Jean Baker Miller's book remains a mainstay for self-in-relation theorists, and this brief chapter in particular focuses this approach on a central theme of the present text: the power and empowerment of women and girls.

Abrams, L. S. (2003). Contextual variations in young women's gender identity negotiations. *Psychology of Women Quarterly, 27*, 64-74.

Laura Abrams interviewed and learned from adolescent girls from two high schools about how they were navigating their gender identity development, underscoring both the central role played by their understandings of power and stereotyping, as well as contextual variations in their different experiences related to their race/ethnicity, social class, and urbanization.

Jack, D. C. (2011). Reflections on the Silencing the Self Scale and its origins. *Psychology of Women Quarterly, 35*, 523–529.

Dana Jack provides a personally engaging and scholarly overview of what it means for young women to silence themselves by looking back at the development of this foundational measure for the area and by reflecting on its impact and future research directions.

Diamond, L. M. (2005). A new view of lesbian subtypes: Stable versus fluid identity trajectories over an 8-year period. *Psychology of Women Quarterly, 29*, 119–128.

Lisa Diamond takes a fresh look at identity development across the lifespan by focusing on the fluidity of lesbian identity and the slower evolving process of its long-term development.

Hyde, J. S., & Kling, K. C. (2001). Women, motivation, and achievement. *Psychology of Women Quarterly, 25*, 364–378.

Janet Hyde and Kristen Kling review psychological research on motivation and achievement, concluding that efforts to substantiate gender differences would be more usefully focused on stereotype threat and peer sexual harassment.

Nentwich, J. C. (2008). New fathers and mothers as gender troublemakers?: Exploring discursive constructions of heterosexual parenthood and their subversive potential. *Feminism & Psychology, 18*, 207–230.

Julia Nentwich describes four scenarios of parenthood that emerged from interviews with 21 employees at the Swiss science institute. Across these scenarios, she explores the gender binary of women mothering and men fathering to identify practices that might challenge these normative role assignments, finding some possibilities in heterosexual couples and not necessarily finding others among nontraditional families.

Calasanti, T. M., & Slevin, K. F. (2001). A gender lens on old age. In T. M. Calasanti & K. F. Slevin, *Gender, social inequalities, and aging* (pp. 13–28). New York: AltaMira.

This opening chapter looks at aging and ageism through a social constructionist perspective that is consistent with our emphases on understanding power and with sensitivity to diversity.

Older Women's League (OWL) *http://www.owl-national.org/*

The Older Women's League is a good resource for up-to-date information about issues relevant to the lives of older women, including political advocacy.

Chapter 6

Individuals and Social Contexts
Looking Beyond Gender Differences

Across the previous three chapters, we have been putting together a puzzle to better understand gender differences (see Box 6.1). Much of our emphasis has been on two distinct groups: biological girls/women and biological boys/men; girls socialized to be girls and boys raised to be boys; and women's and men's development across the life course. The remaining puzzle pieces come from personality and social psychologists whose work seeks to understand human thoughts, feelings, and behaviors by exploring contributions from both the person and the situation (Ross & Nisbett, 2011).

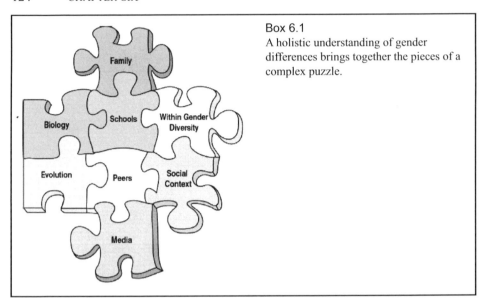

Box 6.1
A holistic understanding of gender differences brings together the pieces of a complex puzzle.

In this chapter, I first want to narrow our focus by looking inside the social category of female and male at both individuals and subgroups in order to make the point that neither gender group is homogeneous. Rather, there's great within-gender, **intragroup diversity** among women and among men both as individuals (**individual differences**) and as diverse subgroups formed by other social markers around the Diversity Wheel (e.g., race/ethnicity and sexual orientation). Although gender differences do capture some consistent **intergroup differences**, we shall see that individuals and subgroups can qualify (**moderate**) these group-level patterns.

Second, I want to expand outward to explore the social context in which each group operates. It is an obvious truism that all human behavior occurs within some **social context** (Rosnow & Rosenthal, 1989); that is, within a social environment that can produce or constrain behavior (Ross & Nisbett, 2011). Social constructionists remind us that we usually work hard to be sure that others know our gender so that gender is always present in our social interactions (Deaux & Major, 1987). Others' expectations about what gender means, as well as the social status we ascribe to gender, play a constant role in influencing how others perceive us. We'll see in Chapter 7 that these perceptions can become self-fulfilling, shaping women into what we expect for women; men, into what's appropriate for men.

AN EXAMPLE: EMPATHETIC ACCURACY

This reasoning will be clearer if we consider a concrete example. The ability to read others' thoughts and feelings is a central part of human interaction, and in social psychology, how skilled people are at reading other people's minds is referred to as **empathetic accuracy**. In popular culture, jokes abound about men who fail to understand the needs and desires of their heterosexual partners, making this "gender difference" a mainstay in television sitcoms and movies.

Research evidence finds that women read their intimate partner's mind better than men do (Fletcher, 2002; Thomas & Fletcher, 2003). Women generally focus more attention on intimate relationships, have more elaborate ideas about what relationships should be like, and talk more about their relationships than do men. Even meta-analysts record a whopping gender difference ($d = -.91$), confirming that women *report* being more empathetic than men (Hyde & Frost, 1993).

Geoff Thomas and Garth Fletcher (2003) conducted a study in which heterosexual dating partners were videotaped trying to resolve a problem with their relationship that both identified as troubling. Afterwards, each separately watched the video and recorded throughout what they were thinking and feeling at the time of the interaction. This provided the researchers with each target's actual thoughts and feelings. This videotape then was played for different viewers who were told to focus on one targeted person and to record what they thought that target was thinking and feeling. Empathetic accuracy thus was measured as how well these two ratings (target's reports and viewer's perceptions) fit together (correlated).

As you might have guessed, gender made a difference. Overall, women were more accurate than men. But individual differences mattered as well. In addition to viewing their own video, each member of the dating couple viewed a second video in which two strangers interacted. These ratings provided a second indicator for each person about their general skills in empathetic accuracy. Both women and men who were accurate in viewing the first video were relatively accurate with the strangers in the second video. Potentially explaining why this may be so, another study found that both women and men who form more complex attributions about what causes another's behaviors are better at mind-reading (Thomas & Maio, 2008). These **individual differences** in mind reading skills remind us that not all women are good at it and not all men are bad at it, even though women as a group outperformed men.

The social context of the relationship also had an effect. For these analyses, the same target was viewed by her or his dating partner as well as by a female or male stranger.[1] As you might expect, strangers were less accurate than dating partners (see Figure 6.2). But more relevant to the point I'm making here, there were contexts in which men (with a dating partner) were comparable mind readers to women (with strangers).[2] In fact, in other studies men were just as accurate as women when they were paid to be accurate (Klein & Hodges, 2001) and when they were motivated to be accurate (Hall & Mast, 2008; Thomas & Maio, 2008). Although men's accuracy never exceeded women's (Hal & Mast, 2008), men are capable of being more empathetically accurate—if the context is right.

Furthermore, women *believe* they are better mind readers than men. Using these expectations, William Ickes and his colleagues (2000) had women and men engage in the same coding task but varied the instructions they first read. When instructions made it clear that their responses indicated how good the respondent was at coding accurately, the **intergroup difference** in women's and men's performance was exaggerated. When the coding

---

[1]Remember that there really are two parts to empathetic accuracy involving accurately reading and effectively displaying one's emotions. There's some evidence that men are better at telegraphing their emotions to dating partners and friends than women are (Thomas & Fletcher, 2003). Interesting, both women and men are faster and more accurate at detecting happy expressions on women's faces and angry expressions on men's faces (Becker et al., 2007).

[2]In marriages, women and men are similarly responsive to their partner's need for support, although wives appear more skilled at giving that support at the time it's most needed (Neff & Karney, 2005).

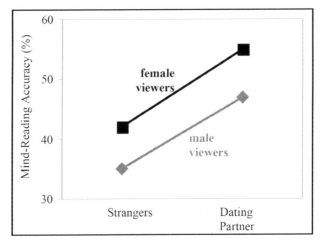

Figure 6.2
How skilled women and men are at judging the thoughts and feelings of others (empathetic accuracy) varies by gender (a gender difference) as well as across individuals (an individual difference) and depends, in part, on the nature of the relationship they have with the target (a social context effect) (Thomas & Fletcher, 2003). In this figure, the same target is viewed by her or his dating partner and by a stranger.

sheet disguised that mind reading was measured, women and men performed more similarly. Thus women's and men's expectations about their abilities affected how well they ultimately performed (also see Koenig & Eagly, 2005).

Across these different studies, individual differences in mind reading skills (particularly attributional complexity) **mediate** the relationship between gender and empathetic accuracy such that skilled women and skilled men preformed similarly.[3] Additionally, variations in social contexts involving relationships, motivations, and expectancies served to both widen and minimize group gender differences in accuracy. These contexts served to **moderate** (or qualify) the relationship between gender and mind reading. (Take another look at Figure 2.2 to refresh your memory of moderation and mediation.) Thus by focusing on both individual differences and social contexts, we begin to move away from **essentializing** explanations that root gender differences inside women and men. As we'll see later in this chapter, this refocusing affects not only how we explain (**socially construct**) gender differences, but also what we might do to bring about social change.

INTRAGROUP DIVERSITY

Starting in Chapter 2, I have presented effect sizes (ds) to summarize intergroup differences between girls/women and boys/men. Although this approach can tell us a lot, it also can gloss over important variations within each group; that is, among women and among men.

---

[3] Another example of mediation in person perception involves remembering others' appearance. Women as a group are better at this than men, but this relationship between gender and appearance recall is mediated by both how important an individual thinks appearance is and appearance knowledge (Mast & Hall, 2006). For example, as a woman I should be good at this task but I have to look down at what I am wearing to remember what I have on, and I can't seem to describe the physical appearance of even my friends. Individual differences …

Take the example of height, a feature of people we observe regularly in everyday life. In 2002, the average height for American women aged 20 to 74 was 5' 4" and for men, 5' 9 ½" (Centers for Disease Control reported in Up and out, 2004). The *d* for height is a huge +2.0 (Hines, 2004b), much bigger than the *d* = ±0.8 minimum that qualifies as very large for social scientists. Look around almost any gathering of adult women and men and you'll readily see this very big intergroup difference.

However, if you begin to focus in on individuals, you'll see some women who are taller than many men. You'll also see large variations among women: a distribution capturing 99% of all U.S. women spans 13 inches, a range that is significantly wider than the 5 or so inches that separate the average women from the average man. Additionally, consider subgroups of women, such as Asian women and basketball players. These comparisons make the average 5' 4" woman seem tall or short. This example illustrates two main aspects of **intragroup difference**: **individual differences** and subgroup diversity.

On every attribute we've examined, there is variability within women as a group and within men as a group. This makes intuitive sense. Just like knowing there are women who are taller than many men, we also know women who are very skilled at spatial tasks and men who read the thoughts and feelings of others quite perceptively. *Oftentimes the diversity within groups is greater than the difference between them.* Thus, if I had to bet money on who would be taller, a randomly chosen woman or a randomly chosen man, I'd be ill-advised to put my money on the woman (given the intergroup difference). But as *d*s shrink, so will my probability of winning any one bet. In this section, I want to step back and look at individual differences and subgroup diversity within women as a group.

Cognitive Abilities: The SAT-M

Nowhere is the impact of group gender differences in math abilities more powerful than on the Scholastic Aptitude Test's math portion (the SAT-M). Men as a group scored as much as 40 points higher than women (Ramist & Arbeiter, 1986). Certainly it's not legal to indiscriminately admit men to college over women. However, if I stressed math abilities and relied on the SAT-M to measure those skills, these scores would make the admission of more men than women likely and arguably defensible (see Leonard & Jiang, 1995).

Not everyone takes the SATs. Rather, students taking the SAT-M self-select so that they come mostly from the high ability tails of various abilities distributions. Thus, our focus changes here from comparing group averages to comparing high-ability women with high-ability men. On this and other "gatekeeper" tests (like the GREs), more men than women score at the high extreme (Ceci et al., 2009).

M. Beth Casey and her colleagues (1997) explored what predicted high scores for women taking the SAT-M. They knew from prior work that **mental rotation skills**, the ability to mentally rotate a two-dimensional object in three-dimensional space, predicted math abilities. In addition, some psychologists suggested that both confidence in one's math abilities and math anxiety contribute to math performance. The purpose of their study was to explore which of these factors predicted how *individuals* scored.

Their data ruled out math anxiety. It also showed that when mental rotation and math confidence were considered, gender was *not* a direct predictor of SAT-M scores. Rather, mental rotation skill and math confidence directly predicted SAT-M scores such that more skilled and confident students, regardless of their gender, scored higher. The better predictor was rotation skill, besting confidence by a 2:1 margin. So, if I wanted to bet my money (or my college scholarship) on the most likely high scorers, I'd be best off selecting names from a pool of students highly skilled in mental rotation rather than simply picking men.[4] Although picking someone highly confident about her or his math skills makes more sense than relying on simple sex, rotation competence would be a better choice than math confidence.

Although I improved my selection chances by choosing individuals based on their mental rotation score over their sex, I'm still relying on a test to make this determination. I might just as well give candidates the SAT-M and choose accordingly. However, if I persist, I can now turn to what predicts mental rotation skills, and again Casey (1996) chimes in. Casey explored the impact of biology (using handedness to predict right hemispheric specialization associated with spatial abilities) and socialization (spatial experiences and college major) to predict mental rotation scores. Indeed, both sets of measures sorted out the highest achieving women. Rather than just picking men, I could now ask a few pointed questions of both women and men and better my odds of selecting the candidates most likely to succeed.

Personality Traits

One of the most widely used measures of personality traits is the NEO-PI-R, which measures self-reports about 30 traits that fall into the "Big Five" personality clusters of neuroticism, extroversion, openness to experience, agreeableness, and conscientiousness. Paul Costa and his colleagues (2001) measured all 30 traits with large samples across 26 cultures globally. They found two consistent patterns of gender differences across cultures, such that women reported being more *agreeable* (trusting, straightforward, altruistic, compliant, modest, and tender-minded) and more *neurotic* (anxious, depressed, self-conscious, impulsive, and vulnerable), on average, than men.[5]

Although the focus of Costa and his colleagues' work is largely on group gender differences, they concluded: "Gender differences, although pervasive [across cultures], appear to be relatively subtle compared with the range of individual differences found within each gender" (p. 326). This quote highlights exactly the point I am making in this section on **intragroup diversity** (also see Lott, 1997). There can be more variability among women than between women and men as groups.

Their data also raise fascinating questions about cross-cultural diversity. Group gender differences in both agreeableness and neuroticism are greater among Europeans and North Americans (in **individualist** cultures) than among Africans and Asians (in **collectivist** cultures). Costa and his associates speculate that this variation may be because their measures of traits fit with an individualistic emphasis on personal qualities and miss the role relationships, which are more central to collectivist thinking. Thus, African and Asian women might not see themselves as that different from men in terms of *traits*, but rather in terms of the different *roles* women and men fill. Indeed, when students read about role changes in a hypothetical society, they shifted their trait assignments for women and men, suggesting that role assignments do predict traits (Diekman & Goodfriend, 2006).

---

[4]Note that gender does predict both math confidence and mental rotation scores, favoring men so that my final pool of highest scoring students likely would still have more men than women.

[5]A more recent study involving 55 countries replicated these findings as well as found that women scored higher in extraversion and conscientiousness (Schmitt et al., 2008).

INDIVIDUAL DIFFERENCES

We have seen above that intragroup diversity can be greater than intergroup differences, making differences among women sometimes larger than a difference between women on average and men on average. Some of this intragroup diversity comes from **individual differences** in how gender itself is viewed, including feminine and masculine gender identity, stereotyping accuracy, and conformity to feminine norms.

Femininity, Masculinity, and Androgyny

We might expect that the most obvious personality traits to distinguish women from men are **femininity** and **masculinity** as forms of **gender identity**. Thus, we might think, quite simply put, that women are more feminine than men, and men, more masculine than women. These expectations, which form our **gender belief system**, originate in our society and rest on two fundamental assumptions that we'll see are faulty (Kite, 2001).

First is the assumption that feminine is defined as *not* masculine, and vice versa. Indeed, femininity and masculinity were once regarded as endpoints on the same continuum so that people (largely women and even gay men[6]) who were high in femininity were, by definition, low in masculinity (Spence, 2011). Notice that this logic reflects **dimorphic** thinking that we already rejected in our discussion of biological sex in Chapter 3. People do not neatly sort into female and male boxes based on biology yet alone psychological identity.

Second, it is assumed that these attributes come in coherent clusters so that nurturing people also are emotional, passive, and so on. As we'll see in what follows, whether there are clusters of traits that truly measure femininity and masculinity is largely open to debate.

Measuring femininity and masculinity. In the 1970s, these assumptions of gender belief systems were called into question by psychologists, leading to the independent development of two new scales. Sandra Bem introduced the *Bem Sex Role Inventory* (BSRI) in 1974, and it has become the most widely used measure (Beere, 1990). At the conceptual heart of the BSRI is the assumption that masculinity and femininity are separate and unrelated dimensions so that an individual can score high on both, low on one and high on the other, etc.

To create the BSRI, college students rated traits according to how desirable they felt each was for women and for men in American society. Twenty items considered significantly more desirable for men defined masculinity; 20 items regarded as more desirable for women described femininity; and 20 filler items were rated as equally desirable. To complete the BSRI, respondents simply indicated if each trait is "never or almost never true" to "always or almost always true" of themselves on 7-point scales. Those who described themselves more strongly on the masculine items than the feminine ones were considered masculine in their gender identity; feminine scorers did the reverse. To label those who described themselves equally strongly as both masculine and feminine, Bem introduced to

---

[6]As amazing as it might now sound, the Mf subscale (Scale 5) of the Minnesota Multiphasic Personality Inventory (MMPI) originally was validated using 13 gay men to establish the feminine pole of the scale (Beere, 1990).

TABLE 6.3
Items in the Personal Attributes Questionnaire

Masculine	*Feminine*
independent	emotional*
active*	able to devote self completely to others
competitive*	gentle
can make decisions easily*	helpful to others*
never gives up easily	kind*
confident*	aware of the feelings of others*
feels superior*	understanding of others*
stands up well under pressure*	warm in relations with others*

* Analyses by Prentice and Carranza (2002) suggest that students still record differences in how desirable these traits are for each sex.

psychology the concept of androgyny. This measure defines **androgyny** as the equal blending of masculine and feminine traits.

Simple to score and also widely used is the *Personal Attributes Questionnaire* (PAQ) developed by Janet Spence and Robert Helmreich in 1978 to measure femininity and masculinity. The PAQ comprises eight masculine and eight feminine items (see Table 6.3). Like the BSRI, separate feminine and masculine scores were calculated, and these were used together to categorize individuals as feminine, masculine, or androgynous (where androgyny involves high levels of both feminine and masculine characteristics).

When women and men actually completed these scales, some women scored high on the masculine items; some women scored low on the feminine items; some men scored high on the feminine items; and so on. *Masculinity, although stereotyped as occurring more frequently in men, was not confined to men nor femininity to women.* Reflecting the dispersion of masculinity and femininity across women and men, the intergroup difference between the scores of women as a group and men as a group was small. Furthermore, *PAQ classifications are unrelated to sexual orientation*; lesbians may be stereotyped as masculine, but there's nothing in the data about gender identity to support this myth (Kite, 2011).

As we saw in Chapter 2, the concept of androgyny took off through the late 1970s and into the 1980s. Androgynous people were expected to be more behaviorally flexible; for example, they played with kittens (a "feminine" task) and did not conform under pressure (a "masculine" task) (Bem, 1975). They were high in self-esteem and psychologically well-adjusted (Bem, 1977; Spence & Helmreich, 1978). Although it hasn't disappeared, the construct of androgyny has faded because of many serious measurement and conceptual problems.

Construct validity. Just what the BSRI and PAQ measure, that is, their **construct validity**, is open to debate. In 1981, Sandra Bem began to conceptualized gender identity in terms of **gender-schematicity** rather than masculinity-femininity. Gender-schematic people see themselves in gendered terms, such that gender-schematic men score high on the masculine items and low on the feminine ones; gender-schematic women do the opposite. In contrast, gender-*a*schematic women and men use a variety of adjectives to describe themselves, rather than relying on gender stereotyping. Note how Bem brings biological labels of women and men into this definition of gender identity.

Janet Spence and Robert Helmreich (1980) have come to think of the PAQ as a measure of **instrumentality** (those who score high on the M items take charge and actively do things) and **expressiveness** (the F items measure caring and nurturing tendencies). Alice Eagly (1987) considers a parallel dichotomy in terms of **agentic** (people who are independent, active agents) and **communal** (people who work with others) orientations. You may want to reexamine the items of the PAQ in Table 6.3 to see if you think they fit with these reconceptualizations.

Whatever the interpretation, these scales remain rooted in their original construction—they measure gender stereotyping (i.e., what people in the 1970s thought were desirable characteristics for women and men) (Morawski, 1987), many of which persist (see Table 6.3) (Prentice & Carranza, 2002). Thus, they may be useful to the extent that they measure how much we stereotype ourselves along gender lines; they may not be as useful as presumed measures of true "inner" femininity or masculinity (Morawski, 1987).

Furthermore, these concepts may be inextricably linked to power (Morawski, 1987). A message that comes through repeatedly in this literature is that masculine traits, alone or in combination with feminine ones, are better. Recent research finds that being **communal** is associated with low status (being female?), and being **agentic**, with high status (being male?) (Conway et al. 1996). For example, is decisiveness (a "masculine" trait) really a better trait than warmth (a "feminine" trait), or is one more closely connected to what we regard as powerful in our culture?

These measures also may mean different things to different people, in different cultures, and at different points in history. Hope Landrine and her colleagues (1992) found that women of color and White women attributed similar adjectives to themselves but interpreted their meaning differently. For example, for women of color, "passive" meant "not saying what I really think"; for White women, "passive" connoted "laid-back/easy-going."

An analysis bringing together over 100 studies using the BSRI and PAQ revealed that the magnitude of differences between women's and men's scores narrowed between 1973 and 1994 (Twenge, 1997). Both women and men showed stability in expressive or feminine scores and increases in instrumental or masculine scores, with especially dramatic increases for women responsible for closing the gap between the sexes. Jean Twenge speculates that these shifts are accounted for by cultural changes resulting from the women's movement and women's participation in the labor force.

Gender identity shifts in importance depending on the situation and intersects with other aspects of identity (Deaux & Stewart, 2001). For example, a woman's sex and gender are likely to be very salient when she is the only woman in her work group; gender may fade into the background when the same woman goes to a movie with her friends. Kay Deaux and Abigail Stewart (2001, p. 88) thus conclude that gender identity is "an inescapable societal process, in which other people, changing situations, and social norms play a major role."

None of this complexity is captured in simple understandings of the BSRI and PAQ as measures of the *traits* of femininity and masculinity. Thus, these scales must be used with caution. You will see that these concepts and their measures continue to crop up in contemporary research, so it is important that you clearly understand what we know—and what we don't know—about these elusive but ubiquitous constructs.

Gender-Stereotype Accuracy

Ironically, the BSRI and PAQ, which did dissociate gender identity from both sex (masculine women) and sexual orientation (feminine lesbians), originally drew on stereotyping about what is desirable for women and men. Judith Hall and Jason Carter (1999) offer an alternative construction that may prove useful. They measured how accurate individuals' gender stereotyping was by correlating participants' ratings of 77 behaviors and traits with data from meta-analyses either confirming or disconfirming these differences. As groups, people's ratings were quite accurate, mapping rather closely onto systematic research evidence. But individuals' accuracy varied widely, making this an **individual differences** measure of gender-stereotype accuracy.

Beginning use of this measure is intriguing. Women and men who were more accurate in their gender stereotyping were less likely to accept and use these stereotypes and were more interpersonally sensitive. As you might expect, more accurate people also possessed a less rigid cognitive style. These patterns suggest that what you are learning in this book may help you to avoid falling back on simplistic overgeneralizations about girls/women and boys/men, and instead to sensitively view individuals as individuals, not stereotyped representatives of social categories.

Conformity to Feminine Norms

Every culture has **social norms** about what constitutes appropriate femininity, and individual women and subgroups vary in how much they conform to these "rules." James Mahalik and his colleagues (2005) focused on dominant U.S. culture, arguing that even if subcultures challenged some of these standards, they still remained generally prescriptive. They asked focus groups of students and community members to describe cultural messages about "how women are supposed to act, think, and feel" (p. 419). Building on this base and after extensive testing (Parent & Moradi, 2010), nine norms emerged (see Table 6.4). My guess is that if you think about these for yourself or for women in general, you'll have individual beliefs about how much you endorse each of these factors. In this way, scores on the Conformity to Feminine Norms Inventory (CFNI) run along a continuum for women respondents from high agreement to high disagreement with traditional statements in each of the nine areas about how women might think, feel, or behave.

As you can see, the CFNI focuses specifically on femininity, not as a trait (like the original BSRI or PAQ), but rather as a cultural construction that may be endorsed to varying degrees by individual women. As a relatively new measure, the promise of this scale and its subscales remains to be seen. Although there is some evidence that the subscales work as projected (e.g., the Thinness subscale predicted symptoms of eating disorders; Green et al., 2008), this measure as a whole may give researchers an opportunity to explore how the set of interrelated feminine norms may function together to oppress women.

SOCIAL CONTEXT

When we explore intragroup diversity, we shift our thinking away from gender as a single cause of intergroup differences between girls/women and boys/men. We begin to see that

TABLE 6.4
Conformity to Feminine Norms Inventory

Subscale	Sample Item
Relational	"I believe that my friendships should be maintained at all costs."
Sweet and Nice	"Being nice to others is extremely important."
Invest in Appearance	"I spend more than 30 minutes a day doing my hair and make-up."
Domestic	"It is important to keep your living space clean."
Romantic Relationship	"Having a romantic relationship is essential in life."
Modesty	"I tell everyone about my accomplishments." (reverse scored)
Sexual Fidelity	"I would feel guilty if I had a one-night stand."
Thinness	"I would be happier if I was thinner."
Care for Children	"I find children annoying." (reverse scored)

Note. Do you 1 (strongly disagree), 2 (disagree), 3 (agree), or 4 (strongly agree) with each item? Higher scores indicate greater conformity to feminine norms. Items taken from Mahalik et al. (2005) using the factor structure suggested by Parent and Moradi (2010).

a phenomenon is more complex than simply saying women do, think, or feel this and men do, think, or feel that. The above exploration took us inside the group of *all* women to focus on individual and subgroup diversity. In this next section, we'll expand our vision outward to the social environment in which girls/women and boys/men operate, and we'll return to our debate about what *causes* gender differences.

Causes and Consequences of Difference

Usually when we search for the possible causes of a reliable intergroup gender difference, two possibilities immediately come to mind: biology and socialization (experiences from childhood). As we saw in Chapter 3, this nature versus nurture distinction typically is artificial because in real life they are inseparably intertwined (sex&gender&sexuality).

At a philosophical level, we can think about comparisons between women and men in one of two opposing ways: from a viewpoint that assumes that differences are real (**alpha bias**) *or* from a perspective that minimizes differences and stresses similarities (**beta bias**) (Hare-Mustin & Marecek, 1988). Here again we seem to have an either/or choice. However, rather than choose between the two and argue over which is correct or more useful, another often overlooked possibility exists (Yoder & Kahn, 2003).

Let's return to the research on empathetic accuracy with which I began this chapter. A biological explanation might suggest that women are better at reading the thoughts and feelings of others because of some better developed regions of their brains (biology), perhaps evolved through thousands of years of rearing children whose survival depended on their mother's ability to recognize the child's needs (evolutionary psychology). Another explanation might be that men are discouraged from getting involved with the feelings of others by socialization practices that punish them for emotional displays (socialization theory). Again, **psychobiosocial models** may focus on the interplay of biology and socialization such that the effects of each are so intertwined that they become functionally inseparable (see McClure, 2000). Whatever the approach, the assumption is that many women possess this ability and men don't because of something *within them*—something that is a part of them and that is relatively permanent. The unavoidable implication is that many men lack this capability so that either they need remedial training to compensate for their restrictive socialization, or they can never truly make up for their biological or evolutionary inadequacy.

Think of the ramifications of this analysis. If empathetic accuracy is something we value in our culture,[7] men are viewed as severely disadvantaged in this arena. If we assume that men's poor mind reading resides exclusively in their biologies (or evolutionary histories), then change becomes virtually impossible, (or frighteningly surrealistic).

Even if we assume that differences in empathetic accuracy are learned, fully or in part, isn't childhood socialization over for adults—so that we then are stuck with whatever we have become? Or we might ask, because socialization explanations acknowledge the role of learning, can adults unlearn and/or relearn? When we speak of such remedies for a gender difference, aren't we implying that the gender to be changed is deficient? Are we blaming members of one gender for their "inadequacies" (Halpern, 1997)? This last process has been dubbed **blaming the victim** (Ryan, 1972).

We see examples of victim blaming in everyday justifications for misfortune: Women are raped because they dress provocatively, and poor people are lazy. This process has at least two noteworthy side effects. First, it serves an **ego protective function**—if I avoid doing whatever the victim presumably did, I will avoid her or his fate. Second, blaming the victim deflects criticism away from larger social forces by pinning the blame squarely on the shoulders of presumably defective individuals. Whatever the reasons for engaging in victim blaming, the result is a victim who may be victimized multiple times. Once we decide an individual caused her or his misfortune, it's a logical step to continue to victimize them because they deserve it (Glass, 1964).

There's a possible explanation for intergroup gender differences beyond biology and socialization that we haven't yet considered and that avoids the pitfalls of victim-blaming. What could make women and men *appear* different are the circumstances or social context in which they find themselves. Our beliefs about sex and gender come into play often as part of this social context.

Thinking Intuitively about Social Context

As I write this chapter, I am 58 years old with many of the responsibilities associated with adulthood in my culture. Along with my partner, we fully support one adult child (paying college tuition!), have another adult child who is largely self-supporting, maintain a house and cars, manage two demanding careers, care for a dog and a cat, etc. Yet I instantly become a child when I visit my parents. There, I sleep in a room surrounded by the white bedroom set from my childhood; I sit down to a dinner my mother prepared and I dry dishes with her afterwards; and I never, ever drive. For better and for worse, I am a kid again, dependent on my parents, with few responsibilities, and with little freedom to structure my own day. They even ask me how things are "at school"!

---

[7] I am making an assumption here that could be easily reversed; that is, one could reasonably argue that we live in a culture that values ignoring the thoughts and feelings of others. The same points follow from this starting point, and these form the crux of the subsequent arguments I make. I purposively elected to put women's behavior at the normative baseline of my argument to reverse more typical **androcentric bias**.

Is this "me"? Yes and no. Away from my routine context, I become a different person, at least for a few days. Put me in a more intense and long-term changed context, and in all honesty, I don't know what I'd become. Indeed, these glimpses into such possibilities form the mainstays of most social psychology classes. Some psychologically well-adjusted college students transformed into submissive prisoners or cruel guards in Phil Zimbardo's (1972) famous prison study, and average adults in New Haven, Connecticut gave dangerous shocks to errant "learners" in Stanley Milgram's (1963) classic shock box studies. As a social psychologist, I can't help but scrutinize photos in newspapers that capture pieces of other people's everyday lives and wonder what I would do if I found myself in their circumstances. This is the power of **social contexts**.

So what if women and men, by simple virtue of their gender, live in different worlds? We already have seen that gender is an omnipresent marker that automatically divides us into two presumably distinct social categories: female and male. What's the social baggage that attaches itself to these designations of female or male?

The Logic of Social Contextual Explanations

This logic of social contextual explorations for a known intergroup gender difference is diagrammed in Figure 6.5. Hypothesis 1 assumes that there is something about women that makes them produce Behavior A (such as superior mind reading), and something about men that leads to a different behavior, Behavior B (such as poor mind reading). Hypothesis 2 proposes that women and men operate in two different *gendered* social contexts. The social context typically associated with women (Social Context W) causes women to do Behavior A, whereas a different social context generally impinging on men (Social Context M) evokes Behavior B.

Hypothesis 2 is supported if the results show the hypothetical pattern diagrammed in Figure 6.4(c). When women and men are exposed to the same social context, they both exhibit the same behavior. Thus, Behavior A is not a "women's reaction," but rather is a human reaction to a contextual factor more typically encountered by women (Social Context W). Similarly, what looks like men's behavior is really a function of the circumstance in which men more commonly find themselves (Social Context M). When we hypothetically "de-gender" (neutralize) the context, the gap between women and men closes. (Alternatively, we could reverse contexts by showing that women "act like men" when in Social Context M, and men behave like women in Social Context W—for example, by motivating men to be empathetic.)

Notice how our focus has shifted. We have moved away from considering internal, dispositional characteristics of women and men (Hypothesis 1) to thinking about the social circumstances in which they find themselves (Hypothesis 2). The key to doing this type of analysis is to identify a contextual factor that is **confounded** with gender; that is, a factor that goes with being female or being male. The critical test is to equalize this factor either by neutralizing it (as in Figure 6.4c) or by exposing men to what typically occurs for women, and vice versa. The keys to this probing of gender comparisons are contextual **moderators** (so that statistically we see their impact in interactions with gender). They *qualify* the conditions under which intergroup gender differences wax and wane.

My overriding point here is that finding a gender difference may be just the start of one's exploration, not the end. To say simply that sex or gender is the cause of the difference ignores other possibilities (James, 1997). The next step should be to explore *why* the

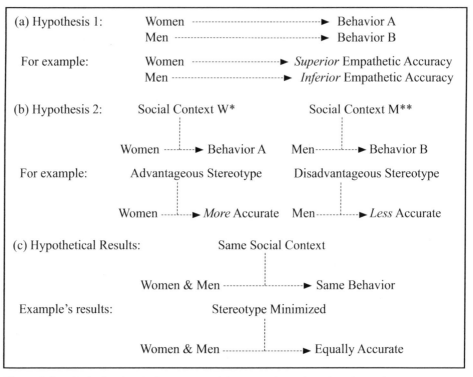

Figure 6.5 The logic of exploring contextual factor (moderated) explanations of apparent gender differences.

*Social Context W = a social context typically encountered by women; **Social Context M, by men.

"difference" exists. All too often, we psychologists have limited our explorations to possibilities internal to women and men—that is, to biology and to past learning (socialization).

Some of this limitation may result because focusing on the presumed internal dispositions of others is a general psychological tendency, referred to by social psychologists as the **fundamental attribution error** (Ross, 1977). One way to avoid this tendency is to think about how you yourself might act and why, because we tend to regard surrounding circumstantial contexts as more salient when we think about ourselves (Taylor & Fiske, 1975). Indeed, research shows that taking the perspective of the other reduces the expression of stereotyping (Galinsky & Moskowitz, 2000) and can help make men more empathetic about the sexist daily hassles women experience (Becker & Swim, 2011). Overall, *a complete understanding of what we think, feel, and do must take into account a combination of biology, socialization (and other historical experiences), as well as present social context* (Riger, 2000a).

THE IMPACT OF SOCIAL CONTEXTS ON WOMEN AND MEN

Now that we understand both intuitively and logically about the reasoning behind social contextual explanations for gender differences, it's time to turn to the growing research evidence about the impact of social contexts on women and men. This research focuses on two different sources for gender-typing social contexts: stereotyping and social status. The literature on **stereotyping** examines how our *expectations* about what is appropriate for women and men affect what women and men ultimately think, do, and feel. Similarly, research on **social status** suggests that women and men operate from different value bases of status and power. Although popular books claim that women are different from men because one comes from Venus and the other from Mars (Gray, 2004), our social contextual approach here explores how women and men may be living day-to-day on different planets—planets made different by our own ways of thinking about and valuing gender.

Stereotyping about Social Variables

Meta-analytic summaries of research in Chapter 2 (Table 2.7) identified a variety of social variables on which intergroup differences were confirmed. Although the possibilities for future research on social contextual explanations remain open since I last revised this text 5 years ago, more and more social contextual research has appeared. In addition to the work on empathetic accuracy with which I began this chapter, the social contexts of women's and men's aggression, helping, and sociability have been explored.

Aggression. Social psychologists define **aggression** as behavior intended to inflict harm (as opposed to accidental injury). Generally, adults' aggression comes in two varieties: **physical aggression** (including delivering shocks and noxious noise in the laboratory as well as outright assault) and **psychological aggression** (including verbal, nonverbal, and written forms). Alice Eagly and Valerie Steffen (1986) uncovered a small difference between women and men on psychological aggression ($d = +0.18$) and an expected moderate effect for physical aggressiveness between strangers ($d = +0.40$).

Eagly and Steffen also found that women and men have different *beliefs* about the consequences of their own physical aggression. Women reported higher fears that their aggressiveness will pose dangers to themselves, perhaps reflecting their awareness that such behavior violates gendered expectations (which indeed exist; Basow et al., 2007; Weaver et al., 2010) as well as attracts retaliation. Women also expected to feel more anxiety and guilt than men as a consequence of behaving aggressively. Thus, women may exercise more control over their expression of aggression because they anticipate more negative consequences (Harris, 1995), or they may seek more indirect outlets. Consistent with this reasoning, systematic observations of soccer games concluded that on those less frequent occasions when women players were aggressive, referees penalized women more than men (Coulomb-Cabagno et al., 2005; Souchon et al., 2009). Overall, this evidence suggests that women are more inhibited than men in expressing aggression.

What would happen if we equalized their inhibitions by lowering women's? College women and men played a violent videogame under anonymous conditions; the experimenters' expectation was that being unidentifiable would make women feel just as comfortable to aggress as men (Lightdale & Prentice, 1994). Indeed, under these circumstances, women opted to drop as many bombs as men. However, women's and men's reports of their own aggressiveness differed—women described significantly less aggressive self-behavior. This pattern is consistent with an explanation based on inhibitions. When inhibitions were lifted, women aggressed like men; but being aware of societal inhibitions based in stereotyping about female nonaggressiveness, women failed to acknowledge their own aggressiveness.[8]

All this argues that a stereotype of nonaggressive women exists (White & Kowalski, 1994). This stereotype comes up as one of five traits believed to distinguish between women and men by respondents from 30 different countries (Williams & Best, 1982).[9] Does this mean that women really are nonaggressive? We all can cite instances when women acted aggressively so that a better summary of this literature is that *women will aggress given the appropriate circumstances* (Richardson & Hammock, 2007). The myth of women's nonaggressiveness sustains men's power by encouraging women's dependence on more powerful men; by bolstering the preconception that women always will lose out to a man's greater strength (misleading women to believe that "resistance is futile"—see Chapter 13); by discounting the potential of assertiveness and competitiveness (believed to be related to aggressiveness); by labeling aggressiveness by women as deviant; and by deflecting research away from understanding the conditions under which women will act aggressively.

What does it take to provoke aggressive behavior in women? Physical attacks, verbal insults, and frustrations (such as cutting ahead in line, losing a competitive game, blockage by a stopped car, and difficult puzzles) all reduce but don't close the gap in aggressive responses between women and men (Bettencourt & Miller, 1996).[10] Moreover, trained women and men coders rated the procedures used in research studies according to the intensity of the provocation used and the likelihood of retaliation. Women perceived less provocation in the procedures and felt more endangered by retaliation. These findings suggest that it may take more to induce aggression in women and that women may exercise greater control over their own aggressiveness because of fears of retaliation.

Extrapolating these findings beyond what is traditionally done in social psychological experiments of aggression, it seems that with significant provocation and reduction of women's stronger inhibitions against aggression, the gap between women's and men's aggressiveness can be narrowed. Indeed, when both violent cues and aversive provocation exist together, women will respond as aggressively as men (Bettencourt & Kernahan, 1997). (A preferable alternative might be to understand the factors that increase men's aggressiveness, with research pointing to the likely roles of higher fear of retaliation and reduced inhibitions in men, not gender differences in anger; Campbell, 2006).

Helping behavior. A hitchhiker stands on the side of a highway, a man collapses on a subway, a brutal fight breaks out—who comes to the rescue? In all likelihood, it's a man. Indeed, when we think about public "heroes," we are more likely to think about men, especially men who perform heroic rescues (Rankin & Eagly, 2008). When we look across a variety of helping studies, there is a small-to-moderate tendency for men to offer help more often than women ($d = +0.34$) and for women to receive help more often than men ($d = -0.46$) (Eagly & Crowley, 1986). Given that the nurturing role is typically ascribed to women, and (as we'll see in Chapter 8) more caregiving is done by women, the finding about who helps seems odd.

---

[8]This reasoning also is consistent with findings of a positive association between alcohol consumption and aggressive behavior in women, indicating that drinking may lower inhibitions (Dougherty et al., 1996).

[9]The others are dominance, autonomy, achievement, and endurance.

[10]Bogus negative feedback seems to make women, but not men, feel unhappy instead of aggressive.

Box. 6.6

When photographed women are not smiling (so that they deviate from our expectations about women's sociability), evaluators rate them negatively by describing nonsmilers as less happy, warm, relaxed, and carefree than the average woman (Deutsch, LeBaron, & Fryer, 1987).

Much of the social-psychological literature on helping behavior relies on settings involving interactions with strangers in short-term relationships. Of course, it is these circumstances that provoke wariness in women and that are likely to reduce their willingness to intervene (Erdle et al., 1992). As women's comfort levels go up, so does their helpfulness. For example, in studies conducted on campus, a presumably safer-feeling environment for women, the gender difference virtually disappears ($d = -0.04$) (Eagly & Crowley, 1986). This difference also evaporates when the appeal for help comes in the form of a direct request ($d = +0.07$). We might expect people to be more responsive to stereotyped expectancies when they are watched than when they act unnoticed by others. Consistent with this reasoning, the gender gap in helping fades when potential helpers feel unobserved ($d = -0.02$).

Sociability. We expect women to be more sociable: to talk about themselves (self-disclosure), to smile, to stand closer, to be sensitive to what others feel and want, to openly express their emotions, and so on. Women's speech is believed to be less direct and more emotional, talkative, and trivial than men's (Popp et al., 2003). As with all stereotyping, a visible way to become aware of their operation is to see what happens when they are violated (see Box 6.6).

As you might have guessed though, there is more to understanding gender and sociability than thinking women are more sociable than men. Campbell Leaper and Melanie Ayres (2007) conducted an extensive meta analysis of different types of speech—including affiliative speech; that is, talking meant to connect with others. They found the overall effect we'd expect ($d = -0.12$), along with specific types of affiliative speech favoring women: active understanding ($d = -0.41$), socioemotional ($d = -0.35$), and supportive ($d = -.016$). However, they also uncovered some **moderators** that qualify this general pattern. Women engaged in more affiliative speech with strangers than did men ($d = -0.18$), but there was no gender difference with close relations, including partners, children, and friends ($d = -0.02$). There was a gender gap in same-sex groups ($d = -0.33$), but not in mixed-sex groups ($d = -0.01$). The topic of conversation also mattered, with wider gender differences when discussing nonpersonal topics (small talk; ($d = -0.44$) and one's self ($d = -0.20$).

An interesting single study showed that even the context in which speech takes place can be important. People tend to dislike both the woman and the man in an intimate couple in which the woman talks a lot and the man is relatively silent (Sellers et al., 2007). In contrast, when the man is more effusive, he is both liked and regarded as more competent. It seems that although women are generally expected to be more sociable than men, women also need to know their "place."

Stereotyping Roles and Occupations

As we'll see in the next chapter, **stereotyping** proscribes what the appropriate roles should be for women and men, and we'll see in Chapter 9 that the workforce (like the school playground we saw in Chapter 4) is characterized by significant gender segregation. Here we'll look at how these expectations for women and men create gender-typed tasks, can be exaggerated by the gender composition of work groups, and can affect people's actual performances on cognitive as well as other gender-typed tasks.

Gender-typed tasks.   Before we examine the impact of gender stereotyping on tasks, let's take a quick look at the basis for task stereotyping. We need to be wary of overgeneralizing about women's and men's task abilities, a trend that is especially common for cognitive tasks. For example, if we asked people to identify who is better at math, girls or boys, most would say "boys," even though the effect size for gender differences in overall math performance among Americans is now negligible (ds = +0.05–.07; Lindberg et al., 2010) and in math achievement across 69 nations is quite small (ds < +0.15; Else-Quest et al., 2010). Additionally, math abilities themselves are not so simply defined. For example, U.S. women benefit when math tests include more algebra items and disadvantaged when they contain more measurements items (questions about measures such as area, perimeters, volume, and angles; Lindberg et al., 2010).

Furthermore, gender differences in U.S. math performance actually vary by age. No differences are documented across elementary and middle school, but small differences favor males in high school (d = +0.23) and into college (d = +0.18) (Lindberg et al., 2010). As we already noted, more boys and men scored at the extreme high tail in distributions of math scores; among the few studies that have used high-level, difficult test items, a gender difference favoring males appears (Lindberg et al., 2010). In sum, although there is some basis for stereotyping math as a male domain, the evidence in support of this conclusion is not all that convincing.

A similar overgeneralization can happen with spatial abilities. Common laboratory tests of spatial abilities tend to tap three specific skills. On **spatial perception** tasks, research participants are asked to determine spatial relationships with respect to the orientation of their own bodies. **Mental rotation** tasks involve the ability to rotate a two- or three-dimensional figure rapidly and accurately. Finally, **spatial visualization** tasks include complicated, multi-step manipulations of spatially presented information. Try doing examples of each of these in Box 6.7.

Here we find the largest and most consistent gender differences in cognitive abilities (Voyer et al., 1995). A d = +0.44 was found for spatial perception, and d = +0.56 for mental rotation (reported elsewhere as +0.90; Masters & Sanders, 1993). Both effects are in the moderate to large range and favor men and boys. The biggest jump in spatial perception differences occurs around age 13 (+0.33 for children under 13; +0.43 for 13 to 18 year-olds; +0.48 for adults over 18). The gap in mental rotation widens consistently with age (+0.33 for children under 13; +0.45 for 13 to 18 year-olds; +0.66 for those over 18). On the

Spatial Perception

Which of the following four tilted glasses has a horizontal water line?

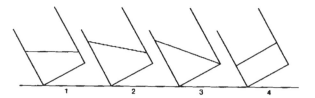

Mental Rotation

Which two of the four choices below show the standard in a different orientation?

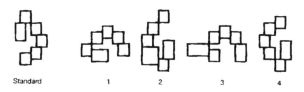

Spatial Visualization: Embedded figures

Find the simple shape above within the more complex pattern below.

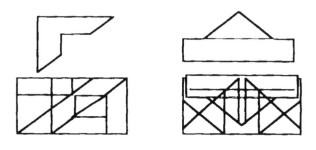

Source: M. C. Linn and A. C. Petersen (1985). University of Chicago Press. Reprinted with permission.

Answers: (1) glass #1; (2) Figures #1 and #4.

other hand, there is only a small gender difference on spatial visualization tasks ($d = +0.19$) (also see Feingold & Mazzella, 1988).

When we turn away from the laboratory to examples of using spatial skills in the real world, a widely cited example describes men's superiority at wayfinding (using maps) (Lawton et al., 1996; Schmitz, 1999).[11] Although most widely used spatial abilities tasks

___

[11]Here again is an example of the impact of context. Although women more often use landmarks and men

favor men or find no differences, there are some exceptions, such as mirror tracing, in which women typically outscore men (Halpern, 1997).

As we noted earlier, some of what turn up as math differences may actually reflect differences in spatial performances, with meta-analytic findings more supportive of a spatial stereotype that favors boys and men over a math stereotype. Yet we will see that although less well grounded, math stereotyping is quite consequential for girls and women.

Task stereotyping. Given that tasks can acquire gender-typing, as we have just seen, we need to watch closely which specific tasks are used to test specific phenomena. A classic example has to do with *influenceability*. Researchers generally concluded that women conformed more readily than men, and eventually meta-analysts found small effect sizes ranging from +0.16 to +0.32 (Eagly & Carli, 1981). Further probing revealed that although masculine, feminine, and neutral content was used across these studies, more masculine topics (such as sports, the military, and technology) produced greater female influenceability. In sum, some of this apparent gender difference had something to do with the task used to measure conformity.

This finding even extends to what participants *believe* the task is measuring. When a task was presented as a spatial task, women who scored as masculine on the BSRI scored high (Massa et al., 2005). When that same task was described as assessing empathy, the performance of feminine women was superior. In another study with a mental rotation task, men for whom the task was described as testing skills necessary for the navigation of naval vessels outperformed men who thought the task had to do with handicrafts (Sharps et al., 1994). When instructions for a mental rotation test stressed accuracy, men outperformed women, but when these instructions were deleted, women's scores equaled men's (Scali et al., 2000). Finally, memory for the same shopping list varied as we'd expect when the list was called a grocery or hardware list and instructions either identified women or men as good at the task (Colley et al., 2002). A sound conclusion then may be that task stereotyping rests more in beliefs than necessarily in documented evidence.

Composition of groups. Like tasks that can arouse gendered expectations, who we are *with* when we perform a task can make gender more or less salient. There is a long-standing body of research exploring what happens when women are in groups of mostly men (see Yoder, 2002, for a review). When **token** women make up 15% or less of a work group, they experience heightened visibility, performance pressures, social isolation, and **role encapsulation**; that is, being perceived as stereotypic women (Kanter, 1977). Thus, a condition that makes it more likely that stereotyping will occur has to do with these contexts of underrepresentation (or **tokenism**).

Stereotype threat. What we know about the gender-typing of tasks and group composition comes together in fascinating and burgeoning work on **stereotype threat**. Stereotype threat is a situational (contextual) threat that generally affects members of any group about which negative stereotyping is aroused (Steele, 1997). For those who seek success in a domain, stereotype threat predicts that negative stereotyping will disrupt performance. Notice that we are not talking about specific tasks, but rather a **domain** or cluster of similar

use cardinal directions ("go north") to give route directions, cardinal directions are favored by people from the Midwest and West and by people living in areas with grid-like road arrangements.

tasks (potentially an overgeneralization about a category, such as all spatial tasks). *It's what test takers believe, and the activation of this stereotyping, that matters.*

For example, stereotype threat posits that for girls and women who have some vested interest in performing well in math, the societal expectation that women aren't good at math will work to undermine their performance on challenging tasks and thus confirm the stereotyping. This cycle can become self-sustaining, leading girls and women to disidentify with math, to withdraw from further testing, and to forego further skill development.

The pattern of activating stereotyping to generate feelings of threat with subsequent disrupted performance has drawn largely on: (1) task beliefs, (2) group composition, and (3) priming a threatened identity. We have seen that even subtle changes in *task beliefs* via instructions given about the task can make a difference in how women and men perform on that task. When experimenters tell test takers straight out that the math task they are about to take is one that can detect men's superiority (Walsh et al., 1999) or is simply diagnostic of true ability (Brown & Josephs, 1999), women do worse than men. This same pattern was found for visuospatial ability, with women's and men's performances equalizing when the stereotype was nullified by telling participants that women generally outperform men on the task at hand (Campbell & Miller, 2009).

When negative stereotyping is pervasive in the domain (as in "men are better at all math"), researchers don't even need to state the stereotype to see its impact. Jessi Smith and Paul White (2002) created three experimental conditions in which they told one-third of the women outright that men do better in math; another third that women and men perform the same on this test; and the last third were told nothing. The last "uninformed" group scored just as poorly as the first group for whom negative stereotyping about women and math was explicitly aroused (and less well than the second, same performance condition). Another part of this study extended the impact of stereotype threat beyond women and math by activating negative stereotyping in White men about Asian men's superior abilities.

Individual differences research also links stereotyping activation to performance. Women who endorsed traditional stereotyping about women's math abilities (and generally regarded women's lower status as legitimate) were more susceptible to stereotype threat than more nontraditional women (Schmader at al., 2004).

Notice in each of the examples above, stereotyping was activated either implicitly or subtly. If stereotypes are boldly made explicit, **stereotype reactance** can be raised so that people will bend over backwards to behave in ways inconsistent with the stereotyping

Box 6.8

Research on stereotype threat tells us that if this woman is taking a math test, both the composition of this group and any instructions that would activate stereotypes about men's superiority in the domain of math will likely undermine her performance. In this way, the presumed objectivity of the test itself is compromised by the context in which it is taken.

(Kray et al., 2001). We'll see this point raised again—highlighting that the power of stereotyping is in its subtly.

Extending the subtly of stereotyping activation to *group composition*, simply completing a task in the presence of others can arouse stereotyping. When women and men completed math problem-solving and verbal tasks in the presence of two other students (of either the same- or other-sex), only women's scores in math and in the presence of two men were negatively affected (Inzlicht & Ben-Zeev, 2000). In a similar study, women were exposed twice to the spatial Ponzo illusion, and the gap between women's and men's scores was greatest when women were with more men (Miller, 2001). Given what we know about **tokenism** and **stereotype threat**, it is likely that being one woman among men is all it takes to arouse debilitating stereotyping.

Denise Sekaquaptewa and Mischa Thompson (2003) brought these two strands of research together in one study by varying both task stereotyping (by describing women as poor performers) and group composition (a lone woman within a group of men). As we'd expect, each condition alone led to performance deficits. Moreover, the combination of both sources of threat resulted in even worse performance. In the everyday world where women encounter all sorts of negative stereotyping about their cognitive abilities, the additive impact of multiple sources of stereotype threat becomes even more troubling.

Finally, researchers have *primed the identity* threatened by a stereotype to explore stereotype threat effects. For example, when women and men were primed to think about the positive characteristics of women, women scored worse than men on a spatial mental rotation task (Ortner & Sieverding, 2008). However, this gap closed when both groups were primed to think about the positive qualities of men. Capturing the subtly of gendering cues, Sapna Cheryan and her colleagues (2009) demonstrated that college women's interest in computer science was negatively affected by simply having masculine-typed objects (Star Wars posters and tech parts) in the room—objects that made salient the masculine-typing of computing. Even the prospect of working on all-women teams did not erase the chilling impact of these masculinizing objects.

In another study, women's leadership aspirations were undermined by prior exposure to gender stereotypic television commercials (Davies et al., 2005). Drawing on task instructions to make women feel safe about their identity (even after watching stereotypic ads) restored women's aspirations to be a leader. Finally, in one of my favorite priming studies, Asian American women primed with their gender identity performed less well than control women on a math test, whereas other Asian American women primed with their ethnic identity did better (Shih et al., 1999).

Note that in this last study (as well as in others) *stereotype "threat" effects can be negative, nullified, or even positive* (beliefs that Asians are good at math) depending on the stereotype activated. This last point raises questions not only about who is unknowingly harmed by stereotyping but also about who is unwittingly benefitted (privileged).

STATUS AND SOCIAL CONTEXT

Stereotyping clearly set up different social contexts for women and men, potentially oppressing or privileging both women and men depending on the stereotype activated. A second way that social contexts can oppress or privilege girls/women and boys/men has to do more directly with the **social status** we culturally ascribe to gender.

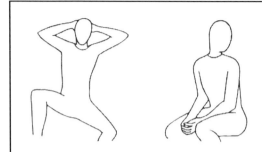

Box 6.9
Body language gives powerful clues about which of these is a woman and which is a man.

Source: Irene H. Frieze et al., *Women and Sex Roles: A Social Psychological Perspective* (New York: W.W. Norton & Company, 1978). Reprinted with permission of W.W. Norton & Company, Inc.

Status construction theory posits that being male, along with other more valued states (e.g., being White and heterosexual), is regarded as both superior in capabilities and **instrumental** (as opposed to **expressive**) in role quality (Berger & Webster, 2006). Thus the social meaning we give to gender includes hierarchical higher status associated with men. We can see the effects of status at work when interactions between peers of equal status and power show few gender differences in behavior, in contrast to most interactions between women and men that are rooted in inequalities in status (Ridgeway & Smith-Lovin, 1999). Because status is so confounded with gender, and because we don't have parallel equal-status interactions with which to compare these unequal relations, we often fail to even notice this fundamental difference. Furthermore, even if we do notice, we are more likely to write it off as differences between women and men than differences between lower- and higher-status individuals.

One of the most researched areas linking hierarchical status to gender in psychology has to do with nonverbal communication—or what Nancy Henley (1977) described as "body politics." This line of reasoning argues that women and lower-status others stake out less territory, wait more, are touched more and touch less, seek eye contact, and smile more in nonintimate relationships. Meta-analysts do find evidence of small-to-moderate differences between women and men on several nonverbal indicators—including recognizing faces ($d = -0.17$), social smiling ($d = -0.30$), greater distance maintained from others ($d = +0.27$) and by others ($d = +0.43$), and expansiveness (taking up space) ($d = +0.46$) (Hall, 1984). Additionally, there is some evidence that these nonverbal signs are linked to dominance (high status) and submissiveness (low status).

For example, Marie Helwig-Larsen and her colleagues (2004) observed attentive head nodding as a gesture of submissiveness. When these researchers observed students interacting with professors and with other students, both women and men students nodded their heads more when professors, than when students, spoke. As we'd predict if status and gender are related, men nodded less when their peers spoke than did women.

Although it is clear that women smile more than men, whether this pattern is related to hierarchical status is less clear. On the one hand, the pattern of women smiling more than men did not completely map onto actual or perceived status (Hall et al., 2002). On the other hand, smiling is more optional among higher-status and more obligatory among lower-status people so that status affects the *propensity* to smile more than actual displays of smiling (Hecht & LaFrance, 1998). For individual women, smiling was related to their dominance preference such that women who wanted to appear subordinate, smiled more (Mast & Hall, 2004).

Status and gender can combine to affect how people are perceived by others. Michael Conway and his associates (2003) examined how people perceived the maladaptive worrying of others. As we might expect, participants both rated and described more worry by women than men. In a follow-up study, participants judged the worry of others who were described, not by their gender, but by their status. Low-status individuals, just like women, were perceived as experiencing more nonproductive worry.

Status construction theory also identifies associations between **status** and **agency** (that is, someone who actively takes control). Michael Conway and his colleagues (1996) asked college students to rate hypothetical characters "Mary Smith" and "Robert Jones," along the dimensions of the Personal Attributes Questionnaire indicating *communal* (warm and able to devote self to others) and *agentic* (aggressive and independent) attributes. Some students read about targets in gender-traditional jobs (Mary as a filing clerk); others, about nontraditional employees (Robert as a filing clerk). The jobs varied by status: high (surgeon) and low (nurse on a surgical ward). The job status of both Mary and Robert made a difference: high-status workers were regarded as more agentic and less communal than low-status workers.

Jobs in the real world are not neatly dispersed for researchers; Higher-status jobs tend to be dominated by White men, and jobs vary according to how much agency and communality they connote. (For example, our expectations that high-status surgeons will help people are unlike our expectations for high-status stockbrokers.) Conway and his colleagues (1996) got around these problems in follow-up studies in which they described fictitious people whose status was varied with social cues such as clothing and access to resources. The pattern noted above persisted: low-status individuals were described using communal/sociable terms in contrast to agentic high-status people.

Other studies systematically vary status cues by gender. I think more research along these lines needs to be developed. My personal favorite is Mary Hogue's and my (2003) study of "depressed entitlement" that we read about in Chapter 2. When women were explicitly told that women typically outperform men on the upcoming task, and even when they were told that the task is usually done by lower-status high school students, these status-enhanced women paid themselves for their work similarly to men. In the control conditions when women and men simply did the task then allocated their self-pay, women gave themselves less than men, reproducing the depressed entitlement effect. Control women didn't know they underpaid themselves, and we didn't know that status played a role until we manipulated these factors in our study.

CHAPTER SUMMARY

The main point that runs across this chapter is that finding a gender difference between women and men, no matter how convincing even a meta-analysis is, doesn't let us automatically jump to the conclusion that intergroup difference is the best way to talk about this finding.

First, the difference between women and men itself may be dwarfed by individual and subgroup diversity that makes intragroup diversity among women greater than the intergroup difference between the average women and the average men. Making this interpretative mistake can restrict individuals and subgroups to living within gender-defined barriers, rather than freeing each of us to realize our own potentials. For example, we have seen that although boys generally are better at spatial tasks than girls, there's no reason to think an individual girl can't excel in this domain.

The stereotyping that can evolve from this misinterpretation of intergroup gender differences though can produce stereotype threat that itself can come to limit individuals. Understanding the power of stereotyping and status takes us to the second point of this chapter that social context is gendered and matters. Stereotyping about social behaviors, roles, and occupations, along with status differentials, can socially construct different worlds for women and men. Thus, what appear to be differences rooted within women's and men's biology and/or socialization histories actually may disappear when the playing field is leveled.

SUGGESTED READINGS

Levitt, H. M., Gerrish, E. A., & Hiestand, K. R. (2003). The misunderstood gender: A model of modern femme identity. *Sex Roles, 48*, 99–113.

Heidi Levitt and her colleagues conducted interviews with femme-identified lesbians about their identity development. Grappling with stereotyping about women and lesbians, their analysis enriches our understandings of femininity, relationships, and privilege.

Lott, B. (1997). The personal and social correlates of a gender difference ideology. *Journal of Social Issues, 53*(2), 279–298.

Bernice Lott makes a case for viewing gender differences with an eye to both within-gender variation and social context. She then takes the next critical step and links this common failure to understand the full complexity of gender differences to a broader political agenda that supports systems of inequality. Her examples help apply my chapter here to the more topical chapters coming up later in this text.

Yoder, J. D., & Kahn, A. S. (2003). Making gender comparisons more meaningful: A call for more attention to social context. *Psychology of Women Quarterly, 27*, 281-290.

This paper actually grew out of this chapter in the second edition of this textbook (then Chapter 5), and it in turn shaped my richer discussion of social context here. Thus, I think it helps contribute to a fuller understanding of a social contextual approach and how it fits across the previous chapters of this text.

Halpern, D. F., Benbow, C. P., Geary, D. C., Gur, R. C., Hyde, J. S., & Gernsbacher, M. A. (2007). The science of sex differences in science and mathematics. *Psychological Science in the Public Interest, 8*, 1–51.

Diane Halpern and her distinguished co-authors respond to then-Harvard University president Lawrence Summer's (2005) speculation that there are few distinguished women in math, science, and engineering because there aren't enough women with the innate abilities necessary to develop the needed advanced skills in these areas. This long and detailed article gives no easy answers but rather provides sound evidence that understanding these patterns requires much more complex thinking than writing off women's potential in these core science domains.

Steele, C. M. (1997). A threat in the air: How stereotypes shape intellectual identity and performance. *American Psychologist, 52*, 613–629.

Claude Steel presents a general overview of stereotype threat in a compelling and reader-friendly form in this important article. Although examples involving gender are peppered throughout this paper, it also provides a broader understanding of how stereotype threat works across different social categories across the Diversity Wheel.

Bohan, J. S. (1993). Regarding gender: Essentialism, constructionism, and feminist psychology. *Psychology of Women Quarterly, 17*, 5–21.

Using the terminology and ideas of essentialist and constructionist thinking, Janis Bohan makes a case for feminist psychology that fits well with the social contextual framework developed in this chapter. Thus, this paper helps integrate the ideas presented in Chapter 2 with our discussions of gender differences and power across the first half of this text.

Chapter 7

Sexism
Sexist Prejudice, Stereotyping, and Discrimination

A boy and his father were in a major car accident. The father was pronounced dead at the scene; meanwhile, the boy was rushed to the nearest hospital. A prominent surgeon was called to perform a life-saving operation. As the boy was being prepared for the surgery, the surgeon saw him and declared: "I can't operate. He's my son." How can this be?

This brain-teaser was widely circulated in the 1970s and baffled many people. Some suggested that the surgeon was a stepfather, an unknown biological father (as opposed to the adoptive father who died in the crash), a reincarnation of the dead father, mistaken about the identity of the boy, and so on. A simple solution eluded many.[1] Yet this simple riddle speaks volumes about how deep-seated sexism can be; we are likely to consider all sorts of outlandish possibilities before we challenge the misleading assumption that the surgeon is male.   ·

In the previous chapter, we explored how gender stereotyping can shape different social contexts for women and men yet make it appear that women and men themselves are essentially different. In this chapter, we'll look at how gender stereotyping moves from being simply descriptive of women and men to proscribing what women and men do, ultimately limiting and oppressing women and girls.[2] In other words, I'll make the case that gender stereotyping can become sexist stereotyping. We'll also see how sexist stereotyping fits within a broader system of sexism that encompasses sexist prejudice, sexist stereotyping, and sexist discrimination.

GENDER STEREOTYPES

We've been talking a lot about gender **stereotyping**, but we haven't yet looked at the content of those stereotypes. Take a few moments and:

> Describe the *typical women*, as viewed by society.
> Describe the *ideal woman*, as viewed by society.

Notice that I'm not really interested in your own views, but rather your perceptions of our general cultural understandings (social norms).

The Contents of Gender Stereotypes

Social norms tell us about how people should behave, in this case defining what is appropriate for girls/women and boys/men. Notice that there are two kinds of social norms: **descriptive norms** (which describe what we perceive to be typical) and **prescriptive or injunctive norms** (which dictate what ought to be ideally) (Eagly & Karau, 2002). These norms are not always the same. For example, the typical American mother is employed, yet the cultural ideal demands that "good" mothers not work outside the home. Overall, the contents of gender stereotypes encompass traits, role behaviors, occupations, and physical characteristics (Deaux & Lewis, 1984).

Stereotyped traits.   Researchers have explored the contents of trait stereotypes about women by asking participants to think about the "typical female student" (Spence & Buckner, 2000), to rate "how desirable it is in American society for a woman to possess" listed

---

[1]The surgeon is the boy's mom.

[2]I do not mean to dismiss prejudice directed against men as inconsequential (see Chapter 1); however, women will take center stage in the present discussion of sexism.

traits (Prentice & Carranza, 2002), to list "things that people in general assume to be true of people the same gender as you" (Oswald & Lindstedt, 2006), and to pick traits from a list that best describe different subgroups of women (Wade & Brewer, 2006). These studies converge on the trait clusters for self-reported gender identity we reviewed in Chapter 6 using the Bem Sex Role Inventory and Personal Attributes Questionnaire (see Table 6.3). The traits stereotypically associated with women and femininity describe a more nurturing, caring, expressive, or **communal** orientation—overall conveying **warmth**. When focusing on men with parallel questions, the traits for men and masculinity draw on a more independent, separate, instrumental, or **agentic** orientation—overall conveying **competence** (Conway et al., 1996).

This linkage of communion/warmth with women and agency/competence with men is quite well ingrained in our thinking. Looking at self-construals, women define themselves as higher in relational interdependence (communion) than men; men, as higher in independence/agency (Guimond et al., 2006). These differences even show up in how women and men are described in letters of recommendation for academic jobs (Madera et al., 2009).

This association of women with communion is so pervasive that when students were first instructed to think about women and then did a modified **Stroop task** in which they had to name the color of words printed in different colors and all referring to sociability, they took longer than with ability words (White & Gardner, 2009). This difference in response time is because participants were distracted by the content of the words that fit women (sociability) and not by words that didn't fit (ability). In other words, there was more interference of word content with the sociability words so that students primed to think about women could less effectively concentrate on the task of identifying each printed word's color.

Stereotypes evoking femininity and masculinity can overpower the sex of the target (Helgeson, 1994a). The "feminine male" is described as more warm than competent; the "masculine female," as more competent than warm. Furthermore, gender stereotypes seem to span cultures (Williams & Best, 1990), all of which are fundamentally patriarchal—but not necessarily historical time periods. College students' perceptions of stereotypes about women are highly dynamic, arguing that contemporary women are more masculine than women of the past, whereas men are regarded as largely unchanged (Diekman & Eagly, 2000).

Stereotyped role behaviors. At least five subcategories of gender stereotypes emerge for women: homemaker, sexy woman, athlete/lesbian, businesswoman, and feminist (Deaux et al., 1985; Wade & Brewer, 2006).[3] The *homemaker* stereotype is characterized as a caregiver who is caring, devoted, loving, and nurturing and who spends time with her family. The subtype of *sexy woman* conjures up a well-dressed woman with a good figure, pretty face, long hair, and nail polish. The third subcategory describes *athletes* who are aggressive, competitive, determined, devoted, driven, energetic, hardworking, healthy, motivated, strong, and talented. The *businesswoman* is aggressive, ambitious, assertive, classy, competitive, confident, driven, hardworking, independent, intelligent, motivated, and professional. A feminist stereotypically is judged to be an aggressive, defensive, political, and opinionated extremist and activist. These five subcategories can be distilled further into two general categories of stereotyping of women:

---

[3]The descriptions used here for all but the sexy woman were generated by college women and men asked to pick traits for these and seven other subgroups of women listed by the researchers (Wade & Brewer, 2006).

traditional (housewife mother and sexy woman[4]), conveying **warmth**, and *nontraditional* (athlete/lesbian, businesswoman, and feminist), conveying **competence** (Glick & Fiske 1997; 1999a; Wade & Brewer, 2006).

Role stereotypes are dependent on **social contexts**. The four role-based stereotypes for women all depend on the social context in which they are evoked. For example, in a business setting, it is unlikely that, upon seeing a woman at a desk with a computer terminal, the housewife/mother stereotype will be activated. We generally look for a good situation-role fit to determine which subtype of role stereotyping to use (Eckes, 1996), making "businesswoman" a better fit in this work context.

In her social role theory, Alice Eagly (1987) sees role stereotypes as the core reason for many gender differences that have been documented by researchers (also see Eagly, Wood, & Diekman, 2000). Because cultures dictate expectations about the role assignments for women (homemaker) and for men (breadwinner), women and men are oftentimes motivated to pursue different goals (Diekman & Eagly, 2008), are expected to exhibit different traits (Diekman & Goodfriend, 2006), hold different political attitudes (Diekman & Schneider, 2010), and envision different near and distant possible selves (Brown & Diekman, 2010).

These authors also project that what is valued in women and men will shift as roles change over time, thus putting changes in women's and men's roles at the heart of social change. For example, in a clever study (Diekman & Goodfriend, 2006), students were presented with one of two hypothetical societies in which the government proactively decided to focus more on caregiving roles (or business competition). Students then rated communal and agentic qualities for how useful and positive they were for individuals. Although agency was generally regarded as useful, communion was rated as more useful and as more positive in the caregiving context; agency, in the competitive context. Thus with a cultural shift in roles came an evaluative shift in values.

Stereotyped occupations. The stereotyping of occupations as appropriate or inappropriate for women or men is intimately tied to actual gender ratios within an occupation. Joyce Beggs and Dorothy Doolittle (1993) created a continuum of people's perceptions of 129 jobs that ran from masculine on one end (anchored by miner) to feminine on the other (manicurist). These perceptions mapped well onto the actual gender ratios of employees in each position. These ratings also were responsive to changing ratios over time. Ratings of the 56 jobs on their list that increased their proportions of women from 1975 to the 1990s became similarly less masculine over time. Despite some movement though, all but 5 of the 129 jobs studied retained their general classification as masculine, feminine, or neutral across the time span of the study,[5] and women ratings in the 1990s were less gender-typed than men's.

The Myth of the Generic Woman

I started this section by asking you to describe society's view of typical and ideal women. Who are these women? Try picturing them. Would your picture change if I added some

---

[4]Although the stereotypes of both housewives and sexy women are similar in their non-threatening warmth, housewives are perceived as high in sexual and moral virtue; sexy women, low (Altermatt et al., 2003).

[5]The 5 exceptions were: sales manager, which moved from masculine to neutral; taxidermist, which shifted from neutral to masculine; and social worker, florist supply sales, and file clerk, which went from neutral to feminine.

qualifications, like picturing the typical African American woman? Elderly woman? Heterosexual woman? For example, who did White American college students rate as loud, religious, talkative, tough, strong, and loyal to family ties? ... as emotional, intelligent, sensitive, educated, family-oriented, and independent? The "typical" Black and White woman, respectively—with no overlap between the dominant traits listed for these two subgroups of women (Donovan, 2011).

Although we might think we can describe women in general, researchers find that this presumably generic version overlaps substantially with some subgroup characterizations and not with others (Irmen, 2006). Not surprisingly, the *unqualified* stereotyping of typical and ideal women parallels the stereotypes for culturally normative (hence privileged) subgroups: White, middle and upper class, heterosexual, younger, physically able, Christian—just take a spin around the Diversity Wheel (Landrine, 1985). The greatest overlap of role stereotypes for "woman" without a qualifier is mother (Eckes, 1994), suggesting that motherhood is the normatively defining feature of womanhood. Additionally, we shouldn't be surprised to find that the more privileged the group, the more positive the content of their stereotyping (Glick, 1997).

Qualifying stereotypes away from the normative moves the content of these stereotypes in a negative direction. For example, consider the most normative role for women: mother. Specifying "African American mothers" brings in conflicting images of mammies, welfare, promiscuity, matriarchy, and superwomen (Sparks, 1996). Think about "lesbian mothers," "unmarried mothers," "stepmothers," "divorced mothers," and "never married mothers" (Burns, 2000; Ganong & Coleman, 1995; Hequembourg & Farrell, 1999). Stepmothers are depicted as less family oriented, uninterested and unskilled in raising children, and less successful in their marriages. Divorced mothers are characterized as lonely, unhappy, stressed, financially poor, and with bleak futures. Never married mothers are portrayed as unpleasant people who are deficient in their childrearing skills, failures as marital partners, and products of dysfunctional families. Overall, the mother stereotype is rosy only if the mom is married, heterosexual, and biologically related to her child(ren).

Before we move to the next section, please go to Box 7.1 and complete the ratings there. Doing this brief exercise will help make the following more concrete.

SEXIST STEREOTYPING

We have seen that both trait and role stereotypes involve two primary dimensions: **warmth** (including the communal expressiveness of feminine traits, the traditional role of homemaker, and female-dominated occupations) and **competence** (including the agentic expressiveness of masculine traits, the roles of athlete and businesswomen, and male-dominated occupations). As simple descriptions, these appear benign, but remember that stereotyping includes prescriptive norms about what women and men *ought* to do. When we culturally dictate rules for what people should do, we open the door to deviations and the costs that go with deviating. As we have seen throughout this text, we slip from simply describing differences to making judgments about deficiency, to disrupting contact, and to losing connection.

Box 7.1

When completing the items below, please note that I am NOT interested in your personal beliefs, but in how you think each group is viewed by others. Read down each column, starting to the left.

As viewed by society, how competent are home-makers?

1	2	3	4	5
not at all ompetent				very competent

As viewed by society, how warm are homemakers?

1	2	3	4	5
not at all warm				very warm

How economically successful have homemakers been?

1	2	3	4	5
not at all successful				very successful

Resources that go to homemakers are likely to take away from the resources of people like me.

1	2	3	4	5
not at all true				very true

As viewed by society, how competent are business-women?

1	2	3	4	5
not at all competent				very competent

As viewed by society, how warm are business-women?

1	2	3	4	5
not at all warm				very warm

How economically successful have business-women been?

1	2	3	4	5
not at all successful				very successful

Resources that go to businesswomen are likely to take away from the resources of people like me.

1	2	3	4	5
not at all true				very true

As viewed by society, how competent are welfare recipients?

1	2	3	4	5
not at all competent				very competent

As viewed by society, how warm are welfare recipients?

1	2	3	4	5
not at all warm				very warm

How economically successful have welfare recipients been?

1	2	3	4	5
not at all successful				very successful

Resources that go to welfare recipients are likely to take away from the resources of people like me.

1	2	3	4	5
not at all true				very true

From Stereotypes to Stereotyping

To make this leap from the simple gendered contents of stereotypes to calling stereotyping sexist, we need first to define what we mean by sexism. **Sexism** directed against women is the oppression or "inhibition" of women "through a vast network of everyday practices, attitudes, assumptions, behaviors, and institutional rules" (Young, 1992, p. 180). If we look at sexism through the eyes of a social psychologist, we see that it has three interrelated, but conceptually distinct, parts: stereotyping, prejudice, and discrimination (Lott, 1995). **Sexist stereotyping** refers to the ascription of both positive and negative traits that characterize women and girls as well suited to restricted, less powerful and/or disliked roles. **Sexist prejudice** refers to negative as well as apparently positive attitudes toward women and girls that serve to oppress them. **Sexist discrimination** describes overt negative acts directed toward women and girls, as well as patronizing acts that assert male superiority. We'll examine each of these forms of sexism in this chapter, focusing our discussion first on stereotyping.

Please notice how my language has shifted from talking about gender stereotypes to considering gender *stereotyping*. As we have seen, the contents of stereotypes are dynamic—changing somewhat over time in response to changes in roles, especially women's (Diekman & Eagly, 2000). However, *stereotyping* is a fundamental process that continues to shape our thinking even if the contents of stereotypes change (Fiske et al., 2002). Most important, this shift away from content toward process lets us look more deeply across all stereotyping to find the common ground that unites stereotypes. This broadened perspective helps us avoid getting bogged down by all the qualifications we have seen can change even the fundamental tone of stereotyping (e.g., from the generally positive tone of stereotyping about "mothers" to the negativity associated with "lesbian mothers").

The Evaluative Meaning of Stereotyping

So far we have distilled all that we know about gender stereotyping down to two dimensions: warmth and competence. Certainly both are positively valued dimensions, and we all would be flattered to have others regard us as *both* warm (likeable) and competent (respected). Using questions like those in Box 7.1, Susan Fiske and her colleagues (2002) asked student and nonstudent samples about all kinds of stereotyped groups. The cluster that scored high on both warmth and competence included Christians, middle-class people, students, Whites, and *women*; that is, mostly culturally dominant groups in the United States. The surprisingly finding is the listing of "women" instead of "men," yet this findings fits with the general favorability of ratings of trait attributions for women (Eagly & Mladinic, 1989).

Based on what we learned above, we already know what's wrong with this simple finding—it assumes a generic woman. There are all kinds of ways we could specify the woman we are talking about, but again turning to what we just learned, it makes sense to consider the major role categories. This is what Fiske and her colleagues did in their Stereotype Content Model, collecting ratings for housewives, sexy women, businesswomen, and feminists. Where these groups fell along the dimensions of warmth and competence, as well as

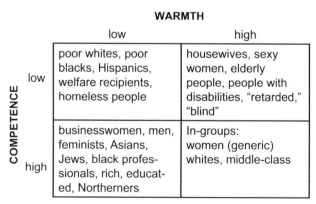

TABLE 7.2
Susan Fiske and her colleagues (2002) found that clusters of groups were similarly stereotyped along two dimensions of warmth and competence.

other groups that clustered with each, can be seen in Table 7.2. (You may want to review your answers in Box 7.1 here to see how they fit into Table 7.2.)

Warmth or Competence

Examining the clusters in Table 7.2, another pattern emerges (Fiske et al., 2002). Housewives, like others in their warm-but-incompetent cluster, are not competitive threats to raters. They aren't expected to make life difficult for raters if they get preferential treatment; their power doesn't lessen raters' perceived power; and the resources they get don't take away from raters' resources.

Businesswomen, like others in their competent-but-cold category, are regarded as high status. They are evaluated by raters as holding prestigious jobs, being well educated, and proving themselves economically successful. To finish out the matrix resulting from crossing warmth with competence, the groups rated as low on both competence and warmth (e.g., the poor and welfare recipients) are regarded as both non-threatening and subordinated in status. In sum, *high warmth is predicted by being non-competitive (non-threatening), and high competence results from privileged status.*

The last point digs deeper to better understand warmth and competence as more than simple descriptions; rather, warmth and competence ultimately are related to non-competitiveness and high status; that is, power (Conway & Vartanian, 2000). Stereotypes about warmth tell us about people's intent, and stereotypes about competence, about people's capabilities to pursue their intentions. People become limited by their traits and in their roles to the extent that they are seen as holding non-threatening intentions and/or powerful capabilities. In Table 7.2, these groups include those high in warmth and low in competence, high in competence and low in warmth, and low on both (i.e., everyone but the culturally dominant groups).

Most, if not all, subtypes of women fall into one of the two mixed cells where groups are stereotyped as high on either warmth *or* competence and low on the other (Eckes, 2002; Fiske et al., 1999, 2002). In other words, all women (except mythical generic women) are either liked *or* respected, but not both liked *and* respected (Goodwin & Fiske, 2001). Given our definition of **sexist stereotyping** as limiting the targets of stereotyping to restricted, less powerful and/or disliked roles, gender stereotypes succumb to sexist stereotyping to the extent that they limit girls and women to choosing between being liked and being respected.

This juggling of warmth *or* competence is made visible in a fascinating naturalistic experiment conducted by Michelle Hebl and her colleagues (2007). Female **confederates** wearing, or not wearing, a pregnancy prosthesis visited retail stores as either customers or job applicants. When apparently pregnant women stayed within a traditional role (customer), they were treated with over-friendliness by store employees relative to non-pregnant women (as we'd expect, given their assumed warmth as mothers-to-be). However, when these seemingly pregnant women turned up as job applicants (who were subtly trying to be both warm—pregnant—and competent—suitable for a job), they were treated with greater rudeness than the non-pregnant controls. In a follow-up study, pregnant women applying for more masculine-typed (likely associated with competence) as compared to feminine-typed (warmth) jobs were treated with more hostility. Across these two studies, friendly and hostile reactions were likely inadvertently used by store employees to keep women "in their place."

This tradeoff between warmth *or* competence for women is also evident in stereotyping about women who try to combine warmth (mothers) with competence (employment). Amy Cuddy and her associates (2004) explored college students' ratings of the stereotyping oxymoron of the "professional mother." When professionally employed women took on the added role of mother, they traded perceived competence for perceived warmth. In contrast, professional men who became fathers gained in warmth yet managed to maintain their perceived competence. Professional mothers not only took a hit in how competent they were regarded, but these declines in competence predicted less interest in hiring, promoting, and educating them. Working mothers' gains in warmth did nothing to help, and instead hurt, them in the workplace.

In sum, we have seen that stereotyping is a process that does more than describe women as warm or competent, but rather actively works to restrict real women to choosing between warmth by being noncompetitive *or* competence by emphasizing status. We can see this process in the no-win examples of women who limit their own opportunities (such as being a contestant on the TV show "Who Wants to Be a Millionaire") because they fear competition where not only does "losing" threaten competence, but "winning" loses warmth (Larkin & Pines, 2003). This linkage of the content of stereotypes to issues of privilege, oppression, and power works to maintain a status quo system of inequality (Glick & Fiske, 2001a). We'll see that this system is maintained through our attitudes of sexist prejudice and that the consequences of this sexist stereotyping are seen in examples of sexist discrimination.

SEXIST PREJUDICE

"Swearing and obscenity are more repulsive in the speech of a woman than a man."

Asking people whether they agree or disagree with statements like the one above (taken from the Attitudes Toward Women Scale; Spence & Helmreich, 1972) used to be all it took to measure individuals' sexist beliefs. Over time, however, respondents, especially from well-educated student samples, stopped varying on items like this one and instead openly and pretty universally expressed egalitarian answers (Spence & Hahn, 1997). Does this change mean that sexist prejudice has disappeared? Read on ....

Explicit and Implicit Attitudes

Recognizing that prejudices in general have become increasingly subtle (but as we'll see, continually powerful), social psychologists distinguish between **explicit attitude**s, measured on self-report scales, and **implicit attitudes,** about which we may be largely unaware (Dovidio et al., 2001). To tap into these implicit attitudes, cognitive psychologists developed the now-popular, computerized **Implicit Associations Test** (IAT; Greenwald et al., 1998). The logic of this test rests on the idea that it will take people longer to process unassociated pairings (flowers and unpleasant) than associated pairings (insects and unpleasant). Using a series of timed tests, experimenters present words or pictures to participants and ask them to make quick judgments. When associated pairs share the same response key on the computer's keyboard, participants can make these judgments more quickly (lower response time) than when they are unassociated. Thus, researchers can explore all kinds of associations involving much more charged pairings (fat/bad) than those involving prejudices toward bugs and preferences for flowers. You might want to Google "implicit associations tests" (or go to *https:/implicit.harvard.edu/implicit*) to participate in an IAT so that you get a feel for how these tests work.

For example, Kelly Malcolmson and Lisa Sinclair (2007) explored college students' explicit and implicit attitudes toward the titles Ms., Miss, Mrs., and Mr. Specifically, they asked students to rate a target person described with one of these titles on communal and agentic traits. On the explicit survey, women addressed as Ms. were judged as less communal than Mrs. and Mr. (but similar to Miss) and as more agentic than all three other targets. Using an IAT, reactions to Ms. (compared to Mrs.) were more agentic than communal, and no implicit differences were found between Ms. and Miss. Given that the title Ms. is associated with being feminist, both types of studies converge on the stereotyping of feminists as competent/agentic but not warm/communal, consistent with what the Stereotype Content Model would predict. Thinking about these findings on a day-to-day level, it is interesting that something as simple as a title of address should force women, but not Mr.-only men, to have to juggle the warmth-or-competence impression they wish to convey (Ms.: competent; Mrs.: warm; Miss: unclear).

You may think that because we cannot easily control our implicit attitudes that they are more "real" measures of our attitudes than traditional self-report measures of explicit attitudes. However, a growing body of research with both types of measures finds that each has its place in helping us understand prejudices (for example, see Petty et al., 2008), especially if self-report measures are less transparent than the item about swearing with which we started this section. At least three more contemporary self-report measures of sexist beliefs have been developed to usefully tap into **explicit attitudes** about women (and men).

Two of these measures capture "hidden" or unacknowledged prejudices against women: the *Modern Sexism Scale* (MS; Swim et al., 1995) and the *Neosexism Scale* (NS; Tougas et al., 1995). Both measure beliefs that discount sexist incidents, contending that such incidents are rare ("Over the past few years, the government and news media have been showing more concern about the treatment of women than is warranted by women's actual experiences"—MS), exhibiting antagonism toward women's demands, and expressing resentment toward efforts to reduce gender equality ("Due to social pressures, firms frequently have to hire underqualified women"—NS). Given that these two measures have to do with being unaware of sexism, making sexist incidents visible to women (by asking them to keep a diary of sexist "daily hassles") can change these beliefs (Becker & Swim, 2011). Interestingly, for men's beliefs to change, men need to both be aware of such incidents and have empathy for the women who are victimized by them. The third measure is the *Ambivalent Sexism Inventory* (ASI; Glick & Fiske, 1996; updated in 2001b), but to fully understand this increasingly used scale, we first need to step back and explore our general ideas about prejudices.

Ambivalent Sexism

We generally think of prejudices as negative, and indeed there are forms of prejudice that are openly and consistently hostile. For example, consider the welfare recipients you rated in Box 7.1. Generally they are regarded with contempt, disgust, anger, and resentment (Fiske

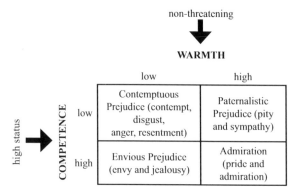

Table 7.3
Raters evidence different types of emotional prejudice for out-groups, but show consistency within clusters (cells). High warmth results from being non-competitive; high competence, from high status (Fiske at al., 2002).

et al., 2002). Indeed, Susan Fiske and her associates find that all groups in the low warmth, low competence quadrant face the same emotional reaction of contemptuous prejudice from others (see Table 7.3). The other three cells of Table 7.3 reveal common emotional prejudices across the groups clustered within them, including favorable reactions of admiration for those culturally dominant members who are regarded as both warm and competent.

However, we have seen that real women generally, if not always, fall into the mixed cells where either warmth *or* competence are high, incurring either paternalistic prejudice with high warmth/low competence or envious prejudice with high competence/low warmth. **Paternalistic prejudice** is characterized by pity and sympathy for those people (e.g., housewives, the elderly) (Cuddy et al., 2005) perceived as unable to control their own outcomes and in need of being cared for, despite their best (non-threatening) intentions. **Envious prejudice** lends grudging admiration to those with high status (e.g., feminists and Black professionals), but this admiration comes with envy and jealousy because the perceiver is threatened by these groups' status.

Neither combination is completely positive nor completely negative, but rather there is a mix of both seemingly positive and negative emotions (captured in the notion of **ambivalence**). Indeed, this ambivalence shows itself in sexist prejudice, which can evoke negative images as well as arguably benign or even revered ones (Glick & Fiske, 1996).

These contrasting attitudes are captured in the Ambivalent Sexism Inventory with its two subscales measuring "**hostile**" (HS) and "**benevolent**" (BS) sexism *targeting women.*[6] To get a sense of these two forms of sexism, especially BS, which is harder to think about and more complex than HS, be sure to check out Box 7.4. The items that compose the hostile subscale conform to what we usually think of when we consider prejudice toward women—the items clearly demean women, especially nontraditional women. As we'll see, the BS items, in contrast, are more prescriptive about what "good" (traditional) women should be like.

As you might suspect, among both students and non-students, American men scored higher than women on both hostile and benevolent sexism, with the difference being greater for HS than BS (Glick & Fiske, 1996). Interestingly though, the structure of these

---

[6]There is an Ambivalence toward Men Inventory (Glick & Fiske, 1999b), although it has attracted far less attention than the ASI.

Box 7.4

Sample Items from the Ambivalent Sexism Inventory (ASI) and from Students' Essays

Hostile Sexism

Most women interpret innocent remarks or acts as being sexist.
Most women fail to appreciate fully all that men do for them.
Women seek to gain power by getting control over men.

Benevolent Sexism

Protective Paternalism: Women should depend on men for protection and should support men

A good woman should be set on a pedestal by her man.
Men should be willing to sacrifice their own well-being in order to provide financially for the women in their lives.
"She sees the husband as the provider and her job is to care for him."

Complementary Gender Differentiation: Women and men are different—gender polarization—and these roles complement each other.

Many women have a quality of purity that few men possess.
"Women are more caring in general and I believe that they instinctively know they are to love and care for their children, perhaps more so than men."

Heterosexual Intimacy: Fulfillment depends on being heterosexually intimate.

People are not truly happy in life without being romantically involved with a member of the other sex.
No matter how accomplished he is, a man is not truly complete as a person unless he has the love of a woman.
"Being a woman also means that you have to get married ... [whereas] a man can be single until the day that he dies, and he's still considered a bachelor, not an 'old maid.'"

Note. Each *italicized* ASI item is rated on a 6-point scale ranging from 0 (*disagree strongly*) to 5 (*agree strongly*). Note that there are three different forms of BS. The statements in quotes come from students asked to write an essay about "What does it mean to be a woman?" Fields and her colleagues (2010) content analyzed these essays, finding examples of ambivalent sexism in 99% of them. These quotes are included here to help you get a richer grasp of what Benevolent Sexism is.

Sources: P. Glick and S. T. Fiske (2001b). An ambivalent alliance: Hostile and benevolent sexism as complementary justifications for gender inequality. *American Psychologist, 56,* 109–118. ASI items printed with permission of Peter Glick. Fields, A. M., Swan, S., & Kloos, B. (2010). What it means to be a woman: Ambivalent sexism in female college students' experiences and attitudes. *Sex Roles, 62,* 554–567.

scales was parallel for women and men, arguing that sexism is alive and well among *both* sexes. Additionally, although HS and BS were correlated (so that individuals who scored high on one tended to score high on the other), we'll see that these subscales function differently—as we might expect if they represent two related but distinguishable forms of sexism. A quick search of PsycINFO turned up 155 journal articles listing "ambivalent" or "benevolent" with "sexism" in their Abstract since this measure was published in 1996. Tiane Lee, Susan Fiske, and Peter Glick (2010a) penned a summary of these studies that captures various research approaches used to study ambivalent sexism.

Given our interest here in a psychology of women, I'm going to focus now on three questions concerning the ASI that have implications for women: (1) What makes men score high in hostile sexism? (2) What makes women score high on benevolent sexism?, and (3) What are the consequences of benevolent sexism for women?

Hostile men.   Hostile sexism is openly negative, and because it targets women as a group, HS potentially unfavorably affects all women. In this way, women have an obvious stake in understanding what causes men to endorse hostilely sexist attitudes. For example, men who endorse HS are more likely to label resistance by women rape victims as wavering ("token resistance") and thus are more accepting of acquaintance rape (Masser et al., 2006). Additionally, men's high hostile sexism is directly related to opposition to policies targeting gender equality (Sibley & Perry, 2010), and high HS men (and women) enjoy sexist humor that belittles women (Greenwood & Isbell, 2002). In fact, the combination of HS men with sexist humor reduces men's willingness to support a women's organization (Ford et al., 2008).

Complicated modeling of the factors that influence men's endorsement of HS show that the most immediate predictor is men's beliefs in intergroup dominance and superiority (or "social dominance orientation"; Christopher & Mull, 2006; Sibley et al., 2007a). Chris Sibley and his co-authors (2007a) further found that what drives men's social dominance orientation is their view of the world as a competitive place and being high in the personality trait of tough-mindedness (being unsympathetic, unfeeling, ruthless, and harsh). Other research adds to the list of antecedents to HS by pointing to men's narcissism (an exaggerated sense of deservingness; Keiller, 2010) and college men's overestimation of their peers' sexism (Kilmartin et al., 2008). In sum, men's HS is driven both by their own personalities and by their perceptions of contexts outside themselves.

Benevolent women.   More intriguing is benevolent sexism, which on the face of it seems positive. People tend to think that benevolent sexism is not all that negative for women (Bosson et al., 2010). Given these perceptions of the "benevolence" of BS, it is not surprising that there are wide individual differences in women's scores, including women who highly endorse BS.

However, the presumed benefits of BS (e.g., being protected and put on a pedestal) are undermined by a growing body of research looking at the causes of women's BS. Across a variety of studies, high levels of BS in women are associated with being in a hostile context, making women's BS appear to be an adaptation to a negative climate.

For example, Peter Glick, Susan Fiske, and a host of colleagues (2000) studied 19 countries, finding that women endorsed BS even more strongly than men in countries with strongly HS men. In contrast, in countries with men who scored lower in HS, women's BS scores were much lower than men's. In a clever experiment with American women, Ann Fischer (2006) created three experimental conditions simply by telling women that research shows that men's attitudes are generally negative, positive, or a no-information control. Women who believed that men hold negative attitudes about women scored significantly higher in BS than women in the other two conditions (and none of the groups differed on HS). In addition, women who held high levels of fear of crime also scored high in BS, and when Julie Phelan and her colleagues (2010) manipulated women's fear of crime in a follow-up study, these fearful women's BS exceeded that of controls. Thus, women's BS not only is associated with being in a hostile climate, but hostile contexts also *cause* women's BS to be elevated.

Consequences of benevolence. So what makes benevolence (by both women and by men) "sexist"; that is, oppressive of girls and women? Actually, BS alone does not "oppress" women; rather, it works in tandem with HS to keep women "in their place." BS provides the "carrot" (rewards) while HS is the "stick" (that doles out punishments).

The bottom line is that the benefits of BS extend only to some (traditional) women (Glick et al., 2002), which then serves to restrict women to the roles "protected" by these benevolent attitudes. For the women who step outside these traditional roles, HS insures negative and limiting outcomes (remember those pregnant women looking for jobs in retail stores). HS targets prejudicial outcomes toward women who break from traditional roles and prescriptive stereotyping, simultaneously sounding a warning to other women not to cross this line, and thus limiting women's favorable options. In sum, there's quite a downside to "benevolence," which *prescribes* what women *ought* to do—be traditional and hence liked (Glick & Fiske, 1999a).

Given this logic, we would predict that women would expect hostility for those nontraditional women who step outside protected roles as well as benevolence for women who conform. Indeed, this pattern is what Julia Becker (2010) found in her study with German women. When these women completed the ASI were told to think about nontraditional women—either feminists or career women—their HS scores were higher. In contrast, women's BS scores were higher when they thought about traditional women (housewives).

But even for the women who adhere to traditional roles and thus reap the immediate benefits of BS, benevolence comes with strings attached. Miguel Moya and his colleagues (2007) explored women's reactions to restrictions imposed "for your own good" across a series of three studies. In the first study, only high BS women accepted their husband's (but not their coworkers') prohibition against driving on a long car trip. In their second study, women's intimate partners objected to their participation in a practicum counseling dangerous men, either with justification ("I am concerned for your safety") or without. Whereas most women deferred to the justified advice, only high BS women accepted the prohibition delivered without any rationale. Their final study paralleled the second, but this time the partner's advice was not specific to the woman: "It is not safe for any woman". In this case, only high BS women accepted the restriction. Overall, when men's dominance is paired with women's BS attitudes, women comply with restrictions to their own pursuits.

There are other studies demonstrating that women's own BS has costs. Women (and men) who endorsed BS had restricted views of what behaviors are appropriate for women to engage in during courtship (Viki et al., 2003). High BS Spanish women were more likely to believe that the husband in a hypothetical vignette would be threatened by his wife's promotion and would react with violence, even when this vignette described the man as supportive (Expsito et al., 2010). Young Spanish women in high school who endorsed BS were more likely to do feminine-typed household chores, perpetuating the gender-typing of these tasks (Silvan-Ferrero & Lopez, 2007). Furthermore, women's own BS is linked to higher endorsement of HS directed at women in general, making these women active participants in maintaining gender inequality (Sibley et al., 2007b). Notice that across all of these studies, women's BS helps to maintain the status quo, thus keeping women "in their place."

Not only does women's own BS affect them, but so does the BS of others. Women exposed to others' BS reacted with higher levels of body shame and appearance monitoring (Shepherd et al., 2011) and by emphasizing their own warmth over their competence (Barreto (2010). Belgian undergraduates confronting BS in the context of a job interview felt more incompetent afterwards, reported intrusive thoughts during a subsequent task, and took longer to complete a simple grammar test (Dumont et al., 2010).

Benoit Dardenne and his colleagues (2007) conducted a fascinating series of four experiments with Belgian students and nonstudents in simulated job interviews in which recruiters expressed benevolent, hostile, or no (control) attitudes. The hostile statement conveyed that women had to be hired despite incompetence and weaknesses, whereas the benevolent statement promised to employ equal performing women and to extend protections and goodwill toward them. Across different tasks described as relevant to the desired job, women consistently performed worse when exposed to BS—showing few effects of HS, which they appeared to discount. Although these women did not identify BS as sexist, they did regard BS (and HS) as unpleasant, but BS, more than HS, caused mental intrusions to interfere with their performance, created self-doubt and anxiety, and decreased women's self-esteem, even though the context ostensibly valued feminine skills. What these experiments convincingly demonstrated after ruling out various alternative possibilities is that the effects of BS are insidious and real. Benevolent sexism truly is sexist!

PERPETUATING SEXIST STEREOTYPING

Given the consistency with which people can identify sexist stereotyping, it likely comes from and is maintained by widely shared processes. Some people suggest that the universality of gender stereotyping reflects a "kernel of truth"; that is, stereotypic images are accurate representations of most women and men. In this way of thinking, even exceptions "prove the rule." However, we saw in the previous chapter how social contexts can minimize or make salient stereotyping and in doing so, reduce or enhance its impact. If stereotyping can be varied across contexts, then this argues that its roots are in contexts, specifically widely shared contexts. Three likely sources and perpetuators of stereotyping are (1) the media, (2) language, and (3) expectancies and behaviors.

Media

There is extensive research evidence pointing to sexualized stereotyping of women's appearance across all forms of media, and we'll explore this research later in Chapter 10. Not surprisingly, content analyses of television commercials continue to document the dominance of traditional images of frivolous, less competent women (Davis, 2003; Rouner et al., 2003), although these images co-exist with a smattering of nontraditional images that emerged throughout the 1990s (Bresnahan et al, 2001; Coltrane & Messineo, 2000). Here I want to concentrate on how persistent patterns in the media work to affect both men's treatment of women and women's own aspirations.

In a clever study exploring how ads affect men, Laurie Rudman and Eugene Borgida (1995) **primed** one group of college men with sexist television ads. These men then prepared for and participated in a simulated job interview with a woman candidate. Their behaviors were compared to those of a control group of men who had not been exposed to sexist ads. Men who had seen the sexist ads selected more sexist and inappropriate questions to ask the woman job candidate, sat closer to her, rated her as more friendly but less competent, and afterwards remembered more about her physical appearance and less about her biographical background. In sum, more primed men stereotyped the woman applicant as a traditional sex object (likeable but incompetent), and they acted accordingly. These findings suggest that sexist media portrayals of women (and men) encourage sexist prejudices and stereotyping that can lead to discriminatory behavior.

Turning to the direct effects of media on women, Paul Davies and his co-authors (2005) first showed that short-term exposure to traditional television advertisements led women to elect to be followers rather than leaders on a subsequent task (Study 1). These researchers then went on to link this effect to the activation of gender stereotyping (Study 2). When women viewed traditional, real-life ads, they were quicker to recognize gender-stereotyped words (housewife and caring)—showing that gender stereotypes had been *automatically* activated by viewing the commercials. These reaction times, in turn, predicted their reduced leadership aspirations. In other words, stereotype activation mediated the relationship between seeing ads and lowered aspirations.

Further speculating that **stereotype threat** was driving their findings, Davies and his colleagues conducted a third study in which they told women that there is no evidence of gender differences on the leadership task. Despite having seen the traditional ads and having stereotypes automatically activated, women in the identity-safe environment in which stereotype threat had been de-activated showed no relationship between stereotype activation and their leadership aspirations. In other words, removal of stereotype threat countered the impact of the traditional ads and restored women's leadership aspirations. In sum, this series of studies tells us a lot about how traditional ads affect women without their awareness of these effects, as well as suggest ways in which we can counteract these negative patterns.

Language

Language becomes sexist when we unnecessarily distinguish between women and men or exclude, trivialize, or diminish either gender (Parks & Robertson, 2000). Often we delimit what is considered to be the exception to the rule (the *woman* engineer and the *male* nurse). We also use gender forms that tend to trivialize women, such as "girl" for an adult woman. Some of this deprecation of women is done by association, for example, by sexualizing terms (madam), and by **objectification**, for example, in demeaning sexual slang which more commonly targets women (Grossman & Tucker, 1997).

Probably the most pervasive form of sexist language is the exclusion of women, sometimes subtly and other times blatantly. For example, when asked to name "famous people," women and men named more men than women (Moyer, 1997). In contrast, when prodded to identify famous "men or women," the gap between men and women named narrowed for male respondents and closed completely for female respondents. Using sexist language also is a good sign that a person also harbors sexist attitudes. For example, individuals scoring as generally sexist (on the Modern Sexism scale) were more likely to use sexist language and not regard sexist language as sexist (Swim et al., 2004).

Language also can shape how we think about topics of critical importance. Sharon Lamb and Susan Keon (1995) examined the language used to describe male partner abuse. Consider the following descriptions of the same events:

"Elizabeth Jones' husband beat her, raped her, and committed gross sexual abuse against her"

versus

"Elizabeth and Charles Jones had an abusive relationship, in which there were beatings, rapes, and gross acts of sexual abuse."

The first version uses the active voice as opposed to shared responsibility in the second. Lamb and Keon found that students assigned the most lenient penalties to the abuser when this shared responsibility form was used. Along these lines, newspapers continue to report more personal information about male crime victims, and researchers found that empathy for a victim increased when more personal information was provided (Anastasio & Costa, 2004).

Recognizing the importance of language, the *Publication Manual of the APA* (2010, pp. 73–77) provides some helpful guidelines about how to reduce bias in language concerning not only gender but also sexual orientation, racial and ethnic identity, disabilities, age, and across history. Thus, paying attention to language is a professional responsibility.

Expectancies and Behavior

In addition to media and language, sexist stereotyping can be perpetuated by the actual behaviors of women and men, suggesting a possible "kernel of truth" to stereotypes. Inherent in this reasoning is the assumption that when women and men act in stereotypic ways, the root cause of their behavior is something internal to them. This assumes that there is something about women and about men that makes them act stereotypically so that their behavior, in turn, verifies the stereotyping.

We already saw in Chapter 6 that gender stereotyping can affect women's and men's social behaviors, roles, and occupations, but we did not explore the mechanisms that drive these outcomes. According to the **self-fulfilling prophecy**, expectations can make anticipated events come true (Jussim, 1986; Merton, 1957; Miller & Turnbull, 1986). A classic example describes "runs" on banks during the Depression of the 1930s; when people feared that their bank would close, they rushed to withdraw their money, panic spread, and the bank soon closed. What people expected to happen, happened.

Extending this logic to gender stereotyping, Berna Skrypnek and Mark Snyder (1982) conducted a clever study. Because the design is complicated, it helps to understand the findings first and then consider the procedure. Skrypnek and Snyder showed that when a man expected to be interacting with a woman, the woman acted like women are supposed to act. When another man thought he was interacting with another man (but his partner was really a woman), the woman acted in line with her partner's expectations by responding in masculine ways. The man's expectations were fulfilled by his partner's behaviors, even when those expectations and behaviors were at variance with the partner's true gender. In the end, the partner's behaviors confirmed the stereotyping *expectations* of the male participant.

Turning to Skrypnek and Snyder's procedure, male-female pairs arrived separately at the lab and were kept away from each other. Some of the men were told that their partner was a man; others were led to believe that their partner was a woman. The pairings always included one man and one woman so that some men were misinformed about the gender of their partner. Which men were misinformed was determined randomly. Each partnered pair was given a list of 12 pairs of tasks. The tasks were masculine (bait a hook), feminine (frost a cake), or neutral (score tests), and the task pairs included all combinations. The participants' job was to agree on who would do each task in a pair. They communicated their preferred choice through signal lights so that the partners never interacted directly.

In the first round, the man selected first, and he understandably treated his partner in accordance with his expectations. For example, he might prefer to bait the hook and leave his partner to frost the cake when he believed his partner to be a woman. On the other hand, for those men informed that their partner was a man, some agreed to ice the cake. All men relied on stereotyping to initiate their interactions with their partner—something we'd expect because the only concrete information these men had about their partner was the gender they were told.

The really interesting findings came in the second round of 12 different task pairs when the woman chose first. Women whose partner believed them to be women made feminine task selections; in contrast, women whose partner believed them to be men chose masculine tasks. These women's seemingly free choices were influenced by their partners' expectations, which must have been subtly conveyed to them through their exchanges in the first round. These women displayed gender-consistent, stereotypic behaviors, not because they were women (in that case, all women would have made feminine selections),[7] but because of what their partners expected. The man's prophecy was fulfilled.

Summing up, even finding apparent confirmation in women's and men's stereotyped behaviors doesn't necessarily verify that stereotypes are true; that is, reflective of genuine, internal characteristics of women and men. When women and men act in concert with sexist stereotyping, it may be because that is what is expected of them, not because there's a "kernel of truth" in stereotyping. In other words, people's stereotypic behaviors may be as much the products of stereotyping itself as the cause of it. A circular pattern that is mutually reinforcing may be established. See Box 7.5 for a more contemporary example and for a diagram of the self-fulfilling prophecy.

REDUCING STEREOTYPING

There is growing evidence that stereotyping is so embedded in our culture that activating stereotyping is virtually automatic (Devine, 1989). Both high- and low-prejudice people know and use negative stereotyping when they can't monitor their behavior. But, given adequate opportunity to think about what they are doing, only low-prejudice people avoid stereotyping. Thus, discrimination does not spring automatically from being non-prejudicial. Rather, *avoiding the pitfalls of knee-jerk stereotyping requires active monitoring,* even by those with open attitudes.

Stereotyping is an attempt to find meaning in unknown circumstances (Fiske, 1993). Thus when people are unknown to us, we can fall back on social categories to try to fill in gaps in our understanding. Thus, it would seem that a key toward reducing stereotyping is to have **individuating information**; that is, knowledge about the specific traits, role behaviors, occupation, and physical characteristics unique to that person (Fiske & Von Hendy, 1992). Getting to know others by being in contact with them makes a differ-

---

[7]If women and men made their choices based solely on what they like to do, their choices would be idiosyncratic and no patterns related to gender would have been found in the data. However, gendered patterns were found, thus ruling out this possibility.

Box 7.5
The Self-Fulfilling Prophecy

Given what we know about stereotype threat, there's nothing we wouldn't have anticipated in the first of two experiments conducted by Amy Kiefer and Margaret Shih (2006). Women were more sensitive than men to negative feedback about their performance on a math test, attributing their own failure to deficits in their math abilities—a domain which we know is male-stereotyped. (The feedback was contrived and randomly provided, with no gender differences in number of math problems attempted and in actual performance.)

Their second study is needed to make the point I want to highlight here about the self-fulfilling prophecy. In this experiment, women (and men) who received negative feedback about their math performance—and then made attributions about the cause of their performance—had a chance to pick the second exam they wanted to take. Just over 80% of the women and just over 60% of the men in this condition elected to switch to a verbal task. Most notably, although gender obviously predicted task choice, this relationship was fully mediated by ability attributions. The more both women and men attributed their alleged failure to their own abilities, the more likely they were to elect to discontinue working on math tests.

Given that women are more likely to internalize math failures because of stereotyping linking math ability to boys and men (Study 1), women are thus more likely to give up on math (Study 2), which in turns confirms that indeed math is a masculine domain. The cycle, depicted below, thus becomes self-sustaining.

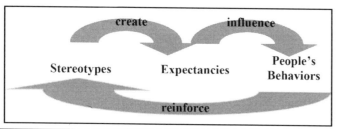

---

ence: For example, a meta-analysis looking at the relationship between contact and sexual prejudice directed at lesbians ($r = -.30$) and gay men ($r = -.27$) documented that increased contact indeed reduced prejudice (Smith, Axelton, & Saucier, 2009).

However, people tend to avoid individuating information that might debunk their stereotyping (Trope & Thompson, 1997). Participants sought out more individuating information about a hypothetical person when their social category (being feminist or Jewish) did *not* match the attitude issue being considered (U.S. support for Israel versus the Equal Rights Amendment, respectively). In other words, people asked less about a feminist target when considering the ERA than they did in the context of thinking about support for Israel.

We might cling to our stereotyping as a way to affirm who we are. Participants in one study were more likely to negatively stereotype a hypothetical woman job candidate when their own self-image was threatened by negative feedback (Fein & Spencer, 1997). Indeed, negative stereotyping paid off in terms of improved self-esteem among those who were threatened. In contrast, those who were exposed to a self-affirmation procedure avoided negative stereotyping. Thus, all patterns across these data point to compensatory benefits derived from negative stereotyping.

Stereotype expression, accessibility, and in-group favoritism all are reduced to the extent that one can take the perspective of the "other" (Galinsky & Moskowitz, 2000).

Box 7.6

How funny are the following jokes?

"How do you recognize a friendly motorbike rider?
    Flies are stuck in his teeth."

"When does a woman lose 99% of her intelligence?
    When her husband dies."

"Why can't women be both good-looking and intelligent at the same time?
    Because then they would be men."

German college men found the second two and other sexist jokes like them funnier when they were forced to rate them under time pressure than when they could take their time and think about them (Eyssel & Bohner, 2007). Time pressure made no difference for nonsexist jokes like the first one. Why might this be?

Paralleling explicit and implicit attitudes, we can process information with either explicit cognition (deliberate judgments about which we are aware) or implicit cognition (automatically activated evaluations occurring outside our awareness; Kahneman & Frederick, 2002). Time pressure may force the male judges in this study to make snap judgments that draw on implicit cognition, which upon more careful thought (explicit cognition) can be overridden.

Applying this point more broadly, then, it takes effort and uses cognitive resources to avoid stereotyping. Given that stereotyping is so ingrained in our culture, it is hard to imagine that even the most non-prejudicial people don't implicitly stereotype sometimes. The key then may be not to assume that because one is not prejudiced, one doesn't stereotype. Rather, we all may be better served by actively working at trying not to engage in stereotyping and to catch ourselves when we unintentionally do.

Source: Eyssel, F., & Bohner, G. (2007). The rating of sexist humor under time pressure as an indicator of spontaneous sexist attitudes. *Sex Roles, 57*, 651–660.

Additional hedges against relying on stereotyping are for the evaluator to be held publicly accountable for her or his judgment (Tetlock, 1992), for standards of evaluation to be clearly delineated (Fiske & Taylor, 1991), and for accuracy to be stressed and given sufficient attentional resources (Biesanz et al., 2001). The more objectively verifiable the standards of assessment are, the less subjective are the judgments, and the less they fall back on stereotyping. Bottom line: Reducing stereotyping takes work!

SEXIST DISCRIMINATION

What we have seen so far is that individuals vary in their attitudes toward the roles and rights of women (prejudice) and that there are different beliefs about women and girls (stereotyping) involving their traits, role behaviors, occupations, and physical characteristics. We have argued that what makes these prejudices and stereotyping sexist is that they work to oppress women and girls by limiting them to traditional roles. A key point in our argument requires that we link these sexist prejudices and sexist stereotyping to overt behaviors with meaningful consequences. This is where **sexist discrimination**, *acts* that serve to oppress women and girls, comes in.

Nijole Benokraitis (1997) insightfully distinguishes among three *forms* of sexist discrimination. **Blatant sexist discrimination** is obvious; it refers to the inequitable and harmful treatment of women that is intentional, highly visible, and can be documented easily. Examples include sexual harassment, sexist language and jokes, and physical violence. **Covert sexist discrimination** is hidden, purposeful, and frequently maliciously motivated; for example, insiders may intentionally try to sabotage women to ensure women's failure when they gain access to formerly all-male jobs. **Subtle sexist discrimination** is typically less visible and obvious; it may go unnoticed; it may be innocent and unintentional or manipulative, intentional, and malicious; and it is difficult to document. Today, it's the most common form of sexist discrimination. Be sure to check out Figure 7.7 for a clear example of subtle sexism that would likely go undetected if we didn't have experimental data.

Given the subtlety of many contemporary examples of sexist discrimination, much of it goes largely unseen and/or unconfronted. Still, there are wide differences in how much sexist discrimination individual women do detect. One frequently used catalogue of these perceptions is the Schedule of Sexist Events (SSE) developed by Elizabeth Klonoff and Hope Landrine (1995). These experiences span general instances of sexist degradation (e.g., the number of times a woman has been called a sexist name or gotten into an argument or fight about something that was done or said) to specific sources of unfair treatment by strangers and acquaintances, friends and family, and in the workplace. In the scale authors' original study with 631 student and community women ranging in age from 18 to

---

Figure 7.7 A Rose by Any Name… ???

Not really. In this simple but very telling study, Millicent Abel and Andrea Meltzer (2007) presented the same written lecture to male and female undergraduates. The topic of the lecture was pay disparities between women and men, and it was written to convey factual information as well as instill a perception of sexist discrimination in the American workforce. The only difference in the two versions (randomly assigned to student evaluators) was the name of the professor alleged to have presented the lecture to their first-year sociology class: Dr. Michael Smith or Dr. Mary Smith. Each of the ratings graphed below is significantly different, capturing usually-hard-to-prove subtle sexist discrimination. In fact, without the comparisons made possible here, we'd never know for sure that sexism was happening.

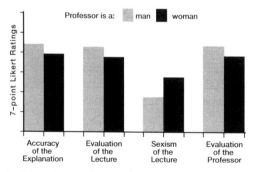

In another study focused on students' ratings of professors, male students were less likely to nominate a woman as their "best" professor, after controlling for the number of female professors they actually had, whereas women's selections of women were representative of their pool of possibilities (Basow et al., 2006). Not surprisingly given the data above, men continued to describe their "worst" female professors as "closed-minded."

73, the lifetime prevalence of such experiences was staggering. For example, fully 82% reported being called sexist names, and two-thirds had gotten into arguments about sexist occurrences. More recent data collections with the SSE continue to document these occurrences in women's lives (Landy & Mercurio, 2009).

As you might expect, women who report more experiences with sexist discrimination also report higher levels of psychological distress (Szymanski et al., 2009) and loss of personal control—with personal control partially, but not fully, explaining the relationship between SSE scores and distress (Landy & Mercurio, 2009). In a sample of college students, women with high scores on the SSE exhibited more mental health problems (including somatization, obsessive-compulsiveness, depression, and anxiety) than both low SSE women and all men (Klonoff et al., 2000). In another study, SSE scores combined with high levels of psychological distress to predict both binge drinking and smoking among college women, and there was a direct relationship between perceived sexism and smoking to control weight for all women (Zucker & Landry, 2007). SSE scores also were related to depression and anxiety among college women (Fischer & Holz, 2007).

These effects are not confined to the SSE. Women scientists who reported experiencing more sexual harassment and gender discrimination also recorded poorer job outcomes (Settles, et al., 2006), and women engineering students who were forced to interact with sexist men experienced threats to their identities and diminished performance on an engineering test (Logel et al., 2009). Latina and White female adolescents who reported hearing sexist comments about girls' and women's math abilities believed that they were less good at math, as well as devalued and disliked it (Brown & Leaper, 2010), and 11-year-old girls who valued egalitarianism and who were purposively discriminated against in an experiment experienced reductions in their social acceptance self-esteem (Brown et al., 2010).

However, sexist discrimination is not typically acknowledged or confronted by many women, not only because of its subtlety but also because there are some good reasons for women not to "see" it. For example, many women believe that men think women are responsible for their own disadvantage (Boeckmann & Feather, 2007), and indeed, unless men are directed to show empathy for targeted women, most men don't think everyday sexist discrimination is all that harmful (Becker & Swim, 2011). A study with college students recruited to keep a diary of their experiences with gender prejudice across 2 weeks resulted in not only a large number of reported incidents (825 from the 81 women and 183 from the 22 men, averaging about 3 incidents each day), but also elevated negative emotions among only the women (Brinkman & Rickard, 2009). In two experiments purposively exposing women and men to a discriminatory person or a discriminatory rule, women and men were both more likely to attribute blame to a rule than to a person, but women were even more reluctant than men to blame the person—especially when that person would be harmed by their accusation (Sechrist & Delmar, 2009).

Exploring some contexts in which women are more likely to confront perpetrators of sexism also can help fill in some of this picture. For example, women college students were more likely to report confronting sexism when they self-labeled as feminist, when the perpetrator was familiar and of equal status (as opposed to unfamiliar and high status), and when they were targeted with sexist comments (rather than unwanted sexual attention or sexual harassment); (Ayres et al., 2009). Although women consider taking more assertive action in response to discrimination than they actually do, when they do confront it, they achieve better outcomes (Hyers, 2007)—including heightened feelings of competence, self-esteem, and empowerment (Gervais, Hillard, & Vescio, 2010).

Looking across this growing literature on sexist discrimination, there is a convergence across different types of data collections to suggest that daily hassles with sexism are common in women's everyday lives. These experiences can be "unseen" and not taken seriously one-by-one; however, over time, they can accumulate so that targets eventually carry a "ton of feathers" (Caplan, 1993). Each "feather" (incident) alone may be light and bearable, but together they still weigh a ton. An example of how such subtle insults or "microaggressions" pile up for women lawyers is documented by Beth Bonniwell Haslett and Susan Lipman (1997), and they have been shown to have serious consequences for people of color (for example, see Sue et al., 2007). There is currently very little research looking at the impact of such repeated exposure to microaggressions targeting women, however; the concept itself helps convey the seriousness with which we need to think about sexist discrimination.

CHAPTER SUMMARY

Sexism includes sexist prejudice, stereotyping, and discrimination, all of which operate to oppress women and girls by limiting their choices. Sexist prejudice appears less blatant now than in the past, taking more subtle forms like denial of continuing discrimination, antagonism toward women's demands, and resentment about special "favors" for women.

Gender stereotyping focuses on traits, role behaviors, occupations, and physical characteristics, which combine to form consistent clusters of stereotyped women. These clusters may be traditional (homemakers and sexy women) or nontraditional (athletes, businesswomen, and feminists). Looking at two fundamental dimensions of stereotyping (competence and warmth), nontraditional women are viewed as competent but unlikeable and are targets of envious prejudice. In contrast, traditional women are regarded as warm but incompetent, engendering paternalistic prejudice. It is the evaluative meaning of stereotypes that moves gender stereotyping away from simple descriptions containing a possible "kernel of truth" to instruments of sexism.

Because most, if not all, stereotyping of real (not presumably generic) women combines either warmth with low competence or competence without warmth, sexist prejudices are ambivalent, mixing hostile negativity with seemingly benevolent attitudes. However, even these apparently benign forms of prejudice serve to maintain sexist stereotyping within a system of inequality that ultimately serves to limit the roles prescribed for girls and women and thus oppresses them.

Sexist stereotyping is perpetuated by the media, language, and even our own behaviors, which are responsive to others' expectancies in a cycle of self-fulfilling prophecies. Researchers have shown that sexist stereotyping can be reduced by vigilant monitoring (even by those without negatively prejudicial attitudes), by individuating targets (when desired), by making evaluators publicly accountable for their actions, and by standardizing assessments.

Sexist discrimination can be blatant, covert, or subtle, with subtle discrimination being the most common and insidious. Although sexist prejudice, stereotyping, and discrimination are not perfectly related so that only the most blatant sexists exhibit all of these aspects of sexism, they generally are mutually supporting. The common link among them, whether they appear on the surface as hostile or benevolent, is that they work together to oppress women and girls. In Chapter 1 we defined feminism as a movement to end sexist oppression. Thus, the elements of sexism discussed in this chapter become critical targets for feminist activism.

SUGGESTED READINGS

Cuddy, A. J. C., Fiske, S. T., & Glick, P. (2004). When professionals become mothers, warmth doesn't cut the ice. *Journal of Social Issues, 60*(4), 701–718.

Amy Cuddy, Susan Fiske, and Peter Glick review the "stereotype content model," which provides the conceptual model used in this chapter for thinking about stereotyping as a process, as well as frames this discussion within an issue important for many students: blending employment with family.

Goodwin, S. A., & Fiske, S. T. (2001). Power and gender: The double-edged sword of ambivalence. In R. K. Unger (Ed.), *Handbook of the psychology of women and gender* (pp. 358–366). New York: Wiley.

Although written in the more dense form appropriate for a handbook, Stephanie Goodwin and Susan Fiske's chapter is approachable and clearly links sexist prejudice and stereotyping to power and gender, cutting to the heart of the present chapter.

Yoder, J. D., Hogue, M., Newman, R., Metz, L., & LaVigne, T. (2002). Exploring moderators of gender differences: Contextual differences in door holding behavior. *Journal of Applied Social Psychology, 32*, 1682–1686.

Our study encourages readers to think about an everyday occurrence (who holds a door for whom) and its subtle, often overlooked meaning for power relations and sexism.

Glick, P., & Fiske, S. T. (2011). Ambivalent sexism revised. *Psychology of Women Quarterly, 35*, 530–535.

In this approachable commentary written to celebrate the 35th anniversary of APA Division 35's journal, Peter Glick and Susan Fiske give readers a behind-the-scenes peak at the development of the concept of ambivalent sexism, discuss its meaning and value, and speculate about some future research directions. (A podcast interview with these authors is available at *pwq.sagepub.com*.)

Rudman, L. A., & Glick, P. (2008). Progress, pitfalls, and remedies. *The social psychology of gender: How power and intimacy shape gender relations.* (pp. 285–310)New York: Guilford Press.

In this chapter of their overall fascinating book, Laurie Rudman and Peter Glick bravely and effectively tackle the tough question raised by social role theory about whether women's and men's roles are fundamentally changing in the 21st century and thus leading the way toward greater gender equality.

Chapter 8

Women's Multiple Roles
Achieving Satisfaction in Close Relationships

Lisa is like thunder.

Imagine what this sentence means to you. When you have an image of Lisa, what occupation is Lisa likely to go into? What kind of hobbies is Lisa likely to enjoy? And what type of household chores is Lisa likely to do?

At first blush, this example seems somewhat odd. The procedure uses similes (a figure of speech in which seemingly unlike things are compared) as a way to get at people's subtle stereotyping. Other combinations used by Ling-yi Zhou and her colleagues (2004) included: Gary is like a rainbow; Karen is like a butterfly; and Brian is like a mountain. These examples cross female and male names with feminine (rainbow and butterfly) and masculine (thunder and mountain) associations, resulting in both gender congruent and incongruent pairings.

Consistent patterns emerged for college students' projections, both in the United States and China. Woman-feminine and man-masculine matches were most commonly assigned to feminine and masculine activities, respectively. More interestingly, gender-typing trumped named sex so that when pairings were mismatched, expected occupations, hobbies, and chores were more likely to fit with gender-typing of the association (feminine or masculine) than the sex connoted by the name. Thus, our thunderous Lisa was more commonly pictured doing masculine activities.

This simple, although somewhat unusual, person perception study captures much of what we have covered so far in this text and will use in the remaining chapters. First, it's unlikely that many people would state outright that some activities are only for men or women. As we have seen, **sexism** today is much more subtle. Second, gender **stereotyping** persists. If it didn't, Zhou and her associates wouldn't find consistent patterns in their data. Although more sensitive, subtle measures may tap into this stereotyping and uncover **implicit attitudes**, more obvious measures often overlook it. Thus, we need to be prepared to find seemingly conflicting patterns, with some data suggesting similarities between women and men; other data, differences.

Third, as we have seen with implicit and **explicit attitudes**, this difference doesn't mean that one finding is necessarily truer than the other, but rather that each has its place in informing our understandings. We need to consider the meaning of our findings within broader systems of inequality, examining how both openly stated and explicit, as well as subtle and often unrealized, expectancies work to maintain or challenge power relations and the status quo.

Nowhere are these patterns more pronounced than in this chapter on multiple roles, friendships, romantic attachments, and caregiving. Repeatedly, we will see that the richest understandings are not simple but rather depend—depend on the measures we use, depend on individual and subgroup **intragroup diversity**, and depend on the specific **social context**.

MULTIPLE ROLES

In this chapter and the next, we examine different roles held by women: friends, intimates, mothers, workers, students, adult children, and so on. We generally believe that the more roles one has, the better. A large-scale study of midlife American women and men

Box 8.1

A popular image of an employed mother pictures her as pulled by multiple roles. Top-selling women's and parenting magazines portray employed mothers as happy, busy, and proud in contrast to confused and overwhelmed at-home mothers (Johnston & Swanson, 2003).

Printed with permission of America's Beef Producers at http://www.beef.org.

holding up to eight roles each documented that greater role involvement was related to enhanced well being—especially when individuals felt in control of their lives (Ahrens & Ryff, 2006). Yet we all have seen advertisements like the one in Box 8.1 that remind us of the costs of being a harried role juggler.

Burnout AND Enhancement?

These contradictory images of time-panicked yet well-adjusted women reflect a tension between two competing views of multiple roles. On the one hand, the **scarcity hypothesis** predicts that holders of multiple roles will be vulnerable to role conflict. This conflict stems from two sources: **time-based conflict** (competing time demands from different roles) and **strain-based conflict** (when one role spills over into another). On the other hand, the **enhancement hypothesis** contends that multiple roles serve as buffers against undesirable consequences in any subset of roles (Crosby & Sabattini, 2006). For example, if things get rough at work, folks who can go home and find solace in strong family ties may be less seriously affected. In their extensive review of work-family research conducted across the first decade of the 21st century, sociologists Suzanne Bianchi and Melissa Milkie (2010, p. 712) concluded that much of this research "implicitly took a role conflict orientation."

Not surprisingly, employed mothers report more role overload than employed fathers, commonly focusing on "time starvation" (Febbraro, 2003; Tiedje, 2004). Some of this difference may result from the different ways that mothers and fathers are expected to fulfill their parental roles. Bianchi and Milkie (2010) cite research linking men's role fulfillment to being breadwinners; for example, dads are more likely to lose contact with their children when they cannot provide for them. In contrast, their review highlights that among women and men with similar jobs and family statuses, women report more work-family conflict; that the links between conflict with reduced well-being and compromised mastery are stronger for women than men; and that feeling a time deficit with children is associated with threatened well-being more so for women than men. Additionally, men are likely to cut back at work when they are experiencing on-the-job problems, whereas women will cut back whether problems originate at work or home. In sum, some of what it means to be a "good" father may be achieved by work itself whereas this appears not to be the case for mothers.

Additionally, Bianchi and Milkie (2010) point to the potentially cyclic nature of work-family conflict. Women may "opt out" of the workforce or assume part-time employment to reduce work-family stress, only to then limit their future employability and work options—trading immediate stress reduction for future stressors. They call for researchers and policymakers to take a more explicit life course perspective that includes understanding that there are periods in life that foster more and less work-family conflict.

For most of us, though, role conflict and enhancement co-exist. For example, in one study of 118 employed mothers of preschoolers aged 23 to 43 months (Rankin, 1993), most women described their lives as stressful—citing lack of time, child-related problems, and maternal guilt. At the same time, these women reported rewards, including personal benefits, financial rewards, and improved family lives as coming from their various roles.

Angela Febbraro (2003) digs deeper into exploring the implications of each perspective. On the one hand, a scarcity perspective can scare women away from taking on too many roles and deny roles to women in the name of paternalistic protection (a form of **benevolent sexism**) (Crosby & Jaskar, 1993). On the other hand, the enhancement hypothesis opens up reasonable options for women to participate fully in the workplace and men in the home (Barnett & Hyde, 2001). The first limits women's roles in ways that we have seen are sexist; but the second may ignore some costs associated with realistic time- and strain-based conflicts. Febbraro resolves this contradiction by reorienting her focus away from individual women's coping to structural changes that work to maximize enhancement outcomes and minimize scarcity ones. This moves our discussion from whether or not to take on multiple roles to the conditions that facilitate their effects. In other words, it encourages us to ask what supports we can provide to make multiple role juggling life-enhancing.

Role Quality and Meaning

Simple role accumulation is not related to self-esteem, but role commitment is (Reitzes & Multran, 1994). A key factor then may not be the number of roles per se, but rather role quality. Grace Baruch and Rosalind Barnett (1986) define **role quality** as the balance of pluses and minuses associated with how one sees a given role. Not surprisingly, it is favorable role quality that Baruch and Barnett find to be positively associated with psychological well-being.

Furthermore, individual differences influence what people want from the roles they enact. Sharon Rae Jenkins (1996) tracked a sample of 118 women college seniors over the next 14 years of their lives. Those who were autonomous in defining their roles, and thus were less bound by conventional dictates, sought excellence in multiple roles with less role conflict. Feeling capable to handle one's roles also is important: Women caregivers who felt competent to handle task demands reported less role-related stress (Franks & Stephens, 1992). Similarly, those women whose attitudes supported their role enactments exhibited enhanced well-being. Employed single mothers of preschool children reported strong psychological well-being when they believed that maternal employment does not harm children and perceived their childcare arrangements as high quality (Goldberg et al., 1992). In contrast, when new mothers' employment status is not what they'd prefer, they are vulnerable to anxiety and anger (Klein et al., 1998).

Other research has focused on **role centrality**; that is, the personal importance of a role to an individual. A study of 296 women—all of whom simultaneously were a mother, wife, employee, and parental caretaker—found that the greater the centrality of all four roles, the better was the woman's psychological well-being (Martire et al., 2000). For women who highly valued their wife role, stress related to that role (e.g., marital conflict) predicted life dissatisfaction. The same pattern was found for employment centrality. Interestingly, women who deeply valued mothering were *less* aversely affected by stresses coming from mothering. In another study of new mothers, long maternity leave was related to depression only for women with strong career centrality (Klein et al., 1998). In sum, the meaning and impact of roles is highly individualized, reflecting individuals' role commitment and centrality as well as the quality of each role (not simply the number of roles one takes on).

Individual and Structural Coping

There also are individual differences in how people cope with multiple roles. Douglas Hall (1972) describes three different coping strategies, paralleling those found more recently (Tiedje, 2004). Women who use **personal role redefinition** change their own expectations and perceptions of their behavior. For example, women employing this strategy in response to work-family conflict may explore time management techniques in order to be more efficient; may try to minimize simultaneous overlap of roles (soccer on weekends only); may reduce their standards (living with unmade beds); may eliminate roles; and may rotate their attention. Overall, the way they cope is by adapting themselves.

In contrast, **structural role redefinition** focuses outward on changing structurally imposed expectations. Women employing this strategy may redefine a role by changing the activities required (e.g., reduce tasks at work); by seeking support from sources beyond themselves, including outsiders (e.g., housekeepers) and insiders to the role (e.g., one's spouse and children); by collaborating with role senders to redefine roles (e.g., encouraging children to accept sending store-bought, not homemade, cookies to school); and by integrating roles so that activities for one role contribute to another (also see Johnston & Swanson, 2006). The third strategy, **reactive role behavior**, doesn't really cope at all; rather, the user attempts to "do it all" ("superwoman").

The type of coping strategy used by women was related to their satisfaction with their career (Hall, 1972). Although most women used combinations of strategies, those who relied most heavily on reactive role behaviors were the least satisfied. Those who used strategies involving structural role redefinition were the most satisfied.

Tamao Matsui, Takeshi Ohsawa, and Mary-Lou Onglatco (1995) explored the structural role redefinition strategies used by 131 Japanese married employed women. They separated this coping strategy into two components: **work-role redefinition**, which involves altering work activities and expectations to meet family-role demands, and **family-role redefinition**, which focuses on changes in the family. Family-role redefinition was more typical of these women's coping than work-role redefinition, and spillover of work into family was more common than from family to work. This pattern is consistent with other research concluding that work interferes more with family life than vice versa, although simultaneous spillover into both spheres is possible, and this pattern may be less true in **collectivist** cultures like Hong Kong (Bianchi & Milkie, 2010).

Multiple roles do not lead inevitably to negative consequences if social supports are strong. Family supports come in two types, both of which reduce role stress. *Instrumental supports* from partners buffer the effects of parental demands on work-family conflict

(Matsui et al., 1995). Elizabeth Ozer (1995) found a woman's belief in her capacity to enlist the help of her spouse for childcare predicted both well-being and reduced distress. Actual responsibility for greater childcare produced the opposite outcomes. The influence of family supports extends beyond immediate partners to a full array of family members (Poole & Langan-Fox, 1992). For example, an unpredictable and ever-present stress for many families involves arrangements for sick children, and African American kin are more likely than White to provide this safety net (Benin & Keith, 1995).

Emotional supports focus on the "degree of commitment, help, and support family members provide to one another" (Moos & Moos, 1994, p. 1). Testing a model of women's work-family conflict, Karyn Bernas and Debra Major (2000) found that family emotional support significantly reduced women's family-related stress and hence the interference of family with work demands. Other research finds that partners' emotional support contributed to women's sense of mastery, which in turn produced favorable well-being (Martire et al., 1998). Similarly, women over 35 years old returning to college experienced less strain when they had high grade-point averages and the support of their children (Novak & Thacker, 1991). Thus, families need not be regarded solely as sources of conflict; rather, they can be sources of support as well.

Looking beyond these interpersonal and individual supports, *structural supports* can moderate the relationships between roles and strain. Globally, the International Labour Conference held in June 2000 recommends that maternity leave be at least 14 weeks long and include cash benefits of at least two-thirds of the woman's previous or insured earnings (reported in United Nations, 2010). In 2009, 85 of 167 countries met or exceeded the time minimum (with 141 having at least 12 weeks), and 73 (37 in developed regions) met or exceeded the payment guideline (United Nations, 2010).

In the United States, the 1993 Family and Medical Leave Act guarantees a minimum of 12 weeks of *unpaid* leave for childbirth, adoption, or sick dependents, from businesses employing over 50 people (thus covering 10.8% of American employers who employed 58.3% of all U.S. workers in 2000; U.S. Department of Labor, 2011). The United States (along with Australia, Lesotho, Papua New Guinea, and Swaziland) is one of only five countries worldwide that does not legislate paid maternity leave (United Nations, 2010). In 1998, Canada provided 17 to 18 weeks with 55% pay for 15 weeks; Japan, 14 weeks with

---

Box 8.2

Which of the following statements was made by a mother and which by a father?

"I'm not here. I'm not watching my kids grow. I'm just getting pieces of their lives. I tell them I love them and hug and kiss them all the time, but I don't think that's enough. Maybe it's just being in the living room when they come in."

"I've missed a lot of my daughter's after-school activities due to my work hours. For me it is stressful. I'm sure that it's important to my daughter that both of us show up to these things, and a lot of times I'm just not able to."

Source: Adapted from R. W. Simon (1995). Gender, multiple roles, role meaning, and mental health. *Journal of Health and Social Behavior, 35*, 182–194.

Answer: The first is from a woman; notice how diffuse her sense of "missing out" is. The second is from a man who describes exactly what he misses—after school activities.

60% pay; and commonly European countries, 14 to 18 weeks at 75% or more pay (with most at 100%) (United Nations, 2000). At the most generous extreme, Sweden offered 14 weeks of maternity leave, with 360 days paid parental leave followed by 90 additional days at a flat rate.

Provocatively, it may be possible for leave to be too long; there is some evidence that long leaves can discourage women's resumption of labor force participation, ghettoize women in deadend jobs, and expand the gap between women's and men's earnings (Bianchi & Milkie, 2010). On the other hand, there's more to consider about family-friendly supports than employment outcomes. For example, a program in Norway that paid parents to care for their young children increased not only parent-child time together, but also enhanced marital stability (Hardoy & Schone, 2008). An ongoing study with employees at one company, Best Buy, in the United States found that when workers had more control over their work schedule, they produced not only less work-family conflict but also better on-the-job workers (Moen et al., 2009).

Is part-time employment a structural solution for women juggling work-family demands? Kathleen Barker (1993) surveyed 315 employed women and found a mixed bag of costs and benefits. Benefits accrued in increased happiness and satisfaction at both home and work. The costs of part-time employment were felt at work, where part-timers reported exclusion from organizational (promotion), interpersonal, and skill-enhancement opportunities, as well as heightened job insecurity. (Think about what employers might do to reduce these costs.) Reduced hours *alone* are not sufficient to successfully balance work and family, and indeed more than half of women who switched to part-time, lower-paid employment actually worked the some workload as previously (Crittenden, 2001).

According to Bianchi and Milkie's (2010) review, two defining trends in the 21st century—the 24/7 economy and the increased flexibility during which and where paid work can occur—create further challenges to work-life balance. As for amount of work, long hours obviously create greater work-family conflict, but conversely, insufficient work can disrupt men's connections with their families as well as undermine the well-being of low-income families. As for job "resources," on the one hand, telecommuting has been linked to better child and family well-being, and having informal supports from co-workers and supervisors (even more so than formal supports) is associated with less work-family conflict. On the other hand, commonly cited work assets, such as flexibility, greater job authority, and self-employment, can also have downsides, such as heightened work-life interference.

In conclusion, multiple roles themselves do not guarantee either role burnout or enhancement. Differences exist in what individuals value and need, in the quality of their roles, in the meaning of roles in the context of their full lives, in how individuals cope with role demands, in the social supports that either value or devalue roles, and in structural supports that either facilitate or inhibit role enactment. It is these variations that ultimately determine whether women's multiple roles work smoothly together or interfere with each other. This evolving perspective, captured in thinking about **work-family role convergence**, takes us away from a simplistic and ultimately useless debate about whether multiple roles are "good" or "bad" toward a richer understanding of multiple roles as central to what all human beings need to find fulfillment (Barnett & Hyde, 2001; Gilbert & Rader, 2001).

CLOSE RELATIONSHIPS

Understanding the previous overview about women's general role patterns, we can now move on to explore specific roles in women's close relationships: friendships, romantic attachments, and caregiving.

Defining Close Relationships

Judith Worell (1988) describes the defining features of a **close relationship**: It is expected to endure over time and to provide an individual with respect, intimacy, caring, concern, support, and affection. **Romantic attachments** include all of this plus sexual passion, exclusiveness, and commitment. **Relationship satisfaction** refers to the degree to which we think and feel a relationship is living up to our expectations, preferences, and conceptualization of what a good, close relationship should be. Thus, how satisfied we are with a relationship depends, to a large extent, on what we expect from a relationship and how well we think our actual, enacted relationship measures up.

There is a substantial body of evidence that relationship satisfaction is positively associated with psychological and physical well-being (Worell, 1988). Supportive relationships enhance our responses to stress, our self-esteem, our feelings of self-efficacy, and our resistance to loneliness, depression, serious illness, and disability. The state of our close relationships also aligns with our general feelings toward life—happy people report having close and supportive relationships.

Gender or Stereotyping?

Try the exercise in Box 8.3.Exchanges like this one describe two kinds of language, women's and men's (Henley, 1995), suggesting irreconcilable differences that ultimately disrupt connection. We usually can spot the stereotype when we see it in examples like the one in Box 8.3 (see the footnote below after reading Box 8.3).[1] Researchers find gender differences in how women and men deal with "troubles talk" in their friendships that are consistent with the patterns we saw here between M and P, but these differences are small, and they seem even smaller in contrast to much bigger **intragroup differences** across women and men (Michaud & Warner, 1997). Separating stereotyping from true gender differences is a major problem for researchers of friendships.

FRIENDSHIPS

Interestingly, the common wisdom about friendships shifted during the 1970s from regarding women's as inferior to men's as superior (Wright, 1982). In a widely cited study, Mayta Caldwell and Anne Peplau (1982) concluded that women emphasized emotional sharing and talking in contrast to men, whose friendships revolved around shared activities. Con-

---

[1]Gender-stereotyped analyses of the conversation above attribute M's statements to a woman and P's to a man, concluding that men maintain autonomy (and hence avoid accountability) in relationships, in contrast to women who seek consideration and understanding.

Box 8.3

Consider the conversation below between a women and man trying to make plans for a dinner party. Which one is the woman, M or P, and which is the man?

M: The only weekend we seem to have free is October tenth.
P: That's the weekend of the tennis tournament.
M: Well, let's do it Saturday or Sunday evening.
P: Okay, make it Saturday.
M: Wouldn't you want to be free to go to the tournament on Saturday?
P: [Annoyed] I said Saturday, so obviously that's the day I prefer.

M: [Now also annoyed] I was just trying to be considerate of you. You didn't give a reason for choosing Saturday.
P: I'm taking off Thursday and Friday to go to the tournament, so I figure I'll have had enough by Saturday night.
M: Well, why didn't you say that?
P: I didn't see why I had to. Why do I have to explain every detail?

Source: Adapted from D. Tannen (1990). *You just don't understand: Women and men in conversations*. New York: Ballentine (pp. 158–159).

---

sistent with this reasoning, researchers found that women's friendships with women were evaluated as more rewarding, reciprocal, disclosing, and close than those between men (Parker & de Vries, 1993; Sheets & Lugar, 2005; Veniegas & Peplau, 1997), yielding a large difference in intimacy favoring women's friendships ($d = -0.85$) (Reis, 1998). Not surprisingly, women who have high quality relationships with their peers also report lower psychological distress (Frey et al., 2006).

Gender Stereotyping

These different images fit well with stereotyping of women seeking **communal** or expressive outcomes in their friendships, in contrast to men's **agentic** or instrumental desires (Morrison, 2009) and of men's friendships being more competitive (Singleton & Vacca, 2007). The impact of gendered stereotyping on images of relationships is further captured in studies showing that stereotypic femininity and masculinity are better predictors of relationship variables than gender itself (Aylor & Dainton, 2004; Basow & Rubenfeld, 2003; Reevy & Maslach, 2001).

These different images of women's and men's friendships widened the gap between the sexes, contributing to the notion that women and men cannot connect meaningfully. This stereotyping is perpetuated in our common wisdom about women's and men's fundamental miscommunications that we saw earlier in Box 8.3 (Tannen, 1990).

We know that gender stereotyping often exists for reasons beyond essential differences between women and men. Even looking back to Caldwell and Peplau's study, they presented evidence that women and men define intimacy similarly. Since then, extensive research concludes that both women and men believe that intimacy involves appreciation,

Box 8.4

How do you use your cell phone? Dafna Lemish and Akiba Cohen (2005) interviewed Israeli women and men and cleverly logged their calls across 5 days. Their actual usage patterns were very similar, mostly calling family and friends from similar locations. In contrast, their self-reported scripts about their usage revealed striking gender differences. Women highlighted the functionality of their cell and saw it as a means for others to reach them. Men viewed their cell as an extension of their body, described it as a technological toy that conveyed status, and valued the power it gave them to reach others. Both data sources tell us something about the behavioral similarity of women and men, as well as their differential conformity to stereotypes of femininity (connection) and masculinity (status and control). Consistent with this interpretation, another study found that women were more likely than men to send images with their cell to further cement their connections with others (Colley et al., 2010).

warmth, and disclosure of personal feelings as well as shared activities (Reis, 1998).[2] Additionally, women and men describe similar **prototypes** for intimacy in friendships (Fehr, 2004), and both value partners with affectively oriented skills (Burleson et al., 1996) and who disclose information (Clark et al., 2004). What women want then is what men want, making them more alike than difference stereotyping would suggest.

Furthermore, both women and men are capable of meeting this goal of intimacy. For example, Karen Walker (1994) conducted 52 in-depth interviews with working-class and professional women and men. Both her data and interviewees' perceptions described women sharing feelings with women and men sharing activities with men. However, when Walker elicited specific experiences in friendships, leaving stereotyping behind, a different picture emerged. Fully 75% of the men she interviewed detailed counter-stereotypic interactions. For example, one man described how he had exchanged details with his closest friend at work about their wives' sexual "courtship" preferences—one liked to be wined and dined and the other valued spontaneity.

Furthermore, there was a wide discrepancy between the activities they said they engaged in with their friends and how much they actually did. Similarly, about 65% of the women's actual friendship **scripts** did not conform to what they had recounted previously. These findings raise serious questions: (1) How much does what we expect for friendships shape our perceptions? and (2) To what extent are our expectancies influenced by gendered beliefs—in this case beliefs that women's and men's friendships are qualitatively different?

A laboratory study of women's and men's exchanges furthers this argument. Harry Reis, Marilyn Senchak, and Beth Solomon (1985) found that undergraduate men described social interactions that were less intimate than those reported by women. This difference held when participants were asked to write down narratives of two recent exchanges. Even when other raters didn't know the gender of the people involved in the written narratives,

---

[2]Although dwarfed by similarities, there are some gender differences in that (1) women mention talk more than men, especially in same-sex interactions; (2) men cite same-sex activities more, and women, more other-sex activities; (3) physical contact, including sexuality, is more central to men's descriptions of other-sex intimacy; and (4) appreciation is greater for male partners, be they same-sex for men or other-sex for women. Each of these highlights how interactions involve two people.

the men's narratives were deemed less intimate than the women's. So far, this fits with stereotyping. However, when participants and their best friends were asked to engage in an intimate conversation in the lab, both self-ratings and ratings by external judges showed no gender differences in the intimacy of the taped conversations. When the setting expressly called for intimacy, men were just as capable of being intimate as women.

Even expectancies about appropriate male behavior can vary across contexts. Mark Morman and Kory Floyd (1998) asked mostly White undergraduate men to imagine themselves in one of six scenarios with either a brother or a close male friend. The scenarios described either a public or private setting and either a neutral (just talking) or emotionally charged (positive = wedding or negative = funeral) exchange. Emotional openness was greater to a brother, in public, and in emotionally charged exchanges. It thus seems plausible to argue that the **social contexts** for men's expression of affection are just more limited than they are for women, rather than arguing that men are incapable of emotional expressiveness.

This insight leads me to believe that women don't corner the market on intimacy in their friendships. Indeed, women and men rate the quality of their same-sex friendships as comparable (Veniegas & Peplau, 1997). Does this mean then that women's and men's friendships are the same? Judith Worell (1988) cites women's disproportionate interest in popular self-help books devoted to understanding relationships and her own and others' experiences in psychotherapeutic practice as evidence that women hunger for information about close relationships. Differential interest, just like differences in stereotyping, does not necessarily signify differences in how relationships are realized, however. *Overall, there are more differences within than between the sexes in same-sex friendships* (Marshall, 2010).

In the remainder of this chapter, we take a fresh look at women's close relationships. Although it would be a disservice to both women and men to ignore differences in what they want from and how they enact their day-to-day relationships, we explore women's *relationships as they are* (rather than looking at how they contrast with those of men)—and with an eye toward understanding how women's satisfaction through their relationships can be maximized.

Friendships between Women

Although women's friendships hardly come in "one size fits all," talk is the centerpiece of most women's friendships (Rose, 1995). Furthermore, friends may offer a safe haven for less inhibited expression. For example, women were videotaped while they viewed emotionally stimulating slides in the presence of either a stranger or a close friend. External judges, identifying the emotions expressed by the viewers, were more accurate for women viewing with friends, suggesting that women were more freely expressive in the presence of friends than strangers (Wagner & Smith, 1991). Women veer away from few topics in friendships, although this varies cross-culturally (for example, British disclosers regard fewer topics as taboo than do Chinese) (Goodwin & Lee, 1994). Generally, women tend to discuss family life, disclose political and religious disagreement, and be demonstrative by hugging or crying with a close friend. They spend time giving quality help to their friends, and they express empathy and sympathy in response to their friends' problems (George et al., 1998).

Fundamentally, women want intimacy and equality in their friendships (Veniegas & Peplau, 1997). Although anywhere from 7 to 57% of women report not having a close friend at some point in their lives (Goodenow & Gaier, 1990), the pattern of having a few close friendships, rather than gangs of acquaintances, tends to begin early for girls (Rose, 1995) and persist into old age (Johnson & Troll, 1994). Women generally look for all-purpose friends with whom they can relate across a variety of dimensions, rather than different friends for different needs (Barth & Kinder, 1988).

A pervasive characterization of women's friendships is that they include a variety of different forms of indirect aggression, such as gossiping and talking negatively behind a friend's back. Across two studies, Lauren Duncan and Ashi Owen-Smith (2006) explored various forms of powerlessness in college students' same-sex friendships. They found that individual differences in deference and lack of control in the relationship did not predict indirect aggression, but rather anxiety about one's status in friendships in general did. Specifically, the more women (and men) expressed fears of being negatively evaluated by their peers and wanted to be accepted by their peers, the more they engaged in indirect aggression. Thus, it appears that the "mean girls" image of young women's friendships is descriptive of only a few students' friendships, and it is *not* confined to "girls."

Suzanna Rose (2000) argues that drawing a clear line between friendship and romantic partners assumes a heterosexist (and possibly masculinist) perspective. For lesbians, this line is often murky. Obviously, lesbians draw female friends and lovers from the same pool of eligible contenders. Companionship typically is highly valued in lesbian partnerships and friendships, further blurring the distinction. Further consideration suggests that the line between friendship and romantic attachment may blur for heterosexual women with female friends as well, although the study of such bonding is often overlooked by researchers (Griffin, 2000). Thus, the division used in this chapter between friends and intimate partners may reflect the state of our research and culture more than the reality of women's close relationships.

"Cross" Friendships

"Cross" friendships involve people of different types, such as cross-gender, cross-orientation, and cross-racial bonds. Although having diverse relationships is associated with heightened cognitive development (Galupo et al., 2010), these relationships openly violate a fundamental characteristic of most close friendships—similarity (Floyd, 1995). Given this, cross friendships are expected to challenge their participants.

Women (and men) have more cross-sex friendships if they believe that these friendships offer benefits beyond those afforded by same-sex friendships and if they hold more flexible gender-role beliefs (Lenton & Webber, 2006). Theorists have speculated that four challenges may confront women and men in close friendships: determining the type of emotional bond to be experienced in the relationship; confronting the issue of sexuality; dealing with equality within a cultural context of inequality; and presenting the friendship as just that, friendship (not romantic involvement), to relevant audiences (O'Meara, 1989). However, researchers conclude that few of these, or any other, challenges are reported by actual casual and close cross-gender friends (Monsour et al., 1994).

In one study of cross-orientation women friends (close for at least one year), Paz Galupo (2007) recruited and interviewed 20 pairs of friends in which one party identified as either bisexual (7 women) or lesbian (13) and the other party as heterosexual. Fundamentally, these friendships looked like other friendships among women in that both parties emphasized talking with and supporting each other. However, only bisexual-heterosexual friendships shifted when the sex of the bisexual woman's partner changed. Although all the heterosexual women were aware of their lesbian friend's sexual orientation, only one bisexual woman shared this information with her heterosexual friend. Finally, bisexual-heterosexual friends were more likely to be integrated into each other's broader social lives than were lesbian-heterosexual friends.

Suzanna Rose (1996) explored obstacles to the formation of friendships between women of color and White women. Rose suggests that these relationships require a thorough analysis of racism as well as well-developed racial identities so that each party is secure in her own identity and open to exploring and valuing differences in that of another. Her research with a handful of existing cross-race friendships suggests that most are initiated by White women, who may dominate the relationship (Scott, 2004) and that work must be actively done to engender trust (Hall & Rose, 1996). Parallel patterns are found for friendships between physically challenged and able women (Fisher & Galler, 1988). The implications of successfully forging such bonds can be extended to diverse groups of women who may learn from these interpersonal exchanges how to unite at a broader level.

ROMANTIC ATTACHMENTS

In her review of "partnering across the life course," sociologist Sharon Sassler (2010) highlights the wide range of heterosexual partnering options that now characterize relationships in the United States. "Individuals select from a veritable smorgasbord of romantic options, including entering into casual, short-term sexual relationships; dating as an end toward finding a long-term partner; entering into shared living with a romantic partner (cohabitation) as an alternative to living alone; forming a cohabiting union as a precursor to marriage; or living with a partner as a substitute for formal marriage" (p. 557). She concludes that even though marriage "remains among the most venerated of options" (p. 557), the "common thread unifying all relationships is a desire for intimacy—whether emotional or sexual" (p. 557)—and that the behaviors and goals associated with partnering typically change across the life course.

Given all this diversity, I need to narrow my focus here to romantic attachments. As we noted at the beginning of this chapter, romantic attachments encompass the same features as close friendships plus sexual passion, exclusiveness, and commitment. Judith Worell (1988) extracted three themes from popular self-help books devoted to women's relationships: Presumably women don't know what will make them happy in relationships (ignorance); women lack the skills or savvy to initiate and maintain satisfying liaisons (incompetence); and in heterosexual relationships, a polarity between women and men creates a rift between them that is difficult, if not impossible, to bridge (illusion). Interestingly, researchers find that the more exposed adults are to this popular media, the more dysfunctional and unrealistic are their beliefs about intimate relationships (Shapiro & Kroeger, 1991). Although Worell goes on to debunk this relationship stereotyping, its residuals often infiltrate our understandings of relationships.

Romance Ideology

Before we explore becoming and being partnered, let's digress for a moment to consider our general beliefs about romance, or what researchers call our *romance ideology* (Rudman & Glick, 2008). These ideas of romance might include sentimentality, unrequited pursuit, and emotional caretaking (Korobov & Thorne, 2009) and include endorsement of thinking about a woman's male lover as "Prince Charming" and a "white knight," as protective, and as a hero—not just an "average" man (Rudman & Heppen, 2003). If you stop to think about these beliefs a bit more, you should recognize much of what we described as **benevolent sexism** in the previous chapter. Women are faithfully adored—just as they are in the valentines commonly selected by women (Gonzalez & Koestner, 2006), and men are "nice guys"—reflecting women's preferences for niceness (Urbaniak & Kilmann, 2006) and for men who express benevolently sexist attitudes (Bohner et al., 2010; Lee et al., 2010b). How could there be a downside to women holding such clearly romantic beliefs?

It turns out that there isn't a downside if we look at **explicit attitudes**; that is, the beliefs women openly express about romance (Rudman & Heppen, 2003). But assessing women's romantic fantasies with questions about Prince Charming might bring their actual relationships to bear, because who wants to admit that their partner doesn't measure up?

To get around this problem, Laurie Rudman and Jessica Heppen (2003) created an **implicit attitudes test** to tap into women's unacknowledged fantasies about romance. They found that the more implicitly romantic a woman was, the *less* likely she was to project high income, educational goals, and a prestigious job for herself, as well as express interest in being a group leader. In sum, these implicitly romantic women bought into the "glass slipper effect," relying on a man, not themselves, to fulfill the Cinderella fantasy of "living happily [or more to the point, successfully/agentically] ever after." Thus it seems that there is a pretty serious downside for women who harbor these types of (unrealistically) romantic images.

Becoming Partnered: Dating

When researchers ask women and men to describe ideal romantic partners or to examine pictures or review vignettes, men rank physical attractiveness higher than women do, and women more strongly value earning potential, setting up the clash of values we often see exhibited on television dating games (Hetsroni, 2000). Paul Eastwick and Eli Finkel (2008) replicated this common finding—but they then went on look more closely at the actual choices of women and men both during and after a speed dating event. No gender differences emerged in these behavioral data, and in fact, none of what people said they were looking for in an ideal partner or speed date predicted what actually inspired their preferences at the event. Not all that surprising to us by now as gender researchers is how poorly gendered expectancies and individuals' behaviors actually match up.

Because many romantic attachments are forged through the courtship process of dating, psychologists have studied the *first-date* expectancies and behaviors of heterosexual women and men. Mary Claire Morr Serewicz and Elaine Gale (2008) asked male and female college students to generate a list of what they expected to happen on a first date, varying who initiated the date (woman or man), the context of the date (keg party or coffee shop), and the relationship between the couple (acquaintance or friend). They then analyzed these lists to identify consistent patterns (as evidence of shared scripts), gauge the amount of redundancy in the items listed, and compare scripts across the different variations in dates.

Interestingly, they found not only that dates are scripted, but also that these 21st century scripts aren't all that different from prior ones. Overall, these first-date scripts included 20 unique actions about which women and men agreed—most commonly including getting ready, picking up the date (by the man), paying (by the man), talking, walking/driving home (directed by the man), kissing, and making future plans. In addition to the general pattern that men controlled more of the elements of the first-date than women, women were more likely to discuss the date with others (both before and after), to show more cognitive complexity (less redundancy) in how they described dates, and to generally regard the date as more romantic (as opposed to sexual). In male-initiated dates, women expected a goodnight kiss, whereas in female-initiated dates, men expected sexual activities beyond kissing. Surprisingly, being a friend or acquaintance beforehand made no difference in the dating script, but the proposed activity did. More sexual behavior, more social networking with others, and less communication intimacy were expected at the keg party than at the coffee shop. Overall then, heterosexual first-dating has not changed much, and college students continue to have clear, well-scripted ideas about what these first dates should be like.

These scripts are so ingrained in our expectancies that they can be reproduced in the laboratory between strangers, and they are resistant to deviations (Gilbert et al., 1999). In a dating simulation, unrelated women and men undergraduates were paired and then asked to role play dating in either a conventional or unconventional context. In the conventional arrangement, the man was told to initiate the date and to later press for sexual intimacy; and the woman was directed to decline his sexual advances. Students were able to re-create this scenario without any trouble. The unconventional context required students to reverse roles, yet the dialogue that followed quickly fell into a conventional script. This study illustrates both the ease with which we use prescriptive dating scripts, as well as the difficulty of challenging these dictates.

Interestingly, there is a substantial amount of overlap between the actual dating scripts of lesbians and heterosexual women (Klinkenberg & Rose, 1994) and in what both groups find romantically attractive (Felmlee at al., 2010), extending to gender similarities in internet personal ads (Groom & Pennebaker, 2005). The most glaring differences point to closer equality in power, more affective/evaluative consideration, and a balance of active and reactive behaviors. Like heterosexual women, lesbians are nervous about their first date, but their preparation focuses more on cleaning up and meal preparation than on appearance. They are likely to engage in the same activities (talking, movies, etc.), but throughout the script, lesbians are more likely to contemplate how they are feeling and assess how things are going. Lesbians also note that they sometimes initiate sexual contact and assume the responsibility for enacting the date (e.g., picking up their partner). These last points suggest something about the power dynamics of dating (see Box 8.5).

Being Partnered

Here, we explore relationship satisfaction in two types of partnerships, lesbian and heterosexual marital, recognizing as we noted above that marriage is not the only context in which romantic attachments are enacted. Undergraduate women's and men's descriptions

Box 8.5

We generally don't think about dating in terms of power relationships between women and men. However, looking across what we just reviewed about heterosexuals' and lesbians' dating scripts and students' resistance to thinking about deviating from these conventional scripts, we shouldn't be surprised that dating men feel more powerful than dating women (Murstein & Adler, 1995), and men are more likely to be named the more powerful party in a dating relationship (Felmlee, 1994).

In a fascinating recent study, Megan Yost and Lauren McCarthy (2012) explored the prevalence and motivations for heterosexual women to engage in a public sexual display (kissing another woman) at a college party. On the face of it, this behavior appears unconventional and empowering for the engaged women; however, further probing suggests that this may not always be the case. Although women reported a complex array of stories, almost all reported being pressured (largely by men), and the most common motivation women reported was to attract men's attention, especially when the party seemed controlled by men. This study, along with others (Nowatzki & Morry, 2009), raises intricate questions about when women's sexuality is empowering and/or objectifying.

of their ideal intimate partner were remarkably similar—valuing, in rank order, warmth, vitality, status, intimacy, and passion (Fletcher et al., 1999). Likewise, Judith Worell (1988) concludes that, despite popular portrayals to the contrary, women know exactly what they want: *intimacy* and *equality*. We'll see that relationship satisfaction is high to the extent that both these desires are met.

Lesbians' relationships. Natalie Eldridge and Lucia Gilbert (1990) conducted an extensive nationwide survey of 275 lesbian couples where both partners were employed full-time. Several patterns emerge from their data. First, relationship was largely *invisible* to outsiders, despite the facts that these women had been in their current relationship for an average of over 5 years, most lived with their partner, and 15% were raising children together. Sizable numbers did *not* tell employers (65%), coworkers (35%), fathers (over half), mothers (one-third), or neighbors and strangers (three-quarters). Coming out to people outside the relationship is unrelated to satisfaction within that relationship (Mohr & Daly, 2008), although lesbians (more so than gay men) report stress related to "outness" to family members (Todosijevic et al., 2005).

Second, despite lack of public acknowledgment of their bond, Eldridge and Gilbert found that *lesbian relationships were stable, enduring, and committed*, and that the women in them displayed high levels of self-esteem and life satisfaction. These data dispel stereotyping that lesbian relationships are fleeting, debilitating, and only sexual in nature, as well as opposite stereotyping of fusion (intense, singular over-reliance on the relationship; Hill, 1999). In addition, lesbian couples who share similar views about their sexual identity have higher-quality relationships (Mohr & Fassinger, 2006). Finally, a large-scale study of childfree lesbian, gay, and heterosexual married and unmarried couples as well as married heterosexual couples with children concluded that close intimate relationships, despite variability in their structure, work in similar ways (Kurdek, 2006).

Third, fully 13 of 14 psychological factors studied were associated with relationship satisfaction; the one exception was career commitment. When partners had divergent career commitments, relationship satisfaction was low. Couples satisfied with their relationship reported high levels of both attachment to their partner and personal autonomy. Relationships generally were characterized by heightened intimacy, especially *recreational* (common interests) and *intellectual* intimacy, with social intimacy lagging last (another potential casualty of secrecy). Couples also reported a clear sense of power or influence in their relationship.

Equality of influence is a central feature for satisfied lesbian couples. Lesbian partners value ideal equality more than do gay men, even though both partnerships are exempted from gender-role disparities (Kurdek, 1995). Compared to heterosexual couples, lesbian couples are more likely to use bilateral influence strategies where both partners participate, and it is these strategies that are associated with more favorable intimacy in both types of relationships (Rosenbluth & Steil, 1995). Psychologically intimate communication also distinguishes long-term lesbian partnerships from other types of enduring attachments (Mackey et al., 2000). Given these values, it is not surprising that lesbian couples tend to report performing an equal number of household tasks, unlike both gay male and heterosexual partners (Kurdek, 2007).

Heterosexual marital relationships. A long-standing conclusion asserts that men report higher levels of marital satisfaction than women (fKaslow et al., 1994), although as we might expect, there are individual variations marked more by personality than by gender (Robins et al., 2000). Love or intimacy is the cornerstone of marriage, at least in Western, individualistic societies (Levine et al., 1995), including a distinct self-disclosure component for women (Culp & Beach, 1998). Women's second desire in relationships, *equality*, may be a potent force that underlies marital satisfaction. Inequality, in both attitudes and behaviors, is related to lower marital satisfaction for women.

Egalitarianism in marriage is more commonly desired today than it was 40 years ago (Apparala et al., 2003), almost reaching levels of consensus among college women and men (Askari et al., 2010). Women who see themselves as equal partners in their marriage are more satisfied, in general, than traditional pairings and are less likely to use power strategies to get their way (Donaghue & Fallon, 2003).

This all seems quite simple: Women want equality, and positive attitudes about equality are associated with strong marital satisfaction. But what about behaviors? It's one thing to value equality, another to realize it. There is an extensive body of data using all kinds of measures that comes to the same conclusion: *women perform a disproportionate share of household labor* (excluding childcare).

For example, drawing on diary data collected from over 25,000 married U.S. women and men across 2003 to 2007, Liana Sayer and Leigh Fine (2011) compiled the average hours per day devoted to *core housework* (cleaning, laundry, cooking, and meal clean-up) and occasional housework (yard work, house and vehicle maintenance and repairs, and household paperwork).

Looking at core housework, how much time women spend varies by race/ethnicity, with Latinas doing the most (2.98 hours/day), followed by Asian American (2.33), White (2.02), and Black (1.81) women. In contrast, men's contributions did not vary significantly across races, ranging from 0.54 to 0.65 hours. As you can readily see from the hours listed,

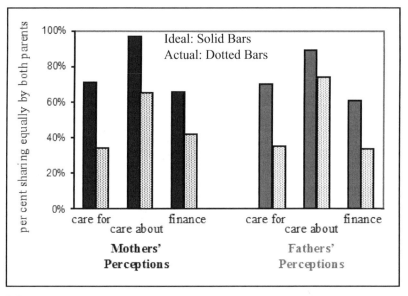

Figure 8.6

Telephone interviews with 234 married parents asked about their ideal and actual sharing in the caring for, emotional caring about, and financial support for their children (Milkie et al., 2002). The figure shows a consistent pattern whereby support for an egalitarian ideal outstrips the reality of actual equal sharing. Furthermore, the reports of actual behaviors not equally shared follow the stereotypes we'd expect with mothers doing more of the caring for (63%; 55%, as perceived by mothers and fathers, respectively) and caring about (34%; 19%) than fathers, as well as with fathers contributing more of the finances than mothers (39%; 60%).

a gender gap remains in women's and men's contributions, intriguingly varying across races. The widest gender gap is between Hispanic couples where women contribute 5.54 times than men, followed by Asian (4.12), White (3.16), and Black (2.79) couples.

Men consistently contribute more time to occasional chores (0.53 to 1.08 hours/day for men; 0.40 to 0.72, for women), but both the amount of time devoted to these chores and the gender gaps in contributions (ranging from 0.52 to 0.85 times more by men) are much smaller than what we saw for core tasks. Follow-up analyses document that these patterns remain unchanged when controlling for household income, education, employment status, parental status, presence of other household adults, age, region of the country, and weekend diary day.

Turning to time use surveys conducted globally, the United Nations (2010) concluded that women throughout the world contribute more domestic labor than men. These surveys estimate that women in developed countries average 5 hours/day on household labor, whereas men contribute less than 2.5 hours/day. By far the greatest daily time demand on women throughout the world involves meal preparation, with little participation from men.

Hold on a minute! We've heard lots about how men are doing more at home. The general pattern in time use studies is that women report doing less and men more, so that, at least in the United States and some other developed countries (United Nations, 2010), time contributions to household tasks are converging (Bianchi & Milkie, 2010). For example, men went from reporting doing only 8% of the housework in 1965, to 20% in 1985 (Robinson, 1988), to a third in the 1990s (Bianchi et al., 2000). There is reason to believe that both conclusions are true: that gender gaps remain as revealed by diary studies *and* that the contributions of men are increasing while women's are decreasing.

Some of this apparent discrepancy may be accounted for by how accurately we all estimate our own contributions to household labor. Julie Press and Eleanor Townsley (1998) calculated a "reporting gap" by comparing self-report survey estimates with arguably more accurate diary data. Both women and men over-report—by 68% and 149%, respectively. This reporting gap appears to be influenced by social desirability. Nontraditional men, traditional women, women with children, upper-class egalitarian men, and poorer "super-moms" are the most flagrant over-reporters. These data should make those of us with egalitarian ideals pause to consider how "good" we truly are. Still, a real gap does exist: Using the diary data, Press and Townsley report that men contribute less than one quarter time (4.2 versus 18.4 hours) to weekly cooking, washing dishes, cleaning the house, and doing laundry.

Pulling these findings together, it is clear that modern family members value egalitarianism and try to portray their contributions as more balanced than diary studies, which actually catalogue activities, document. For those of us who would like to reconcile these differences by making our behaviors more consistent with our equal-sharing values, the central question becomes "Why does this gender gap persist?" In their review of 21st-century research on the division of household labor, Suzanne Bianchi and Melissa Milkie (2010, p. 708) concluded: "Despite the large number of studies, there emerged no dominant consensus on the most persuasive explanation for the persistence of the gender division of labor in the home." This conclusion is shared by other reviewers considering the same time period (Lachance-Grzela & Bouchard, 2010).

However, some explanations are ruled out by the data. As we saw in Sayer and Fine's (2011) diary study, gender gaps in women's and men's contributions persisted despite employment status, parenting status, the presence of other potential helpers in the household, and so on—ruling out the explanations that women contribute more because women have more time or contribute fewer other resources (e.g., income) to the family. Even being raised to do household chores as a child doesn't predict individual men's adult contributions, discounting domestic incompetence as an explanation (Penha-Lopes, 2006). What remains are explanations that focus on gender attitudes and the gendering of domestic labor and household roles as feminine.

The prospects for large-scale changes in this arena are bleak. Sabrina Askari and her colleagues (2010) surveyed 358 unmarried, heterosexual students and non-students about what percentage of work they ideally and actually expected to contribute to doing each of a variety of common household and childcare chores. *Ideally*, men wanted to do 47% of household chores and 47% of childcare, with women averaging 58% of both. This ideal gets close to a 50-50 split, but not fully. As for what they *expected*, the gap expands: men projected doing 45% of household and 47% of childcare chores; women, 69% and 70%, respectively. The gap between women's ideal and expected was significantly different; men's was not. Interestingly, women who wanted to do less ideally wanted a more family-than career-oriented partner, but, not expecting to find one, they then anticipated shouldering a greater domestic load.

In a second study by these same authors led by Mindy Erchull (et al., 2010), we get some further sense of why this discrepancy persists. Simply put, "she wants it more." In this study with 466 college students, the typical man was described as wanting marriage and children less than the typical woman did. Furthermore, desire for marriage and children predicted expected chore involvement such that women (and men) who want it more, do more. The "principle of least interest" generally asserts that the person less interested in a relationship has more power, and indeed these findings fit with that interpretation.

Despite these discouraging prospects for massive change, Shannon Davis (2010) suggests that researchers turn to what we can learn from qualitative studies that explore the lives of albeit select exemplars of equal-sharing couples. For example, a portrayal of *egalitarian men* is provided by Kathleen Gerson's (1993) study of 138 men from diverse social backgrounds. One-third of these men were with work-committed women with whom they shared economic and domestic responsibilities. Half these sharing men expressed egalitarian attitudes before becoming committed to their wives; the remainder developed these attitudes as a result of their commitment. But attitudes can take us only so far; the rest evolved. Some sharing men voluntarily veered away from high-pressure careers; others hit an occupational deadend. As work became less central in their lives, these sharing men became more involved at home. Involvement spawned further involvement because these men reaped benefits from sharing, including a strengthened marriage, bonding with children, increased influence at home, development of expressive qualities, and enhanced personal pride. An upward spiral of participation developed.

This portrait of equal-sharing men highlights both the importance and limits of attitudes. Indeed, couples with more flexible gender role beliefs and egalitarian attitudes do share more equally (Kroska, 2004; Stevens et al., 2006) as do fathers who espouse fewer beliefs in biological **essentialism** (Gaunt, 2006). However, roles and societal expectations about who fills them must change as well because, as we have seen from the very start of this book, we all are embedded within a larger system of gender inequality. Some of this change may rest on nurturing feminist attitudes in both women and men; for example, in Askari et al.'s (2010) study, women and men who endorsed feminist attitudes also ideally and actually expected to contribute more equally.

Other qualitative studies show that some Black men share housework when they define themselves as both caretakers and as breadwinners, as well as regard doing housework as part of being masculine (Penha-Lopes, 2006). Some Mexican American men who are less acculturated into U.S. culture contribute more, suggesting that "Americanized" versions of masculinity may suppress family connections (Coltrane et al., 2004). At least some women may regard housework as less central to their feminine identity as they age (Altschuler, 2004), and some women who out-earn their partner (even sole providers) may justify their domestic contributions as ways to protect their husband's masculinity (Tichenor, 2005). As Shannon Davis (2010) argues, we may learn more about changing gender roles by looking at examples that succeed, shifting our research question from "Why do women do the lion's share of housework?" to "When don't they?"

Egalitarian sharing does not just happen in relationships; rather, it is actively constructed by committed and vigilant partners (Blaisure & Allen, 1995; Mannino & Deutsch, 2007). (We discuss this point further in Chapter 14.) Sandra Tangri and Sharon Rae Jenkins (1997) found that women who expect work-family conflict and prepare accordingly—by asserting their career intentions with their spouse, by postponing childbearing, and by having fewer children—experience less marital conflict than those who fail to acknowledge potential problems. When it comes to being satisfied with intimate relationships, it seems that there is no bliss in ignorance!

CAREGIVING

One of the most fundamental roles to the image of women is that of caregiver. In all likelihood, most women will assume the role of caregiver across their lifetimes—as a caregiver of children, partners, parents, friends, and neighbors, or through volunteer work. Women are expected to be caregivers (Mosher & Danoff-Burg, 2004), and women, more than men, expect to enjoy enhanced mood by both providing and getting help within the context of a relationship (Sprecher et al., 2007). After we briefly explore general patterns in caregiving, we will turn to childcare, including images of mothers and the still evolving image of the employed supermom and her use of nonparental childcare.

General Patterns

With increasing life spans and with the balance of young to older people tipping in the direction of more elderly, caretaking needs for the elderly are on the rise (Etaugh, 2008). Women account for 71% of those devoting 40 hours or more each week to caring for aging parents (Gross, 2005). Care of aging parents can add strain and poor self-care to the lives of midlife women (Remennick, 1999). Additionally, midlife women are increasingly "squeezed" by taking care of both adult children and aging parents (Etaugh, 2008).

Looking at caregiving both inside and outside the family, women give about twice as much help in a month as men (Gerstel & Gallagher, 2001). Women provide about equally for their friends and parents; adult children command as much caregiving as these two groups combined. Men contribute to more volunteer groups, but this difference disappears for local community groups, suggesting that men have more official memberships than women, but women give more time to local groups. Further probing of these data reveals that employed women and homemakers perform practical, labor-intensive caregiving chores equally. Employed husbands help fewer relatives and friends and spend fewer hours than their similarly employed female counterparts. In addition, men defensively distance themselves more than women from others who need their help because of a serious illness or accident (Whitehead & Smith, 2002). In sum, caregiving, even outside of childcare, is expected to be, and is, "women's work."

Caregiving in all its forms provides invaluable social services and gratification to individuals, fundamentally enriching all our lives. Still, our understanding of caregiving would be incomplete if we didn't acknowledge women's disproportionate contributions and that the time and energy caregivers donate rarely, if ever, benefits them with anything exchangeable (Pratto & Walker, 2004). For this reason, caregiving does *not* confer power. Caregiving roles, such as mother (Ridgeway & Correll, 2004), are status characteristics, which we saw in Chapter 7 are linked to likeability and warmth but not to respect and competence. In fact, we might explore our resistance to thinking about caregiving, especially mothering, in status terms as an example of the power of our stereotyping of these activities.

Images of Mothers

Turning to caregiving for children, childcare is considered so much a part of feminine stereotyping that the word we most frequently use to describe it is gender-specific: "mothering."[3] People asked to make judgments about hypothetical post-divorce parental care awarded custody to whichever parent was described with feminine characteristics (Hoffman & Moon, 2000). Furthermore, when the tasks of "mothering" (waking up a child, making dinner, and doing homework together) are done by one parent, students are harsher critics of a non-contributing mother than father (Riggs, 2005).

The dominant cultural images of a "mother" are embodied in two configurations: (1) the traditional, full-time, domestic mother whose sole job is her family and (2) the employed mom with multiple roles—job, self, and family ("supermom") (Thurer, 1994). A defining difference between the two images focuses on caregiving for children. Caregiving for children involves both **caring for** (serving the needs of or caretaking) and **caring about** (loving) children (Traustadottir, 1991). These two features define the traditional mom who provides both forms of caregiving for her children: She is: (1) *continually present* and (2) *exclusive* in that she is expected to be the primary, if not sole, childcare provider (Uttal, 1996). The "supermom" thus differs from the traditional one along both of these dimensions.

One of the most revealing ways to uncover our expectations about motherhood is to explore stereotype violations. Michele Fine and Sarah Carney (2001) do just this by closely examining court cases involving charges of "failure to protect." For example, women have been charged for injury to their children at the hands of a man in the household, even when these women themselves are abused. A charge rarely leveled against men, these cases highlight women's responsibility to care for and about children. Women with few resources and those who violate traditional expectations for women are assigned more responsibility and blame by the courts (and by researchers and mental health professionals; Womack et al., 1999). It seems it is women's responsibility to police their homes and keep transgressions secret.

The underlying message here is not lost on other mothers. All mothers work hard at maintaining their image as "good" mothers by resisting temptations to talk about the downside of their experiences as mothers (Weaver & Ussher, 1997). Indeed, women commonly regarded as "bad" mothers—such as welfare recipients (Croghan & Miell, 1998), substance abusers (Baker & Carson, 1999), teen mothers (Shanok & Miller, 2007), and adoptive single mothers (Ben-Ari & Weinberg-Kurnik, 2007—work especially hard at re-positioning themselves as worthy mothers.

Researchers find a double standard of praise and criticism for mothers and fathers that also speaks volumes about stereotyping (Deutsch & Saxon, 1998). Mothers report being criticized for too much involvement at work and not enough at home, and they describe being praised for successfully combining work and family. Criticisms noted by fathers reverse those for mothers—chiding men for too much family involvement and too little at work. These patterns of external pressures work to discourage nontraditional transitions in family life.

---

[3] A quick glance through *Psychological Abstracts* (PsycINFO) soon reveals that some research purporting to study "parenting" actually includes only mothers so that what really is being studied is "mothering." I have found no reversal of this pattern; "fathering" is clearly meant to be gender-specific.

Cultural variations in mothering.   Images of both traditional mothers and "super-moms," like other global cultural stereotyping, incorporate class and racial/ethnic biases by assuming middle-class and White statuses. Very different images of mothering emerge within African American communities (Collins, 1994). Here, motherhood involves shared and sharing responsibility as African American mothers assume the mothering of others' children and their community, as well as engage others in the mothering of their own bio-logical offspring. The privatized view of mother described by dominant U.S. culture is con-trasted with this more collective orientation in the African American community. Images of family structure in Latina/Latino families often exaggerate traditional images of mothers. These questionable stereotypes rely on simplified explanations involving machismo and submissive roles for women that fail to consider the flexibility of gender roles within fami-lies in response to outside forces (e.g., degree of acculturation, specific country of origin, and the availability and need for dual employment; Vega, 1990).

Pierrette Hondagneu-Sotelo and Ernestine Avila (1997) take a fascinating look at how Latina immigrant women who work as nannies and housekeepers in Los Angeles negotiate mothering their children who reside in their country of origin. They *care for* their absent children's needs by giving them financial security and opportunities that otherwise would be beyond their reach and by monitoring and nurturing positive relationships with their on-site surrogates. These women *care about* their distant children by struggling to maintain lines of communication and emotional connection despite long distances and enduring separations. They report that they are proud of what they do for their children and that their children appreciate their sacrifices. Thus, these immigrant women actively construct caring for and caring about elements of mothering despite extreme violations of both continual presence and exclusivity.

Who mothers?   In part, this basic question asks who does the caretaking chores for children in the home. Mothers average over 11 hours each week more childcare than fathers (Bond et al., 2003). Fathers were more likely to play with children than do the nitty-gritty tasks of caretaking, such as getting up at night (Laflamme et al., 2002). Surprisingly, the time mothers report spending with their children has not changed from 1965 to 1998 (5.8 waking hours per day; Bianchi, 2000).

No single event is more likely to change domestic contributions and role enactments between partners more than the introduction of a first child. Analyzing longitudinal data from 205 first-time and 198 experienced mothers and fathers, who were followed from 5 months into a pregnancy through the child's first year, Sabra Katz-Wise and her colleagues (2010) found that both gender-role attitudes and behaviors became more traditional after the birth of the child. These changes were more pronounced for women than for men and among first-time compared to seasoned parents. Another study concluded that new parent-hood does little to alter men's working or home lives, whereas motherhood commonly increases women's household contributions and reduces their employment hours (Sanchez & Thomson, 1997). Thus, parenthood fosters a gendered division of labor largely by re-shaping women's, not men's, lives.

In fascinating interviews with eight Israeli lesbian couples with 1 to 3 children, Adital Ben-Ari and Tali Livni (2006) concluded that the addition of a biological child challenges the previous equality claimed by both partners. Because the child is legally designated as having a single mother so that the nonbiological mother has no legal ties to the child, these different statuses create a hierarchical imbalance that favors the biological mother, affecting both their enactment of mothering (who makes decisions about the child), their relationship, and their standing in the community (we're now a family). One way that these women elected to level this imbalance was to be pregnant at the same time.

If we move beyond simple caretaking to the full responsibility of caring for and caring about, we ask: Can men "mother"? Barbara Risman (1987) surveyed 55 single fathers of children under 13 whose full-time caretaking resulted from widowhood, desertion, or the mother's disinterest in shared responsibility. Each single father, most of whom were White, was compared to a single mother, a married two-paycheck mother and father, and a married traditional mother and father, all of whom had a youngest child of about the same age. The dual-paycheck families were the most affluent; men tended to work in professional and blue-collar jobs, and women in clerical and sales positions.

Single fathering increased personal household responsibility dramatically; more generally, primary parents (whether women or men) contributed more. Single mothers, as well as traditional fathers (regardless of maternal employment), reported fewer affectionate displays with their children, in contrast to sharing parents of both genders. The best predictor of parent-child intimacy across all groups was **expressiveness**, as measured by the Bem Sex Role Inventory: more expressive (feminine-stereotypic) women *and* men were more intimate (also see Renk et al., 2003).

Risman's point is that "mothering" does not always break down along gender lines— not only women (nor all women) are capable of caregiving. Single fathers "mothered" in the sense that they did the same caretaking work as women mothers, and sharing fathers "mothered" in that they provided the same intimacy as sharing mothers. Also note that not all women mothered in the sense of caring about (intimacy). Thus, *caregiving may best be conceptualized as a role we enact*, rather than as a predilection that we are either born with or are socialized to develop as a function of our sex.

The Supermom and Nonparental Childcare

The notion that men can "mother" challenges both primary dimensions of traditional images of women who are expected to be (1) present at all times and (2) primarily responsible. This leads us to consider the second, still evolving image of the employed supermom and the role nonparental childcare plays in the lives of employed mothers and their children. We begin with data on the prevalence of nonparental childcare and then go on to explore its meaning in women's lives as well as the psychological debate and findings about its effects on children.

Prevalence. Almost all American children are in the care of nonfamily members by the time they reach school age at about age 6,[4] and 63% of children under the age of 5 were in some form of regular childcare arrangement during a typical week (Smith, 2002). Most commonly, care is provided by a relative (41%), most frequently a grandpar-

---

[4]Using data from the National Household Education Surveys conducted by the U.S. Department of Education's National Center for Education Statistics, Stacey Bleeck (2008) estimates that 1.5 million American children were home-schooled in 2007, composing 2.9% of the school-aged population. Kamerman and Kahn (1995) reported that out-of-home care for 3– to 5–year–olds is almost universal in Europe, where day care is more fully subsidized.

ent (21%). When we think of nonparental care, we may picture a day care facility, but only 20% of children under age 5 attend these, with an almost equal percentage (17%) in the care of a nonrelative in their own home or at the provider's. Although both African American and Latina families state preferences for organized day care, they actually more commonly rely on family-based care, especially grandmothers (Johnson et al., 2003). Overall, nonparental care is statistically normative and ultimate inevitability for all but a handful of children.

The meaning of nonparental care. An insightful exploration of the meaning of childcare in employed women's lives is offered by Lynet Uttal (1996), who conducted in-depth interviews with a diverse sample of 31 employed women with preschoolers, toddlers, and infants. She identified three distinct patterns and related each to the core dimensions of traditional mothers' childcare: that is, (1) continued presence and (2) exclusive responsibility.

Women who regarded childcare as **custodial care** separated mothering (caring about) from custodial care (caring for) and retained exclusive rights to the former. They set sharp limits on what providers can and can't do regarding their child's physical, social, and moral development. They often checked in throughout the day to give specific directions and to make caregiving decisions. In this way, these mothers retained sole responsibility for mothering their children, like traditional mothers, but relinquished the traditional mother's provision of continued presence.

A small minority of women who viewed their childcare as **surrogate care** surrendered care to another because the conditions of their employment demanded more separation from their children than they deemed appropriate, or because they felt inadequate as mothers. For these mothers, the provider became the child's "real" preferred mother. These mothers challenged the traditional assumption that only biological mothers can "mother," but they embraced the traditional belief that continued presence is needed to fulfill the demands of true motherhood.

Mothers who embraced **coordinated care** regarded childcare providers as joint contributors to a child's development and well-being. Coordinated arrangements evolved around continuing discussions that sought to synchronize philosophies, values, and practices. Both parties learned from each other and enacted childrearing that was coordinated and consistent. In essence, they developed a cooperative alliance that challenges *both* dictates of traditional mothering, rejecting notions that mothers must be constantly present and exclusively responsible. Thus, although it may seem on the surface that all employed mothers are challenging traditional notions of mothering, only women who embrace a philosophy of coordinated care are fully doing so.

Summing up, we have seen that nonparental care of preschoolers is statistically normative, and that nonmaternal care, both by fathers and by childcare providers, may challenge basic tenets of the image of traditional mothers as the always present and exclusive providers of both care for and care about their children. When fathers provide both custodial and emotional care for their children, their similarity to women who mother discredits biological explanations of women as mothers, instead regarding motherhood as a socially constructed role that can be assumed (and rejected) by anyone. Similarly, when coordinated childcare providers act as extensions of parents in children's lives, traditional images of mothers are reframed and a more realistic picture of a "supermom" develops. One obstacle to the further development of this alternative image of mothers is the often heated debate about the effects of nonparental care on children.

Effects of non-maternal care on children.

Paralleling the always present and exclusive image of mothers is that of the ideal employee who is unencumbered by competing demands and is always available to the employer (Williams, 2001). These two images clash head-on with employed mothers, making non-maternal care a lightning rod for change on the domestic side of this formula. The implicit questions researchers have pursued speak to how politically charged this area is (Scarr & Eisenberg, 1993). The dominant ideology of the 1970s looked for damage to children (see Box 8.7), then shifted in the 1980s to evaluate the quality of care and individual differences among children.

A large body of research has focused on the emotional, social, and intellectual development of children as they relate to maternal employment. One meta analysis of 59 such studies compared maternal (no more than 6 hours of other-than-mother care per week) with supplemented care (Erel et al., 2000). No differences were found across multiple outcomes, including mother-child attachment and interaction, adjustment and well-being, social interaction with peers and with nonparental adults, and cognitive development. Only age of child's entry into day care was significant, such that the older the child, the more *insecure* the child's attachment.

A second meta analysis explored the relationships between maternal employment and children's achievement and behavior problems across 69 studies (Lucas-Thompson et al., 2010). Overall, there were no direct effects; however, variability in the data pointed to the operation of some **moderators**. For example, maternal employment during a child's first year appeared to benefit children challenged by single parenting or low income, whereas some negative effects arose in middle-class and two-parent families(possibly calling for more generous short-term leave policies). In contrast, maternal employment during the child's second and third years was consistently associated with higher achievement.

Bianchi and Milkie's (2010, p. 710) review of research covering the first decade of the 21st century comes to the same conclusion: "The vast majority of studies of maternal employment showed either no or small effects on child outcomes... [In fact, one] area

---

Box 8.7

A contrived laboratory simulation, the "strange situation," labels children as emotionally secure or insecure based on how they react when reunited with their mother, who left them playing with toys in the presence of an adult female stranger (Ainsworth et al., 1978). Kids with employed mothers were somewhat more likely to be classified as insecure, some because they didn't react much to her return (appearing "avoidant"). Rather than using these data to indict day care, critics point out that there's little "strange" about this situation for children in day care who routinely separate from, then return to, their parents and whose apparent avoidance may just as readily be interpreted as independence (Clarke-Stewart, 1989; Hoffman, 1989).

where positive effects were increasingly reported was for young children in low-income families." Interestingly, this review did point to some evidence about academic shortfalls for adolescent children who are charged with caring for younger children when their parents are absent. This last point may say more about having the resources to have appropriate care providers than anything about maternal employment per se.

CHAPTER SUMMARY

In this chapter, we explored a multitude of roles that comprise people's interpersonal lives. We discovered that holding multiple roles can have both overload and enhancement consequences. Role enhancement is facilitated to the extent that each role is of high quality, fulfills needs in an individual's life, and is meaningful and valued. Coping with the demands of multiple roles is enhanced if structural role redefinition is used to redefine otherwise incompatible roles and if social and structural supports are strong.

Close relationships are expected to endure over time and to provide an individual with respect, intimacy, caring, concern, support, and affection. Satisfaction with close relationships is positively associated with psychological and physical well-being. Oftentimes when we consider the role of gender in close relationships, it is difficult to distinguish between genuine gender differences and the self-fulfilling consequences of gendered stereotyping. Although there is no universal recipe for attaining relationship satisfaction, we explored issues involved in working toward such satisfaction in women's friendships, romantic attachments, and caregiving.

An apparent gender difference in friendship patterns evolved in the 1980s suggesting that women share feelings and men share activities with their close friends. Although it is clear that these friendship patterns reflect gender stereotyping, the veracity of this difference is being challenged by recent research that shows men being as intimate as women in settings that call for intimacy. Turning to women's friendships, women seek intimacy and equality from their friends, although how these are realized varies according to the characteristics of friends, including matches and mismatches in gender, race, physical ability, and sexual orientation.

Heterosexual dating scripts reflect gender-typed roles, with men playing the more active and powerful role. Although lesbians' dating scripts parallel heterosexuals' in many ways, the former are characterized by more equality of power, less attention to appearance, and more attention to feelings. Lesbian relationships often are invisible to outsiders, yet in contrast to negative portrayals, frequently offer intimacy and equality in stable, enduring, and committed relationships.

Marital satisfaction is heavily influenced by issues of equality because women generally continue to shoulder the lion's share of domestic responsibilities. This imbalance spills over into caregiving relationships where women often provide a disproportionate share of care for children and other kin. Recent research suggests that the "caring about" part of caregiving, prototypically referred to as "mothering," is not exclusive or universal to women. Furthermore, a new image of mothers is evolving that combines employment with mothering as parts of women's family responsibilities. This image can, but does not always, challenge traditional images of mothers as the always present and exclusive providers of childcare.

Public controversy surrounds debates about "supermom" images and nonparental childcare. Research has become increasingly complex, considering the full array of people involved, individual differences among them, the quality of settings, and the strength of social and structural supports. Broad overgeneralizations about "bad" day care have been replaced by an "it-depends" approach that seeks to understand combinations of factors that best promote an individual woman's satisfaction and health. A clear theme that runs through all of these areas is that relationship satisfaction doesn't come in "one size fits all," nor is it something that one simply has. People do not just "find happiness"; rather, relationship satisfaction is achieved through persistent, everyday work.

SUGGESTED READINGS

Febbraro, A. R. (2003). Alpha and beta bias in research on labour and love: The case of enhancement versus scarcity. *Feminism & Psychology. 13*, 210–223.

Angela Febbraro raises readers' understanding of the meaning of scarcity and enhancement thinking about multiple roles within the context of how we think about gender differences overall.

Marecek, J. (2003). Mad housewives, double shifts, mommy tracks and other invented realities. *Feminism & Psychology, 13*, 259–265.

Jeanne Marecek follows up on Febbraro's (2003) paper above by exploring the implications of scarcity and enhancement thinking. Taken together, these two papers will likely provoke deeper thinking about these issues, how they impact individual women's lives, and the politics of the personal.

Johnston D., & Swanson, D. H. (2006). Constructing the "good mother": The experience of mothering ideologies by work status. *Sex Roles, 54*, 509–519.

Deirdre Johnston and Debra Swanson interview 22 to 51-year-old women—who have full-time employment (30 women), have part-time employment (26 women), and are full-time homemakers (39 women)—about their images of the ideal mother, themselves as mothers, and what they could do to be better mothers. Each group has different ideas about what constitutes "good" mothering, encouraging readers to explore their own definitions.

Rudman, L. A., & Glick, P. (2008). Love and romance. *The social psychology of gender: How power and intimacy share gender relations,* pp. 204–230. New York: Guilford.

Laurie Rudman and Peter Glick do an excellent job in this chapter of laying out how women's and men's ideas about love and romance affect not only relationships but also the power dynamics of gender inequality.

Yost, M., & McCarthy, L. (2012). Girls gone wild?: Heterosexual women's same-sex encounters at college parties. *Psychology of Women Quarterly, 36*, 7–24).

Megan Yost and Lauren McCarthy give voice to women who have engaged in same-sex sexual displays at college parties in order to explore their motivations and goals, raising intriguing questions about women's sexual empowerment and/or objectification and providing fodder for likely lively in-class discussions. A podcast interview with the authors is available at *pwq.sagepub.com.*

Beals, K. P., & Peplau, L. A. (2001). Social involvement, disclosure of sexual orientation, and the quality of lesbian relationships. *Psychology of Women Quarterly, 25*, 10–19.

Kristin Beals and Anne Peplau offer a data-based look at how social relationships affect the quality of lesbian relationships. The quality of their data analyses and literature review make this a good reading for a general audience.

Auchmuty, R. (2004). Same-sex marriage revived: Feminist critique and legal strategy. *Feminism & Psychology, 14*, 101–126.

Rosemary Auchmuty sets the stage for discussion about the uneasy relationship between heterosexual marriage and feminism and what same-sex relationships can model for all intimate partnerships.

Fine, M., & Carney, S. (2001). Women, gender, and the law: Toward a feminist rethinking of responsibility. In R.K. Unger (Ed.), *Handbook of the psychology of women and gender* (pp. 388–409). New York: Wiley.

Set within a broader discussion of the meaning of responsibility, Michelle Fine and Sarah Carney tackle the stereotyping violations of mothers who are blamed for failing to protect their children from abuse.

Chapter 9

Multiple Roles Continued
Work, Wages, and Closing the Gap

 Karen is 21 years old, grew up in Lancaster, PA, and her hobby is weightlifting. Is she graduating from college as an engineering or nursing student?

 Brian is 22 years old, grew up in Springfield, IL, and worked in a day-care center last summer. Is he graduating from college as an engineering or nursing student?

1   2   3   4   5   6
definitely   definitely
engineering   nursing

1   2   3   4   5   6
definitely   definitely
engineering   nursing

Thomas Nelson and his colleagues (1996) asked college students to make the same judgments you just did for 32 photographed students. We might expect that someone with childcare experience would have the personality characteristics to be a good nurse and a weightlifter to be suited for engineering, but gender overrode such information in students' ratings, especially from those students with more traditional attitudes about the roles of women in American society. Students consistently and with confidence pictured women as nurses and men as engineers, ignoring other information that might be expected to influence their perceptions. Gender stereotyping was reduced, but not eliminated, when raters were held publicly accountable for their responses and were given information to invalidate their occupational stereotypes (there's a 50:50 ratio of women to men in both nursing and engineering at the targets' university). In this chapter, we will see how a variety of **social contextual** factors, including stereotyping, influence what jobs women pursue, promotion opportunities, and even wages.

WORK VALUES

Traditionally, social scientists have defined work as the production of goods and services that are of value to others, obviously not confining work to just paid labor (Fox & Hesse-Biber, 1984). Globally, people spend about one-third of their lives doing paid and unpaid work, with women contributing more unpaid labor than men in all countries (averaging 2 hours and 28 minutes per 24-hour day; Miranda, 2011). Generally though, in developed countries, if we are asked what we "do," we commonly define work narrowly as our employment status. The purpose of this chapter is to explore the role of *paid* employment in women's lives.

Around the world from 1990 to 2010, women's participation in the labor market held steady at about 52%, whereas men's declined from 81% to 77 % (United Nations, 2010). In 2009, 59.2% of adult women (72% of adult men) were in the civilian labor force in the United States (*Statistical Abstracts*, 2011) and 61.6% (72.3%) in Canada (*Statistics Canada*, 2011). In other words, about six of every ten women over 16 years old in both the United States and Canada were in the labor force (did some work for pay) (see Table 9.1).

TABLE 9.1
U.S. Labor Force Participation, 2009

	Men	Women
Total	72.0%	59.2%
Ages 20–24	76.2%	69.6%
White	72.8%	59.1%
Black	65.0%	60.3%
Asian	74.6%	58.2%
Latino/a	78.8%	56.5%
Single	68.3%	64.2%
Married	76.3%	61.4%
With children under 6	----	62.0%
With children under 18	----	69.7%

Note. Percentages represent the proportion of civilian men and women, at least 16 years-old, who were classified as "employed." "Employed civilians comprise (a) all civilians, who, during the reference week, did any work for pay or profit (minimum of an hour's work) or worked 15 hours or more as unpaid workers in a family enterprise and (b) all civilians who were not working but who had jobs or businesses from which they were temporarily absent for noneconomic reasons (illness, weather conditions, vacation, labor-management dispute, etc.) whether they were paid for the time off or were seeking other jobs." (p. 374)

Source: U.S. Census Bureau, *Statistical Abstract of the United States*: 2011a. Section 12: *Labor Force, Employment, and Earnings.*

These participation rates in the United States vary by age, race/ethnicity, marital status, and the presence of children (see Table 9.1).

Whereas participation rates look at what percentage of a group does some paid labor, another way to look at these statistics is to count how much of the labor force is made up of women. Since the 1980s, the U.S. labor force has been composed of 45% or more women, coming close to 50% in October of 2009 (49.96%), but then backing away from this milestone (English et al., 2010).

Studies of *why* women are employed conclude that women work for the same reasons as men: for financial compensation, to fulfill identity needs, and to function as competent and productive members of society (Chester & Grossman, 1990). The financial importance of women's employment is obvious when women are the sole support of their families and themselves. However, even in dual-earner families, American women's earnings are playing an increasingly critical role, rising from 29% of total family income in 1983 to 36% in 2008 (U.S. Congress Joint Economic Committee, 2010).

A survey of American college students' work values showed that women and men ranked Lifestyle (having enough time for leisure activities) as their top work priority, followed by Security (knowing that your position will last) among their top three values (Robinson & Betz, 2008). Interestingly, women's ratings were stronger than men's across all 12 work values tapped, with women placing meaningfully higher emphasis on Work Environment (clean), Supervision (having a boss who treats me well), Achievement, Lifestyle, Prestige (others think my work is important), Zariety, and Co-workers.

When we look at women and men doing the same job (business graduates), their work values become even more similar, and, not surprisingly, some values predict work outcomes (the values of wanting recognition and making money predicted actual later salaries for both women and men MBAs; Frieze et al., 2006). Interestingly, and most germane to our focus in much of this chapter on pay, controlling for individual differences in values did not affect the gap between women's and men's salaries (favoring men).

If we turn our attention to expectations about pay, undergraduate men expect to earn higher salaries, and they value power more and family less than women do (Lips & Lawson, 2009). However, this **intergroup difference** between women and men also includes **intragroup variability**. For both sexes, individuals who valued power projected higher salaries for themselves, and individuals who valued family anticipated lower job commitment. This reduced job commitment translated into lower expected pay among women, whereas for men, valuing family heightened their pay expectancies (possibly fulfilling their breadwinner role?). These patterns lead the authors of this study, Hilary Lips and Katie Lawson (2009), to question whether these work values and pay expectations begin to lay the groundwork for a "motherhood penalty" in actual pay.

This last point segues into our main emphasis in this chapter on the gap between women's and men's wages. We start by taking a somewhat detailed look at this intergroup gender difference in earnings, and then go on to the more challenging question of what explanations underlie this persistent gap. In doing so, we tackle many of the key areas explored by psychologists and social scientists in their explorations of women's working lives.

THE WAGE GAP

To gauge this wage gap, we simply take the ratio of women's to men's earnings and subtract it from 1.0. If women's and men's earnings were identical, this ratio would be 1.00; or expressed another way, women would earn, on average, 100% of what men earned. In this case, the wage gap would be zero, indicating no difference between their earnings. However, if this ratio is less than 1.00, there is a gap that disadvantages women. In 2009, the earnings ratio in the United States was .77 (or 77%), yielding a gap between women's and men's wages of 23% (Institute for Women's Policy Research [IWPR], 2010).

$$\text{2009 U.S. Earnings Ratio} = \frac{\substack{\text{median annual earnings} \\ \text{of full-time employed women}}}{\substack{\text{median annual earnings} \\ \text{of full-time employed men}}} = \frac{\$36,278}{\$47,127} = .77$$

In 2009, the earnings ratio in Canada was 74.6% (Statistics Canada, 2011); worldwide, earnings ratios generally range from 70% to 90% (United Nations, 2010).

You may have noticed that different sources report different earnings ratios and gaps, although no one has come close to wiping out the gap by manipulating the figures. The U.S. Census Bureau recommends using the *median annual earnings of year-round, full-time workers* as the most representative way to calculate the earnings ratio, and hence the wage gap. (I will use this too unless I state otherwise.) The median, or the 50th percentile, is the best way to represent incomes, because large outliers (in this case, those who make millions) deceptively pull arithmetic means upward. Restricting incomes to those of full-time workers assures that we compare similar groups, because women are overrepresented among those employed part-time. Finally, annual earnings give a more accurate picture of income than smaller units of measure, which may be affected by variations in bonus and overtime pay, as well as temporary or seasonal work. Smaller time units tend to narrow the gap; for example, the earnings ratio using median *weekly* earnings rises to fully 81.2% in 2010 (IWPR, 2011a).

There are some basic facts about the wage gap we should understand. First, earnings ratios vary by race and ethnicity. In the United States in 2009 using the incomes of White men as the base (denominator), the earnings ratio for White women is 75%; 61.9% for African American women (72.9% for men); 52.9% for Latinas (61.1% for Latinos); and 82.3% for Asian American women (100.1% for Asian men) (IWPR, 2010).

The numbers easily become numbing, so it helps to put them in some perspective. For the average college-educated woman who entered the workforce in 1984, she has accumulated $440,743 less in earnings by 2004 than her male counterpart (IWPR, 2005). In one year, the average full-time employed African American woman earns $12,000 less than the average White man, which when extrapolated over a 35-year career adds up to $420,000. For Latinas, the comparable figures are $17,837/year and $535,100/work life. Black women with college degrees make only $1,545 more each year than White men with high school diplomas (more on this later). Latinas with a high school diploma earn fully one-third less than similarly educated White men. Now the perspective itself becomes numbing.

Second, the gap has narrowed somewhat recently. From 1955, when the earnings ratio was 63.9% to 1987, the earnings ratio in the United States hovered between 58.8% and 65.2%. The 65% U.S. ceiling was exceeded by the end of the 1980s, creeping into the low 70%s through the 1990s and holding in the mid-70s since 2001 (IWPR, 2010). If the earnings ratio is calculated in dollars adjusted for inflation, fully 75% of the narrowing of the wage gap from 1979 to 1995 is accounted for by losses in men's wages. This pattern also holds true within specific occupations (Roos & Reskin, 1992). Although parity can be reached by either advancing women's wages or reducing men's, few labor activists advocate the latter strategy.

Third, the United States does not rank as highly as one might expect among the world's nations (Lopez-Claros & Zahidi, 2005). To compare gender gaps between women and men across 58 countries, the World Economic Forum brought together various indicators of labor force participation and pay to form a single measure of economic participation, as well as a second measure of economic quality (assessing opportunities for upward mobility and supports for employment). The United States ranked 19th of 58 countries on economic participation and 46th for economic opportunity; Canada, 7th and 27th, respectively.

Finally, looking at age differentials in earnings between women and men, the news is mixed. The wage gap varies across workers' age, such that the 2009 *weekly* earnings ratio for the youngest workers, aged 16 to 24, was 93%; for 25 to 34 year-olds, 89% (U.S. Bureau of Labor Statistics, 2010). Does this portend eventual change as the youngest workers mature in the workforce? It might if the gap doesn't expand as the current youngest workers age; however, for past cohorts, the wage gap has increased the longer workers were in the workforce (Arons, 2008).

DISMISSED AND RULED OUT EXPLANATIONS

As I look back over the 30 or so years I have been interested in the wage gap, I am struck by how much the research devoted to exploring pieces of this puzzle has shifted its focus.

At one time, psychologists wrote about women's fears of success (Horner, 1970) and attributions about success as being caused by luck over ability (Deaux & Emswiller, 1974). Some of those ideas were convincingly ruled out by data; others just seemed to succumb to the shift away from such openly negative thinking about women, which didn't fit with the changing times. However, through all these changes, the wage gap itself has been resolute, never getting close to going away.

Just for the record, then (and to keep history from repeating itself), let's start by looking at some explanations for the wage gap that have been dismissed or ruled out. For example, the way we defined the wage gap above (by including full-time workers only) rules out the apples-and-oranges comparison of all employed men and all employed women (who are disproportionately employed part-time). In 1984, 27% of employed women worked part-time, and this proportion has remained largely unchanged (26%) through 2009 (U.S. Congress Joint Economic Committee, 2010). Yet when we make the apple-to-apples comparison of full-time employed women to full-time employed men, we still find a wage gap. Making these matched comparisons is often the most effective way to rule out explanations for the wage gap, and there are a few more of these about which we should be aware.

Not surprisingly, interruptions characterize more women's work histories than men's, and they can be costly to a woman's salary (Eliason, 1995), managerial level (Melamed, 1995a), and self-esteem and sense of accomplishment (Keddy et al., 1993). Using our apples-to-apples comparison to explore the effect of job discontinuity on wages, when statisticians compare the earnings of non-interrupting women to non-interrupting men, the gap in earnings remains unaffected (Rix, 1988). Rule out interrupted career paths.

One commonly held belief about women, especially those with partners and children, is that they are rooted and will not relocate to benefit their careers. However, when women and men managers had "all the right stuff"—they had comparable levels of education, maintained similar levels of family power, kept their names on transfer lists, and even moved within the past 2 years for the purpose of career advancement—gendered salary differences remained (Stroh et al., 1992). Rule out relocation.

How about turnover? In an extensive study of women and men managers in Fortune 500 companies, 26% of the women, compared to just 14% of the men, left their employers (Stroh et al., 1996). Women's reasons for leaving were unrelated to either dual-earner status or number of children. Rather, the best predictors of turnover among women were factors that similarly influence men: lack of opportunity for advancement, job dissatisfaction, and discontent with the present employer. Might we now ask why these job shortcomings were more common among women than men? Turnover per se is not the problem.

Finally, there used to be an education gap between women and men, but it has now closed (and reversed). Following up high school graduates in the Class of 2010, the U.S. Bureau of Labor Statistics (2011) reported that 74% of women and 62.8% of men were enrolled in college. Still, education is linked to better salaries (see Figure 9.2), and there remain many older people in the workforce for whom there was an education gap. However, when we compare American women and men with similar educational attainment in Figure 9.2, the wage gap remains. (Note that these figures from the U.S. Census Bureau are mean earnings, not medians so that they are inflated by extremely high scores, exaggerating the overall gap between women and men. The last time these figures were recorded using median incomes in 2001, however, similar patterns were documented.)

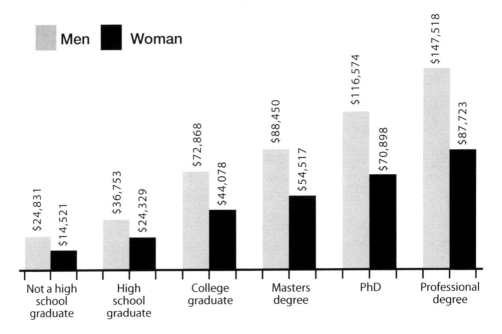

Figure 9.2

Mean annual earnings of U.S. men and women by highest degree earned, 2008. To find updates, go to www.census.gov.

Source: U.S. Census Bureau, *Statistical Abstract of the United States*, 2011b, Table 228.

An apparent paradox of the American labor market is that U.S. women compare favorably to women in other industrialized countries in terms of their education and qualifications, yet the United States lags behind these other countries in closing the wage gap. Economists Francine Blau and Lawrence Kahn (1996) concluded that if the United States had a narrower gap between the wages of high-end, skilled workers and low-end, unskilled workers (wage structure), the U.S. gender gap in wages would look more like Sweden's and Australia's, two countries with the smallest gender differentials in the world. Looked at another way, if U.S. women hadn't expanded their qualifications (by earning higher degrees) as they did throughout the late 1970s and the '80s, the wage difference between women and men would have widened (Blau & Kahn, 1997). In other words, American women's better credentials are keeping the wage gap from widening.

OCCUPATIONAL SEGREGATION AND THE WAGE GAP

The evidence regarding occupational segregation is definitive and unwavering: Women and men are concentrated in different occupations, thus creating a workforce characterized by "women's work," "men's work," and some gender-neutral occupations. The U.S. Bureau of Labor Statistics in 2010 lists 501 different occupations and compiles data on earnings for 111 of them that are big enough to warrant further analyses. (Note that "occupations" refers to general categories of jobs, such as "Managers, all other," which refers to

TABLE 9.3
Top Occupations for American Women and Men, 2010

Most Common: Women	Highest Paying: Women	Most Common: Men
Secretaries and administrative assistants	Physicians and surgeons	Driver/sales workers and truck drivers
Registered nurses	Pharmacists	Managers, all other
Elementary and middle school teachers	Chief executives	First-line supervisors/ managers of retail sales workers
Nursing, psychiatric, and home health aides	Lawyers	Janitors and building cleaners
Customer service representatives	Computer software engineers	Retail salespersons
First-line supervisors/managers of retail sales workers	Computer and information systems managers	Laborers and freight, stock, and material movers, hand
Cashiers	Physical therapists	Construction laborers
First-line supervisors/ managers of office and administrative workers	Speech-language pathologists	Sales representatives, wholesale and manufacturing
Receptionists and information clerks	Computer programmers	Computer software engineers
Accountants and auditors	Human resources managers	Chief executives

Note. The entries in a column are listed in order from the first through tenth ranked occupation. The six highest paying occupations for women that are italicized also appear on the list of men's 10 top paying occupations.

Source: Information taken from report for the Institute for Women's Policy Research (IWPR #C350a), updated April 2011, entitled "The Gender Wage Gap by Occupation."

general business managers.) Of all explanations for the wage gap, occupational segregation—the sorting of women and men into different broad occupational categories—does play a significant role in the wage gap.

As you see in Table 9.3, there is no overlap in the top ten most common occupations that employed American women and men in 2010. These top ten occupations for women employed 28.8% of all full-time women workers (IWPR, 2011b); for men, 20%. The top ten list of commonly "women's work" has been amazingly stable since 1940, and although we have seen women integrate some formerly male-dominated occupations (e.g., lawyer and physician), much of this change is accounted for by the influx of new women workers into the labor force through the 1980s (Cohen, 2004; Sokoloff, 1988). Putting these figures into a more personalized form, for every 1 woman physician in 2000, 83 women held clerical jobs, 15 operated factory machines, 14 worked as sales clerks, 10 were nurses' aides, and 6 served food (Padavic & Reskin, 2002).

Beyond these most common occupations, the full U.S. labor force is amazingly gender segregated. In 2010, fully 41.1% of all employed women worked in traditionally female occupations; 49.3% of men, in traditionally male occupations. To capture the degree to which occupations are gender segregated, an **index of segregation** is calculated to represent the proportion of all female (or male) workers who would have to change occupations to achieve genuine occupational integration (a state of 50-50 representation in every occupation). Zero would denote a fully integrated workforce, in contrast to an index of 100, which would indicate a completely segregated labor force. In 2000, the index of occupational segregation in the United States was 52.1, meaning that over 52% of the female workforce (39 million workers) would have to switch to male-dominated work to achieve full integration (Padavic & Reskin, 2002). Worldwide, half of all workers are employed in occupations with 80% or more of one sex.

The U.S. index does show some favorable changes across time. After hovering between 65 and 69 from 1900 to 1970, the 1970s saw declines in the index into the 50s.[1] This decline continued but at a slower pace in the 1980s (Blau et al., 1998), and it is accounted for more by women moving into "men's work" than by men pursuing nontraditional options, both in the United States (Cotter et al., 1995) and globally (United Nations, 1999).[2] The pace at which U.S. women are entering male-dominated occupations is now decreasing (Jacobs, 2003). In addition, occupational segregation extends within gender to race/ethnicity groupings, and it is not readily explained by differences in the characteristics of workers themselves (Anderson & Shapiro, 1996).

Most germane to our interest in the wage gap, this sorting of women and men into different occupations extends to categorizing occupations as high- and low-paying (IWPR, 2011b). The ten occupations with the highest weekly earnings for full-time workers employ three times more men than women. Of the 10 highest paying occupations for women shown in Table 9.3, women make up a minority of workers in eight (the exceptions being physical therapists and speech language pathologists).

The complement to men's domination of high-pay occupations is women's domination of low-paying ones. Overall, occupations with high concentrations of women and people of color fall at the low end of the pay scale (Catanzarite, 2003; Huffman, 2004). In these low-paying occupations, women outnumber men 2:1, and even within these lowest-paying occupations, women make less than men (IWPR, 2011b). In fact, for three of women's lowest-paying occupations (cafeteria, food concession, and coffee shop attendants), a woman working full-time, every week of the year, would not earn enough to keep a family of three out of poverty.

Employment in different occupations wouldn't produce a wage gap if women's work was paid comparably to men's. Looking across those 111 occupations for which the U.S. Bureau of Labor Statistics collected weekly earnings data in 2010, there were only four in

---

[1]During 1960 to 1980, occupational gender segregation declined in a majority of 56 developed and developing countries (Jacobs & Lim, 1992).

[2]This fits with an analysis of women's labor force participation rates across the twentieth century (Cotter et al., 2001). More and more women entered the workforce in the middle of the century because of expanding opportunities in "women's work" in contrast to the last quarter of the century, when opportunities arose for some women in male-dominated occupations.

which women's earnings were higher than men's: Combined food preparation and serving workers (including fast food), Bill and account collectors, Stock clerks and order fillers, and Counselors (IWPR, 2011b). Even when women and men share the same occupation, gaps in earnings remain and consistently favor men. Even if we try to level the playing field by looking at occupations with similar required skill levels, male-dominated occupations pay more than female-dominated ones (IWPR, 2011b).

This linkage of lower pay with female-dominated jobs is so ingrained that its effects spill over into the entry-level pay expectations of college students. Mary Hogue and her colleagues (2010) surveyed students about their job intentions and expected entry-level pay, finding the predicted gap in men's higher projections than women's. The researchers then coded the job each student expected to pursue according to its gender ratio of who is actually doing that job in the overall U.S. workforce. When they entered this gender-typing of the intended job into their analyses as a **mediator** of the relationship between gender and expected pay, they found full mediation. In other words, pay expectations were muted for both women and men who planned to pursue a job in a female-dominated domain.

In sum, there is no doubt but that the American labor force is largely gendered and segregated and that this sorting relates to pay (both in actuality and in expectancies). The segregation of women and men into different occupations certainly plays a significant, if not definitive, role in maintaining the wage gap. When there were some small declines in both occupational segregation and the wage gap across the 1980s, statisticians estimate that about one-third of the earnings gap was accounted for by gender segregation (Cotter et al., 1995). This pattern holds up within specialties and employment settings (Bird, 1996; Petersen & Morgan, 1995). However, a recent, provocative study finds a relationship between occupational integration and wages across *all* occupations—such that women who work in metropolitan areas with integrated occupations earn more even if they are employed in female-dominated occupations, suggesting a ripple effect (Cohen & Huffman, 2003; Cotter et al., 1997). Although it is not yet clear what mechanisms link occupational integration with enhanced earnings, these findings argue that genuine occupational integration could have far-reaching effects that indeed might narrow the wage gap.

Moreover, even within similar occupations, our apples-to-apples comparisons reveal wage disparities. But occupations are broad categories of similar jobs, not yielding the same *job*-level comparisons of women's and men's wages in which we'd expect to find equal pay for equal work. Although certainly interesting, narrowing our focus to specific jobs leaves those case-specific data open to challenges about their generalizability. Might the problem just be this arguably quirky job?

Still, case examples that track the wage gap can be important both for the data they yield and for the tools they provide to local personnel who want to test their own work setting. For example, Cheryl Travis and her colleagues (2009) explored the gender gap in pay at a large regional university where they were able to converge findings from two different data analyses and to control in these analyses for differences in faculty rank, academic field, and years of service. The gap persisted, both in fields traditionally regarded as female and in science fields where women were under-represented. Although studies with this level of sophisticated data collection and analysis cannot happen everywhere, especially where sample sizes are small, when they are done, they continue to raise questions about job-level wage inequities.

Let's pause for a moment and take stock of what we've learned so far. There is a persistent wage gap in the United States, Canada, and globally, and it is consistently linked to occupational segregation as well as gender itself (within the same occupational category and oftentimes within the same job). We now can refine our question a bit from "What causes the wage gap?" to (1) "Why is there women's and men's work?" (the gendering of work) and (2) "What does being a woman have to do with pay?" (the gendering of pay).

THE GENDERING OF WORK

As we did previously, let's start with what we can rule out. Some social scientists and policymakers have argued that women trade off lower pay for family-friendly employment. Growing up, my parents often extolled the benefits of K-12 teaching because as a woman, I'd presumably have the same work day as my children's school hours. However, predominately female jobs are not necessarily those that accommodate family responsibilities (Budig & England, 2001; Bullock & Waugh, 2004).

Furthermore, these are not the reasons cited by women making seemingly family-friendly choices (Marler & Moen, 2005). Additionally, women who expected to take time out from work and who actually did were no more likely to be in female-dominated occupations than other women (Okamoto & England, 1999). Probing a sample of over 8,000 U.S. scientists and engineers in nonstandard work arrangements (not the usual regular daily and weekly hours), women were indeed over-represented; the wage gap in these jobs not only prevailed but also was worse than in the best arrangements (Prokos et al., 2009).

Family-to-Work Conflict

Although there is little, if any, support for the tradeoff hypothesis, research on the role played by potential family-to-work conflict is much more complex and hence less clear-cut. The stereotyping literature makes it clear that expectations for the role of workers (committed to work and competent; Williams, 2001) clash with the role of mother (committed to home and warm; Cuddy et al., 2004).[3] Not surprisingly then, we expect family-work conflict to limit women's participation and success in the workplace (Fuegen et al., 2004). Management students and executives believe that career success negatively impacts family life (Westman & Etzion, 1990), and some women graduate students self-select away from academic careers because they perceive barriers against blending career with family (van Anders, 2004).

Michelle Budig and Paula England (2001) concluded that U.S. women experience a wage penalty for motherhood that, controlling for other factors like experience, cashes in at 5% less in wages per child—a phenomenon they dubbed the **motherhood penalty**. Further analyses with a large, nationally representative sample of U.S. women concluded that this motherhood penalty was real for White women but had no effect on the Black mothers in the sample (Christie-Mizell et al., 2007).

---

[3]Interestingly, the negative baggage we saw accompany qualified stereotyping of mothers in Chapter 5 may work to the benefit of lesbian workers (stereotyped more positively than heterosexual women workers; Horvath & Ryan, 2003), even lesbian mothers, who do earn more than their heterosexual women counterparts (Peplau & Fingerhut, 2004).

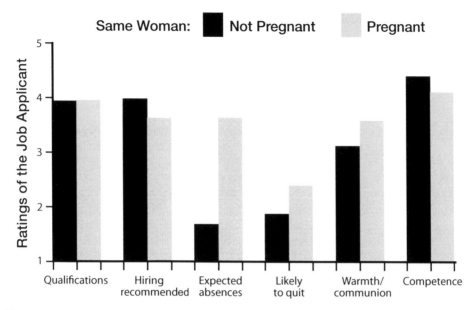

Figure 9.4

Jennifer Cunningham and Therese Macan (2007) asked business students to review a female job candidate's resume and watch a video of her being interviewed for a job as a computer programmer. They created two identical conditions, except in one the same job applicant appeared 7 to 8 months pregnant (using a pregnancy prosthesis) when she entered and left the interview room. Although these two groups of raters saw the candidate in both conditions as equally qualified (which indeed she was!), all the remaining differences diagrammed above were significant. These comparisons uncover not only hiring bias but also stereotyping about family-to-work consequences, warmth, and competence.

Source: Cunningham, J., & Macan, T. (2007). Effects of applicant pregnancy on hiring decisions and interview ratings. *Sex Roles, 57*, 497–508.

In their original study, Budig and England (2001) went on to rule out some possible causes of the motherhood penalty, but two remained standing: sexist discrimination and lower productivity. Are family-committed employees worse workers? The research findings to date are inconsistent. Nancy Betz and Louise Fitzgerald (1987) reviewed this literature and concluded that being married and having children negatively affected career involvement and achievement. This conclusion was supported by other studies showing lesser time commitment from women business owners (Parasuraman et al., 1996) and lower earnings among women with disproportionate responsibility for domestic chores (Cannings, 1991).

On the other hand, a study of women scientists found no difference in the number of research papers published by married women with children and single women without children (Cole & Zuckerman, 1987). Another study with women personnel professionals uncovered no relationship between work-family conflict and career progress (Nelson et al., 1990). Having children is unrelated to women's organizational commitment (Porter, 2001), career salience, and job involvement (van der Velde et al., 2003), and working part-time does not predict lesser commitment (Bianchi, 2000). What may be clearest is that employers *expect* mothers employed part-time to be less committed to work (Crittenden, 2001). We astutely should wonder about the impact of a **self-fulfilling prophecy** here.

An intriguing and consistent finding in this literature is that employed men with employed wives report lower earnings. This finding has been replicated with men MBAs (Schneer & Reitman, 1993) and academic faculty (Bellas, 1992). The literal payoffs of having a nonemployed wife (the "housewife bonus") fit with theories emphasizing the greater economic needs of sole-breadwinner men, fewer distractions for men with homemakers to take care of the domestic front, and the social acceptability of traditional familial arrangements. These data also converge with findings about the relationship between family and work involvement: Men (and women) who are more devoted to family also tend to be less committed to work (Tenbrunsel et al., 1995). This pattern of what has been referred to as the "daddy penalty" (Lewin, 1994) highlights why the wage gap is more than a women's issue.

As we might expect, there are **individual differences** among workers that can overshadow **intergroup differences** between women and men. The implicit assumption throughout many discussions about family-work conflict, rooted in difference thinking (Barnett, 2004), is that women put family first; men, work. We know that stereotyping is rarely, if ever, so universal, and indeed the work and family achievement scripts of women and men tend to be quite similar (Yoder et al., 2008). Women *and* men who highly value work perceive greater family interference with work; women *and* men espousing high levels of family centrality lament work interference with family (Carlson & Kacmar, 2000).

General employment trends make it clear that employed mothers are not an anomaly. Although the media may feature stories about "drop-out moms," women's labor force participation, even among women of childbearing age, has been stable since the 1980s (Boushey, 2005; Outtz, 1996). Rather than questioning if mothers are effective workers or expecting individuals to cope with systemic inequities (Blair-Loy, 2003), both women and employers might be better served if we strive to make the workplace work for women and families (Crosby et al., 2004).

One approach recognizes the disproportionate share of household labor shouldered by women (Chapter 8) and seeks to add workplace supports such as caregiving leave, flextime, job sharing, on-site childcare, and so on (see Williams & Cooper, 2004). There is evidence that such provisions reduce work-family conflict (Nelson et al., 1990) and are valued by women (Heckert et al., 2002). Furthermore, supports like eligibility to take family leave reduce the motherhood wage penalty (by as much as 75%; Kimmel & Amuedo-Dorantes, 2004), and mothers' use of early childcare predicted higher wages and more hours of maternal employment when children reached first grade (Bub & McCartney, 2004). Yet not unexpectedly, evidence is mounting that men who take advantage of family-friendly policies suffer setbacks in their career (Levine, 2000) and how they are perceived by coworkers (Wayne & Cordeiro, 2003). Again, this is more than a "women's problem."

Tokenism

How about women who break into traditionally male-dominated jobs? In 1977, Rosabeth Moss Kanter described the work lives of a few women salesmanagers at a Fortune 500 company. She referred to these women as "**tokens**," who comprised less than 15% of their work group and who faced pressures from their constant visibility and difference from the dominant group of men. Subsequent research with all kinds of women doing all kinds of masculine jobs from West Point cadets to lawyers, coal miners, and auto workers showed that these women faced negative consequences associated with their difference, visibility,

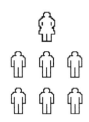

Box 9.5

A laboratory study that Tom Schleicher, Tedd McDonald, and I (Yoder et al., 1998) conducted brings together some ideas we have been exploring related to occupational segregation, task-stereotyping, leadership, tokenism, and the status afforded by legitimacy. All groups in our study were lead by a token woman, included all men as followers, and completed a masculine-typed lost-on-the-moon exercise. We created three different conditions in which:

- the leader was appointed by the male experimenter (the control group).
- the leader was trained before the group met, so she had the answers to the exercise, and then was appointed when the group met.
- the leader was trained and appointed—the male experimenter appointing her legitimated her by telling the group that she had been trained.

We measured how well the group performed the task. Even though the second group was led by a woman who knew the answers, they did no better than the control groups. Only when the leader was legitimated did these groups outperform the control groups.

role violations, and intrusiveness into masculine domains. Unfavorable outcomes include stress, social isolation, role conflicts, sexual harassment, wage inequities, and blocked upward mobility (Yoder, 2002), as well as increased reliance on restrictive gender stereotypes (Ely, 1995). The simple expectation of pressures associated with tokenism may affect women's willingness to be part of male-dominated groups (Cohen & Swim, 1995), although this trend may be reduced by elevating women's status (McDonald et al., 2004).

Some of the most recent work on tokenism processes has expanded definitions of difference to encompass both gender and race/ethnicity, for example, by studying African American women firefighters (Yoder & Aniakudo, 1997), police officers (Martin, 1994), and elite leaders (Jackson et al., 1995). This broadened definition of tokenism highlights both the **intersectionality** of race/ethnicity and gender, as well as subordination through exclusion. For African American women in these White- and male-dominated contexts, they saw their exchanges with their colleagues as perpetually being shaped by intertwined racial and gender oppression. For example, both Black and White women firefighters experienced stereotyping, but this process varied by the content of relevant stereotypes: self-reliant for Black women (thereby over-burdening them by withholding needed help) and fragile for White women (thereby under-burdening and "benevolently" protecting them; Yoder & Berendsen, 2001).

However, there is more to understanding the impact of gender ratios than simply counting how many women and men there are in an organization. Kathi Miner-Rubino and her co-researchers (2009) found that women's perceptions of the organization's climate were strong and important **moderators** of the relationship between gender diversity with job satisfaction and general health. When the organizational climate is regarded as positive, women's job satisfaction and general health are both improved by having all or mostly women above in the organization's hierarchy. However, when the climate is perceived as negative, having advanced women seems to send a chilling message that reduces women's job satisfaction and general health (with health effects also affected by women's high gender-sensitivity). In sum, gender diversity along with positive organizational climate—the degree to which women feel empowered to change things, are freed from sexual harassment, and feel included—is important to women's well-being.

"Unsocialized" Women

In Chapter 5, we explored girls' and young women's channeling into traditional occupations, and indeed, women aspiring to work in predominantly female jobs as children were, 14 years later, more likely to be working in those types of jobs (Okamoto & England, 1999). Nancy Betz (1993) describes some "unsocialized" facilitators that help women break away from prevailing socialization practices typically pressuring girls and women toward traditional occupations. Women who pursue male-dominated occupations tend to exhibit high levels of **agency**, express egalitarian attitudes toward women's roles in society, and feel self-confident. In addition, they often have moms who are employed and well educated.

Occupations may change, but the stereotyping that is part of our socialization may not keep up. Michael White and Gwendolen White (2006) purposively elected to study three occupations, each with similar educational requirements for employees, and that represented a continuum from obviously male (engineering) through neutral (accountant) to obviously female (elementary school teacher). Using an **Implicit Associations Test** to tap into implicit stereotyped associations and explicit ratings of the gender-typing of each task, they found a good match for explicit with implicit attitudes for the two obviously gendered occupations.

However, student raters regarded accounting as more masculine using implicit compared to explicit evidence. *The Statistical Abstracts of the United States* (2011; Table 615) records that 92.2% of "bookkeeping, accounting, and audit clerks" in 2009 were women, yet students explicitly think of accounting as neutral and implicitly react to it as masculine. Given that accounting has change dramatically from being mostly male in the 1970s, these data point to a surprising lag in stereotyping which has failed to keep up with the times and which may still influence potential accountants' (students) occupational perceptions.

Hiring Bias

The opportunity to move outside gendered occupational options must be seen as viable before even the most determined women can make such choices. In studies of hiring stereotyping, raters (typically students or business professionals) review the resumes of job candidates and record their hiring preferences. The general pattern is for women to be preferred for feminine jobs and men for masculine ones (Pratto et al., 1997) and for women and men to be influenced by gender-role expectancies (Cole et al., 2004). For a factory worker position, women candidates were regarded as warmer but less competent (less confident and committed) than male applicants, translating into a lower chance of being hired (Gungor & Biernat, 2009). Obviously, this hiring stereotyping helps maintain a gender-segregated workforce, starting with who even applies for a job.

Not all that surprisingly, the characteristics of job hirers matter, but in some unexpected ways. We would expect student evaluators who scored high in **hostile sexism** to more positively evaluate the resume of a man than a women, but this is not what Amy Salvaggio and her colleagues (2009) found in their first of two studies. Instead, these resumes were evaluated similarly and better than the resume of a candidate ("P.W. Miller") whose sex was unclear. Interestingly, when the applicant's sex was ambiguous, more students defaulted to thinking of the candidate as male.

In their second study, when students, both women and men, scored high in hostile sexism and thought the sex-ambiguous candidate was female, they rated "her" more harshly. It is important to note that these evaluators recorded their projected sex for the ambiguous candidate *after* evaluating the resume. Pulling these two studies together, it seems that hostile sexists can control their negative evaluations when gender is obvious. But when the gender they are rating exists outside their consciousness (not being tapped until later), they disadvantage the candidate perceived as female over the one assumed to be male. Although not what we'd likely expect going into these two studies, the pattern of actual findings does fit well with what we know about the subtlety, and awareness people may have, of their own implicit sexism.

Similarly, we might be surprised to find that how an interviewer acts affects how a third party evaluates a job candidate. Reading transcripts of a job interview, the more students liked a male interviewer who showed hostile sexism toward a female applicant, the lower they rated the competence and hireability *of the applicant*, independent of the observer's own sexist beliefs (Good & Rudman, 2010). Thus, a woman (the applicant) is being penalized for someone else's (the interviewer's) sexism.

Furthermore, this same pattern of reduced perceived competence and less deservingness to be hired appeared when observers liked a male interviewer who showed high **benevolent sexism**. Because benevolent sexism seems to protect and value women, this interviewer should arguably be more likeable than the hostile sexist some students liked above. However, in this context of a job interview, the interviewer's BS played out poorly for the female job candidate—making this type of "benevolence" again sexist in its consequences for women.

Job Queues, Gender Queues

Occupational segregation along gender lines can contribute to the wage gap only if "women's work" is paid less than men's, and indeed we have seen that this is the case. Why is there such a gendered pay differential across occupations? Barbara Reskin and Patricia Roos (1990) compiled case studies of 11 occupations that experienced shifts in their gender composition. A common pattern across these changing occupations can be understood by thinking about two queues: (1) a line of jobs ranked from best to worst by prospective employees (**job queues**) and (2) a line of applicants ordered according to employers' hiring preferences (**hiring queues**). Reskin and Roos propose that people filter into jobs as employers move down their list, and applicants accept or reject offers depending on job availability and where each job ranks on their list of preferences. The result is that the highest ranked candidates monopolize the most desirable jobs. All this seems quite rational. Why hire a high school grad when you can get someone with a BA, and why settle for a less desirable job when the one at the top of a job-seeker's queue is offered?

Reskin and Roos found few differences in how individuals rank jobs, so job queues are pretty universal (also see Corrigall & Konrad, 2006; Konrad et al., 2000). Turning to hiring queues, however, they found that gender, race/ethnicity, and other arguably irrelevant inputs from applicants matter. Employers' hiring queues incorporated demographic factors into their rankings such that men were preferred over women, Whites over people of color,

Box 9.6

The case of women in accounting. Lynn Perry Wooten (2001) drew on 25 interviews with industry experts and employees in public accounting firms to uncover the institutional pressures that have caused more and more accounting firms to adopt women- (family-) friendly policies (e.g., on-site childcare and flexible work hours). Citing shifts in hiring queues (such that the percentage of bachelors degrees in accounting earned by women moved from 10% in 1970 to 56%), high turnover, and competition for experienced talent, she identified five pressures: competition from competitors, government regulation, demographic changes, professional associations, and demands of clients. Given the right conditions, the dynamics of job queues may benefit women (and families.)

and so on. This sets up a system wherein people with less desirable (lower status) demographic profiles move ahead in the employment queue only when more desirable others are unavailable. Thus, when an occupation becomes less lucrative (or jobs within it decline in pay), advancement opportunities and autonomy), highly ranked workers possess the power to move on to the work everyone desires (Pratto & Walker, 2004), leaving a vacuum to be filled by those lower in the queue. Given this logic, women appear disproportionately in low-paying jobs because they start farther down the hiring queue than men. At its root, this queuing analysis focuses on gender (and other) biases in hiring patterns (also see Reskin et al., 1999).

One important part of queuing theory focuses on what Rosabeth Moss Kanter (1977) in her seminal study of tokenism dubbed "homologous reproduction" (the tendency for work groups to prefer **in-group** members because of their perceived good "fit"). Inge Claringbould and Annelies Knoppers (2007) took a look behind the scenes at how board members of Dutch national sports organizations made decisions about bringing in new board members by interviewing male chairs of 12 such boards and 12 high-ranking women members. Although many chairs affirmed their support for affirmatively seeking qualified women, how they framed the processes of recruitment and selection reproduced the male-dominated culture on each board. There were no women chairs of these boards, ten of which represented male-dominated sports and two gender-balanced sports, creating a more masculinized environment on each board. In these environments, women largely worked to distance themselves from their gender, prove their "fit," and thus did not work too openly to support women candidates. So even when there were some women (although 7 of the 12 women were solos), the culture and composition of these boards remained largely male—with dim prospects for change over time.

THE GENDERING OF PAY

Probably the broadest take-away message from the above review of some of the forces that channel many women and men into different occupations is that the gendering of occupations itself matters. Without stereotyping that accompanies both family and employment and without tokenism, socialization pressures, hiring biases, and job queues, people would sort into jobs based on highly individualized and thus idiosyncratic abilities, preferences, and opportunities. If, in this different world, a gendered pattern still emerged, we would have a strong case for the power of **essentialism**. Instead, by noting the power of these forces in shaping the "choices" we all make, we might better argue that the gendering of occupations is **social constructed**, and instead ask what outcomes are served by this arrangement.

Before we move on to this last consideration, let's look more closely at the second question we focused on: "What does being a woman have to do with pay?" Much of what we cover in this section doesn't relate directly to pay, but rather to attitudes and behaviors that may be indirectly associated with pay. One directly related area of research deals with the "salary estimation effect" studied by Melissa Williams and her colleagues (2010). The salary estimation effect refers to the repeatedly documented finding that both women and men tend to make judgments assuming that men earn higher salaries than women. Across a series of four studies, these researchers showed that the salary estimation effect appears in student and community samples, is unaffected by knowing about the real wage gap, and comes up in both descriptive estimates of what women *do* earn as well as in prescriptive estimates of what women *should* earn. Furthermore, this effect is best predicted by an **implicit attitude** that links men, more so than women, with wealth. Thus it appears that money itself is directly associated with men.

In general, we are talking here about an equity issue centered on questions of fair treatment. An arrangement is equitable if people get out what they put in. Given that, at least in terms of pay, if women as a whole arguably get out less than men, then two possibilities arise: (1) women are getting out what they deserve because their inputs are less than (in amount or quality) men's—the argument made by **human capital theorists**—or (2) the system is fundamentally unfair in how it treats women—the argument advanced by **discrimination theorists** (Blau et al., 1998).

Often researchers taking one of these two perspectives examine the same topics, but they do so by asking different questions and/or by exploring different aspects of the topic under scrutiny. For example, human capital theorists might argue that women make irrational choices when they select low-paying occupations. The clearest way to identify this reasoning is to see if you can frame the topic in the form of "If only women ... [did what men do]." Throughout the following section, I'll begin each discussion in this way to see how well that framing holds up.

In contrast, discrimination theorists might argue that women are channeled into these less lucrative occupations by biases in hiring and costs associated with deviating from gendered occupational stereotyping—stereotyping that we just saw extends to pay itself. As you can see, this vantage is more congruent with the reasoning we have pursued so far in this text so that much of the following will explore the impact of stereotyping and different **social contexts** on women's experiences in the workplace (harkening back to the logic of social contexts that we explored in Chapter 6).

Self-Promotion and Negotiation

If only women... stood up for themselves.   As we have already seen, there is a wage gap between the earnings of young women and men who are just launching their careers, and women college students even expect to earn less than men at the start of their careers (Hogue et al., 2010). Why don't women promote themselves better and negotiate for higher salaries?

Are women deficient in their self-promotion skills? In their first of two studies, Corinne Moss-Racusin and Laurie Rudman (2010) found that college men self-promoted more effectively than college women during a staged and videotaped job interview. In their second study, women both believed and actually were (as rated by others) less skilled at promoting themselves than at promoting a peer. So women have these skills when they promote others, but they don't use them to help themselves. Why? This is where the *Backlash Avoidance Model* comes in.

Exploring the processes mediating this gender difference, Moss-Racusin and Rudman measured fears of backlash (thinking that people who watch this interview might think of me as odd) and regulation of locomotion (thinking of one's self as a "go-getter" who wants to get the job started and done; sound like **agency**?). For women charged to promote themselves, the researchers found elevated fears of backlash. Furthermore, having these fears muted locomotion, which, in turn, diminished their actual self-promotion. This backlash activation was not evidenced in the data for men or for the women tasked to promote someone else. In sum, self-promotion, and only *self*-promotion, raises fears of backlash in women.

Are women's fears of backlash realistic? They certainly are. Women who self-promote are regarded as competent, but they incur the costs of being less likeable *and* less hireable (Rudman, 1998). The gender stereotype for women includes modesty, and because self-promotion violates this expectation, there are costs attached to self-promotion for women that make it less likely for them to achieve the desired outcome (getting the job). Also notice the juggling of competence with warmth (liking), that women need (not surprisingly) to manage in these situations.

A parallel backlash avoidance effect exists for women's negotiation styles and the outcomes these styles achieve (Amanatullah & Morris, 2010). When women advocate on behalf of themselves, they anticipate negative gender-role violations (backlash) and thus hold back on their assertiveness by using fewer competitive tactics—so they ultimately achieve lower outcomes. This chain of effects initiated by fears of backlash isn't activated when women negotiate on behalf of others.

This sequence of backlash effects for negotiating is realistically grounded for women because of the gender stereotyping attached to negotiating. Following the logic we explored in Chapter 6 for looking at gender differences and their roots in stereotyping, task instructions matter. When the context of the negotiations was framed in the power language of "opportunities for negotiating," differences between women and men in initiating bargaining were evident (Small et al., 2007). In contrast, when the same task was framed in the more polite and female-congruent language of "opportunities for asking," this gender difference was eliminated.

Similarly, negotiations that take place in a less face-to-face format (through virtual mediums such as email, telephone, or video), where politeness is less expected, might free women to be more aggressive. Reviewing the findings from 43 studies using meta analysis, the expected pattern emerged (Stuhlmacher et al., 2007). Women were more aggressive in virtual than face-to-face negotiations, whereas the context made no difference for men.

Furthermore, taking an **individual differences** approach, the higher women score as self-monitors (they are sensitive to what is happening around them), the more effectively they negotiate (Flynn & Ames, 2006). In contrast, men's self-monitoring skills were less strongly related to their negotiated outcomes, suggesting that managing the juggling act of being a woman with being an effective negotiator is specific to women and varies among women.

The bottom line here is that these studies argue that it's not that women can't stand up for themselves, but rather that they operate in a gendered context in which stereotyping makes it more difficult for women to self-promote and negotiate simply because they are women. Consistent with this conclusion, a review of the literature on impression management concludes that women and men work to fit more closely with gender-role expectations (impression management), and whereas this strategy is advantageous for men, it is not so for women (Guadagno & Cialdini, 2007).

Leadership

If only women... were leaders like men. As you may have guessed, this area of research cannot be reduced to this simple opening statement. In fact, Alice Eagly and her colleagues (1995) meta-analyzed 76 studies and found no differences in the overall *effectiveness* of women and men leaders. Indeed, there are some contexts in which women's leadership skills proved *more* effective than men's (Eagly, 2007). For example, meta analysis documents that women are more likely to exhibit a transformational leadership *style* than men; that is, an approach to leadership that includes developing and mentoring followers, contemplating new ideas for completing tasks, showing excitement about goals, communicating values, and motivating pride and respect (Eagly et al., 2003). Note how this approach to leadership fits with feminized gender-role expectations and thus is confirmed in the expectations people hold for female leaders (Sczesny et al., 2004). Furthermore, a meta analysis 87 studies supported the conclusion that having a transformational leadership style is associated with leaders' effectiveness (Judge & Piccolo, 2004).

So, is there any disadvantage to women in leadership? As you might have guessed, a lingering disadvantage accrues to women when we explore leadership as a *role* that in some specific contexts is incongruent with the gender role of being female (Eagly et al., 1995; Eagly & Karau, 2002) and when incongruent stereotyping is activated. These contexts are not trivial because they encompass tasks that are deemed masculine and settings that evoke agency and masculine stereotyping—in sum, in many of the occupations and jobs with the most prestige and best pay.

Consistent with the role congruity of leadership for specific gender-typed tasks, men were more likely than women to be selected as leader of a mixed-sex dyad doing either a masculine or neutral stereotyped task, even when the female partner exhibited more dominant personality characteristics than the man (Ritter & Yoder, 2004). On the other hand, highly dominant women working with a male partner on a masculine task were encouraged to step up and serve as the leader more often when they were exposed to a female leader model whose presence presumably muted the role incongruity (Carbonell & Castro, 2008). More prejudice was expressed toward female candidates for a leadership position when they worked in a masculine-typed industry (auto manufacturing) as compared to a more feminine-typed industry (clothing manufacturing) (Garcia-Retamero & Lopez-Zafra,

2006). Even the performance expectations for a team were more favorable when the leader's gender was congruent with the industry's gender-typing (Cabrera et al., 2009).

Turning to the link between leadership and **agency**, college students' ratings of purported leaders' masculinity correlated with perceptions of agency (leaders' femininity, with communion) (Johanson, 2008). Indeed, women continue to regard leadership success in both feminine and masculine industries as incompatible with having close relationships (Killeen et al., 2006). Furthermore, when German management students read about a managerial position that pictured a man, a woman, or both, women rated their own suitability for the job lower than men overall (Bosak & Sczesny, 2008). Not surprisingly, the position was regarded as most masculine when just a man was portrayed. However, the most optimistic suitability ratings, for both women and men, occurred when both sexes were pictured. Most germane to our point here about agency, when the self-ascribed agency of students was taken into account, the gender difference in suitability ratings disappeared. Thus, students felt suitable for the position, even the masculinized one showing a man, when they felt strongly about their own agency.

However, the relationships among role incongruence, agency, and a leadership disadvantage for women, as we now have seen many times, is not as simple as incongruent = disadvantage. Ashleigh Shelby Rosette and Leigh Plunkett Tost (2010) tested the role-incongruence model against predictions from the stereotype content model (SCM) we explored in Chapter 7. Both models predict that businesswomen will be regarded as competent (agentic) but not very warm (communal). However, the SCM goes on to allow that for high-status women leaders, it may be possible to be regarded as both competent and warm, because as we saw previously, warmth is connected with not being threatening, and top women leaders, having "made it" to the top, aren't a threat in the way lower-status women might be (also see Parks-Stamm et al., 2008).

Indeed, this pattern is what Rosette and Tost's study found. If organizational success was attributed to the skills of their female CEO, then these women were evaluated as more agentic *and* more communal than male top leaders, thus achieving a female leader advantage suggestive of transformational leadership. Their follow-up study showed that this advantage generalized to high ratings of these top women's leadership effectiveness— but that none of these favorable effects extended to women who were middle managers (for whom these ratings were similar to men's).[4] The overall take-away from Rosette and Tost's study is that women can benefit from a leadership "advantage," but only when they are at the very top of their organization (in this case, CEOs) and are regarded as the cause of the company's successful performance. In sum, then, this advantage, although important to understand, is quite qualified and limited.

Finally, if it is the leadership role that is important, then we'd expect leadership aspirations to be affected by gender stereotyping. Vishal Gupta and his colleagues (2008) explored business students' entrepreneurial intentions (essentially leadership in business) for themselves after reading one of six articles describing successful entrepreneurs. Beyond (1) a control condition of just the basic article, other variations included (2) implicit references to the masculinity of successful entrepreneurs by describing them using indirectly masculine adjectives (aggressive) or (3) implicit feminine characteristics (caring). Building on these implicit bases, the explicit variations added that entrepreneurs were successful

---

[4]I should note that the industry in which these women succeeded was left ambiguous so that we don't have the influence of task gender-typing we saw can create role-incongruence.

specifically because of their (4) masculinity and named male exemplars or emphasized the importance of (5) femininity and named women role models. In the final condition, the control article was amended with a statement to (6) actively nullify the gendering of entrepreneurs by noting that successful ones can be both men and women.

The control condition established a gender difference such that men (M = 3.44) expressed higher entrepreneurial intentions than women (M = 2.66) (compare the leftmost bars in the two graphs in Figure 9.7). Activating the feminine stereotype, whether implicitly or explicitly, made no difference. Both women and men in this condition recorded intentions no different from their same-sex controls. Openly countering the explicitly expressed stereotype, women presented with highly masculinized stereotypes of entrepreneurs raised their own intentions relative to women controls and men muted theirs, showing a boomerang effect. In contrast, the implicit activation of stereotyping, outside the awareness of

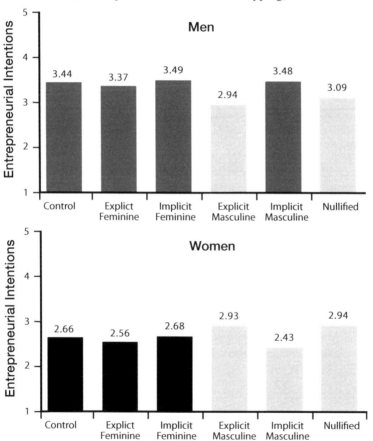

Figure 9.7 Men (top graph) and women (lower graph) business students rated their own entrepreneurial intentions after reading one of 6 descriptions of successful entrepreneurs (captured in the 6 bars within each graph). All comparisons within each sex are against the same-sex control group (the leftmost bar) such that darker bars show no significant difference in intentions and lighter bars show a significant difference from the control.

Source: Data taken from Gupta, V. K., Turban, D. B., & Bhawe, N. M. (2008) The effect of gender stereotype activation on entrepreneurial intentions. *Journal of Applied Psychology, 93*, 1053–1061.

these readers, deflated women's intentions relative to women controls and had no effect on men's. This last finding of no difference between the implicit masculinity and control conditions suggests that the usual stereotyping of entrepreneurship is masculine. Finally, in the nullifying condition, women's ($M = 2.94$) and men's ($M = 3.09$) entrepreneurial intentions converged, both by an increase in women's over control women and a decrease in men's relative to control men. There's obviously a lot going on here, so you might want to consult the graph in Figure 9.7. The bottom line is that entrepreneurship is implicitly stereotyped as masculine, and this stereotyping affects women's and men's aspirations.

Mentoring

If only women... were mentored like men.   It is important in this section to distinguish between role models (who need not be known personally but whose stories can inspire others) and mentors (who actively advise and work with their protégé). Women are more inspired by female than by male role models, whereas the sex of role models makes little difference for men (Lockwood, 2006). As for mentoring, men are more likely than women to serve as a mentor to others, and how men and women typically mentor varies. Men are more likely to focus on career development; women, on psychological and social support (although the heterogeneity of these meta-analytic data call for further research exploring possible moderators; O'Brien et al., 2010).

In a provocative study, George Dreher and Taylor Cox (1996) found that MBA business graduates (including White women, African Americans, and Latina/Latinos) who established mentoring relationships with White men mentors reported an average annual compensation advantage of fully $16,840 over those with mentors with other demographic profiles. Although women and racial/ethnic minority protégés were less likely than their White male counterparts to form mentoring bonds with senior White men, those who did benefited similarly to White male protégés mentored by White men. No compensation differences were found among those without mentors and those with women or minority mentors. This opens up questions about what it is about White men mentors that provides their mentees with better prospects for economic payoffs.

The most probable answer focuses on the power and status of mentors (McIntyre & Lykes, 1998). It seems reasonable to speculate that White men have the strongest links to work networks (thus connecting their protégé as well) and are most likely to be rewarded (thus moving up the ladder and taking their protégé with them). Simply put, more White men tend to hold positions of status and power. The relationship between a mentor's power and the mentee's outcomes is clear: Protégés believe high-ranked mentors can exercise more power (Struthers, 1995) and indeed a mentor's standing in the organizational hierarchy has been associated with her/his effectiveness (Shea, 1994). In addition, the career mentoring more likely to be offered by male mentors may pay off more on work indicators than the more psychosocial mentoring more commonly provided by female mentors (Allen & Eby, 2004).

Perceived Competence

If only women... were as competent as men.   If men were more competent than women, this would justify the wage gap. Psychologists contributed to this debate by exploring *perceived* competence, which we have seen plays a significant role in stereotyping. As we seen for all but the very top echelon of women leaders (such as those CEOs we talked about earlier), women generally face a tradeoff between being regarded as competent/agentic or warm/communal. In the workplace (especially in masculine-typed settings), agentic women are rated as highly competent and capable of leadership, but often are evaluated as socially deficient and thus open to hiring penalties (Heilman & Okimoto, 2007). In short, there can be a backlash effect when women appear competent—affecting women's salary negotiations (Bowles et al., 2007), performance evaluations (Brett et al., 2005), and promotion decisions (Heilman et al., 2004).

We've already explored some hiring biases, but in talking about competence judgments here, we need to understand how **shifting standards** work. For example, evaluators shifted their hiring criteria for a police chief position to more strongly value the strengths of the preferred male candidate (Uhlmann & Cohen (2007). When the male candidate was described as "street smart" and the female applicant as "well educated," raters commonly rated street smarts as more important and then justifiably recommended hiring the male candidate. When these job qualifications were reversed, education took center stage and again the male candidate was preferred. This pattern of shifting standards has been used to justify hiring decisions for both race- and gender-typical candidates (Hodson et al., 2002; Norton et al., 2004).

Julie Phelan and her colleagues (2008) explored the convergence of these two active research strands to see if shifting hiring standards might reflect backlash directed toward agentic women (that is, women perceived as competent). College students watched videotaped interviews staged by the experimenters to present **confederate** male or female interviewees for a computer lab manager position. All interviewees responded to the same question: "What kind of managerial style do you have?" Interviewees trained to appear agentic emphasized that "…I like to be the boss…to get things done well," whereas communal candidates stressed getting "…people together, to talk though…issues" and "…to have plenty of input from the people who work with me." Participants rated the applicants' competence and social skills and then made a hiring recommendation. The experimenters provided guidelines for the job that highlighted the need for successful candidates to both be competent and have social skills.

Importantly, agentic candidates were seen as more competent than communal ones; communal candidates, as more socially skilled than agentic ones. Replicating backlash findings, agentic women were regarded as less socially skilled than agentic men. Hiring preferences favored the agentic man over the agentic woman, with no differences between the two communal candidates (who were rated lower than the agentic ones).

Shifting standards came into play when ratings of candidates' perceived competence, perceived social skills, and hireability were examined together. As we might expect, competence was weighed more heavily than social skills for all candidates, except for the agentic woman whose deficit social skills were more heavily considered. Thus, agentic men were preferred because they were competent—the more "important" job qualification. In contrast, agentic women lost out by being perceived as competent but socially unskilled, with compromised social skills trumping competence. For women, then, there is no way to win here: Be competent and lose out to a competent man, or be socially skilled and lose out to a competent man.

Competence plays a role not only in hiring decisions but also in promotion decisions. Here psychologists have studied **evaluation bias**; that is, whether judges differently evaluate the same work attributed either to a man or to a woman. A meta analysis of 106 such

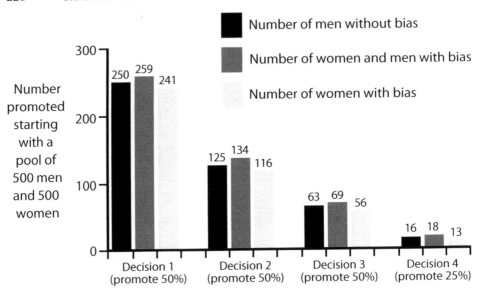

Figure 9.8

Starting with a pool of 500 men and 500 women, the first promotion cycle selecting the top half should promote 250 women and 250 men, but with a small evaluation bias of $d = .07$, 259 men and 241 women would be promoted, resulting in a promoted group that is 48.2% female. As these decisions compound and get tougher across decisions, the percentages of women would drop to 46.4% (at Decision 2), then 44.8% (at Decision 3), and finally 41.9% (at Decision 4). Small biases can compound over promotion cycles, thus putting disproportionately more men at the top and leaving more women behind.

Source: Agars, M. D. (2004). Considering the impact of gender stereotypes on the advancement of women in organizations. *Psychology of Women Quarterly, 28*, 103–111.

studies concluded that such a bias favoring men is actually quite small ($d = .07$), if not statistically insignificant (Swim et al., 1989). However, Mark Agars (2004) argued that even this seemingly small bias can have meaningful effects, both for the individuals affected and for an organization as a whole, if compounded over a series of promotion cycles. He simulated four promotion cycles, without and with the small bias identified by the meta-analysis ($d = .07$), to illustrate this point.

Given that each cycle skims off the best candidates, the numbers of people advancing become smaller and the competition gets stiffer. To take these points into consideration, his simulation selected 50% of the candidate pool to promote at decision points 1 to 3, but got tougher at decision point 4 by selecting only 1 of 4 candidates from the remaining pool. Assuming that the selection process is fair and that the women and men in the pool are equally talented as a group and have similar normal distributions of talent within each group, then we'd expect equal numbers of women and men to be promoted at each stage. This scenario is diagrammed in Figure 9.8 as the black bars.

However, by introducing just the small amount of evaluation bias identified by the meta analysis, the number of men selected at each point exceeded the number of women, and as the pool of workers eligible for further promotion shrank, this gender imbalance grew. From the initial 50:50 pool of men and women, the top echelon—after only four promotion cycles—tips toward about 58% men and 42% women. Evaluation biases, although seemingly small at any one point in the cycle, become consequential across employees' work lives and for the composition of the organizational hierarchy.

Gender Role Orientation

If only women… were more like men.   We already have seen that even when women are more like men (e.g., agentic and perceived as competent), they are not necessarily treated like men (e.g., hired). Even more closely associated with how gender might affect pay is an individual's **gender role orientation** itself—that is, the beliefs one holds about the appropriateness of various social roles for women and men, including those at work and at home. An example is: "Women are much happier if they stay home and take care of children." Individuals record their agreement or disagreement with items like this one, ranging from highly traditional on one end to highly egalitarian on the other.

Timothy Judge and Beth Livingston (2008) investigated the impact gender role orientation might have on actual earnings by using longitudinal survey data collected from thousands of 14 to 22 year-olds in 1979 and again in 2007 when they were 42 to 50 years old. In addition, their dataset allowed them to explore the impact of job complexity and occupational gender segregation as two possible moderators of this relationship between gender role orientation and earnings, as well as to probe for some of the factors that might influence the gender role beliefs that individuals hold.

Most directly relevant to our interests, gender role orientation did predict earnings such that the gap between women's and men's wages was wider (about twice as large) among those with traditional versus egalitarian attitudes. However, the findings get more interesting if we look beyond this overall conclusion. The effect of gender role orientation isn't all that big for women—although the more egalitarian women are, the more money they are likely to earn (also see Stickney & Konrad, 2007). In contrast, the relationship between stronger traditionalism and higher earnings was much more pronounced among men. Thus, men who held more traditional attitudes about the appropriate roles for women in the home and workplace were financially advantaged. Judge and Livingston (2008, p. 1007) speculate that: "This implies that traditional men are rewarded in the workplace for seeking to preserve the social order, whereas traditional women seeking to do the same are not necessarily penalized." Indeed, it is exactly these traditional women and men who react negatively to management programs in organizations designed to tackle diversity issues (Martins & Parsons, 2007).

Turning to the two **moderators** in Judge and Livingston's study, occupational segregation came into play by linking gender role orientation to earnings more strongly in male-dominated than in female-dominated jobs, and, of course, men were more likely to be employed in male-dominated jobs. Job complexity also proved influential, but more so in low-complexity (blue-collar) jobs than in higher ones. This pattern suggests that there's more traditionalism among men in low-complexity jobs and that this traditionalism widens the gender wage gap in these jobs where skills play less of a role in determining pay. This finding fits with the facts we examined about the wage gap at the start of this chapter—specifically the fact that the gap appears even in the lowest paid occupations.

This study adds two more important pieces to our understanding of gender role orientation. First, egalitarianism is more common among women, African Americans, the unmarried, better educated people, more intelligent people, and people raised in households that were less religious, where the father was more educated, and in which the mother was employed. Finally, because these data were longitudinal, changes over time (at least for this **cohort**) could be explored. Participants became less traditional in their gender role attitudes over time, and the gap between women (who were consistently more egalitarian) and men narrowed over time. As we explored in Chapter 5, we can't disentangle aging from all the changes that accompanied this cohort as they aged. However, we can say with confidence that these beliefs can be changed.

Of all the different areas we explored, this one on gender role orientation is most directly tied to gender itself, and it is surprising on some level to find such direct and clear evidence. A lot of what we have seen here documents the subtlety of the forces that may contribute a piece to the puzzle of why the gender wage gap exists and so stubbornly persists. The people whose traditional attitudes are most supportive of keeping things they way they are (some men) are also the people who are directly privileged by the status quo.

SEXIST DISCRIMINATION

Trond Petersen and Ishak Saporta (2004) identify three forms of employment discrimination. **Within-job wage discrimination** captures wage disparities within the same job, but this form has largely disappeared in the United States. **Valuative discrimination** describes lower wages in female-dominated than male-dominated occupations, although skill requirements and other work-relevant factors are comparable. We saw this process when we discussed occupational segregation, and it likely accounts for a substantial amount of the wage gap (Nelson & Bridges, 1999). **Allocative discrimination** involves biases in hiring, promotion, and dismissal. Of these, Petersen and Saporta's review suggests that hiring is the most common site for bias, but other studies point to promotion patterns as well.

Only a handful of studies trace the career progression of individuals over time. For example, Taylor Cox and Celia Harquail (1991) contacted 125 women and 377 men MBAs who graduated from the University of Michigan between 1976 to 1986. They found bigger pay increases and hence higher salaries among the men, even though their samples were comparable in years since graduation, training, ethnicity, seniority with their present employer, and even job performance (participants sent their last two formal evaluations to the researchers). Differences in promotion patterns held the key to understanding their wage differential. Women and men reported similar numbers of promotions, but men's promotions tended to be more substantial, involving movement up the management hierarchy, as opposed to titular but empty promotions for women. Men's promotions of substance brought higher pay with them. Parallel research involving a large sample of women and men scientists came to a similar conclusion (Sonnert & Holton, 1996), as did large-sample research with African American and White women and men managers (Maume, 1999).

The importance of promotions brings us to the concept of the **glass ceiling**. The U.S. Department of Labor studied Fortune 500 companies and in 1991 issued a report concluding that a glass ceiling exists, defined as artificial barriers (based on attitudinal or organizational bias) that prevent qualified individuals from advancing upward in their organization. This glass ceiling was bolstered by reliance on upper management's perceptions rather than formal tracking systems; by informal appraisal procedures that often judged women according to how well they got along with coworkers, in contrast to men's performance evaluations; by segregation of women into staff functions (personnel) instead of the line functions that track toward upper management; and by biased and unmonitored hiring practices that rely on an "old boys' network," (still evidenced; Bragger et al., 2002; Elacqua et al., 2009). One result of the glass ceiling initiative was the appointment of a Federal Glass Ceiling Commission within the Department of Labor, which concluded that women continue to hold disproportionately few senior positions and are underrepresented in the pipelines that lead to these positions (Federal Glass Ceiling Commission, 1995).

A key feature of the glass ceiling is its transparency. Promotions are cloaked in a guise of fairness so that presumably women cannot see the barriers that are holding them back. This is not the case for many racial and ethnic minorities, who realize, quite clearly, that their upward progress is blocked by sexism and/or racism. In recognition of this key difference, the Federal Glass Ceiling Commission captured the perceptions of African Americans with the imagery of a **concrete wall**.

Overall, large-scale studies controlling for a variety of differences between women and men conclude that a substantial portion of the wage gap is explained by discrimination—as much as 55% (Melamed, 1995b). *If only there wasn't sexist discrimination. . .*

If there's so much gender-based discrimination out there, why aren't women (and men) outraged? Some are. However, some research hints that discrimination can remain hidden and thus go unnoticed even by those directly affected by it. Faye Crosby and her associates conducted a series of studies exploring how comparable instances of discrimination were perceived differently according to how information is presented (Crosby & Clayton, 1986; Rutte et al., 1994). They constructed a hypothetical dataset wherein women were substantially undercompensated despite comparable seniority and organizational level to men. They then varied how these data were presented to students, making the differences inconspicuous by avoiding direct comparisons of comparably qualified women and men and by giving piecemeal, case-by-case data (rather than aggregated, intergroup data). Under these circumstances, students noticed the least amount of discrimination, even though, objectively, women were disadvantaged regardless of the presentational method. Given that few people see salary information that directly compares their earnings to equally qualified and situated others and that most of us are privy to only part of an organization's overall wage distributions, it is hard to pinpoint individual wage inequities, even when they exist.[5] *Failure to notice discrimination is not a valid signal that it doesn't exist.*

Finally, discrimination itself may become self-fulfilling as women's sense of **entitlement** is suppressed by low wages. As we saw in Chapter 8, women's sense of entitlement about who should do housework can affect the comparison groups they choose and their assessments of fairness in objectively inequitable arrangements. Parallel reasoning may extend to the wage gap. In a provocative study, undergraduate psychology students reported their earnings from their most recent summer job and described their expectations and entitlement for future wages (Desmarais & Curtis, 1997). Not surprisingly, women earned less during the past summer and believed they deserved less than did men for that job—and future jobs. However, this difference in entitlement disappeared when the researchers controlled for prior wages. This suggests a self-fulfilling, cyclic nature to the wage gap parallel to what we saw with gender stereotypes in general in Chapter 7. Because

---

[5] A fascinating short report on "Pay Secrecy and Wage Discrimination" is available from the Institute for Women's Policy Research, IWPR #C382, June 2011. http://www.iwpr.org/publications/

women earn less, they expect less, encouraging them to accept less, which leads them to continue to make less, and so on...

CLOSING THE WAGE GAP

To close the wage gap, we might best ask: *"Who's got the power?"* This question runs throughout all of the above discussion and indeed may explain much of these findings better, along with stereotyping (Lemons, 2003), than gender per se (Reskin, 1988). Higher-status people are expected to be agentic, to be appropriate for high-status jobs (Smucker et al., 2003), to be evaluated as competent (Smith et al., 2001), to feel responsible (Valentine, 2001), and so on.

Most notably for us here, **social status** is linked to being male and to doing masculine work. Jobs ranked as prestigious by students are described with masculine traits (Glick, 1991). Applicants with mature, not babyish, faces and men were favored for high-status employment (Zebrowitz et al., 1991), as are applicants wearing masculinizing clothing (Forsythe, 1990). Those with high school as opposed to college degrees were preferred by personnel representatives for lower-status jobs as well as female-stereotyped jobs in an electronics firm (Athey & Hautaluoma, 1994). Evaluations of a leader's effectiveness were more strongly affected by how powerful the leader was thought to be by subordinates than by the leader's gender (Ragins, 1991). A clear consequence of discrimination is to disempower (Gutek et al., 1996). The recurrent theme across these studies is that if one thinks of men and masculinity, one thinks of power.

This conclusion hits home even more when we consider the fate of most men who elect to do "women's work" and contrast this with what we know about women in male-dominated occupations. Although men in nursing, elementary school teaching (Cognard-Black, 2004), librarianship, and social work do encounter demeaning stereotypes from the outside public, within these occupations, they do not face hiring discrimination, and they benefit from structural advantages (C.L. Williams, 1992). In contrast to the glass ceiling that characterizes women's nontraditional employment experiences, Christine Williams (1992) concludes that men in female-dominated occupations ride a **glass escalator** to enhanced pay and advancement. Status and power pay off.

How do we bolster women's status and power in the workplace? It is clear that taking a deficiency approach to women doesn't do this. When we dredge up shortcomings in women by asking "if only women...", we are *not* challenging organizational hierarchies that value some types of work and workers over others. Furthermore, we have seen in this chapter that many of these myths about women workers are based more in stereotyping fiction than in workplace fact.

Rather than arguing that women somehow need to shoulder the burden of redressing workplace inequities, three policy positions have been promoted: affirmative action, equal pay for equal work, and comparable worth (Wittig & Lowe, 1989). Each policy is politically charged, and social scientists have played a role in understanding each of them.

Affirmative action targets occupational segregation and thus seeks to close the wage gap by assuring women's fair access to high-paying jobs. There are many popular misunderstandings of what affirmative action means (Crosby, 2004). The U.S. Department of Labor (2002, pp. 2–3) clarifies: "affirmative action refers to the aggressive recruitment programs, mentoring, training, and family programs that work to recruit and retain qualified individuals." Psychological approaches to affirmative action are extensively reviewed in the *Journal of Social Issues* (Skedsvold & Mann, 1996).

Equal pay for equal work defines "equal" as "identical," and it is these forms of readily identified discrimination that have been challenged most successfully through legal action (Pinzler & Ellis, 1989). Although this may redress inequities for some women, the entrenched gender segregation of the workforce we have seen in this chapter works against the widespread use of this approach.

This is where **comparable worth** comes in, emphasizing the role of job content as the critical determinant of compensation (Aaronson, 1995; Steinberg, 1987; Wittig & Lowe, 1989). Jobs are comparable and should be equally compensated to the degree that, looking across a variety of compensable job content dimensions (skill, effort, responsibility, and working conditions), their *total* values are equal. Such job evaluation is designed to provide equity in outcomes without demanding identical job participation (without genuine occupation- and job-level integration). Again, the policy is politically volatile and goes beyond the scope of the present chapter, although social scientists have made significant contributions to this discussion (for example, see the *Journal of Social Issues*, Lowe & Wittig, 1989). Closing the wage gap is not likely to be an easy or quick goal, but social scientists can facilitate efforts toward the realization of this goal by considering the contexts in which women and men work and by working to empower women and men in the workplace.

CHAPTER SUMMARY

Work is experienced almost universally by women and men, even if we narrowly define work in terms of paid employment. Both women and men engage in paid employment for economic reasons, most of which is not optional but necessary, as well as to fulfill psychological needs involving personal identity and competence. One of the largest and most influential differences between employed women and men is reflected in the wage gap—the difference between the earnings of full-time, year-long workers. A gap of 23% between women's and men's earnings persists into the 21st century in the United States. Although no one seriously questions the existence or importance of this gap, there are heated debates about its causes, although some of these possibilities have been ruled out or abandoned (job discontinuity, relocation, turnover, and education). Probably the largest single contributor to the wage gap is occupational segregation, although the separation of women and men into broadly different occupational categories fails to explain why the ones in which women dominate also have low wages.

Dissecting the wage gap refines our original question about what causes this gap into two more specific questions: "Why is there women's and men's work?" (dealing with the gendering of work) and "What does being a woman have to do with pay?" (the gendering of pay). Across research on family-to-work conflict, tokenism, the socialization of girls and women, hiring biases, and the theory of job queues and gender queues, evidence accumulates to suggest that social forces play a significant role in shaping the occupational pursuits of both women and men.

Turning to the gendering of pay, we explored self-promotion and negotiation, leadership, mentoring, perceived competence, and gender role orientation, first within the "if only women..." framework of a human capital approach, and then more fully from the approach of discrimination theory—which focuses on how the sexist prejudice, stereotyping, and discrimination we explored in Chapter 7 play out in the workplace. Across each of these analyses, we saw that pay (and hiring and promotion) truly are gendered, turning out differently for women and men even when women do and believe what men do.

In the final section focused specifically on discrimination, we argued that sexist discrimination subsumes gendered occupational stereotypes, hiring and promotion biases, and prejudicial attitudes that make the workplace environment and access to it qualitatively different for women and men. Situation-centered policies designed to level the playing field include affirmative action, equal pay for equal work, and comparable worth.

Across Chapters 8 and 9, we explored the multiple roles that construct women's lives, including friendships, romantic attachments, caregiving, and employment. None exists in isolation of the others, nor can any be understood fully without examining a complex interplay of personal, interpersonal, and institutional factors within a broader system of power and inequality.

SUGGESTED READINGS

Institute for Women's Policy Research. *www.iwpr.org*

Founded in 1987, IWPR is a think-tank affiliated with the graduate program in Public Policy and Women's Studies at George Washington University. Their multidisciplinary experts pull together academic and government data to write up-to-date reports on the wage gap and other economic and policy issues affecting women. In March or April of each year, you'll find a report here with the latest wage gap data, as well as brief and pointed analyses of these and other data. Check it out.

Watts, J. (2007). Humour as resistance, refuge and exclusion in a highly gendered workplace. *Feminism & Psychology, 17*, 259–266.

Jacqueline Watts explores the uses and meaning of humor among civil engineers in the United Kingdom, a job with some recent increases in women who make up a small minority (about 5%) of the workforce. Her analysis is very approachable and raises intriguing questions about tokenism, prejudice, stereotyping, discrimination, and the perpetuation of occupational segregation.

Williams, J. C., & Cooper, H. C. (2004). The public policy of motherhood. *Journal of Social Issues, 60*(4), 849-865.

Joan Williams and Holly Cohen Cooper propose a legal step toward changing stereotyping about the incompatibility of family and work by forbidding discrimination based on family responsibilities. Their proposal offers a provocative structural approach to family-to-work conflict as well as reviews differences between public policy in the United States and other countries that have implemented creative and effective family-friendly policies.

Smithson, J. (2005). "Full-timer in a part-time job": Identity negotiation in organizational talk. *Feminism & Psychology, 15*, 275–293.

Janet Smithson uses discursive analysis to explore the ways women and men talk about part-time work in financial sector organizations and concludes that this talk is highly gendered, equating part-time employment with women and making it incompatible for men.

Elacqua, T. C., Beehr, T. A., Hansen, C. P., & Webster, J. (2009). Managers' beliefs about the glass ceiling: Interpersonal and organizational factors. *Psychology of Women Quarterly, 33*, 285–294.

Although Tina Elacqua and her co-authors do some complex modeling in this paper, the data come from people in the field (685 managers at a large insurance company) and explore both the explicit and implicit explanations these practitioners hold about why women infrequently reach the top of their own organization. The paper offers as fascinating "behind-the-curtain" look at the glass ceiling.

Padavic, I., & Refskin, B. (2002). Sex segregation in the workplace (Chapter 4). In I. Padavic & B. Reskin, *Women and men at work* (2nd ed.); (pp. 57–95). Thousand Oaks, CA: Pine Forge.

This chapter by Irene Padavic and Barbara Reskin gives the reader a full understanding of the scope and meaning of occupational segregation.

Chapter 10

Women's Bodies
Objects of Appearance

Let's start this chapter with a simple test of your language abilities (Srull & Wyer, 1979). Using 4 of the 5 words on each line below, unscramble the words to make a sentence that makes sense. Note that you will delete one distracting word on each line.

beauty legendary was long their
appears desirable very runs he
horse legs shapely her are
his sea attractive looks body
car slender waist her is
envy inspires good their glamour

There's an obvious theme that runs through the six completed sentences above that relates to the focus of this chapter on women's bodies. Notice how each sentence concerns appearance.

What's stunning about this simple task is that it can have a powerful effect on how women view their own bodies. Tomi-Ann Roberts and Jennifer Gettman (2004) simply presented three different groups of college women and men with three different versions of this task. The first version created 15 of 25 sentences that dealt with appearance, like the examples above, across female (her), male (he), and plural (their) pronouns. The second version also used 15 of 25 sentences related to bodies, but this time focused on body competence (health, stamina, strength, and energy). The third condition was a control using all body-neutral words. Students completed this sentence task before going on to answer a series of questions about how they viewed their own bodies.

Doing the simple appearance task primed thoughts about body shape, size, and appearance in both women and men. When participants were asked after doing the task to give 20 descriptions of themselves in response to the sentence stem "I am _____," both women and men who created the appearance sentences filled in more body appearance responses ("I am overweight") than women and men who unscrambled sentences dealing with body competence.

Although the appearance **prime** worked to focus both women's and men's attention on bodily appearance, only women's body image was negatively affected by this priming. Examining responses from participants who did the appearance task, women reported more body shame, higher appearance anxiety, and less sexual appeal than men. Moreover, women in the appearance condition expressed more body shame, disgust, and appearance anxiety and less sexual appeal than women randomly assigned to do the body competence task. In sum, this very simple appearance prime awakened body concerns among women. Notice that this arousal occurred just for women, even though the appearance sentences referred not only to women but also to men and gender-indeterminate others (using plural pronouns).

Both this chapter and the next will focus on women's bodies. In this chapter we explore women's bodies as *objects* of appearance, both as seen by others and as viewed by women themselves. In the next chapter, we shift our vantage to consider women's bodies as *subjects* of their sexuality and physical health.

GENDER DIFFERENCES IN BODY IMAGE

Psychologists have studied three different ways of thinking about our bodies. The earliest work in this area explored *physical attractiveness*, often focusing on how physical attractiveness affects social interactions. Comparing women and men on physical attractiveness, a meta analysis concluded that observers tended to rate American women overall as being more attractive than men ($d = -.25$), but American men rated themselves as more attractive than women rated themselves ($d = +.17$) (Feingold & Mazzella, 1998). The strongest predictor of women's physical attractiveness is body mass index (weight adjusted for height) (Swami & Tovee, 2006). The research we examine here concentrates on the patterns that these data seem to suggest wherein women are critical of their bodies and thinness plays a dominant role.

A second strand of research looked at **body esteem**, typically by asking respondents to rate how strongly and how negatively or positively they viewed their own body parts and bodily activities (Franzoi & Shields, 1984). Three general patterns emerged from this research. First, an appearance component rested on perceived physical attractiveness for men, whereas for women physical attractiveness was mixed up with their sexual attractiveness. A second component concentrating on weight emphasized getting smaller for girls and women (a thinness ideal) and getting larger for boys and men (a muscularity ideal) (Donaghue & Smith, 2008; Neighbors et al., 2008; Petrie et al., 2010). A third area, focusing on physical conditioning, highlighted how women thought about their body as an object of appearance, in contrast to men, who regarded their body as an instrument of action (Halliwell & Dittmar, 2003).

These two lines of research on physical attractiveness and body esteem have converged into a third stream of research ideas centered on **body image**, or satisfaction with bodily appearance. A large number of studies have measured gender differences in body image, yielding a moderate difference between American women and men ($d = +.53$) as well as the sexes globally ($d = +.51$) (Feingold & Mazzella, 1998). This evidence (Mellor et al., 2010) consistently shows that men are more satisfied than women.

Feingold and Mazzella's (1998) meta analysis also yielded fascinating gender differences across time. Looking across a 30-year span, the gap between women's and men's body satisfaction has widened steadily from a small difference in the 1970s ($d = +.27$) to a larger difference in the 1980s ($d = +.38$), to an even larger difference in the 1990s ($d = +.58$). Across this time period, research in this area blossomed, involving just over 4,000 participants in the 1970s to over 60,000 participants in the 1990s. This trend toward more and more research exploring body image, especially women's, continued into the 21st century, largely driven in the literature on the psychology of women by the introduction of "Objectification Theory" by Barbara Frederickson and Tomi-Ann Roberts (1997; Fredrickson et al., 2011). To get a more personalized "feel" for this theory, think about the items in Box 10. 1.

BODY IDEALS AND BODY DISSATISFACTION

The ideal woman's body is contingent on historical time period, varying across the 19th through 20th century from having a tiny waist and large hips, to being full figured but

Box 10.1
Think about your evaluation of your own body. Which of the following 6 physical qualities is most important to you; next most; and third?

physical attractiveness   stamina   sex appeal
physical fitness   weight   health

Consider how much you agree or disagree with the following statements, if each is applicable to you:

Set 1
During the day, I think about how I look many times.
I think more about how my body feels than how my body looks. (reverse coded)
I often worry about whether the clothes I am wearing make me look good.

Set 2
I feel ashamed of myself when I haven't made the effort to look my best.
When I can't control my weight, I feel like something must be wrong with me.
When I'm not exercising enough, I question whether I am a good enough person.

thin, to being boyishly flat-chested but with womanly lower body curves (Calogero et al., 2007). The 21st century ideal is described as "curvaceously thin," glorifying thinness (a lean figure that includes a flat stomach, thin waist, boyish hips, and long legs) along with well-developed breasts, well-defined muscles, and flawless skin (Calogero et al., 2011, p. 8). Of these historically recent iterations, the current ideal may be the most naturally unattainable (Orbach, 2010). The central tenet of this ideal that takes center stage in the body evaluations of everyday women has to do with thinness.

Nowhere is this thinness ideal more pronounced than in fashion magazines. In the 1960s, models averaged 15 pounds less than the typical American woman; in the 1990s, models averaged 35 pounds less and were 4 inches taller (Spitzer et al., 1999). In a letter published in the *Journal of the American Medical Association*, researchers at Johns Hopkins School of Public Health reported that none of the Miss America winners since 1966 had a body mass index in the healthy range, and many fell to levels indicative of malnutrition (Rubinstein & Caballero, 2000).

Given the importance of weight, we might expect heavier people to harbor greater body dissatisfaction, and in general, this is true for both women and men (Muth & Cash, 1997). However, underweight men express dissatisfaction similar to that of overweight men in a curvilinear relationship between body weight and body image. This relationship is directly linear for women so that underweight women report the highest body satisfaction and overweight women, the least satisfaction. In sum, women seem most satisfied when they are smallest, in contrast to the most satisfied men with average builds.

In a study with over 3,000 adults, body mass index (BMI) was linked to psychological well-being—but only for women, not men (Bookwala & Boyar, 2008). Among women, well-being was highest for normal-weight women and significantly lower for all other higher weight groups, suggesting that there is a stigma associated with higher weight for women. Indeed, such stigma can play out in some fascinating ways. For example, in two longitudinal studies with German and American employees, earnings over a 5-year period were related to weight for women such that earnings dropped rapidly from thin to heavier weights and then flattened out (Judge & Cable, 2011). For men, income and weight rose together up until obesity, where income dropped off. In this last study, thinness seems to literally "pay off" for women.

The relationship between one's *actual* body and satisfaction with it is not simple. Consider the silhouettes of women's and men's bodies in Figure 10.2.[1] Indicate where you think you fall on the scale, where the ideal woman and ideal man are, and where you think the ideals of other peers would be.

Where women place themselves on the scale is pretty accurate; in a study with 87 White college women, trained observers' ratings and self-ratings overlapped by 72 to 85% (Cohn & Adler, 1992). As expected, women did tend to underreport their weight and to think of themselves as overweight (Betz et al., 1994). And not surprisingly, White women's ideal was thinner than themselves; about half the women selected an ideal that was fully one silhouette thinner than themselves (Forbes et al., 2001). The ideal expected by peers was even thinner; indeed, women and men are likely to over-estimate the degree of thinness they think their peers find attractive (Park et al., 2007). Notably, the ideal body image for Black women is curvier than that of White women and includes a larger buttock (Overstreet et al., 2010).

Needless to say, it is this differential between perceived and ideal body size that is consistent with reports of women's body dissatisfaction. In a 1993 survey of 803 adult women across the United States, nearly half reported globally negative evaluations of their appearance and a preoccupation with being or becoming overweight (Cash & Henry, 1995). Most of this dissatisfaction was directed at general weight as well as at the lower-torso (hips, buttocks, thighs, and legs) and mid-torso (waist and stomach). Less than 20% expressed discontent with their face, height, or hair. Even admittedly underweight women reported some degree of body dissatisfaction (Lox et al., 1998). Overall then, *perceptions* of one's body are more predictive of body dissatisfaction and even general self-esteem than actual body size (Miller & Downey, 1999).

There is a general misperception that body dissatisfaction is most troublesome for White women. A meta analysis combining 98 studies concluded that differences among

Figure 10.2

Use these silhouettes of different bodies to identify where you think you fall as well as what your ideal body type is for both women and men.

---

[1]An expanded series of figure drawings of men that extend out to very muscular figures finds that what college women say they want is somewhat more muscular than how men categorize themselves as they currently are but is less than men's more muscular ideal (Lynch & Zellner, 1999).

Asian American, Black, Latina, and White women's body dissatisfaction were small (d = .29 for the largest Black-White contrast) to null (Grabe & Hyde, 2006), although the least globally satisfied group of American college women was Asian American women (Forbes & Frederick, 2008).

Identification with the stereotype for **femininity** as measured by the Personal Attributes Questionnaire was associated with higher body dissatisfaction among women (Forbes et al., 2001). In contrast, women who self-reported more masculine-stereotyped (or **agentic**) traits, both alone or in combination with feminine traits (androgyny), exhibited less dissatisfaction. Additionally, stronger endorsement of thinness ideals and beauty practices among college women and men is associated with both **hostile** and **benevolent sexism** (Forbes et al., 2007). Both patterns suggest some linkages among appearance ideals and traditional attitudes about women.

Finally, there's a prevalent argument made in support of thinness based in presumed health benefits. First, it is important to note that the drive for thinness at one end of the BMI is not the same as promoting obesity. However, even if this were so, there is an intriguing argument made by "fat studies" scholars that the American "obesity epidemic" is more about weight stigmatization and the diet and drug industries than about promoting the health and well-being of people of all sizes (Lyons, 2009).

Second, in most of studies we examine here, participants' actual weight or body mass index was measured and ruled out as the reason why people expressed dissatisfaction with their body. Although, as we have seen, BMI is related to perceived attractiveness by others, people with a full range of body sizes can express dissatisfaction with their body. What we are talking about with objectification theory has much more to do with *self-perceptions* than any objective indicators of attractiveness, weight, or health.

OBJECTIFICATION THEORY

These concepts of physical attractiveness, body esteem, body image, body ideals, and body dissatisfaction all come together in a rich model that includes how we think about our body as well as the antecedents and consequences of this thinking: "Objectification Theory." Since these ideas were first presented by Fredrickson and Roberts in 1997, research to test and expand the theory has burgeoned—so much so that I introduced a new chapter devoted almost entirely to this theory in the third edition of this text. But even since then, the original model has been tested, refined, and expanded beyond its original formulation. I have tried to take a snapshot of this evolving model in Figure 10.3, and it is this model that I will use throughout this chapter to organize and review this literature.

I want to trace this model in detail; however, let me start with a big-picture overview of it. As you can see, the source of our body image rests in our culture and our own individual experiences within that culture. To varying degrees, and in response to what we each experience, we all take on (internalize) some of these body image messages (self-objectification). This process is both individualized and affected by our group memberships, including our gender, age, race/ethnicity, and sexual orientation (which act as moderators). This self-objectification (across Path 1) can lead to psychological consequences (e.g., body shame) that, in turn, can threaten our physical, mental, and sexual health and well-being. Self-objectification (on Path 2) can also affect how strongly we each feel the impact of cul-

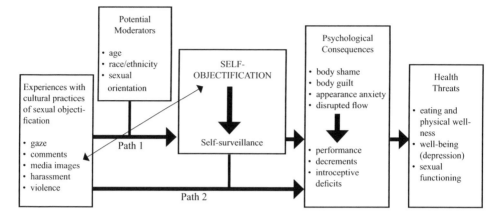

Figure 10.3

A snapshot of an evolving model originated by Objectification Theory (Fredrickson & Roberts, 1997). This model draws on the overview by Calogero, Tantleff-Dunn, and Thompson (2011) and the empirical review by Moradi and Huang (2008).

tural practices related to our body, making these practices most powerful for those people who have internalized high levels of self-objectification.

If you go back to our discussion of **mediation** and **moderation** in Chapter 2 (see Figure 2.2), you'll understand that self-objectification can function both as a mediator (Path 1) leading to psychological consequences and as a moderator (Path 2) along with cultural practices to exaggerate or mute these consequences. The central focus of the model then is **self-objectification**, which functions both as an **individual differences** variable (so that we all score somewhere along a continuum from high to low), and as an outcome that can be induced by exposure to cultural practices that are sexually objectifying.

What Is Self-Objectification?

Let's start to answer this question by thinking about **objectification** in general. What we are talking about here is how we think about objects or things—like the chair you are probably sitting in. It is a tool for your purpose, it has no autonomy, it lacks agency or activity, it is just as good as other chairs in fulfilling its purpose, it is OK for you to break it, it is owned by someone, and you certainly don't need to consider its feelings or its experiences (Nussbaum, 1995, reported in Calogero et al., 2011). For a human being then to be "objectified" is "to be made into and treated as an object that can be used, manipulated, controlled, and known through its physical properties" (Calogero et al., 2011, p. 5). As we'll see, this concept of objectification is important in our discussions both of body image here and of harassment and violence in Chapter 13 (hence, the inclusion of these cultural practices in Figure 10.3).

People become targets of **sexual objectification** when they are treated like things for the sexual gratification of another person. They are fragmented into a collection of body parts, divorced from the individual's personality, and relegated to a subordinated status (Calogero et al., 2011). Sexual objectification occurs in two general life domains: in actual social encounters (being the target of an unreciprocated gaze [ogling] and through comments directed at one's body) and through exposure to the visual media (e.g., magazines and television).

Self-objectification refers to the degree to which an individual internalizes being treated like a thing and turns that perspective on themselves. The body becomes an "it," to be observed from the vantage of an external observer and to be monitored. Rachel Calogero and her colleagues (2011) regard self-surveillance (or habitual body monitoring) as a consequence of self-objectification, whereas Bonnie Moradi and Yu-Ping Huang (2008) conceptualize self-surveillance as a manifestation of self-objectification. In either approach, self-objectification and self-surveillance go hand in hand.

Moradi and Huang (2008) make two important points about self-objectification that will help us throughout the following discussion. First, they point out that researchers commonly talk about self-objectification as both a "state" and as a "trait." Generally though, we think about traits as innate, enduring, and resistant to change—but self-objectification clearly is culturally created (not innate) and, as we'll see, must be targeted for change. The important point for us here is that self-objectification can be both *induced* in individuals by exposing them to body-emphasizing stimuli (making all of us vulnerable to some degree of self-objectification), as well as measured as an *individual difference* variable (with variability along a continuum from high-to-low self-objectification—so that some of us are more self-objectifying than others).

In fact, you can get some sense of self-objectification as an **individual differences** variable by going back to how you responded in Box 10.1. The first part is from the Self-Objectification Questionnaire (SOQ; Noll & Fredrickson, 1998). The full measure includes 12 body-related concepts that participants rank—with half representing appearance-based body attributes (physical attractiveness, weight, sex appeal) and the other half, competence-based body qualities (physical fitness, stamina, health). Higher rankings for the appearance items are indicative of greater self-objectification. Additionally, strong endorsement of the three items in Set 1 in Box 10.1 signals higher levels of self-surveillance (as measured by the Objectified Body Consciousness Scale, OBC) (McKinley & Hyde, 1996).

The second point that Moradi and Huang make defines the two paths that I illustrated in Figure 10.3. The first path treats self-objection as both an outcome of exposure to cultural practices and as a critical **mediator** between these practices and a list of psychological consequences. The second path regards self-objectification as a **moderator** that intensifies the impact of exposure to sexual objectification on psychological consequences. These moderating effects, then, are stronger for individuals who highly endorse self-objectifying attitudes. The point that becomes clear across all these analyses is that self-objectification is the linchpin of the objectification model, making it a prime target for interventions designed to derail both paths.

Objectification Theory Targets Women

Objectification theory largely targets women because, as we have seen, women are more vulnerable than men to threats to their body image and, as we'll see, are more frequently the targets of sexually objectifying cultural practices. In addition, there is evidence that women exhibit greater overall body objectification than men (Strelan & Hargreaves, 2005). However, there is beginning to be some evidence that the objectification model may apply to boys and men as well as to girls and women (see Choma et al., 2010; Slater & Tigge-mann, 2010). A key point in extending the model to men may be in better understanding some potential differences in what drives men's body image as compared to women's (for example, see Chen & Russo, 2010) as well as in recognizing diversity among men.

A series of three studies conducted by Nathan Heflick and his colleagues (2011) further explains why objectification theory is applied largely to women. Participants in these studies were instructed to focus solely on the appearance of targeted women and men. Only the appearance-emphasized women were then rated as less competent, warm, and moral, taking away three key signs of being "human," and thus treating these women more like objects. In another study, women's and men's memories about the appearance of women were more accurate than their memories about the appearance of men, suggesting that appearance itself is more salient when it is about women (Horgan et al., 2004).

Finally, self-objectification appears to be better understood by women than by men, suggesting that women have more experience with self-objectification than do men (Newheiser et al., 2010). When college women and men were lead to regard a female target as engaging in self-objectification, only the women perceived more negative emotions in her (independent of their own state of self-objectification). In a follow-up study, when an online sample of women and men was asked to identify with a self-objectifying target, again women reported stronger negative reactions suggestive of greater empathy. In sum, there is much about objectification theory that makes it especially well targeted to understanding women's body concerns.

CULTURAL PRACTICES TARGETING WOMEN

Let's start working our way through Figure 10.3, starting with an overview of cultural practices identified by objectification theorists that target women, specifically the sexualized gaze, comments, and media images. We'll also explore the impact of these cultural practices on women's self-objectification and self-surveillance. Situating each of these cultural practices within the puzzle we outlined in Chapter 6 (in Box 6.1), each represents a piece of women's general **social context**. It is this environmental context that is the root of women's self-objectification, making the logic we developed about social contexts in Chapter 6 applicable here.

The most global point that we shouldn't lose track of is that *culture matters*. Women's body image is embedded within a culture that socially constructs appearance ideals. However, the effects of something as broad as culture are necessarily complex. On the one hand, Polish women desired a larger body ideal than American women (Forbes et al., 2004). More Ghanaian than U.S. women rated larger body sizes as ideal (Cogan et al., 1996), as did Ugandan as compared to British women (Furnham & Baguma, 1994).

On the other hand, body image and change concerns were similar among Indigenous and mostly Anglo-Saxon White Australians (Ricciardelli et al., 2004). Arab and Jewish Israeli women expressed more body dissatisfaction than their male counterparts, like American women, but unlike American women, these Israeli women reported dissatisfaction when they thought they were too thin (Safir et al., 2005). For an ethnically diverse sample of women, neither how acculturated they were into American culture nor how long their family's generations lived in the United States predicted body satisfaction (Petrie et al., 2002). However, a study with Japanese and Chinese students studying in the United

States suggests that it is not acculturation per se that predicts disordered eating, but rather awareness and internalization of Western appearance norms (Stark-Wroblewski et al., 2005). Thus, there's more going on here than a simple, blanket characterization of Western culture as bad for women's body image.

Still, there is reason to be concerned specifically about Western body ideals. For example, interviews with Tanzanian women about their use of damaging skin bleach documented that colonialism and Westernization played important roles (Lewis et al., 2011). Most fascinating is a naturalistic experiment that involves girls and women living on the Fiji islands in the Pacific after the introduction of Western television in 1995. Among both adolescent girls and adult women a cultural body image that previously centered on robustness came to include thinness (Williams et al., 2006)—bringing with it a desire to lose weight and disordered eating (Becker, 2004; Becker et al., 2005).

The Sexualized Gaze

Ask almost any woman if she has ever felt that someone, especially a man, was looking at her in an unwanted sexualized way, and she'll likely tell a story or two. These cultural images are easy to picture: women being whistled at on the street or people making open comments about women's bodies, clothing, etc. Think about words like "ogling" and "leering," and what images come to your mind? This sense is backed up by research evidence documenting that women are gazed at more than men; that women feel looked at more than men; that men direct more unreciprocated gaze at women in public places than women do in turn; and that men's gaze is often accompanied by sexually evaluative commentary (the common 10-point rating scale; reviewed by Fredrickson and Roberts, 1997, and captured provocatively in the film "War Zone").

The gaze targets women. Men continue to objectify women more than other women do (Strelan & Hargreaves, 2005). American men's reported preference for the highly sexualized breast size of women is consistently larger than women's ideal, and the variety of positive characteristics thought to accompany larger breasts has grown from 1992 to 1998 (Tantleff-Dunn, 2001). Women and men in 1998 associated larger breasts with greater intelligence, success, and popularity for women than did raters in 1992.

Not surprisingly, there's evidence that the media play a significant role in leading men to sexualize women's bodies. A study with 13 to 15-year-old boys exposed half to 20 commercials that epitomized the thin ideal for women and the reminder to 20 neutral ads (Hargreaves & Tiggemann, 2003). The researchers also measured how much importance each boy placed on appearance as part of his general **schema** for choosing a partner or girlfriend. Interestingly, the commercials most affected the boys with *moderate* appearance schemas by making them more sensitive to the appearance characteristics of girls. Exposure is not enough to affect body perceptions, but rather for some people, even brief exposure can have significant effects. It doesn't take a giant leap to move from this relatively small amount of exposure to 20 sexist ads to their virtual omnipresence in many boys' lives.

Turning to adult men, men originally expressing egalitarian attitudes about women moved toward becoming more traditional after viewing stereotypic *masculine* models (Garst & Bodenhausen, 1997). Men exposed to magazines and action movies that targeted male audiences not only expressed greater concerns about their own muscularity and fitness, but also overvalued thinness in women (Hatoum & Belle, 2004). Thus, growing trends about valuing "bigness" for men have implications for men themselves and for men's images of women.

Before we blame men as the cause of women's self-objectification, two other pieces of information qualify this blanket statement. First, men are not alone in their objectification of women; rather, women objectify women as well. In fact, White women are harsher critics of their own bodies than White men are: fully 69% of women considered the thinnest silhouettes as most attractive to men, yet only 25% of men actually selected these options (Cohn & Adler, 1992).

Women are also more likely to objectify other women than they objectify themselves (Strelan & Hargreaves, 2005). Furthermore, women objectify men more than men do. What may eventually sort this all out is the power relations involved in the sexualized gaze. Surely few people wouldn't mind being sexually appreciated, *if* that appreciation did not demean them as objects, but rather empowered them as equal subjects in their own sexuality.

A second piece of this puzzle has to do with women's misunderstanding of men's desires. Women greatly overestimated men's preferences for thin women (Forbes et al., 2001), and wives exaggerated their husband's presumed dissatisfaction with their wife's body (Markey et al., 2004). Obviously the blame for this misunderstanding could just as easily reside in the misperceptions of women as in miscommunication from men.

However, the simplicity of this conclusion becomes muddied when we consider that the above findings involve mostly White women and men. African American and Latino men prefer to date larger women than do White men (Glasser et al., 2009). Not only are Black men less demanding of thinness, African American women are more accurate in estimating Black men's preferences (Patel & Gray, 2001). Thus, women and men can convey their desires accurately—when they are Black.

I don't want to let men fully off the hook here. It just makes some sense to me that men play some role in heterosexual women's concerns about their bodies. Indeed, heterosexual men's personals ads generally emphasize the physical attractiveness of prospects (Miller et al., 2000), sending a clear message that looks matter. However, when a phenomena is this pervasive (affecting women and men) and targeted (affecting most acutely younger, White, heterosexual, middle class and affluent women more than others), we need to think about larger systems than any one of us as individuals controls.

Indeed, some authors talk about a "culture of thinness" to capture this systemic perspective (White, 1992). For example, there appears to be a **halo effect** for women centered on their weight. Joel Wade and Cristina DiMaria (2003) asked participants to rate as heavy or thin, Black or White women not only for their perceived attractiveness, but also for their expected life success and personality. The perceived attractiveness of the thin White woman didn't stop there, but rather extended to projections for a successful life and a more favorable personality. In contrast, the halo effect with its positive glow surrounded the heavy Black woman in contrast to the thin one.

The gaze affects women.   Peggy Evans (2003) took this finding about a halo effect a step farther by linking it to internalized thinking. She hypothesized that White women may internalize the thin ideal because they associate this ideal not only with attractiveness but also with a halo of other positive outcomes. She tested this prediction by exposing one group of women to a thin ideal described as successful, while another group saw the same women but described as having an unsuccessful life. Only the successful ideal led to reduced self-satisfaction in observers (as well as suppressed optimism about observers' future life prospects). In another study, the more women linked positive outcomes to being like a media ideal, the more they internalized these ideals and subsequently reported heightened appearance dissatisfaction (Engeln-Maddox, 2006). Thus, it appears that weight serves as a central trait that globally affects not only how we see others, but also ourselves.

A core point of objectification theory is that women's repeated exposure to this direct sexualized gaze can affect women's own self-objectification. More research is needed to directly make this link, but one study does confirm objectification theory's predictions. Rachel Calogero (2004) recruited college women to participate in a study on "mind, body, and health issues" (p. 17). After completing a packet of questionnaires gathering demographic, self-objectification, and health information, women were randomly told that for the next part of the study, they would engage in "small talk" with a stranger for 5 minutes. Their partner was described as either male, female, or not at all. All participants then completed a second packet of surveys that included measures of body shame and social physique anxiety. Simply anticipating interacting with a male stranger was enough to affect women's body image. Women expecting to talk with a male stranger reported more body shame and more anxiety about their bodies than women who thought they would interact with another woman. In sum, women's mere *anticipation* of the potential male gaze was enough to elevate their body concerns.

Additionally, as objectification theory would predict, the more women acknowledged experiencing the sexualized gaze, the more internalization of thin ideals and self-surveillance they reported (Kozee et al., 2007). Furthermore, women actually talked less when a camera was focused on their bodies (compared to their face or just their voice), suggesting some muted performance in response to appearance concerns (Saguy et al., 2010).

Some of the earliest and most provocative studies coming from objectification theory used a swimsuit versus sweater experimental manipulation to raise women's *anticipation* of the sexualized gaze (Fredrickson et al., 1998). Under the pretext of sampling and evaluating consumer products, women were randomly assigned to either try on a one-piece bathing suit or a sweater. While wearing the garment in a private, mirrored room where they were seen by no one, they completed questionnaires measuring body shame. Women simply wearing the swimsuit, even though they were not observed, recorded higher body shame scores than women wearing a sweater. Presumably, wearing a more revealing bathing suit is enough to raise concerns about body image that are a response to the context, not any personality characteristics of the women involved.

Furthermore, the effects of this experimentally induced body shame linger. In another study (Quinn et al., 2006), even after the swimsuit women got dressed, they continued to have body-related thoughts intrude into a free response task (unlike the women who had tried on the sweater). In fact, the more body shame these swimsuit women had reported predicted how many body thoughts they continued to experience.

Other research finds that women don't even need to put on a bathing suit to elevate their body concerns. Simply imagining both social and nonsocial body-focused situations (like being on a beach or in a dressing room) is all it takes to raise women's body dissatisfaction (Tiggemann & Slater, 2001). In sum, these studies begin to argue that varying the situation people are in can affect how much bodily objectification they experience. Thus objectification can be a *state* that can be induced by the social context in which women find (or even imagine) themselves—a context that can affect most randomly assigned women, thus capturing the pervasiveness of exposure to objectification.

Finally, Sarah Gervais, Theresa Vescio, and Jill Allen (2011) actually created the sexualized gaze in the laboratory by training women and men **confederates** to stare briefly but repeatedly at the chest of the other-sex undergraduate man or women they were interviewing. (You can actually see this gaze as well as hear Dr. Gervais talk about this study in a video and podcast posted at *pwq.sagepub.com*.) To reinforce the sexual connotations of this gaze, these confederates also provided appearance feedback after the interview. In contrast, these same confederates simply made eye contact with randomly assigned control participants. Participants then went on to complete a math test, indicated if they would like to interact again with their interviewer, and filled out measures of body surveillance, body shame, and body dissatisfaction.

Women exposed to the sexualized gaze scored significantly lower on the math test than both men exposed to the gaze and control women. Intriguingly, sexualized women were most likely to want to interact with their partner in the future, suggesting that women found his attraction flattering. Indeed, this positive reaction may explain why being exposed to this sexualized gaze from a man had no impact on these women's body evaluations. The authors speculate that "the objectifying gaze may simultaneously convey to women that their appearance is valued while their other qualities [their competence and abilities] are devalued, which may cause **stereotype threat**" (p. 13) and hence lower math performance.

What strikes me as most chilling about this experiment is that these sexualized women left the experiment feeling good about themselves and the male interviewer without realizing that their performance had suffered. Thus, the effect of the sexualized gaze remained subtle and outside their awareness, although clearly documented in their math test scores. Without the comparison to the control group afforded by this experiment, these women would have never known that their performance was lowered by simply being randomly assigned to the "wrong" interviewer.

Comments and "Fat Talk"

Like the sexualized gaze, body-related comments more commonly target girls and women than boys and men. For example, in-depth interviews with adolescent girls and boys documented that girls receive more negative and positive messages about their body than do boys (McCabe et al., 2006). In fact, boys reported almost none of these types of messages. Similarly, a "Health and Wellness Survey," emailed to over 4,000 adult women and men, found that women reported hearing more body-related talk and felt pressured to engage in it (Martz et al., 2009).

Given the centrality of weight-related concerns in objectification theory, it is not surprising that much of this body-related talk focuses negatively on the size and shape of women's bodies and thus has been dubbed "fat talk." Think about how you'd respond to a friend beginning a conversation with "Ugh, I feel so fat." Then take a look at Box 10.4 to see how undergraduate women typically responded.

Rachel Salk and Renee Engeln-Maddox (2011) went beyond just looking at the content of fat talk (in Box 10.4) to also explore the meaning of fat talk to women by asking

TABLE 10.4

Fat Talk: How college women respond to the conversation-starter from another woman saying "Ugh, I feel so fat."

Theme Mentioned	Sample Response	Percentage
Denial	"Oh, come on! You're not fat at all!"	87%
Evidence	"Yes I am, look at my thighs."	37%
Causes	"Me too. I ate so much last night."	30%
Empathy	"I feel that way too sometimes."	26%
Action together	"We should diet together!"	23%
I'm fat, you're not	"If you're fat, then I'm humongous."	13%
Probing	"Why do you think like that?"	8%

Note. A podcast interview with these authors about this study is available at pwq.sagepub.com.

Source: R. H. Salk & R. Engeln-Maddox. (2011). "If you're fat, then I'm humongous!": Frequency, content, and impact of fat talk among college women. *Psychology of Women Quarterly, 35*, 18–28.

these women to consider what they want to get from fat talk dialogues with their friends. Most women (69%) want their friend to deny their assertion that they are fat; other desired responses include fishing for a direct compliment, looking for strategies to be healthier or lose weight, and seeking emotional support. As for women's reactions to having a friend initiate fat talk, the most common reaction was to believe that such talk could relieve their friend's distress (often considered temporary), although this reaction was followed by annoyance and feeling manipulated to say something nice. Only a few women thought that engaging in fat talk made them feel worse about their own body. Most notably, fully 149 (93%) of the women in the study indicated that they engaged in "body-related talk… [in which] women express dissatisfaction with their bodies (e.g., feeling fat or expressing disappointment in a body part)" (p. 20).

Furthermore, Salk and Engeln-Maddox found that the more frequently women reported engaging in fat talk, the more body dissatisfaction they expressed. Interestingly, the woman these participants imagined talking with was most commonly of average or below average weight, suggesting that fat talk is more about body perceptions than about actual body size. Indeed, in another study of fat talk with preadolescent and adolescent girls, the initiators of these conversations were typically not overweight (Nichter (2000). Finally, college women reported feeling pressured to engage in fat talk, which ultimately serves "to reinforce the thin body ideal and the notion that disliking one's body is normative for women" (Salk & Engeln-Maddox, 2011, p. 26).

Fat talk focuses negatively on women's bodies, and indeed it is commonsensical that repeated exposure to body *criticisms* reflects poorly on body image. As we might then expect, overweight adult women had poorer body image and psychosocial functioning to the degree that they were stigmatized for their weight throughout their lives (Annis et al., 2004). What, however, is surprising about findings related to body comments is that even *compliments* appear to have a downside.

Rachel Calogero and her colleagues (2009) explored whether experiences with body-related criticisms and compliments over the past 2 years were related to an ethnically and weight-diverse sample of college women's self-objectification, self-surveillance, and body dissatisfaction. As we would expect given our weight-driven culture, women with higher body mass index scores were more frequently targeted and felt the negative impact of criticisms more than lower BMI women. Not surprisingly, regardless of body size, the more negatively these women felt about experiencing criticism, the higher they scored on all three body measures. Furthermore, the more positively these women felt about being complimented, the higher were their scores on all three troubling body measures—so that *compliments functioned no differently than criticisms*. Challengingly our intuition that body compliments are "nice," this finding of **complimentary weightism** suggests that drawing attention to women's bodies, even in a seemingly positive way, is not good for women's body image.

Expressed comments, both negative and positive, then have a downside for women. We might also think about "comments" as those subtle, unexpressed indicators of a general climate. Indeed, Rachel Calogero and John Jost (2011) conducted the first study about which I am aware to consider this unspoken **social context** in which women and men are embedded. Specifically, they subtly manipulated college women's and men's exposure to sexism by setting up a bogus "proofreading task" that asked students to rate their agreement with, and then the clarity of, four items taken from the Ambivalent Sexism Inventory (see Chapter 7). They randomly assigned participants to one of four conditions in which all four items came from the Benevolent Sexism (BS) portion of the ASI, all from the Hostile Sexism (HS) scale, two from each scale, and four neutral items (the control).

Across three studies conducted by Calogero and Jost, their results consistently indicated that exposure to two or four BS items caused women, but not men, to exhibit negative body image effects. For example, in Study 2, BS exposure predicted women's self-surveillance, body shame, and intention to engage in some form of appearance management (e.g., dieting or exercise for weight loss) in the next week. Interestingly, HS exposure had no more impact on women's body image than did the control condition—indicating that these women's body image attitudes and intentions were not created in response to openly sexist hostility, but rather they were insidiously affected by subtle benevolent sexism. Just like body compliments, nice-appearing benevolent sexism is not so nice in its consequences for women's own body image.

Sexualized Media

There are two strands of research that combine to make the case that the visual media is a major source of objectification leading to self-objectification for women (and possibly men). The obvious place to start is to examine how women's bodies are portrayed in the media. A piece of this analysis also looks at the status afforded women in the media and how women are treated in the media as they age. Although the media indeed may be sexist and ageist, to support objectification theory we then need to link these portrayals to women's body image. We are all exposed to lots of media images, but what are the conditions that encourage internalization of these images (self-objectification)?

The media targets women. You probably aren't taken aback by the assertion that the media present thin and sexualized images of women's bodies, so I'll just sample a few recent research examples. A content analysis of almost 2,000 print ads from 59 popular U.S. magazines documented that one of every two ads that featured women portrayed them as sex objects (Stankiewicz & Rosselli, 2008). Even the printed content of women's magazines focuses on bodily appearance: 78% of popular women's magazines, and none of

Box 10.5

Lessons about women's beauty can be found in many popular fairy tales. Lori Baker-Sperry and Liz Grauerholz (2003) found that references to women characters' beauty outstripped references to men's handsomeness across all Brothers Grimm fairy tales. Even more interestingly, the 25% of these stories that made it into contemporary children's books and movies have more themes about women's beauty than those that haven't been reproduced. Why these choices?

men's, spotlighted appearance content on their covers (Malkin et al., 1999). Men's magazines offered entertainment and information about general knowledge, hobbies, and activities, in contrast to popular women's magazines, that promised to improve women's lives by changing their appearance.

Just as sobering, print images of women have not changed significantly from 1955 to 2002 (Lindner, 2004), although, not surprisingly, what did change from 1985 (more) to 1994 (less) was how clothed women were (Plous & Neptune, 1997). Looking at over 200 photos from the top fashion magazines (Cosmo, Glamour, and Vogue), White women models were more likely than Black to strike sexually explicit poses, whereas Black women models were more often shown in submissive poses (Millard & Grant, 2006). In fact, women in print magazines were most often shown in passive poses and were airbrushed to appear flawless, and the objectifying tendency to dismember women into their body parts continues (Conlesy & Ramsey, 2011). Not surprisingly, younger models were more prevalent than older ones, especially in magazines targeting young women, and were thinner and less clothed (Bessenoff & Del Priore, 2007).

These types of thinness and attractiveness messages are not confined to adults. Rather, a look at the top 150 top-selling video games revealed that games rated for children featured even thinner female characters than games targeting adults (Martins et al., 2009). Another study examining the 25 top children's movie videos listed by Amazon and the American Film Institute for ages 4 to 8 recorded an average of 8.7 body image-related messages per video (topped by *Cinderella* and the *Little Mermaid*, each with 14)—the majority of which targeted women's thinness and physical attractiveness (Herbozo et al., 2004).

The media affects women. For the media to affect women, women obviously need to pay attention to it, and indeed college women are more likely than college men to compare themselves to professional models (Franzoi & Klaiber, 2007). Similarly, the more Black adolescent girls identify with sexualized portrayals of Black women, the more these girls emphasize the importance of their own appearance (Gordon, 2008).

Beyond these baseline data, there are two empirical ways to study the impact of media message on women. The first are correlational designs, which document associations between media choices and body outcomes. For example, among Australian female high school students, choosing to view appearance magazine and Internet content was highly related to internationalizing thin ideals, making appearance comparisons of one's self with others, and reporting weight dissatisfaction and a drive for thinness (Tiggemann & Miller,

2010). In another study with middle-aged Australian women (age 35 to 55 years-old), television and magazine exposure was associated with internalization, body comparisons, appearance investment, and aging anxiety, which in turn were related to body dissatisfaction and disordered eating (Slevec & Tiggemann, 2011). A meta analysis by Shelly Grabe and her colleagues (2008) established that women's media exposure was associated with more internalized self-objectification ($d = .42$ across 16 studies) and disordered eating behaviors and beliefs ($d = .28$ across 12 studies).

A key shortcoming of these correlational studies, though, is that we don't know whether media choices are affecting women or if women with body interests self-select specific media (a directionality problem). Jennifer Stevens Aubrey (2006) tackled this problem in her 2-year panel study with undergraduate women, finding that the patterns go in both directions. The more women were exposed to sexually objectifying images at Time 1, the more they self-objectified at Time 2, indicating the impact of media. Additionally, self-objectification, appearance anxiety, and body shame at Time 1 all predicted media choices at Time 2, signifying a self-selection factor. In sum, then, correlational studies argue for a small-to-moderate impact of media exposure on women's body image that appears to exist within a self-sustaining cycle (captured by the thin two-headed arrow between media images and self-objectification in Figure 10.3).

The second approach to studying media exposure is experimental, allowing for clear causal statements as well as suggesting that most women, randomly assigned, can be affected. Overall, Grabe et al.'s (2008) meta analysis concluded that experimental demonstrations were similar in small-to-moderate size as correlational evidence: for internalization, $d = .21$ (7 studies); for disordered eating behaviors and beliefs, $d = .36$ (8 studies); and for body dissatisfaction, $d = .28$ (across 90 correlational and experimental studies).

Studies published subsequent to this meta analysis repeatedly confirm this pattern of media effects across a wide range of outcomes as well as among girls and women. For example, 6 to 10 year-old Dutch girls randomly assigned to play for just 10 minutes with an average-sized doll ate more in a subsequent "taste test" than girls who played with a thin doll (Anschutz & Engels, 2010). A similar pattern was demonstrated with German college women who chose a diet snack after viewing thin models, regardless of their own BMI (Krahé & Krause, 2010). Australian college women who viewed thin-idealized magazine ads reported higher self-objectification, appearance anxiety, negative mood, and body dissatisfaction (Harper & Tiggemann, 2008). Turning to video game exposure, college women who played games with thin female characters exhibited lower body esteem (Barlett & Harris, 2008); others who played games with sexualized women figures showed reduced self-efficacy (Behm-Morawitz & Mastro, 2009). Highlighting how these effects extend to many women, appearance-based ads reduced White women's body satisfaction independent of their BMI and across varying degrees of objectified body consciousness (Hamilton et al., 2007).

Bianca Loya and her colleagues (2006) documented that college women exposed to images of attractive models recorded higher levels of hostility directed toward women than control women whose hostility was measured prior to exposure. Interestingly, this hostility did not reflect competition with the attractive models, but rather was expressed by discounting the models' attractiveness. Furthermore, the higher an individual woman's hostility score, the more self-surveillance and body shame she reported—demonstrating that the hostility aroused by attractive models negatively targets not only other women but also the woman doing the viewing herself.

Finally, there's more to a print ad than the image of the woman herself. The surrounding copy (words) frames the image and presumably can affect its meaning. For example, ads in women's health magazines frequently present idealized models along with copy that promotes health, although not to the extent that we might think. A content analysis of over 400 cover headlines in the five highest circulating women's U.S. health magazines found an equal representation of health and appearance messages (Aubrey, 2010). Ironically, undergraduate women exposed to *appearance*, not health, framing reported more body shame and *more* motivation to exercise.

There's a sizable, but still not dominant (Conley & Ramsey, 2011) trend in the framing of print ads to project models as active and powerful. Emma Halliwell and her co-authors (2011) captured these themes in how they framed the same idealized images of women. For example, one ad for a push-up bra featured a woman holding a ribbon on the strap she is wearing accompanied by the sexually agentic slogan "I pull the strings"—versus the passively objectifying copy "For a beautiful figure." The former characterization is meant to be empowering; however, just like the objectifying version, the agentic framing increased college women's weight dissatisfaction compared to a non-exposed control. Furthermore, women rated the agentic version no more positively than the appearance one, and intriguingly, the agentic version created more self-objectification in viewers than did the appearance-based one. These authors conclude: "…what on the face of it appears to be a positive step forward toward empowering women consumers of sexualized advertising actually appears to be a step backward" (p. 43).

POTENTIAL MODERATORS

Cultural practices like the sexualized gaze, comments, and the media certainly affect different individuals in various ways—a point we address later. As we saw in Chapter 6, women are not a monolithic group, but rather vary by subgroupings defined by the multiple social representations we explored around the Diversity Wheel in Chapter 1. In objectification theory, three potential moderating variables have attracted researchers' attention: age, race/ethnicity, and sexual orientation. Returning to Figure 10.3 in this chapter, we'll see here that although the model may vary across these diverse subgroups of women by showing somewhat different patterns and by considering additional variables, the general variables that make up objectification theory affect diverse women.

Age

As we might expect, girls aren't born with body dissatisfaction. Preschool girls and boys showed similar body image satisfaction as measured with same-gender silhouettes (Hendy et al., 2001). Sadly though, even girls as young as age 3 show signs of being emotionally invested in the thinness ideal (Harriger et al., 2010). By about age 9, clear gender differences begin to emerge (Thompson et al., 1997) and peak in high school (Frost & McKelvie, 2004). Likewise, girls' physical self-concept declines across the school years (Klomsten et al., 2004). Not surprisingly, Feingold and Mazzella's (1998) meta analysis revealed that the most vulnerable periods in the life course appear to be during adolescence (when gender differences ranged from $ds = +.41$ to $+.57$) and through the traditional college ages of 18 to 22 ($d = +.42$). This difference narrows in early adulthood (23 to 34 years old; $d = +.23$), then revives a bit in midlife onward (over 35; $d = +.36$).

A longitudinal study of seventh- to tenth-grade girls and boys captures both the process of how this change occurs and why it is more pervasive for girls than for boys (Jones, 2001). Many girls' increasing body dissatisfaction reflected the effects of more and more appearance conversations with friends, more frequent comparisons of one's body with those of peers, and gaining body mass.

At every age, women's concerns about appearance are greater than men's, and women's appearance esteem is lower than men's (Pliner at al., 1990). Looking across the life course, the importance of appearance declines with aging, and appearance self-esteem improves. Among the elderly, body dissatisfaction shifts away from weight-related issues toward concerns about facial attractiveness and body functioning (Franzoi & Koehler, 1998). Still, body concerns remain a life-long issue, with the predicted relationships among media exposure, body dissatisfaction, and disordered eating extending to middle-aged women (Slevec & Tiggemann, 2011).

Race/Ethnicity

A meta analysis (Grabe & Hyde, 2006) and a large-scale study of over 2,000 undergraduates (Frederick et al., 2007) converge on the general conclusion that racial/ethnic differences in body satisfaction among Asian American, Latina, Black, and White women are small to moderate. Although there are variations in the body ideals projected by different racial/ethnic groups, sexually objectifying experiences, self-objectification, body self-surveillance, and body shame characterize all groups of women (Harrison & Fredrickson, 2003; Kozee et al., 2007; Moradi et al., 2005). Women who base their self-worth on their weight, regardless of their race/ethnicity, are vulnerable to objectification outcomes—indicating that race/ethnicity itself is not a sufficient buffer against objectification (Sabik et al., 2010).

As we have seen, much of objectification theory is based on evaluations of bodily size and shape, ignoring other features that may be significant to women of color. For example, Taneisha Buchanan and her colleagues (2008) found support for objectification theory in regards to thinness with their sample of African American college women (also see Mitchell & Mazzeo, 2009) as well as skin-tone specific surveillance linked to skin-tone dissatisfaction.

Maya Poran (2002; also 2006) compared the body image perceptions of Black, Latina, and White college women. Black women exhibited the highest body esteem and described cultural standards of beauty as racist, in contrast to White women, who, ignoring race, regarded these standards as solely sexist. Latinas scored lowest in body esteem and emphasized consumerism in their conceptualization of body standards. Poran concluded that beauty is a *racialized* experience such that diverse women perceive the same cultural stimuli differently. Indeed, capturing the richness of diverse women's body experiences may rest in more open-ended approaches such as this one.

Sexual Orientation

Although lesbians reported feeling more fit, fewer negative body attitudes, and less internalization of cultural norms related to negative body attitudes than heterosexual women

(Bergeron & Senn, 1998), conflict between mainstream valuing of thinness and lesbians' acceptance of women's bodies is a recurring theme in interviews with young lesbian women (Beren et al., 1997). It is not surprising then that objectification theory applies to lesbians—but in a somewhat different way than for heterosexual women.

Holly Kozee and Tracy Tylka (2006) recruited sizable samples of both lesbian and heterosexual college women to complete a survey that included the central concepts of objectification theory: self-objectification, self-surveillance, body shame, interoceptive awareness, and disordered eating. Although they found in heterosexual women's data a good fit to the model, a different model emerged for their lesbian respondents. Lesbians reported low levels of disordered eating but high levels of self-surveillance (although other research may challenge the latter finding). However, consistent with the general objectification model, lesbians were just as prone to self-objectification, body shame, and deficits in interoceptive awareness as heterosexual women.

In another study, the inclusion of a measure of lesbians' internalized heterosexism ("If I could change to being heterosexual, I would") adds richness to our understanding (Haines et al., 2008). The higher individual women scored in internalized heterosexism, the higher were their self-surveillance, body shame, and depression (which was linked both to body shame and directly to their internalized heterosexism). As we just saw with age and race/ethnicity, the variables that make up objectification theory can play out differently for lesbians as well as suggest additional variables and further qualifications of the overall model. Watch for more research with these potential moderators.

CONSEQUENCES OF SELF-OBJECTIFICATION

If we continue Path 1 in Figure 10.3 beyond self-objectification, we see that the model predicts a set of psychological consequences which, in turn, predict some specific threats to women's health and well-being. There is ample research evidence in support of the linkages modeled by objectification theory and reviewed by Bonnie Moradi and Yu-Ping Huang (2008). We already noted some of this research above when we traced cultural practices not only to self-objectification and self-surveillance but also to these other outcomes. My goal, then, is this section is not to explore these established linkages, but rather to describe what these psychological consequences and health threats are—mindful that their sources are cultural practices and women's internalization of their objectifying messages.

Psychological Consequences

Both *body shame* and *body guilt* are related forms of regulating one's self, but in somewhat different and complementary ways (Calogero & Pina, 2011). Body shame captures women's sense of feeling ashamed about their body when they don't measure up to societal standards (and to their own ideal; Bessenoff & Snow, 2006). You responded to three items designed to tap body shame in the final segment of Box 10.1 earlier in this chapter (items from McKinley & Hyde, 1996). Feelings of shame cue us as to what we should *proscriptively* do in order to be more like our body ideal. In contrast, body guilt tells us how we should go about *prescriptively* "fixing" ourselves; that is, what corrective action we can take in response to tension, remorse, or regret over specific body-related behaviors. An example item tapping body guilt is: "You are watching a television show and you notice that all the actors have perfect bodies. How likely is it that you would decide to stop eating junk food from now on?" (p. 431). Both outcomes result from self-surveillance and predict restrained eating.

At least five additional studies link self-objectification by women to body shame, both directly (Greenleaf, 2005; Fingeret & Gleaves, 2004; Muehlenkamp et al., 2005; Slater & Tiggemann, 2002) and as mediated by body surveillance (Moradi et al., 2005). One of these studies also associated self-objectification by women to appearance anxiety (Slater & Tiggemann, 2002), and other research extends this finding to general anxiety and depression (Davison & McCabe, 2005). Elevated body shame (Greenleaf, 2005; Slater & Tiggemann,) and appearance anxiety (Slater & Tiggemann) were then related to disordered eating. Furthermore, body shame predicted depression that was then linked to vulnerability to engage in self-harm (Muehlenkamp et al., 2005). Additionally, internalized thinness pressures were associated with smoking for weight control (Zucker et al., 2001).

Anxiety is a generalized reaction to threat—as opposed to more concrete and specific fears. *Appearance anxiety* refers to generalized negative reactions in response to body threats. An example of appearance anxiety concerns worrying about how others might think one looks (as opposed to self-surveillance, which monitors how one *thinks* one looks). Becky Choma and her colleagues (2010) found that the more self-surveillance Canadian college women did, the more body shame and appearance anxiety they reported, which together then predicted lower overall self-esteem. Heightened appearance anxiety has also been linked with depression (Szymanski & Henning, 2007), and worrying about others' evaluations has deterred women from trying weightlifting (a good hedge against losing bone density; Salvatore & Marecek, 2010).

Flow refers to the optimal experience of being uninhibited in one's involvement in accomplishing something difficult and worthwhile. As an academic, I live for such moments of peak motivational experience when I am so immersed in what I'm doing that I don't attend to anything going on around me. Self-objectification interrupts flow, both by diverting attention toward bodily worries about appearance and by distracting one away from the loss of self-consciousness that is part of being in a state of flow (Frederickson & Roberts, 1997).

Recall the swimsuit study we talked about previously in which women expressed more body shame when wearing a one-piece bathing suit compared to other women wearing a sweater, even though both were unobserved (Fredrickson et al., 1998). A second experiment tested both women and men, with men wearing swim trunks[2] or a sweater. Women's body shame differed according to what they wore as it did in the first experiment, but men's did not. However, even more strikingly, randomly assigned women who took a math test in a private dressing room wearing a bathing suit did worse than women wearing a sweater!

This last finding speaks to the re-direction of cognitive energies when worries about how one looks are activated. It also should sound familiar given what we know about ste-

---

[2] A discerning reader may question whether swim trunks are sufficiently threatening to men's body image. In another study, wearing a scanty Speedo heightened gay and heterosexual men's self-objectification over control men, and those who felt increased body shame also reported dissatisfaction with their lower body parts (Martins et al., 2007). However, gay men reported more overall body shame than did heterosexual men, and only gay men subsequently ate less Chex mix than men in the control group. Thus the body effects of the swimsuit manipulation play out differently for women and heterosexual men and vary across subgroups of men (gay versus heterosexual).

reotype threat. Might the context of wearing a swimsuit raise appearance demands that are linked for women to stereotyping about femininity which then raises negative expectations about women's math abilities?

However, the link between objectification and flow is not confined to tasks for which negative stereotyping of women is evident. Using the gender-neutral Stroop task in which test takers name the color or the name of colors printed, in unmatched versions (the word purple printed in red), Diane Quinn and her colleagues (2006) found that women who simply thought about wearing a swimsuit took longer to perform the task than women told to think about wearing a sweater. Furthermore, the effects of disrupted flow are not confined to task performance; indeed, they can extend to depression (Szymanski & Henning, 2007).

In their original formulation of objectification theory, Fredrickson and Roberts (1997) speculated that by treating one's body as an object separate from one's self, a woman can become alienated and distant from "it." Thus, the day-to-day signals that our body may send (for example, reminding us to eat) may be actively suppressed and ignored, paving the way for dieting and restricted eating. Also, the attention one directs toward maintaining external appearances can be channeled away from internal needs—again making one out of touch with one's own body, including one's own sexuality. Limited research to date on these *interoceptive deficits* starts to clarify some these ideas.

Taryn Myers and Janis Crowther (2008) concluded that interoceptive deficits might best be captured by looking at both reduced awareness of hunger and satiety (being full) cues and lower emotional awareness. In their study, both resulted from self-objectification and predicted disordered eating, but neither alone fully explained troubled eating. In a subsequent study, Sarah Shouse and Johanna Nilsson (2011) concluded that higher levels of emotional awareness can combine with not expressing these emotions (self-silencing) to increase disordered eating and reduce positive, intuitive eating by college women. The deficit thus shifts in this study from being about emotional unawareness to being aware of emotions but unable to express them. Both studies are provocative and call for further research in this area, especially with regard to disordered eating.

Health Threats

The original formulation of objectification theory described these ultimate outcomes mainly in terms of mental health risks (see Moradi & Huang, 2008, for a review). However, the outcomes linked to objectification have since expanded to generally threaten women's holistic physical, mental, and sexual health.

The most obvious consequence of self-objectification we'd expect is pathologically disordered eating, and indeed research evidence does make a case for linking self-objectification to severe eating disorders meriting residential treatment (Calogero et al., 2005). **Anorexia** and **bulimia** are important topics that we'll address in Chapter 12. However, making this leap to such extreme cases can overshadow how pervasive threats to women's body image can be. Objectification theory helps us to stay focused on the harm that self-objectification can produce in large numbers of women's everyday lives, including restricted eating by college women (Muehlenkamp & Saris-Baglama, 2002) as well as disordered eating attitudes ("I think about bingeing"; Morrison & Sheahan, 2009) and behaviors (extensive dieting) (Harrell et al., 2006).

In Figure 10.3, I included "physical wellness" in this category of outcomes to capture studies that look at body-relevant behaviors and attitudes beyond those tied directly to eating. For example, women smokers scored higher in self-objectification and disordered eating than nonsmokers (Harrell et al., 2006), and body shame has been implicated in weight control motives for smoking (Fiissel & Lafreniere, 2006). In addition, body image variables are all linked to British college women's (Calogero et al., 2010) and Australian middle-aged women's (Slevec & Tiggemann, 2010) attitudes toward having cosmetic surgery, which we'll see in the next chapter can carry health risks.

The most thoroughly studied mental health risk associated with high levels of self-objectification is depression. For example, Shelly Grabe and her colleagues (2007) found that adolescent girls scored higher than boys on self-objectification, body shame, rumination (continually thinking about a problem), and depression. In support of the theory, they showed that among adolescent girls, self-objectification predicted both mediators of body shame and rumination, which, in turn, each lead to depression. Furthermore, testing these adolescents at age 11 and again at age 13, they demonstrated that the gender difference in self-objectification appeared before gender differences in rumination and depression, suggesting that self-objectification was indeed a root cause in the chain between rumination and depression.

Moreover, self-objectification appears to lead to additional mental health risks that cut to the very core of women's well-being. Testing multiple mediated paths, Andrea Mercurio and Laura Landry (2008) concluded that among college women, self-objectification created body shame, which in turn lowered self-esteem, which in turn reduced overall life satisfaction.

Finally, when we consider sexual functioning as an outcome of objectifying processes, it is important to understand that we aren't necessarily talking about pathological levels of dysfunction. Rather, self-objectification has been linked to compromised sexual self-esteem, that, along with body shame leads to disordered eating (Calogero & Thompson, 2009). Additionally, common sexual functioning itself can be affected. For example, Marika Tiggemann and Elyse Williams (2012) found that appearance anxiety negatively affected Australian college women's normal sexual functioning, including their reported desire, arousal, orgasm, and satisfaction. In another study, heterosexual college women's body dissatisfaction was related to a set of sexual functioning variables, including elevated sexual anxiety, sexual un-assertiveness, lower sexual esteem, and more sexual problems (Weaver & Byers, 2006).

SELF-OBJECTIFICATION AS A MODERATOR

Path 2 in Figure 10.3 diagrams self-objectification as a moderator affecting the link between cultural practices with psychological consequences and their subsequent health outcomes. The emerging research I want to capture with this path shows that women who score chronically high in self-objectification (as a trait) are affected more powerfully by exposure to cultural practices (the gaze, comments, and media) than less self-objectifying women. This point should make some intuitive sense—we all realize that not all women are similarly affected by these social contextual factors. However, it is important to realize that few, if any, women are immune. As we saw earlier, randomly assigned groups of women internalize objectification beyond what control groups do—arguing that these cultural practices are powerful elements of our social context.

Let me give a few examples here for each of the cultural practices we reviewed, starting with the gaze. The more strongly college women endorsed thinness ideals (alone or in combination with being overweight), the more comparison to peers and evaluation by another affected their appearance anxiety (Darlow & Lobel, 2010).

Turning to comments, not surprisingly criticisms hit high objectifiers harder, increasing their self-surveillance and body dissatisfaction (Calogero et al., 2009). The pattern with compliments though gets more complex. Chronically self-objectifying women were more strongly affected by a compliment, which increased both their state objectification and body shame (Tiggemann & Boundy, 2008). Even more complicated, Rachel Calogero and her colleagues (2009) considered women's reactions to compliments as well as their levels of chronic self-objectification. Even when high objectifiers felt good about a compliment, it aroused body dissatisfaction in them. For generally low objectifiers, feeling good about a compliment produced *more* body dissatisfaction than reacting negatively to a compliment. Further specifying the impact of **complimentary weightism**, even compliments that are perceived as complimentary by their recipient have a downside.

As for the media, the more discrepant women's actual and ideal body images were, the more likely they were to engage in body comparisons after exposure to thin-ideal advertisements which then led to increased body dissatisfaction, negative mood, lower self-esteem, and depression (Bessenoff, 2006). In another study, exposure to sexually objectifying images or conversations more strongly affected highly objectifying college women (Henderson-King et al., 2001). Research with 6 to 12-year-olds who were shown images of objectified women and men showed that exposure alone was not sufficient to lower body esteem. Rather, girls who actively rejected the pictures were unaffected; only girls who weren't sure how to react were affected negatively (Murnen et al., 2003).

In another study, how much exposure women aged 18 to 49 years old had to body shape images in magazines they routinely read was coded by the researchers (Cusumano & Thompson, 1997). Simply seeing these pictures did not predict body image disturbance, eating dysfunction, or overall self-esteem. What did significantly predict these outcomes was, not surprisingly, self-objectification. In other words, only women who showed evidence of internalization were negatively influenced by exposure to these objectifying images. Similarly, the impact of viewing ads featuring idealized images was most powerful for young women with high self-objectification scores (Monro & Huon, 2005; also see Botta, 2003).

RESISTING SELF-OBJECTIFICATION

Overall, I know of no research to suggest that self-objectification works *for* women. Rather, resisting self-objectification seems like a much more defensible path. Objectification theory and research begins to offer some clues about how women can avoid falling into a self-objectifying trap. Furthermore, as more and more media images emphasize men's muscularity and body size, some men too are showing signs of objectification that may best be thwarted.

We have seen that negative consequences follow from both internalized self-objectification and cultural practices that sexualize people. These two components point to sources both internal and external to the person, respectively. This naturally leads to solutions that are both internally (individually) and externally (contextually) focused.

Individual Resistance

We all need to examine our own attitudes about our bodies and those of others (Maine, 2000). Both avoidance coping ("I eat something to help me deal with the situation") and appearance fixing ("I spend extra time trying to fix what I don't like about my looks") don't work; rather, they link self-objectification and body shame to negative outcomes for women (Choma et al., 2009). We need to watch our attitudes about food and eaters; for example, both women and men who ate a low-calorie "feminine" diet were regarded more favorably by others (Mooney & Lorenz, 1997). Adopting a model of *intuitive eating* (that is, eating in response to physiological hunger and satiety cues coupled with little preoccupation with food) leads to better body acceptance and less self-objectification by women (Augustus-Horvath & Tylka, 2011).

When we compliment others for losing weight and looking good, we are reinforcing some dangerous cultural norms, and as we saw with the research on **complimentary weightism**, compliments turn out to be not that complimentary. We need to buffer our daughters from harmful cultural standards of thinness (Frank, 1999), as well as avoid (especially maternal; Rodgers et al., 2009) comments about weight and shape (Wertheim et al., 1999). Listen to women's concerns; when women were exposed to minimizing messages that trivialized their body image concerns, they became more vulnerable to an appearance threat (Bosson et al., 2008).

We need to exercise for health and fitness, not weight control (Strelan et al., 2003; Tiggemann & Williamson, 2000). Yoga practice seems to derail the unresponsiveness to bodily sensations that we saw can result from self-objectification (Daubenmier, 2005). Participation in any sport is not a simple panacea. Generally, both female and male athletes have more positive body images (Greenleaf et al., 2009; Hausenblas & Downs, 2001), and physical activity is consistently related to greater **instrumentality** and feeling in control (**agency**), both of which predict favorable self-esteem and fewer symptoms of psychological distress (Parsons & Betz, 2001). However, women's participation in both physical activities and sports, especially those that emphasize appearance, was associated with greater body shame. This may be because body shame has to do with acceptance of traditional images of feminine bodies that may be challenged when active women develop their musculature.

Watch what you watch. Black-oriented television was unrelated to body image for both Black and White women (Schooler et al., 2004); in contrast, viewing mainstream television was related to poor body image among White, but not Black, women. Comparing ourselves to others is an automatic process that takes active, conscious processing to avoid (Want, 2009). For example, I know that I feel a lot better about my own body when I avoid reading fashion magazines.

Developing one's feminist thinking (or more specifically, feelings of empowering) (Peterson et al., 2008), may help to some degree. A meta analysis summarizing 26 studies found a small relationship between women's feminist identity and body attitudes ($d = +.28$) that was strongest among older women (Murnen & Smolak, 2009). Additionally, lower endorsement of **benevolent sexism** was related to higher perceived sexual attractiveness

(Franzoi, 2001). Documented feminist strategies for resisting body dissatisfaction include celebrating bodily diversity and maintaining critical awareness about cultural messages and the consequences these can have (Rubin et al., 2004). However, knowing that cultural messages are demeaning and objectifying doesn't necessarily make women immune to their impact. In fact, some feminists report feeling guilty about "buying into" pervasive cultural ideals. This ambivalence by feminists points to the fact that resistance is not an endpoint to be achieved, but rather entails an ongoing and active process of seeking new and better ways to live comfortably within one's complete self, including one's body. It also points to how appearance issues are part of systems of oppression that exist well beyond any single individual.

Contexts That Promote Resistance

To resist this broader system of appearance, we need to explore structural changes. The most obvious target is the media. A wider diversity of images could derail much of what we reviewed earlier about the sexism and ageism of the media. One study of the 1999 to 2000 prime-time television season revealed that shows involving women writers included fewer appearance insults, but focused more on appearance comments (Lauren & Dozier, 2002). For better and for worse, writers make a difference. Maybe media creators will get the message from research showing that readers did not like newspaper articles about athletes, both female and male, that focused on attractiveness (Knight & Giuliano, 2001). I think more research along these lines might help compel those who control media images to respond more proactively to calls for more diverse and realistic body images.

Media itself isn't necessarily the culprit; rather, media itself can be used to raise awareness about the realism of typical media images and real women's dissimilarity from these popular images (Irving & Berel, 2001). Various interventions that encourage media literacy can derail otherwise negative media effects (Strahan et al., 2008). For example, Heidi Posavac and her colleagues (2001) exposed women to information either about the artificiality of beauty created by make-up and air brushing or about genetic predispositions that make most women constitutionally ineligible to ever meet the exacting standards for media models. Both educational approaches were effective at preventing women, especially women likely to internalize objectification (Yamamiya et al., 2005), from expressing body dissatisfaction after exposure to thin-and-beautiful media images.

Think more expansively about the media models you see. Ann-Marie Lew and her colleagues (2007) asked college women to write essays about thin-model images they just perused. The experimental group was instructed to consider aspects of themselves that they valued but didn't see in the models, as well as things they might be better at than the models. Compared to control women (who were simply reminded that advertisers use attractive models to sell products and whose essays focused on common features across models), the experimental women showed positive shifts in their body and weight satisfaction, appearance anxiety, and desire to lose weight.

Renee Engeln-Maddox and Steven Miller (2008) developed a measure, the Critical Processing of Beauty Images Scale, that may help us be more critical consumers of idealized media images. The scale focuses our attention in three areas: Fake ("That kind of perfection isn't real"), Questioning/Accusing ("Images like that make women feel like they have to look perfect"), and Too Thin ("She looks malnourished").

Interestingly, being in a trusting intimate relationship enhanced women's self-confidence and body esteem (Ambwani & Strauss, 2007), and women primed to think about relationships exhibited less self-objectification when they were in a relationship than when they were single (Sanchez & Broccoli, 2008). Among a racially diverse sample of college women and men, those who felt agentic and authentic in their relationships also felt more positively about their body (Gillen & Lefkowitz, 2006). On the flip side, the higher women scored in relationship contingency (feeling that their self-worth was tied up in having a relationship), the higher was their body shame and, in turn, their symptoms of disordered eating (Sanchez & Kwang, 2007). It appears that having secure and positive relationships establishes a context in which women (and men) can feel good about their body.

Women and girls themselves can band together effectively to share and change their experiences of body dissatisfaction (Piran, 2001). In fact, this linking of the personal to broader political issues is effective for encouraging fat acceptance (McKinley, 2004) as well as dealing with physical impairments (Olkin, 1999).

Body Politics and Power

Throughout this book, we have talked about power, privilege, and oppression. There's power in bodies (Johnson & Lennon, 1999). Privileges do accrue to those who are deemed attractive. We saw the **halo effect** of perceived beauty, and social psychologists have documented advantages of attractiveness, from being liked to being more effective in changing others' attitudes (Chaiken, 1979). Thus, there's both a carrot (the halo effect) and a stick (discrimination) to appearance that makes it difficult not to monitor and try to control our own looks (Rubin et al., 2004).

Physical discrimination becomes clearest when we observe the consequences of deviating from stereotyped perceptions of women's bodies, including social pressures to be thin and able-bodied. Stigmatization of obesity is evidenced as early as preschool (Cramer & Steinwert, 1998) and carries with it strict proscriptions about women's eating behaviors. Women who eat smaller meals are considered more physically desirable (Bock & Kanarek, 1995), interpersonally attractive (Mooney & Lorenz, 1997), and socially appealing (Basow & Kobrynowicz, 1993). Fully 14% of American college women admit to being embarrassed when they bought a chocolate bar (Rozin et al., 2003). Weight may even play

Box 10.6

Both photos are of me, but which makes me look more powerful? Dress is an important part of conveying power and status. Think of how you dress for an important job interview compared to just coming to class every day. Indeed, researchers frequently use dress, defined as modifications and supplements to the body, to convey information about

power (see Johnson & Lennon, 1999). Often one function of uniforms (think about the military and police) is to lend power to the wearer. Look again at my pictures. Are there limits to how far dress can take me toward conveying power? Why is that?

into employment. Actors of normal weight who were dressed in theatrical prostheses to appear overweight were videotaped during a mock employment interview; hiring preferences were biased against the "job applicants" when they appeared overweight (Pingitore et al, 1994). As we saw earlier, thinness even predicted higher earnings for women (Judge & Cable, 2011).

The halo effect we saw for attractiveness reverses for obese women (Breserman et al., 1999). Overweight women were described as lazy, stupid, and unfriendly, and they were perceived as "slow moving" and thus "slow thinking." Much of this negativity comes from beliefs that obese people lack discipline, flaunting the control beliefs that we have seen are part of body image. Being out of control furthermore is associated with powerlessness, coming full circle to link obesity with lack of power. Indeed the corollary of this relationship bears it out: feeling powerful and feeling good about one's self are closely connected (Rudd & Lennon, 1999).

Fat stigmatization is so strong that guilt by simple association exits. Michelle Hebl and Laura Mannix (2003) found that male job applicants were regarded less favorably simply by being pictured sitting next to a heavy (as compared to an average-weight) woman. In a follow-up study, participants were induced to rate an apparent participant who was actually part of the experiment (a **confederate**). Before completing these ratings, they observed the male confederate either with a heavy or average woman with whom it was clear he was either intimately involved or a stranger. The girlfriend/stranger—average (size 8) or heavy (wearing an obesity prosthesis to look like a size 22) woman—was the same woman across all participants. The *man* was evaluated less favorably when he was seen with the heavy woman, even when they were strangers, and even when the female and male raters expressed unbiased attitudes about obesity.

Theorists argue that a "myth of bodily perfection" dominates American culture and creates misperceptions of those who deviate from this standard by virtue of physical impairments (Stone, 1995). Stereotyping of people who are physically challenged includes victimization, dependence, helplessness, and social isolation—stereotyping that is exaggerated for women (Hanna & Rogovsky, 1991). As we'll see in the next chapter, a feminist model of (dis)ability is beginning to emerge (Olkin, 1999).

We have seen that surveillance and control beliefs underlie self-objectification and the negative consequences that continue from there. Bodies can be sources of both privilege and oppression, leading to body shame and guilt, anxiety, loss of flow, and dissociation from internal and emotional states, as well as threats to our physical, mental, and sexual health. Understanding the power of our bodies may be a big first step toward coming to terms with this very visible part of ourselves.

CHAPTER SUMMARY

Fundamental aspects of our bodies involve appearance, sexuality, and health. We have seen in this chapter that it takes active resistance to think about women's bodies, both women's own and others', as parts of people's subjective being rather than as distant, detached objects. Bodies need not be regarded this way; indeed, many men commonly think of their bodies as instruments for action (**agency**). Researchers have consistently documented a fundamental gender difference in body consciousness wherein women report more body dissatisfaction than men, engage in more body surveillance, and endorse stronger beliefs about control over body appearance.

Objectification theory offers the concept of self-objectification as a way to bring these ideas together. Self-objectification refers to the degree to which an individual internalizes cultural messages that view bodies as objects. Although women as a group self-objectify themselves more than men (**intergroup differences**), there are wide variations among individuals and subgroups of both women and men (**intragroup differences**). Although objectifying messages originate in our culture—indirectly through the media and directly through the sexualized gaze and comments—exposure alone doesn't explain internalized self-objectification. Whereas some groups, such as young, White, heterosexual, middle class and affluent women, appear most vulnerable to the negative consequences of self-objectification, individuals vary in how much they internalize the lessons conveyed through cultural practices.

For individuals with high levels of self-objectification, many of whom are women, the consequences of repeated and pervasive exposure to idealized images of thinness and bodily perfection can lead to negative consequences, including body shame, body guilt, and appearance anxiety, disrupted peak motivational experiences (flow), and detachment from bodily states and emotions. The evidence is ample and clear that media images, especially of thin and perfect women (and increasingly of muscular men), are largely unrealistic and unattainable. Furthermore, it is clear that these sources produce pressures even active resistors can identify. Surely the research argues that a de-emphasis on thinness and perfection in both mass culture and in our everyday interactions would help derail objectification pathways.

Yet objectification theory and research make it clear that resistance is *not* futile. Both individuals and contexts can promote health over appearance, leading active resistors down a path toward bodily empowerment. In the next chapter, we'll extend our call for understanding the power of our bodies by exploring empowerment in the determination of our own sexuality, health, and physical well-being.

SUGGESTED READINGS

Fredrickson, B. L., & Roberts, T. (1997). Objectification theory: Toward understanding women's lived experiences and mental health risks. *Psychology of Women Quarterly, 21,* 173–206.
Fredrickson, B. L., Hendler, L. M., Nilsen, S., O'Barr, J. F., & Roberts, T.-A. (2011). Bringing back the body: A retrospective on the development of objectification theory. *Psychology of Women Quarterly, 35,* 689–696.

The original article summarizes the thinking that lead Barbara Fredrickson and Tomi-Ann Roberts to propose objectification theory, as well as fully lays out the theory as a good supplement to this chapter. The subsequent retrospective look at the theory's development provides a fascinating behind-the-curtain peek at theory development and the importance of bringing together and listening to diverse voices.

McKinley, N. M. (2004). Resisting body dissatisfaction: Fat women who endorse fat acceptance. *Body Image, 1,* 213–219.

Rather than give in to the process of body objectification, Nita McKinley seeks out women who resist falling into this cultural trap.

Lyons, P. (2009). Prescription for harm: Diet industry influence, public health policy, and the "obesity epidemic." In E. Rothblum & S. Solovay (Eds.), *The fat studies reader* (pp. 75–87). New York: New York University Press.

Many chapters in this path-breaking reader are worth reading, but this one by Pat Lyons struck me as especially thought-provoking because she offers an alternative interpretation of the "obesity epidemic" that undermines some of the health justifications for fat bias.

Ahern, A. L., Bennett, K. M., Kelly, M., & Hetherington, M. M. (2011). A qualitative exploration of young women's attitudes toward the thin ideal. *Journal of Health Psychology, 16*, 70–79.

Amy Ahern and her colleagues describe a series of focus groups with 41 women, 16 to 26 years old, about how they think about the thin ideal, revealing diverse and multifaceted perspectives.

New Moon Magazine
This bimonthly, advertising-free magazine is edited by and for girls aged 8 to 14. It delivers on its pledge to be "the magazine for every girl who wants her voice heard and her dreams taken seriously." *http://www.newmoon.org*

Johnson, K. P., & Lennon, S. J. (Eds.) (1999). *Appearance and power.* New York: Berg.

This edited book offers an array of chapters that converge on the social constructionist theme of how we dress to modify our appearance, and in doing so shape how much power we feel and actually do have. The implications of dress extend to rape survivors, images of police, and power in the workplace, the popular press, and television. They also connect women's appearance management with social power and obesity with powerlessness.

Chapter 11

Women's Physical Health and Well-Being
Understudied, Mythologized, but Changing

Health Psychology
   Gender as a Marker
   Mortality and Morbidity
Women's Sexuality
   "Machines without Motors"?
   Attitudes and Behaviors: A Double Standard?
   Consequences of the Remaining Double Standard
   Women's Sexual Well-Being
Reproductive Health
   The Case of Breast Cancer
   Menstruation
   Childbirth
   Miscarriage
   Abortion
   Section Conclusion
Chronic Diseases
   Cardiovascular Diseases
   HIV/AIDS
Health Care Practice
   Surgeries
   Health Care Policy
Chapter Summary

The line between physical and mental health has become increasingly blurred as more and more evidence accumulates linking the two. The purpose of this chapter is to take a holistic look at women's physical health and well-being from the perspective of health psychologists who have studied women's sexuality and reproductive health, chronic diseases, and the impact of health care practice and policy on women. We turn out attention here from women's bodies as objects of appearance (Chapter 10) to women's bodies as agents of physical health and subjective well-being. Before you read any farther, please complete the checklist in Box 11.1. We'll refer back to your answers later in this chapter.

HEALTH PSYCHOLOGY

More and more evidence suggests that conditions typically believed to be largely medical—such as heart disease, cancer, AIDS, and menstruation—are social as well as biological (Travis, 1988a). For example, consider the debate about when to limit medical intervention; that is, when to pull the proverbial "plug" on medical technology. Few people focus exclusively on biological signs of being alive without also considering the "quality of life" a patient is likely to face. At a less dramatic level, whenever dietary and lifestyle changes are indicated for treatment or prevention, the prescription calls for behavioral changes by individuals. Evidence is accumulating that psychological well-being, such as being optimistic, predicts health (Jones et al., 2004). Both the definition of health itself and the activities indicated for health maintenance or recovery benefit from the knowledge base amassed by health psychologists. A strong example of such a holistic approach to health is

---

Box 11.1
Stress Inventory

Put a check next to each of the following signs of stress that you have experienced in the past 4 to 5 weeks.

Weight gain _____	Insomnia _____
Crying _____	Lowered performance _____
Muscle stiffness _____	Forgetfulness _____
Confusion _____	Taking naps _____
Headache _____	Feeling out of control _____
Loneliness _____	Feelings of suffocation _____
Orderliness _____	Restlessness _____
Irritability _____	Dizziness, faintness _____
Accidents _____	Decreased efficiency _____
High spirits _____	Increased sexual desire _____
Vibrant activity _____	Revolutionary zeal _____
Intense concentration _____	Feelings of affection _____
Self-confidence _____	Sense of euphoria _____
Creativity _____	Feelings of power _____

the Women's Health Initiative (WHI), a 15-year project sponsored by the National Institutes of Health targeting 164,500 postmenopausal women (Matthews et al., 1997).[1]

Gender as a Marker

Why do we need a special focus on women's health (Chrisler, 2001)? Some health issues disproportionately affect women as compared to men (e.g., osteoporosis and eating disorders) as well as different segments of the population of women (e.g., breast cancer and lupus). Some illnesses (e.g., coronary heart disease and AIDS) function differently for women and men. Other health concerns are unique to women (e.g., hysterectomy and menstruation). Although interest in women's reproductive health is important, all too often women's health is framed almost exclusively by a myopic focus on these unique capacities of women (Stanton, 1995). Being a healthy woman involves a lot more than being reproductively fit, and as we saw in Chapter 5, life doesn't end when reproductive capacities cease.

The **androcentric** assumption that men's bodies are normative still appears in the field; for example, gender bias in how information is presented in medical textbooks persists (Dijkstra et al., 2008). Additionally, women were routinely excluded from clinical trials (the gold standard of medical research) into the 1990s because men are at greater risk of dying younger, because women's variable hormonal levels may confound findings, and because of concerns about pregnancy during data collection. Ironically, these same differences may be some of the reasons why findings from men might not readily generalize to women (see Hamilton, 1996, for an overview).

However, there have though been praiseworthy improvements into the 21st century; for example, the overall participation by women and men in clinical trials for new drugs approved by the USA's Food and Drug Administration equalized (Yang et al., 2009), and the number of studies looking separately at data from women and men has risen across 1990 to 2005 (Aulakh & Anand, 2007). Still, there is room for continued improvements—specifically targeting better representation of women in early phase trials and in critical areas (such as the development of heart drugs; Yang et al., 2009), more and better done gender-segregated analyses (Aulakh & Anand, 2007), and within-gender analyses focused on race and ethnicity (Mak et al., 2007).

Mortality and Morbidity

There's an intriguing paradox about women's health: women generally live longer than men (lower **mortality**) but are sicker (higher **morbidity**). On one end of the life course, about 125 male embryos are conceived for every 100 female embryos, and 27% more boys than girls die during their first year of life (Strickland, 1988). On the other end of the spectrum, for those who reach 100 years old, only one man is alive for every five women (Rodin & Ickovics, 1990). Overall, an American baby born in 2007 is expected to live until *she's* 80.4 years old (76.8 for Black women: 80.8 for White women) or *he's* 75.4 years old

---

[1]For more information about the Women's Health Initiative visit *http://www.nhlbi.nih.gov/whi/* (Retrieved September 2011).

(70.0 for Black men; 75.9 for White men) (CDC, 2011a).[2] The life expectancy advantage for women has shrunk from 7 years in 1990 to 5 years in 2007.

Life expectancy and infant mortality are often used to gauge the overall health of a population, and there has been a generally steady drop in infant mortality in the United States (from 26 infant deaths per 1,000 live births in 1960 to 6.75 in 2007; CDC, 2011a). However, wide disparities in infant mortality remain across racial and ethnic groups: highest among non-Hispanic Black (13.31), Indigenous Native American (9.22), and Puerto Rican (7.71) mothers. Compared to 58 countries globally, the United States ranks 42nd in health and well-being; Canada, 14th (Lopez-Claros & Zahidi, 2005).

Table 11.2 compares mortality trends for American women and men on diseases that rank among women's top ten killers, as well as a handful of select other causes of death that will come up later in our discussions (CDC, 2011a). The death rate for the total population has declined 42% since 1950, driven largely by fewer deaths from heart disease, stroke, and accidents (although deaths from accidents have been rising since 1992). For both women and men, note that heart disease and cancers top the list.

TABLE 11.2
Top Causes of Americans' Deaths in 2007 from the
U.S. Centers for Disease Control and Prevention (CDC, 2011)

Multiply numbers by 1000; ranked for women	*Women*	*Men*
Overall	**1,219.7**	**1,203.9**
1. Heart diseases	306.2	309.8
2. Cancers (malignant neoplasms)	270.0	292.9
(Breast / Prostate)	(40.6)	(29.1)
3. Cerebrovascular (brain)diseases	81.8	54.1
4. Chronic lower respiratory (breathing) diseases	66.7	61.2
5. Alzheimer's disease	52.8	21.8
6. Unintentional injuries (accidents)	43.9	79.8
(Motor vehicle-related injuries)	(8.2)	(20.9)
7. Diabetes mellitus	35.9	35.5
8. Influenza and pneumonia	28.6	24.1
9. Nephritis, etc. (Kidney diseases)	23.8	22.6
10. Septicemia (Infections)	19.0	15.8
Others of Special Interest:		
Suicide	4.7	18.4
Homicide	2.5	9.6
HIV	2.1	5.4
Black	11.3	24.5
Latina/o	1.8	6.3
White	0.7	3.1

[2]The at-birth life expectancy for women in the United States in 2007 (80.4) is lower than in 22 of 28 other developed countries sampled by the CDC, with Japanese women topping the list at 86.0 years (CDC, 2011a). Canada, at 82.6 for women, is topped by 13 other countries.

The second half of our medical paradox has to do with being sicker (**morbidity**). Women are more likely to report illness and to seek medical attention through telephone calls and office visits than are men, although hospitalization rates are similar when childbirth is excluded (Leventhal, 1994; Woods, 1995). In a general health survey, 36% of women and 42% of men rated their health as excellent (Woods, 1995). Does this mean that women are more biologically predisposed to illness than men? Not necessarily; there are a host of other possibilities to explain this **intergroup difference**, including differential socialization about help-seeking and admission of weakness, gender stereotyping that fits better with being sick for women than for men, and the stresses of women's roles.

The flip side of this disparity between the health of women and men has to do with behaviors, attitudes, and expectations for men. Men are less likely to seek health care for illness, injuries, and prevention and to practice everyday health-protective behaviors from wearing sunscreen to seatbelts (reviewed in Courtenay, 2000, and Good & Sherrod, 2001). Men also are bigger risk-takers than women (Byrnes et al., 1999), likely contributing to men's much higher mortality from unintentional injuries. Physicians average less time with male patients and are less likely to issue health-risk warnings to men. Indeed, men's health knowledge is worse than women's (Beier & Ackerman, 2003). Images of masculinity involving independence, invulnerability, and powerfulness mediate against help-seeking, especially in areas directly tied to manhood (e.g., prostate exams). Thus, both images of femininity and masculinity serve to widen the health gap between women and men.

The femininization of health care does not extend to all women. For example, stereotyping of African American women as strong and long-suffering, combined with a common distrust of the medical system, works against their use of the medical system and encourages delays in seeking medical treatment (Collins, 1996). Latinas are less likely than other women to seek out regular pelvic and breast exams (Ramirez de Arellano, 1996), and lesbians may restrict medical contact to maintain privacy and to avoid anticipated homophobia. Even when treatment is sought by women, the tendency to regard a woman's complaints of physical maladies as "all in her mind," when there is little or no evidence to justify a psychological over a medical diagnosis (referred to as **psychologization**), may interfere with effective treatment of women by the medical system (Grace, 2001).

Consistent with what we have seen in previous chapters, Elaine Leventhal (1994) proposed that *gender be considered a marker for further analysis of health patterns rather than a cause in and of itself.* In this chapter, we take Leventhal's suggestion and think of gender as a *lens* through which we can view women's health. The answers won't rest in biology alone, but rather in how being female interacts with other aspects of women's lives. As we have seen in earlier chapters, contextual factors play a significant role in affecting women's attitudes and behaviors. With this in mind, we'll explore what we know about the psychology of women's sexuality and then turn to psychologists' roles in reproductive health, chronic diseases, and health care practice and policy.

WOMEN'S SEXUALITY

To put sexuality in context, a large-scale survey of American's sexual behavior identified 17.7 years as the average age of first intercourse, with first vaginal intercourse being premarital for 82.9% of the sample (Else-Quest et al., 2005). As for the frequency of sexual intercourse reported by women, as we might expect, there are large variations across ages, study designs, and countries (Schneidewind-Skibbe, et al., 2008). Higher rates are reported by women from the United States and Europe, with declining rates after age 50. Interestingly, changes across age were not found in African and South American studies, highlighting the role of culture in affecting sexual norms. But getting accurate data is difficult. In a study with an American sample, retrospective reports collected at the end of the study *under*-reported participants' sexual activities relative to the daily dairies they kept during the preceding 3 months (McAuliffe et al., 2007).

We might consider it reasonable to think about sexual behaviors as natural acts that are normal and instinctive, should be uninhibited, and can be expressed in diverse ways across humans and animals. Leonore Tiefer (1994) argues that such thinking can reduce sexuality to **biological essentialism**—a biological imperative that *drives* people to act. By overemphasizing the biological, this view can discount how sexual attitudes and behaviors are shaped within a **social context**. When that social context changes over time, attitudes and behaviors also change—an evolution that sexologists have charted across historical periods. Furthermore, viewing sexuality as a natural drive absolves us of working at being sexual—of teaching it to our children and of making it work as only one aspect of our more-than-biological relationships. Sexuality, like women's health in general, is more than biology; it is filled with social meanings and feelings.

"Machines without Motors"?

William Masters and Virginia Johnson (1966) conducted pathbreaking and detailed observations of the stages of sexual responsiveness experienced by heterosexual women and men during intercourse. Despite their attempts to provide a gender-neutral model of sexuality, critics have pointed to fundamental assumptions that suggest instead a model of male dominance and female passivity (Tiefer, 2000; White et al., 2000). Although Masters and Johnson do describe detailed physiological reactions to sexual stimulation, they tell us little about the totality of sexuality by ignoring what the person is thinking and feeling (like "machines without motors"). Sexuality is implicitly, exclusively, and narrowly defined by heterosexual genital contact (Christina, 1997; Rothblum, 1994).[3] Furthermore, all women and all men are lumped together, ignoring their individual differences (Townsend, 2002), gender stereotyping about female and male sexuality, and stereotyping for different subgroups of women. For example, consider the diverse expectations we have about Asian women as presumably passive, Indigenous Native American women as property, mothers as asexual, Jewish women as uninterested, and so on (Reid & Bing, 2000).

This tendency to medicalize women's sexuality to the exclusion of psychological and social components spills over into treatment for women's sexual problems. The *Diagnostic Statistical Manual of the American Psychiatric Association* (DSM–IV, 1994) identifies four categories of female and male sexual "dysfunction": sexual desire disorders, sexual arousal disorders, orgasmic disorders, and sexual pain disorders. Each reflects a disturbance in the assumed universal sexual response cycle described by Masters and Johnson. A working group of noteworthy sexologists charge that such a mechanical view of women's sexuality fails to acknowledge differences between women's and men's views of sexuality

---

[3]Even female-female sexuality can be co-opted into male-defined models of sexuality by playing to male voyeuristic fantasies (Diamond, 2005).

and sociopolitical conditions, to distinguish psychological "desire" (for intimacy, to please one's partner, etc.) from physiological "arousal," and to recognize differences among individual women's sexual needs and satisfactions (New View, 2011). The result is the pharmaceutical search for the female version of Viagra (a widely publicized drug to treat male erection problems) as a simple (and likely profitable) way to treat women's problems. Reducing remedies for women's (and men's) problems to a pill fails to acknowledge the full meaning of sexuality in women's and men's lives.

A complete picture asks what women and men want from sexuality. Folk wisdom holds that men seek pure pleasure from sexuality, in contrast to women who seek emotional connection (Hatfield et al., 1988), but this really is too simple an overgeneralization. A well-done survey of 445 women and 477 men in San Francisco did find that women attached less importance to pure pleasure, conquest, and relief of tension than did men (Leigh, 1989). In contrast to men, who ranked pleasure first, women cited emotional closeness as their top reason for engaging in sexual behaviors, regardless of their sexual orientation. Digging deeper into the data, men ranked attachment as a close second to pleasure and even considered pleasing their partner more important than did women. Indeed, other research concludes that how one thinks about one's own sexuality (our sexual self-**schema**) (Andersen et al., 1999) as well as sexuality related terms (Noland et al., 2004) are remarkably similar for women and men.

Attitudes and Behaviors: A Double Standard?

The traditional **double standard** of heterosexual sexuality suggests that sexuality is more socially acceptable for men than for women. Indeed, young women report receiving more restrictive messages from their parents about sexuality than do young men (Morgan et al., 2010). This logic would further predict that men would be more sexually experienced than women, men would hold more permissive attitudes about sexuality than women, and women would be more openly sexualized by men than men by women. Although a meta analysis of 30 sexual behaviors and attitudes found mainly similarities between women and men, there was some support for these predictions (Petersen & Hyde, 2010). Men reported slightly more sexual experience than women, as well as moderately more pornography use, masturbation, and casual sex. Men generally held slightly more permissive attitudes than women overall, with a medium difference in men's more accepting attitudes about casual sexuality. Looking across the 1960s to 1980s, gender differences in sexual attitudes and behaviors narrowed (Oliver & Hyde, 1993) and then stabilized across the 1990s and into the 21st century (Petersen & Hyde, 2010).

Notice that the gender differences identified by this meta analysis largely have to do with casual sex encounters—exactly the focus of the double standard. Indeed, when women's and men's beliefs about sexuality are examined within the context of intimate relationships, they are more mutual and more alike than different (Seal et al., 2008; Tiegs et al., 2007). When it comes to casual sex, though, a long-standing finding that garnered lots of public attention came from an experiment in which women and men were propositioned by an other-sex **confederate**; some men took her up on her offer, but all women declined his (Clark & Hatfield, 1989). More recently, Terri Conley (2011) conducted a series of four studies to explore this finding more fully. She found that both women and men agreed that the woman proposer was a better prospect than the man, and that the gap in interest closed when the proposer was made more appealing (a famous person, sexually skilled). Thus Conley concluded that decision making about casual sex has less to do with the gender of the decider and more to do with the attractiveness of the opportunity (also see Epstein et al., 2007).

As for the greater sexualization of women by men (as opposed to of men by women), there is continuing evidence that men over-sexualize unacquainted women (Levesque et al., 2006) and even show stronger associations between women and sexuality on an **Implicit Associations Test** (Lindgren et al., 2007). As we might expect, there are individual differences in men's sexualization of women. College men most likely to sexualize women exhibit more risk factors (hostile masculinity, desire for impersonal sex, and drinking on dates and in sexual situations; Jacques-Tiura et al., 2007) and are generally more interested in casual sex (the same goes for women; Lenton et al., 2007). Furthermore, the media (*Cosmopolitan* magazine, television dating programs) promote this sociocultural message about men's hyper-sexuality (Farvid & Braun, 2006; Zurbriggen & Morgan, 2006). Not so surprising to us, power comes into play here. When college women and men had power over another student, they expected and perceived greater sexual interest from their subordinate (Kunstman & Maner, 2011).

Consistent with patterns we have seen with other stereotyping, evidence of a double standard of sexuality is not always clear-cut (Fugre et al., 2008); instead, its existence appears in more subtle forms. For example, students reading others' "journals" recalled more information consistent with the double standard than countering it (Marks & Fraley, 2006); alcohol consumption by women (but not by men) was linked with sexual disinhibition (Young et al., 2007). Intoxication is more strongly linked with sexual behaviors among sexual minority than other youth (Herrick et al., 2011).

Margaret Gentry (1998) asked undergraduates to evaluate a hypothetical woman or man described as either monogamous or engaged in multiple heterosexual relationships and enacting low, moderate, or high levels of sexual activity. On direct, obvious measures, women targets were treated similarly to men, such that all promiscuous and highly active targets were downgraded (also see Marks & Fraley, 2005). Opposing the double standard, an aura of being liberal and assertive surrounded the more active woman target, who also was most appealing to men. In contrast, women preferred the woman target described as below average in sexual activity, consistent with the double standard's dictate that "good" women should be sexually reticent. Thus, newly evolving images of sexuality include a complex mixture of similarly permissive expressed attitudes for women's and men's sexuality, some overt acceptance of the sexually assertive woman, and some subtle signs of clinging to the old stereotyping of men as sexually dominant and women as not virginal but selective.

Additional signs about the subtlety of what remains of the double standard appear in people's reactions to sexual transgressions by women and men. Undergraduate students concocted a stronger justification of love for an extramarital partner when marital cheating was done by a woman than by a man (Sprecher et al., 1998) and evaluated female pornography actors more negatively than male (Evans-DeCicco & Cowan, 2001). Unobtrusive observations of Wisconsin's procedures to establish paternity and child support revealed that non-married women were questioned far more extensively about their sexual practices and partners than were men (Monson, 1997). In prime-time television, depictions of sexually negative consequences were more common when women, rather than men, initiated sexual activities (Aubrey, 2004). Although students reacted negatively to both male and female targets described as having a sexually transmitted infection (STI) compared to a non-sexual infection control, they did express more social rejection toward the STI woman than the STI man (Smith et al., 2008).

Consequences of the Remaining Double Standard

Residuals of the double standard continue to impact women's knowledge and communication, decision making, token resistance, risk taking, and what research is and isn't done. Both possessing adequate sexual knowledge and being able to communicate about sexuality are inhibited by double-standard expectations that women who are informed and assertive are sexually promiscuous ("sluts" as opposed to "studs") (Wyatt & Riederle, 1994). Furthermore, lack of knowledge is part of a complex mix that predicts risky sexual behaviors (Ayoola et al., 2007; Marston & King, 2006).

Exploring decision making, Charlene Muehlenhard and Marcia McCoy (1991) surveyed 403 mostly White college women about being in situations where they wanted to engage in first-time intercourse with a man and either overtly declined or openly acknowledged their desire. The former women gave in to a double-standard **script** that asserts that women, irrespective of their desires, refuse. The researchers included individual difference measures of the woman's traditionalism, acceptance of the double standard, and attitudes about sexuality. None of these measures predicted how each woman reacted—nor did her sense of her partner's actual belief in the double standard. Women who pursued their desires were more likely to *think* their partner disavowed the double standard than did women who went along with the double-standard script, despite their desire to do otherwise. This speaks volumes about how women's immediate interpersonal context influences their decision making above and beyond even their own personalities, attitudes, and desires.

One of the most dangerous offshoots of a sexual double standard has to do with "**token resistance**." Token resistance reflects the notion, fueled by a double standard stressing women's purity, that women will say "no" to sexual activity when they really mean "yes." Most seriously, token resistance is a risk factor for sexual victimization (Krahe et al., 2000).

When respondents thought about token resistance in the abstract, women and men reported similar rates of token resistance (Muehlenhard & Rodgers, 1998). However, when asked to give real-life examples of token resistance, both women and men wrote stories that didn't fit the scenario of saying "no" when meaning "yes." Rather, they wrote true stories about saying "no," possibly waffling a bit in their mind, but ultimately meaning "no" with certainty and without regrets. Although belief in women's reliance on token resistance may be a way for sexual predators to justify sexual assault (and even rape), research evidence suggests that women and men most often say what they mean: *"no" means "no."*

Remnants of the double standard continue to influence women's sexual risk-taking behaviors, involving exposure to pregnancy, sexually transmitted diseases, and even HIV infection (Wyatt & Riederle, 1994). For example, insisting on condom usage may conflict with some women's beliefs that sexuality is natural and spontaneous, that condoms are uncomfortable for men and that women should be passive and let men control heterosexual encounters (Gavey & McPhillips, 1999). Being "swept away" is a common theme in romance novels, and women who read lots of these books are more likely to hold negative attitudes about condoms (Diekman et al., 2000). Most distressingly, young people continue to regard a woman who is carrying a condom negatively (Frankel & Curtis, 2008), as well as more sexually willing and less justified in claiming sexual assault (Hynie et al., 2003; Kelly & Bazzini, 2001).

College women report that they failed to plan contraceptive precautions prior to a date because to do so would admit that sexual pursuits are expected (Wright, 1992). Indeed when women read a hypothetical diary entry by a woman who provided the condom in a casual relationship, they rated the writer less positively than when she introduced a condom in a committed relationship (Hynie et al., 1997). Undergraduate women also over-rely on questioning their partner as a way to reduce HIV risk (Mays & Cochran, 1993). These patterns converge to suggest that accurate knowledge of adequate prevention alone, without sufficient understanding of the potent role still played by the double standard of sexuality, is not sufficient to reduce sexual risk-taking behaviors (Cochran & Mays, 1993).

Finally, the double standard portrays women as passive and without sexual desire, making sexual desire a topic largely ignored by researchers (Jackson, 2005). In a controversial paper, Roy Baumeister (2000) concluded that women are more "erotically plastic" than men by engaging in a wider array of sexual behaviors over time, by being more responsive to sociocultural variables, and by showing less consistency across attitudes and behaviors. Although subsequent commentary about these conclusions didn't question their validity (Baumeister et al., 2000), questions were raised about what these differences mean. Most consistent with the approach we have taken in this book, Janet Hyde and Amanda Durik (2000) argue that gender roles that privilege men allow men to be more sexually open, consistent, and focused on themselves than women, making men less "plastic" (contextually variable) than women.

Women's Sexual Well-Being

Not surprisingly, a woman's sexual well-being depends on her body satisfaction and sense of agency and personal control. As we saw in Chapter 10, self-objectification can affect sexual functioning. Interestingly, it is not a woman's overall body dissatisfaction—but rather her context-specific negative body image during sex—that predicts ambivalence in sexual decision making, lower sexual self-efficacy, and less engagement with her partner (Yamamiya et al., 2006). Sexually satisfied women initiate sexual contact more often, express their sexual needs clearly in their primary relationships, and exhibit high levels of **agency** (Mosher & Danoff-Burg, 2005). Furthermore, personal control and self-efficacy are associated with safer sexual behavior (Pearson, 2006). Conversely, women who implicitly associate sexuality with submission report less sexual satisfaction (Kiefer et al., 2006), and this relationship is mediated by women's compromised feelings of sexual autonomy (Sanchez et al., 2006). Consistent with this reasoning, women who hold feminist beliefs report higher sexual satisfaction and condom-use self-efficacy (Schick et al., 2008). Interestingly, only women who both held feminist beliefs and adopted the label of being feminist rejected the **double standard** of sexuality (Bay-Cheng & Zucker, 2007).

REPRODUCTIVE HEALTH

Make a list of the medical personnel with whom you interact on a routine basis. You might see a dentist, a general practitioner, an optometrist, and so on. If you are a woman, you might visit a gynecologist.[4] What's the comparable physician for a man? Only women's health care is so routinely divided.

The Case of Breast Cancer

Cancer presents an ideal opportunity to address this division of women's health care because it can develop in any body part, including women's and men's reproductive structures. Beth Meyerowitz and Stacey Hart (1995) analyzed the contents of medical and psychological publications reporting cancer research in 1983 and 1992. In the leading medical journal, *Cancer*, more studies focused on breast and reproductive cancers in women than their incidence would warrant. In contrast for men, studies of reproductive cancers were under-represented. Paralleling this pattern in the psychology literature, breast cancer survivors dominated samples of research participants, even beyond what we would expect, given their optimistic survival rates. Not surprisingly, middle-aged and older women overestimate their risk of dying from breast cancer (Wilcox & Stefanick, 1999). Although breasts indeed are the leading site for cancer in women (with a 2007 rate of 120.4 in 100,00 women), occurring more than twice as often in women's breasts than lungs (54.5), the *top cancer killer is lung cancer*. In 2007, lung cancer (with a death rate of 40.0 in 100,000 women) claimed about as many women's lives as breast (22.8, ranked #2) and colon (14.1, #3) cancers combined (CDC, 2011a).

My point is not to diminish the importance of research on breast cancer, the seriousness of being diagnosed with breast cancer (Fischer, 2001; Petersen & Benishek, 2001), the body image threats raised by breast cancer (Helms et al., 2008; Rubin & Tannenbaum, 2011), or the importance of monthly self-examination and routine mammograms. Rather, we might ask: Why this obsession with breasts? The question itself suggests an answer, but let's go beyond the obvious sexual possibility (see Wilkinson & Kitzinger, 1994). The incidence of breast cancer in the United States is highest among White women (121.0 in 100,000 in 2007), followed by Black (117.0), Latina (88.2), Asian (83.4), and Indigenous Native American (67.3) women (CDC, 2011a). However, Black women are most likely to die from breast cancer (31.4 per 100,000 women), followed by White (22.2) and then Latina (14.6), Indigenous Native American (12.8), and Asian (11.2) women.

Breast cancer is detected most frequently in a select subset of privileged women whose survival surpasses others', raising questions about the amount of attention afforded breast cancer detection and treatment. Are the women most susceptible to breast cancer as influential as Latina women, for example, who are at highest risk for cervical cancer, a disease that disproportionately strikes Indigenous Native American (Tom-Orme, 1995) and African American women as well (Leigh, 1995)? Or, what about African American women, of whom almost one of every 250 will struggle with lupus, a blood disorder in which the immune system becomes overactive (Sullivan, 1996)? Issues of power and privilege are raised here, not between women and men, but among women (**intragroup differences**).[5]

---

[4]A thought-provoking feminist critique of gynecology as a specialty practiced on women by and for men is offered by Diana Scully and Pauline Bart (2003).

[5]The point that we are tackling here has to do with broad racial disparities in health in the United States. For a look at how culture, gender, and power all play into this problem, as well as a look at some examples of community-based interventions, see Airhihenbuwa and Liburd (2006).

A questionable belief that may underlie psychologists' apparent obsession with breast cancer assumes that breast vulnerability is especially devastating for women. However, research evidence indicates that even complete breast loss, although certainly traumatic, is no more psychologically debilitating than other amputations or serious cancers (Wilkinson & Kitzinger, 1994). The three most common concerns reported by mastectomy patients focus on difficulty in engaging in strenuous activity, fear of reoccurrence of the cancer, and obtaining high quality medical care—none of which focus on breast loss itself.

As you read this chapter and other texts in the field, you will encounter this division of women's health into reproductive and nonreproductive concerns. Still, some recent developments are starting to strain this artificial separation. For example, is HIV a sexually transmitted disease for women and thus a sexual/reproductive threat? Or is it a general threat to women's health and well-being? We'll discuss it along with other chronic diseases later. For now, let's explore the psychology of a sampling of reproductive concerns including menstruation, pregnancy and miscarriage, and abortion.

Menstruation

Elissa Koff and her colleagues (1990) asked 80 college women, recruited from introductory and intermediate psychology classes, to simply describe the causes of menstruation. To be graded as correct, an answer must include information that the uterine lining is shed if fertilization has not taken place. Only 41% of the answers met this criterion, and fully 24% provided incorrect or irrelevant information.

The menstrual cycle. Menstruation is the shedding of the lining of the uterus, approximately 2 to 3 ounces of menstrual blood and uterine tissue, typically over 3 to 5 days on a 28-day cycle (Klebanov & Ruble, 1994). The menstrual cycle is characterized by changing hormone levels, the development and release of an ovum by the ovaries, and preparation of the uterus for possible implantation of an ovum, if it is fertilized. If fertilization does not occur, declines in estrogen and progesterone levels signal the shedding of the endometrial lining, or the start of the menstrual flow.

The *menstrual cycle* begins on the first day of menstruation when one of the many immature ova begins to mature in one of the two ovaries. Over the next 2 weeks (the **fol-**

Box 11.3

Sexual scripts are cognitive frameworks we each construct that guide our sexual behaviors, help us plan for sexual encounters, and organize our memories. We all have our own script, which is affected by our gender, our individual characteristics, and our culture (Schneider & Gould, 1987), including the magazines we read (Kim & Ward, 2004). There are five components to our sexual script, so you might want to think about your own views about each of the following before you read on.

- Who is and isn't an appropriate sexual partner for you?
- What acts are on and off limits?
- When is sexuality appropriate: time of day, across your life course?
- Where is sexuality appropriate: in what setting and under what circumstances?
- Why do people have sex (e.g., pleasure, reproduction, form bonds)?

licular phase), the follicle grows and matures as a new lining replaces the one just shed. By about the 16th day, estrogen reaches its peak and the ovary releases the fully developed ovum (**ovulation**), which survives about 2 days during which it can be fertilized. Over the remaining 2 weeks (the **luteal phase**), progesterone levels rise and stimulate the ovaries to release a mucus-like substance to prepare the uterus for a fertilized egg. If fertilization has not occurred on or around the 24th day, estrogen and progesterone *decline* rapidly, marking the **late luteal** or premenstrual phase, as the uterus again prepares to shed its lining and thus initiate a new menstrual cycle.

Although many college women may be misinformed about menstruation, Koff and her colleagues found considerable agreement about physical and emotional stereotyping associated with menstruation. These women attributed four categories of *physical* changes to menstruating—all of them unpleasant: general discomfort (cramps, aches, and pains); water retention and weight gain; tender or swollen breasts; and a variety of autonomic signs (nausea and temperature changes). This negativity extended to *emotional* changes focusing on depression, emotional lability (mood swings), and irritability. Finally, women agreed that there were few, if any, changes in their cognitive or *intellectual* abilities (e.g., reduced concentration) related to menstruation. Interestingly, much of what these women described about the physical and emotional changes associated with menstruation are not really about menstruation itself, but rather about the late luteal or premenstrual phase.

Students' emphasis on the late luteal phase, which typically lasts about 4 days, is shared by both the popular media and the scientific community.[6] The assumption underlying much of this attention is that the marked hormonal changes that accompany this normal phase of the menstrual cycle account for physical, emotional, and cognitive changes in women—an assumption captured in popular references to "raging hormones" (Davis, 1996)—although in reality hormone levels are falling. The common discourse for this phase uses the term "premenstrual syndrome" (PMS) or the more benign term, "premenstrual *symptoms*." The *Diagnostic and Statistical Manual of Mental Disorders* (DSM) of the American Psychiatric Association (which, in essence, defines abnormality) described Late Luteal Phase Dysphoric Disorder (LLPDD) as a bona fide disorder in its 1987 third edition, but renamed and relegated Premenstrual Dysphoric Disorder (PDD) to the appendix as a syndrome in need of further testing and to a subsection under depression in its 1994 fourth edition (Caplan, 1995).

"Premenstrual syndrome."   In the popular media, both medical experts and women's testimony are used to establish PMS as a medical malady (Kissling, 2002). Sometimes these messages are mixed, following negative, sensationalized headlines with text that works to dispel myths (Merskin, 1999). Still, stereotyping of maladjusted women comes through loud and clear, with PMS suffering estimated to affect from 5% to 95% of women according to these articles, with most converging on estimates between 30% and 60%. When college students read just the basic fundamentals of PMDD as a psychiatric disorder, their perceptions of how problematic menstrual changes are for women in general increased (Nash & Chrisler, 1997).

---

[6]Carol Tavris (1992, p. 140) reports that researchers' interest in PMS, Premenstrual Syndrome, or Premenstrual Tension grew from one article in a medical journal in 1964 to 305 articles in medical journals and 120 in psychological journals in 1988–89. How might this attention fit with the emerging women's movement across this same time period?

Box 11.4

Stereotyping about "PMS" can be seen in the story about Sarafem, a drug approved by the U.S. Federal Drug Administration (FDA) and marketed by Eli Lilly, generating $2.6 billion in sales in 2000. Now marketed by Warner Chilcot (2005), their website claims that it "relieves both the mood and physical symptoms of PMDD (Premenstrual Dysphoric Disorder). Many physicians believe that Sarafem helps to correct the imbalance of serotonin that could contribute to PMDD."

Sarafem actually is a lower dose of the antidepressant, Prozac, re-packaged in a pink capsule and costing 13 cents more per daily dose (Rebensdorf, 2001). In November of 2000, the FDA released a letter sent to the Lilly Corporation regarding an advertisement that the company was airing on television. The ad featured a frustrated woman irritably pulling at a shopping cart that was interlocked with other carts (FDA Warning Letters, 2000). The ad diagnosed her with PMDD and offered Sarafem for relief. The FDA charged that this message confused the serious DSM diagnosis of PMDD with general stereotyping about PMS. The FDA warned that this confusion both broadened the scope of pathologizing women's normal behavior and trivialized the seriousness of genuine PMDD, urging the company to withdraw this and other similar promotions. It seems interesting to me that since the FDA effectively limited the market for Sarafem, it has moved to a smaller, specialty pharmaceutical company focused on women's health care and dermatology.

The story of Sarafem speaks about our readiness to biologize women's problems and treat them simply with a pill, raising questions about who profits from such an approach (Gurevich, 1995). Furthermore, some feminists argue that this pattern serves to deflect women's efforts for social change away from political activities inward and toward individualized clinical treatment (Nicholson, 1995; also see Gannon, 1998).

To be clinically diagnosed with **Premenstrual Dysphoric Disorder**, a woman must present at least five symptoms from a list of 11 during the week before and a few days after the onset of menses (DSM-IV, 1994, p. 717). At least one of these must include markedly depressed mood, anxiety, affective lability (sadness), and anger or irritability. Furthermore, "the disturbance seriously interferes with work or with usual social activities or relations with others," is not "merely an exacerbation of the symptoms of another disorder... ," and is "confirmed by daily self-ratings during at least two symptomatic cycles" (DSM-IV, 1994, p. 718). Researchers estimate that about 5% of American women do suffer with such intense perimenstrual symptoms (Klebanov & Ruble, 1994).

For a less clinical diagnosis of PMS, over 150 popular indicators have been identified (Gurevich, 1995). Many of these are negative (Moos, 1968) but some are positive (Delaney et al., 1988). You checked off some of them in Box 11.1 at the start of this chapter. My experience with this checklist is that men, like women, check many items, raising questions about how moods are related to menstruation if men have them. These checklists also raise important questions about what truly does define PMS (Parlee, 1993) and how broad its scope legitimately is. Some definitions are so broad that almost all women (and likely some men) would be diagnosed with PMS (Caplan, 1995).

Separating physical fact from stereotyping fiction is challenging. Pamela Kato Klebanov and Diane Ruble (1994) conclude that *physical* changes involving pain, water retention, and weight gain have enjoyed consistent support, at least when based on women's self-reports. In a few cases where more objective measures (actual weight checks) have been employed, the validity of even these effects becomes questionable. On the other hand, in studies where women are given **placebos**, reports of physical symptoms persist. Moving from physical to cognitive and *intellectual* consequences, there is no consistent evidence to conclude that women's abilities change across the menstrual cycle.[7]

Conclusions become fuzzier when we focus on *emotional* changes. Hypotheses involving hormones have received, at best, modest support, and linkages with other physiological mechanisms (e.g., neurotransmitters) have not been established convincingly (Klebanov & Ruble, 1994). Sociodemographic characteristics, social environments, and individual differences among women may each play a role in constructing PMS. In sum, PMS is experienced differently by different women, if at all.

Looking at sociodemographic subgroup variations, race and ethnicity seem to play a role in PMS reports. For example, none of the African American women nurses studied by Kathryn Lee and Amanda Rittenhouse (1991) reported mood swings, and fewer Asian American women indicated experiencing cramps or weight gain. Controlling for socioeconomic levels, Anglo-Saxon women appear to be at greatest risk for premenstrual symptomatology (Maluf & Ruble, 1993, cited in Klebanov & Ruble, 1994). In a large-scale study of women in 10 countries, patterns and beliefs about menstruation varied widely according to country of residence, religion, literacy, age, work environment, and social status (Severy et al., 1993). For a long time, the impact of gender was not even considered, yet there is evidence that men's general moods cycle too in weekly patterns that may synchronize with women's (Gallant et al., 1991; McFarlane et al., 1988). Although menstruation is unique to women, mood cycles are not (which is why our opening checklist may apply similarly to women and men).

Turning to women's **social context**, stress and social support may affect reports of premenstrual symptomatology. For example, women nurses who acknowledged less satisfaction with their social lives and low levels of social support also reported more perimenstrual symptoms (Lee & Rittenhouse, 1992). Heightened exposure to work, familial, and financial stress was related to reports of negative moods during the late luteal phase (Gallant & Derry, 1995). Similarly, more symptomatic women reported lower marital quality and less perceived support from their spouses. Interestingly, the relationship between symptomatology and employment was moderated by choice, such that homemakers who chose their role reported the lowest symptom ratings in contrast to the highest ratings from women for whom employment was unwanted (Coughlin, 1990).

Personality, attitudes, and expectancies (**individual differences**) may influence women's perceptions of premenstrual moods. Although only a few studies have focused on personality correlates with PMS, emotionally symptomatic women may be higher in external locus of control, lower in self-esteem (Gallant & Derry, 1995) and optimism (Chrisler et al., 2006), and higher in fear of anxiety symptoms (Sigmon et al., 2000). Premenarcheal girls, who picked up their attitudes toward menstruation from sources stressing negative aspects, expected more distressed symptomatology (Brooks-Gunn & Ruble, 1982), and daughters continue to describe communications with their mothers about menstruation as negative in tone (Costos et al., 2002). Women who held more sexually objectified views of their body exhibited more disgust and shame about their menstruation (Roberts, 2004).

---

[7]Because physical indicators are the only "symptoms" of PMS confirmed by research, I elected to discuss this topic here under physical health rather than in the next chapter on mental health.

Finally, whether or not an individual woman's expectancies become self-fulfilling remains unclear (Gallant & Derry, 1995). For example, Pamela Kato Klebanov and John Jemmott (1992) used a fictitious saliva test, presumably measuring hormonal levels, to convincingly persuade actually premenstrual White women to *believe* they were premenstrual or in the middle of their cycle. As predicted, those who believed this reported more pain, but the finding did not extend to negative affect. Similarly, although fully 40% of 101 employed women said they experienced PMS, none exhibited actual premenstrual affective change across the two cycles studied (Hardie, 1997). What is clear is that what women report can be **primed**. If we labeled the items in Box 11.1 as responses to menstruation and put "distressful" items first and then "joyful" ones later, women's reports would be more negative than if we flipped them and put the positive items first (Aubeeluck & Maguire, 2002). Expectations surely affect reporting, but it's unclear if they influence actual experiences.

Although the existence of PMS may be more medical fiction than fact, societal beliefs about menstruation still may impact women's lives. Tanith Oxley (1998) asked British undergraduate and professional working women to describe how they manage their own menstruation. Although women reported mastery at managing their pain and discomfort, dominant themes involved being highly self-conscious of their bodies and avoiding situations that might expose their menstruation. These themes of disruption and fear of exposure appear in another study in which 18 to 22 year-old menstruating and non-menstruating women interacted with a male interviewer (Kowalski & Chapple, 2000). Menstruating women who believed the interviewer knew of their condition felt less liked by the interviewer and made less of an attempt to positively impress him than did menstruating women who believed the interviewer to be unaware. Furthermore, menstruating women, regardless of interviewer's perceived knowledge, were less motivated to be impressive and felt less liked than non-menstruating women. These findings suggest that menstruation has a psychological impact on women that probably has linkages to societal taboos about menstruation.

Women's fears about societal taboos are not unfounded. Both women and men, especially those scoring high in **hostile sexism**, rated a menstruating, compared to the "average," woman more negatively (Forbes et al., 2003). In a clever laboratory study, participants interacted with a **confederate** who appeared to accidentally drop a hair clip or a tampon from her purse (Roberts et al., 2002). When the woman dropped a tampon, she was rated as less likeable and competent, and participants even tended to avoid sitting close to her. Among participants holding more traditional gender stereotypes, the reminder of menstruation was associated with increased body **objectification** of women in general. The social meaning of menstruation comes through loud and clear in Box 11.5.

Childbirth

Health psychologists have contributed to our understanding of the medicalization of childbirth and the postpartum period. The use of technology in childbirth, such as electronic fetal monitoring and an epidural shot for pain reduction, has become expected and routine, but it affects mothers and fathers differently. Kristi Williams and Debra Umberson (1999) interviewed 15 married couples with a firstborn 2 to 4 months after childbirth. For women, medical technology transferred some of their ownership of control not only onto medical personnel but onto fathers as well. For fathers, medical intervention enhanced their per-

Box 11.5
If Men Could Menstruate--
(Steinem, 1978)

What would happen, for instance, if suddenly, magically, men could menstruate and women could not?
The answer is clear—menstruation would become an enviable, boast-worthy, masculine event:

- Men would brag about how long and how much.
- Boys would mark the onset of menses, that longed-for proof of manhood, with religious ritual and stag parties.
- Congress would fund a National Institute of Dysmenorrhea to help stamp out monthly discomforts.
- Sanitary supplies would be federally funded and free. (Of course, men would still pay for the prestige of commercial brands such as John Wayne Tampons, Muhammad Ali's Rope-a-dope Pads...)
- Street guys would brag ("I'm a three pad man")...
- Lesbians would be said to fear blood and therefore life itself—though probably only because they needed a good menstruating man...

In fact, if men could menstruate, the power justifications could probably go on forever.

If we let them.

ceived involvement and importance in the birthing process, mainly by providing access to the baby. In sum, medicalization seems to level the playing field by involving men more, sometimes providing fathers with medical information not readily disclosed to the mother.

Debate surrounding the medicalization of childbirth has often crystallized around the alleged overuse of Cesarean sections (Stanton & Danoff-Burg, 1995). C-section rates for U.S. women have spiraled upward from 23% of births in 1991 to 32% in 2007 (Menacker & Hamilton, 2010). Although lower infant mortality rates have been attributed, in part, to C-sections, maternal mortality is 4 times higher for Cesarean than vaginal deliveries. In addition, at least one-third of these women suffer postoperative infections, and almost all experience abdominal pain. The medical justification for many C-sections has been undermined by provocative patterns in their incidence: C-section rates are inflated among women of higher socioeconomic status, among those who are privately insured, and in hospitals with high malpractice claims and employing physicians fearful of legal entanglements. Women having C-sections show no differences in depression, anxiety, or confidence in mothering, but they do tend to be less satisfied with their delivery experiences (DiMetteo & Kahn, 1997). Thus, there appear to be no atypical psychological consequences for mothers delivering by C-section; however, there are medical and pragmatic bases from which to suggest their overuse.

We hear a lot in the popular press about postpartum blues and depression, and unlike their use as synonyms in the media, they refer to different syndromes (Stanton & Danoff-Burg, 1995). **Postpartum blues** may occur in the 10-day period after childbirth during which time the new mother may experience depressed mood, tearfulness, mood swings, anxiety, and other symptoms. Estimates of incidence vary widely, from 26% to 85% of new mothers. Comparing these women to other women, there is evidence that mood fluctuations are more pronounced for postpartum women. However, compared to other women who are recovering from elective gynecological surgery, new mothers' symptoms may be milder. Furthermore, an expanded look at women's affect during this period shows heightened positive feelings as well, suggesting that the "blues" exist within a context of enhanced happiness. No definitive link has been established between these so-called "blues" and hormonal markers.

Postpartum depression refers to a period of at least 2 weeks in duration during the first year after giving birth when symptoms of clinical depression appear (Stanton & Danoff-Burg, 1995). Incidence rates of 8% to 26% have been offered, at least for mild depression. Evidence does suggest that rates of mild depression are higher in new mothers than in other women; however, these postpartum levels are no higher, and possibly even lower, than depression levels during pregnancy and appear lower in women with strong partner support (Thorp et al., 2004). No biological markers have been linked to postpartum depression. The predictors for postpartum depression appear no different than those for depression during other periods of women's lives, hence calling into question the usefulness of this concept.

Another perspective on postnatal depression regards it as a relatively safe way to express concerns about motherhood, especially feelings of inadequacy and a disjunction between what the new mother expected and is actually experiencing (Mauthner, 1998). Additionally, other emotions may come into play postpartum, such as anger, which also may depend on childcare stress (Graham et al., 2002).

Miscarriage

About 10 to 25% of clinically recognized pregnancies in the United States end in miscarriage (American Pregnancy Association, 2011). Reviewing the psychological literature on women's reactions to miscarriage and drawing on interviews with 65 women 4 months after their miscarriages, Margaret Madden (1994) concluded that reactions are individualized. At the time of their miscarriage, most women reported feeling sad, with frustration, disappointment, anger at one's self, fright, and feeling troubled being expressed by more than one of every five women. Only 10% recalled feeling relieved, and much of this came from an end to uncertainties initiated by physical troubles rather than relief to see the pregnancy terminated. As one might expect, immediate emotional distress was more intense when the woman had become attached to the fetus (regardless of the length of the pregnancy), held herself responsible for her loss, and was unable to talk to anyone. Distress was reduced by sensitive health care providers who provided information and involved a woman in her own treatment decisions as much as possible (Geller et al., 2010).

Women's reports at the time of Madden's interviews 4 months after their miscarriages are a tribute to their resilience, coping, and acceptance. Still, most expressed concerns about a recurrence, and many described feeling blue on occasion when something triggered their memory, when they were upset about something else, and when they were fatigued. However, these feelings lessened with time and did not dominate their lives. The most frequent emotion expressed by these women was hope, and as many women expressed sadness as happiness. In sum, there are **individual differences** in women's reactions to miscarriage. Because a woman is not devastated with depression and grief, as folk wisdom and the popular media might suggest, does not mean that she is uncaring or even deviant from what most women typically report.

Abortion[8]

Globally, an estimated 42 million women induced abortion in 2003, ending one of every five pregnancies (World Health Organization, 2011). The World Health Organization (2011) concluded that legal restrictions on abortion do not affect its incidence, but they do limit its safety. Unsafe abortions conducted by insufficiently skilled persons or in unsafe conditions accounted for 48% of all abortions worldwide. In the United States, about 1.2 million legal abortions were reported in 2007 (compared to 4.3 million live births). The rate of abortion is 19.5 for every 1,000 American women ages 15 to 44 (48.2 for Black and 13.8 for White women; *Statistical Abstracts of the United States*, 2011, Table 101).

In the United States, abortion is a hotly debated moral and political issue that extends into the arena of public health policy (Russo & Denious, 1998). It is clear that the legalization of abortion has reduced abortion-related deaths of women in the United States: between 1975 and 1982, mortality from induced abortions declined 89%, compared to a decline in mortality of 35% associated with pregnancy and contraception (Rosenberg & Rosenthal, 1987). The risk of a woman's death from abortion during the first 9 weeks of gestation is estimated at one death per half million abortions (National Center for Health Statistics, 1988, cited in Travis, 1993). Based on data such as these, Surgeon General Koop concluded in 1989 that abortion can be a medically safe procedure with no greater health risks than carrying a pregnancy to term (Wilmoth, 1992). His declaration of medical safety shifted interest toward psychology and the possibility of a "postabortion syndrome." Since then, psychologists have addressed questions about who seeks abortions, what the immediate consequences are for women, and the effects of denied abortion on women and children.

Brenda Major and her colleagues (2009) critically reviewed this vast and oftentimes flawed body of research and came to the following conclusions. "First, the relative risk of mental health problems among adult women who have a single, legal, first-trimester abortion of an unwanted pregnancy for nontherapeutic [not health-threatening] reasons is no greater than the risk among women who deliver an unwanted pregnancy" (p. 885). Second, abortion because of a fetal abnormality is no more traumatic for women than miscarriage, having a stillborn, or losing a newborn. Because it is virtually impossible to control for all pre-existing and co-existing threats to a woman's mental health beyond having experienced one or more abortions, the link between abortion per se and mental health risks cannot be convincingly substantiated. Not surprisingly, the strongest predictor of a woman's post-abortion mental health is her pre-abortion mental health.

Although "the majority of adult women who terminate a pregnancy do not experience mental health problems" (p. 885), this does not mean that all women avoid these outcomes. There are wide **individual differences** among women who experience a range of positive, negative, and ambivalent emotions and outcomes. These variable reactions suggest that **social contexts** make a difference—including the degree to which a woman wanted and felt committed to her pregnancy, secrecy and perceptions about the stigma of abortion, low

---

[8]For a fuller discussion of psychological and health issues related to abortion, see Beckman and Harvey (1998). For ideas about how to teach the topic of abortion, see Greene (1995).

self-efficacy for coping with abortion, low actual or expected social support, and use of avoidance or denial coping strategies (Major et al., 2009).

Section Conclusion

In each of the areas we explored so far, including women's sexuality, menstruation, and reproduction, the tendency to biologize each function has detracted from our ability to see each as a normal process that is part of women's broader lives, including their psychological well-being and social and interpersonal contexts. "Raging hormones," alleged to accompany routine menstruation and the postpartum period, lose their force when we consider men's mood cycles and the trauma of any medical procedure, respectively. Presumably universally devastating miscarriages and "post-abortion syndrome" also dissolve when held up to scientific scrutiny. Across each area, there are diverse **individual differences** in women's experiences and outcomes, as well as influences from their **social contexts** (also see Hinchliff et al., 2010, on menopause). Why then is there so much misinformation about women's sexuality and reproductive health? Just asking this question itself is an important insight to take away.

CHRONIC DISEASES

Chronic diseases are defined as irreversible, accumulative, or latent illnesses or impairments that require continued medical and personal care to avoid further disability (Lubkin, 1995). As we saw, the two leading causes of women's (and men's) death are cardiovascular diseases (#1) and cancer (#2). A wide range of chronic diseases in women has been studied by psychologists including diabetes (Butler & Wing, 1995), autoimmune disorders (Chrisler & Parrett, 1995), and chronic pain (Reading, 1994). Here, we look at the leading killer of women, cardiovascular diseases, and a recent addition to women's list of significant health threats, HIV. Both are important examples because they typically play out differently for women and men, making what we know about men's developments of questionable utility for women.

Cardiovascular Diseases

Cardiovascular diseases, encompassing coronary heart disease, stroke, hypertension, and congestive heart failure, are the leading cause of women's death in the United States, accounting for about 25% of all women's deaths (26% of men's; see Table 11.2). Over the past 35 years, death from coronary heart disease has *decreased* for men at the same time that it has *increased* for women (reviewed by Chrisler, 2001). Surprisingly, fully 36% of women surveyed in 2005 did not think women were at major risk for heart disease , and almost two-thirds of women who die suddenly from coronary heart disease reported no previous symptoms (CDC, 2010a). In 2006, about 8.8% of African American women, 6.6% of Mexican American women, and 6.9% of U.S. White women were living with coronary heart disease.

Sally Shumaker and Teresa Smith (1995) reviewed research on cardiovascular diseases in women from the perspective of health psychologists. There were differences in who, when, and how women and men present themselves to medical personnel for heart disease. Women tended to be of lower socioeconomic status and possessed less formal education than presenting men. African American women are especially prone to hypertension, which afflicts about 39% of Black women (compared to 25% of White women) between the ages of 18 and 74 (Crawford-Green, 1996). Related to both hypertension and cardiovascular heart disease for a disproportionate number of African American women is obesity, a common outcome of diets high in fat and low in fruits and vegetables—in other words, "diets of poverty" (Leigh, 1995).

The recognized onset of women's heart disease appears to lag 7 to 10 years behind that of men, but this could be confounded by differences in presenting symptoms. More men are likely to seek treatment because they suffered a heart attack (myocardial infarction) as compared to the majority of women, who initially present with complaints of chest pains (angina pectoris). Follow-ups of women with chest pain are less likely to show narrowing of their arteries, suggesting that this may not be as accurate a marker for heart disease in women as it is for men. Similarly, noninvasive procedures like stress tests may more accurately identify male sufferers than female. When women do present with myocardial infarction, these attacks are more likely to be misdiagnosed and to prove fatal.

The combination of different presenting symptoms, different markers for the disease, and expectations that heart disease is restricted to men (among women themselves, family and friends, as well as physicians) all may lead to misdiagnosis. Even more disturbing, when an African American woman and a White man presented identical symptoms, heart-trained medical students were more likely to misdiagnose the woman and treat her symptoms as less severe (Rathore et al., 2000). Once diagnosed, referral and aggressive treatments are more common for men, even controlling for women's older age of diagnosis, their disease severity, and their preoperative status. One study found that men were twice as likely to have bypass surgery as women with similar medical profiles (Travis, 2005). Looking at prognosis, heart attacks are more deadly for women; 38% of women (and 25% of men) die within one year after a heart attack (American Heart Association, 2005). Women are more likely to experience stroke and less likely to recover than men, with poorer functional outcomes and lower quality of life (Reeves et al., 2008). There is also limited evidence suggesting that women experience less health-related quality of life and more depression following bypass surgery than men, although this procedure generally is physically beneficial for both.

Although risk factors for women have been understudied, research has identified coronary-prone behavior characterized by: a sense of time-urgency, hostility, and impatience (Weidner, 1994), being overweight, and cigarette smoking[9] as risk factors. Recent comparisons suggest that anxiety may be more of a risk factor for women; hostility, for men (Consedine et al., 2004). Greater exposure to chronic stressors (including PTSD; Kubzansky et al., 2009), higher sensitivity to interpersonal stress, and internalizing coping styles are associated with heightened risk for cardiovascular diseases in women (Möller-Leimkhler, 2010).

After diagnosis, cardiac rehabilitation programs are equally effective for women and men when they are used, but some researchers suggest that these typically are designed to better accommodate men so that women's participation may be structurally discouraged

---

[9]Although ceasing to smoke may contribute to weight gain, on average this amounts to 4 to 8 pounds, which generally does not enhance the risk associated with being overweight.

(Shumaker & Smith, 1995). Although social supports have proved protective for men, initial research with women suggests that women derive both strain and support from their social networks, possibly making them less beneficial. Finally, lack of exercise, depression, and anxiety have been associated with heightened risk in men, but their relationship for women is yet to be fully researched.

HIV/AIDS[10]

Across 2006 to 2009, the overall incidence of new HIV infections in the United States has been stable at about 50,000 cases annually, with over half these cases accounted for by men who have sex with men. Heterosexuals made up 27% of new cases in 2009, with 8,800 women accounting for 68% of these cases. The remaining general group is injection drug users who represented 9% of new infections and with similar numbers of men (2,400) and women (1,960). By far, *the most common form of transmission of HIV to women is through heterosexual contact*, and race/ethnicity matters: Black women (39.7 per 100,000) were infected at a rate 15 times higher than that for White women (2.6); Latinas (11.8), over 4 times higher than White women. The U.S. Centers for Disease Control and Prevention (2011b) estimates that about one million Americans (25% women) are living with HIV, with 21% unaware of their infection, and reports that more than 18,000 people with AIDS (28% women) die each year.

The most common paths of transmission in the United States are anal or vaginal sex (although oral sex is also a possible route) or sharing needles with an infected person (CDC, 2011b). For transmission to occur, blood, semen, vaginal secretions, or breast milk must come in contact with a mucous membrane or damaged tissue or be directly injected into the blood stream. Female-to-female transmission is rare, although possible. A good resource for information about the transmission of HIV in the United States can be found on the CDC's (2011a) website.

Globally, the prevalence of HIV infection appears to have stabilized between 2001 and 2007, estimated at 33 million adults (half women) and children living with HIV (United, Nations, 2010). About 2 million people worldwide die each year due to AIDS. The hardest hit region continues to be Sub-Saharan Africa, where two-thirds of people living with HIV reside, where women account for almost 60% of all HIV-positive adults, and where the most common mode of transmission is heterosexual sex. HIV also disproportionately affects women and girls, who most frequently are the caregivers to stricken family members and who assume parenting responsibilities for orphaned children.

Psychologists have played two major roles in dealing with HIV: devising and implementing models of prevention and helping infected people live with HIV infection and its stigma. The image of who has HIV has changed away from thinking about at-risk groups to at-risk *behaviors* (Batchelor, 1988). For example, a monogamous gay man practicing safe sexual behavior is at lower risk than a lesbian injected-drug user who shares needles.

Reducing women's risk.   Effective risk-reduction interventions to cut down on high-risk behaviors typically involve risk education, risk sensitization, self-efficacy building, and skills training as core components (Kalichman et al., 1996). Although education is a start,

---

[10]For more information about psychology and HIV, check out the Office of AIDS at the American Psychological Association (*http://www.apa.org/pi/aids/index.aspx*).

understanding HIV transmission is not enough to ensure protective behavior (Morokoff et al., 1995). For poor ethnic-minority women, risks associated with daily living—including exposure to the elements among the homeless, care of dependent children, hunger, drug withdrawal or acquisition, acute illness or trauma resulting from physical or sexual assault, threat of withdrawal of emotional and financial support from sexual partners, and loss of loved ones—often outweigh the risks believed to be associated with HIV-risky behaviors (Mays & Cochran, 1988; Thomas, 1994). Physically abused women also are more likely to engage in risk-enhancing behaviors (Beadnell et al., 2000). To undercut transmission through shared needles, needle exchange programs must be responsive to the special needs of women (Brown & Weissman, 1993), and researchers must be sensitive to gender differences in injection behavior—starting with women's greater likelihood of sharing drug paraphernalia (Morokoff et al., 1995).

As for heterosexual transmission, the proper use of *latex* condoms reduces the risk of exposure, and college students are most favorably inclined to condom introducers who express a care and responsibility theme (Castaneda & Collins, 1998). However, unflagging condom use is rare, even among women engaged in high-risk behaviors (Morokoff et al., 1995), but having a reminder cue (wearing a bracelet) has been shown to increase compliance (Dal Cin et al., 2006). A variety of factors are implicated in the inconsistent use of condoms including race/ethnicity (Leonardo & Chrisler, 1992). For example, Spanish-speaking women report having fewer sexual partners as well as reduced condom use (Zambrana & Ellis, 1995).

Patricia Morokoff, Lisa Harlow, and Kathryn Quina (1995) summarize their review of barriers to condom use: Infrequent and irregular usage is associated with being married and monogamous, being less educated, drinking alcohol, sexuality with a main partner rather than a client, beliefs that there is little one can do to protect one's self from sexually transmitted disease, distaste for condoms, and lack of control over decision making. A fascinating study of the role played by alcohol found that women who either consumed or expected to consume alcohol reported elevated confidence that they could detect a partner's potential for HIV infection through simple interaction—a detection strategy known to be ineffective (Monahan et al., 1999).

The need to seek information about one's sexual partners is clear. Fully 5% of women surveyed for the National AIDS Behavioral Surveys described a high-risk sexual partner (Grinstead et al., 1993). For Latina women, higher education was associated with having a riskier partner, whereas the reverse was true for White women. Fully 17% of women in this study who reported no high-risk behaviors for themselves were unsure of the risk status of their partners. Such uncertainty is especially common among ethnic-minority women, older women, and less-educated women. In another study of men injected-drug users, half reported a relationship with a woman non-user who was unaware of the man's drug habit (Rhodes et al., 1990). African American women's heterosexual risk is further aggravated by higher rates of bisexuality among Black as compared to White men (Leigh, 1995). In a study of 105 HIV-positive women in New York City, fully 54% reported engaging in unsafe sexual behavior during the past 90 days (Simoni et al., 2000).

Thus, interest among psychologists in the role played by interpersonal power and sexual communication in relationships has grown substantially (for example, see Quina et al., 2000). As we saw previously, the sexual **script** outlined by the **double standard** portrays men as sexually assertive and women as passive. Power to negotiate safe sexual practices is implicated in condom usage among African American (Bowleg et al., 2004) and European American heterosexually active adolescents (Gutierrez et al., 2000) and Mexican-born married women (de Snyder et al., 2000). In one study of decision making, if the man made the decision, only 12% of these couples used condoms more than half the time. This figure jumped to 49% when women made the decision, and to 32% when both partners decided (Osmond et al., 1993). Through all these factors runs a strand of power—the more powerful person, both personally and interpersonally, controls how sexuality is practiced (Amaro et al., 2001; Pulerwitz & Dworkin, 2006).

Power in an intimate relationship involves two key dimensions that may be important in communication about safe sexual practices: *Relationship Control* and *Decision-Making Dominance* (Pulerwitz et al., 2000). Two central indicators of relationship control are women's projections of their male partner's response (of violence and anger) to a request to use a condom, but it is not confined to the sexual arena. For example, other signs are doing what one's partner wants to do most of the time and having a partner dictate what one wears. Decision-making dominance includes deciding whose friends the couple interacts with, whether they engage in sexual relations, and what they do together. In a study with 388 mostly Latina women, women with higher levels of these types of relationship power were 5 times as likely as less powerful women (matched on a variety of sociodemographic and psychosocial factors) to report consistent use of condoms (Pulerwitz et al., 2002).

Prevention programs aimed at women must foster women's empowerment in negotiating sexual encounters and in ending those that put them at risk (Croteau et al., 1993). They must also be sensitive to the social context in which risky behavior is enacted, especially regarding cultural differences related to race/ethnicity and socioeconomics (Scott-Sheldon et al., 2010). Technological advances (such as the female condom and a microbiocide that kills the HIV virus but that can be used safely as a vaginal gel, foam, or sponge) would help to give women direct control of their own protection.

Living with HIV. The second focus of health psychologists studying HIV-related behaviors has been on women infected with HIV. For example, women delay seeking medical care for themselves 1.6 times more often than men, often because women are caring for others (including a child in the household) and are without insurance (Stein et al., 2000). HIV-infected women commonly struggle with depression, apprehension, sadness, helplessness, anger, and fear (Morokoff et al., 1995), as well as social discrimination and stigmatization (Teti et al., 2010). Even women's participation in the workplace can be affected (Barkey et al., 2009). The potential and need for interventions (Webel, 2010) to help HIV-infected women improve the quality of their lives is critical.

HEALTH CARE PRACTICE

Although women are disproportionately heavy users of the medical system, the medical system has not been a consistent health promoter for women. We have seen that women have been excluded from research central to their health needs, although women-centered work is in progress. We also have seen that misperceptions of women's bodies that overemphasize reproduction and ignore other symptomatology, such as gender-specific signs of cardiovascular disease, have biased women's interactions with the health care system. Probably the most egregious example of women's questionable treatment centers on surgeries.

Surgeries

Leslie Laurence and Beth Weinhouse (1994) detail how current surgical practice affects women's health. They acknowledge that surgery performed appropriately and skillfully saves many lives, and their purpose is not to undermine surgery itself. However, there are patterns of surgical use that raise some very serious questions. Of the top ten inpatient surgeries, one is unique to men (prostatectomy) and three to women: episiotomies (an incision between the vagina and rectum meant to speed childbirth), Cesarean sections, and hysterectomies.

Hysterectomy. Approximately 600,000 hysterectomies are performed in the United States every year, costing more than $5 billion and affecting more than one of every four American women by the time they are 60 years old (CDC, 2005).[11] This makes hysterectomy the second most frequent major surgical procedure among women of reproductive age. However, experts report that anywhere from 20% to 90% of them are medically unnecessary (Laurence & Weinhouse, 1994). Looked at another way, 80 to 85% of hysterectomies are elective in that other treatment options are available and untried. Only 15% of hysterectomies are performed because of uterine cancer, the most compelling reason for removal. At this rate, it is projected that 40% of American women will have their uterus removed during their lifetime; more than one-third will not have their uterus by age 50.

The most common reasons for hysterectomy before age 50 are uterine fibroids and endometriosis (a disease of the uterine lining). Fully one-third of premenopausal women have fibroids, most of which naturally shrink as menopause approaches. An American woman is two- to three-times more likely to have a hysterectomy than her counterpart in England, France, or West Germany, and her chances increase if she sees a male physician. Hysterectomy is more likely among poor women, women without a college education, and African American women, and it even was abused as a form of involuntary sterilization for poor Black women. There are complications possible with this surgery that make it a choice that should not be approached casually.

Cosmetic surgery. We typically think of medicine as promoting health and of surgical procedures as serious, invasive activities with risks made acceptable by pressing health threats. Elective cosmetic surgery stands in contrast to this image if its outcomes are considered trivial or not worth the risks of intervention. Diana Dull and Candace West (1991) interviewed both cosmetic surgeons and their clients to understand how they reconcile this apparent contradiction. They found that both physicians and their patients justify their involvement by thinking of cosmetic surgery as a form of reconstructive surgery that legitimately is designed to improve physical functioning and minimize disfigurement. These procedures ignore women's psychological problems that may underlie their endorsement, such as excessive approval seeking (David & Vernon, 2002) and media exposure to idealized body images (Harrison, 2003).

---

[11]An informative website for information on hysterectomy can be found at http://womenshealth.gov (retrieved October 2011).

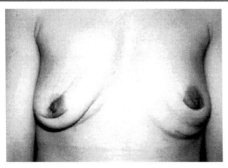

Box 11.6

Breast implants have an outer shell of silicone that is filled with either silicone or saline (sterile salt water). Although silicone-filled implants had been used since 1964, the FDA didn't request that manufacturers register reports of serious health problems with implants until 1984, still didn't require manufacturer's safety data until as late as 1991, and then virtually banned their use in 1992. Such "correction" for small breasts is a medically named deformity ("micromastia"). The most common complications include capsular contracture (a buildup of scar tissue that made breasts hard and misshapened), implant rupture or deflation, and the need for follow-up surgeries (Bren, 2000). Implants interfere with mammography, making breast cancer harder to detect. Most American women who seek breast implants do so for cosmetic reasons (Latteier, 1998).

These cosmetic motivations are compromised when implants collapse (as in the photograph). The U.S. Food and Drug Administration offers a handbook with information for consumers about breast augmentation at: http://www.fda.gov/ cdrh/breastimplants/indexbip.html (Retrieved October 2011).

Photograph copied with permission of Walter Peters, Ph.D., M.D., F.R.C.S.C., University of Toronto, as posted on the FDA's website: http://www.fda.gov/cdrh/breastimplants/breast_implants_photos.html

The American Society of Plastic Surgeons (ASPS, 2011) released a press statement in February of 2011 reporting that 13.1 million cosmetic procedures were performed in the United States in 2010, up 5% from 2009. Their list of invasive procedures (totaling 1.6 million) was topped by breast augmentation (296,000; up 2%), nose reshaping (252,000), eyelid surgery (209,000), liposuction (203,000), and tummy tuck (116,000); their list of less invasive procedures (totaling 11.6 million) was led by botox injections ("botulinum toxin type"; 5.4 million).

The targets for much of these surgeries are middle-aged women whose attitudes about cosmetic surgery are shaped by body dissatisfaction, appearance investment, aging anxiety, and television exposure (Slevec & Tiggemann, 2010). Not surprising, anti-aging fears fuel many women's purchase and use (ironically with skepticism) of anti-aging products (Muise & Desmarais, 2010). However, interest in cosmetic surgeries is not confined to older women. College women's interest is increased with their weight, body dissatisfaction, internalization of media messages, and being teased about their physical appearance (Markey & Markey, 2009). Negative consequences, such as threatened sexual esteem, even extend to young women's dissatisfaction with the appearance of their genitals (Schick et al., 2010).

Although cosmetic surgery may be a more dramatic health risk than many of us are willing to take, most women (including myself, I confess) engage in arguably health-threatening practices (Saltzberg & Chrisler, 1995). Make-up can cause allergic reactions in as many of one-third of its users; fashionable shoes (along with weighty purses) are related to foot and back problems; allergies are common from scented products; long hair and dangling earrings get caught in machinery; fashionable clothing can restrict movement, including escape from danger; body piercing and tattooing can lead to infections; and so on.

Indeed, one can (although rarely) contract HIV from tattooing, yet I myself have a tattoo on my ankle. At some level, we might begin to think of these as forms of self-mutilation, to question who does and who doesn't routinely do these things, to think about how they maintain stereotyping about acceptable femininity (Tiggemann & Hodgson, 2008; Toerien et al., 2005), to consider how these practices might be related to the social standing of the groups most likely to engage in them (Jeffreys, 2000; Lienert, 1998), and to link these practices with pressures related to finding intimate partners (Hill & Durante, 2011).

Health Care Policy

All of this leaves us with a very basic question: Does the health care system promote women's health? We know that health care policy in the United States is in crisis and is a major economic and political issue hotly and repeatedly debated at the federal level. Two central problems confronted by health-policy reformers focus on cost and access. In 2009, over 23 million American women (15% of all women) were not covered by health insurance (*Statistical Abstracts of the United States*, 2011, Table 155). Over 5 years, the number of women without health care coverage grew three times faster than the number of uninsured men, and older women are 20% more likely to be uninsured than men of their age (Lambrew, 2001). About half of all uninsured women work part-time and are married, with many older women being ineligible for Medicaid in contrast to their covered spouse.

Disparities exist by race and ethnicity. For example, a higher percentage of Hispanics (32.4%) and Blacks (21%) were not covered by health insurance in 2009 than Whites (15.8%) and Asian Americans (17.2%; *Statistical Abstracts of the United States*, 2011, Table 155). Obviously, household income also makes a difference, with the uninsured rate rising to 31.9% of Americans living below the poverty line. Cheryl Travis and her colleagues (1995) considered how insurance coverage affects women and women's health (also see Travis & Compton, 2001).Underemployment, part-time employment, and employment in small businesses not offering health insurance are associated with being uninsured, and women (especially racial and ethnic minority women, older women, and single heads of households) hold a disproportionate number of these jobs. Most disturbing is the finding that insurance may affect treatment. For example, Travis and her colleagues reviewed 400,000 records of patients with heart disease and found that those with private insurance were twice as likely to receive heart bypass surgery as those on Medicaid (reported in Travis et al., 1995).

Health care policy in general has revolved around three major conceptual strategies: single-payer government-based systems (like Canada's), employer-mandated plans, and market reform (Travis et al, 1995). All strive toward universal coverage at reduced cost. Single-payer systems cover everyone, with the government picking up the tab; employer programs require employers to pay into a general public pool (pay) or provide minimum coverage for employees (play); and market reforms rely on tax deductions, credits, or vouchers. Employer plans are especially likely to miss women because coverage is determined by employment in regulated settings.

Travis and her associates conclude that for reform to truly benefit women, health care policy must adequately define what needs and treatments are legitimate; empower individuals to take control of their own health; and value diversity, inclusiveness, and equity in health care provision. Furthermore, it is clear that this debate must be informed by health psychologists.

A recurrent theme that silently hovers in the background of some of the health literature blames women for failing to promote their own health. For example, it is frustrating to find high rates of cervical cancer among groups of women who avoid regular Pap smears; to record late breast-cancer detection rates for women who fail to do routine breast exams and shun mammography;[12] and to find condom avoidance and needle sharing even among those who know better. Who's to blame? It's tempting to point wagging fingers at women, but this reflects the person-blaming perspective we rejected earlier.

A fuller picture needs to view women within the contexts of their lives (for example, see Sheffer et al., 2002), and we saw examples of this perspective throughout this chapter. Is a poor woman to blame for inadequate gynecological care when 44% of ob/gyns don't accept Medicaid patients (Travis et al., 1995)? Is a woman to blame for not using a condom when the expectation is that women control contraception but its practice depends on a partner's cooperation? Is risk of HIV contraction such a big threat when one lives in a crime-ridden neighborhood and can barely put food on the table? Is liposuction worth the pain and cost if it relieves the shame of being viewed as fat and out of control? Even the very definitions of what it means to be fit and healthy vary among women and men, with women's definitions more conflated with having an "appropriate body shape" (Wright et al., 2006).

Not surprisingly, power, control, and agency play important roles in women's health. For example, **agency** was associated with better health outcomes for women with rheumatoid arthritis (Trudeau et al., 2003); feelings of having little control were related to negative birthing experiences (Baker et al., 2005); and self-efficacy beliefs predicted responses to pain (Jackson et al., 2002). As the field of health psychology burgeons, a fuller contextual account of women's lives must be understood to simultaneously empower women to promote their own health and give them the means to do so.

CHAPTER SUMMARY

Psychology plays an indispensable role in understanding and promoting the physical health and well-being of women. A feminist focus on women's health is needed to ensure adequate research of those health issues that disproportionately or uniquely affect women; to provide a holistic understanding of women's sexual, reproductive, and general health needs; to counter androcentric assumptions about disease, prevention, and health; and to explore the apparent paradox of women's longer life spans and greater morbidity. A key to doing this is to consider gender as a marker from which to launch further explorations of health patterns, rather than a cause in and of itself.

Turning to women's sexual well-being, a mechanical view of human sexuality ignores the socioemotional function sexuality plays in the lives of both women and men. Although residuals of a subtle double standard in sexual attitudes and behaviors may persist, there

---

[12]A review of studies with U.S. ethnic-minority women documents various barriers to mammography use, including low income and lack of health insurance, lack of physician recommendation, lack of trust, language barriers, and transportation difficulties (Alexandraki & Morradian, 2010). Not surprisingly then, interventions that are culturally tailored and that address logistical barriers prove most effective (Masi et al., 2007).

are substantial individual differences, subgroup sociodemographic factors, and contextual variations, making this a more complex area than simple intergroup gender comparisons can capture. Parallel complexities emerge in discussions of menstruation, "PMS," and reproduction, including childbirth, miscarriage, and abortion. Folk wisdom evoking psychological disturbance is debunked, or at least called into question, by growing bodies of research evidence.

Less thoroughly studied than women's reproductive health, women's mortality and morbidity, like men's, are affected by a wide array of chronic diseases, with cardiovascular diseases and cancers topping the charts. Research on cardiovascular diseases challenges the simple extension of findings from men to women, beginning with differences as fundamental as onset (later for women), presenting symptoms (fewer myocardial infarctions), different markers (missed by stress tests and searches for narrowed arteries), expectations (leading to misdiagnosis), and risk factors. HIV has risen to become a leading cause of death for American women aged 25 to 44, and is most commonly transmitted to women worldwide through heterosexual relations. Effective prevention strategies need to be sensitive to women's social contexts, including their disempowered status in interpersonal relationships.

The mission of health care practice, to heal, is seriously undermined by questionable patterns in rates of hysterectomy and by the expanding popularity and invasiveness of cosmetic surgery. As health care policy reform continues to be a pressing sociopolitical and economic issue, the input of health psychologists will be integral to the development of women-friendly and inclusive health care policies. The themes that run through each of these areas are that women's health is understudied and mythologized, but this is changing as fundamental understandings of power and empowerment come to the forefront of our theories and research.

SUGGESTED READINGS

McHugh, M. C. (2006). What do women want?: A new view of women's sexual problems. *Sex Roles, 54*, 361–369.

In this engaging and accessible paper, Maureen McHugh provides a women-centered view of women's sexual desire and problems that expands on the perspective taken in this chapter about the over-"medicalization" of women's sexuality.

Chrisler, J. C. (2011). Leaks, lumps, and lines: Stigma and women's bodies. *Psychology of Women Quarterly, 35*, 202–214.

Joan Chrisler uses ideas from feminist and terror management theories and about stigma to take a closer look at women's bodies when menstruating (leaking), fat (lumpy), and old (lined).

Bobel, C. (2006). "Our revolution has style": Contemporary menstrual product activists "doing feminism" in the Third Wave. *Sex Roles, 54*, 331–345.

Chris Bobel's in-depth content analysis of websites and "zines" provides a provocative look at how young feminists take action against the control of women's menstruation (and more broadly) women's health. This paper can serve as a jumping-off reading for further exploration of the web on this and other topics (e.g., safer sexual practices; Noar et al., 2006) related to women's physical health and well being.

Simoni, J. M., et al. (2010). HIV/AIDS among women of color and sexual minority women. In H. Landrine & N. F. Russo (Eds.), *Handbook of diversity in feminist psychology* (pp. 335–366). New York: Springer.

Jane Simoni and five of her colleagues take a more targeted and insightful look at women and HIV that expands upon the general overview provided in this chapter. Additionally, one of the authors, Keren Lehavot, is part of a podcast discussion with Caroline Huxley and Lisa Rubin about three studies they conducted with sexual minority women (published in *Psychology of Women Quarterly*, 35[3]) available at *pwq.sagepub.com*.

Toerien, M., Wilkinson, S., & Choi, P. Y. L. (2005). Body hair removal: The "mundane" production of normative femininity. *Sex Roles, 52*, 399-406.

The meaning of an often unexplored, everyday part of many women's lives is discussed by Merran Toerien and her colleagues in ways that are challenging and thought-provoking.

Chapter 12

Women's Mental Health and Well-Being
From "Mental Disorders" to Feminist Practice

Consider each of the following recognized mental disorders. Fill in each blank with your guess about the gender ratio for each; that is, does each occur more frequently in men (F < M), more frequently in women (F > M), or equally in each (F = M)?

- Trichotillmania (compulsively pulling out one's own hair): F ___ M
- Gambling Disorder: F ___ M
- Alcohol Abuse: F ___ M
- Schizophrenia: F ___ M
- Childhood and Adolescent Conduct Disorder: F ___ M
- Inhibited sexual desire and orgasm: F ___ M

Definitions of what each of these disorders is, as well as a determination about their occurrence in women and men, appear in the *Diagnostic and Statistical Manual of Mental Disorders* published by the American *Psychiatric* Association (DSM–IV, 1994[1]). The gender information provided about each disorder is based on experts' readings of published research about each disorder, but I'd be willing to bet that your guesses fit pretty well with their more informed reports (see the answers in the footnote below[2]). Cynthia Hartung and Thomas Widiger (1998) reviewed 125 disorders and found gender information about 101 (81%) of them in the DSM, with most arguing for gender differences. As we have seen throughout this text, such strong interest in gender differences probably means that there's a lot going on here that deserves a closer look.

I don't mean to suggest that there's intentional malfeasance here, but rather that the picture is likely more complex than what laypeople like us are able to guess and that the concerns we have seen previously about individual differences, stereotyping, status, and power are probably implicated. Hartung and Widiger help us out by drawing our attention to some interesting patterns across the examples above.

First, systematic explorations for gender differences in any disorder are affected by biases in reporting. For example, more women than men might seek treatment for Trichotillmania because appearance is culturally more important to women and because hair loss is more socially acceptable among adult men. Women may be under-represented in treatment programs for gambling because of the social stigma attached to public acknowledgement of this problem for women.

Second, these gender differentials may reflect biases in who is recruited for research studies on a given topic. For example, over 70% of studies on alcohol abuse recruited mostly male participants, and only 6% recruited mostly women. Although the DSM describes schizophrenia as occurring equally in women and men, Hartung and Widiger summed across reviews of participation rates and concluded that 69% of research partici-

---

[1]DSM–5 is expected in May of 2013. For information, visit the American Psychiatric Association at *www.psych.org.*

[2]Trichotillmania and inhibited sexual desire/orgasm are reported to occur more often in women; gambling disorder (2:1), conduct disorder, and alcohol abuse, more frequently in men; and schizophrenia, equally.

pants were men. Beyond simple counting, women and men vary in the onset of schizophrenia (women later), in their personal histories prior to diagnosis, in the severity of their symptoms (milder in women), in their responsiveness to treatment, and even possibly in relevant brain patterns (also see Taylor & Langdon, 2006).

Third, more boys are diagnosed with childhood disorders, and women dominate more of the adult disorders. Some of this may have to do with who makes the referral (others, like parents and teachers, or one's self) and who is harmed by the person's behaviors. Contrast the aggressiveness and disruption of conduct disorders with the self-injury of Trichotillmania. Overall, childhood disorders tend to be more **externalizing** (affecting others); adult disorders, **internalizing** (affecting one's self). This shift in what is considered disordered behavior by age may itself be gendered, and interestingly, much of what is disordered for boys (e.g., reading disorders) has no parallel in later life.

Finally, the very definitions of some disorders may lean toward stereotyping of one gender. Inhibited sexual desire and orgasm is a good example. It may be more difficult for men to meet the criteria for this diagnosis, and there certainly are differences in cultural acceptance of women's and men's sexual arousal. These last points make us consider issues surrounding the very definition of disorders, a topic to which we'll return.

Our obvious starting point will be the DSM and how clinical diagnoses are done. Notice that I embedded overviews of specific diagnoses with gendered patterns— agoraphobia, alcohol and substance abuse, depression, eating disorders, and three personality disorders (borderline, histrionic, and dependent)—within this disucssion. After critiquing how diagnosis is done within a DSM-based medical model, we'll take a proactive approach and review the theory of feminist practice.

DIAGNOSIS: THE DSM-IV

The DSM defines a "**mental disorder**" as:

> ...*a clinically significant behavioral or psychological syndrome or pattern* that occurs in an individual and that is associated with *present distress* (e.g., a painful symptom) or *disability* (i.e., *impairment* in one of more *important* areas of functioning) or with a significantly increased risk of suffering death, pain, disability or an important loss of freedom. In addition, this syndrome or pattern *must not be merely an expectable and culturally sanctioned response* to a particular event, for example, the death of a loved one. Whatever its original cause, it must currently be considered a manifestation of a behavioral, psychological, or biological dysfunction in the individual. Neither deviant behavior (e.g., political, religious, or sexual) nor conflicts that are primarily between the individual and society are mental disorders unless the deviance or conflict is a symptom of a dysfunction in the individual, as described above (DSM–IV, 1994, p. xxi–xxii, italics added by Caplan, 1995).

Although this definition may sound reasonable and definitive on the face of it, a closer look reveals that all the italicized portions are compromised by subjectivity, and therefore vulnerable to biases (Caplan, 1995). For this reason, some therapists have questioned whether we should even think in terms of diagnostic labels.[3] A key question to ask may focus on how labels, once applied, will be used. Despite these very serious objections, labeling is at the heart of the DSM; is widely used (over 1 million copies of DSM–III–R were sold in less than 6 years [Caplan, 1995]); and assumes that a line can be established such that crossing it moves an individual from normality to abnormality.

The DSM claims that it classifies symptoms, not people, but in reality, a DSM diagnosis labels a person. Each disorder is assigned a number with decimal (e.g., 302.73 for "Female Orgasmic Disorder") that becomes a handy referent for insurance companies and lends a scientific aura to the diagnosis. A list of diagnostic criteria outlines the symptoms for each disorder, usually specifying cut-off points: how many symptoms must be present to merit each classification and its duration. There even are decision trees at the back of the volume to walk one through the choices possible within a general diagnostic category.

As early as 1977, a task force of the American *Psychological* Association questioned the conceptual basis of the DSM by highlighting its limitations. The DSM reflects a disease-based model extrapolated from medicine; the specific categories are unreliable (and continue to be so with low agreement rates even among trained therapists; Garfield, 1986); categories are deleted and added based on committee vote with little research backing; the labels can lead to biased treatment; and there is little evidence that such categorization facilitates treatments or predicts outcomes (Task Force, 1977, cited in Lerman, 1996; also see Hyman, 2010). Furthermore, the DSM imposes sharp boundaries between normal and abnormal as well as between disorders (Marecek, 2001). One estimate concluded that 60% of clients who seek help from a professional describe problems that fit none of the DSM categories (Wylie, 1995, cited in Marecek, 2001).

GENDERED PATTERNS IN DSM DIAGNOSES

Data collected from 2001 to 2003 in the United States demonstrate that fewer women than men (a ratio of 0.7:1.0) were *un*affected by DSM-defined mental disorders (Kessler et al., 2005). Women were consistently more likely to report internalizing disorders (both alone and in combination with other disorders; that is, co-morbid) as well as highly co-morbid major depressive episodes than men; men, more externalizing disorders (including social phobia and attention-deficit/hyperactivity disorder). The one area where no gender difference was found, bipolar disorder, also shows few gender differences in its expression, severity, and treatment (Diflorio & Jones, 2010). These general patterns for the lifetime **prevalence** of mental disorders extend to 15 countries surveyed by the World Health Organization (Seedat et al., 2009).

Table 12.1 catalogues some specific disorders identified in DSM-IV as occurring more frequently in one gender than the other (**intergroup differences**). American boys are more vulnerable than girls; adult women are more susceptible to major mood, anxiety, and eating disorders; men dominate in substance-abuse disorders; and women and men are diagnosed with some different personality disorders.

---

[3]Labeling opponents argue that labels are stigmatizing; labeling proponents argue that labels result in the provision of needed services. For a good overview of this debate, as well as data linking both lower stigma and high quality services to quality of life and enhanced self-concept, see Rosenfield (1997).

TABLE 12.1
Differential Diagnosis by Gender

More Common in Women	More Common in Men
CHILDHOOD	
Selective Mutism	Mental Retardation (1.5:1)
	Reading Disorder
	Language Disorders
	Autistic Disorders
	Attention Deficit/Hyperactivity
	Conduct Disorder
	Oppositional Defiant Disorder
	Feeding Disorder
	Tourette's Disorder (motor/vocal tics)
	Stereotypic Movement Disorder
	Elimination Disorders

ADOLESCENCE AND ADULTHOOD

Substance-Related Disorders

Alcohol Abuse and Dependence (5:1)
Drug Abuse and Dependence

Mood Disorders

Major Depression (2:1)
Dysthymic Disorder (2:1) (long-term depression

Anxiety Disorders

Agoraphobia (3:1)
Specific Phobia
Social Phobia

Somatoform Disorders

Somatization Disorder
Conversion Disorder

Dissociaative Disorders

Dissociative Identity Disorder (3-9:1)

Eating Disorders

Anorexia Nervosa (9:1)
Bulimia Nervosa (9:1)

Impulse-Control Disorders

Kleptomania	Explosive Disorder
Trichotillomania	Pyromania
	Pathological Gambling (3:1)

(continued)

TABLE 12.1
Differential Diagnosis by Gender (cont.)

More Common in Women	More Common in Men
Personality Disorders	
Borderline Personality Disorder (7.5:1)	Paranoid Personality Disorder
Histrionic Personality Disorder	Schizoid/Schizotypal Personality Disorder
Dependent Personality Disorder	Antisocial Personality Disorder
	Narcissistic Personality Disorder
	Obsessive-Compulsive Personality Disorder

Note. Compiled from the *Diagnostic and Statistical Manual of Mental Disorders*, 4th ed. (1994). Other categories of disorders include: cognitive disorders, mental disorders due to a medical condition, psychotic disorders (e.g., schizophrenia), factitious disorders (feigned ailments), sexual and gender identity disorders, sleep disorders, and adjustment disorders.

Although non-Hispanic Blacks and Hispanics overall were less likely to be affected by a mental disorder than Whites (Kessler et al., 2005), some patterns differ along racial and ethnic lines for specific disorders (**intragroup differences**). Major depression appears most commonly in White Americans and least in African Americans. Among women, alcohol abuse and dependence is highest for African Americans and lowest for Latinas. Panic disorders are most pronounced for White women and least common among Latinas, and **somatization disorders** occur more frequently in the lifetimes of non-Black women (.78%) than African American women (.17%).

Summing up, gender differences emerge in a variety of areas. Five of these have attracted the attention of clinical researchers and will be described in this chapter: agoraphobia, alcohol and substance abuse, depression, eating disorders, and a set of three personality disorders (borderline, histrionic, and dependent). Rather than focus on each of these "mental disorders" separately, as a DSM-based approach might dictate, our discussion will proceed as a critique of the DSM, using each of these five gendered areas as examples to illustrate points made in this argument. My argument will focus on three areas: (1) on definitions of what is pathological and what is normal; (2) on biological explanations for gender differences in diagnosis; and (3) on problems with exclusively intrapsychic explanations.

DSM DEFINITIONS

We saw at the start of this chapter that determining the gender ratio within any diagnosis is complicated by sampling and definitional biases. Fundamentally, there's a logical tautology here that draws on circular reasoning: Because research on DSM classifications starts with these classifications, it confirms itself. If the DSMs recorded psychopathologies that existed independent of it, we might expect revisions to be relatively minor. However, the DSMs have grown remarkably over time. The first edition appeared in 1952, was 129 pages long, and described about 79 different diagnostic categories. The most recent version, published in 1994, extends to 886 pages and defines 374 categories (Lerman, 1996). Disorders come and go, take on different names and defining criteria, and move from presumably legitimate status in the text back into the appendices, where they hang in limbo until further research either re-establishes them in the text or removes them. These flip-flops seem most common for controversial disorders involving sexual orientation and gender. In sum, we need to explore what *legitimates* a disorder so that it is included in the DSM, as well as what remains excluded, and thus "normal."

What's Pathological?

Picture the following client who is being assessed by a therapist:

> Within less than 10 minutes of talking with a therapist, *Terry* is sweating profusely, trembling, having trouble breathing, and feeling lightheaded and out of control. When things settle down, Terry says that fears of these sorts of attacks make leaving the house difficult. Terry goes to great lengths to avoid being in a crowd, crossing a bridge, or traveling, preferring to stay home or venture out only occasionally with a companion. Terry always needs to know that escape is possible.

Is Terry a woman or a man? If you slipped a pronoun into the description as you read it, was it "she" or "he"?

The description of Terry illustrates the two defining criteria for diagnosing **agoraphobia** (with or without a history of panic disorder). In all likelihood, you pictured Terry as a woman. Fully 85 to 95% of diagnosed agoraphobics are women, the typical age of onset is the mid-twenties to early thirties, the majority are married (Gelfond, 1991), and symptoms are more severe in women than men (Turgeon et al., 1998). Prevalence rates for panic disorder are comparable across Latina, African American, and White women (Katerndahl & Realini, 1993). It is estimated that only about one-quarter of phobics seek treatment (Fodor, 1992), and fully 26% of normal college students report experiencing panic attacks in the past year (Brown & Cash, 1990). In a study of average women, 55% scored at or near the clinical range for agoraphobia (Gelfond, 1988, cited in Gelfond, 1991). These findings suggest that there's a lot more agoraphobia in the general population of women than has been diagnosed as a mental disorder, raising red flags about how "abnormal" some agoraphobia really is.

Agoraphobic women differ from agoraphobic men in that women are more sensitive to others, fear being alone more, and avoid going out alone (Bekker, 1996). Married women's agoraphobia may be sustained by a symptom-supportive spouse (Hafner & Minge, 1989) who generally is more critical of his wife than control husbands (Chambless et al., 2002). Thus agoraphobia is expressed by women as fears of solitary and anonymous situations. Agoraphobia also may be easier for women than men to admit—it may be compromising for a guy to admit fears of being away from home (Bekker, 1996). When an antipanic pill was introduced in Holland, signaling that panic was biologically based and hence chemically correctable, significantly more phobic men called a hot line for help and advice than before.

Majorie Gelfond (1991) interviewed, tested, and observed 21 women diagnosed as agoraphobic, 20 average women, and 21 independent women (who scored highest on a measure of autonomy reflecting how often in the past year they traveled more than 50 miles alone, traveled at night, and ate alone in a restaurant). Overall, independent women differed from the other two groups who had many qualities in common. Agoraphobic and average women shared less **agentic** gender-role orientations, were less confident in their way-finding abilities, used less detail in the neighborhood maps they drew, and had restrictive parents (although the agoraphobics' parents were even more anxious). All women considered home a safe haven, although the agoraphobic women lived in the most highly personalized, carefully decorated houses. All shared similar experiences with crime, but only the independent women were confident in their abilities to respond to criminal occurrences. The overriding finding is that agoraphobic women, although quite different from independent women, weren't that different from women in general.

All this suggests that agoraphobia represents the extreme end of a continuum reflecting many women's concerns about a not-so-women-friendly world. If a continuum of such fears does exist, where do we draw the line between reasonable fears and psychopathology? Also, how much does it help Terry to classify her/him as an agoraphobic? There is no doubt but that Terry is experiencing hardship, but is this lessened by labeling this pain as an abnormality? We might ask similar questions of other presumably pathological disorders, calling into question the whole basis of the DSM by asking, What's abnormal? There are no definitive answers, but our discussion certainly suggests that these concerns cannot be dismissed lightly.

What's "Normal"?

Maybe we can get a better sense of what's pathological by defining what is normal. Again, consider the following profile of a client coming for therapy:

> *Lee* can't stay in a relationship—friends, relatives, and lovers fence Lee in. Lee doesn't like talking about feelings, stays withdrawn from others, and doesn't want to know what others are feeling. Lee thinks there's a place for men and women; feels confident to do anything, especially perform sexually; and thinks others should respect and praise this sexual prowess and omnipotence. Lee is threatened by women who seem more intelligent and derives little, if any, pleasure from helping others.

Did you picture Lee as a woman or a man?

Lee doesn't fit neatly into any of the 374 DSM classifications, so by default, Lee is normal. In contrast, Lee might be labeled as exhibiting "Delusional Dominating Personality Disorder," according to DSM critic Paula Caplan (1995). If Lee sounds like a man, he's meant to. He represents an exaggeration of masculine stereotyping. Caplan finds that audiences respond knowingly to this caricature, granting it some legitimacy if we define abnormality by popular acclaim. Expecting to be rebuffed, she submitted it to the DSM committee for consideration where their initial reaction questioned her sincerity.

However, evidence is growing which suggests that the kind of **hypermasculinity** attributed to our hypothetical "Lee" negatively impacts men's mental health and well being. Popular media descriptions of threats to men's mental health focus on the suppression of emotion, gender role changes in employment and sexual expression, and the advancement of women (Coyle & Morgan-Sykes, 1998). Some of these may indeed prove problematic. A study with 98 men seeking counseling found connections between unfavorable well-being and intense competitive strivings, restricted affection, and work-family conflict (Hayes &

Mahalik, 2000). Emotional restriction was related to relationship problems among college men (Blazina & Watkins, 2000). Similarly, mildly depressed men differed from non-depressed men on gender-role conflict (Mahalik & Cournoyer, 2000). Among Mexican American men, high levels of machismo, gender-role conflict, and restrictive emotionality went together and predicted depression and stress (Fragoso & Kashubeck, 2000). Hyper-masculinity may belong in the DSM!

Contrast Caplan's proposal with **self-defeating personality disorder**. This "mental disorder" appeared in DSM-III, was intended for inclusion in DSM-IV despite serious empirical shortcomings (Caplan & Gans, 1991), but it was withdrawn at the last minute in response to a public outcry (Caplan, 1995). In essence, this "disorder" blamed women for being abused: "chooses people and situations that lead to disappointment, failure, or mistreatment…"; "rejects or renders ineffective the attempts of others to help him or her"; "incites angry or rejecting responses from others…"; "rejects opportunities for pleasure…" ; "engages in excessive self-sacrifice"; and so on. The inclusion of this category would have provided a sanctioned way to blame people (in most instances, women) for their own victimization.

What I am asking you to think about here is what may be missing from the DSM. Might the columns of Table 12.1 tip in the direction of more disorders ascribed to women because more disorders in the DSM fit women, whereas those that might describe men are missing? This is the question Paula Caplan is raising with her proposal for a Delusional Dominating Personality Disorder. Although Caplan surely does not want to expand the DSM by adding more "disorders," her proposal does raise questions about what makes the grade and what doesn't.

In conclusion, we raised questions in the preceding section about what is included and excluded from classification in the DSM-IV. In the next two sections, we examine specific diagnoses within the DSM with an eye to understanding why gendered patterns exist within them. Why is it that more women than men are diagnosed as depressed, eating disordered, and characterologically different with borderline, histrionic, and dependent personality disorders? Why are more men diagnosed for alcohol and substance abuse? One explanation relies on biological differences; another, on intrapsychic differences which can ignore broader contextual influences in women's lives.

NOT ALL BIOLOGY

The DSM system best fits with the assumptions of a medical model. Adherents of this model envision mental disorders as similar to physical ones—the role of therapists, paralleling that of physicians, is to catalog symptoms, diagnose, and subsequently treat as the diagnosis dictates. The strongest evidence in support of a medical model comes from explorations of the etiology (origins) of disorders in biology. There is evidence that biology plays a role in some disorders, although never an exclusive or even dominant role. Also, as we saw in Chapter 3, it is important to remember that causal relationships between biology and behavior run both ways: Biology not only influences behavior but is influenced by it as well.

For example, in a series of studies with female twins, Kenneth Kendler and his associates found greater **concordance rates** in **monozygotic twins** than in **dizygotic twins** for major depression (Kendler et al., 1992a), generalized anxiety disorder (Kendler et al., 1992b), phobias (Kendler et al., 1992c), and alcoholism (Kendler, Health et al., 1992b).

Estimating the proportional contribution of genetics to the presence of each disorder (**heritability**) for women and men, these researchers reported heritability estimates of 60% for agoraphobia, 52% for alcohol abuse and dependence, 43% for depression, 42% for eating disorders, and 49% for borderline, 32% for histrionic, and 37% for dependent personality disorders (Kendler et al., 2011). Be sure to note that none of these percentages is close to 100%, and understand that a specific genetic marker has not been identified for any. Genetics, like other biological explanations such as hormonal changes, may trigger depression in women but always as part of a complex confluence of social, psychological, and biological factors (Nolen-Hoeksema & Hilt, 2009).

Differing intragroup patterns across the life course, across race and ethnicity, and across cultures suggest that more than biology is at work. In pre-adolescents, rates of depression are low and likely equal for girls and boys, but then a gap emerges and peaks from ages 15 through 30 years old (Parker & Brotchie, 2010). From the late thirties onward, rates of depression decline for both women and men but the numbers never equalize. This gender difference is even more pronounced among Black and Latino/a adults than among White, and this gender difference holds up across many cultures and countries (Nolen-Hoeksema & Hilt, 2009).

Focusing on biological causes leads to the treatment of disorders with medical treatments (drugs), the domains of psychiatrists and physicians (not psychologists and other mental health professionals), although these exclusive rights are being challenged. Over half of physician visits where patients are diagnosed with a mental disorder result in a prescription for mood-altering **psychotropic drugs**: tranquilizers, sedatives/hypnotics, antidepressants, and stimulants (Travis, 1988b). In the United States, adult use of antidepressants almost tripled between 1988 to 1994 and 1999 to 2000 so that 10% of women and 4% of men were taking antidepressants in 2000 (CDC, 2004).

It has been argued that women receive more drug prescriptions because they suffer from more psychiatric distress and are more willing to report psychological symptoms to physicians. There is evidence that doctors are more likely to believe that women's physical illnesses encompass a psychological component and dismiss women's complaints of undesirable side effects of medication (Shapiro, 1995). Furthermore, advertisements for drugs in professional magazines more commonly feature women (Hansen & Osborne, 1995), and drug ads appeal directly to women consumers through women's magazines (Sokol, 2010).

Although biology does appear to play some role in the etiology of certain mental disorders, these studies urge us to look beyond biology for a fuller picture. The medical model that underlies the DSM may not foster such expansive exploration. Furthermore, the possible over-reliance of medical practitioners on psychotropic drugs to treat women's complaints, both physical and psychological, suggests needs for further research and cautious vigilance on the part of consumers. It also raises questions about the potential psychological treatment of truly physiological maladies—problems that if left untreated could jeopardize women's lives (Brozovic, 1989). All this underscores the need for a feminist approach to psychopharmacology (Marsh, 1995) that considers biochemical treatment as an adjunct to, not a replacement for, psychotherapy (Rosewater, 1988).

NOT ALL INTRAPSYCHIC

Jeanne Marecek (2001) argues that the conventional DSM system identifies the individual as the locus of pathology without taking into consideration the **social contexts** of women's and men's lives. This assumption removes the family, the community, and other social factors from consideration in both diagnosis and treatment. Feminist critiques have challenged this exclusive focus on intrapsychic factors presumably internal to, and controlled by, the client. Apparent gender differences in specific diagnoses might be influenced by gender stereotyping, involving both the definition of disorders and therapists' judgments in assigning diagnostic labels, as well as from contextual factors differentially affecting the lives of women and men.

Stereotyping and DSM Definitions

Try picturing two more clients seeking therapy:

> Over the past two weeks, *Chris* has been depressed most of nearly every day, feeling sad and empty and appearing tearful to others. Chris, who usually isn't like this and who is not experiencing bereavement, doesn't get pleasure from or feel interested in what had been pleasurable activities. Chris doesn't feel like eating, resulting in weight loss across the past month, and wakes up in the middle of the night and can't get back to sleep. Thus Chris is fatigued so that even the smallest tasks, like washing and getting dressed, seem exhausting. Chris appears agitated during the interview, having trouble sitting still, speaks in low, labored tones, and has trouble concentrating. Chris reports feeling worthless and keeps thinking morbid thoughts. What's wrong with Chris?

> *Pat* shows up reeking of alcohol. Pat has been referred for counseling because of repeated driving violations and for picking fights with coworkers. Pat knows that drinking creates problems but feels terrible if a day goes by without a drink—nauseous, agitated, sweating, and just plain nervous. At these times, it seems easier to take a drink (or two, or more—it seems to take more and more to help), even though obtaining and consuming alcohol takes up lots of Pat's time. What's wrong with Pat?

The argument proposed here is that the DSM system, as conceived, draws on gendered stereotyping to define syndromes. For example, is the list of symptoms that defines major depression gender-neutral, or does it, at its core, rely on images of women as depressive and thus describes gender-biased versions of this disorder? Chris fits the DSM definition of major depression. Did you imagine her as a woman (specifically a White, middle class woman)? Similarly, does the image of an alcoholic as a man shape how alcohol dependence and abuse are presented in the DSM? Pat presents the symptoms of alcohol abuse and dependence—do you picture "him"? Parallel logic applies to the scenario for Terry, our agoraphobic earlier in the chapter. Hope Landrine (1988; 1989) found these patterns in the responses of students who made consistent determinations regarding the gender of targets diagnosed with depression, dependent personality disorders (White, middle class, married women), and antisocial personality disorders (poor, young men). Notice how *stereotyping of these disorders is consistent with gender stereotyping.*

Throughout this book, we have seen that gender stereotyping goes not only with the sex category of participants (women are expected to be depressed), but also with gender-typing (femininity is associated with depression). Melissa Hoffman and her colleagues (2004) tested both these linkages by looking at how sex categories (being female or male) as well as femininity (expressiveness or **communion**) and masculinity (instrumentality or **agency**) affected the mental health symptoms reported by high school students. They classified these symptoms broadly as **internalizing** (causing problems for the student her/himself; e.g., feeling depressed) or **externalizing** (causing difficulties for others; e.g., lying and cheating). As sex category would predict, girls reported higher femininity and internalizing; boys, more masculinity and externalizing; but this is just the start.

Differences between girls and boys in externalizing closed when gender-typing was considered. Rather, both girls and boys high in masculine agency or low in feminine communion were more likely to report externalizing symptoms. Thus, gender-typing, not being female or male per se, predicted externalizing. In contrast, being female was associated with high internalizing, but so was low agency combined with low social attractiveness and self-worth (for both girls and boys). In other words, girls did report more internalizing symptoms than boys, but so did girls *and boys* with low agency, social attractiveness, and self-worth.[4]

Stereotyping and Therapists' Judgments

We have asked many questions about the validity of the DSM itself. Here we will focus on how the DSM is *used*. Might therapists themselves bring biases to the DSM that are justified, reinforced, and further entrenched by biases within the DSM system so that their combination further compounds the effects of gender stereotyping? In a classic study, Inge Broverman and her colleagues (1970) asked clinically trained psychologists to rate one of three clients described as a "healthy, mature, socially competent adult" (1) "man," (2) "woman," or (3) "person."

There was remarkable consensus among the therapists about what constitutes psychological health for women, for men, and for adults in general, when each was considered separately. Healthy "men" and "persons" were described similarly to each other and differently from the "woman." Healthy women, relative to men, were portrayed as being more submissive, less independent, less adventurous, more easily influenced, less aggressive, less competitive, more excitable in minor crises, more emotional, more conceited about their appearance, less objective, having their feelings more easily hurt, and disliking math and science—not a very flattering picture of women's mental health.

Given what we have learned about contemporary stereotyping, we might expect such explicit linkages of mental health to being male/adult and not to being female to have ceased. They haven't. Susan Seem and Diane Clark (2006) updated their list of stereotypic traits and repeated the above research design with Masters'-level counseling students. They found that the healthy man was still generally masculine stereotyped, that the healthy man and adult overlapped more than each did with the healthy woman and that the healthy woman continued to be generally feminine, but with three new, masculine-typed expectations: to be "strong" and "independent" and to "enjoy a challenge."

There also is some evidence of the more subtle bias we might expect in contemporary stereotyping studies. For example, a study of gender-typing by 554 psychotherapists found that they typically stereotyped women as more communal and less agentic than male

---

[4]Similarly, other studies link gender-typing with specific mental disorders—depression: Broderick & Korteland, 2002; eating disorders: Klingenspor, 2002; self-sacrificing: Dear & Roberts, 2002; and general psychological health and well-being: Woodhill & Samuels, 2003.

targets (Turner & Turner, 1991). Another study of 229 therapists reported that they were more likely to view men's problems with a utilitarian, let's-fix-it approach (Fowers et al., 1996). Both studies suggest that therapists approach male clients expecting a more favorable prognosis.

We saw in Chapter 11 that physicians' expectations about who has heart disease may affect how women are diagnosed. A similar pattern regarding therapists' biases appears here. In a clever analogue study by John Robertson and Louise Fitzgerald (1990), 47 practicing counselors-therapists were shown one of two videos in which the same male actor described symptoms of depression (poor appetite, boredom, and sleeplessness). In half the tapes, the actor described his marriage as a traditional one in which he was employed as an engineer and his wife was a homemaker and primary caretaker of their children. In the other version, only these segments were altered to describe a nontraditional arrangement in which domestic and employment roles were reversed.

Not surprisingly, practitioners rated the nontraditional client as less masculine (**agentic**) on 14 of 20 items of the Bem Sex Role Inventory. Most notably for us, the nontraditional client was diagnosed significantly more frequently with severe mood disorder, and more therapists planned to probe for marital problems as the source of his depression—despite the client's expressed belief that his marital arrangement was satisfactory. This speaks volumes about the mental health implications of breaking gendered occupational and domestic norms. More to the point here, depression, with its feminine connotations, was a more likely diagnosis for a less "masculinized" client.

Other analog studies present the same written description of a case to practitioners and then ask for their diagnosis. For example, Douglas Samuel and Thomas Widiger (2009) shared the case of "Madeline G" with practicing therapists—a case widely regarded as a prototypical example of narcissistic and histrionic personality disorder. Their participants largely agreed with this assessment, but not when "Madeline" was framed as "Matthew." Their diagnosis of Matthew veered away from histrionic toward antisocial personality disorder. This shift reflects the general framing of histrionic as more common in women; antisocial, as more typical of men (Lynam & Widiger, 2007), suggesting that therapists' expectations about the gendering of each personality disorder influenced their judgments.

What happens when we look at the opposite scenario, such as when a woman presents the symptoms of a male-dominated disorder such as **alcohol abuse and dependence**? Alcoholism may not be suspected when it indeed exists (Vogeltanz & Wilsnack, 1997). A review of 90 studies on substance abuse found that fully 65 of the researchers (72%) failed to probe their data for potential gender differences, even though these analyses were feasible (Toneatto et al., 1992). This oversight results in a gap in our understanding of alcoholism (Wilsnack et al., 1994) and reinforces **androcentric bias** (Wilke, 1994).

Reflecting stronger societal linkages of drinking with men (LaBrie et al., 2008) and complementary disapproval of drinking by women (Gomberg, 1993), except when the context permits (bachelorette parties; Montemurro & McClure, 2005), women alcoholics are thought to require more therapy sessions (Hardy & Johnson, 1992). Given this, alcoholic women are more likely to be considered co-morbid, combining alcohol abuse with additional diagnoses of mental disorders, most often depression and anxiety (Haver & Dahlgren, 1995) and eating disorders (Harrop & Marlatt, 2010). In keeping with these co-diagnoses, women report that they drink to reduce anxiety (Dunne, et al., 1993) and alter their moods (Olenick & Chalmers, 1991). This perspective then tends to view women's, but not men's, alcoholism as symptomatic of another underlying disorder.

Many adult American women (43%) and men (61%) drink alcohol (at least 12 drinks in the past year), with more White (51%) than both Black (31%) and Hispanic (28%) women drinkers (CDC, 2010b, Tables 26 & 27). Cross-culturally and across age groups, men drink larger quantities, drink more frequently, and report more drinking-related problems (Wilsnack et al., 1994). Young women generally have higher rates of intoxication, drinking problems, heavy episodic drinking, and alcohol dependence than older women, who are often characterized by moderate but more frequent drinking. Binge drinking by women is more common in coeducational colleges than women's colleges (Dowdall et al., 1998). Alcohol abuse is sanctioned more in African American than White women (Rhodes & Johnson, 1997), and their patterns of drinking differ. Among Black women, alcoholism rates rise from 18 to 44 years of age and remain high until after 65. In contrast, incidence among White women peaks early (18 to 29 years) and then declines steadily (Caetano, 1994). Patterns of alcohol problems among lesbians, like those of African American women, do not decline with age and are at rates two times higher than those for the general population (Hughes & Wilsnack, 1994).

Factors putting women at risk for drinking-related problems include a family history of problem drinking, depression, trauma, employment in male-dominated occupations, unwanted statuses (e.g., being involuntarily unemployed), stress, and peer and spousal pressure (Gomberg, 1994; Wilsnack et al., 1994). Although linked to marital dissolution for some women with no prior history of alcohol abuse, drinking problems may abate for women who leave reinforcing relationships in which the partner is a heavy drinker (Sandoz, 1995; Wilsnack et al., 1991). Women with alcoholic parents will offer more help to an exploitative man, suggesting that high-risk women are prone toward developing nonsupportive relationships (Lyon & Greenberg, 1991). In sum, just as there are male depressives, there are female alcoholics, regardless of gendered stereotyping of these two (and presumably other) disorders.

Neglected Contextual Factors

The DSM and its use have been criticized for focusing solely on individual causes and expressions of disorders, to the exclusion of contextual influences (Brown & Ballou, 1992; Kaschak, 1992; Lerman, 1996; Marecek & Hare-Mustin, 1991). For example, in the American Psychological Association's "Task Force Report on Women and Depression" (McGrath et al., 1990), a variety of moderating variables is identified (such as family and employment roles, victimization, and poverty) that may combine with an individual's personality to predict depression. To focus on individual personality factors alone implies a personal deficit model that ignores history, human spirit, and a life span perspective (Root, 1992).

Such an individualistic focus is most pronounced in the DSM for personality disorders which are stable over time and hence presumed to be characterological; that is, coming from within the person regardless of external stressors (Brown, 1992). These disorders are afforded heightened attention by "multiaxial assessment" in the DSM-IV whereby clients are assessed over five axes, including Axis II specifically for personality disorders and mental retardation.[5] Looking at Table 12.1, women dominate in the diagnoses of borderline, histrionic, and dependent personality disorders. The most extensively studied dif-

---

[5]The other axes are: Axis I: Clinical Disorders; Axis III: General Medical Conditions; Axis IV: Psychosocial and Environmental Problems; and Axis V: Global Assessment and Functioning.

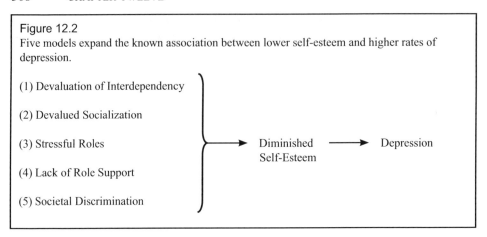

Figure 12.2
Five models expand the known association between lower self-esteem and higher rates of depression.

(1) Devaluation of Interdependency

(2) Devalued Socialization

(3) Stressful Roles   Diminished   ⟶   Depression
                         Self-Esteem

(4) Lack of Role Support

(5) Societal Discrimination

ferential diagnosis on Axis I (Clinical Disorders) is major depression, estimated as two times more common in women. Each of these disorders will help paint a picture about the importance of **social context**.

To be classified as exhibiting **major depression**, a client must experience at least two depressive episodes, each of which entails at least five symptoms from a list of nine, present over at least a 2-week period, and at least one of which must be either depressed mood or loss of interest or pleasure. (If depression is chronic over the course of at least 2 years, the diagnosis changes to **dysthymic disorder**, which also tips toward higher prevalence in women.) The only mentions of causes external to the person in this presentation are the disqualifying exceptions of depression due to physiological effects of a substance (street drugs or a medication), a general medical condition, or bereavement. Beyond these exceptions, external threats to self-esteem, interpersonal stress, body dissatisfaction, physical illness, finances and employment, acculturation, and trauma are ignored.

Self-esteem and depression. A link between low self-esteem and depression has been well established (Katz et al., 2002) and has been accounted for by at least five interrelated models (Woods et al., 1994). Each of these models explores what causes the client's self-esteem to be low, considering factors outside the woman herself for the root cause of diminished self-esteem. Self-esteem then becomes a **mediator** in these models, holding for Asian, African American, and White women (Woods et al., 1994).

First, *self-in-relation* theorists posit that lowered self-esteem results from the devaluation of women's learned desires for interdependency and intimacy. Indeed, undergraduate women who reported lack of mutuality in their relationships were more prone to depression (Sperberg & Stabb, 1998), as were eighth-grade girls who reported low authenticity in their relationships (Tolman et al., 2006). Both self-esteem and relationship harmony are tied to women's well-being (Reid, 2004) and to rumination and depression (Cambron et al., 2009), especially when women feel responsible for the emotional tone of their relationships (Nolen-Hoeksema & Jackson, 2001). Whereas women seek validation through relationships, our individualistic society values the opposite—autonomy. This creates a double bind for women, who have to choose between being good, caring women or independent, agentic "men."

A second, *socialization* model extends this reasoning to all feminine socialization—arguing that most feminine traits are devalued, causing women who hold these characteristics to feel inadequate relative to the cultural (masculine) ideal. Consistent with this logic, instrumentality/**agency** is linked to stronger self-esteem and lower depression (Hermann & Betz, 2004), and women who constantly put concerns for others ahead of concern for themselves ("**unmitigated communion**") are more likely to report depression (Katz et al., 2002).

The third and fourth social role models emphasize the differing roles women and men enact. One model highlights the *stresses* that accompany women's roles, and the other concentrates on the *lack of support* afforded women in the fulfillment of their roles. Interpersonal stress plays a role in depression for some women and girls—more commonly than for men (Davis et al., 1999) and boys (Moran & Eckenrode, 1991). Although women typically derive support from their more expansive social networks than do men, these networks can also be sources of interpersonal stress (Turner, 1994) and criticism (Gruen et al., 1994). Involvement in conflicted networks is associated with depression for both African American and White women (Woods et al., 1994). The potential supports and risks of social networks are evident in a study of college women who were asked to describe the expressiveness of their families (Cooley, 1992). Women were more prone to depression when their families were more negatively than positively expressive, in contrast to depression-resistant women in families showing net positive expressiveness.

A fifth model argues that women are vulnerable to depressed self-esteem and hence depression because of societal *discrimination*, which blocks their achievement of personal mastery and is related to women's lesser power and status (Nolen-Hoeksema & Keita, 2003). For example, women who reported more exposure to sexist treatment also exhibited more symptoms of depression, anxiety, and **somatization** (Klonoff et al., 2000), and psychological distress (Moradi & Funderburk, 2006). Furthermore, sexism predicted African American women's psychological distress (Szymanski & Stewart, 2010), and among college women, this relationship between sexism and distress was partially mediated by reduced feelings of control (Landry & Mercurio, 2009).

Two reviews link gender inequality across cultures with women's heightened mental health disorders (Andermann, 2010)—specifically identifying poverty, limited access to resources (nutrition, education, employment, and health care), workplace harassment, and exposure to disasters as major threats to women's mental health (Chandra & Satyanarayana, 2010). Most provocatively, Soraya Seedat and her colleagues (2009) concluded that the narrowing of gender differences in major depression across generations (**cohorts**) worldwide is linked to changes away from the traditionalism of women's roles.

Distress that results from other forms of discrimination also impacts some women's mental health. For example, race-related stress increases anxiety and obsessive-compulsive symptoms for African American women (Greer et al., 2009; Greer, 2011); (Go to *pwq. sagepub.com* to listen to a podcast interview with Dr. Tawanda Greer.) Racism serves to undermine African American women's sense of mastery and thus makes them feel less psychologically resilient (Keith et al., 2010). Similarly, internalized homophobia is associated with heightened psychological distress among sexual minority women (Szymanski & Owens, 2008), as well as mental health problems and substance use (Lehavot & Simoni, 2011).

Body image and mental disorders. We saw in Chapter 10 that some women report greater dissatisfaction with their bodies than do men. Among both depressed outpatients and general college students, body image is the single most influential factor in distinguishing women's from men's depression (Santor et al., 1994). Specifically, among women and girls who emphasize the importance of appearance, body dissatisfaction predicts depression (Koenig & Wasserman, 1995). The root of this dissatisfaction for White women is concern about weight as a central component of how their femininity is physically enacted (Bay-Cheung et al., 2002). Given this centrality of weight, at least in some women's psyches, it is no surprise that depression and eating disorders appear together (Harrell & Jackson, 2008).

Two specific diagnoses compose the category of eating disorders in the DSM-IV. **Anorexia nervosa** is characterized by a refusal to maintain a minimally acceptable body weight. **Bulimia nervosa** is distinguished by recurrent episodes of binge overeating followed by inappropriate compensatory purging behaviors such as self-induced vomiting; laxative, diuretic, or other medicinal abuse[6]; fasting; and/or excessive exercise. An essential feature of both disorders is a disturbance in perception of body shape and weight. Bulimia occurs at least five times more often than anorexia (Marecek, 2001). Both are described in DSM-IV as disorders with greatest incidence in young women. As we expected, researchers narrow these demographics even further to mostly White women (Lucero et al., 1992) and heterosexual women (Herzog et al., 1992).

Characterological approaches emphasize the personality traits associated with eating disorders. Some examples include ambivalence about emotional expressivity (Krause et al., 2000), dissociative experiences (from daydreaming to blocking out thoughts; Lyubomirsky et al., 2001), underidentification with masculine/agentic qualities (Klingenspor, 1994) and over-identification with femininity (Burns, 2004), adherence to a superwoman ideal (Mensinger et al., 2007), strong desires for perfectionism (Minarik & Ahrens, 1996) and hyper-competitiveness regarding appearance (but not academic or career achievement; Burckle et al., 1999), and beliefs that dieting and thinness lead to overall self-improvement (Hohlstein et al., 1998).

As we saw in Chapter 10, **objectification** theory posits that personality predispositions in women like those above prepare them to internalize messages from a "culture of thinness," that values a thin physique, sets up dieting as normative, links thinness to some athletic and occupational pursuits, and stresses thinness in media and medical advice (Fredrickson & Roberts, 1997; White, 1992). It comes as no surprise to us that researchers find evidence in support of objectification theory's prediction that self-objectification is associated with disordered eating (Calogero et al., 2005; Noll & Fredrickson, 1998; Tylka & Hill, 2004).

Objectification theory adds cultural contributions to our understanding of eating disorders, as well as expands our thinking beyond pathological disorders like anorexia and bulimia to include more normalized and pervasive symptomatology. For example, one study of 167 mostly White women at a western U.S. university found that 7% were diagnosable with a DSM-level eating disorder and 28% were symptomatic for some form of disordered eating (Mintz et al., 1997). In a larger, more diverse sample of 334 women from a southwestern U.S. university, about 10% tested as diagnosable and fully 39% were symptomatic (Cohen & Petrie, 2005).

---

[6]Medicinal abuse differs by race/ethnicity such that African American women typically prefer laxatives; Latinas, diuretics (Cachelin et al., 2000).

Such evidence of a "culture of thinness" shifts our focus away from characterologically deficient women to **social contexts** that encourage disordered eating. However, a few recent feminist analyses, although supportive of such refocusing outward and on objectification, argue that an exclusive emphasis on weight, attractiveness, and thinness may miss the mark for some women with eating disorders (see Thompson, 1995). Both anorexia nervosa and bulimia are found in women of color and outside Western culture (Dolan, 1991), although detecting these problems may be obstructed by stereotyping of who does and who doesn't suffer with eating disorders (Root, 1990).

Among Asian American (Hall, 1995; Lee, 1995), African American, Latina (Thompson, 1992), and lesbian (Brown, 1987) women, eating disorders may be psychological responses, not to body dissatisfaction alone, but to sexual abuse, racism, classism, heterosexism, and poverty. Along these lines, college women's eating disturbances have been linked to psychological aggression from male partners in dating relationships (Skomorovsky et al., 2006). This perspective regards eating disorders as more than seemingly narcissistic attempts to conform to cultural standards of beauty. It regards eating as a way to handle emotional distress and reassert control; for example, by changing body parts that may be considered responsible for attracting abuse or by turning to food for comfort.

Other external sources of disorders. Women's susceptibility to chronic but non-life-threatening illnesses makes physical complaints and functional limitations a source of depression (Betrus et al., 1995). Also associated with women's depression are financial strain (Mendes-de-Leon et al., 1994), poverty (van der Waerden et al., 2011), unemployment (Hauenstein & Boyd, 1994), nonemployment (Bromberger & Matthews, 1994), homelessness (Ingram et al., 1996), and physical inactivity (Wang et al., 2011). These patterns extend to other disorders as well. Alcohol and drug-related problems are exacerbated by poverty (Thomas, 1995) and homelessness (Geissler et al, 1995). Exposure to sexism predicts disordered eating among women (Sabik & Tylka, 2006). Schizophrenia is diagnosed more frequently in people with lower socioeconomic status (Greenwald, 1992). At times these risk factors may be too narrowly defined in line with stereotyping. For example, Karen Wyche (1993) contends that poor, single-parenting women are overrepresented in applied research exploring factors that affect African American women's lives.

Acculturation of women into American society may create two risks. One results from the added stresses that accompany pressures to blend in. One example is found among some Korean American women who are vulnerable to depression resulting from acculturation pressures (Shin, 1994). The second makes strongly acculturated women more vulnerable to the gendered patterns of disorders that permeate our culture. For example, stronger adoption of American culture has been related to risks of depression among Mexican American women (Masten et al., 1994) and of eating disorders among African (Pumariega et al., 1994) and Asian (Cummins & Lehman, 2007) American women.

Violence and mental disorders. Finally, there is a growing body of research linking women's depression to violence and trauma (Cutler & Nolen-Hoeksema, 1991; Hamilton & Jensvold, 1992; Howard et al., 2010). This relationship holds across a diversity of women, including African American (Barbee, 1992), Asian American (Ho, 1990), and lesbian (Rothblum, 1990) women, although each may express this connection in unique ways (Rosewater, 1990). The neglected role of trauma in women's lives comes through more clearly when we turn our attention to the personality disorders in which women dominate: borderline ($d = -.09$), histrionic ($d = -.13$), and dependent ($d = -.24$); Lynam & Widiger, 2007).

Borderline personality disorder is characterized by attention seeking, manipulative behavior, rapidly shifting emotions, self-destructiveness, angry disruptions in close relationships, and chronic feelings of deep emptiness and loss of identity. **Histrionic personality disorder** is distinguished by pervasive and excessive emotionality and attention-seeking behavior. The essential feature of **dependent personality disorder** is an excessive need to be taken care of, leading to submissive and clinging behaviors and fears of separation. Think of each of these three personality disorders in the context of child sexual abuse, rape, intimate partner abuse, and so on. Researchers find that sexual and physical abuses occur in women diagnosed with personality disorders at very high rates—as much as 81% (Bryer et al., 1987; Herman et al., 1989).

Maria Root (1992) distinguishes among three forms of trauma, all of which are stressful. The most obvious forms are **direct trauma**, such as rape and abuse, which are identified by maliciously perpetrated violence. Direct traumas encompass experiences not only of being targeted for, but also of being forced to commit, atrocities (e.g., military orders to kill civilians). **Indirect trauma** is produced through secondary effects, including experiences such as pulling bodies from wreckage, watching one's mother being beaten, and witnessing homicide. **Insidious trauma** results from being devalued because of an individual characteristic intrinsic to one's identity, such as one's gender, race and ethnicity, sexual orientation, physical ability, age, and so on. Examples include women's general fear of rape (Riger & Gordon, 1981), the "terrorism of racism" (Wyatt, 1989), the legacy of racism and sexism (Greene, 1990), and fears of genocide by children of Holocaust survivors (Danieli, 1985).

DSM-IV includes one diagnosis specifically designed to deal with direct and some indirect trauma survivors: **Posttraumatic Stress Disorder** (PTSD). To meet the diagnostic criteria for PTSD, a person must have been exposed to a traumatic incident in which the "the person experienced, witnessed, or was confronted with an event or events that involved actual or threatened death or serious injury, or a threat to the physical integrity of self or others" and "the person's response involved intense fear, helplessness, or horror" (DSM-IV, 1994, pp. 427–428). For at least one month, the traumatic event is persistently re-experienced in recollections, dreams, flashbacks, symbolic cues, or similar settings, and attempts are made to avoid stimuli associated with the trauma. Persistent symptoms of increased arousal are present, such as difficulty falling or staying asleep, irritability or angry outbursts, difficulty concentrating, hypervigilance, and exaggerated startle responses.

PTSD entered the pages of the DSMs in DSM–III, mostly in response to veterans' groups and others dealing with the aftermath of military service on young men (Lerman, 1996). It is one of a handful of disorders that recognizes the importance of social factors outside the individual. Needless to say, it immediately became useful to therapists treating women survivors of rape as well as other physical and verbal abuses (Koss et al., 2003; Stovall-McClough & Cloitre, 2006), traumatic events more likely to be experienced by women than by men[7] (Tolin & Foa, 2006). Indeed, Lilia Cortina and Sheryl Pimlott Kubiak (2006) tested two models: one that looked at gender as the key determinant of PTSD symptom severity and the other that used gender as a marker for sexual victimization history.

---

[7]Men are more likely than women to experience traumatic events like accidents, nonsexual assault, witnessing death or injury, disaster, or fire, and combat or war (Tolin & Foa, 2006).

Their data supported the second explanation, confirming that it is sexual victimization, not gender per se, that makes women vulnerable to PTSD.

In DSM–III, the external stressor triggering PTSD was described as "outside the range of usual human experience" and as "markedly distressing to almost anyone" (quoted in Lerman, 1996, p. 49). This verbiage painted a picture of PTSD as a normal reaction to an abnormal event. This assurance disappeared in the language of DSM–IV, where "threat" takes center stage—a tightening of the criteria that some feminists fear may limit its usefulness to women surviving traumatic occurrences that aren't life threatening (such as most date rape) and that may shift our focus toward validating the veracity of the threat (Caplan, 1995; Lerman, 1996).

Does it matter so much that an abuse survivor, for example, is labeled as having a borderline personality or as experiencing PTSD? The former presumes a characterological deficiency (there's something wrong with the woman); the latter, especially in its original formulation, sees the abnormality in the precipitating event(s). This difference can play into how therapists feel about their clients. Hannah Lerman (1996) describes the label of personality disorder as one of the most stigmatizing of the DSM categories, making those who receive it different from everyone else. Therapists typically find clients so classified as difficult to work with, obnoxious, and unlikeable. However, when practitioners recognize that many of these women clients are struggling with traumatic histories, they empathetically come to regard them as distressed and in legitimate need of help. Thus, it seems that there's a lot more to a label than just a name.

Given the importance of labeling, two feminist theorists and practitioners, Laura Brown and Lenore Walker, have proposed alternative classifications to facilitate diagnosis and treatment of abused women (Brown, 1992; Walker, 1986). Both seek to capture the repetitive exposure to trauma that differentiates interpersonal violence from the discrete events that presumably underlie PTSD. For example, "Abuse and Oppression Artifact Disorder" seeks to identify the nature of the stressor by distinguishing between interpersonal (from intimates, acquaintances, or strangers) and cultural environmental stressors (overt, punitive phenomena; covert, systematic phenomena; lack of protection/denial of opportunity). This latter category recognizes the insidious forms of trauma catalogued by Maria Root.

Trauma affects more than diagnoses of depression and personality disorders. Histories of sexual abuse and other violence are overrepresented in women in substance abuse programs (Teets, 1995) and in prison (Bradley & Davino, 2002; Marcus-Mendoza & Wright, 2004), and these have been related to the development of alcoholism (Miller et al., 1987). Incest rates are higher among alcoholic than nonalcoholic women (Beckman, 1994). In studies of eating disorders, sexual abuse and/or rape are reported in half or more cases, with sexual assault experiences occurring at even higher levels (75%+) in inpatient samples (Root, 1991; also see Tripp & Petrie, 2001). Sexual abuse has been associated with **somatization disorders** (Morrison, 1989), **psychotic disorders** (Darves-Bornoz et al., 1995), and bodily self-harm (Shaw, 2002). Even when evaluated many years after a physical assault, survivors were more likely to qualify for psychiatric diagnoses than women without such histories (Koss, 1990), and recovery from eating disorders is lower among women with a history of chronic physical and sexual abuse (Hesse-Biber et al., 1999).

All of this makes a strong case for the importance of factors external to the individual. To consider an individual without considering social context confines diagnosis to presenting symptoms. This seems to miss much of what we'd expect follow-up therapy to consider, and also to pathologize the person without taking into account the possibility that *normal* people are coping with *pathological* settings. Combined with therapists' biases, the result has been a checkered history of psychiatric treatment of women, with egregious examples of misogynous treatment appearing in women's autobiographical accounts. (About 175 of these are thematically reviewed by Jeffrey Geller, 1985). The remedy to this failure, taking a holistic look at psychological difficulties, has led some practitioners and scholars to propose feminist approaches to doing therapy—our next topic.

THE THEORY OF FEMINIST PRACTICE

The above critique of the DSM implies a lot about what feminist therapy should *not* be, but it doesn't tell us much about what feminist therapy is. We need to explore the theory of feminist therapy—*not* to describe specific techniques of therapy, but rather the conceptual underpinnings of a feminist *approach* to doing therapy. Feminist therapy is not a stand-alone technique, but rather is an approach to doing therapy that can be applied widely across techniques such as cognitive-behavioral (Hill & Ballou, 1998) and humanistic (Morris, 1997). Furthermore, it is not practiced in any single, standard way (Marecek & Kravetz, 1998a).

Principles for Doing Feminist Psychotherapy

The defining elements of feminist therapy are outlined comprehensively and clearly in a series of 11 guidelines developed for the American Psychological Association's Practice Directorate (American Psychological Association, 2007). These guidelines were developed by a task force created jointly by two APA Divisions (Counseling [Div. 17] and Psychology of Women [Div. 35]) that was charged to update and consolidate earlier work in this area by creating guidelines that honor the complexity of the lives of girls and women across multicultural contexts. For our purposes, these guidelines encompass most, if not all, of the points developed in other expositions of feminist therapy theory (Enns & Byars-Winston, 2010; a special issue of *Women and Therapy*, 2011, 34[1-2]).

The guidelines are organized into three clusters focusing on: (1) diversity, social context, and power (Guidelines 1–3), (2) professional responsibility (Guidelines 4 and 5), and (3) practice applications (Guidelines 6-11). The first section draws on what we have learned in this book about gender as a social identity and about gender-role socialization, laying the groundwork for the applied principles outlined in the remaining two sections. Because we all have a gender, these guidelines as recommended practices apply to both women and men across all their diversity. Their purpose is not to dictate what therapists do in practice, but rather to raise awareness and sensitivity so that all consumers of psychological practice (not just clients and health professionals, but also students and research participants) benefit.

My goal is not to offer a rationale for each of these points,[8] but rather to understand how each is conceptually linked to putting feminism into psychotherapy practice. Each of these points views therapy as a process that is negotiated between therapist and client, not as some technique that is used on a passive recipient. Throughout the following I draw heavily on illustrative examples as a way to link theory with practice.

---

[8]A careful and thorough rationale for each of these principles is documented in the *American Psychologist* article that introduced them (American Psychological Association, 2007). They also should be evident from much of our earlier discussions throughout this book.

Guideline 1: Psychologists strive to be aware of the effects of socialization, stereotyping, and unique life events on the development of girls and women across diverse cultural groups.

This opening recommendation draws on two of the key concepts we have developed throughout this book: (1) recognizing the importance of **social context** (socialization, stereotyping, and experiences) and (2) girls' and women's diversity. We have seen that individualism without context (assuming that pathology resides in characterological defects within a person) ignores many social forces that have been implicated in women's mental health, such as body dissatisfaction, poverty, acculturation, and trauma. Thus, the first part of this guideline puts gender front and center in understanding and working with clients.

It is important to understand that being nonsexist is not the same as being gender-sensitive. A nonsexist approach presumably is gender-neutral or gender-inclusive: being gender-neutral ignores gender; being gender-inclusive fails to be responsive to differences between the experiences and social contexts of women and men. In contrast, feminist therapy puts gender at the core of our analyses.

Carol Mowbray (1995) uses examples from actual cases contributed by members of a Michigan state committee on women's mental health issues to illustrate how practices by ostensibly nonsexist therapists inadvertently can be *nonfeminist* in their effect by ignoring the contexts of women's lives, imbalances of power between therapists and clients, and the importance of self-determination for women. Consider the following woman's frustration with her therapy which ignores the context of her life:

> We were a two-career couple. I had a 50-hour a week job that was responsible, stressful, and demanding. Yet, I also had the major responsibility for childcare and family functioning in economic and social arenas. A major part of the communication problems that brought us into marital therapy was a smoldering resentment over these inequities that kindled into explosive anger in conflicted or stressful circumstances. Yet we never had a discussion in therapy or set goals around redistributing the inequities and lowering my underlying hostility. When I raised these concerns, the discussion always reverted back to how I could better communicate my feelings. Yet, no matter how much I worked on better communication, the inequities in the relationship still did not change (Mowbray, 1995, pp. 15–16).

The structure and function of the family, especially regarding gender roles and power, go unanalyzed and pass without confrontation in this gender-neutral approach. This creates an outcome (maintenance of gendered inequities in this interpersonal relationship) that is far from feminist. In contrast, a feminist therapist would ask questions that simultaneously challenge the domestic arrangements of this couple, the patriarchal hierarchy that has come to characterize the American family, and the devaluation of household work.

This initial guideline, emphasizing a core point that permeates all 11 guidelines, requires a full multicultural understanding to capture the diversity of women's lives. For example, the roles of ritual and spirituality in women's lives may be overlooked by some therapists. Teresa LaFromboise and her colleagues (1994) describe how a Navajo woman's interpersonal problems and alcohol abuse declined remarkably after she ritually disposed of her mother's ashes, freeing her mother's, as well as her own, spirit. Julia Boyd (1990) cites

Latina women who return to using their native language, American Indian women who turn to purification rights, and African American women who find solace in religion as sources of personal strength that should not be discounted by feminist therapists (Mattis, 2002).

Similarly, Boyd (1990) describes the case of a young Southeast Asian woman, recently immigrated, who was ordered by the American courts to therapy for shoplifting. After several nonproductive sessions with a White therapist in which the client refused to detail her reasons for stealing, the therapist remanded her back to the judge with the labels of withdrawn, non-communicative, and depressed. An Asian paralegal took note of the case and realized that the same product (sanitary napkins) was being stolen repeatedly from the same store. In the context of her culture, her actions didn't reflect depression but rather embarrassment, both from the prospect of publicly purchasing this needed product and from discussing it with strangers. Cultural context, not characterological pathology, explained all.

Guideline 2: Psychologists are encouraged to recognize and utilize information about oppression, privilege, and identity development as they may affect girls and women.

From the first chapter of this text, we have talked about the importance of understanding oppression, privilege, and power. Not surprisingly, then, a key component of feminist therapy revolves around issues of power, both generally in girls' and women's lives and specifically in the therapist-client relationship.

The therapist's role encompasses the power to label and to act as an authority, both in reality and symbolically. The well-educated and often relatively affluent position of the therapist may contribute to status differences, and other sociodemographic differences can tip the balance of power. The therapist-client relationship can be used to explore issues of unequal power that then can be generalized to other settings. This process may be especially poignant for women with physical disabilities, many of whom experience powerlessness in their interactions with institutional, medical, and bureaucratic settings, as well as within interpersonal relationships (Olkin, 1999; Prilleltensky, 1996). Ironically, failure to acknowledge one's power as a therapist can be related to the abuse of this power (Brown, 1994a).

The point that may be even more difficult to realize about this guideline's challenges concerns exploring privilege. Indeed, it is this charge that seems central to engaging in feminist approaches with male clients. Jack Kahn (2011) discusses the usefulness of feminist approaches with men when practitioners reject essentializing men, understand that men's gender identity is diverse, help men sort out how to deal with pressures to conform to limiting norms defining masculinity, and confront the **unearned entitlements** of male privilege.

Guideline 3: Psychologists strive to understand the impact of bias and discrimination upon the physical and mental health of those with whom they work.

In Chapter 7, we explored the combination of prejudice, stereotyping, and discrimination (**sexism**) in girls' and women's lives. The additional point that is important to consider here is that sexism is experienced differently by diverse women because it can combine with other forms of oppression. This understanding is so central to doing feminist therapy that I have purposively selected an example that incorporates multiple, intertwined forms of oppression to illustrate it.

Consider the case of "Maria," a 30-year-old woman of Cuban American descent involved in a physically abusive relationship with her lesbian partner, "Susana" (Kanuha, 1994). Violence was hard for outsiders to see in this relationship both because the nature of the relationship itself was disguised as non-intimate to avoid homophobic reactions and because women are stereotypically regarded as nonviolent. Susana maintained power over Maria by threatening to "out" her to her employer and family, potentially disrupting the strong family bonds of Maria's Latina culture. Sensitivity to multiple forms of oppression and how they worked together in Maria's life were needed by this therapist to work effectively with her.

Guideline 4: Psychologists strive to use gender and culturally sensitive, affirming practices in providing services to girls and women.

The remaining guidelines apply the general principles of diversity, social context, and power that we saw developed across the first three guidelines. Guideline 4, along with 5, focuses on the responsibilities of health practitioners—looking first at what they do with their clients. A somewhat less obvious point concerns the responsibility of therapists, not clients, to provide such training. Feminist therapists agree that the responsibility for continuing education rests on the shoulders of the therapist, not the client (Porter, 1995).

Julia Boyd (1990), an African American therapist, describes the "homework" she did in advance of sessions with a Southeast Asian woman. Her background work paid off because she was able to integrate what the client revealed with what she had learned about the value of family loyalty and harmony between self and nature in Asian culture. The result was a more culturally sensitive and ultimately effective treatment for this client's depression. The National Multicultural Summit, held every two years since 1999, is an excellent resource for practitioner training in these areas (*www.multiculturalsummit.org*).

Guideline 5: Psychologists are encouraged to recognize how their socialization, attitudes, and knowledge about gender may affect their practice with girls and women.

This second practice recommendation directed at health professionals concentrates on the practitioner herself or himself. One important aspect of dealing with the intrusion of one's own perspectives into a therapist's relationship with her or his client concerns setting and maintaining boundaries. Indeed, ethical questions arise about what constitutes appropriate behavior. Is it right to ask a client to take her or his therapist to pick up a car at the repair shop? Should a therapist hug a distraught client? Laura Brown (1994b) explores such *boundary confusion* by first debunking three myths, concluding instead that (1) there are no clear, universal rules detailing appropriate and inappropriate behavior; (2) that boundary violations are not always easy to detect; and (3) it is possible to violate boundaries even if rigid rules are followed to the letter.

Rather than constructing lists of do's and don'ts, Brown argues that we must understand the basic characteristics of unethical boundary violations to lessen the risks of committing them. Although clients ultimately determine when lines have been crossed, they are not the sole arbitrators of this decision. Rather, the responsibility for maintaining appropriate boundaries rests with therapists.

Boundaries are crossed when the client is **objectified**, when the therapist acts from impulse, and when the needs of the therapist come before those of the client. Clients can be objectified when they are used by therapists to teach them (for example, about their different cultural experiences), to entertain them, and to listen to the emotional disclosures of the therapist. Therapists act impulsively, not when they draw on intuition, but when they act without diagnostic clarity; that is, without thinking through the impact of their actions on their client.

Regarding therapists' needs, therapists always must play a supporting role in relation to their clients, relinquishing center stage. For example, Julia Boyd (1990) relates how a White woman therapist's preoccupation with her African American woman client's rape alienated the client, whose most pressing, immediate concern was the robbery that accompanied her rape and stripped her of her last $25. Brown offers this conceptual analysis of boundaries as a means from which therapists and each of their clients can work together to define and maintain appropriate boundaries specific to their own relationship.

> *Guideline 6*: Psychologists are encouraged to use interventions and approaches that have been found to be effective in the treatment of issues of concern to girls and women.

The remaining six guidelines apply the principles of diversity, social context, and power to the services provided by health practitioners. The first of these, Guideline 6, challenges researchers to establish the effectiveness of feminist approaches and charges practitioners to continually expand their repertoire of therapeutic techniques so that they can tailor their use to specific clients.

There is no one-size-fits-all approach to doing feminist therapy, nor is there an agreed upon set of outcomes that are specific to doing effective feminist therapy. Although these understandings certainly complicate researchers' lives, there is building evidence that taking a gender-sensitive approach to practice benefits clients. For example, Charlene Senn and her colleagues (2011) documented that having women explore their own sexual values and desires as part of a sexuality education program increased women's confidence that they could defend themselves if attacked. In another study, career interventions targeting women survivors of intimate partner violence effectively promoted these women's career-search efficacy (Chronister & McWhirter, 2006). The key understanding, then, for practitioners who wish to comply with this recommendation is to seek out research on interventions specific to the client they seek to help and the outcomes they mutually value.

As for expanding therapists' toolboxes, Lillian Comas-Díaz (1994) explores the concept of womanhood for many women of color who define themselves as women, not as autonomous individuals, but rather within the contexts of extended units such as family and community. Given this understanding, she finds *family narratives* to be a useful therapeutic technique. These cultural stories include family history as well as describe values, lessons, the client's place in their social network, and so on. In one example, Comas-Díaz describes a client who reported sudden fears of falling (among other problems), part of which could be traced to a family "lesson" learned from a beloved sister who fell to her death. Part of the therapy process allowed this client to grieve for her sister and provided reassurances about the likely safety of the client's daughter, now the age of the client's sister when she died.

> *Guideline 7*: Psychologists strive to foster therapeutic relationships and practices that promote initiative, empowerment, and expanded alternatives and choices for girls and women.

This recommendation raises serious questions about the goals of therapy: what are the desirable outcomes and who sets them—the client or the therapist? Feminist therapists have reacted strongly to a history of misogynous practice wherein women were expected to adjust to oppressive situations, rather than work to change them or leave them. The most egregious examples came in settings of abuse where women were urged to "stand by their man," learn not to aggravate him, and, in essence, to be a "good wife." These pressures are especially strong for women of color who want to avoid becoming just another oppressor in their men's already oppressed lives (Greene, 1994).

This history speaks to some outcomes that should be avoided, whereas this important guideline directly addresses goals to be achieved. Drawing on a social justice agenda that unites feminist psychology with critical and positive psychologies and is consistent with the general dictum for practitioners to maximize positive psychological functioning and minimize distress (American Psychological Association, 1999), the general goals of counseling are to promote individual well-being and liberation, both from oppression and toward empowerment (Lopez & Edwards, 2008; Prilleltensky & Prilleltensky, 2003). Furthermore, there is developing evidence to link these positive outcomes with women's endorsement of feminist beliefs (Yoder et al., in press).

As for who sets these goals, what happens when the client's goals conflict with the therapist's? Consider the following woman's disappointment with her therapist:

> One time, after I had recounted a recent incident of my husband's unpredictable and explosive anger, my therapist asked me, "Why do you stay in this relationship?" I explained quite calmly that I had thought about this a lot and decided that in another relationship things could be a lot worse, e.g., substance abuse, violence, physical absence and abandonment, etc. My therapist breathed a deep sigh and almost seemed to bow and shake his head in disgust, disbelief, or sorrow. There was no verbal support for my statement, not even acknowledgment! I felt robbed and cheated. If this was my decision, why didn't I get help to better carry it out? Instead, I felt that I was being castigated by my therapist for not being more independent or assertive in my relationship (Mowbray, 1995, p. 18).

Does this mean that feminist therapists have to accept client's wishes regardless of their beliefs, (and arguably, regardless of what many would say are in the best interests of the client)? Additionally, might a therapist's revulsion toward violence conflict with cultural settings that find such behavior "acceptable," or at least widespread enough to be almost normative? Although feminist therapists agree that violence against women is oppressive and intolerable regardless of a woman's social or cultural background, therapists' approaches to dealing with it need not be rooted in American, masculine models of self-determination and autonomy (Ho, 1990). Rather, a feminist model must embrace ethical decision-making that empowers the client (Hill et al., 1998).

Guideline 8: Psychologists strive to provide appropriate, unbiased assessments and diagnoses in their work with women and girls.

We talked about **androcentric bias** at the start of this book, so it is not surprising that feminist therapy should react against this bias as well. A revealing tale of how this bias can infiltrate therapy is told through some uses of psychological tests (Brown, 1994a, Chapter 7). The most widely used psychological test, the Minnesota Multiphasic Personality Inventory (MMPI), routinely over-diagnoses people of color, especially African Americans, as paranoid; raises questions about sexual orientation based on deviations from gender stereotyping; and can label people with progressive political views as pathologically deviant. Although feminist therapists have used the MMPI as a diagnostic tool for uncovering some cases of abuse by intimates (M.A. Dutton, 1992), some common interpretations can support androcentric bias.

Laura Brown (1994a) describes how the MMPI and other androcentric biases influenced the custody case of "Alina," a Middle Eastern woman married to a White American man. Although he had verbally abused both Alina and their children, he came across fine on the MMPI and Rorschach (inkblot) tests; in court he appeared cool, calm, and collected. In contrast, Alina expressed anger that her husband left her for another woman; she tested as a "mixed personality disorder with histrionic and borderline features." The custody case was swinging toward the abusive father. The feminist therapist consulted by Alina convinced the courts to initiate another series of obviously more relevant tests by sending observers to watch parent-children interactions. Even knowing that he was being observed, the father verbally berated his children, disparaged their mother to them, used age-inappropriate language, allowed them to play with potentially dangerous objects, and failed to respond appropriately to their needs. In contrast, the presumably mentally disordered woman behaved as a loving and responsive mother. The court's final judgment favored the mother.

This guideline also raises concerns about the sociodemographic match between a therapist and a client. Some feminist therapy theorists have argued quite persuasively that women clients should see women therapists (Cammaert & Larsen, 1988), even arguing that therapists and clients be matched on other qualities, such as sexual orientation and race and ethnicity.[9] Oliva Espín (1994) notes that such specific matches are advantageous because they facilitate firsthand understanding, promote the therapist as a role model, reduce some unequalizing status differences, and heighten the therapist's investment in the client's success. Indeed, she provides a case in point whereby a Latina client was empowered by her Latina therapist's aversion to domestic violence. For this client, having a Latina challenge what the client regarded as pervasive acceptance of violence in her community benefited her therapeutic progress.

The reality, though acknowledged by Espín, is that matches are not always available nor do they ensure cultural sensitivity. In these cases, feminist therapists must work with these differences. For example, a major obstacle that may stand in the way of White women therapists' effectiveness with clients of color is a misunderstanding of the role of racism in their clients' everyday lives. For many White women, the impact of race on their own lives, while far from nonexistent, is invisible and privileged (Frankenberg, 1993; Roman, 1993). For White women therapists to work sensitively with clients of color, they must understand the privileges afforded by their own race in American culture, acknowledge the role of racism in their clients' lives, and actively engage in self-education (Espín, 1994).

---

[9]Also often implicit in these discussions is the assumption that clients in feminist therapy should be restricted to women, although feminist therapy with men has been described (for example, see Worell & Johnson, 2001). Additionally, researchers conclude that the sex of one's therapist does not directly affect treatment outcomes; rather, the story, as I argue here, is more complex (Blow et al., 2008).

The point here is not to confuse the issues of the therapist with those of the client. Lillian Comas-Díaz (1994) describes a case in point. A Jewish woman Holocaust survivor as therapist was matched with an American Indian woman as client on the basis of their shared cultural experience as targets of genocide. The client elected not to continue this relationship beyond initial contact because the therapist drew so many parallels between their ethnic commonalties that she failed to acknowledge differences, such as the role alcoholism played in the American Indian woman's community. This therapist did not move beyond her own issues to relate to the uniqueness of her client.

Guideline 9: Psychologists strive to consider the problems of girls and women in their sociopolitical context.

Approaching therapy with the realization that "the personal is political" highlights the view that individual experience does not take place in a vacuum, but rather is informed by the social and cultural context in which it takes place (Brown, 1994a). In this framework, what happens to individual women often reflects broader sociopolitical forces that devalue women and women's experiences, including racism (Comas-Díaz, 1988), ableism (Prilleltensky, 1996), classism, ageism, and so on. Making linkages between individual experiences ("the personal") and general trends that affect many women ("the political") connects women to other women and makes public these common bonds. *Consciousness raising* becomes a legitimate and important part of individual and group therapy designed to help women relate their personal difficulties to social context (Marecek & Hare-Mustin, 1991).

Although the common bonds that associate one woman's experiences with others' are critical for making connections between the personal and the political, this linkage must be balanced against honoring each client's unique experiences of reality (Brown, 1994a). Just as individualism without context can limit our understanding of women's full lives, so can context without the individual serve to invalidate the personal. Just because other women experience rape, for example, raising serious questions about who has power and how it is used, an individual woman's experience of and coping with such trauma cannot be discounted because of these broader connections. A critical dynamic in feminist therapy is to negotiate this balance between individuals and social context.

Guideline 10: Psychologists strive to acquaint themselves with and utilize relevant mental health, education, and community resources for girls and women.

Psychotherapy doesn't take place in a vacuum; rather, it is embedded within a potentially supportive environment upon which this guideline challenges the practitioner to draw. For example, Melba Vasquez (1994) describes how she used a Latina woman's wanting to care for others, not *against* her by labeling her dependent, but *for* her by encouraging her to extend these community-based principles of caring toward herself (and, through herself, toward her children) (also see Weiner, 1999). This approach validated her caring and connection to others and simultaneously enhanced her self-esteem and personal empowerment—necessary ingredients to terminating abuse from within the relationship or by leaving it. Similarly, Christine Ho (1990) suggests that strong family ties and a hierarchy of elders in Asian communities can be employed to abused women's advantage by drawing on these resources for support and to intercede on their behalf.

Guideline 11: Psychologists are encouraged to understand and work to change institutional and systemic bias that may impact girls and women.

As we have seen, a central goal for feminist psychotherapy is to empower women—to help women gain control of their lives (Espín, 1994; Worell, 2001). Such empowerment assists women to be aware of the deleterious effects of sexism and other forms of oppression; to perceive themselves as agents for solving their own problems; to understand how the personal is political; and to work toward broader, societal change. This last part of empowerment moves both the therapist and the client beyond individual change (psychotherapy) to social change. A distinguishing feature of feminist therapy is the realization not only that the personal is political, but also that the political is personal.[10] In other words, with personal empowerment comes the responsibility to actively work for social changes that promote the well-being of women in general (Barrett, 1998; Morrow & Hawxhurst, 1998; Weiner, 1998). How feminists do this depends on the form of feminism they espouse because there are multiple approaches to doing feminism, as we discussed in Chapter 2 (Brown, 1994a). This challenge will be the major focus of the final chapter of this book.

Summary of Therapy Theory

These 11 guidelines organize ideas about feminist theory of therapy, and the examples described throughout this section link this theory to actual practice. One way to bring this all together is to explore the common ground that unites feminist practitioners doing feminist therapy. Bonnie Moradi and her colleagues (2000) examined the therapy behaviors reported by 101 self-identified, practicing feminist therapists (also see Chester & Bretherton, 2001; Marecek & Kravetz, 1998b; Szymanski, 2003). Strongly identified feminists (1) emphasized an understanding that the personal is political, (2) recognized issues of oppression and their interrelationships, and (3) paid attention to experienced socialization. They engaged in these behaviors with both women and men clients.

Additionally, practitioners did not have to endorse a feminist label to report using some of these core identifiers of feminist therapy. This suggests that some therapists who don't think of themselves as feminist draw on feminist approaches as simply good ethical practice. Thus, key elements of feminist theory may infuse more of actual practice than the self-labeling of therapists might imply. This is a good example of how psychology is transformed, often without overt acknowledgement of the root causes of the adopted changes.

CHAPTER SUMMARY

Throughout this chapter, we have taken a critical look at the existing medical model of "mental disorders" as embodied in the DSMs. We saw that this model yields similar overall prevalence rates for women and men, but that gendered patterns emerge for specific diagnoses, including agoraphobia, alcohol and substance abuse, depression, eating disorders, and three personality disorders (borderline, histrionic, and dependent).

---

[10]For a fuller discussion of how individual "psychological" problems can mask broader sociopolitical oppression, see Prilleltensky & Gonick (1996).

In contrast to the assumptions of the DSMs, which root the causes for these gender differences primarily in women's and men's biologies or within their psyches, a feminist perspective expands our focus to consider definitional ambiguities surrounding what is and is not deemed pathological, to move beyond exclusively biological explanations and drug treatments, and to explore extra-psychic influences such as the infiltration of gender stereotyping into definitions of disorders, stereotyped therapists' judgments, and neglected contextual factors. These contextual influences may include threats to women's self-esteem, interpersonal stress, body dissatisfaction, physical illness, finances and employment, acculturation, and direct, indirect, and insidious forms of trauma.

We also reviewed a general feminist approach to practice that encompasses practice recommendations explicated by a variety of feminist therapy theorists. Throughout this review of theory of feminist practice and exemplary cases, we have stressed the importance of making the personal political and vice versa, of linking gender with other forms of oppression and to power, and of privileging women's experiences so that they move from the margins of therapy theorizing to center stage. By both critiquing traditional approaches to "mental disorders" and offering an alternative approach (feminist therapy), we are striving to develop theory and practice in psychology that will work effectively and sensitively for all women whose true psychological pain must be considered at the heart of these discussions.

SUGGESTED READINGS

Widiger, T. A. (1998). Invited essay: Sex biases in the diagnosis of personality disorders. *Journal of Personality Disorders, 12*, 95–118.

In this accessible essay, Thomas Widiger makes a case for the role sex biases (including biased thresholds for diagnosis, biased diagnostic constructs, biased applications of diagnostic criteria, etc.) play in creating and sustaining gender differences in the prevalence of personality disorders (differences confirmed by meta analysis; see Lynam & Widiger, 2007), making arguments that underlie the general propositions about such biases made in this chapter.

McHugh, M. C. (2008). A feminist approach to agoraphobia: Challenging traditional views of women at home. In J. C. Chrisler, C. Golden, & P. D. Rozee (Eds.), *Lectures on the psychology of women* (4th ed., pp. 393–417). New York: McGraw-Hill.

Maureen McHugh makes the personal political by exploring the case of her mother, highlighting how an understanding of social context can normalize what otherwise can appear to be pathological behavior.

Kranz, K. C., & Long, B. C. (2002). Messages about stress in two North American women's magazines: Helpful? We think not! *Feminism & Psychology, 12*, 525–530.

Karen Kranz and Bonita Long's brief commentary explores how women's stress is simultaneously normalized and problematized in women's magazines and how the advice these magazines offers promotes internalizing stress and individualism and, by ignoring the political in the personal, helps maintain the status quo.

Koss, M. P., Bailey, J. A., Yuan, N. P., Herrera, V. M., & Lichter, E. L. (2003). Depression and PTSD in survivors of male violence: Research and training initiatives to facilitate recovery. *Psychology of Women Quarterly, 27*, 130–142.

Mary Koss and her colleagues illustrate the limitations of the DSM using the examples of depression and PTSD in the context of male violence against women and link these shortcomings to broader public policy issues.

Walsh, E., & Malson, H. (2010). Discursive constructions of eating disorders: A story completion task. *Feminism & Psychology, 20*, 529–537.

Eleanore Walsh and Helen Malson report their analyses of British undergraduates' responses to an incomplete story about a woman exhibiting either anorexic or bulimic eating behaviors. (Students may be encouraged to first complete the task on their own.) The authors' analysis raises provocative questions about the normalizing of dieting and about how women with eating disorders "should" be treated (e.g., involuntary hospitalization and their personal responsibility for recovery).

Geller, J.L. (1985). Women's accounts of psychiatric illness and institutionalization. *Hospital and Community Psychiatry, 36*, 1056–1062.

Jeffrey Geller puts a human face on diagnosed women, setting the stage for engaging discussions about the way things were, continue to be, and should be.

Chapter 13

Male Violence Against Girls and Women
Linking Fears of Violence, Harassment, Rape, and Abuse

Anita wants to take a class at a local community college but it's scheduled at night in a neighborhood with which she is unfamiliar and which would require a long bus ride. She calls her friends to see if she can recruit someone to take the class with her, but no one is both available and interested. She decides to take something different (based on Riger & Gordon, 1981).

Barbara was on the subway the other day and a man kept making insulting remarks to her, calling her a snobbish Black slut. He didn't touch her, but Barbara left the train feeling sick, fearful, and disgusted (adapted from Kelly & Radford, 1996, p. 24).

Mary was a first year science major at a large university. She took a student assistant position in a science department to support herself financially. One of her professors began stopping by her desk, leaning over and touching her breasts "accidentally" while talking about her course work. Fearing for her grade and her job, she remained silent. At the end of the semester she filed a letter of complaint and quietly left school (Quina & Carlson, 1989, p. 8).

Irene recalled, "While I was a little girl of nine, my mom went into the hospital, and it became up to me to run the household. My father drank for the two weeks Mom was away. During this time, my father first began to sexually abuse me. He told me that if I did Mom's work, I had to sleep in her place. This continued until I finally left the house at age eighteen. I tried several times to tell my mom but she never believed me" (Quina & Carlson, 1989, p. 6).

Carol was seventeen and a virgin. She had dated Andrew for two years when he was drafted into military service. The night before he left, she visited his home. Although she didn't normally drink, he persuaded her to share a "toast." Soon she felt dizzy and had to lie down. With his sister and mother in another part of the house, Andrew raped her (Quina & Carlson, 1989, p. 4).

Elaine married a man she had dated for 7 months. He had been rough physically on occasion before they were married, but now he seemed more aggressive. One night, he hid in the house when she came home from work and viciously attacked her. He held a gun while he raped her, saying he "performed better." The next day he was gentle and sweet. This assault was to be repeated every few months until Elaine left him (Quina & Carlson, 1989, p. 4).

A man fired eight bullets at two women backpacking on the Appalachian Trail in south central Pennsylvania in 1988. The lone survivor describes the murderer: "He shot from where he was hidden in the woods 85 feet away, after he stalked us, hunted us, spied on us. . . He shot us because he identified us as lesbians. He was a stranger with whom we had no connection. He shot us and left us for dead" (Brenner, 1992, p. 12).

On December 6, 1989, a 25-year-old man carrying a hunting rifle burst into an engineering school at the University of Montreal. In some classes, he forced women to line up against one wall; men against another. He clearly expressed his intent to kill feminists. He left a three-page statement blaming feminists for his problems and targeting 15 women, none of whom he found at the school. In the end, he left 14 women dead before he killed himself (Stato, 1993).

Each of the examples above can be subsumed under the working definition of male violence against women used by a task force formed by the American Psychological Association in 1991: "physical, visual, verbal, or sexual acts that are experienced by a woman or girl as a threat, invasion, or assault and that have the effect of hurting her or degrading her and/or taking away her ability to control contact (intimate and otherwise) with another individual" (Koss, Goodman et al., 1994). Each involves increasing physical harm, ranging from restricted activity for Anita because of fear of violence to the outright murder of women for being lesbian and/or women. In between, we find women victimized by other forms of abuse: Barbara by sexist and racist verbal abuse; Mary by sexual harassment at school and work; Irene by childhood sexual abuse; Carol by acquaintance rape; and Elaine by intimate partner abuse and rape.

Although each experience is unique to the woman who undergoes it, each type of violence against women is linked by common threads that weave a broader tapestry of violence and its consequences for all women. Thus, violence is not a singular experience; rather, it connects all women through their universal vulnerability (Griffin, 1971). This theme of *interconnections*—among these different forms of violence, among women as targets and potential targets of violence, and between violence and societal-wide male dominance over women—will be echoed throughout this chapter.

We will examine four forms of male violence against women: sexual harassment, rape, male intimate partner abuse, and childhood sexual abuse.[1] We shall see that these are linked by four general themes: (1) problems with defining and talking about male violence against women; (2) debates about incidence and prevalence; (3) invisibility resulting in claims of invalidation; and (4) serious physical and psychological consequences, not only for victims themselves but for women in general.

By limiting our focus to male violence against women, I do not invalidate violence directed at men or perpetrated by women. However, violence by women against men or women in general is not sustained by societal power differences (White & Kowalski, 1998); indeed, college students regard male-on-female violence as the most frightening form (Hamby & Jackson, 2010). What happens to individual men does not seep over into men's awareness; it doesn't create general fears of violence and thus restrict their behaviors. Many more women can relate to Anita's experience at the start of this chapter than can men. As for men's victimization of other men, both the targeting of vulnerable men (Uggen & Blackstone, 2004) and use of de-masculinizing tactics (Pino & Meier, 1999) highlight the connection between the power and gender themes we'll emphasize here. All of this directly links such violence with misogyny (woman-hating) as well as homophobia.

DEFINING AND TALKING ABOUT VIOLENCE

All forms of male violence against women share some definitional ambiguities that blur the cutoff between acceptable and abusive behaviors. These ambiguities carry over into discussions of how often violence occurs because, without consensus about what constitutes each form of violence, measurement gets bogged down in a quagmire of competing defini-

---

[1] A more comprehensive, global perspective might include bride burnings, genital mutilation, forced prostitution and trafficking, skewed birth patterns resulting from aborted female fetuses and infanticide, forced sterilization, rape in war, and so on (United Nations Population Fund, 2000). For example, there would be over 60 million more women in the world if demographic trends in birth rates were followed without intervention.

tions. Sexual harassment, rape, and male intimate partner violence provide good examples of this process. For all, psychologists' thinking has shifted from an initial emphasis on measuring behavioral indicators to looking at how each is *experienced* by those involved.

Definitions of Violence as Experienced

Sexual harassment is a violation of Sec. 703 of Title VII of the U.S. Civil Rights Act. According to the U.S. Equal Employment Opportunity Commission (EEOC, 2011a), sexual harassment can include unwelcome advances, requests for sexual favors, and other verbal or physical contact of a sexual nature when submission is made, implicitly or explicitly, a condition of employment; when submission or rejection affects employment decisions; and when such conduct interferes unreasonably with work performance or creates an intimidating, hostile, or offensive working environment. It does not have to be sexual in nature, extending to offensive comments made about a person's sex.

This legal definition sets up two distinct types of **sexual harassment**: **quid pro quo**, which is characterized by the dominant power position occupied by the perpetrator who can reward or punish the target, and **hostile work environment**, which involves unwanted behavior that creates a chilling work or educational climate. The most commonly used survey measure of exposure to sexually harassing behaviors is the *Sexual Experiences Questionnaire* (SEQ) developed by Louise Fitzgerald and her colleagues (1988; 1995). The SEQ documents *sexual coercion* (being treated badly by a coworker or supervisor for refusing sexual advances, paralleling quid pro quo harassment), *unwanted sexual attention* (staring and leering), and **gender harassment** (offensive sexual and sexist remarks). Gender harassment can take on qualitatively unique forms for African American women that draw on racial stereotyping and racially specific physical features (Mecca & Rubin, 1999) and can combine with racial harassment (Buchanan & Fitzgerald, 2008).

Definitions of rape have changed over time (Hengehold, 2000). The traditional common-law definition of rape is: "carnal knowledge of a female forcibly and against her will" (cited in Koss, Goodman et al., 1994, p. 159). The definition of **rape** used by the APA Task Force on Male Violence Against Women is: "nonconsensual oral, anal, or vaginal penetration, obtained by force, by threat of bodily harm, or when the victim is incapable of giving consent" (Koss, 1993). All definitions include some notion that the sexual acts are nonconsensual (Muehlenhard et al., 1992).

Finally, measures of male intimate partner violence (IPV) often simply count up incidents. Counting behaviors alone draws our attention to events (not people) ignores their meaning to the victim and perpetrator, and takes them out of the **social context** in which they occurred (Smith et al., 1999). In contrast, by bringing the people involved into consideration, by understanding the fundamental role of gendered relations, and by viewing battering as a repeated cycle, measurement moves away from behavior to look at both how battering is *experienced* and the *gendered context* in which it occurs. To understand male IPV, then, we must understand how it is lived in the everyday lives of everyday people.

Perceptions of Violence

The inclusion of "unwanted" and "nonconsensual" elements in all conceptualizations of violence also moves our discussion beyond behaviors themselves. This takes us into the realm of *perceptions* asking questions about (1) the criteria for establishing nonconsent, (2) the relationship of the victim to the assailant, and (3) who decides whether or not sexual assault has occurred (Muehlenhard et al., 1992).

Regarding criteria for establishing consent in sexual relations, college students generally supported a definition that assumes "yes" until "no" is stated and that when nonconsent is verbalized, "no" means "no," not "maybe" (Gross et al., 1998; Livingston et al., 2004). Women generally prefer a more cautious approach to establishing consent; yet some college students continue to assume consent as the default (Humphreys & Herold, 2007); and some men appear insensitive to verbal and nonverbal cues of nonconsent that are not clear (as opposed to actually saying "no") and forceful (O'Byrne et al., 2006). Other factors can render consent questionable (intoxication), meaningless (consent given under duress), or impossible (a drugged victim).[2] The meaning of consent becomes even more blurred by findings that women who fear that their partner will lose interest in them are most willing to consent to unwanted sexual behaviors (Impett & Peplau, 2002).

Turning to the relationship between victim and perpetrator, since 1976 (when marital rape was expressly exempted from some legal definitions of rape), every U.S. state has made marital rape illegal (Wellesley Centers for Women, 1998). Still, some college students persist in believing that the same offense committed by a husband is less troubling than by a stranger (Simonson & Subich, 1999). Acknowledgement of rape can become clouded when the perpetrator is an intimate or even an acquaintance of the victim.

The third point focuses on who decides whether or not sexual harassment or rape has occurred. Fears of false reporting fuel arguments against relying on victims' claims alone; however, objective evidence concludes that false accusations are relatively rare,[3] especially when compared to much higher levels of legitimate under-reporting. How others respond also makes a difference; when people are exposed to negative reactions toward a rape victim by others, they too make less supportive judgments (Brown & Testa, 2008). Additionally, what happens when the views of victims and perpetrators conflict? Let's explore how psychologists have addressed each of these three still unresolved issues.

Victims know. As surprising as it may seem on first blush, sometimes victims of violence fail to acknowledge their victimization. Some women check off behavioral indicators of sexual harassment but deny having ever been harassed (Saunders, 1992, cited in Koss, Goodman et al., 1994). Because some battered women don't feel helpless, or they hit back, or they are ambivalent about their lover and their relationship, they don't fit their own stereotyping about IPV. Although these women might even admit to being physically harmed, some still won't label themselves as "battered women" (Fine, 1993).

---

[2]The National Institute of Drug Abuse (NIDA) describes three "club drugs" that are reportedly being used in sexual assault incidents: rohypnol, ketamine, and gamma hydroxbutyrate (GHB). All are central nervous system depressants that have a sedative effect, including amnesia, muscle relaxation, and slowing of psychomotor performance. Because they are virtually colorless, tasteless, and odorless, they can be slipped into the target's beverage. Some universities are warning students not to drink from open beverages, and this is a reasonable self-protective strategy to heed. For more information, contact your local Women's Center or try NIDA at *http://www.nida.nih.gov/* (Retrieved October 2011).

[3]David Lisak and his colleagues (2010), combining their data across a 10-year period with findings from other studies, conclude that false allegations of sexual assault fall between 2-10% of reported cases. These fears may be fueled by the media; for example, the more women watched TV, the more likely they were to believe that rape allegations were false (Kahlor & Morrison, 2007).

It is not uncommon for victims of rape by known assailants not to name their experiences as rape (Warshaw, 1994). Stereotyping of rape includes images of strangers using excessive aggression and force—features that often do not characterize acquaintance rape (Parrot & Bechhofer, 1991). Still these atypical rape scripts continue to be generated by college women (Clark & Carroll, 2008) and other women (Littleton et al., 2007), and they affect their willingness to report a rape (Turchik et al., 2009). In one sample of college students, for example, fully 43% of women who met the behavioral criteria for rape did not label their own experience as such (Koss, 1985). In a vignette study describing physical resistance and intercourse, fully 47% of college students did not label the date's aggressive behavior as rape (Hannon et al., 1996). In a survey with over 3,000 employed women, rates of unacknowledged rape or attempted rape ran as high as 59% of the cases meeting these definitions (Koss et al., 1996).

Comparing acknowledged and unacknowledged rape victims, no differences were found in dating behaviors, different aspects of their rape experience, victims' personality, attitudes about rape (Koss, 1985), resistance strategies (Levine-MacCombie & Koss, 1986), or recovery (McMullin & White, 2006). The key difference is that unacknowledged rape victims were more likely to possess more violent, stranger-perpetrated, "blitz" rape scripts (Kahn et al., 1994) that emphasized extreme force (Bondurant, 2001). They also were more likely to accept rape myths that unless women fight back it isn't rape, and they have restricted definitions of what constitutes "sex" (Peterson & Muehlenhard, 2004). Given this stereotyping, it is not surprising that unacknowledged rape victims were younger than women who named their experiences as rape, knew their assailant better, reported less force, and had weaker emotional reactions (Kahn et al., 2003). All this points to the power of rape stereotyping in framing even victims' own perceptions of rape. Extending this logic to marital rape, attitudes about sexuality in marriage that stress husbands' sexual rights and domination compromise women's acknowledgment of marital rape (Muehlenhard & Schrag, 1991).

Victim-perpetrator discrepancies.   Generally there is consensus among women and men about harassment that involves severe behaviors and is perpetrated by an authority with power over the victim (quid pro quo harassment) (Gutek & O'Connor, 1995), and penalties here tend to be harsh (Wayne, 2000). However, definitional ambiguities arise in the murky area of hostile work environment harassment and with milder behaviors. There are **intragroup differences** among women and among men regarding how they evaluate specific incidents. For example, sexist attitudes predict less sensitivity to "seeing" both sexual harassment (Ohse & Stockdale, 2008) and childhood sexual abuse (Cromer & Freyd, 2007), and college-aged samples are less likely to "see" sexual harassment than are older-aged samples (Ohse & Stockdale, 2008).

Turning to **intergroup differences** between women and men, men overall tend to hold a narrower definition of what constitutes bona fide harassment (Burian, et al., 1998; Rotundo et al., 2001) and may even regard some mild forms of harassment (e.g., offensive email) as somewhat enjoyable (Khoo & Senn, 2004). Women are more likely to attend to power relations between a target and perpetrator in contrast to men, who focus on the sexual aspects of interchanges (Perry et al., 1998).

Barbara Gutek and Maureen O'Connor (1995) describe three conditions that reduce agreement among observers. First, the gender composition of one's work group matters. In male-dominated occupations where the harassment of women is more commonplace, women and men are similarly sensitive to harassment; but women in female-dominated occupations are more likely to label an (unexpected) event as harassing than their male co-workers are (Maeder et al., 2007). Second, the *perceived* complicity of the victim decreases consensus. Third, when evaluators aren't **primed** to think about harassment, more disagreement between women and men arises.

All these conditions point to contextual cues that make people more or less sensitive to the possibility of harassment (Fiske & Glick, 1995). Although these contextual cues are likely to distinguish women's from men's perceptions, they certainly do not need to do so. If men are sensitized to what women consider harassing, these contextually created differences could well disappear. Indeed, an educational intervention designed to sensitize participants to incidents of sexual harassment evened out initial gender differences (Bonate & Jessell, 1996), and workers become less skeptical about claims of harassment when they were encouraged to empathetically take the complainant's point of view (Wiener & Hurt, 2000).

The line between sexual seduction and date rape readily blurs around what constitutes women's sexual interest and men's coercion (see Box 13.1). Generally, men perceive more sexual intent in others than do women (Abbey, 1991), and individual men who reported engaging in sexually aggressive behavior misperceived women's sexual intent more than other men (Bondurant & Donat, 1999). These ambiguities often are used by convicted rapists to justify their actions (Lea & Auburn, 2001). Although Box 13.1 does suggest that the difference between seduction and rape can be vague, it also identifies areas in which the difference is clear (using violent tactics). Indeed, in 40 scenarios of coercive sexuality described by college women and men, no gender differences in their perceptions emerged (McCaw & Senn, 1998). Thus, miscommunication is not as valid a rationale for perpetrating violence as some assailants might like us to believe.

Box 13. 1

Heather Littleton and Danny Axsom (2003) asked 42 women and 8 men college students to "write a description of what happens before, during, and after a typical rape (or seduction)." Below are examples of the separate rape scripts (left) and seduction scripts (right) they described. Systematically content analyzing and comparing these scripts, they differed in that in rape scripts the man more often felt powerful and in control as well as used violent tactics, and the woman felt negative emotions and resisted. However, they also shared some chilling commonalties: in both, men used manipulative and coercive tactics (complimenting, stalking, and persuading) and women displayed behaviors suggesting sexual interest (e.g., going on a date, dressing provocatively, flirting, and consensual kissing/petting). The line between seduction and rape blurs.

Rape	Seduction
The man would probably pick out a female who is either drunk or drinking. Their victim is probably someone they think is vulnerable…. The man would end up coaxing the girl away from the crowd. During the rape, the rapist is feeling control and sexual pleasure as he rapes his victim. Eventually, she will give up hope and just let it happen without fighting back. She is probably tied up or held by her attacker with ripped or torn clothing.	A person who is going to seduce someone also knows that the other person is vulnerable and lonely…. You try to say "no" but the person persists and keeps giving you a disappointed look and keeps saying how beautiful you are…. You finally give in even though you feel really uncomfortable…. The more you try to say no to his requests, you can't seem to say no to him, ending up doing things you don't want to do.

Naming Violence

Without the right words to describe what has happened, victims can be left without a way to talk, or even think, about their victimization, and research is compromised by lack of conceptual clarity (Cook & Parrott, 2009). The terms "battered woman," "sexual harassment," "marital rape," and "date rape" were all coined in the past 30 or so years to help women label their experiences (McHugh et al., 1993).

Of key concern to feminists working in this area is how to think about women who are targeted for violence (Koss, Goodman et al., 1994). The term "victim" rightfully places responsibility for violence on the perpetrator and captures the severity of the violence that has occurred. However, it also implies that the recipient is passive and irreparably damaged by the violation. The term "survivor" overcomes the latter problem, but implies that the violence has passed, ignoring the repetition of violence in some women's lives (e.g., women who are chronically terrorized by their partners) and the long-term consequences of violence. Furthermore, people survive acts of nature as well as acts of violence, but only violent acts are purposively perpetrated. First, I acknowledge these shortcomings with the terminology. Second, in terms of women's coping with violence, self-labeling that moves from victim to survivor may be an important step toward recovery (Quina & Carlson, 1989). I will keep this second point in mind throughout the present chapter in my use of these terms.

How we talk about the physical abuse of women by male intimates offers a case in point. Overall, two different approaches to male IPV have dominated this literature (Kurz, 1989): the family violence perspective offered by Murray Straus, Richard Gelles, and Suzanne Steinmetz (1980) and a feminist approach (for example, see Stanko, 1985; Yllö & Bograd, 1988; L.E.A. Walker, 1994).

Family violence theorists consider what they call "spouse abuse" or "family violence" to be part of a general pattern involving violence among all family members. Central to their thesis are data suggesting equivalent amounts of violence committed by heterosexual partners against each other and toward their children, by children against parents, and among siblings (Straus, 1997). This approach focuses on the family as the central unit of analysis; highlights stresses faced by contemporary families; regards the family as accepting of violence as a means for solving conflict; and cites the power of men over women in the family, as well as in society at large, as a cause of violence. Furthermore, they believe that power in the family can be shared equally by women and men. In support of their proposed relationship between egalitarianism and nonviolence, they cite evidence that abuse occurs least frequently in democratic households. The policy recommendations they offer concentrate on changing societal norms that legitimate and glorify violence—a generally laudable goal.

Feminist refinements to family violence theory have challenged their basic assumptions (Berns, 2001). Central to this challenge are interpretations of data suggesting equal rates of violence by heterosexual partners (Archer, 2000). These findings largely rely on surveys of participation rates and measurement of violence using the Conflict Tactics Scale, which simply counts violent acts ranging from swearing to brandishing a gun. Given this framework, a woman who pushes is labeled as violent, just as a man who chokes. Nothing is recorded about intent to harm, amount of harm inflicted, who initiated the exchange, what was done in self-defense, and how much risk was perceived by each party (Koss, Goodman et al., 1994; Kurz, 1997; Gordon, 2000).

When these qualifiers are factored in, men engage in more severe forms of violence and are more likely to perpetrate multiple aggressive acts; in contrast, women sustain more injuries (Frieze, 2000) and often feel more threatened. Although much of women's violence (e.g., self-defense, escape, and retaliation) responds to men's physical violence and verbal abuse, some (e.g., anger expression and alcohol-induced violence) does not (Langhinrichsen-Rohling, 2010). Still, a feminist reconceptualization of the full context of violence reframes it from a gender-neutral view to put male-female power relations front and center in our analyses, consistent with what we have done throughout this book.

This highlighting of gendered relationships raises questions about power dynamics and the use of violence as a means for establishing and maintaining control and dominance. It also questions why women are the more frequent targets of domestic abuse. This reframing moves the discourse about adult abuse by intimates from the family (where violence against women is thought of as just another example of family violence), into discussions of other forms of male violence against women. Such refocusing paves the way for inclusion of male IPV in discussions such as the present one focused on rape, sexual harassment, and other forms of social control and male dominance (Kurz, 1989).

The language we use to describe psychological, physical, and sexual abuse in intimate relationships must reflect the basic assumptions of the feminist perspective outlined above. Such a perspective dismisses gender-neutral terms such as "spousal abuse" and "family violence." An improved (but still far from satisfactory) compromise has been to use the term "wife abuse" to capture both the gendered nature of the violence and its harm. The obvious difficulty with this terminology is that it doesn't include nonmarital abuse in heterosexual cohabiting and dating relationships. This suggests the term "partner abuse." Aggression among lesbian couples is far from nonexistent; estimates as high as 40% have been offered (Bologna et al., 1987). However, lesbian relationships are free of gendered cultural differences in power that characterize the types of violence reviewed in this chapter so that violence within lesbian relationships does not produce generalized fears among women (Koss, Goodman et al., 1994).[4] Women do not restrict their behaviors from fear of being attacked by lesbians. For all these reasons, throughout this chapter I selected the terminology most representative of the research or ideas being presented, using the term "male intimate partner violence" or male IPV.

Language also can be used to sanitize, and hence minimize, violence that is inflicted against women when it relies on the passive voice (she was beaten) or suggests shared responsibility (domestic violence) (Lamb & Koen, 1995). Such language covers up the psychological and physical harm delivered by pushing, shoving, slapping, kicking, hitting, beating, choking, stabbing, brandishing guns and knives, and so on, as well as the fact that another person is responsible for these behaviors.

Section Summary

One common thread that runs through different forms of male violence against women is definitional ambiguity—what exactly defines sexual harassment, rape, and male intimate partner violence and who decides that such abuse has occurred? Behaviors alone are insufficient to make these determinations. At an individual level, these uncertainties may

---

[4]For reviews of abuse in lesbian relationships, see Stahly and Lie (1995) and Renzetti (1997) as well as research (Bernhard, 2000).

interfere with women's ability to name and recover from victimization. They also may be used by perpetrators to excuse their behavior, as in "I didn't sexually harass her; can't she take a joke?" and "I didn't rape her; she liked it." A key to reducing victim-perpetrator misperceptions is to educate and sensitize men and boys about what women and girls regard as sexually threatening behavior and how they react to it. At a societal level, definitional ambiguities cloud discussions and disrupt research on male violence against women, starting with fundamental debates about how widespread each of these forms of violence is—the topic to which we next turn.

INCIDENCE AND PREVALENCE

There are two measures of scope that are important not to confuse: incidence and prevalence. **Incidence** refers to the number of victimizations that occur within a given time period, typically one year. **Prevalence** captures an individual's exposure to at least one assault any time during her lifetime. Extrapolating one from the other can lead to gross mis-estimates (Muehlenhard et al., 1997).

Although we talk about different forms of male violence against women as conceptually distinct phenomena, they often overlap in women's lives. Many women who are raped also are viciously physically assaulted; beaten women may be raped by their male partners; sexually harassed women may be physically threatened, assaulted, and raped; and so on (Campbell et al., 2008). In real life, different forms of violence co-occur, succeed one another, and blend together to create a pervasive culture of male violence against women. Such *co-occurrences* thus challenge classification schema that try to sort individuals into discrete, non-overlapping categories.

Sexual Harassment

The U.S. Equal Employment Opportunity Commission (EEOC, 2011b) reported that 11,717 sexual harassment cases were filed and resolved under Title VII in 2010, with fully 83.6% of these incidents being filed by women. We know that filing and experiencing are not the same, yet despite definitional challenges and variations in measures, studies with different populations of women give us some sense of the overall **prevalence** of sexual harassment. Overall, Louise Fitzgerald (1993; Fitzgerald & Ormerod, 1993) estimates that *one of every two women will be subjected to some form of sexual harassment during her academic or working life.*

For example, a large-scale phone survey that asked SEQ questions about sexual harassment experiences in the workplace across the past year recorded that over 50% of women reported at least one incident of being treated differently because of her gender, of unwanted sexual attention, or of sexual coercion (Rospenda et al., 2009). Women's retrospective reports of their service in the U.S. military reserves recounted over 10 incidents of sexual harassment experiences—over 5 times the rate recalled by men (Street et al., 2007). Gender harassment extends to behaviors by clients and customers (Gettman & Gelfand, 2007) and by strangers (Wesselmann & Kely, 2010). It also expands to racial and ethnic harassment (Berdahl & Moore, 2006; Raver & Niskii, 2010) and to the heterosexist harassment of sexual minorities (Silverschanz et al., 2008).

Rape and Sexual Assault

Two major sources of federal statistics on rape **incidence** are the FBI's Uniform Crime Reports, which compile crimes reported to local authorities, and the Bureau of Justice Statistics' National Crime Victimization Survey (NCVS), which conducts a nationwide household poll (Koss, 1993). The former is heavily jeopardized by the underreporting of rape, considered the most underreported crime of personal violence (Koss, Goodman et al., 1994). The latter relied on an ambiguous question about general attacks and threats to elicit reports of rape and asked questions in front of other family members, violating confidentiality (Koss, 1992). In 1992–93, NCVS changed their format and instead privately asked direct questions about rape and sexual assault, following up with questions about whether or not the assailant was known to the victim. The one-year incidence of reported rape doubled from the previous survey to 310,000 cases, fully 80% of which were committed by someone known to the victim (Schafran, 1995). In comparison, this figure for 2010 was 188,380 cases, representing a steady decline in victimizations since 2001, with 169,370 (90%) involving women victims, and of these, 73% perpetrated by a non-stranger (Truman, 2011).

Turning to **prevalence**, *estimates of rape or sexual assault among adult women typically settle around 15%* (Kolivas & Gross, 2007). One survey found that up to eight of every ten rape victims reported that the attack occurred before they were 30 years old (National Victims Center, 1992), and fully 13% of 834 college women surveyed reported being raped between the ages of 14 and 18 (Humphrey & White, cited in White et al., 2001). The prevalence of sexual assault appears to be equivalent among African American and White women (Wyatt et al., 1992) and lower among Latinas (Sorenson & Siegel, 1992). Rape is reported disproportionately by unemployed, poor, and unmarried women (Avakame, 1999).

Not surprisingly, a gap exists between women's reports of victimization and men's reports of perpetration, ranging between two-thirds to three-quarters less (Kolivas & Gross, 2007). Men are more forthcoming on anonymous self-administered scales than in interviews, which arouse social anxiety (Ouimette et al., 2000; Rubenzahl & Corcoran, 1998). Men's admission of acquaintance rape jumps substantially under disinhibiting reporting conditions (e.g., a male experimenter, exposure to a sexually explicit story, or private testing room) such that gap between perpetration and victimization rates closes. This convergence strengths the validity of women-based estimates of prevalence.

Intimate Partner Violence (IPV)

Integrating data from a variety of prominent studies of **prevalence**, *it is estimated that between 21% and 34% of women in the United States will be physically assaulted*—slapped, kicked, beaten, choked, or threatened or attacked with a weapon—by an intimate adult partner (Browne, 1993; Coker et al., 2002; Randall & Haskell, 1995). These rates are consistent with nationwide surveys in nine other developed countries, which estimate prevalence rates of 17 to 38% (United Nations, 1995); these country-wide rates extend to over 70% at the highest extreme (Alhabib et al., 2010). The World Health Organization (reported in Alhabib et al., 2010) further estimates that 15-to-44-year-old women globally lose 5 to 20% of the healthy years of their lives to IPV. The U.S. **incidence** of IPV reported by women in 2010 was 407,700 cases, representing a rate of 3.1 women for every 1,000 women over age 12— four times the number of cases reported by male victims (101,530) (Truman, 2011).

Reviewing studies of prevalence rates by race and ethnicity, Casey Taft and her colleagues (2009) concluded that higher and more violent prevalence rates among African American women level out to levels comparable for White Americans when income is controlled. Rates of male IPV appear lower among Latina women (Sorenson & Siegel, 1992), and Christine Ho (1990) warns that low reporting rates by Asian American women may reflect cultural prohibitions against reporting rather than truly lower prevalence rates. Only anecdotal evidence is available for Native American women (Allen, 1990). Intimate abuse occurs across social classes (Sheffield, 1989), may be intensified for women with disabilities (Curry et al., 2001), and as the photo shows, has horrifying consequences.

Childhood Sexual Abuse (CSA)

A meta analysis of **prevalence** rates using 65 articles and covering 22 countries concluded that women are 3 times more likely than men to have been sexually abused as children (Pereda et al., 2009). Across 19 U.S. studies, the mean prevalence rate for women was 25.3% (with 95% of estimates falling between 19.7% to 31.8%); 7.5% (5.1% to 11.1%) for men. These rates become even more stunning for sexual minorities: 76% for lesbian and bisexual women; over 59% for gay and bisexual men (Rothman et al., 2011). One survey established the median age of onset for girls (9.6 years) and boys (9.9 years), and it noted that the perpetrator was more likely to be a family member for girls and a stranger for boys (Boney-McCoy & Finkelhor, 1995). Given that CSA is reported retrospectively by adults, there are no incidence rates available.

Sexually abusive families commonly share three distinguishing features (Draucker, 1996). First, family members often are emotionally distant, limiting displays of affection. Second, these families generally are traditionally hierarchical, with fathers as the undisputed head of household, mothers subordinated to fathers, and children subordinated to both parents. Obedience and control permeate these parent-child relationships. Finally, many of these families are marked by frequent open conflict, most typically between parents.

INVISIBILITY AND INVALIDATION

These estimates become numbing, but despite attempts to dismiss them as "advocacy numbers" (Gilbert, 1997), the numbers hold (Muehlenhard et al., 1997). At a personal level, it is tempting to ask incredulously, like then-graduate student Katie Roiphe (1993, p. 52): "If 25 percent of my female friends were really being raped,[5] wouldn't I know it?" This asks a question about invisibility and validation—if we don't see something, does it mean it isn't there? It also raises concerns about **positivity bias**; that is, women's tendency to *under*estimate their own vulnerability relative to other women (Norris et al., 1999).

We already have seen that even victims themselves may not define their experiences as sexual harassment, rape, male IPV, or CSA, although their experiences meet the criteria for defining them. In addition to having experiences that don't fit with abuse stereotyping, women may fail to name their victimization because of concern for the perpetrator, self-

---

[5]This 25% figure comes from a highly publicized and well done study of 3000 college women across 32 campuses that reported that 15.4% of women experienced rape and an additional 12.1% attempted rape (Koss et al., 1987).

blame and shame, and desires not to think about the events (Parrot & Bechhofer, 1991)—processes that are reinforced by sociocultural myths. Finally, women themselves, having internalized societal disregard for their hurt, may come to minimize the severity of their own abuse (Kelly & Radford, 1996). We'll review each of these processes and use different forms of violence to highlight the general point that *invisibility does not invalidate* the prevalence and incidence estimates we just documented.

Excusing Perpetrators

Sexual harassment may be trivialized by outside observers. For example, the media adopted a boys-will-be-boys attitude toward the harassment of U.S. Navy women at the Tailhook convention until female Congressional representatives became involved (Kasinsky, 1998). Gender harassment is trivialized in television situation comedies (Montemurro, 2003) and more in collectivist cultures (Sigal et al., 2005). Male perpetrators typically are judged more harshly than are women (Cummings & Armenta, 2002); attractive (Golden et al., 2001; LaRocca & Kromrey, 1999) or wealthy (Black & Gold, 2003) perpetrators are excused more readily; and **in-group** assailants are judged less harshly (Harrison et al., 2008). Sexual harassment between Black men and Black women is minimized compared to similar behavior enacted between White men and Black women (Shelton & Chavous, 1999). At least in the military, sexual harassment is most likely to be tolerated by male soldiers who express hostility toward women, exhibit negative masculinity, and reject women as equals (Rosen & Martin, 1998). Among psychology faculty, weak ethical perceptions were related to more frequent occurrences (Rubin et al., 1997).

It is hard to imagine excusing perpetrators of the severest forms of physical and sexual abuse. However, we may be more tolerant of some forms of male IPV than others; for example, when the perpetrator is an African American husband (Locke & Richman, 1999). Additionally, both myths and researched data have focused on biological and personality characteristics of individual men who perpetrate these abuses. They paint images of men out of control and responding to their own victimization.

A long-standing myth about male perpetrators of violence against women is that these men are psychopathic. Indeed, a handful of killers are, such as Ted Bundy, who targeted attractive, middle-class women, and the less publicized serial killers who brutally murder unprotected and less socially valued women (prostitutes) (Caputi, 1993). The stereotype of disordered men originated in early studies of convicted rapists who, in reality, represent a very select and small subset of all rapists (Sorenson & White, 1992). It also was fostered by erroneous beliefs that rape is sexually motivated, rather than an expression of male dominance and control (Brownmiller, 1975). It is perpetuated by film (Bufkin & Eschholz, 2000) and television (Cavender et al., 1999) depictions and remains active in some women's images of criminals (Madriz, 1997).

This stereotyping of psychopathic rapists is challenged by admissions from some men that they would rape a woman if they were assured they wouldn't be caught (studies reviewed by Lonsway & Fitzgerald, 1994). In one of these studies (Koss et al., 1987), 69% of 371 male college students reported they would never, under any circumstances, force someone to engage in a sexual act, even if they were guaranteed to be free from reprisals. This leaves fully 31%—that's almost one of every three—to contemplate such an act with or without reprisals! Looked at more behaviorally, of the more than 2,900 men who responded to Koss's survey of college students nationwide, 4.4% admitted to behaviors fulfilling the legal definition of rape, an additional 3.3% attempted these behaviors, 7.2% acknowledged using sexual coercion, and 10.2% admitted to forced or coerced sexual contact such as kissing and touching.

Further data suggest a great deal of heterogeneity among rapists (Prentky & Knight, 1991), with only a handful manifesting deviant arousal patterns and personality disorders (Sorenson & White, 1992). Among college students, men who heavily use alcohol (or none at all; Abbey et al., 2002), who have an athletic connection (Murnen & Kohlman, 2007), affiliate with a fraternity (Lackie & deMan, 1997; Robinson et al., 2004), and who are sexually predatory (Kanin, 1985) are more likely to engage in sexual aggression against women and endorse rape-supportive statements (Boeringer, 1999), but aggressors certainly are not limited to heavy drinkers, jocks, "frat boys," and flagrant "wolves" (just as all men are not sexually aggressive). In sum, *many rapists appear normal* (White et al., 2001).

The gap between cultural mythology and research reality about rapists undermines women's readiness to label their assailant as a rapist. Given this logic, it is no surprise that far more rapes by strangers (estimated at 21%) are reported than are the more common acquaintance rapes (2%) (Koss et al, 1988; also see Pino & Meier, 1999). Complement this pattern with the onset of abuse toward women intimates, which is most likely to begin when the couple becomes committed to each other (for 75 to 85% of abused wives, the abuse didn't start until after they were married), and women often care about the perpetrators of their victimization (Koss, Goodman et al., 1994). In an experiment where women's responses to sexual coercion in a hypothetical relationship vignette were measured, women took longer to terminate the relationship when it was described as long-term (Faulker et al., 2008). Indeed, it is greater perceived investment that distinguishes women in sexually coercive relationships from women in other relationships (Katz et al., 2006) so that shifting perceptions of a woman's partner from good to bad is an important part of being able to leave him (Enander, 2011).

Other research focuses on the victimization of abusers themselves. Extensive research finds higher rates of witnessing domestic violence or being targeted for childhood abuse among abusive men as compared to non-abusive men (Lichter & McCloskey, 2004; Whitaker et al., 2008). However, a distinction needs to be made between being socialized toward violence and excusing responsibility for perpetrating violence (Ptacek, 1988). Not all abusers were socialized toward abuse, and not all of those reared in abusive families grow up to be abusers themselves (Widom, 1989). Although male drunkenness is associated with battering by men (Hutchison, 1999), excusing perpetrators because they "lack impulse control" ignores the intended use of violence by many perpetrators as a means for controlling women's behavior (Dutton & Goodman, 2005).

Rather than regarding individual male abusers as rare, obviously pathological, and ultimately unlovable, some researchers focus on the pathology of exaggerations of the male gender role. Looking across societies, **hypermasculinity** was found to be related to higher rape rates across states (Jaffe & Straus, 1987) and across cultures (Sanday, 1981b). On an individual level, there is a growing body of evidence relating male sexual aggressiveness to exaggerations of the masculine gender role (Driscoll et al., 1998; Franchina et al., 2001; Weisbuch et al., 1999), re-asserting masculinity (Eisler et al., 2000; Messerschmidt, 2000), and the masculine ideal of control and dominance (Anderson & Umberson, 2001; Reitz, 1999).

For example, violent husbands tend to control what the couple does, whose friends they see, and what major household purchases they make (Frieze & McHugh, 1981, cited in McHugh et al., 1993). Similarly, violent dates ascribe to more traditional, controlling **dating scripts**—initiating the date, paying all expenses, driving the car (Muehlenhard & Linton, 1987). Fascinating research establishes a link between masculinity and rape-related attitudes through **entitlement**—both men's general expectation that they should have their needs met and their specific expectations about having sexual urges fulfilled (Hill & Fischer, 2001). This paints a picture of some men who believe that sexual coercion is justifiable because they deserve to have their needs fulfilled. Combine this belief with rape myths that promote the image of uncontrollable, animalistic sexual urges in men, and men's responsibility for their actions is even more excused to a point whereby some evolution theorists even justify rape as men's adaptive mandate for reproduction (Thornhill & Palmer, 2000).

Self-Blame and Shame

Sexual harassment, male IPV, and rape all share an aura of misunderstanding arising from the misogynous belief that, because of characterological deficiencies, women bring such abuse on themselves and contribute to its continuation. In no other crime do we heap such blame on the victim (see Box 13.4). Both characterological and behavioral self-blame are associated with heightened symptomatology in victims of non-stranger sexual assault (Arata & Burkhart, 1998), and self-blame remains evident even in women who prosecute sexual harassment charges (Wright & Fitzgerald, 2007).

"The Rape" of Mr. Smith (Box 13.4) was first published in April 1975 in the *American Bar Association Journal* to expose legal bias against rape victims based in rape myths. Students still can report the contents of these myths but confine their personal beliefs to victims' reactions to rape (Buddie & Miller, 2001). Given what we know about contemporary stereotyping, we shouldn't expect to find much blatant endorsement of rape myths; instead, we might expect these myths to linger in more subtle and harder to detect forms. For example, a content analysis of media coverage of a high profile rape case found that fully 10% of the headlines subtly endorsed rape myths, and that male readers exposed to these myths were more likely to think the accused was innocent (Franiuk et al., 2008). Research designed to uncover such potentially subtle stereotyping has used mock juries or has randomly assigned research participants to react to a single vignette describing an incident and then compared these responses across systematically varied vignettes.

Given what we already know about the subtlety of modern **sexism**, we shouldn't be surprised to find that the subtle stereotyping that reinforces rape myths persists. Like Mr. Smith's "deservingness," women's suggestive attire remains linked to perceived sexual intent (Farris et al., 2008; Maurer & Robinson, 2008), and knowing one's attacker is still associated with more victim blame (Grubb & Harrower, 2008). Respondents high in **benevolent sexism** who believe in protecting "good women" were more likely to blame women for marital rape (Dum et al., 2010) and for bringing on date rape by inviting the relationship with the man (thus violating heterosexual dating scripts that assign women a passive role) (Abrams et al., 2003) and by not being a stereotypic victim (Masser et al., 2010). Mock jurors viewed complainants who had prior sexual intercourse with the defendant as less credible (Schuller & Hastings, 2002), and a woman who experienced acquaintance rape

---

Box 13.4. "The Rape" of Mr. Smith

"Mr. Smith, you were held up at gunpoint on the corner of 16th and Locust?"
　　"Yes."
"Did you struggle with the robber?"
　　"No."
"Why not?"
　　"He was armed."
"Then you made a conscious decision to comply with his demands rather than to resist?"
　　"Yes."
"Did you scream? Cry out?"
　　"No. I was afraid."
"I see. Have you ever been held up before?"
　　"No."
"Have you ever given money away?"
　　"Yes, of course—"
"And did you do so willingly?"
　　"What are you getting at?"
"Well, let's put it like this, Mr. Smith. You've given away money in the past—in fact, you have quite a reputation for philanthropy. How can we be sure that you weren't contriving to have your money taken from you by force?"
　　"Listen, if I wanted—"
"Never mind. What time did this holdup take place, Mr. Smith?"
　　"About 11 p.m."
"You were out on the streets at 11 p.m.? Doing what?"
　　"Just walking."
"Just walking? You know that it's dangerous being out on the street that late at night. Weren't you aware that you could have been held up?"
　　"I hadn't thought about it."
"What were you wearing at the time, Mr. Smith?"
　　"Let's see. A suit. Yes, a suit."
"An expensive suit?"
　　"Well—yes."
"In other words, Mr. Smith, you were walking around the streets late at night in a suit that practically advertised the fact that you might be a good target for some easy money, isn't that so? I mean, if we didn't know better, Mr. Smith, we might even think you were asking for this to happen, mightn't we?"
　　"Look, can't we talk about the past history of the guy who did this to me?"
"I'm afraid not, Mr. Smith. I don't think you would want to violate his rights, now, would you?"

From Unknown, 1975.

---

during an act of infidelity was blamed more than a similar victim whose marital status was unknown (Viki & Abrams, 2002).

Students were most favorably inclined toward victims who reported immediately and espoused an altruistic motive ("so he doesn't do it to someone else") (Balogh et al., 2003). Both Black and White women who were victims of *inter*racial rape were blamed more than victims of *intra*racial rape (George & Martinez, 2002). Gay men and heterosexual women were blamed more for being raped by a man, presuming sexual attraction on the part of the victim, than lesbian and heterosexual men (Wakelin & Long, 2003).

Cultural expectations about the influences of alcohol—as a disinhibitor for the man, as an excuse for his behavior, and as a strategy for reducing victims' resistance—also contextually support violence (Koss, Goodman et al., 1994). They send the double messages that "he's *not* responsible, *he was drinking*" and "she *is* responsible, *she was drinking*." College students associated more blame and derogated a victim of male IPV if she drank before the assault (Harrison & Esqueda, 2000); student mock jurors considered an alleged victim of acquaintance rape as more credible if she was sober at the time of the rape (Wenger & Bornstein, 2006); and police were less likely to arrest when victims were drunk (Stewart & Maddren, 1997). All of these factors combine to set up a **social context** that both reflects and reinforces male violence against women.

Blame for victimization. The tendency to blame women for bringing on their abuse runs through common *myths* about sexual harassment (e.g., she was seductive), male IPV (e.g., she must have provoked him), rape (e.g., all women want to be raped), and CSA (e.g., the child imagined it) (Sheffield, 1989). Acceptance of these myths has not disappeared fully (Cowan, 2000a; Hinck & Thomas, 1999; Johnson et al., 1997). A meta analysis of 72 studies of beliefs in rape myths found more acceptance among men, older people, people from lower socioeconomic backgrounds, and among those espousing traditional gender role attitudes, adversarial sexual beliefs, needs for power, dominance, aggressiveness and anger, and conservative political beliefs (Anderson et al., 1997). Beliefs about sexual aggression are shared in families (Quinones et al., 1999). Latina women perceive the most victim-blaming for rape in their communities, White women, the least (Lefley et al., 1993).

Looking across a wide range of rape myths, researchers uncover four distinct themes underlying them: disbelief of rape claims, victim responsibility for rape, rape reports as manipulation of a man by a woman, and the belief that rape happens only to deserving women (Briere et al., 1985). All of these undermine the truthfulness and victimization of the recipient. For those of us who dismiss these myths for the hogwash they are, we may think that we wouldn't blame ourselves if we were so victimized. Indeed, people who read cases of sexual harassment and then are asked to describe what they would do in those situations (analog studies) rarely relate that they would blame themselves (Fitzgerald, 1990). Yet, reports from actual victims provide evidence to the contrary:

> I was ashamed, thought it was my fault, and was worried that the school would take action against me (for "unearned" grades) if they found out about it. . . .

> When I came to, I wanted to die, the guilt and depression were so bad. Your whole sense of worth is tied up with being a successful wife and having a happy marriage. If your husband beats you, then your marriage is a failure, and you're a failure. It's so horribly the opposite of how it is supposed to be (Sheffield, 1989, p. 15).

> I felt guilty. I felt it was my fault because I had been drinking. I felt angry at myself for not having fought or screamed louder (Hanmer & Saunders, 1984, p. 37).

Knowing of this inconsistency between what we think we'd do and what others actually do raises serious questions about what each of us really would do if confronted with these kinds of abuse.

Furthermore, these myths, regardless of their veracity, help to sustain violence. There is well established evidence linking acceptance of rape myths with the men who perpetrate these acts (Anderson et al., 1997). Additionally, some women help perpetuate rape myths through their own distrust of and hostility toward other women (Cowan, 2000b). Surveying various professionals, Colleen Ward (1995) concluded that many doctors, police, and lawyers were misinformed; they accepted these faulty myths, including beliefs that women provoke rape by their dress, that women cannot be believed and that men are not responsible (also see Lea, 2007). **Priming** viewers with the promiscuous female stereotype (by simply having them watch a talk-show television segment) led to perceptions of less trauma and more responsibility attributed to a victim of sexual harassment (Ferguson et al., 2005).

Male violence against women does not take place in a vacuum. Rather, it occurs within a sociocultural context that subtly promotes violence or turns away from it. We have seen that exaggerations of the masculine gender role and male-dominant dating scripts help support violence. So does sexualized media violence. When exposed to both X-rated and R-rated materials that portrayed violence directed at women in sexualized contexts, college men expressed callous attitudes toward husband-perpetrated sexual abusiveness and were themselves more aggressive in the laboratory (Donnerstein et al., 1987). Similarly, men who watched slasher films showed less sensitivity toward rape victims (Linz, 1989). Media violence affects women as well, making college women feel disempowered (Reid & Finchilescu, 1995). In general, depictions of sexual violence can promote antisocial attitudes and behavior (Linz et al., 1992) and can desensitize both women and men (Krafka et al., 1997).

Blame for "inappropriate" responding. We tend to think of male violence against women as a one-time event. How many women confidently have claimed: "If a man ever hit me, it would be over between us"? But much of male violence against women is cyclic. Sexual harassment typically encompasses a long-term barrage of offensive behaviors (Fitzgerald et al., 1995). Once the cycle of partner abuse begins, it tends to spiral upward, becoming increasingly dangerous for the victim (Short et al., 2000). CSA usually cycles as well (Stanko, 1985).

We have stereotypic images about how women should respond to violence, and this often erroneous stereotyping affects how we react toward victims. The courts have sent a message that a victim's behavior will be closely scrutinized in sexual harassment cases and that a "real" victim will speak out against her harassment, both publicly and privately, when it is happening (Fitzgerald et al., 1995). Women themselves tend to think hypothetically that if they confronted sexual harassment, they should and *would* respond assertively to make it stop (Fitzgerald, 1993). Not surprisingly, consistent and persistent assertiveness is believed to be most effective toward thwarting unwanted sexual attention (Yagil et al., 2006), and college students evaluate victims who confront their harasser as most effective and appropriate (Sigal et al., 2003). In fact, students are most likely to "see" harassment if the target resists and the perpetrator subsequently persists (Osman, 2007). Similarly, we expect abused women to leave their relationships, implying that their failure to do so is indicative of some inexplicable characterological shortcoming. In sum, we stereotype how victims *should* respond, and we evaluate the genuineness of victimization against this stereotype.

Louise Fitzgerald and her colleagues (1995) described how real-life victims of sexual harassment actually did respond. *Internally focused responses* include endurance (ignoring the situation, pretending it is not happening, not caring), denial (of information, threat, vulnerability, or negative feelings), reattribution (reinterpreting the events as non-harassment, such as, "he was just joking"), illusory control, and detachment. Thus, seemingly "doing nothing" is a form of responding—one that is used quite frequently by some women, especially if the harassment is less severe (Chan et al., 1999; Cochran et al., 1997).

Externally focused responses include avoidance, appeasement, assertiveness, looking for social support, and seeking institutional or organizational relief. Of these, avoidance is the most common, followed by appeasement (an attempt to put off the harasser without direct confrontation). Avoidance coping is negatively related to reporting sexual harassment (Goldberg, 2007), and it is used most often by rape survivors who blame themselves and received negative reactions from others (Littleton & Breitkopf, 2006), which in turn predicts PTSD symptoms (Ullman et al., 2007).

The *most infrequent* response, seeking institutional relief, is probably *most* effective in terminating sexual harassment, but unless strong organizational supports exist (e.g., an effective union; Bulger, 2001), targets are fearful of doing this—fearing retaliation, disbelief, harm to one's career, shame, and humiliation.[6] Reviewing the literature, there is substantial evidence to verify that all of these fears are real (Campbell & Raja, 2005). A large-scale study with federal employees found that both women and men who experienced frequent sexual harassment and used confrontational coping experienced worse job outcomes than others (Stockdale, 1998). Although reporting women are regarded by others as assertive, they also are considered less feminine and trustworthy (Marin & Guadagno, 1999)—reminiscent of the competence versus warmth quandary we explored for women in Chapter 7.

Note how what we think a harassment victim should do (that is, be assertive or report him) differs from what victims really do. Are being a silent tolerator or an instigator-in-kind (someone who appeases harassers by "playing along") forms of consent or forms of coping (Fitzgerald et al., 1995)? Compared to what we stereotypically think victims should do, these typical responses look like consent. But in light of what we have presented here, these responses look more like coping. Furthermore, the **coping perspective** suggests that, rather than concentrate on what victims do and don't do to make their dissent known, women would be better served if the burden of demonstrating that sexual overtures were welcomed by a woman in the workplace was put squarely on the shoulders of the initiator. Additionally, organizations can be proactive by taking steps to address harassment, such as setting strong and clear policies (Gruber, 1998).

Turning to male IPV, few women fail to seek some form of help (Hutchison & Hirschel, 1998), although battered woman have mixed views about the effectiveness of the criminal justice system (Barata, 2007). For example, 44% of women murdered by their intimate partner had visited an emergency room within the past 2 years (NCIPC, 2005). Because battering is an extreme attempt to exert control and is associated with men's fears of abandonment (Conrad & Morrow, 2000), a woman's escape is often thwarted by threats of escalated violence (extending even to pets; Flynn, 2000) and homicide/suicide should she try to leave (NCIPC, 2005). These threats often are credible; fully one-third of 135 women

---

[6]Reporting is less likely when the proportion of women in a woman's overall occupation or specific job is small (Goldberg, 2001).

were abused by former partners within 2 years of leaving a shelter (Fleury et al., 2000).[7] Overall, laws and social norms limit women's power to leave abuse relationships (Pratto & Walker, 2004).

Although this may make entrapment understandable, how can we understand a woman who escapes and then returns? One study that followed a group of beaten women across 2.5 years found that 23% were in an abusive relationship at the start and at the end of the study (Campbell et al., 1994). (The average duration of an abusive marriage is 6 years—the same as the average marriage [L.E.A. Walker, 1994.]) Reviewing data from a variety of sources, Michael Strube (1988, p. 238) concludes that "about half of all women who seek some form of aid for spouse abuse can be expected to return to their partners." This pattern holds across different races, social classes, marital statuses, educational levels, and the presence of children in the home.

What does seem to distinguish women who don't return from those who do is that the former are more likely to be employed (and thus can afford to leave,)[8] are in shorter-term relationships (less invested?), think of themselves as better off financially, are less in love, are less likely to be White (and possibly have wider kinship networks to take them in) and feel they have somewhere to go (Strube & Barbour, 1984). The absence of these facilitators fits with a psychological profile of a returner who feels entrapped; the presence of these facilitators describes women who have less to lose by leaving. In sum, for a woman to leave an abusive relationship she has to answer two questions affirmatively: "Will I be better off?" and "Can I do it?" (Choice & Lamke, 1997).

Understanding the cycle of partner abuse also helps frame women's apparent choices to stay and even return. Lenore Walker (1979) describes a three-stage **cycle of battering**. In the first phase, *tension builds* as minor battering incidents are seemingly controlled and rationalized by the woman, who does her best to avoid "provoking" an outburst. (It is during this first phase that Walker [1989] reports women are most likely to kill their abusers.)

In the second phase, *the acute battering incident*, violence escalates and the woman feels that she has lost control and cannot predict her partner's behavior. The trigger is rarely something the battered woman does, although Walker describes how some women may move things toward this outburst as a way to relieve the intolerable pressure mounting during the tension-building phase. The second phase typically lasts between 2 to 24 hours, after which most women tend to stay isolated for several days before seeking any help.

Phase three can be the hook for many women—after the explosion, the batterer exudes *kindness and contrite, loving behavior*. At the exact time when we would expect the woman to be most motivated to leave, he stops the abuse and steps up the charm. The pressure to stay at this point also is bolstered by societal valuation of "standing by one's man," a common component of descriptions of "perfect love" (Towns & Adams, 2000). When things return to "normal," tension building begins anew and the cycle continues. Walker describes these women as *survivors* who learn to control inevitable violent out-

---

[7]One possible counter-offensive to threats of retaliation is to file assault charges. One study of 90 women found that filing charges was an effective deterrent to future violence, even though only 37% resulted in a successful arrest (McFarlane et al., 2000).

[8]A trap of financial dependency may disrupt women's ability to leave. For example, extremely poor women who had experienced partner violence in the past 12 months also had trouble maintaining their own employment (Browne et al., 1999; also see Riger et al., 2004).

bursts so as to survive the violence, not as passive victims helplessly out of control (also see Bergen, 1995).

Control is a repeated theme throughout descriptions of battering (Eisikovits & Buchbinder, 1999). In contrast to the control exerted by women, noted above by Walker, to cope with violence, men describe how they paradoxically lose control in order to reassert their control, wanting ultimately to be Bigger, Better, and Winning over their partner (Reitz, 1999). Nine men described the acute battering incident as one in which they lost control—failing to remember what they did and feeling out-of-body as they did it. The aftermath of contrite, loving behavior reflects their attempt to live up to their ideal of being Big, Good, and Winning, but pressure to achieve these ideals rebuilds anew. Thus from both the women's and men's sides of this pattern, *the cycle perpetrates itself.*

In sum, both myths about what brings on male violence against women (e.g., women who are "asking for it") and stereotyping of how "genuine" victims should react differ from reality for many women. Until we let go of these false and misleading myths and stereotyping, we will fail to understand many women's victimization and ultimately will contribute to their second victimization as they struggle to cope and survive.[9] At a societal level, these myths and this stereotyping keep alive a culture that largely ignores, and ultimately accepts, violence.

Cognitive Coping Strategies

First writing this chapter revived memories for me of being sexually harassed in my first job. I can recall many of the details of the 3-hour session that took place in my office at a deserted university on a Sunday afternoon. However, I am struck by the fact that I'd have to review a roster of the faculty to remember the name of the senior professor who threatened me—and the idea of doing this is quite unnerving. My feelings parallel those of other women asked to reconstruct their experiences with sexual harassment (Kidder et al., 1995). Denial, avoidance, and numbing are adaptive, especially when the event in question involves a betrayal of trust (Freyd, 1997). Many women have vague, sketchy memories of actual abusive incidents by male partners (Kelly, 1988). Although women certainly remember a past rape experience, their descriptions are characterized by less detail and a numbing of emotion common to memories of other unpleasant experiences—but very different from pleasant memories (Koss et al., 1996).

One of the most controversial areas to explore memories of trauma focuses on recovered memories of childhood sexual abuse (see Pope & Brown, 1996). On the one side, the False Memory Syndrome Foundation, founded in 1992 by accused parents and independent of any recognized organization of mental health professionals, coined a "syndrome" they believe befits DSM-IV as a personality disorder (described in Pope, 1996). People afflicted with this presumed disorder obsess about a false, implanted memory so much that their entire life revolves around it. They argue that this memory is the product of suggestive psychotherapists who, through naiveté, greed, incompetence, or zealotry, convince the client that she (usually a woman) has been sexually abused by a family member (although subsequent research disputes these charges of therapists' implantation; Sullins, 1998).

---

[9]Support services for victims of all forms of violence vary by locales. Good resources on college campuses for these services or referrals for services include women's centers, women's studies offices, psychology clinics, and health facilities. Be clear that you are looking for feminist-oriented services.

These assertions resonate with a general distrust of children's reports of sexual abuse within Western society (Scott, 1997) and serve to silence women and children who are struggling to be believed (Saraga & MacLeod, 1997). The scientific foundation for these claims rests on a series of studies in which a presumably untrue "memory" is suggested by an older family member to research participants, who eventually report that they believe the implanted event actually happened. The original procedure created a "memory" of being lost in a shopping mall (Loftus & Ketcham, 1994). Other suggestions tested by researchers have included earaches, trips to the hospital at night, and words that did not appear in a list.

Ken Pope (1996) points to some compelling shortcomings in this research. Being lost in a mall is offered as analogous to being sexually abused in that both are arguably traumatic. However, being lost is a more common experience than abuse, contains no sexual content, seems less stressful, and is a singular incident. It also fails to capture the betrayal that is so central to understanding the trauma of CSA (Freyd, 1997). These differences raise serious questions about the relevance of everyday memory processes toward our understanding of the traumatic memories of childhood abuse (Kristiansen et al., 1996).

A somewhat closer analog may be having a mother give her child an enema. When researchers tried to implant this memory, they were successful with *none* of their participants (Pezdek, 1995, 1996). Also, having an older family member suggest the false "memory" in these studies is a lot different from having a therapist do so, in that only the relative is presumed to have first-hand experience, making her or him more credible. (I know I tell my children lots of stories about their childhood that they don't recall on their own.) Contrary to the false memory agenda, these studies suggest that if family members can alter their children's memories, then abusers feasibly might convince their victims that "nothing really happened"—or at least insure that they keep events hidden.

We might think of traumas as life-altering events (which indeed they are) that are too powerful to be put aside. However, an approach focused on "recovered" memories asks us to reframe our thinking around the concept of coping. Taking a **coping perspective**, our expectations change—we expect victims to remember but to do so in ways that let them go on with their lives. Such *cognitive adaptation* might include talking less about these events, numbing the emotions they engender, and letting go of disturbing details (Koss et al., 1996). Adopting this orientation, Laura Brown and Erica Burman (1997) ask us to reframe our point of view by thinking in terms of "delayed," instead of "recovered," memories. There is provocative evidence to support such rethinking. For example, follow-up studies with women known to have been sexually abused as children (because they were treated in emergency rooms) found that 38% (almost 200 women) were unable to vividly recall the index event. Paralleling these findings, studies of crime victims show that some seem to report hazy memories of even fairly serious attacks (Block & Block, 1984).

Minimization of Violence

Again, if we take a coping perspective, it is understandable that some survivors will seek to minimize their abuse (Kelly, 1988). Combine this with the well-documented tendency for abusive men to underreport their violent actions and their impact (reviewed by McHugh et al., 1993) and for harassers in court cases to try to minimize outrage (McDonald et al., 2010), and abuse may be reported by those directly involved as being not as bad as a third-party observer might document. Note the italicized contradictions in the following examples from British women:

> I was molested by a man who grabbed hold of me and pushed himself against me in the tube when it was crowded. I screamed as loudly as I could. He *slapped my face*, but then got off as we got to a station. I suppose I was lucky that *nothing actually happened*....

> The men in the office are forever having a go—sort of half joke/half propositioning me. They know I don't like it, but they never give up. It's *nothing really*. I can handle it, or I have so far, but it pisses me off. I'm *exhausted by the end of the day*....

> I've been attacked in the library—young White boys fooling around in a threatening and racist way. *Nothing's actually happened* to me, but I've had to *call the police* to have them removed... (Kelly & Radford, 1996, p. 26; italics added).

As Liz Kelly and Jill Radford (1996) point out, although these women insist that nothing really happened, something really did. That "something" has more to do with women's feelings than with any documented physical hurt per se. The evidence is minimized not only by these women in parts of their stories (and contradicted in other parts), but probably by outsiders as well. Furthermore, these stories illustrate how, when women say nothing really happened, they may be considering a much worse scenario than what they experienced, such as he slapped but didn't rape me. In contrast, when the law says nothing really happened, violation is invalidated.

Section Summary

We have seen that there are many factors that conspire to keep male violence against women hidden, even at times from victims themselves. It is noteworthy that some critics who wish to invalidate women's experiences require that victims appropriately label their abuse before it can be characterized as abuse. Must clients come to therapy calling themselves survivors of childhood abuse to be legitimately treated for its aftermath? Or may conscientious therapists pursue diagnostic leads based on observed signs and testing that may be indicative of abuse?

Most advocates of a recovered memory model note that clients don't come to therapy without showing any signs of abuse and then spontaneously report it during the course of therapy, as false memory advocates suppose (Polusny & Follette, 1996). Most fundamentally, psychologists are in the habit of assigning labels to people based on their adherence to established criteria, without requiring that they self-report the label given. For example, how many diagnosed alcoholics would we miss if we required self-identification? Similarly, why should a researcher give research participants the Ambivalent Sexism Inventory if she or he could simply ask them to classify themselves? Such demands are immediately absurd; yet we seem to accept parallel demands as legitimate for women survivors of abuse.

Even knowing in the abstract why abuse is invisible, at some basic level I admit to being overwhelmed by these prevalence rates—it's just too depressing to be true. While taking a break from first writing this chapter, I bumped into a retired friend, and she asked about my progress with this book. I shared how gut-wrenching this topic was, and she proceeded to tell me about her own experience with attempted date rape—her date ripped her brand new dress and then called her the next day, oblivious to why she was "acting funny." I was stunned. This nice, White-haired woman recalled vivid images of an attempted date rape that happened over 40 years ago. Somehow this made these prevalence rates more concrete for me. As students and as caring human beings, I urge you to be open to women's experiences. Sexually assaulted women cope better if they are believed and listened to by others (Ullman et al., 2007).

We have reviewed different strategies used to invalidate women's experiences—strategies that are simultaneously fueled by the hiddenness of violence as well as ultimately maintaining this invisibility. By excusing perpetrators, we place the burden for establishing nonconsent squarely on the shoulders of women victims alone, and we ultimately come to blame victims for bringing about their own victimization. One theme that runs through this section is a call for men to assume responsibility for establishing consent before engaging in sexual relations. At the root of this call is the need to respect and listen to women—a fundamental ingredient that could reduce other forms of violence, like physical assault, as well. A second theme challenges us to replace a victim-blaming perspective with a coping approach to better understand women's responses to violence, including appearing to play along with sexual harassment; staying and even returning to abusive intimates; denying, avoiding, and numbing; and abuse minimizations.

CONSEQUENCES

Consistent with the previous sections of this chapter, common threads run through what we know about the consequences for women of sexual harassment, rape, male IPV, and CSA. Here we will explore some immediate and long-term physical and psychological consequences for individual women (Ullman & Brecklin, 2003). The patterns we will review argue that the pervasive threat of male violence against women serves to unite all women, differentiates women from men, and is used to maintain social control in a male-dominated, **patriarchal** society.

Physical Sequelae

Both immediate and long-term physical harm results from all forms of male violence against women. For women coping with sexual harassment, common responses include anxiety attacks, headaches, sleep disturbances, disordered eating, gastrointestinal disorders, nausea, weight loss or gain, and crying spells (Crull, 1982; Gutek, 1985). A meta analysis established the predicted associations between sexual harassment and health dissatisfaction ($r = .26$) and negative health symptoms ($r = .29$) (Chan et al., 2008). Sophisticated statistical modeling argues that body dissatisfaction and eating disturbances are results of, not antecedents to, harassment (Harned, 2000).

One-half to two-thirds of rape survivors escape without physical trauma (Koss & Heslet, 1992), and only half of the injured receive formal medical treatment (Koss et al., 1991). Survivors are more likely to contact a physician than a mental health professional, and gross underfunding of rape crisis intervention programs has limited their utility (Koss, 1993). The U.S. National Center for Victims of Crime (NCVC, 2005) reported a national study finding that only 13% of rape victims receiving emergency room treatment were both screened and received medication for sexually transmitted diseases. Physical problems persist for a disproportionate number of women beyond the immediate aftermath. Survivors report more physical health problems, perceive their health less favorably, and visit physicians twice as often as women in general (Koss, 1993).

The most obvious consequences of male IPV are physical, yet the range of violent acts is stunning. Lenore Walker (1979) sums up the stories of 120 women:

> Major physical assaults included: slaps and punches to the face and head; kicking, stomping, and punching all over the body; choking to the point of consciousness loss; pushing and throwing across a room, down the stairs, or against objects; severe shaking; arms twisted or broken; burns from irons, cigarettes, and scalding liquids; injuries from thrown objects; forced shaving of pubic hair; forced violent sexual acts; stabbing and mutilation with a variety of objects, including knives and hatchets; and gunshot wounds. The most common physical injuries reported are those inflicted by the man's hands and feet to the head, face, back, and rib areas. Broken ribs and broken arms, resulting from the woman's raising her arm to defend herself, are the most common broken bones.
>
> Several women in this sample have suffered broken necks and backs, one after being flung against objects in the room. One woman suffered the loss of a kidney and severe injury to her second kidney when she was thrown against a kitchen stove. Others suffered serious internal bleeding and bruises. Swollen eyes and nose, lost teeth, and concussions were all reported. Surgery was required in a large number of cases. Women were often knocked unconscious by these blows. Many others were choked nearly unconscious (pp. 79–80).

About 17% of all violence-related injuries treated in emergency rooms resulted from IPV (Bureau of Justice Statistics, 1997). Whereas it is typical for adults to make one injury visit to an emergency service in their lifetime, abused wives average more than one such visit each year (Stark & Flitcraft, 1996). In a clinical study of 691 pregnant women, 17% reported physical and sexual abuse during their pregnancy (MacFarlane et al., 1992), and 25% of women using a community-based family practice reported injuries inflicted by an intimate (Hamberger et al., 1992).

Psychological Sequelae

Given our premise that different forms of male violence against women are linked, it comes as no surprise that survivors' reactions to these victimizations share much in common—but with a few noteworthy exceptions. All violence poses threats to normal psychological well-being and challenges survivors' fundamental beliefs about the world.

Disrupted psychological well-being. Throughout these explorations, what is cause and what is effect often have been confused. For example, low self-esteem characterizes victims of male IPV. For those who assume that women's low self-esteem predated their abuse, presumed helplessness has been cited as a preexisting characterological flaw in women that makes them more vulnerable to battering. However, researchers who have questioned this causal chain have concluded instead that low self-esteem, like other signs of helplessness and entrapment, results from the abuse itself (Hotaling & Sugarman, 1986; Margolin, 1988). The psychological aftermath we will describe here is more accurately conceptualized as a result of the trauma these women experienced, rather than as something that was germinating in these survivors prior to their assault.

College women who have experienced sexual harassment show signs of posttraumatic stress, clinical psychological symptoms, and reduced satisfaction with life (Rederstorff et al., 2007). The consequences of sexual harassment in high school may carry over into college as general doubts about romantic relationships (Duffy et al., 2004) and are more severe than the effects of being bullied (Gruber & Fineran, 2008). Among women taking part in a class-action suit, their degree of psychological distress was most related to the severity of the harassment and how much they blamed themselves (Collinsworth et al., 2009).

As for the psychological consequences of rape survival, women's responses generally change over time (Koss & Figuredo, 2004). For many survivors, distress levels are severely elevated during the first week, and then peak in severity by about 3 weeks. For an average of 12 days after a rape, fully 94% of survivors meet the criteria for **posttraumatic stress disorder** (PTSD). This continues at an elevated level for about the next month, and then begins to diminish. By 2 to 3 months post-assault, many differences between survivors and women in general disappear, with the exceptions of persistent reports of fear, anxiety, self-esteem problems, and sexual dysfunction among survivors. Fully 46% still meet the criteria for PTSD 3 months afterwards. These patterns cut across Latina, African American, and White women (Wyatt et al., 1992) for whom issues of race, ethnicity, and class must enter into effective counseling (Bryant-Davis et al., 2009).

When does a rape survivor go back to her pre-assault self? Possibly never. Even years after a rape, survivors are more likely to be diagnosed for major depression, alcohol and drug abuse and dependence, generalized anxiety, obsessive-compulsive disorder, and PTSD (Koss, 1993), and they often have difficulties in relationships, especially around nurturing and trust (McMullin et al., 2007). Looking across a wide array of post-assault consequences, the most important overall factor appears to be *self-blame*: the more women blame themselves, the worse their recovery (Campbell et al., 2009).

Women raped by an acquaintance typically delay disclosing their experience and often experience more negative reactions than those attacked by a stranger (Sudderth, 1998). Alcohol consumption may increase women's vulnerability to assault (Davis et al., 2004). College women raped when intoxicated are just as emotionally affected and engage in more self-blame than those raped by force (Schwartz & Leggett, 1999). Anti-lesbian rape, which targets lesbians and is designed to degrade lesbian sexuality, often threatens women's general sense of safety, independence, and well-being (Garnets et al., 1993).

For women survivors of male IPV, common reactions include shock, denial, withdrawal, confusion, psychological numbing, fear (Browne, 1987; D.G. Dutton, 1992), depression, anxiety, stress, and low self-esteem (Haj-Yahia, 2000). These survivors frequently are characterized by high levels of negative health symptoms, gynecological problems, and risk of homicide (Campbell & Soeken, 1999). Chronic fatigue and tension, intense startle reactions, disturbed sleep and eating patterns, and nightmares also may result (Goodman et al., 1993; Herman, 1992). More severe symptomatology is likely for women who experience more violent forms of abuse (Abbey et al., 2004) and for victims of both physical and sexual aggression (Browne, 1987).

The psychological effects of CSA may be long-term for survivors. Given the hidden nature of this form of victimization, it is hard to gauge its consequences. For example, a highly controversial article attributed more problems to dysfunctional family environments than abuse per se (Rind et al., 1998), but subsequent commentaries called into question the merits of this conclusion (Dallam et al., 2001; Ondersma et al., 2001). In contrast, it is estimated that fully 40% of survivors will need therapy some time during their adulthood (Browne & Finkelhor, 1986). Documented sequelae include depression, self-destructive behavior, feelings of isolation and stigma, poor self-esteem, sexual maladjustment, difficulty trusting others, PTSD symptoms, and symptoms of dissociation (Browne & Finkelhor, 1986; Lemieux & Byers, 2008; Roesler & McKenzie, 1994).

Disrupted world views. We all possess views of how the world works—who can be trusted, what's fair, and who deserves what, as well as hopes expressed by "it just can't happen to me" (Janoff-Blumen & Frieze, 1983). A woman's fundamental beliefs about the world, including feelings of safety, power or efficacy, trust, esteem, and intimacy (McEwan et al., 2002), may be challenged by experiencing rape (Koss, 1993). Even those of us not immediately affected by sexual violence may suffer just-world consequences. In the United States, conviction rates for sexual assault are persistently low. If the world is just, we might begin to question the veracity or severity of these charges. Indeed, H. Colleen Sinclair and Lylce Bourne (1998) found that after reading a summary of a rape trial in which a verdict of "not guilty" was handed down, both women and men exhibited greater acceptance of rape myths than others randomly assigned to read the same case but with a "guilty" verdict.

Diagnosis. A common diagnosis for victims/survivors of sexual and male IPV is **posttraumatic stress disorder** (PTSD). As we saw in Chapter 12, PTSD has advantages over characterological diagnoses like borderline and histrionic personality disorders, because PTSD focuses diagnosis and hence treatment on traumatic events outside the individual. However, PTSD was developed for war survivors and, as such, has several noteworthy limitations (Koss, Goodman et al., 1994). First, responses to sexual assault go beyond PTSD's focus on fear and anxiety, missing common violence after-effects, such as relational disturbances, isolation, and sexual dysfunction. Second, PTSD ignores the cognitive disruptions we examined above to survivors' views of the world, as well as the chronic and seemingly inescapable risks inherent in many women's daily lives (e.g., living in violent neighborhoods or with abusive partners). Third, PTSD responds better to single traumatic events rather than the recurrent ones that tend to characterize male IPV and CSA. Finally, one might philosophically ponder why the DSM-IV considers victimization a mental disorder whereas perpetrating such violence, except in egregious "sociopathic" cases, goes undiagnosed.

Unique Consequences

lthough there are many commonalties across women's responses to violence, some consequences are unique to specific types of violence. For example, sexual harassment produces specific education- or work-related consequences not directly attributable to other forms of violence, such as decreased academic satisfaction (Huerta et al., 2006), lowered job satisfaction, reduced organizational commitment, and withdrawal from work (Willness et al., 2007).

There is a myth unique to IPV: once a victim, always a victim. As we've seen, 23% of abused wives at the start of a study were still in abusive relationships over 2 years later (Campbell et al., 1994), and we examined the factors that mediated such persistence. However, these data also highlight the majority who successfully changed their lives. The myth that battered women simply will trade one abusive relationship for another was discredited many years ago (Walker, 1979).

A different pattern emerges for survivors of rape and CSA whose histories appear to make these women more vulnerable to re-victimization. For example, sexual assault survivors were less likely to project responding to a hypothetical sexually aggressive man with effective resistance, and CSA survivors were more likely to anticipate responding with ineffective passivity (Stoner et al., 2007). College women actually victimized over an 8-month follow-up period were more likely both to have been victimized previously and to delay leaving a potentially risky situation than non-victimized women (Messman-Moore & Brown, 2006). Additionally, women with a history of CSA conveyed more nonverbal vulnerability in a videotaped session in which they interacted with a man they just met in a laboratory "bar" that served alcohol (Parks et al., 2008), and prior victimization predicted women's own aggressiveness in dating relationships (Edwards et al., 2009). In sum, a woman's history of adult and childhood sexual assault can combine with subsequent risky behaviors to sustain a continuing cycle of victimization.

Consequences for All Women

The consequences of male violence against women are not limited to the women who survive these attacks. All women are affected, every day of their lives, by the threat of psychological, physical, and sexual abuse (Hollander, 2001). Every time a woman restricts her activities because of fear, sits in a locked car in sweltering heat, feels her heart beat faster as someone runs up behind her, wears clothes that restrict her means of escape, drops a course when a professor points her out as the only woman in the class..., she is reacting to her fear of attack and vulnerability created by the simple fact that she is a woman in a **patriarchal** culture. These consequences are what distinguish male violence against women from women-perpetrated violence, and what link some forms of male violence against men, as well as homophobic violence against lesbians, to our discussion here.

Fully one-third of urban women reported fear of physical harm, especially rape, as their most common concern (Gordon & Riger, 1989). Although women are less likely than men to be victimized by violent crime overall, more than half of the women surveyed admit to using self-isolation as a form of protection—in stark contrast to only 10% of men in the same neighborhoods who admitted to taking steps to reduce their vulnerability to crime. *Living with the burden of threat of physical and sexual violation unites all women and is limited to them* (Thompson & Norris, 1992).

One of the strongest forms of social control is not force itself, but rather the threat of it (Wrong, 1979, p. 43). In this way, every example we read at the beginning of this chapter, from fear of rape through femicide, is a form of *social control*. This intent to control is made clear in a clever laboratory experiment. Elena Dall'Ara and Anne Maass (1999) gave 120 male Italian university students an opportunity to send pornographic material over the computer to a female stranger; that is, a chance to engage in gender harassment. The alleged recipient was described to the male sender as either traditional or egalitarian. These materials were sent more often to the egalitarian woman, especially by men with a high propensity to sexually harass, with sexist attitudes, with a strong masculine identity, and with low self-monitoring. Parallel findings were confirmed among American college men sending sexist jokes (Siebler et al., 2008), and they fit with findings that highly agentic women in male-dominated professions experience high levels of harassment (Berdahl, 2007). In sum, gender harassment was used as a tool by some men to punish undesirable (egalitarian, feminist, agentic) women.

CHALLENGING GENDER-BASED VIOLENCE

Before we conclude this chapter, let's step back to look at a point that permeates this chapter so fully that it can be largely taken for granted—gender. *"Gender shapes the meaning of violent acts ..."* (Russo & Pirlott, 2006, p. 179; italics added). What is your automatic image of an incident of sexual harassment, rape, or partner abuse? You might argue, as I have done here, that each most commonly involves a male perpetrator and female target so that your images are simply statistically normative. But this response begs the question of why these prevalence rates tip against women, why we take for granted that they do, and, most important, why we "accept" that they do?

My last point takes us back to the first chapter of this text where we talked about a system of inequality, and it leads us to ask whether gender-based violence reflects and helps to maintain this interlocking system of male privilege and female oppression. Simply put, would there be more outrage if we saw a spike in female-perpetrated violence against men? Or is violence less jarring when it harms the less powerful? There are two ways to approach this last question: by looking at (1) how power is involved in perpetration of violence and (2) how disempowerment is part of victimization.

A fascinating series of two experiments by John Bargh and his colleagues (1995) begins to address the first of these points. In their first study, they showed that college men who self-reported an above average likelihood to either sexually harass or behave sexually aggressively toward women demonstrated an unconscious link between sexuality and power on a task similar to the **Implicit Associations Task**. In their second experiment, they exposed college men (who scored either above or below average in sexual aggressiveness) to primes that were either about power or were neutral. For example, authority-power primes consisted of completing word fragments like BO_S (boss); physical-power primes such as STRO_ _ (strong). Sexually aggressive men exposed to the power primes found one of two female **confederates** much more attractive than similarly aggressive men exposed to the neutral primes. Thus, their first study established a link between power and sexuality for some men, and their second study put this association into practice (also see Hitlan et al., 2009). The long-held feminist contention (Brownmiller, 1975) that gender-based violence against women is about men's power and its link to sexuality, not about sexuality per se, is supported by this experimental evidence.

One of the most powerful ways to morally justify violence toward other human beings is to dehumanize them by denying them human attributes (thus making them animal-like) and/or by denying them human nature (thinking of them as objects) (Haslam, 2006). Women's bodies are not uncommonly portrayed as disgustingly animal-like (Citrin et al., 2004; Chrisler, 2011). Fredrickson and Roberts' (1997) **objectification** theory described how women can be treated as objects (including by sexual harassment and violence; see Chapter 10 and Figure 10.2), as well as can come to internalize that objectification into their own self-image. Such objectification includes treating others as tools and commodities, regarding them as without autonomy and agency, seeing people as interchangeable and with fluid boundaries that can be violated, and believing that their experiences and feelings don't matter (Nussbaum, 1999).

Although the role of dehumanization in gender-based violence calls for more research evidence, their conceptual connection seems intuitively defensible. More intriguing for us here and now are the connections between dehumanization and everyday psychological processes. For example, Nck Haslam (2006) points out that objectification may reflect not seeing a connection between one's self and others; that is, regarding some other people as "not like me." When we put this point into the context of what we have reviewed in this book, we are talking about **gender polarization** (the idea that women and men are fundamentally different and with little in common). Additionally, **social categorization** includes seeing **out-group** members as all alike and with one member as good as any other (**out-group homogeneity**).

It may be easy to walk away from this chapter safe in the conviction that as a man, I'd never be violent toward a woman, or that as a woman, I don't perpetrate these forms of violence. However, these linkages of violence to some of the ordinary processes we have repeatedly considered in this text (power, objectification, and gender polarization) suggest otherwise. They suggest that power inequities, objectification of others and ourselves, and gender polarization work together to make gender-based violence possible, normalized (tolerated), and largely invisible (Russo & Pirlott, 2006). Understanding these interconnections makes us all part of the ultimate solution to ending gender-based violence by building empathy in place of objectifying others and agency in place of objectifying ourselves; by challenging essentialism, hypermasculinity, gender stereotyping and rigid role prescriptions, and sexism (gender polarization); and by exposing the linkage between gender and power.

CHAPTER SUMMARY

The major point I have argued throughout this chapter is that the threat of male violence against women and its various realized forms are connected so that each reinforces the others. As we have seen, sexual harassment, rape, male intimate partner violence, and childhood sexual abuse all are linked by definitional ambiguities, language that masks their severity, high prevalence rates, invisibility and efforts to invalidate women's experiences so that they remain hidden, and serious immediate and long-term consequences that extend beyond direct victims to all women.

SUGGESTED READINGS

Kristof, N. D., & WuDunn, S. (2009). *Half the sky: Turning oppression into opportunity for women worldwide*. New York: Knopf.

This haunting, but ultimately inspiring, book detailing cases and statistics about women's lives (including sex trafficking and forced prostitution, IPV, and rape) and fills in large gaps in this chapter by exploring male violence against women globally and by pragmatically directing readers to "make a difference."

Walton, M. D., Harris, A. R., & Davidson, A. J. (2009). "It makes me a man from the beating I took": Gender and aggression in children's narratives about conflict. *Sex Roles, 61*, 383–398.

Marsha Walton and her colleagues coded stories about aggression written by 364 4th to 6th graders from two U.S. poor inner-city schools according to type and severity of violence, explanations, and mental and emotional states. They conclude that children's aggression is gendered, with boys' aggression being seen as more normative and requiring less explanation. Beyond their findings, their analysis raises critical issues about how research questions are framed and the power of social contexts in creating gender differences.

Kurth, S. B., Spiller, B. B., & Travis, C. B. (2000). Consent, power, and sexual scripts: Deconstructing sexual harassment. In C. B. Travis & J. W. White (Eds.), *Sexuality, society, and feminism* (pp. 323–354). Washington, DC: American Psychological Association.

Suzanne Kurth, Bethany Spiller, and Cheryl Travis sagely deconstruct issues surrounding consent and the misuse of power in sexual harassment.

Hamby, S. L., & Koss, M. P. (2003). Shades of gray: A qualitative study of terms used in the measurement of sexual victimization. *Psychology of Women Quarterly, 27*, 243–255.

Sherry Hamby and Mary Koss examine the meaning of coercion with an ethnically diverse sample of women in focus groups, finding that "unwanted," "nonvoluntary," and "forced" have distinct meanings that can cloud our research and thus our understanding of sexual victimization.

Jackson, S. (2001). Happily ever after: Young women's stories of abuse in heterosexual love relationships. *Feminism & Psychology, 11*, 305–321.

Sue Jackson relates the stories of dating abuse told by 23 16 to 18-year=old women and explores how these relate to cultural narratives of romance as well as feminist alternatives.

Kahn, A. S., Jackson, J., Kully, C., Badget, K., & Halvorsen, J. (2003). Calling it rape: Differences in experiences of women who do or do not label their sexual assault as rape. *Psychology of Women Quarterly, 27*, 233–242.

Arnie Kahn and his associates provide insights into rape stereotyping and how rape can go unacknowledged by victims.

Langhinrichsen-Rohling, J. (2010). Controversies involving gender and intimate partner violence in the United States. *Sex Roles, 62*(3–4), 179–193.

Jennifer Langhinrichsen-Rohling considers five controversies that surround the "domestic violence" and feminist approaches to IPV that we touched on here, concluding that IPV is based in relationships, bidirectional, and dynamic and offering a more detailed and nuanced analysis likely to spark discussion (as it did in this issue of *Sex Roles*).

Chapter 14

Making a Difference
Transforming Ourselves, Our Relationships, and Our Society

Power and Empowerment
Personal Empowerment
   Gender-Role Transcendence
   Feminist Identity
Empowered Relationships
   Heterosexual Dating
   Heterosexual Marriage
   On the Job
   Responses to Violence
Activism
   Definition and History
Being an Activist

How much progress do you think has been made toward gender equality in terms of wage and opportunities for career advancement in the United States?

1	2	3	4	5	6	7
no real						a great deal
progress						of progress

The subtitle of this text and the title of this final chapter are "Making a Difference," so a good place to start might be to think about where things now stand regarding gender equality. Stop for a moment and reflect on how you answered this opening question. Did you base your judgment (1) on how current levels of gender equality compare to where they were in the past or (2) on how well they stack up against an ideal goal of true gender equality? This difference captures a glass half-full (as in look-at-how-far-we've-come) versus glass half-empty (as in look-at-how-far-we've-yet-to-go) mentality. Both perspectives make sense, but each suggests something different about work yet to be done.

These are the questions Richard Eibach and Joyce Ehrlinger (2010) explored with college women and men. Although their participants recorded generally positive views of progress, women ($M = 5.28$, $SD = 1.10$) were significantly less positive than men ($M = 5.85$, $SD = 1.28$), with no differences across ethnic minority and White raters. Whereas women reported using both frames to make their judgments, men more commonly relied on measuring progress relative to the past. Importantly, it is this past referent that **mediated** the difference in men's and women's judgments. In other words, men's overall assessment was that we have made more substantial progress because men relied more singularly on thinking about the past and how far we have come (not on how far we have yet to go). In a follow-up study, when women and men were given a specific reference point (past or ideal) to consider, their judgments merged—demonstrating conclusively that seeing the glass as half-full or half-empty matters.

As I argued in Chapter 2, psychology has been irrevocably transformed by feminist thinking and research. However, here in this chapter, I am asking you to use the frame of ideal gender equality to think about the work yet to be done and what you can do to make a difference.

As we look back over this book and contemplate how we might make a difference, there are at least four major themes that recur. The first overriding theme finds meaning in our psychological theories and research by drawing on a social justice agenda based in feminist values. At the heart of this understanding is **gender** differences, not as explanations, but rather as these differences relate to broader issues of **power**, **privilege**, **oppression**, and a **patriarchal system of inequality**. Thus, the ultimate value of our efforts will be judged by their usefulness in contributing to feminist goals for women and men. The purpose of this final chapter is to explore some concrete ways you can use what you've learned throughout this book to "make a difference."

A second repeated theme across these chapters contends that our **socially constructed** and continually changing psychology has been irrevocably transformed by feminist questions that critique, refine, and expand what we do, how we do it, what we've found, and how we interpret our findings. Within this framework, gender too is socially constructed—enacted in what we do, think, and feel, and thus open to change. Moving away from more **essentialist** toward more social constructionist thinking gives us a base from which to "make a difference" because it allows for the possibility of realist change. Indeed, it is the shift in thinking that is empirically connected to believing in the possibility of social change and that is a big part of what students take away from psychology of women and gender courses (Yoder et al., 2007a).

Our third point takes a holistic approach to understanding women and gender by bringing together biology, socialization, **individual differences**, and **social context**. Awareness of how these are intertwined moves us away from an **androcentric**, deficit model that blames women for their presumed shortcomings and lays the groundwork for social activism directed at eliminating unfair external constraints. It also opens up a wide array of possibilities for individuals who are not limited by gendered stereotyping or prescriptions dictating what they *should* do as women and as men.

Our fourth recurrent theme extends our analysis of **social categorization** beyond gender to consider other markers of **social status** and power, including race and ethnicity, physical (dis)ability, sexual orientation, socioeconomic class, religion, age, and so on. Each of these **intersects** with gender so that how one plays out her or his gender is inseparably and always intertwined with these other social markers. Additionally, these social indicators cannot be left unexplored as final explanations for differences. For example, when racial and ethnic differences are found, a full analysis must examine the cultural settings that are related to these markers. We cannot simply accept race and ethnicity itself as an explanation; rather, we need to **"do" difference** as part of **"doing" gender**. This book only begins this process by focusing mostly on gender.

The immodest hope I have for this book is that when you have finished it, you will take something important away from it. This book falls short of its usefulness in a movement toward social justice if we don't examine its impact on you and what you can do with what you've learned and considered. Feminist psychologists have looked at making a difference in three realms: (1) within ourselves as individuals, (2) within our relationships, and (3) throughout our society through social activism. Each is informed by our general understanding of power and **empowerment**. We first will take another look at how psychologists in general, and feminist psychologists in particular, have approached the concepts of power and empowerment, and then we'll go on to discuss how we can become empowered individually and in our relationships, as well as simultaneously work toward social change as activists.

POWER AND EMPOWERMENT

From the very start of this book, we have talked about power in relation to gender differences such that men and what is associated with men (masculinity or **agency**) is generally privileged, and women and that which is regarded as feminine (or communal) is devalued—leading to the oppression of women and supporting a patriarchal system of inequality. The core concept underlying this process is power—power to be considered normative (as in **androcentric bias**), to be distinct from the "other" (**gender polarization**), and to control relationships (despite an ultimate loss of connection).

Feminist psychologists have had an uneasy relationship with the concept of power. Traditionally, psychologists have conceptualized power as dominance, control, or influence over others (see Unger, 1986, for a review of social psychological approaches to studying power). From this tradition emerged six distinct bases of direct power: **reward, coercive, expert, information, legitimate authority** (derived from one's position), and **referent** (derived from others wanting to emulate or identify with the powerful person) (French & Raven, 1959). Although these direct forms of using power are often regarded as masculine and are ascribed to men, a clever computerized protocol in which women and men served as "advisors" to an unseen confederate trying to solve difficult puzzles found that women used these forms of power as much as men when they were in high- (but not in low-) status positions (Keshet et al., 2006). Thus, using power may be more about having status than about gender per se.

It is these forms of direct power that underlie feminist analyses of male dominance or **patriarchy**: ending sexist oppression ultimately means righting unjust power relationships. Yet Celia Kitzinger (1991) points to the paradoxes accompanying such a feminist critique of power in psychology (and in **feminism** as a whole). In psychology, the concept of power is rarely mentioned, and when it is used, it often summarizes power differentials in gender relationships without explaining how those differences arose. Although power may be as invisible and all-encompassing as the air we breathe (Henley, 1977), this description does little to inform us about what it is. Joan Griscom (1992) details four components of a good definition of power: power must involve more than coercion or dominance; it must be understood as relational (one has power over another:—t cannot exist in isolation of others); it is sustained at an individual and relational level by broader societal forces; and it is a process that dynamically changes over time (rather than exists as a stable trait).

In addition to defining what power is, feminist analyses of male dominance necessarily portray women as powerless, engendering disempowered feelings in women who acknowledge the extent and pervasiveness of their oppression:

> My entry into the women's movement has led to feelings of vulnerability, despair, and shock. That cannot be denied. For identifying with women, instead of men, means taking on, in part, the notion of one's powerlessness, victimisation, and lack of resources. In my own head, for example, I was much less exposed to the danger of rape when I believed that the women who were raped contributed to it in some way, for after all there was no way I would provoke or initiate such an attack. Recognising now that all women are potentially rape victims, that most rapists are known to their victims, that the object of rape is domination, I no longer have that (false) security that it won't happen to me (Spender, 1984, p. 211).

Attributing the powerlessness of women to conditioning or socialization ultimately underestimates the power of male dominance by suggesting that if only women understood they were free, they would be—ignoring the social consequences of deviance and the strong normative pressures that enforce conformity (Kitzinger, 1991). Paradoxically, a feminist analysis of power that defines power solely in terms of dominance and control and that assigns such power exclusively to (some) men renders women both powerless and blame-worthy.

One potential solution to this quandary is a reconceptualization of power as **empowerment** or power-to, rather than power-over (Yoder & Kahn, 1992). This approach regards empowerment as more of a *process* than a thing, focusing on power as energy, potential, and competence—not as domination, coercion, and competition (Browne, 1995). Such an analysis of power recognizes the forces of patriarchal domination *and* turns to the empowerment of women and men not only to empower themselves (develop personal **agency**), but also to change broader social structures (activism) (Kitzinger, 1991). This form of empowerment is articulated by Colette Browne (1995) as:

> a process of liberation of self and others, as a life force, a potential, a capacity, growth, and energy, where one works toward community and connection

responsibly as opposed to working primarily toward one's individual good (p. 360).

Note that this definition meets all four of Griscom's (1992) criteria: **empowerment** is more than coercion, is relational, is sustained by societal forces, and is a dynamic process. Throughout the research we have reviewed in this book, we have seen that the concept of masculinity, instrumentality, or agency comes into play. This concept has been measured as an individual difference variable [commonly using the Bem Sex Role Inventory (BSRI) or Personal Attributes Questionnaire (PAQ)] such that each person falls somewhere along a continuum from reporting low to high levels. It's easy to regard empowerment as simple personal agency, but empowerment goes beyond this to add concerns for activism (Kitzinger, 1991; Riger, 2000c).

This point about individual agency versus empowerment with activism is at the core of contemporary debates about women's self-sexualizing behavior versus **objectification**. The central argument made in support of women's self-sexualizing behaviors (e.g., catwalks at dance clubs and wearing clothing with sexualized statements) is that women choose and control their own behavior, are taking an active role in its production, and may, in fact, gain power over men by exploiting their own sexuality. However, a developing body of research challenges this portrayal.

Two studies looked at women's attitudes about self-sexualization and their correlates. In the first, the more women reported enjoying being sexualized, the higher was their endorsement of both hostile and benevolent sexism (Liss et al., 2011)—attitudes that we saw in Chapter 7 don't serve women very well. In the second study, the more strongly women accepted self-sexualizing behavior, the more extremely they adhered to the feminine role (Nowatzki & Morry, 2009)—that is, "hyperfemininity," which had previously been linked to women's beliefs in adversarial sexual relations (including some acceptance of sexual coercion and rape myths as well as destructive self-blame when coercion occurs) and in putting a traditional marriage ahead of career aspirations (Murnen & Byrne, 1991). Both studies document that self-sexualization isn't all that good for women.

Turning to the sexualization of women in the media, Emma Halliwell and her colleagues (2011) modified magazine advertisements that depicted sexualized women as passive (e.g., a woman holding a ribbon on the bra she is wearing along with the slogan "For a beautiful figure") to convey powerfulness ("I pull the strings"). These presumably empowering images had the same effect on women (felt objectification and weight dissatisfaction) as the more typical passive version of the same ads. Connecting media images with attitudes, exposure to sexualized media is related to women's acceptance of self-sexualizing behavior (Nowatzki & Morry, 2009).

Finally, Megan Yost and Lauren McCarthy (2012) explored the prevalence and meaning of heterosexual women kissing one another publicly at a college party. Surveying students at a private residential U.S. college, they found that one-third of women had engaged in this behavior and over two-thirds of women and men had observed it. In follow-up surveys and interviews with women who had engaged in this behavior, many women's motivations appeared far from empowering—citing pressures from men who controlled the party, intoxication, and desires to avoid men's unwanted sexual attention and to bond with women friends. Although some women did use this behavior to get something from a man at the party (the presumably power wielding benefit of self-sexualization), this strategy targeted a resource he controlled (e.g., alcohol) and thus ultimately acknowledged his, not her, power. Given this analysis, it is not surprising that only a small minority of women did not feel pressured and reported feeling empowered by the experience. In contrast, one woman summed up the more common sentiments of felt objectification:

> It makes me feel cheap, it makes me feel like I'm kind of betraying those friends that I have that are lesbian because when I make out with girls at parties, I think that it's making women's sexuality not about ourselves but about the other people around us. (p. 18–19)

These findings argue, then, that true empowerment entails more than simply doing whatever one wants to do without inhibition. Given this understanding about what empowerment is not, let's take a look in the next section at what psychologists know about how to develop genuine personal empowerment.

PERSONAL EMPOWERMENT

Our emphasis in this section will be on empowering individual women. We saw in Chapter 12 that individual empowerment is a primary goal of feminist therapy (Worell & Remer, 2003). For psychologists, personal **empowerment** is defined as helping a woman "to become more independent and assertive about attaining her goals and achieving change and psychological growth" (Wyche & Rice, 1997, p. 60). Tied to personal empowerment are psychological well-being, self-esteem, and **agency** (Yoder et al., in press). For example, agency has been associated with reduced depression, lower anxiety, elevated self-esteem, fewer health complaints, and decreased distress (reviewed by Helgeson, 1994b). Similarly, well-being includes autonomy (agency), personal growth, and self-acceptance (Ryff, 1989).

My goal in this section on personal empowerment is to explore how women might achieve some genuine personal empowerment, starting at an individual level. Specifically, we'll explore gender-role transcendence as well as what it means to have a feminist identity and the outcomes associated with feminist labeling and beliefs. However, personal empowerment cannot reside in an individual-level model alone that stresses autonomy, self-control, and independence from others. Rather, a feminist reassessment enlarges the scope of what defines mental health to include self and others. Descriptions by 51 feminist women of a fully functioning woman integrate both agentic independence and communal interdependence—women who feel empowered by themselves and in their relationships (Crowley-Long & Long, 1992). We'll then turn to empowered relationships in the next section.

Gender-Role Transcendence

Strict adherence to gender-role prescriptions limits the full expression of human behavior in both women and men (Philpot et al., 1997) and disrupts their human connection. As we've seen throughout this book, gender-schematic thinking that holds fast to gendered **stereotyping** and **scripts** constrains thinking and social interaction. We further explored in Chapter 4 some ways to counteract sexist socialization processes; however, we noted that this approach was compromised by the pervasiveness of sexist societal influences. It also gives up on adults whose childhood socialization is complete. A supplement to **gender-aschematic** socialization is offered by **gender-role transcendence**—an approach that views people simply as people who often operate in gender-laden contexts.

Gender-role transcendence does not ignore gender; rather, it *reflects the final stage in a developmental progression that grapples with gendered norms in increasingly complex ways* (Eccles, 1987; Rebecca et al., 1976). At the simplest stage, people are undifferentiated by gender. A person who ignores gender might claim to treat individuals without regard to their sex, claiming to be gender neutral (for example, by claiming to be a "humanist" rather than a feminist). Such a position is made untenable by the simple fact that we automatically categorize people by sex. Furthermore, it avoids grappling with sexist oppression and ultimately is a form of passive resistance to feminism. It defines a starting point for the development of gender-role transcendence, not its endpoint.

In response to repeated exposure to a universal system of **social categorization** that divides people into female and male, a polarized view emerges that regards the sexes as opposite and distinct. This **gender polarization** may mellow somewhat, but gendered stereotyping continues to have a prescriptive quality by defining what women, girls, men, and boys *should* do. Both gender-neutrality and gender-polarized thinking must be rejected to move toward true gender role transcendence.

For this movement to happen, four psychological shifts are critical (Eccles, 1987, p. 236). First, we must break the link between gender identity and gender stereotyping so that our gender identity is independent from what is culturally prescribed. Here is a trivial personal example: I harbored a distaste for pink clothing for a long time in reaction to the feminizing quality it represented. My feminist identity was somehow compromised by the thought of wearing this color, even though I knew at a fundamental level that my self-concept need not be so fragile.

This relates to the second necessary ingredient for gender-role transcendence—the differentiation of **descriptive** (what is) from **prescriptive** or injunctive (what should be) **norms**. Pink may describe some women's clothes, but it need not prescribe or dictate them. Men's clothes can be pink, and women's can vary endlessly (although I still recoil from putting pink on a baby, probably because it is used to demarcate the often indeterminable gender of infants). Put on a more substantial level, nursing describes more women's than men's employment, but it certainly need not be this way.

Understanding the difference between description and prescription, the third step is to question the validity of the prescriptive functions of norms and stereotyping, both for individuals and for society at large. Why should women be nurses and not surgeons; and why should men be surgeons and not nurses? On the face of it, these questions seem simplistic, but when we dig deep to explore them, they open up lots of challenges to gendered stereotyping, beginning with who benefits from (is **privileged** by) and who loses out from (is **oppressed** by) such restrictions. They also reveal a host of **social contexts** that channel women and men in different directions.

The fourth shift in thinking toward gender-role transcendence moves away from gender as a defining property of one's self-image and evaluations of others, refocusing our understanding of gender outward to social, contextual factors that influence women's and men's lives. This takes us beyond feeling secure as a woman or man (**gender identity**) to how we feel about ourselves as people, about others, and about the settings in which we live. Now we might think it's appropriate for a person to be tender toward a baby, directive with subordinates, warm and expressive with friends, cool and detached with opponents, and so on. The situation, not **essentialist** gender, dictates the appropriateness of a full range of behaviors. This fits well with our discussion of **gender aschematicity** in Chapter 6.

Summing up, **gender-role transcendence** is the opposite of rigid **gender polarization**, including **hypermasculinity** and hyperfemininity. It also rejects gender-neutrality as well as attempts to overlook gender. Throughout this book, we have seen the pitfalls of exaggerations of stereotyping, both feminine (e.g., vulnerability to agoraphobia, Ch. 12) and masculine (e.g., tendencies toward violence, Ch. 13). However, gender-role transcendence can take us only so far toward social change. Even if we each manage to better understand the role gender plays in our own lives and in our interactions with others, we often will be opposing broad societal norms and will face the not-so-trivial consequences of deviance (remember the **sexist discrimination** of Chapters 7 and 9). This is where the activism part of this chapter comes into play.

Feminist Identity

Are you a feminist: NO   YES

Do you agree or disagree with each of the following statements:

(1) Girls and women have not been treated as well as boys and men in our society.
(2) Women and men should be paid equally for the same work.
(3) Women's unpaid work should be more socially valued.

Alyssa Zucker (2004, pp. 426-427) considers these three items the core "cardinal beliefs" of feminism, and she uses agreement with all three of them to indicate endorsement of feminist beliefs. She then combines these beliefs with the opening labeling as feminist or not to designate three groups of women: (1) feminists (who adopt the label and all three beliefs), (2) egalitarians (who do not self-label as feminist but who endorse all three cardinal beliefs), and (3) nonfeminists (who do not self-label and disagree with at least one cardinal belief). In this way, she captures a group between feminists and nonfeminists who in essence say "I'm not a feminist, but ..." (going on to advocate feminist positions). Women college students (Yoder et al., 2011) and college graduates (Zucker, 2004) spread across these three groupings.

My colleagues Ann Tobias and Andee Snell and I dissected the impact of labeling and beliefs on women's reports of engaging in feminist activism (signing a petition and giving money "on behalf of women's rights"), psychological well-being, and endorsement of equal-sharing intimate relationships (Yoder et al., 2011). We concluded that it is labeling alone that is important for predicting feminist activism—a point to which we'll return later. On the other hand, beliefs were the more potent predictor of both personal well-being and interpersonal egalitarianism. Thus, it appears that both labeling and beliefs are important parts of feminist identification but they are linked to different outcomes. Given our interest in personal empowerment here, let's turn our attention now to feminist beliefs and their outcomes for the women who hold them.

Feminist beliefs.   Psychologists have developed an array of different ways to capture an individual woman's feminist beliefs. These measures include the Feminist Perspectives Scale (Henley et al. 1998), which taps women's sociopolitical beliefs; Fassinger's (1994) Attitudes Toward Feminism and the Women's Movement Scale, which explores women's emotional ties to both feminists and the women's movement; a sense of common fate (Gurin & Townsend, 1986), which captures a woman's feelings of connection with other women as a collectivity; and the Feminist Identity Composite (FIC; Fischer et al., 2000), which takes a snapshot of a woman's evolving feminist identity over time. Other measures, such a Janet Helms' (1990) **womanist identity** model, propose that women's gender and racial identities intersect; for example, by including black identity for African American women and anti-racism for White women.

As we have already seen, feminist identity is complicated by including both labeling and beliefs. This wide array of measures of beliefs further complicates the picture. Let's focus in on one of these measures (the widely cited FIC) and the model of feminist identity development that underlies it, and then we'll explore whether holding feminist beliefs works to personally empower women.

Feminist identity development.   Before you read on, you'll find it helpful to complete the brief scale in Box 14.1.

Nancy Downing and Kristin Roush (1985) presented a five-stage model of feminist identity development. The Feminist Identity Composite (FIC) identifies the degree to which a woman endorses each of the five stages with items such as those in Box. 14.1. According to this model, respondents high in **passive acceptance** are either unaware of or deny individual, institutional, and cultural prejudice and discrimination against women (the first item labeled "PA"). High scorers believe that traditional roles are advantageous for women and men and that men are superior to women. For example, women endorsing passive acceptance would agree that men should be masculine and women, feminine. After taking a women's studies course (Bargad & Hyde, 1991) or psy-

---

Box 14.1

Please express your feelings by indicating how much agree or disagree with each statement.

PA.   I don't see much point in questioning the general expectation that men should be masculine and women should be feminine.
strongly disagree   disagree   neutral or undecided   agree   strongly agree

Rev.   Gradually, I am beginning to see just how sexist society really is.
strongly disagree   disagree   neutral or undecided   agree   strongly agree

EE.   I am very interested in women writers.
strongly disagree   disagree   neutral or undecided   agree   strongly agree

Syn.   I feel like I have blended my female attributes with my unique personal qualities.
strongly disagree   disagree   neutral or undecided   agree   strongly agree

AC.   I am very committed to a cause that I believe contributes to a more fair and just world for all people.
strongly disagree   disagree   neutral or undecided   agree   strongly agree

chology of women class (Yoder et al., 2007a), students were likely to disagree with items like these both more than before taking the course and more than control students taking other courses.

A second dimension involves **revelation** (Rev)—a series of crises or contradictions disrupt one's passive acceptance so that ignoring and denying are no longer possible. Potential disruptions include this book and the course you are taking (as well as other women's studies classes which tend to stress critical thinking, open-mindedness, and participatory learning; Stake & Hoffmann, 2000) as well as being targeted for **sexist discrimination** (Anthis, 2002). These challenges typically result in open questioning of one's self and one's roles, often accompanied by feelings of anger and guilt. Often this stage is characterized by dualistic thinking in which women are seen as positive and men are vilified. Again, students agreed with these revelation-type items after taking a feminist course—more than they did beforehand and more than control students.

Nancy Downing and Kristin Roush (1985) drew upon a model of racial-identity development (Cross, 1971) that projected stages of development. A central assumption of stagewise models is that individuals pass through and resolve prior stages before moving to more advanced stages in a stepwise progression. Such a progression is evident from passive acceptance to revelation as earlier attitudes are rejected in the face of an intervening crisis. However, moving from revelation to some resolution does not seem to follow a simple, linear progression from rudimentary to more advanced forms of feminist identity, as Downing and Roush originally theorized. A better conceptualization based on subsequent research considers the next three configurations as *dimensions* of feminist identity that co-exist in varying degrees in many post-revelation women (Worell, 1996) and through which an individual may recycle (Henderson-King & Stewart, 1997). For our purposes, you probably will find parts of each of the remaining three dimensions in your own post-revelation identity.

In the third dimension of the model, **embeddedness-emanation** (EE), feminists immerse themselves in feminist culture, seeking both affirmation and strengthening of their new identity. Their newfound feminist identity may begin as somewhat rigid, but openness to alternative viewpoints grows. A more relativistic approach to men appears, making it worthwhile to engage in cautious interaction with a select few. In the fourth **synthesis** (Syn) dimension, women are able to transcend traditional gender roles, celebrate and value the positive aspects of femininity, make choices based on personal values, and evaluate men on an individual, not a stereotyped, basis. The final dimension emphasizes **active commitment** (AC), integrating personal feminist identity with plans for meaningful and effective action aimed at social change. Men are viewed as equal to, but not the same as, women. These five stages/dimensions are summarized in Table 14.2.

Interestingly, subsequent research showed that synthesis, not active commitment, best predicted feminist activism (Liss et al., 2004). As we might expect, each of these last three dimensions was affected by taking a women's studies or psychology of women/gender course such that students expressed stronger agreement with each dimension after taking a course than they did beforehand. As one student commented:

> I feel I have a better understanding of feminist issues so I can argue for the feminist cause more effectively, making me more confident in identifying myself as a feminist (Bargad & Hyde, 1991, p. 193).

TABLE 14.2
Feminist Identity Development According to Downing and Roush

Passive Acceptance Stage	Revelation Stage	Embeddedness-Emanation Dimension	Synthesis Dimension	Active Commitment Dimension
Passive acceptance of traditional gender roles and discrimination; belief that traditional roles are advantageous; men are considered superior.	Catalyzed by a series of crises, resulting in open questioning of self and roles and feelings of anger and guilt; dualistic thinking; men are perceived as negative.	Characterized by connectedness with other select women, affirmation and strengthening of new identity. Eventually more relativistic thinking and cautious interaction with men.	Development of an authentic and positive feminist identity; gender-role transcendence; "flexible truce" with the world; evaluate men on an individual basis.	Consolidation of feminist identity; commitment to meaningful action; to a nonsexist world. Actions are personalized and rational. Men are considered equal but not the same as women.

Other studies have documented the positive influence of psychology of women and other women's studies classes on students' feminist identity development (Gerstmann & Kramer, 1997; Worell et al., 1999), sexist and feminist beliefs (Katz et al., 2004), performance self-esteem and occupational aspirations (Stake & Gerner, 1987), activism (Stake & Rose, 1994; Stake et al., 1994), self-concept and assertiveness (O'Connell, 1989), and progressive gender role orientation and empowered locus of control (Harris et al., 1999). All of this research predicts that this book and the course you are taking are likely to have some impact on how you think, feel, and act toward feminism and feminist psychology.

Feminist identity and personal empowerment. Studies of feminist identity find that women with strong feminist identities are personally and collectively empowered (Carpenter & Johnson, 2001), see the world through feminist lenses (Liss et al., 2001), and exhibit high levels of psychological well-being (Saunders & Kashubeck-West, 2006; Yakushko, 2007). Feminist beliefs, even without self-labeling, are related to self-efficacy (Eisele & Stake, 2008), and they are linked to rejecting pressures to be thin, attractive, and in a romantic relationships (Hurt et al., 2007).

College women who scored high on the feminist identity scale followed less traditional dating scripts than did women high on passive acceptance (Rickard, 1989) and internalized less **heterosexism** (Szymanski, 2004). Women's feminist views influenced political voting choices when candidates held divergent views on feminist issues (Cook, 1993); predicted perceptions of gender discrimination on a college campus (Fischer & Good, 1994) and in general (Kobrynowicz & Branscombe, 1997); helped women faculty cope with discrimination (Klonis et al., 1997); and eliminated evaluation bias such that feminist college women did not devalue the work of women artists (Rickard, 1990).

A feminist orientation can affect occupational aspirations in that feminist adolescent girls exhibited enhanced confidence in their abilities to pursue career-related tasks (Ahrens & O'Brien, 1996), and feminist African American women placed greater value on blending career and family (Weathers et al., 1994). Non-bulimic women were more likely to endorse a feminist ideology than bulimics (Brown, et al., 1990), and women who identified with feminist values reported less body dissatisfaction, fewer bulimic symptoms, and strength-ened feelings of effectiveness (Ojerholm & Rothblum, 1999; Snyder & Hasbrouck, 1996). Feminist adult women survivors of childhood sexual abuse expressed more anger toward their parents in therapy and were less likely to blame themselves for bringing on their own abuse (Newman & Peterson, 1996).

However, these generally positive conclusions are muddied by some negative corre-lates with feminist identification. For example, some women equate feminism with dishar-mony in heterosexual intimate relationships (Rudman & Farchild, 2007). Only egalitarian women scored higher than self-labeling feminists and nonfeminists in their sexual asser-tiveness regarding condom use (Bay-Cheng & Zucker, 2007). Most consistently, scoring high on the revelation stage has been linked to psychological distress (Moradi & Subich, 2002), lower self-esteem, and anger (Fischer & Good, 2004).

These inconsistencies point to the likelihood that the picture we are exploring about how feminist identity relates to various psychological outcomes is even more complicated. Making this argument, my colleagues Andee Snell and Ann Tobias and I examined how a set of multiple measures of women's feminist beliefs might be related to a complex set of psychological outcomes, including the individual indicators we are considering here of personal empowerment, self-esteem, well-being, and agency, as well as measures of inter-personal (egalitarianism and sexual assertiveness) and collective (feeling entitled to social justice) empowerment (Yoder et al., in press).

We found strong evidence that the more firmly established college women's feminist beliefs were ("established feminism"), the more they exhibited optimal psychological functioning across this wide array of outcomes. Conversely, the more actively anti-feminist a woman's beliefs were, the most compromised were her psychological outcomes, topped by low levels of both personal empowerment and egalitarianism (endorsement of equal-sharing relationships). Additionally, a configuration we called "awakening feminism" that was characterized by high levels of revelation was related to less optimal functioning, con-firming that the revelation stage is a period of vulnerability (but with hope, a step toward established feminism).

Most fascinating was a final configuration of beliefs and outcomes that we called "woman-identified traditionalism." Women who connected with other women but did so while also endorsing passive acceptance rather than feminist beliefs showed high levels of self-esteem and moderate levels of personal empowerment and self-acceptance. However, this positive picture was tainted by compromised autonomy well-being and low levels of seeking social justice (justice entitlement). Although certainly not a negative configura-tion for a woman (unlike anti-feminism), these traditionalists (like established feminists) benefit from their connection with women as a collective but (unlike established feminists) falter both in their own well-being and toward promoting women's rights.

Feminist men. Given the complexity we have seen in defining feminist beliefs for women, it is not surprising that we know relatively little about men and feminism. Can men develop a feminist identity? One approach to men and masculinity, often acclaimed in the popular media, mimics the claims of the women's movement by lamenting the oppression of men vis-à-vis the restrictions of the masculine gender role (Allen, 1997). The fundamental goal of this movement of "weekend warriors" is to de-feminize, then re-masculinize, men and boys (Kimmel & Kaufman, 1997). At its heart, it is a defensive reaction to the presumed male-bashing of the feminist movement. (As we saw in our model of feminist identity devel-

Box 14.3
How is it that we intuitively know the sex of the person in the closet? Who has more power in this exchange?

opment, male-bashing may play a temporary role in women's movement toward a more advanced feminist identity that ultimately brings in men as partners in activism.) At its core, this approach to understanding men and masculinity fails to recognize the privileges attached to the masculine gender role, seeks to reaffirm it, and is thus fundamentally anti-feminist.

A second strand of men's studies emerges from a profeminist stance (Brod, 1987a; Clatterbaugh, 1990; Messner, 1997, 1998). From this perspective, men's lives become a focal point for study because leaving men's lives unexamined ignores male privilege (Brod, 1987b, p. 57). For example, an often-cited drawback of the masculine stereotype is the demand for strength that eschews weakness (operationalized as not being able to cry and express emotions). A profeminist perspective would approach this gendered expectation to see if its enactment privileges men and boys in some ways; for example, by empowering them by hiding vulnerability and withholding information (Brod, 1987a, p. 8).

Such a perspective envisions an end to **sexism** that ultimately liberates both women and men, rather than re-entrenches male-dominance. It also provides a framework from which men can join women in developing feminist identities. For example, feminist values may serve as an antidote to male violence against women. Men who endorsed feminist ideology possessed a lower proclivity to perpetrate sexual harassment (Bartling & Eisenman, 1993; Wade & Brittan-Powell, 2001), exhibited less rape myth acceptance (Cowan & Quinton, 1997), and reported less acceptance of interpersonal violence overall (Truman et al., 1996).

Summary. As we saw, *a strong feminist identity involves both a sense of personal empowerment and a commitment to social activism.* Indeed, empowerment mediates the relationship between feminist beliefs and activism (Stake, 2007). We also argued throughout this book that a psychology of women was valuable to the extent that it is useful—that it works *for* women. It is clear that effective activism relies on individual empowerment and optimal psychological functioning (a configuration we identified as "established feminism").

However, we shall see that personal empowerment without social activism falls short of an active commitment to social change and hence misses the mark for this final dimension of feminist identity development. Too often, psychologists have focused on personal empowerment without making this necessary connection to social activism (Kravetz & Marecek, 1996; Marecek & Hare-Mustin, 1991; Parvin & Biaggio, 1991). Although we began here by exploring personal empowerment, this section cannot stand alone without the one that follows later on social activism. The need for this broader definition of empowerment becomes even clearer when we next consider empowerment in women's relationships with men.

EMPOWERED RELATIONSHIPS

A general model for how gender is enacted in interpersonal exchanges was proposed by Kay Deaux and Brenda Major (1987). They think of gender as one aspect of ongoing relationships in which one member expects certain behaviors from another, the other member negotiates her or his own identity, and the **social context** in which the interaction occurs shapes what behaviors are emitted. Given this model, we would expect to find lots of stereotype-confirming behavior if both parties in an interaction hold traditional beliefs, and these beliefs are activated by the situation.

For example, consider a manager who has two subordinates, Joan and John. If that manager held traditional beliefs about the male-appropriateness of leadership, those beliefs might prompt the manager to describe a performance appraisal exercise quite differently to the two employees: say as an opportunity for John to take charge and for Joan to display cooperative skills. To further maximize the gender-typing here, assume that Joan and John have different histories and expectations about leadership that also conform to gender stereotyping. Combine these with what the manager conveys (either openly or subtly), and an observable gender difference between the behaviors of Joan and John is likely to result: John is likely to take charge and Joan is likely to work cooperatively with her group. Joan and John behave differently, confirming everyone's original beliefs and making the roles played by these original beliefs invisible.

Consider the same scenario with all components working synchronously to minimize gender differences. We would expect to find few differences between the behaviors of Joan and John if: (1) the manager believed that women and men enact leadership similarly; (2) gender-related beliefs were not activated in the manager; (3) Joan and John thought similarly about leadership and shared similar past experiences; and (4) similar **schema** about leadership were activated in Joan and John.

We saw in Chapter 7 that gender expectations can become a **self-fulfilling prophecy**. Deaux and Major's model both can explain how this happens and can offer an alternative scenario to short-circuit the process. The important point here is that *gendered enactments are dependent on ourselves, the others with whom we interact, and the social context in which this occurs.* With this in mind, we'll explore empowerment in heterosexual dating, marital and working relationships, and in responses to violence. We saw in Chapter 8 that gendered issues of imbalanced power are influential in heterosexual intimate relationships, so our discussion here is purposively confined to heterosexual dating and marriage.

Heterosexual Dating

One intervention designed for high school girls and college women in abusive heterosexual dating relationships formed support groups to help empower them (Rosen & Bezold, 1996). Participants reported that the groups were effective in providing a safe environment to share experiences; in encouraging thoughtful consideration of their relationship; in inspiring self-efficacy; in developing communication, problem-solving, and assertiveness skills; and in recognizing their own personal rights. The heterosexual **dating scripts** we saw in Chapter 8 were associated with dating violence in Chapter 13 in part because these scripts serve to disempower women. Support groups such as this one, as well as the development of a feminist identity, serve to better balance these power dynamics.

Heterosexual Marriage

A similar effect of women's empowerment emerges from our discussion in Chapter 8 of the division of domestic labor. We saw that there is some evidence, although far from conclusive, that the balance of power in a heterosexual relationship may make a difference. We also saw that egalitarian attitudes do not automatically translate into domestic sharing. Some clues regarding how to empower women and men in marriage (and other intimate heterosexual relationships) can be gleaned from studies of feminist couples (Choi & Bird, 2003; Laennec & Syrotinski, 2003). Indeed, having a feminist partner is associated with healthier relationships for women (Rudman & Phelan, 2007), and women scoring high in passive acceptance (low feminist beliefs) had low egalitarian expectations for their intimate relationships (Yoder et al., 2007b).

In one such study, Karen Blaisure and Katherine Allen (1995) conducted in-depth interviews with 10 self-identified feminist married couples. All participants stressed the importance of **vigilance** and the dynamic nature of their exchanges as they *continually worked* to define and redefine their participation in their marriages (also see Knudson-Martin & Mahoney, 2005). All couples monitored their relationship in three ways. First, they spent time together exploring the **sexism** faced by women in their everyday lives. They analyzed life events from a feminist framework:

> DAN: I was mad because I felt Barb wasn't valued for what she was. She worked just as hard as anyone else, and she wasn't appreciated. It made me more supportive of her (Blaisure & Allen, 1995, p.11).

Second, they worked hard to demonstrate publicly their concern for the wife's status in marriage, most often through different last names (also see Hoffnung, 2006) and joint involvement in financial decisions:

> LARRY: Well, the world we're in still expects to see the male making all the decisions about what the family is going to do. So people ranging from a car salesman to everything else expect me to make any decision that is confronting what we should do. They talk to me, and I don't like that. I don't want them to talk to me, I want them to talk to both of us (Blaisure & Allen, 1995, p. 12).

Third, all participants stressed the importance of supporting the woman's activities, including employment and feminist activism.

Six of the ten couples interviewed justified their unequal division of household labor by pointing to either gendered (cooking is women's work) or personality (she enjoys cooking) explanations. In contrast, four claimed to share equally in domestic responsibilities, and only these four reported two additional processes of vigilance. First, the equal-contributing subset continually monitored their contributions:

> PATRICK: I think it is really possible to have equality or a nonoppressive marriage but it is not something that sort of happens and you say "Zap, now we got it" and you go on. You have to constantly communicate and sometimes it swings a little bit more toward the other.... You have to ensure that equality maintains itself (Blaisure & Allen, 1995, p. 13).

Second, although all couples noted the importance of feeling close to their partner, the four equal-sharers worked together to meet each other's emotional needs:

> MIRIAM: He's my soul mate, and I know I would never find anyone as perfect for me as he is. Other friends are for spice, for variety, for flavor, for a fuller emotional range (Blaisure & Allen, 1995, p. 15).

The message that comes through loud and clear is that equal sharing is not a given, but rather reflects a continual process involving vigilance and painstaking work to bring feminist ideology to life in everyday practice (also see Knudson-Martin & Mahoney, 2009).[1]

On the Job

Almost all of what we discussed in Chapter 9 points to broad macrostructural factors (e.g., occupational segregation) and more narrow microstructural factors (e.g., tokenism) that work together to restrict women's and men's participation in the workforce. One small form of personal empowerment that emerged from this discussion focused on using individuating information on job resumes, most notably by masculinizing an applicant's background for a male-defined job. Others have noted the value of making earnings public to highlight, and ultimately undermine, wage inequities (Steinem, 1983). Beyond the individual worker, I believe that it is important for employers to ask what they can do to level the playing field; for example, by training and legitimating women leaders (Yoder, 2001). In the classroom, feminist educators report feeling empowered to bring about political and social change (Sinacore et al., 2002).

Responses to Violence

Feminists have discussed personal empowerment as an impetus for recovery and as a component of violence prevention. Both themes appear in discussions of sexual harassment (Anonymous, 1991; Charney & Russell, 1994), male intimate partner violence (Dutton-Douglas, 1992; Frieze & McHugh, 1992; Webb, 1992), and childhood sexual abuse (Liem et al., 1992; Nelson, 1991).

Resilience.   Box 14.4 catalogues the reactions survivors of sexual assault reported from others. Sarah Ullman (2000, 2010) not only clustered these into categories of posi-

---

[1]For sound, practical advice on how to realize gender equality in dual career relationships, see Lucia Gilbert's work (1993). For ideas about equal-sharing parenting, see Deutsch (1999).

Box 14.4: Tangible Aid

Sarah Ullman (2000) collected reactions that sexual assault survivors reported from others and found that they sorted into the seven categories identified below, fully five of which are negative. She then explored the effectiveness of these reactions with 323 survivors. Combining these data gives us a list of do's and don't's to guide us if a woman discloses her experiences to us.

Positive Social Reactions	*Negative Social Reactions*
Emotional Support/Belief	*Blame*
Told you that you were not to blame	You could have done more
Told you that you did not do anything wrong	*Control*
Told you that it was not your fault	Made decisions for you
Reassured you that you were a good person	
Held you or told you that you are loved	*Egocentric*
Comforted you by telling you it would be all right or by holding you	Others' own anger and revenge dominate
Spent time with you	*Distraction*
Listened to your feelings	Told you to stop talking and thinking about it; try to supply alternatives
Showed understanding of your experiences	
Reframed the experience as a clear case of victimization	*Treat Differently*
Saw your side of things and did not make judgments	Includes withdrawal and avoidence.
Was able to really accept your account of your experience	
Told you that s/he felt sorry for you	
Believed your account of what happened	
Seemed to understand what you were feeling	

**Lower self esteem
Greater PTSD symptom
severity**

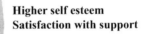

**Higher self esteem
Satisfaction with support**

Tangible Aid and Information/Support
Helped you get medical care
Provided information and discussed
options
Helped you get information of any kind
about coping with the experience
Took you to the police
Encouraged you to seek counseling

tive and negative reactions, but also showed that only positive reactions were associated with better self-esteem and greater satisfaction among survivors. This list informs all of us about how we can best react when a woman does choose to disclose her victimization. A study with 102 rape survivors documented that most (nearly 75%) turned to informal support providers, and over one-third of these contacts were not initiated by the survivor herself (Ahrens et al., 2007). Over half reported receiving positive reactions from informal supporters, in contrast to the more commonly negative reactions garnered by women who sought support from formal providers.

Seeking self-defense or assertiveness training after an assault, especially when social supports failed, may help survivors regain their sense of control (Brecklin & Ullman, 2004) and may reduce women's chances of re-victimization (Orchowski et al., 2008). As for therapy, key features of an effective approach include avoidance of blaming the victim; a nonstigmatizing view that regards rape as criminal victimization; support to overcome cognitive and behavioral avoidance; information about the normality of trauma reactions; expectations that symptoms will improve (Resick & Markaway, 1991); and building on positive sexual self-perceptions (Offman & Matheson, 2004; see Russell & Davis, 2007, for a review of treatment evidence).

The resilience of some abuse survivors is attested to in in-depth interviews conducted by Linda DiPalma (1994). In childhood, some girls imagined sunny but realistic futures to relieve their pain and to escape their victimization. Some put their energy into academic success to obtain personal validation; others drew on creative outlets such as writing, drama, and music. Their stories testify to their unflagging determination and inner strength.

> Being a survivor means being able to feel again, not to repress, not to forget, not to run away from, but to be able to stand still, remember what happened, claim all of that experience, claim the feelings, and still be able to hang on to this new person that I am (DiPalma, 1994, p. 87).

Rape resistance and avoidance. Overall violence prevention takes two interrelated forms: resistance/avoidance and prevention. On an individual level, empowerment of individual women can help them resist and avoid being victimized. For example, comparisons of women who were raped by a *stranger* with those who escaped focus on situational characteristics, offender aggression, and victim resistance. Higher completion rates have been found when the rape takes place indoors, when environmental interruptions (someone driving by) are absent, when a weapon is present, when the attack occurs at night, and when it is a blitz attack (a surprise physical assault) (reviewed by Ullman & Knight, 1993).

Offender aggression can fall into one of four categories: nonviolent verbal aggression (the attacker tells the victim what to do); violent verbal aggression (the perpetrator yells and/or swears at the victim); violent physical aggression (using physical assault or a weapon); and use of other items (blindfolds, ropes, and sticks) (Ullman & Knight, 1991). *Victim resistance* can be classified as none; nonforceful verbal (pleading or crying); forceful verbal (screaming); physical (pushing, wrestling, striking, and biting); and fleeing (Zoucha-Jensen & Coyne, 1993). The effectiveness (defined as rape escape, minimal physical harm, and less sexual abuse) of each of these depends on the type of offender aggression and on some *situational characteristics*.

Sarah Ullman and Raymond Knight (1991, 1993) found that forceful verbal and physical responses were equally efficacious across all rape locations. In contrast, nonforceful verbal strategies were ineffective in escaping rape in both dangerous and less dangerous situations. *Forceful verbal, physical, and fleeing responses were most effective for escaping rape by a stranger*, especially in dangerous settings. Physical resistance proved effective in thwarting a rape attempt even in the presence of a weapon, although more rapes are completed with the presence of a weapon (Bart & O'Brien, 1997).

Physical injury to the victim resulted more from the stranger's violent physical aggressiveness than from the physicality of the victim's resistance and is more likely if the attacker has been drinking (Martin & Bachman, 1998). In other words, most physical injury appears to result from the sexual assault itself, not the victim's resistance. Women tend to confine their use of physical resistance to offenders who use violent physical aggressiveness (so it is hard to say if this would work with other forms of attack). Sexual abuse was most severe when the assailant used violent verbal aggression or executed a con assault (in which the victim was duped into trusting her more sadistic attacker or stalker-like assault). Both offender propensity to abuse alcohol (Martin & Bachman, 1998; Tests & Livingston, 1999) and victim's preassault use of alcohol are associated with greater sexual aggression severity (Ullman et al., 1999). In sum, crying and pleading don't seem to help; rather *meeting the offender's violence with an equal level of resistance is generally most effective.*

The above discussion was generated by research with survivors of stranger rape and attempted rape, ignoring a more likely threat to women from acquaintances and intimates. Recognizing this point, Joyce Levine-MacCombie and Mary Koss (1986) compared college women who either escaped date rape or were victimized. All reported feeling angry during the attack, but only successful resistors recalled less fear and guilt during the attack. Women who succeeded in escaping rape retrospectively perceived their assault as less violent, and they reported running away and screaming for help more often than unsuccessful resistors.

This resistance pattern with acquaintances parallels what we saw above with stranger rape. Quarreling with the offender contributed significantly to the *completion* of date rape, making this a strategy to avoid. In contrast to stranger escape, women who escaped date rape reported that crying and reasoning contributed to their success, probably because they had some relationship with the attempted perpetrator. However, these nonforceful verbal strategies were less effective than more active patterns of resistance—*still making screaming, physical attacking, and fleeing the most effective responses.* Furthermore, women who resisted rape by using forceful physical strategies exhibited less post-assault depression than other survivors (Bart & O'Brien, 1997).

Ironically, these effective response strategies involve actions many women have been socialized to avoid as "unfeminine," "impolite," and hurtful (Rozee, 1996; Quina & Carlson, 1989) and are not what most women expect to do in the face of an impending sexual assault (Masters et al., 2006). This is where empowerment programs come in. There is research evidence documenting that a self-defense class can help most women show improvements in their assertiveness, self-esteem, perceived control, self-efficacy, and physical competence, as well as declines in anxiety, helplessness, fear, and avoidance behaviors such as restricting their own behaviors (Brecklin, 2008). In heterosexual dating relationships, communication and assertiveness skills are linked to successful date-rape resistance (Rosen & Bezold, 1996).

Some avoidance advice argues for developing "assertive wariness," whereby women recognize risky behaviors and plan alternative escape and avoidance strategies (Greene & Navarro, 1998). An example is carrying one's purse tucked securely under one's arm rather than holding it loosely—a strategy that reflects "street savvy." More fundamentally, physical empowerment can encourage women to reclaim their bodies as instruments of action and sources of confidence, instead of as passive objects for others' oppression (McCaughey, 1998).

However, these strategies, taken alone, fail to challenge the faulty ideas that women alone are responsible for preventing violence; that women who are unsuccessful at resisting rape are blame-worthy; that confine rape scenarios to the less likely occurrence of stranger rape; and that (taken to an extreme) fit with the pattern of borderline agoraphobia we examined in Chapter 12. In fact, they may contribute to a pattern whereby women engage in more precautionary behaviors designed to thwart stranger rape even though acquaintance rape is, and is understood by women to be, much more common (Hickman & Muehlenhard, 1997).

Successfully escaping rape and avoiding rape attempts are positive outcomes, the importance of which should not be minimized for individual women. However, an avoidance approach is fundamentally individualistic; it does not protect women in general (Lonsway, 1996). Rapists tend to seek out vulnerable women so that the success of one woman in deterring rape is offset by the likely victimization of another. Because of this, no matter how well trained women are in avoidance, escape, and self-defense, they remain vulnerable to sexual assault to the extent that men continue to commit these acts (Schewe & O'Donohue, 1993). It is this key point that distinguishes rape avoidance from our next topic—rape prevention.

Rape prevention. Rape prevention focuses on men as the perpetrators of these acts *and* on cultural beliefs and institutions that, intentionally or not, support the victimization of women. Kimberly Lonsway (1996) reviewed educational programs, most of which target women or mixed-sex audiences. One increasingly popular program designed to target men's attitudes and empathy is "The Men's Program" (Foubert, 2005), which has been shown to induce self-reported, positive changes in some men (Foubert & Cremedy, 2007). Targeting the misinformation of rape mythology is widely used by educational programs and has been linked to desirable attitude change (Pinzone-Glover et al., 1998). Similarly, participant interaction, typically in the forms of group discussion, role play, and interactive dramatic performances, generally is found to co-occur with favorable attitude change.

Improved communication skills appear effective only when they incorporate explicit understandings of gender roles and the subordinated status of women. Simple enhancements to interpersonal exchanges without these broader societal linkages indeed may make communication clearer, but men who perpetrate sexual aggression seem to ignore, not misunderstand, women's intentions and desires (Hanson & Gidycz, 1993). Evidence about the effectiveness of getting men to empathize with their targets and of previous experiences with either victimization or perpetration is inconclusive, warranting further research. Researchers are beginning to realize the importance of multicultural sensitivity in violence interventions (Oliver, 2000; Preisser, 1999). Finally, confrontational approaches induce alienation and defensiveness, both of which run contrary to prevention. It is clear that educational programs using effective approaches are likely to encourage positive attitude change. However, a causal link between rape-rejecting attitudes and reduced sexually aggressive behavior has not been established definitively, although these factors clearly are correlated (Lonsway & Fitzgerald, 1994).

At the end of Chapter 13, I argued that gender-based violence is more than acts confined to individual women and men; for this reason, solutions must look beyond individuals as well. Some broader possibilities include supporting and participating in "take back the night" events (where supporters march in unison in settings individual women usually find disturbing); pressuring organizations to establish policies and set up an atmosphere in which they'll be enforced (Nelson et al., 2007; Ormerod et al., 2008); boycotting products that rely on violent advertising; raising nonviolent children (Warner & Steel, 1999);

making violence visible by speaking out (Quina & Carlson, 1989); educational programs targeting young children (Tulloch & Tulloch, 1992) and college students (Berkowitz, 1994; Earle & Nies, 1994); interventions designed for male batterers (Dutton, 1988) and rape perpetrators (Pollard, 1994); multifaceted community-based programs and services for incest survivors (Wisconsin Coalition Against Sexual Assault, 1989) and campus rape (Adams & Abarbanel, 1988; Bohmer & Parrot, 1993); organizations for men against rape (see the appendix of Beneke, 1992, for a beginning list), including fraternities (Egidio & Robertson, 1981); expanded feminist coverage of violence against women in the media (Kozol, 1995; Stone, 1993); and so on.

However, the true key to violence prevention may rest in expanding our vision beyond ending acts of violence themselves to looking more closely at the building blocks that lead up to violence. Box 14.5 offers a step toward such an expanded vision.[2] Much of how we commonly think about gender supports two general cognitive processes: **gender polarization** (viewing women and men as basically different) and **objectification** (treating different others as objects). Simply viewing others as fundamentally different takes a step toward disconnection that *can* lead to objectification, which in turn *can* lead to violence. Gender polarization and objectification become building blocks upon which violence becomes more likely.

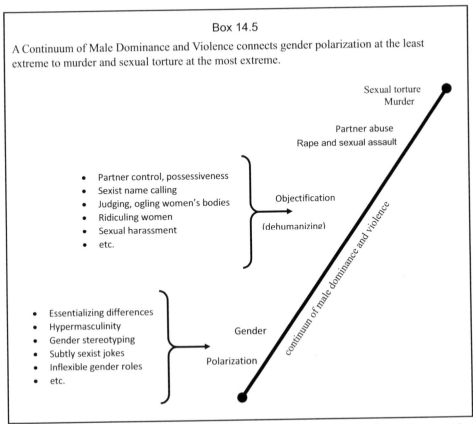

Box 14.5

A Continuum of Male Dominance and Violence connects gender polarization at the least extreme to murder and sexual torture at the most extreme.

[2] I am indebted to my colleague Ann Fischer for first encouraging me to think about this continuum and for laying out much of the contents of Box 14.5.

On first blush you may object that I am making mountains out of molehills. For example, what's so harmful about a funny but sexist joke? Researchers found that college men who enjoyed sexist humor also were more likely to harbor destructive rape attitudes and report a greater likelihood of using sexual coercion (Ryan & Kanjorski, 1998). The reverse also is true in that what peers do can set the stage for accepting sexist humor. A study that exposed a college man to a male confederate who engaged in sexual harassment or was generally sexist found that the participant subsequently told more sexually oriented jokes to a female student (Angelone et al., 2005).

Hypermasculinity has been linked to sexual aggression (Murnen et al., 2002) as well as **hostile sexism** to tolerance of sexual harassment (Russell & Trigg, 2004), to men's rape proclivity and misperceptions that rape victims really wanted it (Abrams et al., 2003), and to rape myth acceptance (Chapleau et al., 2007). Interestingly, what has been found to underlie men's hostile sexism is their own feelings of inadequacy (Cowan & Mills, 2004) and threats to men's "precarious manhood" (Vandello et al, 2008).

Thus a climate that disinhibits sexist behaviors can be established subtly by others' behaviors or overtly by outspoken objections. Women who confront sexist remarks tend to be liked and respected by other women, but can be disliked by college men (Saunders & Senn, 2009). Furthermore, although women hypothetically believe they will confront male perpetrators of **sexist prejudice**, they actually are unlikely to do so when the social costs are high (Shelton & Stewart, 2004). Pro-feminist men can play a supportive role here by addressing incidents of sexism themselves as well as by openly supporting women who do.

Objectification of women also has been tied to violence. For example, men who viewed R-rated movie scenes that portrayed women enjoying or responsible for either stranger or date rape felt that a subsequent magazine account of rape was less objectionable (Millburn et al., 2000). Taking one step does not necessarily lead to the others, but each step does set up the possibility of moving up the continuum of male dominance and violence. By avoiding those first steps, and by challenging ourselves and others when we do, we *all* could get at the root causes of violence against women.

ACTIVISM

In each of the examples of personal and relationship empowerment we explored here, we saw that the picture was incomplete if we didn't expand our vision beyond the individual or relationship levels. Gender-role transcendence indeed moves individuals away from gendered-typed thinking and behaviors, but when enacted within a gender-schematic social context, different behaviors easily can be regarded as deviant, rather than as models for social change. Similar scenarios emerged from our discussions of empowerment in heterosexual dating, marital, and working relationships; empowered well-being; and violence avoidance. Individual solutions cannot exist alone without consideration of broader societal forces. Here's where activism enters the scene.

Definition and History

In the 1970s and through the defeat of the Equal Rights Amendment (ERA) in 1982, it was clear what the mainstream, large-scale U.S. feminist issues were. Feminist organizations (the National Organization for Women, National Abortion Rights Action League, Women's Equity Action League, Women's Legal Defense Fund, and the National Women's Political Caucus) flourished, as did grass-roots consciousness raising and political and social action groups (battered women's shelters, rape-crisis centers, and job-training programs). Women's Studies programs spread on college campuses, the Supreme Court's 1973 *Roe v. Wade* decision seemed to protect abortion rights, the Equal Rights Amendment[3] sailed through both houses of Congress after a long dormancy (it was first introduced in 1923) and racked up the support of 35 states (needing just three more for final ratification), affirmative action laws passed, and so on. Doing feminist activism seemed clear during this period, considered the heyday of the contemporary wave of feminism (Ryan, 1992; Taylor & Whittier, 1997).

After the defeat of the ERA, some political analysts argued that **feminism** died, offering contradictory arguments that it both outlived its usefulness and succumbed to its whimsy. It is not uncommon to now hear about a "post-feminist" period. Indeed, the 1980s saw a decline in both formal and informal feminist organizations, and the political climate shifted away from values of equality, human rights, and social justice—igniting a backlash directed against feminism and its gains during the 1970s (Faludi, 1991; Taylor & Whittier, 1997). Recognizing all this complexity, feminist analysts, like Verta Taylor and Nancy Whittier (1997), are not so pessimistic (or so naively optimistic to think that a feminist agenda is no longer necessary). Instead, they describe a post-heyday period of abeyance.

Taylor and Whittier (1997) argue that social movements go into **abeyance** in order to hold out during periods of hostility toward their ideology. Applied to contemporary feminism, this is reflected in the lower profile recently adopted by many feminists, although there have been significant exceptions—the 300,000 to 600,000 person-strong march in Washington in 1989 to protest restrictions on abortion and women's participation internationally in sociopolitical movements in Arab countries. U.S. feminism in the 1990s has established strong links to other political causes, ranging from peace to environmental, lesbian and gay, AIDS, anti-violence, and labor union movements) (Paul, 1993). It offers within each an approach that includes and empowers women and men. Consciousness-raising activities continue in classes, in books such as this one, and from one generation to the next. Additionally, some of the tenets of feminism have so permeated Western cultures that we barely notice them, taking for granted everything from married couples with different last names and separable credit ratings to the viability of women political candidates. A parallel pattern of changing foci describes the recent history of feminist psychology (Rutherford et al., 2010). Feminism isn't dead; it's just not as visible as it was at other times. With a little digging, feminist activism comes within one's reach—both within psychology and beyond.

Being an Activist

There obviously are women and men who are committed to feminist causes in the sociopolitical arena. However, politics itself is stereotyped as male (see Box 14.6), and indeed women's leadership in politics is often more precarious than men's (Ryan et al., 2010). Women tend to come into politics through more circuitous routes than men, often starting with local community participation (Bond et al., 2008). Indeed, women's political partici-

---

[3]The full text of the ERA states: "Equality of rights under the law shall not be denied or abridged by the United States or by any state on account of sex. The Congress shall have the power to enforce, by appropriate legislation, the provisions of this article. The amendment shall take effect two years after the date of ratification."

Box 14.6

Do you know the answers to the following questions about U.S. politics?

- Whose responsibility is it to determine if a law is constitutional or not: The president, the Congress, or the Supreme Court?

- How many years is the term of office for a U.S. Senator?

Matthew McGlone and his colleagues (2006) asked college students questions about their political knowledge like these general ones as well as more time-specific ones (Name one U.S. senator from your home state). They activated stereotype threat by telling participants that their test is diagnostic of gender differences and by using a male phone interviewer. As they predicted, men scored higher than women on the test, and this overall effect was moderated both by how the test was described and by the interviewer's sex. Women scored significantly lower than men in the diagnostic condition and when interviewed by a man, but they found no differences in women's and men's scores in the non-diagnostic condition and with a female interviewer. Their findings confirm their speculation that indeed politics is stereotyped as a male-appropriate domain.

Answers: Supreme Court; 6 years

---

pation is likely to be more private than men's more direct and active participation in political parties (Coff & Bolzendahl, 2010).

Comparing rank-and-file political activists to nonactivists, feminist activists tend to be better educated, not live in the South, belong to voluntary organizations, work in the labor force, have fewer children, and believe in nontraditional political roles for women, abortion rights, the importance of women's rights, and the trustworthiness of others (Dauphinais et al., 1992). Interestingly in this study, there were a few activists who weren't strongly committed feminists, but rather who were pulled into supporting the women's movement by friends, their affiliation with voluntary organizations, and their experiences in the workforce.

Beyond being politically active, what else can we each do to contribute to feminist activism? First steps obviously involve developing, expanding, and refining our own feminist identity and personal empowerment. Part of this includes adopting the simple label of "feminist" to describe one's self (Zucker, 2004). As we have already seen, adopting the label of being feminist is more important than holding feminist beliefs per se in predicting participation in feminist activities (Yoder et al., 2011), and this relationship between self-labeling and activism holds up across Baby Boomers (born between 1943 and 1960) and Generation Xers (1961 and 1975) (Duncan, 2010). Additionally, self-labeled feminists are more likely to acknowledge the existence of sexism, see injustice in the present gender system, and believe that women should join together to bring about social change (Liss & Erchull, 2010). Having an elevated sense of women's entitlement to social justice is strongly associated with awakening to feminism (as part of the revelation stage of feminist identity development) (Yoder et al., 2011).

As we saw in Chapter 1, there are some strong negative cultural stereotypes that can make acceptance of the feminist label a risky proclamation. Women's feminist identity is threatened by homophobia, which links feminism with homosexuality as a means to disparage both (Frye, 1992); by stereotyping that predicts family-role failure for feminist activists (Rickabaugh, 1995); by sanctions against women's expression of anger, which is a key emotional ingredient for motivating activism (Hercus, 1999); and by justifiable fears that claiming a feminist identity will make one an outsider in some contexts (Griffin, 1994). (The last of these is offset by becoming an insider in feminist contexts; Smith, 1999.) Women who take notice of discrimination are women who are willing to risk losing social approval (Kobrynowicz & Branscombe, 1997) and who are more politically engaged (Bernstein, 2005). For men, feminist identification is undermined by de-masculinizing stereotyping, but this process may be counteracted by men's positive **communion** (Toller et al., 2004) as well as women's expectations that feminist men will be favorably oriented toward family (Rickabaugh, 1995).

Gloria Steinem (1983) offers an amazingly empowering yet simple strategy for individuals to do—engage in "outrageous acts and everyday rebellions" for the cause of social justice. She contends, and I agree, that having done one act, the world will seem different and you'll want to do more. She gives some examples to get the ball rolling (e.g., making public your salary; challenging some bit of woman-hating, homophobic, or racist humor), but feel free to brainstorm and try out your own. For example, use nonsexist language (Parks & Robertson, 2000), consider hyphenating your last name (Forbes et al., 2002), and routinely use "Ms." as a title that, like "Mr.," doesn't make assumptions about age and marital status (Lawton et al., 2003). A resource for such ideas is Donna Jackson's (1992) intriguing book, *How to Make the World a Better Place for Women in Five Minutes a Day.*

There are plenty of outrageous acts you can do as a student. In psychology, some examples include doing a paper on a "forgotten" woman psychologist for your history course; giving a presentation on sexist bias in therapy in a psychopathology course; joining a professional organization for women (see Chapter 2 for ideas); and generally resisting the aspects of the discipline that run counter to feminist ideology and practice (see Kitzinger, 1990). At a more involved level, you can help out with feminist research being conducted by your faculty and graduate students.[4] By taking women's studies classes, you cast a vote for their inclusion in the curriculum (Coulson & Bhavnani, 1990). Challenge the discipline of psychology, as well as the general academic curriculum, to be feminist (see Ussher, 1990). As you can see, many of these acts are simple things that don't consume time or financial resources. Rather, they simply require some attention to details in your everyday life that can make a difference.

A major point repeated throughout this chapter is the need to see activism beyond the individual level to encompass the collective. However, as Erika Appelbaum (1999) points out in a reprinted article, this is easier said than done. Fundamental to understanding power differences between women and men is the recognition that although women are marked and identifiable as women, women (because they are subordinated) do not share a common identity as a unified group. Within such **androcentric** dictates, THE group is men. Women exist as a deviation from this norm, not as a group in and of themselves. This "de-grouping" of women mediates against the collective unification needed to bring about change.

Critics, overlooking Appelbaum's point about the basic nature of domination, often blame feminists themselves for undermining the unification of women. The heyday of American feminism was remiss in acknowledging and learning from differences among feminist women and men (Taylor & Whittier, 1997). Since then, feminists have become

---

[4]Look for research with activist roots; that is, research that specifies how specific situations and social structures treat women and men differently, that suggest ideas for social change (Riger, 2000c), and that gives back to the community in which it was conducted (Russell & Bohan, 1999).

more tuned into a paradox of difference; that is, recognition that awareness of diversity can lead to better understandings and, ultimately, to unity (or "re-grouping" in Appelbaum's terms) (see Greenwood, 2008). It also is this understanding that makes feminism more of an approach, a way of seeing the world that can permeate many arenas—personal, political, social, economic, educational, organizational, and so on—as well as unify diverse women (Settles et al., 2008). There are a wide range of examples of how women working together change things (see for example, Bookman and Morgen, 1988; Fonow, 1998; Taylor & Whittier, 1998; 1999). This is true in psychology as well (Tiefer, 1991; Wilkinson, 1990; Unger et al., 2010).

Thus, my ultimate challenge to you (and for me as well) is to take what we talked about here and to be mindful about making a difference. We can follow the path of least resistance by giving in to the powerful systems of inequality that privilege and oppress us, that divide us into in-groups and out-groups, and that serve to disrupt our fundamentally human connections. Or we can empower ourselves—personally, in our relationships, and by working collectively to challenge and change these social structures. Each of us CAN make a difference.

The Welder
Cherríe Moraga

I am a welder.
Not an alchemist.
I am interested in the blend
of common elements to make
a common thing.

No magic here.
Only the heat of my desire to fuse
what I already know
exists. Is possible.

We plead to each other,
we all come from the same rock
we all come from the same rock
ignoring the fact that we bend
at different temperatures
that each of us is malleable
up to a point.

Yes, fusion is possible
but only if things get hot enough—
all else is temporary adhesion,
patching up.

It is the intimacy of steel melting
into steel, the fire of our individual
passion to take hold of ourselves
that makes sculpture of our lives,
builds buildings.

And I am not talking about skyscrapers,
merely structures that can support us
without fear
of trembling.

For too long a time
the heat of my heavy hands
has been smoldering
in the pockets of other
people's business—
they need oxygen to make fire.

I am now
coming up for air.
Yes, I *am*
picking up the torch.
I am the welder.
I understand the capacity of heat
to change the shape of things.
I am suited to work
within the realm of sparks
out of control.

I am the welder.
I am taking the power
into my own hands.

SUGGESTED READINGS

Schreiber, R. (2002). Injecting a woman's voice: Conservative women's organizations, gender consciousness, and the expression of women's policy preferences. *Sex Roles, 47,* 331–342.

Ronnee Schreiber explores how two conservative political groups talk about women, gender differences, and gender consciousness while pursuing political goals antithetical to a feminist agenda, raising questions about how gender consciousness relates to feminism and is translated into political action.

Bart, P. B., & O'Brien, P. H. (1997). Stopping rape: Effective avoidance strategies. In L. Richardson, V. Taylor, & N. Wittier (Eds.), *Feminist Frontiers IV* (pp. 410-420). New York: McGraw Hill.

This reprint of an article originally published in 1984 remains germane. Pauline Bart and Patricia O'Brien present data from 94 interviews with women, who when attacked either avoided being raped or were raped to give women realistic advice about what to do, and not do, if threatened with sexual assault.

Hydén, M. (2005). "I must have been an idiot to let it go on": Agency and positioning in battered women's narrative of leaving. *Feminism & Psychology, 15,* 169–188.

Margareta Hydén followed 10 battered Swedish women who came to a women's shelter across 2 years to explore how they talked about their decisions to stay or leave, highlighting individual variations in their narratives and the importance of their own agency or empowerment.

Sharpe, S. (2001). Going for it: Young women face the future. *Feminism & Psychology, 11,* 177–181.

Twenty years later, Sue Sharper revisits the schools she studied in the 1970s and again explores girls' and boys' views about feminism, careers, and relationships. She not only provides a barometer about contemporary attitudes, but also describes how these have changed and remained the same across two generations. This article is a good springboard to discuss how realistic some of their expectations are.

Steinem, G. (1983). Far from the opposite shore. In *Outrageous acts and everyday rebellions* (pp. 341–362). New York: Holt.

I still find this chapter from Gloria Steinem's book inspiring because it makes doing feminism a part of everyday life.

Psychology's Feminist Voices http://www.feministvoices.com

This project, directed by Alex Rutherford at York University, is a great resource for reading about (in "Women Past") and for actually hearing the voices of (through videotaped interviews published online in "Feminist Presence"). influential women in the history of the psychology of women and gender *Pray the Devil Back to Hell praythedevilbacktohell.com*

This award-winning documentary chronicles the women's movement in Liberia, Africa, which is credited with helping to bring an end to that country's long and bloody civil war in 2003 and usher in the election of Africa's first modern woman president, Ellen Johnson Sirleaf (a 2011 recipient of the Nobel Peace Prize). This video speaks to the empowerment of women and tells an inspiring story of how diverse women can come together to make an important difference.

Glossary

Abeyance   A period during which a social movement becomes less visible in response to a hostile climate

Accommodation   The cognitive process whereby an existing cognitive schema (framework) is adjusted to take in new, otherwise discrepant, information

Activational effects   Within a neuroendrocrine approach, research seeking to understand how concentrations of hormones affect specific activities of the adult brain

Active commitment   The fifth dimension of feminist identity development in which the personal becomes political, presumably leading to activism

Affirmative action   A range of programs designed to recruit and retain a diversity of qualified individuals

Ageism   Prejudicial attitudes and discriminatory behavior directed toward the aged and the process of aging

Agency (instrumentality)

How much an individual believes s/he can take charge of and accomplish things independently

Agoraphobia   A DSM diagnosis primarily defined by fears of losing control, being trapped, and panicking

Alcohol abuse and dependence   A DSM diagnosis primarily identified by overuse of alcohol

Allocative discrimination   Biases in hiring, promotion, and dismissal

Alpha bias   A philosophical world view that assumes that differences between girls/women and boys/men are real (essential)

Ambivalent sexism   Prejudicial attitudes, combing both hostile and benevolent aspects, that work together to oppress women and girls

Androcentric bias (androcentrism)   Privileging men and what is associated with men as normative (that is, the standard against which others are judged)

Androgens   Often referred to as reproductive hormones, these growth hormones tend to be more highly concentrations in males

Androgyny   An equal blending of feminine and masculine traits

Anorexia nervosa   A DSM diagnosis marked by refusal to maintain a minimally acceptable body weight

Assimilation   The cognitive process whereby new information is added to an existing cognitive schema

B

Benevolent sexism   Seemingly benign or complimentary attitudes that serve to oppress women and girls

Beta bias   A philosophical world view that assumes that differences between girls/women and boys/men are minimal and instead stresses similarities

Bilateralization   Regarding verbal and visospatial processing as occurring equally across both brain hemispheres

Biological essentialism   An assumption that differences between women and men are rooted in their biological differences

Bipotential   The flexibility of a human fetus until 6–7 weeks gestation to develop female or male gonads

Blaming the victim   Regarding oppressed people as the cause of their own oppression

Blatant sexist discrimination   Intentional, highly visible acts that are easily documented and that serve to oppress women and girls

Body consciousness   An individual's behaviors and attitudes about their body (physical) experiences

385

Body esteem How strongly and positively an individual rates their own body parts and bodily activities

Body image Satisfaction with one's own bodily appearance, blending physical attractiveness with body esteem

Body shame An individual's feelings of failure for not achieving the cultural ideal for one's body

Borderline personality disorder A DSM diagnosis characterized by attention seeking, anger, and manipulative behavior

Brain organization research A term preferred by Jordan-Young (2010) to describe the "organization-activation hypothesis" or "neurohormonal theory" that prenatal hormone exposure causes sexual differentiation of the human brain as well as predispositions that can be activated by hormones later in life.

Bulimia nervosa A DSM diagnosis marked by binge eating and compensatory purging

C

Caring about Providing emotional connection for another

Caring for Providing caretaking work for another

Caring orientation A approach to making moral judgments focused on minimizing the harm done to those involved

Chromosomes Every human cell contains 23 pairs of chromosomes which carry a large number of genes; one pair, the sex chromosomes, are XX for females; XY for males (a X from the mother and either a X or a Y from the father)

Close relationships Interpersonal connections expected to endure over time and provide individuals with respect, intimacy, caring, concern, support, and affection

Coercive power The ability to directly influence others by threatening punishment

Cognitive crowding hypothesis The prediction that specialization is better for specific tasks (e.g., spatial processing) and bilaterality is better for global tasks (e.g., verbal)

Cohort A generation with a shared cultural history

Collectivism (collectivist) A broad cultural philosophy that values group harmony over individual needs

Communion (expressiveness) How much an individual is caring and nurturing toward others and works cooperatively

Comparable worth A program to insure that jobs with similar skill requirements are paid similarly

Comparative approach to research Research that seeks to understand one group (e.g., women) by examining them relative to another group (e.g., men)

Compensatory expectancies The tendency for individuals when faced with a nonstereotypic out-group member to believe that another member of the out-group will behave in ways consistent with stereotyping for that group

Competence Conveyed by a cluster of traits associated with masculinity, instrumentality, and agency and implicitly associated with men and masculine attributes

Complete Androgen Insensitivity Syndrome (CAIS) A developing XY fetus cannot capture and use testosterone so its genitals appear female at birth; at adolescence, breasts and a feminine body shape develop but no menstruation occurs

Complimentary weightism Drawing attention to another's body in a seemingly favorable way

Concordance rates A positive correlation between amount of genetic similarity and another behavior (e.g., sexual orientation)

Concrete wall An upper limit in promotion opportunities that is visible, largely impenetrable, and based on being a member of an outgroup

Confederate A person in an experiment who was trained to play a role that is part of the study's goals but appears to other participants to be another participant

Conferred dominance The power that comes with privilege that grants the beneficiary access to rewards and resources

Confound Two or more intertwined factors (explanations) that operate together

Construct validity How well a measure assesses what it claims to measure

Control beliefs How much an individual believes they can control the appearance of their body

Coordinated care Regarding child care as the joint contribution of the mother and the provider to both caring for and caring about a child

Coping perspective to violence Interpreting victims' reactions to violence as adaptive strategies for surviving trauma

Core gender identity Whether an individual regards her or himself as basically female or male

Corpus callosum A mass of nerve fibers that connects the left and right hemispheres of the brain

Counting review   An approach to summarizing a body of research by tallying findings, assuming that the most frequently occurring pattern is strongest

Covert sexist discrimination   Hidden yet purposive and often intentionally malicious acts that serve to oppress women and girls

Cross-over-model   The prediction that women will become more masculine and men, more feminine, as they age

Cultural preparedness for powerlessness   A subtle meta-message targeting girls that conveys lower status and reduced self-efficacy

Cultural-relativism schema   A cognitive framework that regards events as reflective of the cultural and historical time period in which they occur

Custodial care   Regarding child care by those other than the child's mother as providing caring for, but not caring about

Cycle of battering   A self-sustaining pattern of tension building, then battering, then contrite, loving behavior

D

d statistic   An effect size resulting from a meta-analysis that indicates the size of a difference between groups, summarizing across multiple studies

Dating script   A step-by-step sequence of events expected to describe a prototypic first date

Dependent personality disorder   A DSM diagnosis involving submissiveness and excessive needs to be taken care of

Depressed entitlement   The tendency for women to allocate less pay to themselves for work of similar quality to men's and to consider their pay fair

Descriptive norms   Social behaviors we perceive as typical within our culture

Dialectical model   A model that regards nature and nurture as intertwined and reciprocal (with each affecting the other), making the separation of the two meaningless

Diethylstilbestrol   A synthetic estrogen that can masculinize a fetus's brain development without affecting its genitals

Dimorphism   An assumption that biology consistently sorts animals into two distinct and opposite sexes

Direct trauma   Reactions to maliciously perpetuated violence (e.g., rape and abuse)

Direct tutoring   Telling children what is culturally expected of them (as a part of their socialization)

Discrimination Theory   Roots causes for the wage gap in prejudices, stereotyping, and inequitable treatment

Discursive analysis   A research approach that looks for patterns in participants' everyday speech that reflect the underlying meaning of concepts, that is, that expose how people think about things

Diversity   Multiculturalism; recognition that no one social category is created in isolation from other social categories, creating heterogeneity in how any one social category is expressed

Dizygotic twins   Two separate fertilized eggs develop together in the same prenatal environment, making these twins no more genetically similar than siblings

Doing difference   The social construction of multiple social categories combining privileges and oppressions

Doing gender   The processes through which we construct our gender in our everyday lives

Domain   A cluster of similar tasks or abilities

Double standard of sexuality   Attitudes that are more permissive about men's than about women's sexual expressiveness

Dysthymic disorder   A DSM diagnosis of major depression extending over at least 2 years

E

Effect size   How much variability in an outcome a researcher can explain with a specific variable

Ego protective function   Using the logic of blaming the victim to regard one's self as invulnerable to the oppression of the victim

Electra complex   Within the psychoanalytic phallic stage, girls presumably sexually desire their fathers and resent their mothers, resolving this conflict by identifying with the mother and thus developing their own femininity and heterosexual desire for a baby

Embeddedness-Emanation   The third dimension of feminist identity development in which one immerses one's self in feminist culture

Empathetic accuracy   How skilled an individual is in reading the feelings of others

Empowerment   A dynamic process, sustained by societal forces, that nurtures the potential and growth of one's self and others, encompassing both personal agency and activism toward social change

Enactive experience   Teaching children cultural expectations by rewarding and punishing their behaviors (as a part of their socialization)

Enhancement hypothesis Predicts that when women hold multiple roles, some roles may buffer them from stresses coming from other roles

Entitlement One's personal sense of deservingness

Envious prejudice Associated with perceptions of others as high in competence and low in warmth and characterized by grudging admiration

Epigamic selection The tendency to choose mate(s) with features linked to reproductive success

Episodic memory Recollections about events in one's own life

Essentialism A world view that assumes that differences between women/girls and men/boys are rooted in their natures

Estradiol Estrogen in a woman's bloodstream

Estrogens Often referred to as reproductive hormones, these growth hormones tend to be more highly concentrated in females

Evaluation bias Judgments about the quality of a person (e.g., a worker to be promoted) or a product (e.g., artwork) influenced by the gender of the person or creator

Evolutionary psychology The theory that human psychological development reflects adaptive solutions to problems of survival and reproduction

Experimenter effects The expectations a researcher holds about how participants should behave affects what participants actually do (creating a type of self-fulfilling prophecy within research)

Expert power The ability to directly influence others by drawing on one's own task-relevant knowledge or training

Explicit attitude A consciously held belief that an individual can self-report

Expressiveness (communion) How much an individual is caring and nurturing toward others and works cooperatively

External genitalia The clitoris, labia minora, and vaginal orifice for females; the penis and scrotum for males

Externalizing Mental disorders that affect others

F

Family-role redefinition coping Managing work-family conflict by changing family demands

Femininity Conceptualized by psychologists as a personality trait on which individuals differ and which is defined by cultural understandings of what accompanies being female

Feminism Although complexly defined in multiple ways, common elements include valuing women and their experiences, concern for equality of power, need for social change and activism, and adoption of a social constructionist world view

Feminist experiential research An approach to doing research on gendered systems of inequality that stresses individuals' experiences and provides a medium for participants to express themselves on their own terms

Feminist positivist empiricism An approach to doing research on gendered systems of inequality that draws on conventional research methodologies (e.g., experiments and surveys)

Feminist social constructionists An approach to doing research on gendered systems of inequality that explores language as a way to uncover deeper meanings (see discursive analysis)

Follicular phase About a 2-week period during the menstrual cycle when a new egg (ovum), as part of a group of cells called the follicle, and the lining of the uterus grow

Fundamental attribution error The tendency to explain other people's behavior by assuming stable personality dispositions, ignoring social context

G

Gender A social construction of biological sex that is rooted in cultural meanings

Gender belief system An individual's network of expectations about what constitutes femininity and masculinity

Gender constancy A key developmental, cognitive understanding that being biologically female or male cannot be changed by changing one's appearance

Gender differentiation The socialization process through which girls and boys presumably learn gender-typing

Gender harassment Offensive sexual and sexist remarks targeting people because of their sex category

Gender identity How each person perceives her/himself as female or male

Gender identity disorder Persistent, disruptive discomfort with one's assigned sex and its gender role

Gender polarization Thinking about women/girls and men/boys as opposites with little in common

Gender role orientation The beliefs that an individual holds about the appropriateness of various social roles for women and men, especially at home and in the workplace

Gender schematicity (schema)   How rigidity one regards traits, roles, occupations, and physical characteristics as divided into female- and male-appropriate (ranging from rigid schematicity to flexible aschematicity); a cognitive schema about gender

Gender-role transcendence   Understanding that gender matters by establishing a gendered social context and then trying to rise above that context

Glass ceiling   An upper limit in promotion opportunities that is largely invisible to a worker and results from one's membership in an outgroup

Glass escalator   Privileging men's status in female-dominated occupations through enhanced promotion opportunities and pay

Gonadal hormones   A balance of more estrogens and less androgens for females; less estrogens and more androgens for males

Gonads   Ovaries for females; testes for males

H

Halo effect   The packaging of traits and judgments into psychologically consistent clusters

Hemispheres   The two structurally similar halves of the brain, split from top to bottom along the corpus callosum, that control opposite sides of the body

Hemispheric dominance (laterality)   The relatively greater importance of one brain hemisphere in processing information

Heritability   How much a trait in a population can be accounted for by genetics; for individuals, a predisposition that may or may not develop

Heterosexism   Assuming heterosexuality

Hippocampus   A part of the human brain that is involved in estrogen feedback loops

Hiring queues   Employers' hiring preferences from most to least desirable candidates

Histrionic personality disorder   A DSM diagnosis characterized by pervasive, excessive emotionality and attention-seeking

Hormones   Chemical messengers that allow cells to communicate

Hostile sexism   Overtly negative attitudes that serve to oppress women and girls

Hostile work environment sexual harassment   Unwanted behaviors that create a chilling educational or work climate for members of an outgroup

Human Capital Theory   Roots the causes for the wage gap in differences in workers' qualifications and personal investments

Hypermasculinity   Exaggerated displays of characteristics associated with men and being male

Hypospadius   The opening for urination is not at the tip of a penis

Hypothalamus   A part of the human brain, located just above the brain stem, that plays a role in regulating the amount of hormones in the body

I

Implicit Association Test (IAT)   A computerized test that uses response times to gauge whether two concepts (e.g., homemaker and warmth) are automatically associated or not, oftentimes outside the awareness of the test taker

Implicit attitude   A prejudice or preference that is activated automatically, often without the holder's awareness

Incidence   The number of events (e.g., victimizations) that occur within a given time period

Index of segregation   The proportion of female (or male) workers who would need to change occupations to achieve full occupational gender-integration

Indifferent gonad   The gonadal tissue of a human fetus for its first 6-7 weeks of gestation that can develop either into female (ovaries) or male (testes) gonads

Indirect trauma   Secondary effects from witnessing violence

Individual differences   Variations (heterogeneity) within a social category

Individual-differences schema   A cognitive framework that sees individuals as unique and resists social categorization

Individualism   A broad cultural philosophy that values individual needs over group harmony

Individuating information   Information (e.g., one's name) that identifies a specific person

Information power   The ability to directly influence others by sharing or withholding information

In-groups   Social categories to which one belongs

Injunctive (prescriptive) norms   Dictates about what ought to be ideally

Innateness   Characteristics people are born with; not a predisposition that may or may not develop (heritability)

Insidious trauma   Being devalued because of membership in an oppressed social category

Instrumentality (agency) How much an individual believes s/he can take charge of and accomplish things independently

Intergroup differences Variations between groups, summing over intragroup diversity

Internal accessory organs The Fallopian tubes and uterus for females; the vas deferens and seminal vesicles for males

Internalization Incorporating information from external sources into one's own ways of thinking (internalizing: affecting one's self)

Intersectionality An analytic approach that takes in account the meaning and the consequences of multiple categories of social group membership

Intersexuality Physically falling between being completely biologically female or male

Intragroup differences/diversity Variations within groups (heterogeneity), reflecting individual differences and/or subgroup diversity

Intrasexual selection Competition among members of the same sex for mates likely to successfully reproduce

J

Job queues Workers' priority rankings of jobs from most to least desirable

Justice orientation A approach to making moral judgments using the logic of rights or justice

K

Klinefelter Syndrome A designated male with an extra X chromosome (XXY), leading to breast enlargement at puberty and infertility

L

Late luteal phase The premenstrual phase of the menstrual cycle in which estrogen and progesterone levels drop rapidly, preparing the uterus to shed its lining

Laterality (hemispheric dominance) The relatively greater importance of one brain hemisphere in processing information

Legitimacy Entitles the holder to compliance from others

Legitimate authority power The ability to directly influence others by virtue of the position one holds

Life course A cultural ideal of an age-related sequence of roles and group memberships across an individual's life

Longitudinal study A research design that tracks the same individuals across time

Luteal phase The last 2 weeks of the menstrual cycle during which progesterone levels rise and the uterus is prepared for the possibility of a fertilized egg

M

Major depression A DSM diagnosis marked primarily by depressed mood or loss of interest or pleasure

Male bashing Belittling men and boys for simply belonging to the social category of male

Masculinity Conceptualized by psychologists as a personality trait on which individuals differ and which is defined by cultural understandings of what accompanies being male

Mediation (mediator) An intervening or process variable that fully or partically links a cause to an effect

Menarche The first onset of menstruation

Menopause One full year without menstruating permanently

Menses The time during a woman's menstrual cycle when she is menstruating

Menstrual synchrony The tendency for women in close social interaction to menstruate together on the same cycle

Mental disorder A DSM classification reflecting a cluster of clinically diagnosed symptoms

Mental rotation skills The ability to picture an object in three-dimensional space from different perspectives

Mentor A co-worker who serves as a role model, shares their success, and plays an active role in connecting their protégé to organizational networks

Meta-analysis A statistical approach to summarizing a body of research that can identity homogeneous measures, weight individual studies by their sample size, and yield an overall statistic (effect size) that captures the strength of a finding

Meta-message An unspoken, broad, pervasive message that is conveyed subtly through consistent, repeated patterns

Modeling Learning through observation of others (as a part of socialization)

Moderators Contexts or individual differences that qualify an effect, that is, limit the effect to specified circumstances or individuals, respectively

Monozygotic twins The same fertilized egg separates into twins giving each identical chromosomes as well as a shared prenatal environment

Morbidity   A measure of quality of life; how sick or incapacitated one is

Mortality   Death rate; how long one lives

Motherhood penalty   The finding that mothers earn less than childless women

N

Narrative review   An approach to summarizing a body of research by reading it and reporting general trends

Naturalistic study   A non-manipulational research approach in which the independent variable under study occurs on its own (naturally)

Neuroendrocrine approach   An area of study that explores the relationship between reproductive hormones in the brain and human behavior

Norm of reaction   The understanding that genes express themselves differently in different environments

O

Objectification   Treating one's own or others' bodies as objects (things) without feelings of their own

Oedipal complex   Within the psychoanalytic phallic stage, boys presumably sexually desire their mother and want to be rid of their father, resolving this conflict by identifying with the father and thus developing their own masculinity and heterosexuality

Oppression   Losing something of value, not because it is deserved, but simply because of membership in a social category

Organization effects   Within a neuroendrocrine approach, research seeking to look at how prenatal exposure to hormones during fetal brain development affect behaviors after birth

Out-group   A social category to which one does not belong or that is under-represented and/or oppressed within a group, organization, or culture

Out-group homogeneity effect   Thinking of members of groups to which one does not belong (out-groups) as all alike

Ovulation   The point in the menstrual cycle when a fully developed egg (ovum) is released by the ovary

P

Parental investment   Speculation that women's reproductive success depends more heavily than men's on the survival of a few children for whom she cares

Passive acceptance   The least developed stage of feminist identity development in which an individual is unaware of or denies sexism

Paternalistic prejudice   Associated with perceptions of others as high in warmth and low in competence and characterized by pity and sympathy

Patriarchy   A system of inequality that privileges men and boys over women and girls

Personal role redefinition coping   Changing one's own expectations and perceptions to manage multiple roles

Phallic stage   A theorized psychoanalytic stage, at about age 5, where pleasure is derived from one's genitals and the resolution of which produces one's superego (as well as gender identity)

Physical aggression   Defined by social psychologists as behavior intended to cause harm to another person

Physical discrimination   Stigmatized treatment based on bodily appearance and conformity to cultural ideals

Placebo   A treatment appearing to be genuine but without the agent under study (e.g., a sugar pill without the drug being tested)

Plasticity   The capability of the brain to pick up functions lost with brain damage

Positivism   A philosophical approach to doing science that assumes that the goal of science is to discover truth

Positivity bias   Women's tendency to underestimate their own vulnerability to violence relative to other women

Postpartum blues   Depressed mood following childbirth, often combined with enhanced happiness

Postpartum depression   A period of over 2 weeks following giving birth when a woman develops symptoms of clinical depression

Posttraumatic Stress Disorder (PTSD)   A disruptive reaction to exposure to a traumatic incident that included personal threat and resulted in fear or horror

Power   The capability to influence the behaviors of others

Premenstrual Dysphoric Disorder   A DSM classification of severe mood disturbance linked to a woman's menstrual cycle

Prescriptive (injunctive) norms   Dictates about what ought to be ideally

Prevalence   An individual's exposure to an event (e.g., assault) any time during their lifetime

Prime   A manipulation in an experiment designed to make a thought cognitively salient

Principle of reciprocal determinism The circular relationship between biology and behavior; not only does biology influence behavior, but experiences also alter biology

Privilege Getting something of value, not because it is earned, but simply because of membership in a social category

Prototype A representative image of a hypothetical person whose traits, roles, occupations, and physical characteristics reflect specific stereotyping

Psychoanalysis Rooted in the work of Freud, psychoanalysts theorize that personality (an id, ego, and superego) develops across stages of psychosexual development (oral, anal, phallic, latent, and genital)

Psychobiosocial model The intertwining of psychological, biological, and social factors such that they become inseparable (also see intersectionality)

Psychological aggression Behaviors, including verbal, nonverbal, and written, intended to cause mental harm

Psychologization The tendency to regard medical maladies as coming from psychological problems

Psychotic disorders A class of DSM disorders marked by social dysfunction and withdrawal from reality

Psychotropic drugs Mood-altering pharmaceuticals, such as tranquilizers, sedatives, antidepressants, and stimulants

Q

Quasi-experimental design Research that compares groups (e.g., women and men) that are naturally occurring and therefore not open to random assignment

Quid pro quo sexual harassment Sexual coercion characterized by the dominant power position of the perpetrator

R

Rape Nonconsensual oral, anal, or vaginal penetration, obtained by force, threat of bodily harm, or when the victim is incapable of giving consent

Rape prevention Interventions designed to reduce the incidence of rape

Rape resistance and avoidance Individual strategies for escaping attempted rape

Reactive role behavior coping Attempts to manage all role demands

Referent power The ability to directly influence others by being a model to emulate or identify with

Relationship satisfaction Degree to which an interpersonal connection lives up to one's expectations, preferences, and ideals

Revelation The second stage of feminist identity development during which crises call into question an individual's passive acceptance

Reward power The ability to directly influence others by controlling resources others want

Role centrality The personal importance of a role to an individual

Role encapsulation Confining members of a social category to play roles consistent with stereotyping

Role quality High quality roles produce fewer negative and more positive consequences

Romantic attachments Close relationships that also include sexual passion, exclusiveness, and commitment

S

Scarcity hypothesis Predicts that the more roles women hold, the more conflict they will experience

Schema An internalized, cognitive framework giving social/cultural meaning to a social category such as being female and male (see gender schematicity)

Scripts Expected social sequences that we learn from our culture

Selection bias Recruitment procedures that make groups different along dimensions not considered by a researcher (and confounded with the variable of interest to the researcher)

Self-defeating personality disorder A rejected DSM diagnosis that blames the client for being vulnerable to abuse by others

Self-efficacy The belief that one is able to produce positive outcomes for one's self

Self-fulfilling prophecy Expectations that help make anticipated events come true

Self-in-relation theorists An approach that roots individual identity development through connections with others

Self-objectification The degree to which an individual internalizes being treated like a thing and turns that perspective on themselves. Can be a chronic individual difference (like a trait) or induced by a social context (a state).

Semantic memory Recollections of facts, general historical events (not experienced personally), and word knowledge

Sex Connotes biological causation of female and male

Sexism   The oppression of women through everyday practices, attitudes, assumptions, behaviors, and institutional rules (encompasses prejudice, stereotyping, and discrimination)

Sexism schema   A cognitive framework that labels discriminatory treatment as sexist and resists assimilating (internalizing) it

Sexist discrimination   Overt negative acts that serve to oppress women and girls and/or work to privilege men and boys

Sexist prejudice   Attitudes about women and girls that serve to oppress them

Sexist stereotyping   Expectations about both positive and negative traits assigned to women and girls that serve to oppress them

Sexual harassment   See quid pro quo sexual harassment and gender harassment

Sexual objectification   Treating others' bodies as objects without feelings for one's own sexual pleasure

Sexual orientation hypothesis   The expectation that feminine boys will be gay (resulting in stronger prohibitions for boys' socialization than girls')

Sexual selection   How individuals chose a mate

Sexuality   Refers to sexual activities or reproduction

Sexualized gaze   Treating someone else's body as a object for one's own sexual pleasure

Shifting standards   The tendency when making selection decisions (e.g., hiring) to weigh the qualifications of a desired candidate more heavily in order to justify a preferred choice

Social categorization   The cognitive tendency to sort people into groups based on perceived common properties

Social Cognitive Theory   Bussey and Bandura's model of gender differentiated development

Social constructionism   A world view that assumes that differences between women/girls and men/boys are created by what we actively do within a specific culture to define our gender

Social context   The social environment in which behavior occurs that can work to either produce or constrain behavior

Social justice   An agenda that works to eliminate systems of inequality, privilege, and oppression

Social norms   Culturally defined dictates for behavior

Social representations   External characteristics of people that are used by others to sort them into groups

Socialization theorists   The common ground on which various socialization theories are based hypothesizes that personality is learned in childhood

Socializing agents   Mechanisms for passing culture on to children (typically parents, schools, peers, and the media)

Somatization disorders   A class of DSM diagnoses in which psychological problems are expressed through physical ailments

Spatial perception   Orienting objects in three-dimensional space in relation to one's own body

Spatial visualization   Complex manipulations of spatial information requiring multiple steps

Specialization   Refers to automatically relegating verbal processing more to the left hemisphere of the human brain and visospatial processing more to the right hemisphere

Standard deviation   A measure of variability within a group around its mean (arithmetic average)

Status (social)   An individual's position along a socially determined hierarchy of power, prestige, and resources

Status Construction Theory   This theory predicts that privileged members of a social category will be regarded as superior and instrumental/agentic

Stereotype reactance   Purposively reacting in counter-stereotypic ways

Stereotype threat   Reduced performance on tasks on which the test taker perceives negative stereotyping

Stereotyping   The cognitive processing of information about a social category creating expectations for members of that category; attempts to find meaning in unknown circumstances by attributing traits, roles, occupations, and/or physical characteristics to another person

Stimulus variable   Using a social category as an independent variable to study stereotyping related to that variable. Studies doing this expose all participants to the same materials (often vignettes), which they evaluate, but vary the social category membership of the targeted individual.

Strain-based conflict   Stress from having one role spill over into another

Stroop task   A classic psychology task in which participants must name the color or name of printed words that are either consistent (e.g., the word "purple" printed in purple ink) or inconsistent (e.g., the word "purple" printed in red ink) so that inconsistent words take longer to identify.

Structural role redefinition coping   Changing externally imposed, structural expectations to manage multiple roles

Subtle sexist discrimination   Less visible acts that may go unnoticed, that may or may not be intentional, and that serve to oppress women and girls

Surrogate care   Relinquishing both caring for and about to a care child provider

Surveillance   The degree to which an individual watches and thinks about their own body, putting appearance above feelings and action

Synthesis   The fourth dimension of feminist identity development in which gender-role transcendence occurs

System of inequality   A status hierarchy built on privilege and oppression and maintained by social categorization

T

Testosterone   An androgen; a growth (or reproductive) hormone typically found in higher concentrations in males

Time-based conflict   Stress from competing time demands from multiple roles

Token resistance   An expectation rooted in the sexual double standard that women will resist sexual activities even when they desire them

Tokenism (token)   The proportional underpresentation of a social category (less than 15%) within a larger group

Transformational leadership   Leadership emphasizing the nurturing and development of followers

Triangulation   Bringing research evidence from different methodologies and across disciplines together to focus on a specific problem

Turner's Syndrome   A designated female missing a second X chromosome (XO) whose ovaries and secondary sex characteristics (e.g., breasts) do not develop and whose stature is short

U

Unearned entitlements   Core, fundamental valuables that all people deserve (e.g., a sense of safety)

Unmitigated agency   Exaggerations of agency/instrumentality where one fails to connect with others (i.e., agency without communality)

Unmitigated communion   Exaggerations of communal/expressiveness where one continually puts the needs of others ahead of their own needs (i.e., communality without agency)

V

Valuative discrimination   Lower wages in female-dominated compared to male-dominated occupations with similar skill requirements

Values   Core principles in an individual's belief system

Vigilance   Continually monitoring and working toward an ideal (e.g., an egalitarian intimate relationship)

Visual dominance   Power expressed by looking at one's partner more when speaking than when listening

W

Warmth   Conveyed by a cluster of traits associated with femininity, expressiveness, and communality

Within-job wage discrimination   Wage disparities within the same job

Womanist identity   The intersection of racial and gender identity for African American women

Work-family role convergence   A model for making work and family roles more compatible

Work-role redefinition coping   Managing work-family conflict by changing work demands

References

Aaronson, S. (1995, January). *Pay equity and the wage gap: Success in the states.* Washington, DC: Institute for Women's Policy Research.

AAUW. (1992). *The AAUW report: How schools shortchange girls.* Washington, DC: The American Association of University Women Educational Foundation.

AAUW. (1996). *Girls in the middle: Working to succeed in school.* Washington, DC: AAUW.

AAUW. (1999). *Voice of a generation: Teenage girls on sex, school, and self.* Washington, DC: AAUW's Educational Foundation.

Abbey, A. (1991). Misperception as an antecedent of acquaintance rape: A consequence of ambiguity in communication between women and men. In A. Parrot & L. Bechhofer (Eds.), *Acquaintance rape: A hidden crime* (pp. 96–112). New York: Wiley.

Abbey, A. et al. (2002). Alcohol-involved rapes: Are they more violent? *Psychology of Women Quarterly, 26,* 99–109.

Abbey, A. et al. (2004). Similarities and differences in women's sexual assault experiences based on tactics used by the perpetrator. *Psychology of Women Quarterly, 28,* 323–332.

Abel, M.H., & Meltzer, A.L. (2007). Student ratings of a male and female professors' lecture on sex discrimination in the workforce. *Sex Roles, 57,* 173–180.

Abrams, D. et al. (2003). Perceptions of stranger and acquaintance rape: The role of benevolent and hostile sexism in victim blame and rape proclivity. *Journal of Personality and Social Psychology, 84,* 111–125.

Adams, A., & Abarbanel, G. (1988). *Sexual assault on campus: What colleges can do.* Santa Monica, CA: Rape Treatment Center of Santa Monica Hospital Medical Center.

Addis, M.E., & Mahalik, R. (2003). Men, masculinity, and the contexts of help seeking. *American Psychologist, 58,* 5–14.

Adler, D.N., & Johnson, S.B. (1994). Sample description, reporting, and analysis of sex in psychological research: A look at APA and APA division journals in 1990. *American Psychologist, 49,* 216–218.

Agars, M.D. (2004). Reconsidering the impact of gender stereotypes on the advancement of women in organizations. *Psychology of Women Quarterly, 28,* 103–111.

Ahrens, C.E. et al. (2007). Deciding whom to tell: Expectations and outcomes of rape survivors' first disclosures. *Psychology of Women Quarterly, 31,* 38–49.

Ahrens, C.J.C., & Ryff, C.D. (2006). Multiple roles and well-being: Sociodemographic and psychological moderators. *Sex Roles, 55,* 801–815.

Ahrens, J.A., & O'Brien, K.M. (1996). Predicting gender-role attitudes in adolescent females: Ability, agency, and parental factors. *Psychology of Women Quarterly, 20,* 409–417.

Ainsworth, M.D.S. et al. (1978). *Patterns of attachment: A psychological study of the strange situation.* Hillsdale, NJ: Erlbaum.

Airhihenbuwa, C.O., & Liburd, L. (2006). Eliminating health disparities in the African American population: The interface of culture, gender, and power. *Health Education and Behavior, 33,* 488–501.

Aldrich, N.J., & Tenenbaum, H.R. (2006). Sadness, anger, and frustration: Gendered patterns in early adolescents' and their parents' emotional talk. *Sex Roles, 55,* 775–785.

Alexandraki, I., & Mooradian, A.D. (2010). Barriers related to mammography use for breast cancer screening among minority women. *Journal of the National Medical Association, 102,* 206–218.

Alhabib, S. et al. (2010). Domestic violence against women: Systematic review of prevalence studies. *Journal of Family Violence, 25*, 369–382.

Allen, L. et al. (1989). Two sexually dimorphic cell groups in the human brain. *Journal of Neuroscience, 9*, 497–506.

Allen, M. (1997). We've come a long way, too, baby. And we've still got a ways to go. So give us a break! In M.R. Walsh (Ed.), *Women, men, and gender: Ongoing debates* (pp. 402–405). New Haven, CT: Yale.

Allen, P.G. (1990). Violence and the American Indian woman. *The speaking profits us: Violence in the lives of women of color.* Seattle, WA: SAFECO Insurance Company.

Allen, T.D., & Eby, L.T. (2004). Factors related to mentor reports of mentoring functions provided: Gender and relational characteristics. *Sex Roles, 50*, 129–139.

Altermatt, T.W. et al. (2003). Agency and virtue: Dimensions underlying subgroups of women. *Sex Roles, 49*, 631–641.

Altschuler, J. (2004). Meaning of housework and other unpaid responsibilities among older women. *Journal of Women & Aging, 16*, 143–159.

Amanatullah, E.T., & Morris, M.W. (2010). Negotiating gender roles: Gender differences in assertive negotiating are mediated by women's fear of backlash and attenuated when negotiating on behalf of others. *Journal of Personality and Social Psychology, 98*, 256–267.

Amaro, H. et al. (2001). Women's sexual health: The need for feminist analyses in public health in the Decade of Behavior. *Psychology of Women Quarterly, 25*, 324–334.

Ambwani, S., & Strauss, J. (2007). Love thyself before loving others? A qualitative and quantitative analysis of gender differences in body image and romantic love. *Sex Roles, 56*, 13–21.

American Heart Association. (2005). Women and coronary heart disease. http://www.amhrt.org (Retrieved November 2005).

American Heritage Dictionary. (2006). Second College Edtion. Boston, MA: Houghton Mifflin.

American Pregnancy Association. (2011). http://www.americanpregnancy.org/pregnancycomplications/miscarriage.html (Retrieved October 2011)

American Psychological Association. (1999). Archival description of counseling psychology. *The Counseling Psychologist, 27*, 589–592.

American Psychological Association. (2007). Guidelines for psychological practice with girls and women. *American Psychologist, 62*, 949–979.

Anastasio, P.A., & Costa, D.M. (2004). Twice hurt: How newspaper coverage may reduce empathy and engender blame for female victims of crime. *Sex Roles, 51*, 535–542.

Andermann, L. (2010). Culture and the social construction of gender: Mapping the intersection with mental health. *International Review of Psychiatry, 22*, 501–512.

Andersen, B.L. et al. (1999). Women's sexual self-schema. *Journal of Personality and Social Psychology, 76*, 645–661.

Anderson, D., & Shapiro, D. (1996). Racial differences in access to high-paying jobs and the wage gap between Black and White women. *Industrial and Labor Relations Review, 49*, 273–286.

Anderson, D.A., & Hamilton, M. (2005). Gender role stereotyping of parents in children's picture books: The invisible father. *Sex Roles, 52*, 145–151.

Anderson, K.B. et al. (1997). Individual differences and attitudes toward rape: A meta-analytic review. *Personality and Social Psychology Bulletin, 23*, 295–315.

Anderson, K.L., & Umberson, D. (2001). Gendering violence: Masculinity and power in men's accounts of domestic violence. *Gender & Society, 15*, 358–380.

Angelone, D.J. et al. (2005). The influence of peer interactions on sexually oriented joke telling. *Sex Roles, 52*, 187–199.

Annis, N.M. et al. (2004). Body image and psychosocial differences among stable average weight, currently overweight and formerly overweight women: The role of stigmatizing experiences. *Body Image, 1*, 155–167.

Anonymous. (1991). Sexual harassment: A female counseling student's experience. *Journal of Counseling and Development, 69*, 502–506.

Anshultz, D.J., & Engels, R.C.M.E. (2010).The effects of playing with thin dolls on body image and food intake in young girls. *Sex Roles, 63*, 621–630.

Anthis, K.S. (2002). The role of sexist discrimination in adult women's identity development. *Sex Roles, 47*, 477–484.

APA. (2010). *Publication manual of the American Psychological Association* (6th ed.). Washington, DC: American Psychological Association.

Apfelbaum, E. (1999). Relations of domination and movements for liberation: An analysis of power between groups (abridged). Reprinted in *Feminism & Psychology, 9*, 267–272. (Originally published in 1979.)

Apparala, M.L. et al. (2003). Cross-national comparison of attitudes toward fathers' and mothers' participation in household tasks and childcare. *Sex Roles, 48*, 189–203.

Arata, C.M., & Burkhart, B.R. (1998). Coping appraisals and adjustment to nonstranger sexual assault. *Violence Against Women, 4*, 224–239.

Arber, S., & Ginn, J. (1994). Women and aging. *Reviews in Clinical Gerontology, 4*, 349–358.

Archer, J. (2000). Sex differences in aggression between heterosexual partners: A meta-analytic review. *Psychological Bulletin, 126*, 651–680.

Arons, J. (2008). *Lifetime losses: The career wage gap.* Washington, DC: Center for American Progress Action Fund. http://www.amercianprogressaction.org

Arthur, A.E. et al. (2009). An experimental test of the effects of gender constancy on sex typing. *Journal of Experimental Child Psychology, 104*, 417–446.

Askari, S.F. et al. (2010). Men want equality, but women don't expect it: Young adults' expectations for participation in household and child care chores. *Psychology of Women Quarterly, 34*, 243–252.

ASPS. (2011). Plastic surgey rebounds along with the economy. http://www.plasticsurgery.org/news-and-resources/press-release-archives/2011–press-release-archives/plastic-surgery-rebounds-along-with-recovering-economy.html (Retrieved October 2011).

Atchley, R.C. (1994). *Social forces and aging: An introduction to social gerontology* (7th ed.). Belmont, CA: Wadsworth.

Athey, T.R., & Hautaluoma, J.E. (1994). Effects of applicant overeducation, job status, and job gender stereotype on employment decisions. *Journal of Social Psychology, 134*, 439–452.

Aubeeluck, A., & Maguire, M. (2002). The Menstrual Joy Questionnaire items alone can positively prime reporting of menstrual attitudes and symptoms. *Psychology of Women Quarterly, 26*, 160–162.

Aubrey, J.S. (2004). Sex and punishment: An examination of sexual consequences and the sexual double standard in teen programming. *Sex Roles, 50*, 505–514.

Aubrey, J.S. (2006). Exposure to sexually objectifying media and body self-perceptions among college women: An examination of the selective exposure hypothesis and the role of moderating variables. *Sex Roles, 55*, 159–172.

Aubrey, J.S. (2010). Looking good versus feeling good: An investigation of media frames of health advice and their effects on women's body-related self-perceptions. *Sex Roles, 63*, 50–63.

Augustus-Horvath, C.L., & Tylka, T.L. (2011). The acceptance model of intuitive eating: A comparison of women in emerging adulthood, early adulthood, and middle adulthood. *Journal of Counseling Psychology, 58*, 110–125.

Aulakh, A.K., & Anand, S.S. (2007). Sex and gender subgroup analyses of randomized trials: The need to proceed with caution. *Women's Health Issues, 17*, 342–350.

Avakame, E.F. (1999). Females' labor force participation and rape: An empirical test of the backlash hypothesis. *Violence Against Women, 5*, 926–949.

Avis, N.E. (2003). Depression during the menopausal transition. *Psychology of Women Quarterly, 27*, 91–100.

Aylor, B., & Dainton, M. (2004). Biological sex and psychological gender as predictors of routine and strategic relational maintenance. *Sex Roles, 50*, 689–697.

Ayoola, A.B. et al. (2007). Reasons for unprotected intercourse in adult women. *Journal of Women's Health, 16*, 302–310.

Ayres, M.M. et al. (2009). Individual and situational factors related to young women's likelihood of confronting sexism in their everyday lives. *Sex Roles, 61*, 449–460.

Bailey, J.M. et al. (1993). Hereditable factors influence sexual orientation in women. *Archives in General Psychiatry, 50*, 217–223.

Bailey, J.M., & Pillard, R. (1991). A genetic study of male sexual orientation. *Archives of General Psychiatry, 48*, 1089–1096.

Bailey, W.T. (1991). Knowledge, attitude, and psychosocial development of young and old adults. *Educational Gerontology, 17*, 269–274.

Baird, C.L. (2008). The importance of community context for young women's occupational aspirations. *Sex Roles, 58*, 208–221.

Baker, P.L., & Carson, A. (1999). "I take care of my kids": Mothering practices of substance-abusing women. *Gender & Society, 13*, 347–363.

Baker, S.R. et al. (2005). "I felt as though I'd been in jail": Women's experiences of maternity care during labour, delivery and the immediate postpartum. *Feminism & Psychology, 15*, 315–342.

Baker-Sperry, L., & Grauerholz, L. (2003). The pervasiveness and persistence of the feminine beauty ideal in children's fairy tales. *Gender & Society, 17*, 711–726.

Balogh, D.W. et al. (2003). The effects of delayed report and motive for reporting on perceptions of sexual harassment. *Sex Roles, 48*, 337–348.

Barata, P.C. (2007). Abused women's perspectives on the criminal justice system's response to domestic violence. *Psychology of Women Quarterly, 31*, 202–215.

Barbee, E.L. (1992). African American women and depression: A review and critique of the literature. *Archives of Psychiatric Nursing, 6*, 257–265.

Barer, B.M. (1994). Men and women age differently. *International Journal of Aging and Human Development, 38*, 29–40.

Bargad, A., & Hyde, J.S. (1991). Women's studies: A study of feminist identity development in women. *Psychology of Women Quarterly, 15*, 181–201.

Bargh, J.A. et al. (1995). Attractiveness of the underling: An automatic power→sex association and its consequences for sexual harassment and aggression. *Journal of Personality and Social Psychology, 68*, 768–781.

Barker, K. (1993). Changing assumptions and contingent solutions: The costs and benefits of women working full- and part-time. *Sex Roles, 28*, 47–71.

Barkey, V. et al. (2009). Barriers and facilitators to participation in work among Canadian women living with HIV/AIDS. *Canadian Journal of Occupational Therapy/ Revue Canadienne D'Ergothrapie, 76*, 269–275.

Barlett, C.P., & Harris, R.J. (2008). The impact of body emphasizing video games on body image concerns in men and women. *Sex Roles, 59*, 586–601.

Barlow, M.R., & Becker-Blease, K. (in press). Caring for our students in course with poetentially threatening content. *Psychology of Women Quarterly.*

Barnett, R., & Rivers, C. (2004). *Same difference: How gender myths are hurting our relationships, our children, and our jobs.* New York: Basic.

Barnett, R.C. (2004). Preface: Women and work: Where are we going, where did we come from, and where are we going? *Journal of Social Issues, 60*(4), 667–674.

Barnett, R.C., & Hyde, J.S. (2001). Women, men, work, and family: An expansionist theory. *American Psychologist, 56*, 781–796.

Barreto, M. et al. (2010). How nice of us and how dumb of me: The effect of exposure to benevolent sexism on women's task and relational self-descriptions. *Sex Roles, 62*, 532–544.

Barrett, S.E. (1998). Contextual identity: A model for therapy and social change. *Women & Therapy, 21*, 51–64.

Bart, P.B., & O'Brien, P.H. (1997). Stopping rape: Effective avoidance strategies. In L. Richardson, V. Taylor, & N. Wittier (Eds.), *Feminist Frontiers IV* (pp. 410–420). New York: McGraw Hill.

Barth, R.J., & Kinder, B.N. (1988). A theoretical analysis of sex differences in same-sex friendships. *Sex Roles, 19*, 349–363.

Bartling, C.A., & Eisenman, R. (1993). Sexual harassment proclivities in men and women. *Bulletin of the Psychonomic Society, 31*, 189–192.

Baruch, G.K., & Barnett, R. (1986). Role quality, multiple role involvement, and psychological well-being in midlife women. *Journal of Personality and Social Psychology, 51*, 578–585.

Basow, S.A. et al. (2006). Gender patterns in college students' choices of their best and worst professors. *Psychology of Women Quarterly, 30*, 25–35.

Basow, S.A. et al. (2007). Perceptions of relational and physical aggression among college students: Effects of gender of perpetrator, target, and perceiver. *Psychology of Women Quarterly, 31*, 85–95.

Basow, S.A., & Kobrynowicz, D. (1993). What is she eating? The effects of meal size on impressions of a female eater. *Sex Roles, 28*, 335–344.

Basow, S.A., & Rubenfeld, K. (2003). "Troubles talk": Effects of gender and gender-typing. *Sex Roles, 48*, 183–187.

Batchelor, W.F. (1988). AIDS 1988: The science and the limits of science. *American Psychologist, 43*, 853–858.

Baumeister, R.F. (2000). Gender differences in erotic plasticity: The female sex drive as socially flexible and responsive. *Psychological Bulletin, 126*, 347–374.

Baumeister, R.F. et al. (2000). Nature, culture, and explanations for erotic plasticity: Reply to Andersen, Cyranowski, and Aarestad (2000) and Hyde and Durik (2000). *Psychological Bulletin, 126*, 385–389.

Bay-Cheng, L.Y. et al. (2002). Linking femininity, weight concern, and mental health among Latina, Black, and White women. *Psychology of Women Quarterly, 26*, 36–45.

Bay-Cheng, L.Y., & Zucker, N. (2007). Feminism between the sheets: Sexual attitudes among feminists, nonfeminists, and egalitarians. *Psychology of Women Quarterly, 31*, 157–163.

Beadnell, B. et al. (2000). HIV/STD risk factors for women with violent male partners. *Sex Roles, 42*, 661–689.

Becker, A.E. (2004). Television, disordered eating, and young women in Fiji: Negotiating body image and identity during rapid social change. *Culture, Medicine and Psychiatry, 28*, 533–559.

Becker, A.E. et al. (2005). Changes in prevalence of overweight and in body image among Fijian women between 1989 and 1998. *Obesity Research, 13*, 110–117.

Becker, D.V. et al. (2007). The confounded nature of angry men and happy women. *Journal of Personality and Social Psychology, 92*, 179–190.

Becker, J., & Breedlove, S.M. (1992). Introduction to behavioral endrocrinology. In J.B. Becker, S.M. Breedlove, & D. Crews (Eds.), *Behavioral endocrinology* (pp. 3–37). Cambridge, MA: MIT Press.

Becker, J.C. (2010). Why do women endorse hostile and benevolent sexism? The role of salient female subtypes and internalization of sexist contents. *Sex Roles, 62,* 453–467.

Becker, J.C., & Swim, J.K. (2011). Seeing the unseen: Attention to daily encounters with sexism as a way to reduce sexist beliefs. *Psychology of Women Quarterly, 35,* 227–242.

Beckman, L.J. (1994). Treatment needs of women with alcohol problems. *Alcohol Health and Research World, 18,* 206–211.

Beckman, L.J., & Harvey, S.M. (Eds.). (1998). *The new civil war: The psychology, culture, and politics of abortion.* Washington, DC: American Psychological Association.

Beere, C.A. (1990). *Gender roles: A handbook of tests and measures.* New York: Greenwood.

Beggs, J.M., & Doolittle, D.C. (1993). Perceptions now and then of occupational sex typing: A replication of Shinar's 1975 study. *Journal of Applied Social Psychology, 23,* 1435–1453.

Behm-Morawitz, E., & Mastro, D. (2009). The effects of the sexualization of female video game characters on gender stereotyping and female self-concept. *Sex Roles, 61,* 808–823.

Beier, M.E., & Ackerman, P.L. (2003). Determinants of health knowledge: An investigation of age, gender, abilities, personality, and interests. *Journal of Personality and Social Psychology, 84,* 439–447.

Bekker, M.H.J. (1996). Agoraphobia and gender: A review. *Clinical Psychology Review, 16,* 129–146.

Bellas, M.L. (1992). The effects of marital status and wives' employment on the salaries of faculty men: The (house) wife bonus. *Gender & Society, 6,* 609–622.

Bem, D.J. (2000). Exotic becomes erotic: Interpreting the biological correlates of sexual orientation. *Archives of Sexual Behavior, 29,* 531–548.

Bem, S.L. (1974). The measurement of psychological androgyny. *Journal of Consulting and Clinical Psychology, 42,* 155–162.

Bem, S.L. (1975). Sex-role adaptability: One consequence of psychological androgyny. *Journal of Personality and Social Psychology, 31,* 634–643.

Bem, S.L. (1977). On the utility of alternative procedures for assessing psychological androgyny. *Journal of Consulting and Clinical Psychology, 45,* 196–205.

Bem, S.L. (1981). Gender schema theory: A cognitive account of sex-typing. *Psychological Review, 88,* 354–364.

Bem, S.L. (1983). Gender schema theory and its implications for child development: Raising gender-aschematic children in a gender-schematic society. *Signs, 8,* 598–616.

Bem, S.L. (1989). Genital knowledge and gender constancy in preschool children. *Child Development, 60,* 649–662.

Bem, S.L. (1993). *The lenses of gender: Transforming the debate on sexual inequality.* New Haven, CT: Yale.

Ben-Ari, A., & Livni, T. (2006). Motherhood is not a given thing: Experiences and constructed meanings of biological and nonbiological lesbian mothers. *Sex Roles, 54,* 521–531.

Ben-Ari, A., & Weinberg-Kurnik, G. (2007). The dialectics between the personal and the interpersonal in the experiences of adoptive single mothers by choice. *Sex Roles, 56,* 823–833.

Beneke, T. (1992). *Men on rape: What they have to say about sexual violence.* New York: St. Martin's Press.

Benenson, J.E. et al. (1998). Gender differences in emotional closeness between preschool children and their mothers. *Sex Roles, 38,* 975–985.

Benin, M., & Keith, V.M. (1995). The social support of employed African American and Anglo mothers. *Journal of Family Issues, 16,* 275–297.

Benokraitis, N.V. (1997). Sex discrimination in the 21st century. In N.V. Benokraitis (Ed.), *Subtle sexism: Current practice and prospects for change* (pp. 5–33). Thousand Oaks, CA: Sage.

Berdahl, J.L. (2007). The sexual harassment of uppity women. *Journal of Applied Psychology, 92,* 425–437.

Berdahl, J.L., & Moore, C. (2006). Workplace harassment: Double jeopardy for minority women. *Journal of Applied Psychology, 91,* 426–436.

Beren, S.E. et al. (1997). Body dissatisfaction among lesbian college students: The conflict of straddling mainstream and lesbian cultures. *Psychology of Women Quarterly, 21,* 431–445.

Berenbaum, S.A., & Hines, M. (1992). Early androgens are related to childhood sex-typed toy preferences. *Psychological Science, 3,* 203–206.

Bergen, R.K. (1995). Surviving wife rape: How women define and cope with the violence. *Violence Against Women, 1,* 117–138.

Berger, J., & Webster, M. (2006). Expectations, status, and behavior. In P.J. Burke (Ed.), *Contemporary social psychological theory* (pp. 268–300). Stanford, CA: Stanford University Press.

Bergeron, S.M., & Senn, C.Y. (1998). Body image and sociocultural norms: A comparison of heterosexual and lesbian women. *Psychology of Women Quarterly, 22*, 385–401.

Berkowitz, A.D. (1994). A model acquaintance rape prevention program for men. In A. Berkowitz (Ed.), *Men and rape: Theory, research, and prevention programs in higher education* (pp. 35–42). San Francisco, CA: Jossey-Bass.

Bernas, K.H., & Major, D.A. (2000). Contributors to stress resistance: Testing a model of women's work-family conflict. *Psychology of Women Quarterly, 24*, 170–178.

Bernhard, L.A. (2000). Physical and sexual violence experienced by lesbian and heterosexual women. *Violence Against Women, 6*, 68–79.

Berns, N. (2001). Degendering the problem and gendering the blame: Political discourse on women and violence. *Gender & Society, 15*, 262–281.

Bernstein, A.G. (2005). Gendered characteristics of political engagement in college students. *Sex Roles, 52*, 299–310.

Bessenoff, G.R. (2006). Can the media affect us? Social comparison, self-discrepancy, and the thin ideal. *Psychology of Women Quarterly, 30*, 239–251.

Bessenoff, G.R., & Del Priore, R.E. (2007). Women, weight, and age: Social comparison to magazine images across the lifespan. *Sex Roles, 56*, 215–222.

Bessenoff, G.R., & Snow, D. (2006). Absorbing society's influence: Body image self-discrepancy and internalized shame. *Sex Roles, 54*, 727–731.

Betrus, P.A., et al. (1995). Women and somatization: Unrecognized depression. *Health Care for Women International, 16*, 287–297.

Bettencourt, B.A., & Kernahan, C. (1997). A meta-analysis of aggression in the presence of violent cues: Effects of gender differences and aversive provocation. *Aggressive Behavior, 23*, 447–456.

Bettencourt, B.A., & Miller, N. (1996). Gender differences in aggression as a function of provocation: A meta-analysis. *Psychological Bulletin, 119*, 422–447.

Betz, N.E. (1993). Women's career development. In F.L. Denmark & M.A. Paludi (Eds.), *Psychology of women: A handbook of issues and theories* (pp. 627–684). Westport, CT: Greenwood Press.

Betz, N.E. et al. (1994). Gender differences in the accuracy of self-reported weight. *Sex Roles, 30*, 543–552.

Betz, N.E., & Fitzgerald, L.F. (1987). *The career psychology of women*. Orlando, FL: Academic Press.

Bianchi, S. (2000). Maternal employment and time with children: Dramatic change and surprising continuity. *Demography, 37*, 401–414.

Bianchi, S.M. (2000). Maternal employment and time with children: Dramatic change or surprising continuity? *Demography, 37*, 401–414.

Bianchi, S.M. et al. (2000). Is anyone doing the housework? Trends in the gender division of household labor. *Social Forces, 79*, 191–228.

Bianchi, S.M., & Milkie, M.A. (2010). Work and family research in the first decade of the 21st century. *Journal of Marriage and Family, 72*(3), 705–725.

Biblarz, T.J., & Stacey, J. (2010). How does the gender of parents matter? *Journal of Marriage and the Family, 72*, 3–22.

Biesanz, J.C. et al. (2001). When accuracy-motivated perceivers fail: Limited attentional resources and the reemerging self-fulfilling prophecy. *Personality and Social Psychology Bulletin, 27*, 621–629.

Bird, C.E. (1996). An analysis of gender differences in income among dentists, physicians, and veterinarians in 1987. *Research in the Sociology of Health Care, 13*, 31–61.

Bishop, K.M., & Wahlsten, D. (1997). Sex differences in the human corpus callosum: Myth or reality. *Neuroscience and Biobehavioral Reviews, 12*, 581–601.

Black, K.A., & Gold, D.J. (2003). Men's and women's reactions to hypothetical sexual advances: The role of initiator socioeconomic status and level of coercion. *Sex Roles, 49*, 173–178.

Blair-Loy, M. (2003). *Competing devotions: Career and family among women executives*. Cambridge, MA: Harvard.

Blaisure, K.R., & Allen, K.R. (1995). Feminists and the ideology and practice of marital equality. *Journal of Marriage and the Family, 57*, 5–19.

Blakemore, J.E. (1998). The influence of gender and parental attitudes on preschool children's interest in babies: Observations in natural settings. *Sex Roles, 38*, 73–94.

Blakemore, J.E. (2003). Children's beliefs about violating gender norms: Boys shouldn't look like girls, and girls shouldn't act like boys. *Sex Roles, 48*, 411–419.

Blakemore, J.E., & Centers, R.E. (2005). Characteristics of boys' and girls' toys. *Sex Roles, 53*, 619–633.

Blau, F.D. et al. (1998). Continuing progress? Trends in occupational segregation in the United States over the 1970s and 1980s. *Feminist Economics, 4*(3), 29–71.

Blau, F.D., & Kahn, L. (1996). Wage structure and gender earnings differentials: An international comparison. *Economica, 63,* S29–S62.

Blau, F.D., & Kahn, L. (1997). Swimming upstream: Trends in the gender wage differential in the 1980s. *Journal of Labor Economics, 15,* 1–42.

Blazina, C., & Watkins, C.E. (2000). Separation/individuation: Parental attachment, and male gender role conflict: Attitudes toward the feminine and fragile masculine self. *Psychology of Men and Masculinity, 1,* 126–132.

Bleier, R. (1984). *Science and gender: A critique of biology and its theories on women.* New York: Pergamon.

Bleleck, S. (2008). *1.5 million homeschooled students in the United States in 2007.* Issue Brief NCEC 2009–030. Retrieved from http://nces.ed.gov/pubs2009/2009030.pdf, July 2011).

Block, C.R., & Block, R.L. (1984). Crime definition, crime measurement, and victim surveys. *Journal of Social Issues, 40*(1), 137–160.

Blood, P. et al. (1995). Understanding and fighting sexism: A call to men. In M.L. Andersen & P.H. Collins (Eds.), *Race, class, and gender: An anthology* (2nd ed) (pp. 154–161). Belmont, CA: Wadsworth.

Blow, A.J. et al. (2008). The role of the therapist in therapeutic change: Does therapist gender matter? *Journal of Feminist Family Therapy: An International Forum, 20,* 66–86.

Bock, B.C., & Kanarek, R.B. (1995). Women and men are what they eat: The effects of gender and reported meal size on perceived characteristics. *Sex Roles, 33,* 109–119.

Bock, J.D. (2000). Doing the right thing? Single mothers by choice and the struggle for legitimacy. *Gender & Society, 14,* 62–86.

Boeckmann, R.J., & Feather, N.T. (2007). Gender, discrimination beliefs, group-based guilt, and response to affirmative action for Australian women. *Psychology of Women Quarterly, 31,* 290–304.

Boeringer, S.B. (1999). Associations of rape-supportive attitudes with fraternal and athletic participation. *Violence Against Women, 5,* 81–90.

Bohmer, C., & Parrot, A. (1993). *Sexual assault on campus: The problem and the solution.* New York: Lexington.

Bohner, G. et al. (2010). How sexy are sexist men? Women's perception of male response profiles in the Ambivalent Sexism Inventory. *Sex Roles, 62,* 568–582.

Bologna, M.J. et al. (1987, July). *Violence in gay male and lesbian relationships: Implications for practitioners and policy makers.* Paper presented at the Third National Conference for Family Violence Researchers, Durham, NH.

Bonate, D.L., & Jessell, J.C. (1996). The effects of educational intervention on perceptions of sexual harassment. *Sex Roles, 35,* 751–764.

Bond, J.T. et al. (2003). *Highlights of the 2002 national study on the changing workforce* (No. 3). New York: Families and Work Institute.

Bond, L.A. et al. (2008). Movers and shakers: How and why women become and remain engaged in community leadership. *Psychology of Women Quarterly, 32,* 48–64.

Bondurant, B. (2001). University women's acknowledgement of rape. *Violence Against Women, 7,* 294–314.

Bondurant, B., & Donat, P.L.N. (1999). Perceptions of women's sexual interest and acquaintance rape: The role of sexual overperception and affective attitudes. *Psychology of Women Quarterly, 23,* 691–705.

Boney-McCoy, S., & Finkelhor, D. (1995). Psychosocial sequelae of violence victimization in a national youth sample. *Journal of Consulting and Clinical Psychology, 63,* 726–736.

Bookman, A., & Morgen, S. (Eds.). (1988). *Women and the politics of empowerment.* Philadelphia, PA: Temple.

Bookwala, J., & Boyar, J. (2008). Gender, excessive body weight, and psychological well-being in adulthood. *Psychology of Women Quarterly, 32,* 188–195.

Boring, E.G. (1951). The woman problem. *American Psychologist, 6,* 679–682.

Bosacki, S.L., & Moore, C. (2004). Preschoolers' understanding of simple and complex emotions: Links with gender and language. *Sex Roles, 50,* 659–675.

Bosak, J., & Sczesny, S. (2008). Am I the right candidate? Self-ascribed fit of women and men to a leadership position. *Sex Roles, 58,* 682–688.

Bosscher, R.J. et al. (1995). Physical performance and physical self-efficacy in the elderly: A pilot study. *Journal of Aging and Health, 7,* 459–475.

Bosson, J.K. et al. (2008). The affective consequences of minimizing women's body image concerns. *Psychology of Women Quarterly, 32,* 257–266.

Bosson, J.K. et al. (2010). The emotional impact of ambivalent sexism: Forecasts versus real experiences. *Sex Roles, 62,* 520–531.

Botta, R.A. (2003). For your health? The relationship between magazine reading and adolescents' body image and eating disturbances. *Sex Roles, 48,* 389–399.

Boushey, H. (2005, Nov.). *Are women opting out? Debunking the myth.* Washington, DC: Center for

Economic and Policy Research. http://www.cepr. net (Retrieved December 2005)

Bowen, D.J. et al. (2010). Gender diverse recruitment to research projects. In J.C. Chrisler & D.R. McCreary (Eds.), *Handbook of gender research in psychology* (Vol. 1, pp. 179–190). New York: Springer.

Bowker, A. et al. (2003). Sports participation and self-esteem: Variations as a function of gender and gender role orientation. *Sex Roles, 49,* 47–58.

Bowleg, L. et al. (2004). "The ball was always in his court": An exploratory analysis of relationship scripts, sexual scripts, and condom use among African American women. *Psychology of Women Quarterly, 28,* 70–82.

Bowles, H.R. et al. (2007). Social incentives for gender differences in the propensity to initiate negotiations: Sometimes it does hurt to ask. *Organizational Behavior and Human Decision Processes, 103,* 84–103.

Boyd, J.A. (1990). Ethnic and cultural diversity: Keys to power. In L.S. Brown & M.P.P. Root (Eds.), *Diversity and complexity in feminist therapy* (pp. 151–167). New York: Harrington Park Press.

Boysen, G.A., & Vogel, D.L. (2007). Biased assimilation and attitude polarization in response to learning about biological explanations of homosexuality. *Sex Roles, 56,* 755–762.

Brabant, S., & Mooney, L.A. (1997). Sex role stereotyping in the Sunday comics: A twenty year update. *Sex Roles, 37,* 269–281.

Bradley, R.G., & Davino, K.M. (2002). Women's perceptions of the prison environment: When prison is "the safest place I have ever been." *Psychology of Women Quarterly, 26,* 351–359.

Bragger, J.D. et al. (2002). The effects of the structured interview on reducing biases against pregnant job applicants. *Sex Roles, 46,* 215–226.

Brecklin, L.R. (2008). Evaluation outcomes of self-defense training for women: A review. *Aggression and Violent Behavior, 13,* 60–76.

Brecklin, L.R., & Ullman, S.E. (2004). Correlates of post-assault self-defense/assertiveness training participation for sexual assault survivors. *Psychology of Women Quarterly, 28,* 147–158.

Bren, L. (2000, July-Aug.). Saline implants stay on market as experts warn about risks. *FDA Consumer Magazine,* http://www.fda.gov/fdac/features/2000/400_implant.html (Retrieved November 2005).

Brenner, C. (1992). Survivor's story: Eight bullets. In G.M. Herek & K.T. Berrill (Eds.), *Hate crimes: Confronting violence against lesbian and gay men* (pp. 11–15). Newbury Park, CA: Sage.

Breserman, B.C. et al. (1999). Obesity and powerlessness. In K.P. Johnson & S.J. Lennon (Eds.), *Appearance and power* (pp. 153–172). New York: Berg.

Bresnahan, M.J. et al. (2001). Changing gender roles in prime-time commercials in Malaysia, Japan, Taiwan, and the United States. *Sex Roles, 45,* 117–131.

Brett, J.F. et al. (2005). Effective delivery of workplace discipline: Do women have to be more participatory than men? *Group and Organization Management, 30,* 487–513.

Bridges, J. (1993). Pink or blue: Gender-stereotypic perceptions of infants as conveyed by birth congratulations cards. *Psychology of Women Quarterly, 17,* 193–205.

Bridges, J.S. et al. (2002). Trait judgments of stay-at-home and employed parents: A function of social role and/or shifting standards? *Psychology of Women Quarterly, 26,* 140–150.

Bridges, J.S., & Etaugh, C. (1995). College students' perceptions of mothers: Effects of maternal employment-childrearing pattern and motive for employment. *Sex Roles, 32,* 735–751.

Briere, J. et al. (1985). Sexuality and rape-supportive beliefs. *International Journal of Women's Studies, 8,* 398–403.

Brinkman, B.G., & Rickard, K.M. (2009). College students' descriptions of everyday gender prejudice. *Sex Roles, 61,* 461–475.

Brod, H. (Ed.). (1987a). *The making of masculinities: The new men's studies.* Boston, MA: Unwin.

Brod, H. (1987b). The case for men's studies. In H. Brod (Ed.), *The making of masculinities: The new men's studies* (pp. 39–62). Boston, MA: Unwin.

Broderick, P.C., & Korteland, C. (2002). Coping style and depression in early adolescence: Relationships to gender, gender role, and implicit beliefs. *Sex Roles, 46,* 201–213.

Bromberger, J.T., & Matthews, K.A. (1994). Employment status and depressive symptoms in middle-aged women: A longitudinal investigation. *American Journal of Public Health, 84,* 202–206.

Brooks-Gunn, J., & Ruble, D.N. (1982). The development of menstrual-related behaviors during early adolescence. *Child Development, 53,* 1567–1577.

Broverman, I.K. et al. (1970). Sex-role stereotypes and clinical judgments of mental health. *Journal of Consulting and Clinical Psychology, 34,* 1–7.

Brown, A.L., & Testa, M. (2008). Social influences on judgments of rape victims: The role of the negative and positive social reactions of others. *Sex Roles, 58,* 490–500.

Brown, C.S. et al. (2010). An experimental study of the correlates and consequences of perceiving oneself to be the target of gender discrimination. *Journal of Experimental Child Psychology, 107,* 100–117.

Brown, C.S., & Leaper, C. (2010). Latina and European American girls' experiences with academic sexism and their self-concepts in mathematics and science during adolescence. *Sex Roles, 63,* 860–870.

Brown, C.S. et al. (2011). Ethnicity and gender in late childhood and early adolescence: Group identity and awareness of bias. *Developmental Psychology, 47,* 463–471.

Brown, E.R., & Dickman, A.B. (2010). What will I be? Exploring gender differences in near and distant possible selves. *Sex Roles, 63,* 568–579.

Brown, J.A. et al. (1990). Sex-role identity and sex-role ideology in college women with bulimic behavior. *International Journal of Eating Disorders, 9,* 571–575.

Brown, L.M. (1998). *Raising their voices: The politics of girls' anger.* Cambridge, MA: Harvard University Press.

Brown, L.M., & Gilligan, C. (1993). Meeting at the crossroads: Women's psychology and girls' development. *Feminism & Psychology, 3,* 11–35.

Brown, L.S. (1987). Lesbians, weight, and eating: New analyses and perspectives. In Boston Lesbian Psychologies Collective (Eds.), *Lesbian psychologies* (pp. 294–309). Urbana, IL: University of Illinois Press.

Brown, L.S. (1992). A feminist critique of the personality disorders. In L.S. Brown & M. Ballou (Eds.), *Personality and psychopathology: Feminist reappraisals* (pp. 206–228). New York: Guilford.

Brown, L.S. (1994a). *Subversive dialogues: Theory in feminist therapy.* New York: Basic.

Brown, L.S. (1994b). Boundaries in feminist therapy: A conceptual formulation. *Women & Therapy, 15,* 29–38.

Brown, L.S., & Ballou, M. (Eds.). (1992). *Personality and psychopathology: Feminist reappraisals.* New York: Guilford.

Brown, L.S., & Burman, E. (Eds.). (1997). Editor's introduction: The delayed memory debate: Why feminist voices matter. *Feminism & Psychology, 7,* 7–16.

Brown, R.P., & Josephs, R.A. (1999). A burden of proof: Stereotype relevance and gender differences in math performance. *Journal of Personality and Social Psychology, 76,* 246–257.

Brown, T.A., & Cash, T.F. (1990). The phenomenon of nonclinical panic: Parameters of panic, fear, and avoidance. *Journal of Anxiety Disorders, 4,* 15–29.

Brown, V., & Weissman, G. (1993). Women and men injection drug users: An updated look at gender differences and risk factors. In B.S. Brown & G.M. Beschner (Eds.), *Handbook of risk of AIDS: Injection drug users and sexual partners* (pp. 173–194). Westport, CT: Greenwood Press.

Browne, A. (1987). *When battered women kill.* New York: Macmillan/Free Press.

Browne, A. (1993). Violence against women by male partners: Prevalence, outcomes, and policy implications. *American Psychologist, 48,* 1077–1087.

Browne, A. et al. (1999). The impact of recent partner violence on poor women's capacity to maintain work. *Violence Against Women, 5,* 393–426.

Browne, A., & Finkelhor, D. (1986). The impact of child sexual abuse: A review of the research. *Psychological Bulletin, 99,* 66–77.

Browne, C.V. (1995). Empowerment in social work practice with older women. *Social Work, 40,* 358–364.

Brownmiller, S. (1975). *Against our will: Men, women and rape.* New York: Simon & Schuster.

Brozovic, M. (1989). With women in mind. *British Medical Journal, 299,* 689.

Bryant-Davis, T. et al. (2009). From the margins to the center: Ethnic minority women and the mental health effects of sexual assault. *Trauma, Violence, & Abuse, 10,* 330–357.

Bryer, J.B. et al. (1987). Childhood sexual and physical abuse as factors in adult psychiatric illness. *American Journal of Psychiatry, 144,* 1426–1430.

Bub, K.L., & McCartney, K. (2004). On childcare as a support for maternal employment wages and hours. *Journal of Social Issues, 60*(4), 819–834.

Buchanan, C.M. et al. (1992). Are adolescents the victims of raging hormones? Evidence for activational effects of hormones on moods and behavior at adolescence. *Psychological Bulletin, 111,* 62–107.

Buchanan, N.T., & Fitzgerald, L.F. (2008). Effects of racial and sexual harassment on work and the psychological well-being of African American women. *Journal of Occupational Health Psychology, 13,* 137–151.

Buchanan, T.S. et al. (2008). Testing a culture-specific extension of objectification theory regarding African American women's body image. *The Counseling Psychologist, 36,* 699–718.

Buddie, A.M., & Miller, A.G. (2001). Beyond rape myths: A more complex view of perceptions of rape victims. *Sex Roles, 45,* 139–160.

Budig, M.J., & England, P. (2001). The wage penalty for motherhood. *American Sociological Review, 66,* 204–225.

Bufkin, J., & Eschholz, S. (2000). Images of sex and rape: A content analysis of popular film. *Violence Against Women, 6,* 1317–1344.

Bulger, C.A. (2001). Union resources and union tolerance as moderators of relationships with sexual harassment. *Sex Roles, 45,* 723–741.

Bullock, H.E., & Waugh, I.M. (2004). Caregiving around the clock: How women in nursing manage career and family demands. *Journal of Social Issues, 60*(4), 767–786.

Burckle, M.A. et al. (1999). Forms of competitive attitude and achievement orientation in relation to disordered eating. *Sex Roles, 40,* 853–870.

Bureau of Justice Statistics. (1997). *Violence-related injuries treated in hospital emergency departments.* Washington, DC: US Department of Justice. http://www.ojp.usdoj.gov/bjs/abstract/vrithed.htm. (Retrieved November 2005). Publ no. NCJ-156921.

Burgess, M.C.R. et al. (2007). Sex, lies, and video games: The portrayal of male and female characters on video game covers. *Sex Roles, 57,* 419–433.

Burian, B.K. et al. (1998). Group gender composition effects on judgments of sexual harassment. *Psychology of Women Quarterly, 22,* 465–480.

Burke, H.L., & Yeo, R.A. (1994). Systematic variations in callosal morphology: The effects of age, gender, hand preference, and anatomic asymmetry. *Neuropsychology, 8,* 563–571.

Burleson, B.R. et al. (1996). Men's and women's evaluations of communication skills in personal relationships: When sex differences make a difference—and when they don't. *Journal of Social and Personal Relationships, 13,* 201–224.

Burns, A., & Leonard, R. (2005). Chapters of our lives: Life narratives of midlife and older Australian women. *Sex Roles, 52,* 269–277.

Burns, D. (2000). Feminism, psychology and social policy: Constructing political boundaries at the grassroots. *Feminism & Psychology, 10,* 367–380.

Burns, M. (2004). Eating like an ox: Femininity and dualistic constructions of bulimia and anorexia. *Feminism & Psychology, 14,* 269–295.

Buss, D.M. (1989). Sex differences in human mate preferences: Evolutionary hypotheses tested in 37 cultures. *Behavioral and Brain Sciences, 12,* 1–49.

Bussey, K., & Bandura, A. (1999). Social cognitive theory of gender development and differentiation. *Psychological Review, 106,* 676–713.

Bussey, K., & Bandura, A. (2004). Social cognitive theory of gender development and functioning. In A. Eagly et al., *The psychology of gender* (2nd ed.) (pp. 92–119). New York: Guilford.

Butler, B.A., & Wing, R.R. (1995). Women with diabetes: A lifestyle perspective focusing on eating disorders, pregnancy, and weight control. In A.L. Stanton & S.J. Gallant (Eds.), *The psychology of women's health: Progress and challenges in research and application* (pp. 85–116). Washington, DC: American Psychological Association.

Butler, J. (1990). *Gender trouble: Feminism and the subversion of identity.* New York: Routledge.

Byrnes, J.P. et al. (1999). Gender differences in risk taking: A meta-analysis. *Psychological Bulletin, 125,* 367–383.

Cabrera, S.F. et al. (2009). The evolving manager stereotype: The effects of industry gender typing on performance expectations for leaders and their teams. *Psychology of Women Quarterly, 33,* 419–428.

Cachelin, F.M. et al. (2000). Disordered eating, acculturation, and treatment-seeking in a community sample of Hispanic, Asian, Black, and White women. *Psychology of Women Quarterly, 24,* 244–253.

Cacioppo, J.T., & Berntson, G.G. (1992). Social psychological contributions to the decade of the brain: Doctrine of multilevel analysis. *American Psychologist, 47,* 1019–1028.

Caetano, R. (1994). Drinking and alcohol-related problems among minority women. *Alcohol Health and Research World, 18,* 333–341.

Cahill, B., & Adams, E. (1997). An exploratory study of early childhood teachers' attitudes toward gender roles. *Sex Roles, 36,* 517–529.

Caldwell, M.A., & Peplau, L.A. (1982). Sex differences in same-sex friendship. *Sex Roles, 8,* 721–732.

Calogero, R.M. (2004). A test of objectification theory: The effect of the male gaze on appearance concerns in college women. *Psychology of Women Quarterly, 28,* 16–21.

Calogero, R.M. et al. (2005). The role of self-objectification in the experience of women with eating disorders. *Sex Roles, 52,* 43–50.

Calogero, R.M. et al. (2007). The impact of Western ideals on the lives of women and men: A sociocultural perspective. In V. Swami & A. Furnham (Eds.), *Body beautiful: Evolutionary and sociocultural perspectives* (pp. 259–298). New York: Palgrave Mcmillan.

Calogero, R.M. et al. (2009). Complimentary weightism: The potential costs of appearance-related commentary for women's self-objectification. *Psychology of Women Quarterly, 33,* 120–132.

Calogero, R.M. et al. (2010). Objectification theory predicts college women's attitudes toward cosmetic surgery. *Sex Roles, 63*, 32–41.

Calogero, R.M. et al. (2011). *Self-objectification in women: Causes, consequences, and counteractions.* Washington, DC: American Psychological Association.

Calogero, R.M., & Jost, J.T. (2011). Self-subjugation among women: Exposure to sexist ideology, self-objectification, and the protective function of the need to avoid closure. *Journal of Personality and Social Psychology, 100*, 211–228.

Calogero, R.M., & Pina, A. (2011). Body guilt: Preliminary evidence for a further subjective experience of self-objectification. *Psychology of Women Quarterly, 35*, 428–440.

Calogero, R.M., & Thompson, J.K. (2009). Sexual self-esteem in American and British college women: Relations with self-objectification and eating problems. *Sex Roles, 60*, 160–173.

Cambron, M.J. et al. (2009). Explaining gender differences in depression: An interpersonal contingent self-esteem perspective. *Sex Roles, 61*, 751–761.

Cammaert, L.P., & Larsen, C.C. (1988). In M.A. Dutton-Douglas & L.E. Walker (Eds.), *Feminist psychotherapies: Integration of therapeutic and feminist systems* (pp. 12–36). Norwood, NJ: Ablex.

Campbell, A. (2006). Sex differences in direct aggression: What are the psychological mediators? *Aggression and Violent Behavior, 11*, 237–264.

Campbell, D.W., & Eaton, W.O. (1999). Sex differences in the activity level of infants. *Infant and Child Development, 8*, 1–17.

Campbell, J.C. et al. (1994). Relationship status of battered women over time. *Journal of Family Violence, 9*, 99–111.

Campbell, J.C., & Soeken, K.L. (1999). Forced sex and intimate partner violence: Effects on women's risk and women's health. *Violence Against Women, 5*, 1017–1035.

Campbell, K.T., & Evans, C. (1993, November). *Gender issues and the math/science curricula: Effects on females.* Paper presented at the annual meeting of the Mid-South Educational Research Association, New Orleans, LA.

Campbell, R. et al. (2008). The co-occurrence of childhood sexual abuse, adult sexual assault, intimate partner violence, and sexual harassment: A meditational model of posttraumatic stress disorder and physical health outcomes. *Journal of Consulting and Clinical Psychology, 76*, 194–207.

Campbell, R. et al. (2009). An ecological model of the impact of sexual assault on women's mental health. *Trauma, Violence, & Abuse, 10*, 225–246.

Campbell, R., & Raja, S. (2005). The sexual assault and secondary victimization of female veterans: Help-seeking experiences with military and civilian social systems. *Psychology of Women Quarterly, 29*, 97–106.

Canetto, S.S. et al. (1995). Typical and optimal aging in women and men: Is there a double standard? *International Journal of Aging and Human Development, 40*, 1–21.

Cannings, K. (1991). An interdisciplinary approach to analyzing the managerial gender gap. *Human Relations, 44*, 679–695.

Caplan, P.J. (1993). *Lifting a ton of feathers: A woman's guide for surviving in the academic world.* Toronto, ON: University of Toronto Press.

Caplan, P.J. (1995). *They say you're crazy: How the world's most powerful psychiatrists decide who's normal.* Reading, MA: Addison-Wesley.

Caplan, P.J., & Gans, M. (1991). Is there empirical evidence for the category of "self-defeating personality disorder"? *Feminism & Psychology, 1*, 263–278.

Caputi, J. (1993). The sexual politics of murder. In P.B. Bart & E.G. Moran (Eds.), *Violence against women: The bloody footprints* (pp. 5–25). Newbury Park, CA: Sage.

Carbonell, J.L., & Castro, Y. (2008). The impact of a leader model on high dominant women's self-selection for leadership. *Sex Roles, 58*, 776–783.

Carlson, D.S., & Kacmar, K.M. (2000). Work-family conflict in the organization: Do life role values make a difference? *Journal of Management, 26*, 1031–1054.

Carnevale, A.P. et al. (2009). *What's it worth: The economic value of college majors.* Washington, DC: Georgetown University Center on Education and the Workforce.

Carpenter, C. (2012). Meta-analyses of sex differences in responses to sexual versus emotional infidelity: Men and women are more similar than different. *Psychology of Women Quarterly, 36*, 25–37.

Carpenter, S., & Johnson, L.E. (2001). Women derive collective self-esteem from their feminist identity. *Psychology of Women Quarterly, 25*, 254–257.

Carroll, M.P. (1998). But fingerprints don't lie, eh? Prevailing gender ideologies and scientific knowledge. *Psychology of Women Quarterly, 22*, 739–749.

Case, K.A. (2007). Raising male privilege awareness and reducing sexism: A evaluation of diversity courses. *Psychology of Women Quarterly, 31*, 426–435.

Casey, M.B. (1996). Understanding individual differences in spatial ability within females: A nature/nurture interactionist framework. *Developmental Review, 16*, 241–260.

Casey, M.B. et al. (1997). Mediators of gender differences in mathematics college entrance test scores: A comparison of spatial skills with internalized beliefs and anxieties. *Developmental Psychology, 33*, 669–680.

Cash, T.F., & Henry, P.E. (1995). Women's body images: The results of a national survey in the U.S.A. *Sex Roles, 33*, 19–28.

Cassell, J., & Jenkins, H. (Eds.). (1998). *From Barbie to Mortal Kombat: Gender and computer games.* Cambridge, MA: MIT Press.

Castaneda, D.M., & Collins, B.E. (1998). The effects of gender, ethnicity, and a close relationship theme on perceptions of persons introducing a condom. *Sex Roles, 39*, 369–390.

Cataldi, S. (1995). Reflections on "male bashing." *National Women's Studies Association Journal, 7*, 76–85.

Catanzarite, L. (2003). Race-gender composition and occupational pay degradation. *Social Problems, 50*, 14–37.

Cavender, G. et al. (1999). The construction of gender in reality crime TV. *Gender & Society, 13*, 643–663.

CDC. (2004, Dec. 2). Almost half of Americans use at least one prescription drug, annual report on nation's health shows. Centers for Disease Control and Prevention's Statistics Press Office. http://www.cdc.gov/media/pressrel/r041202.htm

CDC. (2005). Centers for Disease Control and Prevention: *Women's reproductive health: Hysterectomy fact sheet.* http://www.cdc.gov/reproductivehealth/WomensRH/FS_Hysterectomy.htm (Retrieved November 2005).

CDC. (2010a, January). Women and heart disease fact sheet. http://www.cdc.gov/dhdsp/data_statistics/fact_sheets/docs/fs_women_heart.pdf (Retrieved October 2011).

CDC. (2010b, December). Summary health statistics for U.S. adults: National Health Interview Survey, 2009. Centers for Disease Control and Prevention. http://www.cdc.gov/nchs/data/series/sr_10/sr10_249.pdf

CDC. (2011a). Centers for Disease Control. www.cdc.gov

CDC. (2011b, August). Estimates of new HIV infections in the United States, 2006–2009. http://cdc.gov/nchhstp/newsroom/docs/HIV-Infections-2006–2009.pdf (Retrieved October 2011).

Ceci, S.J. et al. (2009). Women's underrepresentation in science: Sociocultural and biological considerations. *Psychological Bulletin, 135*, 218–261.

Chaiken, S. (1979). Communicator physical attractiveness and persuasion. *Journal of Personality and Social Psychology, 37*, 1387–1397.

Chambless, D.L. et al. (2002). Marital interaction of agoraphobic women: A controlled, behavioral observation study. *Journal of Abnormal Psychology, 111*, 502–512.

Chan, D.K. et al. (1999). Sexual harassment: A preliminary analysis of its effects on Hong Kong Chinese women in the workplace and academia. *Psychology of Women Quarterly, 23*, 661–672.

Chan, D.K-S. et al. (2008). Examining the job-related, psychological, and physical outcomes of workplace sexual harassment: A meta-analytic review. *Psychology of Women Quarterly, 32*, 362–376.

Chandra, P.S., & Satyanarayana, V.A. (2010). Gender disadvantage and common mental disorders in women. *International Review of Psychiatry, 22*, 513–524.

Chapleau, K.M. et al. (2007). How ambivalent sexism toward women and men supports rape myth acceptance. *Sex Roles, 57*, 131–136.

Charney, D.A., & Russell, R.C. (1994). An overview of sexual harassment. *American Journal of Psychiatry, 151*, 10–17.

Chatham-Carpenter, A., & DeFrancisco, V. (1998). Women construct self-esteem in their own terms: A feminist qualitative study. *Feminism & Psychology, 8*, 467–489.

Chen, F.F., & Russo, N.F. (2010). Measurement invariance and the role of body consciousness in depressive symptoms. *Psychology of Women Quarterly, 34*, 405–417.

Cherney, I.D., & London, K. (2006). Gender-linked differences in the toys, television shows, computer games, and outdoor activities of 5- to 13-year-old children. *Sex Roles, 54*, 717–726.

Cheryan, S. et al. (2009). Ambient belonging: How stereotypical cues impact gender participation in computer science. *Journal of Personality and Social Psychology, 97*, 1045–1060.

Chester, A., & Bretherton, D. (2001). What makes feminist counseling feminist? *Feminism & Psychology, 11*, 527–545.

Chester, N.L., & Grossman, H.Y. (1990). Introduction: Learning about women and their work through their own accounts. In H.Y. Grossman & M.L. Chester (Eds.), *The experience and meaning of work in women's lives* (pp. 1–9). Hillsdale, NJ: Lawrence Erlbaum.

Chick, K. et al. (2003). The impact of child care on gender role development and gender stereotypes. *Early Childhood Education Journal, 29*, 149–154.

Chisholm, J., & Greene, B. (2008). Women of color: Perspectives on "multiple identities" in psychological theory, research, and practice. In F.L. Denmark & M.A. Paludi (Eds.), *Psychology of women: A handbook of issues and theories* (2ⁿᵈ ed). (pp. 40–69). Westport, CT: Praeger.

Chodorow, N. (1978). *The reproduction of mothering.* Berkeley, CA: University of California Press.

Choi, P.Y.L. (2001). Genes and gender roles: Why is the nature argument so appealing? *Psychology, Evolution, and Gender, 3*, 279–285.

Choi, P.Y.L., & Bird, S. (2003). Feminism and marriage: To be or not to be Mrs. B. *Feminism & Psychology, 13*, 448–453.

Choice, P., & Lamke, L.K. (1997). A conceptual approach to understanding abused women's stay/ leave decisions. *Journal of Family Issues, 18*, 290–314.

Choma, B.L. et al. (2009). Assessing the role of body image coping strategies and mediators or moderators of the links between self-objectification, body shame, and well-being. *Sex Roles, 61*, 699–713.

Choma, B.L. et al. (2010). Self-objectification, self-esteem, and gender: Testing a moderated mediation model. *Sex Roles, 63*, 645–656.

Chrisler, J.C. (2001). Gendered bodies and physical health. In R.K. Unger (Ed.), *Handbook of the psychology of women and gender* (pp. 289–302). New York: Wiley.

Chrisler, J.C. (2008). The menstrual cycle in a biopsychosocial context. In F.L. Denmark & M.A. Paludi (Eds.), *Psychology of women: A handbook of issues and theories* (2ⁿᵈ ed., pp. 400–439). Westport, CT: Praeger.

Chrisler, J.C. (2011). Leaks, lumps, and lines: Stigma and women's bodies. *Psychology of Women Quarterly, 35*, 202–214.

Chrisler, J.C. et al. (2006). The PMS illusion: Social cognition maintains social construction. *Sex Roles, 54*, 371–376.

Chrisler, J.C., & Parrett, K.L. (1995). Women and autoimmune disorders. In A.L. Stanton & S.J. Gallant (Eds.), *The psychology of women's health: Progress and challenges in research and application* (pp. 171–195). Washington, DC: American Psychological Association.

Christie-Mizell, C.A. et al. (2007). Gender ideology and motherhood: The consequences of race on earnings. *Sex Roles, 56*, 689–702.

Christina, G. (1997). Are we having sex yet? In A. Soble (Ed.), *The philosophy of sex: Contemporary readings* (pp. 3–8). Lanham, Md. : Rowman & Littlefield.

Christopher, A.N., & Mull, M.S. (2006). Conservative ideology and ambivalent sexism. *Psychology of Women Quarterly, 30*, 223–230.

Chronister, K. M., , & McWhirter, E. H. (2006). An experimental examination of two career interventions for battered women. *Journal of Counseling Psychology, 53*, 151–164.

Cichy, K.E. et al. (2007). Generational differences in gender attitudes between parents and grown offspring. *Sex Roles, 57*, 825–836.

Cinamon, R.G., & Rich, Y. (2002). Gender differences in the importance of work and family roles: Implications for work-family conflict. *Sex Roles, 47*, 531–541.

Citrin, L.B. et al. (2004). Objectification theory and emotions: A feminist psychological perspective on gendered affect. In L.Z. Tiedens & C.W. Leach (Eds.), *The social life of emotions* (pp. 203–223). Cambridge England: Cambridge University Press.

Claringbould, I., & Knoppers, A. (2007). Finding a "normal" woman: Selection processes for board membership. *Sex Roles, 56*, 495–507.

Clark, M.D., & Carroll, M.H. (2008). Acquaintance rape scripts of women and men: Similarities and differences. *Sex Roles, 58*, 616–625.

Clark, R. et al. (2003). Two steps forward, one step back: The presence of female characters and gender stereotyping in award-winning picture books between the 1930s and the 1960s. *Sex Roles, 49*, 439–449.

Clark, R.A., et al. (2004). Initial encounters of young men and women: Impressions and disclosure estimates. *Sex Roles, 50*, 699–709.

Clark, R.D., & Hatfield, E. (1989). Gender differences in receptivity to sexual offers. *Journal of Psychology and Human Sexuality, 2*, 39–55.

Clarke-Stewart, K.A. (1989). Infant day care: Maligned or malignant? *American Psychologist, 44*, 266–273.

Clatterbaugh, K. (1990). *Contemporary perspectives on masculinity: Men, women, and politics in modern society.* Boulder, CO: Westview.

Clearfield, M.W., & Nelson, N.M. (2006). Sex differences in mothers' speech and play behavior with 6–, 9–, and 14–month old infants. *Sex Roles, 54*, 127–137.

Cochran, C.C. et al. (1997). Predictors of responses to unwanted sexual attention. *Psychology of Women Quarterly, 21*, 207–226.

Coff, H., & Bolzendahl, C. (2010). Same game, different rules? Gender differences in political participation. *Sex Roles, 62*, 318–333.

Cogan, J.C. et al. (1996). A comparison of the United States and African students on perceptions of obesity and thinness. *Journal of Cross-Cultural Psychology, 27*, 98–113.

Cognard-Black, A.J. (2004). Will they stay, or will they go? Sex-atypical work among token men who teach. *Sociological Quarterly, 45*, 113–139.

Cohen, D.L., & Petrie, T.A. (2005). An examination of psychosocial correlates of disordered eating among undergraduate women. *Sex Roles, 52*, 29–42.

Cohen, J. (1977). *Statistical power analysis for the behavioral sciences* (Rev. ed.). San Diego, CA: Academic Press.

Cohen, L.L., & Swim, J.K. (1995). The differential impact of gender ratios on women and men: Tokenism, self-confidence, and expectations. *Personality and Social Psychology Bulletin, 21*, 876–883.

Cohen, P.N. (2004). The gender division of labor: "Keeping house" and occupational segregation in the United States. *Gender & Society, 18*, 239–252.

Cohen, P.N., & Huffman, M.L. (2003). Individuals, jobs, and labor markets: The devaluation of women's work. *American Sociological Review, 68*, 443–463.

Cohen-Bendahan, C.C.C. et al. (2005). Prenatal sex hormone effects on child and adult sex-typed behavior: Methods and findings. *Neuroscience and Biobehavioral Reviews, 29*, 353–384.

Cohn, L.D. (1991). Sex differences in the course of personality development: A meta-analysis. *Psychological Bulletin, 109*, 252–266.

Cohn, L.D., & Adler, N.E. (1992). Female and male perceptions of ideal body shapes: Distorted views among Caucasian college students. *Psychology of Women Quarterly, 16*, 69–79.

Coker, A.L. et al. (2002). Physical and mental health effects of intimate partner violence for men and women. *American Journal of Preventive Medicine, 23*, 260–268.

Cole, E.R. (2009). Intersectionality and research in psychology. *American Psychologist, 64*, 170–180.

Cole, E.R. et al. (2007). Vive la difference? Genetic explanations for perceived gender differences in nurturance. *Sex Roles, 57*, 211–222.

Cole, E.R., & Rothblum, E. (1990). Commentary on "Sexuality and midlife woman." *Psychology of Women Quarterly, 14*, 509–512.

Cole, J.R., & Zuckerman, H. (1987). Marriage, motherhood and research performance in science. *Scientific American, 256*, 119–125.

Cole, M.S. et al. (2004). Interaction of recruiter and applicant gender in resume evaluation: A field study. *Sex Roles, 51*, 597–608.

Collaer, M.L., & Hines, M. (1995). Human behavioral sex differences: A role for gonadal hormones during early development? *Psychological Bulletin, 118*, 55–107.

Colley, A. et al. (2002). Gender-linked differences in everyday memory performance: Effort makes the difference. *Sex Roles, 47*, 577–582.

Colley, A. et al. (2010). Communication using camera phones among young men and women: Who sends what to whom? *Sex Roles, 63*, 348–360.

Collins, C.F. (Ed.). (1996). *African-American women's health and social issues*. Westport, CT: Auburn House.

Collins, P.H. (1994). The meaning of motherhood in Black culture. In R. Staples (Ed.), *The Black family* (5th ed.). Belmont, CA: Wadsworth.

Collinsworth, L.L. et al. (2009). In harm's way: Factors related to psychological distress following sexual harassment. *Psychology of Women Quarterly, 33*, 475–490.

Coltrane, S. et al. (2004). Complexity of father involvement in low-income Mexican American families. *Family Relations, 53*, 179–189.

Coltrane, S., & Messineo, M. (2000). The perpetuation of subtle prejudice: Race and gender imagery in 1990s television advertising. *Sex Roles, 42*, 363–389.

Colwell, M.J., & Lindsey, E.W. (2005). Preschool children's pretend and physical play and sex of play partner: Connections to peer competence. *Sex Roles, 52*, 497–509.

Comas-Díaz, L. (1988). Feminist therapy with Hispanic/Latina women: Myth or reality? *Women & Therapy, 6*(4), 39–61.

Comas-Díaz, L. (1994). An integrative approach. In L. Comas-Díaz & B. Greene (Eds.), *Women of color: Integrating ethnic and gender identities in psychotherapy* (pp. 287–318). New York: Guilford.

Condit, C.M. et al. (2003). Lay understandings of sex/gender and genetics: A methodology that preserves polyvocal coder input. *Sex Roles, 49*, 557–570.

Confer, J. C. et al. (2010). Evolutionary psychology: Controversies, questions, prospects, and limitations. *American Psychologist, 65*, 110–126.

Conley, T.D. (2011). Perceived proposer personality characteristics and gender differences in acceptance of casual sex offers. *Journal of Personality and Social Psychology, 100*, 309–329.

Conley, T.D., & Ramsey, L.R. (2011). Killing us softly? Investigating portrayals of women and men in contemporary magazine advertisements. *Psychology of Women Quarterly, 35,* 469–478.

Conrad, S.D., & Morrow, R.S. (2000). Borderline personality organization, dissociation, and willingness to use force in intimate relationships. *Psychology of Men and Masculinity, 1,* 37–48.

Considine, N.S. et al. (2004). Hostility and anxiety differentially predict cardiovascular disease in men and women. *Sex Roles, 50,* 63–75.

Conway, M. et al. (1996). Status, communality, and agency: Implications for stereotypes of gender and other groups. *Journal of Personality and Social Psychology, 71,* 25–38.

Conway, M. et al. (2003). Are women perceived as engaging in more maladaptive worry than men? A status interpretation. *Sex Roles, 49,* 1–10.

Conway, M., & Vartanian, L.R. (2000). A status account of gender stereotypes: Beyond communality and agency. *Sex Roles, 43,* 181–199.

Cook, E.A. (1993). Feminist consciousness and candidate preference among American women, 1972–1988. *Political Behavior, 15,* 227–246.

Cook, S., & Parrott, D. (2009). Exploring a taxonomy for aggression against women: Can it aid conceptual clarity? *Aggressive Behavior, 35,* 462–476.

Cooley, E.L. (1992). Family expressiveness and proneness to depression among college women. *Journal of Research in Personality, 26,* 281–287.

Corral., I., & Landrine, H. (2010). Methodological and statistical issues in research with diverse samples: The problem of measurement equivalence. In H. Landrine & N.F. Russo (Eds.), *Handbook of diversity in feminist psychology* (pp. 83–134). New York: Springer.

Corrigall, E.A., & Konrad, A.M. (2006). The relationship of job attribute preferences to employment, hours of paid work, and family responsibilities: An analysis comparing women and men. *Sex Roles, 54,* 95–111.

Corrigall, E.A., & Konrad, A.M. (2007). Gender role attitudes and careers: A longitudinal study. *Sex Roles, 56,* 847–855.

Cortina, L.M., & Kubiak, S.P. (2006). Gender and posttraumatic stress: Sexual violence as an explanation for women's increased risk. *Journal of Abnormal Psychology, 115,* 753–759.

Costa, P.T. et al. (2001). Gender differences in personality traits across cultures: Robust and surprising findings. *Journal of Personality and Social Psychology, 81,* 322–331.

Costos, D. et al. (2002). Recollections of menarche: Communication between mothers and daughters regarding menstruation. *Sex Roles, 46,* 49–59.

Cotter, D.A. et al. (1995). Occupational gender desegregation in the 1980s. *Work and Occupations, 22,* 3–21.

Cotter, D.A. et al. (1997). All women benefit: The macro-level effect of occupational integration on gender earnings equality. *American Sociological Review, 62,* 714–734.

Cotter, D.A. et al. (2001). Women's work and working women: The demand for female labor. *Gender & Society, 15,* 429–452.

Coughlin, P.C. (1990). Premenstrual syndrome: How marital satisfaction and role choice affect symptom severity. *Social Work, 35,* 351–355.

Coulomb-Cabagno et al. (2005). Players' gender and male referees' decisions about aggression in French soccer: A preliminary study. *Sex Roles, 52,* 547–553.

Coulson, M., & Bhavnani, K. (1990). Making a difference-questioning women's studies. In E. Burman (Ed.), *Feminists and psychological practice* (pp. 62–75). Newbury Park, CA: Sage.

Courtenay, W.H. (2000). Engendering health: A social constructionist examination of men's health beliefs and behaviors. *Psychology of Men and Masculinity, 1,* 4–15.

Covey, L.A., & Feltz, D.L. (1991). Physical activity and adolescent female psychological development. *Journal of Youth and Adolescence, 20,* 463–474.

Cowan, G. (2000a). Beliefs about the causes of four types of rape. *Sex Roles, 42,* 807–823.

Cowan, G. (2000b). Women's hostility toward women and rape and sexual harassment myths. *Violence Against Women, 6,* 238–246.

Cowan, G., & Mills, R.D. (2004). Personal inadequacy and intimacy predictors of men's hostility toward women. *Sex Roles, 51,* 67–78.

Cowan, G., & Quinton, W.J. (1997). Cognitive style and attitudinal correlates of the Perceived Causes of Rape Scale. *Psychology of Women Quarterly, 21,* 227–245.

Cox, D.L. et al. (2000). Anger and depression in girls and boys: A study of gender differences. *Psychology of Women Quarterly, 24,* 110–112.

Cox, T.H., & Harquail, C.V. (1991). Career paths and career success in the early career stages of male and female MBAs. *Journal of Vocational Behavior, 39,* 54–75.

Coyle, A., & Morgan-Sykes, C. (1998). Troubled men and threatening women: The construction of "crisis" in male mental health. *Feminism & Psychology, 8,* 263–284.

Cramer, P., & Steinwert, T. (1998). Thin is good, fat is bad: How early does it begin? *Journal of Applied Developmental Psychology, 19,* 429–451.

Crandall, C.S. et al. (1999). Newsworthy moral dilemmas: Justice, caring, and gender. *Sex Roles, 40*, 187–209.

Crawford, M.C. (1989). Agreeing to differ: Feminist epistemologies and women's ways of knowing. In M. Crawford & M. Gentry (Eds.), *Gender and thought* (pp. 128–145). New York: Springer-Verlag.

Crawford, M.C., & Marecek, J. (1989). Psychology reconstructs the female, 1968–1988. *Psychology of Women Quarterly, 13*, 147–166.

Crawford-Green, C. (1996). Hypertension and African-American women. In C.F. Collins (Ed.), *African-American women's health and social issues* (pp. 59–73). Westport, CT: Auburn House.

Crittenden, A. (2001). *The price of motherhood: Why the most important job in the world is still the least valued.* New York: Metropolitan Books.

Crocker, J. et al. (2003). When grades determine self-worth: Consequences of contingent self-worth for male and female engineering and psychology majors. *Journal of Personality and Social Psychology, 85*, 507–516.

Croghan, R., & Miell, D. (1998). Strategies of resistance: "Bad" mothers dispute the evidence. *Feminism & Psychology, 8*, 445–465.

Crombie, G. et al. (2005). Predictors of young adolescents' math grades and course enrollment intentions: Gender similarities and differences. *Sex Roles, 52*, 351–367.

Cromer, L.D, & Freyd, J.J. (2007). What influences believing child sexual abuse disclosures? The role of depicted memory persistence, participant gender, trauma history, and sexism. *Psychology of Women Quarterly, 31*, 13–22.

Crosby, F., & Jaskar, K.L. (1993). Women and men at home and at work: Realities and illusions. In S. Oskamp & M. Costanzo (Eds.), *Gender issues in contemporary society* (pp. 143–171). Newbury Park, CA: Sage.

Crosby, F.J. (2004). *Affirmative action is dead; Long live affirmative action.* New Haven, CT: Yale.

Crosby, F.J. et al. (2004). The maternal wall. *Journal of Social Issues, 60*(4), 675–682.

Crosby, F.J., & Clayton, S. (1986). Introduction: The search for connections. *Journal of Social Issues, 42*(2), 1–10.

Crosby, F.J., & Sabattini, L. (2006). Family and work balance. In J. Worell & C.D. Goodheart (Eds.), *Handbook of girls' and women's psychological health: Gender and well-being across the lifespan* (p. 350–358). New York: Oxford.

Cross, W.E. (1971). Negro-to-Black conversion experience: Toward a psychology of Black liberation. *Black World, 20*(9), 13–27.

Croteau, J.M. et al. (1993). Social and cultural sensitivity in group-specific HIV and AIDS programming. *Journal of Counseling and Development, 71*, 290–296.

Crouter, A.C., & Booth, A. (Eds.).(2003). *Children's influence on family dynamics.* Mahwah, NJ: Erlbaum.

Crouter, A.C., & Crowley, M.S. (1990). School-age children's time alone with fathers in single- and dual-earner families: Implications for the father-child relationship. *Journal of Early Adolescence, 10*, 296–312.

Crowley-Long, K., & Long, K.J. (1992). Searching for models of fully functioning women. *Women & Therapy, 12*, 213–225.

Crull, P. (1982). Stress effects of sexual harassment on the job: Implications for counseling. *American Journal of Orthopsychiatry, 52*, 539–544.

Cuddy, A.J.C. et al. (2004). When professionals become mothers, warmth doesn't cut the ice. *Journal of Social Issues, 60*(4), 701–718.

Cuddy, A.J.C. et al. (2005). This old stereotype: The pervasiveness and persistence of the elderly stereotype. *Journal of Social Issues, 61*(2), 267–285.

Culp, L.N., & Beach, S.R.H. (1998). Marriage and depressive symptoms: The role and bases of self-esteem differ by gender. *Psychology of Women Quarterly, 22*, 647–663.

Cummings, K.M., & Armenta, M. (2002). Penalties for peer sexual harassment in an academic context: The influence of harasser gender, participant gender, severity of harassment, and the presence of bystanders. *Sex Roles, 47*, 273–280.

Cummins, L.H., & Leman, J. (2007). Eating disorders and body image concerns in Asian American women: Assessment and treatment from a multicultural and feminist perspective. *Eating Disorders: The Journal of Treatment & Prevention, 15*, 217–230.

Cunningham, G.B. et al. (2004). Gender representation in the NCAA news: Is the glass half full or half empty? *Sex Roles, 50*, 861–870.

Cunningham, J., & Macan, T. (2007). Effects of applicant pregnancy on hiring decisions and interview ratings. *Sex Roles, 57*, 497–508.

Cunningham, M. (2001). Parental influences on the gendered division of housework. *American Sociological Review, 66*(2), 184–203.

Curry, M.A. et al. (2001). Abuse of women with disabilities: An ecological model and review. *Violence Against Women, 7*, 60–79.

Cusumano, D.L., & Thompson, J.K. (1997). Body image and body shape ideals in magazines:

Exposure, awareness, and internalization. *Sex Roles, 37*, 701–721.

Cutler, S.E., & Nolen-Hoeksema, S. (1991). Accounting for sex differences in depression through female victimization: Childhood sexual abuse. *Sex Roles, 24*, 425–438.

Dal Cin, S. et al. (2006). Remembering the message: The use of a reminder cue to increase condom use following a safer sex intervention. *Health Psychology, 25*, 438–443.

Dallam, S.J. et al. (2001). The effects of child sexual abuse: Comment on Rind, Tromovitch, and Bauserman (1998). *Psychological Bulletin, 127*, 715–733.

Dall'Ara, E., & Maass, A. (1999). Studying sexual harassment in the laboratory: Are egalitarian women at higher risk? *Sex Roles, 41*, 681–704.

Dalton, S.E., & Bielby, D.D. (2000). "That's our kind of constellation": Lesbian mothers negotiate institutionalized understandings of gender within the family. *Gender & Society, 14*, 36–61.

Dancey, C.P. (1992). The relationship of instrumentality and expressiveness to sexual orientation in women. *Journal of Homosexuality, 23*, 71–82.

Danieli, Y. (1985). The treatment and prevention of long-term effects and intergenerational transmission of victimization: A lesson from Holocaust survivors and their children. In C.R. Figley (Ed.), *Trauma and its wake: The study and treatment of post-traumatic stress disorder* (pp. 295–313). New York: Brunner/Mazel.

Daniels, E., & Leaper, C. (2006). A longitudinal investigation of sport participation, peer acceptance, and self-esteem among adolescent boys and girls. *Sex Roles, 55*, 875–880.

Dardenne, B. et al. (2007). Insidious dangers of benevolent sexism: Consequences for women's performance. *Journal of Personality and Social Psychology, 93*, 764–779.

Darlow, S., & Lobel, M. (2010). Who is beholding my beauty? Thinness ideals, weight, and women's responses to appearance evaluation. *Sex Roles, 63*, 833–843.

Darves-Bornoz, J.M. et al. (1995). Sexual victimization in women with schizophrenia and bipolar disorder. *Social Psychiatry and Psychiatric Epidemiology, 30*, 78–84.

Daubenmier, J.J. (2005). The relationship of yoga, body awareness, and body responsiveness to self-objectification and disordered eating. *Psychology of Women Quarterly, 29*, 207–219.

Dauphinais, P.D. et al. (1992). Predictors of rank-and-file feminist activism: Evidence from the 1983 General Social Survey. *Social Problems, 39*, 332–344.

Davenport, D.S., & Yurich, J.M. (1991). Multicultural gender issues. *Journal of Counseling & Development, 70*, 64–71.

Davey, F. H. (1998). Young women's expected and preferred patterns of employment and child care. *Sex Roles, 38*, 95–102.

David, D., & Vernon, M.L. (2002). Sculpting the body beautiful: Attachment style, neuroticism, and use of cosmetic surgeries. *Sex Roles, 47*, 129–138.

Davies, P. G. et al. (2005). Clearing the air: Safety moderates the effect of stereotype threat on women's leadership aspirations. *Journal of Personality and Social Psychology, 88*, 276–287.

Davis, D. (1996). The cultural constructions of the premenstrual and menopausal syndromes. In C.F. Sargent & C.B. Brettell (Eds.), *Gender and health: An international perspective* (pp. 57–86). Upper Saddle River, NJ: Prentice Hall.

Davis, M.C. et al. (1999). Is life more difficult on Mars or Venus? A meta-analytic review of sex differences in major and minor life events. *Annals of Behavioral Medicine, 21*, 83–97.

Davis, S. (2010). The answer doesn't seem to change, so maybe we should change the question: A commentary on Lachance-Grzela and Bouchard (2010). *Sex Roles, 63*, 786–790.

Davis, S.N. (2003). Sex stereotypes in commercials targeted toward children: A content analysis. *Sociological Spectrum, 23*, 407–424.

Davison, T.E., & McCabe, M.P. (2005). Relationships between men's and women's body image and their psychological, social, and sexual functioning. *Sex Roles, 52*, 463–475

De Beauvoir, S. (1952). *The second sex.* New York: Alfred A. Knopf.

de Snyder, V.N.S. et al. (2000). Understanding the sexuality of Mexican-born women and their risk for HIV/AIDS. *Psychology of Women Quarterly, 24*, 100–109.

Dean, A. et al. (1992). The influence of living alone on depression in elderly persons. *Journal of Aging and Health, 4*, 3–18.

Dear, G.E., & Roberts, C.M. (2002). The relationships between codependency and femininity and masculinity. *Sex Roles, 46*, 159–165.

Deaux, K. (1984). From individual differences to social categories: Analysis of a decade's research on gender. *American Psychologist, 39*, 105–116.

Deaux, K. et al. (1985). Level of categorization and content of gender stereotypes. *Social Cognition, 3*, 145–167.

Deaux, K. et al. (1995). Parameters of social identity. *Journal of Personality and Social Psychology, 68*, 280–291.

Deaux, K., & Emswiller, T. (1974). Explanations of successful performance on sex-linked tasks: What is skill for the male is luck for the female. *Journal of Personality and Social Psychology, 29,* 80–85.

Deaux, K., & Lewis, L.L. (1984). Structure of gender stereotypes: Interrelationships among components and gender label. *Journal of Personality and Social Psychology, 46,* 991–1004.

Deaux, K., & Major, B. (1987). Putting gender into context: An interactive model of gender-related behavior. *Psychological Bulletin, 94,* 369–389.

Deaux, K., & Stewart, A.J. (2001). Framing gender identities. In R.K. Unger (Ed.), *Handbook of the psychology of women and gender* (pp. 84–97). New York: Wiley.

Delaney, J. et al. (1988). *The curse: The cultural history of menstruation* (rev. ed). Champaign, IL: University of Illinois Press.

Denmark, F.L. et al. (2008). Historical development of the psychology of women. In F.L. Denmark & M.A. Paludi (Eds.), *Psychology of women: A handbook of issues and theories* (2nd ed., pp. 3–39). Westport, CT: Praeger.

Denner, J., & Dunbar, N. (2004). Negotiating femininity: Power and strategies of Mexican American girls. *Sex Roles, 50,* 301–314.

Desmarais, S., & Curtis, J. (1997). Gender differences in pay histories and view on payment entitlement among university students. *Sex Roles, 37,* 623–642.

Deutsch, F.M. (1999). *Having it all: How equally shared parenting works.* Cambridge, MA: Harvard University Press.

Deutsch, F.M. et al. (1987). What is a smile? *Psychology of Women Quarterly, 11,* 341–351.

Deutsch, F.M., & Saxon, S.E. (1998). The double standard of praise and criticism for mothers and fathers. *Psychology of Women Quarterly, 22,* 665–683.

Devine, P.G. (1989). Stereotypes and prejudice: Their automatic and controlled components. *Journal of Personality and Social Psychology, 56,* 5–18.

Devos, T. et al. (2008). The role of parenthood and college education in the self-concept of college students: Explicit and implicit assessments of gendered aspirations. *Sex Roles, 59,* 214–228.

Diamond, L.M. (2005). "I'm straight, but I kissed a girl": The trouble with American media representations of female-female sexuality. *Feminism & Psychology, 15,* 104–110.

Diamond, L.M., & Butterworth, M. (2008). Questioning gender and sexual identity: Dynamic links over time. *Sex Roles, 59,* 365–376.

Dickman, A.B. et al. (2000). Love means never having to be careful: The relationship between reading romance novels and safe sex behavior. *Psychology of Women Quarterly, 24,* 179–188.

Diekman, A.B., & Eagly, A.H. (2000). Stereotypes as dynamic constructs: Women and men of the past, present, and future. *Personality and Social Psychology Bulletin, 26,* 1171–1188.

Diekman, A.B., & Eagly, A.H. (2008). Of men, women, and motivation: A role congruity account. In J.Y. Shah & W.L. Gardner (Eds.), *Handbook of motivation science (*pp. 434–447). New York: Guilford.

Diekman, A.B., & Goodfriend, W. (2006). Rolling with the changes: A role congruity perspective on gender norms. *Psychology of Women Quarterly, 30,* 369–383.

Diekman, A.B., & Murnen, S.K. (2004). Learning to be little women and little men: The inequitable gender equality of nonsexist children's literature. *Sex Roles, 50,* 373–385.

Diekman, A.B., & Schneider, M.C. (2010). A social role theory perspective on gender gaps in political attitudes. *Psychology of Women Quarterly, 34,* 486–497.

Diflorio, A., & Jones, I. (2010). Is sex important? Gender differences in bipolar disorder. *International Review of Psychiatry, 22,* 437–452.

Dijkstra, A.F. et al. (2008). Gender bias in medical textbooks: Examples from coronary heart disease, depression, alcohol abuse and pharmacology. *Medical Education, 42,* 1021–1028.

Dill, K.E., & Thill, K.P. (2007). Video game characters and the socialization of gender roles: Young people's perceptions mirror sexist media depictions. *Sex Roles, 57,* 851–864.

DiMatteo, M.R., & Kahn, K.L. (1997). Psychosocial aspects of childbirth. In S. Gallant, G.P. Keita, & R. Royak-Schaler (Eds.), *Health care for women: Psychological, social and behavioral influences* (pp. 175–186). Washington, DC: American Psychological Association.

Dindia, K., & Allen, M. (1992). Sex differences in self-disclosure: A meta-analysis. *Psychological Bulletin, 112,* 106–124.

Dion, K.K., & Dion, K.L. (2001). Gender and relationships. In R.K. Unger (Ed.), *Handbook of the psychology of women and gender* (pp. 256–271). New York: Wiley.

DiPalma, L.M. (1994). Patterns of coping and characteristics of high-functioning incest survivors. *Archives of Psychiatric Nursing, 8,* 82–90.

Dolan, B. (1991). Cross-cultural aspects of anorexia nervosa and bulimia: A review. *International Journal of Eating Disorders, 10,* 67–79.

Donaghue, N., & Fallon, B.J. (2003). Gender-role self-stereotyping and the relationship between equity and satisfaction in close relationships. *Sex Roles, 48*, 217–230.

Donaghue, N., & Smith, N. (2008). Not half bad: Self and others' judgements of body size and attractiveness across the life span. *Sex Roles, 58*, 875–882.

Donnerstein, E. et al. (1987). *The question of pornography: Research findings and policy implications*. New York: Free Press.

Donovan, R.A. (2011). Tough ot tender: Dis(similarities) in White college students' perceptions of Black and White women. *Psychology of Women Quarterly, 35*, 458–468.

Dougherty, D.M. et al. (1996). The effects of alcohol on the aggressive responding of women. *Journal of Studies on Alcohol, 57*, 178–186.

Dovidio, J.F. et al. (1988). The relationship of social power to visual displays of dominance between men and women. *Journal of Personality and Social Psychology, 54*, 233–242.

Dovidio, J.F. et al. (2001). Implicit and explicit attitudes: Examination of the relationship between measures of intergroup bias. In R. Brown & S.L. Gaertner, S.L. (Eds.), *Blackwell handbook of social psychology: Intergroup relations* (Vol. 4, pp. 175–197). Oxford, UK: Blackwell.

Dowdall, G.W. et al. (1998). Binge drinking among American college women: A comparison of single-sex and coeducational institutions. *Psychology of Women Quarterly, 22*, 705–715.

Downing, N.E., & Roush, K.L. (1985). From passive acceptance to active commitment: A model of feminist identity development for women. *The Counseling Psychologist, 13*, 695–709.

Draucker, C.B. (1996). Family-of-origin variables and adult female survivors of childhood sexual abuse: A review of the research. *Journal of Child Sexual Abuse, 5*, 35–63.

Dreher, G.F., & Cox, T.H., Jr. (1996). Race, gender, and opportunity: A study of compensation attainment and the establishment of mentoring relationships. *Journal of Applied Psychology, 81*, 297–308.

Driesen, N.R., & Raz, N. (1995). The influence of sex, age, and handedness on corpus callosum morphology: A meta-analysis. *Psychobiology, 23*, 240–247.

Driscoll, D.M. et al. (1998). Can perceivers identify likelihood to sexually harass? *Sex Roles, 38*, 557–588.

DSM-IV: Diagnostic and statistical manual of mental disorders. (1994). (4th ed.). Washington, DC: American Psychiatric Association.

Duffy, J. et al. (2004). Psychological consequences for high school students of having been sexually harassed. *Sex Roles, 50*, 811–821.

Dull, D., & West, C. (1991). Accounting for cosmetic surgery: The accomplishment of gender. *Social Problems, 38*, 54–70.

Dum, M. et al. (2010). Social perception of rape victims in dating and married relationships: The role of perpetrators' benevolent sexism. *Sex Roles, 62*, 505–519.

Dumont, M. et al. (2010). Be too kind to a woman, she'll feel incompetent: Benevolent sexism shifts self-construal and autobiographical memories toward incompetence. *Sex Roles, 62*, 545–553.

Duncan, L. et al. (2002). Midlife educational, career, and family outcomes of women educated at two single-sex colleges. *Sex Roles, 47*, 237–247.

Duncan, L., & Owen-Smith, A. (2006). Powerlessness and the use of indirect aggression in friendships. *Sex Roles, 55*, 493–502.

Duncan, L.E. (2010). Women's relationship to feminism: Effects of generation and feminist self-labeling. *Psychology of Women Quarterly, 34*, 498–507.

Dunne, F.J. et al. (1993). Gender differences in psychiatric morbidity among alcohol misusers. *Comprehensive Psychiatry, 34*, 95–101.

Dunne, G.A. (2000). Opting into motherhood: Lesbians blurring the boundaries and transforming the meaning of parenthood and kinship. *Gender & Society, 14*, 11–35.

Dutton, D.G. (1988). *The domestic assault of women: Psychological and criminal justice perspectives*. Boston, MA: Allyn and Bacon.

Dutton, D.G. (1992). Assessment and treatment of PTSD among battered women. In D. Foy (Ed.), *Treating PTSD: Cognitive and behavioral strategies* (pp. 69–98). New York: Guilford.

Dutton, M.A. (1992). *Empowering and healing the battered woman*. New York: Springer.

Dutton, M.A., & Goodman, L.A. (2005). Coercion in intimate partner violence: Toward a new conceptualization. *Sex Roles, 52*, 743–756.

Dutton-Douglas, M.A. (1992). Treating battered women in the aftermath stage. *Psychotherapy in Private Practice, 10*, 93–98.

Eagly, A.H. (1987). *Sex differences in social behavior: A social-role interpretation*. Hillsdale, NJ: Erlbaum.

Eagly, A.H. (1995). The science and politics of comparing women and men. *American Psychologist, 50*, 145–158.

Eagly, A.H. (2007). Female leadership advantage and disadvantage: Resolving the contradictions. *Psychology of Women Quarterly, 31*, 1–12.

Eagly, A.H. et al. (1995). Gender and the effectiveness of leaders: A meta-analysis. *Psychological Bulletin, 117*, 125–145.

Eagly, A.H. et al. (2000). Social role theory of sex differences and similarities: A current appraisal. In T. Eckes & H.M. Trautner (Eds.), *The developmental social psychology of gender* (pp. 123–174). Mahwah, NJ: Erlbaum.

Eagly, A.H. et al. (2003). Transformational, transactional, and laissez-faire leadership styles: A meta-analysis comparing women and men. *Psychological Bulletin, 129*, 569–591.

Eagly, A.H., & Carli, L.L. (1981). Sex of researcher and sex-typed communications as determinants of sex differences in influenceability: A meta-analysis of social influences studies. *Psychological Bulletin, 90*, 1–20.

Eagly, A.H., & Crowley, M. (1986). Gender and helping behavior: A meta-analytic review of the social psychological literature. *Psychological Bulletin, 100*, 283–308.

Eagly, A.H., & Johnson, B.T. (1990). Gender and leadership style: A meta-analysis. *Psychological Bulletin, 108*, 233–256.

Eagly, A.H., & Karau, S.J. (1991). Gender and the emergence of leaders: A meta-analysis. *Journal of Personality and Social Psychology, 60*, 685–710.

Eagly, A.H., & Karau, S.J. (2002). Role congruity theory of prejudice toward female leaders. *Psychological Review, 109*, 573–598.

Eagly, A.H., & Mladinic, A. (1989). Gender stereotypes and attitudes toward women and men. *Personality and Social Psychology Bulletin, 15*, 543–558.

Eagly, A.H., & Steffen, V.J. (1986). Gender and aggressive behavior: A meta-analytic review of the social psychological literature. *Psychological Bulletin, 100*, 309–330.

Earle, J.P., & Nies, C.T. (1994). Resources for developing acquaintance rape prevention programs for men. In A. Berkowitz (Ed.), *Men and rape: Theory, research, and prevention programs in higher education* (pp. 73–82). San Francisco, CA: Jossey-Bass.

Eastwick, P.W., & Finkel, E.J. (2008). Sex differences in mate preferences revisited: Do people know what they initially desire in a romantic partner? *Journal of Personality and Social Psychology, 94*, 245–264.

Eccles, J.S. (1987). Adolescence: Gateway to gender-role transcendence. In D.B. Carter (Ed.), *Current conceptions of sex roles and sex typing: Theory and research* (pp. 225–241). New York: Praeger.

Eccles, J.S. (1994). Understanding women's educational and occupational choices: Applying the Eccles et al. model of achievement-related choices. *Psychology of Women Quarterly, 18*, 585–609.

Eccles, J.S., & Harold, R.D. (1992). Gender differences in educational and occupational patterns among the gifted. In N. Colangelo, S.G. Assouline, & D.L. Ambroson (Eds.), *Talent development: Proceedings from the 1991 Henry B. and Jocelyn Wallace National Research Symposium on Talent Development* (pp. 3–29). Unionville, NY: Trillium Press.

Eccles, J.S., & Jacobs, J.E. (1986). Social forces shape math attitudes and performance. *Signs, 11*, 367–380.

Eckes, T. (1994). Explorations in gender cognition: Content and structure of female and male subtypes. *Social Cognition, 12*, 37–60.

Eckes, T. (1996). Linking female and male subtypes to situations: A range-of-situation-fit effect. *Sex Roles, 35*, 401–426.

Eckes, T. (2002). Paternalistic and envious gender stereotypes: Testing predictions from the stereotype content model. *Sex Roles, 47*, 99–114.

Edwards, K.M. et al. (2009). College women's aggression in relationships: The role of childhood and adolescent victimization. Psychology of Women Quarterly, 33, 255–265.

EEOC. (2011a). Sexual harassment. http://www.eeoc.gov/ laws/types/sexual_harassment.cfm (Retrieved October 2011).

EEOC. (2011b). Sexual harassment charges EEOC & FEPAs combined: FY 1997–FY 2010. http://www.eeoc.gov/eeoc/statistics/enforcement/sexual_harassment.cfm

Egidio, R.K., & Robertson, D.E. (1981). Rape awareness for men. *Journal of College Student Development, 22*, 455–456.

Eibach, R.P., & Ehrlinger, J. (2010). Reference points in men's and women's judgments of progress toward gender equality. *Sex Roles, 63*, 882–893.

Eisele, H., & Stake, J. (2008). The differential relationship of feminist attitudes and feminist identity to self-efficacy. *Psychology of Women Quarterly, 32*, 233–244.

Eisikovits, Z., & Buchbinder, E. (1999). Talking control: Metaphors used by battered women. *Violence Against Women, 5*, 845–868.

Eisler, R.M. et al. (2000). Masculine gender role stress and intimate abuse: Effects of gender relevance of conflict situations on men's attributions and affective responses. *Psychology of Men and Masculinity, 1*, 30–36.

Elacqua, T.C. et al. (2009). Managers' beliefs about the glass ceiling: Interpersonal and organizational factors. *Psychology of Women Quarterly, 33*, 285–294.

Eldridge, N.S., & Gilbert, L.A. (1990). Correlates of relationship satisfaction in lesbian couples. *Psychology of Women Quarterly, 14*, 43–62.

Eliason, S.R. (1995). An extension of the Sorensen-Kalleberg theory of the labor market matching and attainment processes. *American Sociological Review, 60*, 247–271.

Ellis, J. (1993). Supporting giftedness in girls in the classroom. *Proceedings of the Society for the Advancement of Gifted Education Annual Conference*, EC 303, 142.

Else-Quest, N.M. et al. (2005). Context counts: Long-term sequelae of premarital intercourse or abstinence. *Journal of Sex Research, 42*, 102–112.

Else-Quest, N.M. et al. (2010). Cross-national patterns of gender differences in mathematics: A meta-analysis. *Psychological Bulletin, 136*, 103–127.

Ely, R.J. (1995). The power in demography: Women's social constructions of gender identity at work. *Academy of Management Journal, 38*, 589–634.

Enander, V. (2011). Leaving Jekyll and Hyde: Emotion work in the context of intimate partner violence. *Feminism & Psychology, 21*, 29–48.

Engeln-Maddox, R. (2006). Buying a beauty standard or dreaming of a new life? Expectations associated with media ideals. *Psychology of Women Quarterly, 30*, 258–266.

Engeln-Maddox, R., & Miller, S.A. (2008). Talking back to the media ideal: The development and validation of the Critical Processing of Beauty Images Scale. *Psychology of Women Quarterly, 32*, 159–171.

English, A. et al. (2010, April). *Are women now half the labor force? The truth about women and equal participation in the labor force.* IWPR Report #C374 http://www.iwpr.org

Enns, C.Z., & Byars-Winston, A.M. (2010). Multicultural feminist therapy. In H. Landrine & N.F. Russo (Eds.), *Handbook of diversity in feminist psychology* (pp. 367–388). New York: Springer.

Epstein, J. et al. (2007). Perceived physical attractiveness, sexual history, and sexual intentions: An internet study. *Sex Roles, 56*, 23–31.

Epstein, S. (1987). Gay politics, ethnic identity: The limits of social constructionism. *Socialist Review, 17*, 9–53.

Erchull, M.J. et al. (2010). Well…she wants it more: Perceptions of social norms about desires for marriage and children and anticipated chore participation. *Psychology of Women Quarterly, 34*, 253–260.

Erdle, S. et al. (1992). Sex differences in personality correlates of helping behavior. *Personality and Individual Differences, 13*, 931–936.

Erel, O. et al. (2000). Maternal versus nonmaternal care and seven domains of children's development. *Psychological Bulletin, 126*, 727–747.

Erikson, E. (1959). *Identity and the life cycle.* New York: Norton.

Espín, O. (1994). Feminist approaches. In L. Comas-Díaz & B. Greene (Eds.), *Women of color: Integrating ethnic and gender identities in psychotherapy* (pp. 265–286). New York: Guilford.

Etaugh, C.A. (2008). Women in the middle and later years. In F.L. Denmark & M.A. Paludi (Eds.), *Psychology of women: A handbook of issues and theories* (2nd ed., pp. 271–302). Westport, CT: Praeger.

Etaugh, C.A., & Bridges, J.S. (2006). *Women's lives: A topical approach.* Boston, MA: Allyn & Bacon.

Etaugh, C.A., & Folger, D. (1998). Perceptions of parents whose work and parenting behaviors deviate from role expectations. *Sex Roles, 39*, 215–223.

Etaugh, C.A., & Liss, M.B. (1992). Home, school, and playroom: Training grounds for adult gender roles, *Sex Roles, 26*, 129–147.

Etaugh, C.A., & Moss, C. (2001). Attitudes of employed women toward parents who choose full-time or part-time employment following their child's birth. *Sex Roles, 44*, 611–619.

Etaugh, C.A., & Nekolny, K. (1990). Effects of employment status and marital status on perceptions of mothers. *Sex Roles, 23*, 273–280.

Etaugh, C.A., & Poertner, P. (1991). Effects of occupational prestige, employment status, and marital status on perceptions of mothers. *Sex Roles, 24*, 345–353.

Evans, L., & Davies, K. (2000). No sissy boys here: A content analysis of the representation of masculinity in elementary school reading textbooks. *Sex Roles, 42*, 255–270.

Evans, P.C. (2003). "If only I were thin like her, maybe I could be happy like her": The self implications of associating a thin female ideal with life success. *Psychology of Women Quarterly, 27*, 209–214.

Evans-DeCicco, J. A., & Cowan, G. (2001). Attitudes toward pornography and the characteristics attributed to pornography actors. *Sex Roles, 44*, 351–361.

Expsito et al. (2010). Don't rock the boat: Women's benevolent sexism predicts fears of marital violence. *Psychology of Women Quarterly, 34*, 36–42.

Eyer, D.E. (1992). *Mother-infant bonding: A scientific fiction.* New Haven, CT: Yale.

Eyssel, F., & Bohner, G. (2007). The rating of sexist humor under time pressure as an indicator of spontaneous sexist attitudes. *Sex Roles, 57,* 651–660.

Faludi, S. (1991). *Backlash: The undeclared war against American women.* New York: Doubleday.

Farris, C. et al. (2008). Sexual coercion and the misperception of sexual intent. *Clinicial Psychology Review, 28,* 48–66.

Farvid, P., & Braun, V. (2006). "Most of us guys are raring to go anytime, anyplace, anywhere": Male and female sexuality in Cleo and Cosmo. *Sex Roles, 55,* 295–310.

Fassinger, R E. (1994). Development and testing of the Attitudes toward Feminism and the Women's Movement (FWM) scale. *Psychology of Women Quarterly, 18,* 389–402.

Faulkner, G.E. et al. (2008). Sex role ideology, relationship context, and response to sexual coercion in college females. *Sex Roles, 59,* 139–150.

Fausto-Sterling, A. (1992). *Myths of gender* (2nd ed.). New York: Basic.

Fausto-Sterling, A. (1993, March/April). The five sexes: Why male and female are not enough. *The Sciences,* p. 20–24.

Fausto-Sterling, A. (2000). *Sexing the body: Gender politics and the construction of sexuality.* New York: Basic.

FDA Warning Letters. (2000, November 16). http://www.pharmcast.com/WarningLetters/November2000/EliLilly1100.htm (Retrieved November 2005).

Febbraro, A.R. (2003). Alpha and beta bias in research on labour and love: The case of enhancement versus scarcity. *Feminism & Psychology. 13,* 210–223.

Federal Glass Ceiling Commission. (1995, March). *Good for business: Making full use of the nation's human capital.* Washington, DC: U.S. Department of Labor.

Fehr, B. (2004). Intimacy expectations in same-sex friendships: A prototype interaction-pattern model. *Journal of Personality and Social Psychology, 86,* 265–284.

Fein, S., & Spencer, S.J. (1997). Prejudice as self-image maintenance: Affirming the self through derogating others. *Journal of Personality and Social Psychology, 73,* 31–44.

Feingold, A. (1988). Cognitive gender differences are disappearing. *American Psychologist, 43,* 95–103.

Feingold, A. (1992). Gender differences in mate selection preferences: A test of the parental investment model. *Psychological Bulletin, 112,* 125–139.

Feingold, A. (1995). Gender differences in personality: A meta-analysis. *Psychological Bulletin, 116,* 429–456.

Feingold, A., & Mazzella, R. (1998). Gender differences in body image are increasing. *Psychological Science, 9,* 190–195.

Feldman, D.C. (1994). The decision to retire early: A review and conceptualization. *Academy of Management Review, 19,* 285–311.

Felmlee, D.H. (1994). Who's on top? Power in romantic relationships. *Sex Roles, 31,* 275–295.

Felmlee, D.H. et al. (2010). Fairy tales: Attraction and stereotypes in same-gender relationships. *Sex Roles, 62,* 226–240.

Ferguson, T. et al. (2005). Variation in the application of the "promiscuous female" stereotype and the nature of the application domain: Influences on sexual harassment judgments after exposure to the Jerry Springer Show. *Sex Roles, 52,* 477–487.

Fields, A.M. et al. (2010). What is means to be a woman: Ambivalent sexism in female college students' experiences and attitudes. *Sex Roles, 62,* 554–567.

Fiese, B.H., & Skillman, G. (2000). Gender differences in family stories: Moderating influence of parent gender role and child gender. *Sex Roles, 43,* 267–283.

Fiissel, D.L., & Lafreniere, K.D. (2006). Weight control motives for cigarette smoking: Further consequences of the sexual objectification of women? *Feminism & Psychology, 16,* 327–344.

Fine, M. (1993). The politics of research and activism: Violence against women. In P.B. Bart & E.G. Moran (Eds.), *Violence against women: The bloody footprints* (pp. 278–287). Newbury Park, CA: Sage.

Fine, M., & Carney, S. (2001). Women, gender, and the law: Toward a feminist rethinking of responsibility. In R.K. Unger (Ed.), *Handbook of the psychology of women and gender* (pp. 388–409). New York: Wiley.

Finegan, J. et al. (1989). A window for the study of prenatal sex hormones influences on postnatal development. *Journal of Genetic Psychology, 150,* 101–112.

Fingeret, M.C., & Gleaves, D.H. (2004). Sociocultural, feminist, and psychological influences on women's body satisfaction: A structural modeling analysis. *Psychology of Women Quarterly, 28,* 370–380.

Finlay, B., & Love, G.D. (1998). Gender differences in reasoning about military intervention. *Psychology of Women Quarterly, 22,* 481–485.

Fischer, A.R. (2006). Women's benevolent sexism as reaction to hostility. *Psychology of Women Quarterly, 30,* 410–416.

Fischer, A.R. at el. (2000). Assessing women's feminist identity development: Studies of convergent, discriminant, and structural validity. *Psychology of Women Quarterly, 24,* 15–29.

Fischer, A.R., & Good, G.E. (1994). Gender, self, and others: Perceptions of the campus environment. *Journal of Counseling Psychology, 41,* 343–355.

Fischer, A.R., & Holz, K.B. (2007). Perceived discrimination and women's psychological distress: The roles of collective and personal esteem. *Journal of Counseling Psychology, 54,* 154–164.

Fischer, A.R., & Good, G.E. (1994). Gender, self, and others: Perceptions of the campus environment. *Journal of Counseling Psychology, 41,* 343–355.

Fischer, A.R., & Good, G.E. (2004). Women's feminist consciousness, anger, and psychological distress. *Journal of Counseling Psychology, 51,* 437–446.

Fischer, P.C. (2001). Putting theory into practice: A psychologist's story. *Women & Therapy, 23,* 101–109.

Fisher, B., & Galler, R. (1988). Friendship and fairness: How disability affects friendship between women. In M. Fine & A. Asch (Eds.), *Women with disabilities* (pp. 172–194). Philadelphia, PA: Temple.

Fisher-Thompson, D., & Burke, T.A. (1998). Experimenter influences and children's cross-gender behavior. *Sex Roles, 39,* 669–684.

Fiske, S.T. (1993). Social cognition and social perception. *Annual Review of Psychology, 44,* 155–194.

Fiske, S.T. et al. (1999). (Dis)respecting versus (dis)liking: Status and interdependence predict ambivalent stereotypes of competence and warmth. *Journal of Social Issues, 55,* 473–489.

Fiske, S.T. et al. (2002). A model of (often mixed) stereotype content: Competence and warmth respectively follow from perceived status and competition. *Journal of Personality and Social Psychology, 82,* 878–902.

Fiske, S.T., & Glick, P. (1995). Ambivalence and stereotypes cause sexual harassment: A theory with implications for organizational change. *Journal of Social Issues, 51*(1), 97–115.

Fiske, S.T., & Taylor, S.E. (1991). *Social cognition* (2nd ed.). New York: McGraw-Hill.

Fiske, S.T., & Von Hendy, H.M. (1992). Personality feedback and situational norms can control stereotyping processes. *Journal of Personality and Social Psychology, 62,* 577–596.

Fitzgerald, L.F. (1990). Sexual harassment: The definition and measurement of a construct. In M. Paludi (Ed.), *Ivory power: Sexual harassment on campus* (pp. 21–44). Albany, NY: State University of New York Press.

Fitzgerald, L.F. (1993). Sex harassment: Violence against women in the workplace. *American Psychologist, 48,* 1070–1076.

Fitzgerald, L.F. et al. (1988). The incidence and dimensions of sexual harassment in academia and the workplace. *Journal of Vocational Behavior, 32,* 152–175.

Fitzgerald, L.F. et al. (1995). Why didn't she just report him? The psychological and legal implications of women's responses to sexual harassment. *Journal of Social Issues, 51*(1), 117–138.

Fitzgerald, L.F., & Ormerod, A.J. (1993). Breaking the silence: The sexual harassment of women in academia and the workplace. In F.L. Denmark & M.A. Paludi (Eds.), *Psychology of women: A handbook of issues and theories* (pp. 553–581). Westport, CT: Greenwood.

Fitzpatrick, M.J., & McPherson, B.J. (2010). Coloring within the lines: Gender stereotypes in contemporary coloring books. *Sex Roles, 62,* 127–137.

Flannagan, D., & Perese, S. (1998). Emotional references in mother-daughter and mother-son dyads' conversations about school. *Sex Roles, 39,* 353–367.

Fletcher, G.J.O. (2002). *The new science of intimate relationships.* Oxford, England: Blackwell.

Fletcher, G.J.O. et al. (1999). Ideals in intimate relationships. *Journal of Personality and Social Psychology, 76,* 72–89.

Fleury, R.E. et al. (2000). When ending the relationship does not end the violence: Women's experiences of violence by former partners. *Violence Against Women, 6,* 1363–1383.

Floyd, K. (1995). Gender and closeness among friends and siblings. *Journal of Psychology, 129,* 193–202.

Flynn, C.P. (2000). Woman's best friend: Pet abuse and the role of companion animals in the lives of battered women. *Violence Against Women, 6,* 162–177.

Flynn, F.J., & Ames, D.R. (2006). What's good for the goose may not be as good for the gander: The benefits of self-monitoring for men and women in task groups and dyadic conflicts. *Journal of Applied Psychology, 91,* 272–281.

Fodor, I.G. (1992). The agoraphobic syndrome: From anxiety neurosis to panic disorder. In L.S. Brown & M. Ballou (Eds.), *Personality and psychopathology: Feminist reappraisals* (pp. 177–205). New York: Guilford.

Fonow, M.M. (1998). Protest engendered: The participation of women steelworkers in the

Wheeling-Pittsburgh steel strike of 1985. *Gender & Society, 12*, 710–728.

Forbes, G.B. et al. (2001). Body dissatisfaction in women and men: The role of gender-typing and self-esteem. *Sex Roles, 44*, 461–484.

Forbes, G.B. et al. (2002). Perceptions of married women and married men with hyphenated surnames. *Sex Roles, 46*, 167–175.

Forbes, G.B. et al. (2003). The role of hostile and benevolent sexism in women's and men's perceptions of the menstruating woman. *Psychology of Women Quarterly, 27*, 58–63.

Forbes, G.B. et al. (2004). Association of the thin body ideal, ambivalent sexism, and self-esteem with body acceptance and the preferred body size of college women in Poland and the United States. *Sex Roles, 50*, 331–345.

Forbes, G.B. et al. (2007). Sexism, hostility toward women, and endorsement of beauty ideals and practices: Are beauty ideals associated with oppressive beliefs? *Sex Roles, 56*, 265–273.

Forbes, G.B., & Frederick, D.A. (2008). The UCLA Body Project II: Breast and body dissatisfaction among African, Asian, European, and Hispanic American college women. *Sex Roles, 58*, 449–457.

Ford, T.E. et al. (2008). More than "just a joke": The prejudice-releasing function of sexist humor. *Personality and Social Psychology Bulletin, 34*, 159–170.

Forsythe, S.M. (1990). Effect of applicant's clothing on interviewer's decision to hire. *Journal of Applied Social Psychology, 20*, 1579–1595.

Foubert, J.D. (2005). *The men's program: A peer education guide to rape prevention* (3rd ed.). New York: Routledge.

Foubert, J.D., & Cremedy, B.J. (2007). Reactions of men of color to a commonly used rape prevention program: Attitude and predicted behavioral changes. *Sex Roles, 57*, 137–144.

Fowers, B.J. et al. (1996). His and her individualisms? Sex bias and individualism in psychologists' responses to case vignettes. *Journal of Psychology, 130*, 159–174.

Fox, M., & Hesse-Biber, S. (1984). *Women at work*. Palo Alto, CA: Mayfield.

Fragoso, J.M., & Kashubeck, S. (2000). Machismo, gender role conflict and mental health in Mexican American men. *Psychology of Men and Masculinity, 1*, 87–97.

Franchina, J.J. et al. (2001). Masculine gender role stress and intimate abuse: Effects of masculine gender relevance of dating situations and female threat on men's attributions and affective responses. *Psychology of Men and Masculinity, 2*, 34–41.

Franiuk, R. et al. (2008). Prevalence of rape myths in headlines and their effects on attitudes toward rape. *Sex Roles, 58*, 790–801.

Frank, M.L. (1999). Raising daughters to resist negative cultural messages about body image. *Women & Therapy, 22*, 69–88.

Frankel, A., & Curtis, D.A. (2008). What's in a purse? Maybe a woman's reputation. *Sex Roles, 59*, 615–622.

Frankenberg, R. (1993). *White women, race matters: The social construction of Whiteness*. Minneapolis, MN: University of Minnesota Press.

Franks, M.M., & Stephens, M.P. (1992). Multiple roles of middle-generation caregivers: Contextual effects and psychological mechanisms. *Journals of Gerontology, 47*, S123–S129.

Franzoi, S.L. (2001). Is female body esteem shaped by benevolent sexism? *Sex Roles, 44*, 177–188.

Franzoi, S.L., & Klaiber, J.R. (2007). Body use and reference group impact: With whom do we compare our bodies? *Sex Roles, 56*, 205–214.

Franzoi, S.L., & Koehler, V. (1998). Age and gender differences in body attitudes: A comparison of young and elderly adults. *International Journal of Aging and Human Development, 47*, 1–10.

Franzoi, S.L., & Shields, S.A. (1984). The body esteem scale: Multidimensional structure and sex differences in a college population. *Journal of Personality Assessment, 48*, 173–178.

Frederick, D.A. et al. (2007). The UCLA Body Project I: Gender and ethnic differences in self-objectification and body satisfaction among 2,206 undergraduates. *Sex Roles, 57*, 317–327.

Fredrickson, B.L. et al. (1998). That swimsuit becomes you: Sex differences in self-objectification, restrained eating, and math performance. *Journal of Personality and Social Psychology, 75*, 269–284.

Fredrickson, B.L. et al. (2011). Bringing back the body" A retrospective on the development of objectification theory. *Psychology of Women Quarterly, 35*, 689–696.

Fredrickson, B.L., & Roberts, T. (1997). Objectification theory: Toward understanding women's lived experiences and mental health risks. *Psychology of Women Quarterly, 21*, 173–206.

French, J.R.P., & Raven, B. (1959). The bases of social power. In D. Cartwright (Ed.), *Studies in social power* (pp. 150–167). Ann Arbor, MI: Institute for Social Research, University of Michigan.

Frey, L.L. et al. (2006). Relational health, attachment, and psychological distress in college women and men. *Psychology of Women Quarterly, 30*, 303–311.

Freyd, J.J. (1997). Violations of power, adaptive blindness and betrayal trauma theory. *Feminism & Psychology, 7*, 22–32.

Frieze, I.H. (2000). Violence in close relationships—development of a research area: Comment on Archer (2000). *Psychological Bulletin, 126*, 681–684.

Frieze, I.H. et al. (2006). Work values and their effect on work behavior and work outcomes in female and male managers. *Sex Roles, 54*, 83–93.

Frieze, I.H., & McHugh, M.C. (1992). Power and influence strategies in violent and nonviolent marriages. *Psychology of Women Quarterly, 16*, 449–465.

Frost, J., & McKelvie, S. (2004). Self-esteem and body satisfaction in male and female elementary school, high school, and university students. *Sex Roles, 51*, 45–54.

Frye, M. (1992). Willful virgin or do you have to be a lesbian to be a feminist? In *Willful virgin: Essays in feminism* (pp. 124–137). Freedom, CA: Crossing Press.

Fuegen, K. et al. (2004). Mothers and fathers in the workplace: How gender and parental status influence judgments of job-related competence. *Journal of Social Issues, 60*(4), 737–754.

Fugre, M.A. et al. (2008). Sexual attitudes and double standards: A literature review focusing on participant gender and ethnic background. *Sexuality and Culture: An Interdisciplinary Quarterly, 12*, 169–182.

Fulcher, M. et al. (2008). Individual differences in gender development: Associations with parental sexual orientation, attitudes, and division of labor. *Sex Roles, 58*, 330–341.

Fuller-Iglesias, H. et al. (2008). *Theories of aging from a life course and life span perspective: An overview and outlook.* New York: MacArthur Foundation Aging Society Network.

Furnham, A., & Baguma, P. (1994). Cross-cultural differences in the evaluation of male and female body shapes. *International Journal of Eating Disorders, 15*, 81–89.

Furnham, A., & Twiggy, M. (1999). Sex-role stereotyping in television commercials: A review and comparison of fourteen studies done on five continents over 25 years. *Sex Roles, 41*, 413–437.

Furumoto, L., & Scarborough, E. (1986). Placing women in the history of psychology: The first American women psychologists. *American Psychologist, 41*, 35–42.

Fyre, M. (1983). *The politics of reality: Essays in feminist theory.* Trumansburg, NY: Crossing Press.

Gagne, P. et al. (1997). Coming out and crossing over: Identity formation and proclamation in a transgender community. *Gender & Society, 11*, 478–508.

Galinsky, A.D., & Moskowitz, G.B. (2000). Perspective-taking: Decreasing stereotype expression, stereotype accessibility, and in-group favoritism. *Journal of Personality and Social Psychology, 78*, 708–724.

Gallant, S.J. et al. (1991). Daily moods and symptoms: Effects of awareness of study focus, gender, menstrual-cycle phase, and day of week. *Health Psychology, 10*, 180–189.

Gallant, S.J., & Derry, P.S. (1995). Menarche, menstruation, and menopause: Psychosocial research and future directions. In A.L. Stanton & S.J. Gallant (Eds.), *The psychology of women's health: Progress and challenges in research and application* (pp. 199–259). Washington, DC: American Psychological Association.

Galupo, M.P. (2007). Women's close friendships across sexual orientation: A comparative analysis of lesbian-heterosexual and bisexual-heterosexual women's friendships. *Sex Roles, 56*, 473–482.

Galupo, M.P. et al. (2010). Cross-category friendships and postformal thought among college students. *Journal of Adult Development, 17*, 208–214.

Gannon, L. (1998). The impact of medical and sexual politics on women's health. *Feminism & Psychology, 8*, 285–302.

Ganong, L.H., & Coleman, M. (1995). The content of mother stereotyping. *Sex Roles, 32*, 495–512.

Garcia-Retamero, R., & Lopez-Zafra, E. (2006). Prejudice against women in male-congenial environments: Perceptions of gender role congruity in leadership. *Sex Roles, 55*, 51–61.

Garfield, S.L. (1986). Problems in diagnostic classification. In T. Millon & G.L. Klerman (Eds.), *Contemporary directions in psychotherapy: Toward DSM-IV* (pp. 99–114). New York: Guilford.

Garnets, L.D. et al. (1993). Violence and victimization of lesbians and gay men: Mental health consequences. In L.D. Garnets & D.C. Kimmel (Eds.), *Psychological perspectives on lesbian & gay male experiences* (pp. 577–597). New York: Columbia University Press.

Garst, J., & Bodenhausen, G.V. (1997). Advertising's effects on men's gender role attitudes. *Sex Roles, 36*, 551–572.

Gaucher, D. et al. (2011). Evidence that gendered wording in job advertisements exists and sustains job inequality. *Journal of Personality and Social Psychology, 101*, 109–128.

Gaunt, R. (2006). Biological essentialism, gender ideologies, and role attitudes: What determines parents' involvement in child care. *Sex Roles, 55,* 523–533.

Gavey, N., & McPhillips, K. (1999). Subject to romance: Heterosexual passivity as an obstacle to women initiating condom use. *Psychology of Women Quarterly, 23,* 349–367.

Geary, D.C. (1998). *Male, female: The evolution of human sex differences.* Washington, DC: American Psychological Association.

Geary, D.C. et al. (2003). Evolution and development of boys' social behavior. *Developmental Review, 23,* 444–470.

Geissler, L.J. et al. (1995). Women, homelessness, and substance abuse: Moving beyond the stereotypes. *Psychology of Women Quarterly, 19,* 65–83.

Gelfond, M. (1991). Reconceptualizing agoraphobia: A case study of epistemological bias in clinical research. *Feminism & Psychology, 1,* 247–262.

Geller, J.L. (1985). Women's accounts of psychiatric illness and institutionalization. *Hospital and Community Psychiatry, 36,* 1056–1062.

Geller, P.A. et al. (2010). Satisfaction with pregnancy loss aftercare: Are women getting what they want? *Archives of Women's Mental Health, 13,* 111–124.

Gentry, M. (1998). The sexual double standard: The influence of number of relationships and level of sexual activity on judgments of women. *Psychology of Women Quarterly, 22,* 505–511.

George, D.M. et al. (1998). Gender-related patterns of helping among friends. *Psychology of Women Quarterly, 22,* 685–704.

George, L.K. (1996). Missing links: The case for a social psychology of the life course. *The Gerontologist, 36,* 248–255.

George, W.H., & Martinez, L.J. (2002). Victim blaming in rape: Effects of victim and perpetrator race, type of rape, and participant racism. *Psychology of Women Quarterly, 26,* 110–119.

Gergen, K. (1985). The social constructionist movement in modern psychology. *American Psychologist, 40,* 255–265.

Gergen, K., & Gergen, M. (2010). Positive aging: Resilience and reconstruction. In P.S. Prem & C.L.M. Corey (Eds.), *New frontiers in resilient aging: Life-strengths and well-being in late life* (pp. 340–356). New York: Cambridge.

Gergen, M.M. (1990). Finished at 40: Women's development within the patriarchy. *Psychology of Women Quarterly, 14,* 471–494.

Gerson, K. (1985). *Hard choices: How women decide about work, career and motherhood.* Berkeley, CA: University of California Press.

Gerson, K. (1993). *No man's land: Men's changing commitments to family and work.* New York: Basic.

Gerstel, N., & Gallagher, S.K. (2001). Men's caregiving: Gender and the contingent character of care. *Gender & Society, 15,* 197–217.

Gerstman,, E.A., & Kramer, D.A. (1997). Feminist identity development: Psychometric analyses of two feminist identity scales. *Sex Roles, 36,* 327–348.

Gervais, S.J. et al. (2010). Confronting sexism: The role of relationship orientation and gender. *Sex Roles, 63,* 463–474.

Gervais, S.J. et al. (2011). When what you see if what you get: The consequences of the objectifying gaze for women and men. *Psychology of Women Quarterly, 35,* 5–17.

Gettman, H.J., & Gelfand, M.J. (2007). When the customer shouldn't be king: Antecedents and consequences of sexual harassment by clients and customers. *Journal of Applied Psychology, 92,* 757–770.

Gilbert, L.A. (1993). *Two careers/one family.* Newbury Park, CA: Sage.

Gilbert, L.A. et al. (1999). Challenging discourse themes reproducing gender in heterosexual dating: An analog study. *Sex Roles, 41,* 753–774.

Gilbert, L.A., & Rader, J. (2001). Current perspectives on women's adult roles: Work, family, and life. In R.K. Unger (Ed.), *Handbook of the psychology of women and gender* (pp. 156–169). New York: Wiley.

Gilbert, N. (1997). Advocacy research exaggerates rape statistics. In M.R. Walsh (Ed.), *Women, men, and gender: Ongoing debates* (pp. 236–242). New Haven, CT: Yale.

Gillem, A.R. (1996). Beyond double jeopardy: Female, biracial, and perceived to be Black. In J.C. Chrisler, K. Golden, & P.D. Rozee (Eds.), *Lectures on the psychology of women* (pp. 199–209). New York: McGraw-Hill.

Gillen, M.M., & Lefkowitz, E.S. (2006). Gender role development and body image among male and female first year college students. *Sex Roles, 55,* 25–37.

Gillespie, R. (2003). Childfree and feminine: Understanding the gender identity of voluntary childless women. *Gender & Society, 17,* 122–136.

Gilligan, C. (1982). *In a different voice: Psychological theory and women's development.* Cambridge, MA: Harvard.

Ginorio, A., & Huston, M. (2000). ¡Si, Se puede! *Yes, We can: Latinas in school.* Washington, DC: American Association of University Women's Educational Foundation.

Glascock, J., & Preston-Schreck, C. (2004). Gender and racial stereotypes in daily newspaper comics: A time-honored tradition? *Sex Roles, 51*, 423–431.

Glass, D. (1964). Changes in liking as a means of reducing cognitive discrepancies between self-esteem and aggression. *Journal of Personality, 32*, 531–549.

Glasser, C.L. et al. (2009). Internet daters' body type preferences: Race-ethnic and gender-differences. *Sex Roles, 61*, 14–33.

Glick, P. (1991). Trait-based and sex-based discrimination in occupational prestige. *Sex Roles, 25*, 351–378.

Glick, P. (1997, October). *Allport's afterthought: Why prejudice cannot be defined as an antipathy.* Paper presented at the meeting of the Society of Experimental Social Psychology, Toronto.

Glick, P. et al. (2000). Beyond prejudice as simple antipathy: Hostile and benevolent sexism across cultures. *Journal of Personality and Social Psychology, 79*, 763–775.

Glick, P. et al. (2002). Ambivalent sexism and attitudes toward wife abuse in Turkey and Brazil. *Psychology of Women Quarterly, 26*, 292–297.

Glick, P., & Fiske, S.T. (1996). The Ambivalent Sexism Inventory: Differentiating hostile and benevolent sexism. *Journal of Personality and Social Psychology, 70*, 491–512.

Glick, P., & Fiske, S.T. (1997). Hostile and benevolent sexism: Measuring ambivalent sexist attitudes toward women. *Psychology of Women Quarterly, 21*, 119–135.

Glick, P., & Fiske, S.T. (1999a). Sexism and other "isms": Interdependence, status, and the ambivalent content of stereotypes. In W.B. Swann, Jr., J. Langlois, & L.A. Gilbert (Eds.), *Sexism and stereotypes in modern society: Essays in honor of Janet Taylor Spence.* Washington, DC: American Psychological Association.

Glick, P., & Fiske, S.T. (1999b). The Ambivalence toward Men Inventory: Differentiating hostile and benevolent beliefs about men. *Psychology of Women Quarterly, 23*, 519–536.

Glick, P., & Fiske, S.T. (2001a). Ambivalent sexism. In M.P. Zanna (Ed.), *Advances in experimental social psychology* (Vol. 33, pp. 115–188). San Diego, CA: Academic Press.

Glick, P., & Fiske, S.T. (2001b). An ambivalent alliance: Hostile and benevolent sexism as complementary justifications for gender inequality. *American Psychologist, 56*, 109–118.

Goldberg, C.B. (2001). The impact of the proportion of women in one's workgroup, profession, and friendship circle on males' and females' responses to sexual harassment. *Sex Roles, 45*, 359–374.

Goldberg, C.B. (2007). The impact of training and conflict avoidance on responses to sexual harassment. *Psychology of Women Quarterly, 31*, 62–72.

Goldberg, W.A. et al. (1992). Role demands in the lives of employed single mothers with preschoolers. *Journal of Family Issues, 13*, 312–333.

Golden, J.H. et al. (2001). Sexual harassment in the workplace: Exploring the effects of attractiveness on perception of harassment. *Sex Roles, 45*, 767–784.

Golombok, S. (2000). *Parenting: What really counts.* New York: Routledge.

Golombok, S., & Tasker, F. (1996). Do parents influence the sexual orientation of their children? Findings from a longitudinal study of lesbian families. *Developmental Psychology, 32*, 3–11.

Gomberg, E.L. (1993). Women and alcohol: Use and abuse. *Journal of Nervous and Mental Disease, 181*, 211–219.

Gomberg, E.S.L. (1994). Risk factors for drinking over a woman's life span. *Alcohol Health and Research World, 18*, 220–227.

Gomez, M.J., & Fassinger, R.E. (1994). An initial model of Latina achievement: Acculturation, biculturalism, and achieving styles. *Journal of Counseling Psychology, 41*, 205–215.

Gonzalez, A.Q., & Koestner, R. (2005). Parental preference for sex of newborn as reflected in positive affect in birth announcements. *Sex Roles, 52*, 407–411.

Gonzalez, A.Q., & Koestner, R. (2006). What Valentine announcements reveal about the romantic emotions of men and women. *Sex Roles, 55*, 767–773.

Good, G.E., & Sherrod, N.B. (2001). The psychology of men and masculinity: Research status and future directions. In R.K. Unger (Ed.), *Handbook of the psychology of women and gender* (pp. 201–214). New York: Wiley.

Good, J.J., & Rudman, L.A. (2010). When female applicants meet sexist interviewers: The costs of being a target of benevolent sexism. *Sex Roles, 62*, 481–493.

Good, J.J. et al. (in press). When do we confront? Perceptions of costs and benefits predict confronting discrimination on behalf of the self and others. *Psychology of Women Quarterly.*

Goodenow, C., & Gaier, E.L. (1990, August). *Best friends: The close reciprocal friendships of married and unmarried women.* Paper presented at the meeting of the American Psychological Association, Washington, D.C.

Goodman, L.A. et al. (1993). Violence against women: Physical and mental health effects: Part

1. Research findings. *Applied and Preventive Psychology, 2,* 79–89.

Goodwin, R., & Lee, I. (1994). Taboo topics among Chinese and English friends: A cross-cultural comparison. *Journal of Cross-Cultural Psychology, 25,* 325–338.

Goodwin, S.A., & Fiske, S.T. (2001). Power and gender: The double-edged sword of ambivalence. In R.K. Unger (Ed.), *Handbook of the psychology of women and gender* (pp. 358–366). New York: Wiley.

Gordon, M. (2000). Definitional issues in violence against women: Surveillance and research from a violence research perspective. *Violence Against Women, 6,* 747–783.

Gordon, M.K. (2008). Media contributions to African American girls' focus on beauty and appearance: Exploring the consequences of self-objectification. *Psychology of Women Quarterly, 32,* 245–256.

Gordon, M.T., & Riger, S. (1989). *The female fear.* New York: Free Press.

Gough, B. (1998). Men and the discursive reproduction of sexism: Repertoires of difference and equality. *Feminism & Psychology, 8,* 25–49.

Gould, S.J. (1981). *The mismeasure of man.* New York: Norton.

Gowaty, P.A. (2001). Women, psychology, and evolution. In R.K. Unger (Ed.), *Handbook of the psychology of women and gender* (pp. 53–65). New York: Wiley.

Grabe, S. et al. (2007). Body objectification and depression in adolescents: The role of gender, shame, and rumination. *Psychology of Women Quarterly, 31,* 164–175.

Grabe, S. et al. (2008). The role of the media in body image concerns among women: A meta-analysis of experimental and correlational studies. *Psychological Bulletin, 134,* 460–476.

Grabe, S., & Hyde, J.S. (2006). Ethnicity and body dissatisfaction among women in the United States: A meta-analysis. *Psychological Bulletin, 132,* 622–640.

Grace, V. (2001). Critical encounters with the medical paradigm: Encouraging dialogue. *Feminism & Psychology, 11,* 421–428.

Grady, K.E. (1981). Sex bias in research design. *Psychology of Women Quarterly, 5,* 628–636.

Graham, J.E. et al. (2002). Anger after childbirth: An overlooked reaction to postpartum stressors. *Psychology of Women Quarterly, 26,* 222–233.

Gray, J. (2004). *Men are from Mars, women are from Venus: The classic guide for understanding the opposite sex.* New York: HarperCollins.

Gray-Little, B., & Hafdahl, A.R. (2000). Factors influencing racial comparisons of self-esteem: A quantitative review. *Psychological Bulletin, 126,* 26–54.

Green, M.A. et al. (2008). Femininity and eating disorders. *Eating Disorders: The Journal of Treatment & Prevention, 16,* 283–293.

Greene, B. (1990). What has gone before: The legacy of racism and sexism in the lives of black mothers and daughters. *Women & Therapy, 9,* 207–230.

Greene, B. (1994). African American women. In L. Comas-Díaz & B. Greene (Eds.), *Women of color: Integrating ethnic and gender identities in psychotherapy* (pp. 10–29). New York: Guilford.

Greene, D.M., & Navarro, R.L. (1998). Situation-specific assertiveness in the epidemiology of sexual victimization among university women. *Psychology of Women Quarterly, 22,* 589–604.

Greene, E. (1995). Teaching about psychological perspectives on abortion. *Teaching of Psychology, 22,* 202–204.

Greenleaf, C. (2005). Self-objectification among physically active women. *Sex Roles, 52,* 51–62.

Greenleaf, C. et al. (2009). High school sport participation and subsequent psychological well-being and physical activity: The mediating influences of body image, physical competence, and instrumentality. *Sex Roles, 61,* 714–726.

Greenwald, A.G. et al. (1998). Measuring individual differences in implicit cognition: The Implicit Association Test. *Journal of Personality and Social Psychology, 74,* 1464–1480.

Greenwald, D. (1992). Psychotic disorders with emphasis on schizophrenia. In L.S. Brown & M. Ballou (Eds.), *Personality and psychopathology: Feminist reappraisals* (pp. 144–176). New York: Guilford.

Greenwood, D., & Ibell, L.M. (2002). Ambivalent sexism and the dumb blonde: Men's and women's reactions to sexist jokes. *Psychology of Women Quarterly, 26,* 341–350.

Greenwood, R.M. (2008). Intersectional political consciousness: Appreciation for intragroup differences and solidarity in diverse groups. *Psychology of Women Quarterly, 32,* 36–47.

Greenwood, R.M., & Christian, A. (2008). What happens when we unpack the invisible knapsack? Intersectional political consciousness and inter-group appraisals. *Sex Roles, 59,* 404–417.

Greer, T.M. (2011). Coping strategies as moderators of the relation between individual race-related stress and mental health symptoms for African American women. *Psychology of Women Quarterly, 35,* 215–226.

Greer, T.M. et al. (2009). Gender as a moderator of the relation between race-related stress and mental health symptoms for African Americans. *Psychology of Women Quarterly, 33*, 295–307.

Griffin, C. (2000). Absences that matter: Constructions of sexuality in studies of young women's friendships. *Feminism & Psychology, 10*, 227–245.

Griffin, G. (1994). The desire for change and the experience of women's studies. In G. Griffin (Ed.), *Changing our lives: Doing women's studies* (pp. 13–45). Boulder, CO: Pluto Press.

Griffin, S. (1971). Rape: The all-American crime. *Ramparts, 10*, 26–35.

Grinstead, O.A. et al. (1993). Sexual risk for human immunodeficiency virus infection among women in high-risk cities. *Family Planning Perspectives, 25*, 252–256, 277.

Griscom, J.L. (1992). Women and power: Definition, dualism, and difference. *Psychology of Women Quarterly, 16*, 389–414.

Groom, C.J., & Pennebaker, J.W. (2005). The language of love: Sex, sexual orientation, and language use in online personal advertisements. *Sex Roles, 52*, 447–461.

Gross, A.M. et al. (1998). Magnitude scaling of intensity of sexual refusal behaviors in a date rape. *Violence Against Women, 4*, 329–343.

Gross, J. (2005, Nov. 24). Forget the career. My parents need me at home. *New York Times*, pp. A1, A20.

Grossman, A.L., & Tucker, J.S. (1997). Gender differences and sexism in the knowledge and use of slang. *Sex Roles, 37*, 101–110.

Grubb, A., & Harrower, J. (2008). Attribution of blame in cases of rape: An analysis of participant gender, type of rape and perceived similarity to the victim. *Aggression and Violent Behavior, 13*, 396–405.

Gruber, J.E. (1998). The impact of male work environments and organizational policies on women's experiences of sexual harassment. *Gender & Society, 12*, 301–320.

Gruber, J.E., & Fineran, S. (2008). Comparing the impact of bullying and sexual harassment victimization on the mental and physical health of adolescents. *Sex Roles, 59*, 1–13.

Gruen, R.J. et al. (1994). Support, criticism, emotion and depressive symptoms: Gender differences in the stress-depression relationship. *Journal of Social and Personal Relationships, 11*, 619–624.

Guadagno, R.E., & Cialdini, R.B. (2007). Gender differences in impression management in organizations: A qualitative review. *Sex Roles, 56*, 483–494.

Guimond, S. et al. (2006). Social comparison, self-stereotyping, and gender differences in self-construals. *Journal of Personality and Social Psychology, 90*, 221–242.

Gungor, G., & Biernat, M. (2009). Gender bias or motherhood disadvantage? Judgments of blue collar mothers and fathers in the workplace. *Sex Roles, 60*, 232–246.

Gupta, V.K. et al. (2008). The effect of gender stereotype activation on entrepreneurial intentions. *Journal of Applied Psychology, 93*, 1053–1061.

Gurevich, M. (1995). Rethinking the label: Who benefits from the PMS construct? *Women & Health, 23*, 67–98.

Gurin, P., & Townsend, A. (1986). Properties of gender identity and their implications for gender consciousness. *British Journal of Social Psychology, 25*, 139–148.

Gutek, B.A. (1985). *Sex and the workplace*. San Francisco, CA: Jossey-Bass.

Gutek, B.A. et al. (1996). Reactions to perceived sex discrimination. *Human Relations, 49*, 791–813.

Gutek, B.A., & O'Connor, M. (1995). The empirical basis for the reasonable woman standard. *Journal of Social Issues, 51*(1), 151–166.

Guthrie, R.V. (1976). *Even the rat was white: A historical view of psychology*. New York: Harper & Row.

Gutierrez, L. et al. (2000). Toward an understanding of (em)power(ment) for HIV/AIDS prevention with adolescent women. *Sex Roles, 42*, 581–611.

Gutmann, D. (1987). *Reclaimed powers: Toward a new psychology of men and women in later life*. New York: Basic.

Hackett, G., & Byars, A.M. (1996). Social cognitive theory and the career development of African American women. *Career Development Quarterly, 44*, 322–340.

Hafner, R.J., & Minge, P.J. (1989). Sex role stereotyping in women with agoraphobia and their husbands. *Sex Roles, 20*, 705–711.

Haines, M.E. et al. (2008). Predictors and effects of self-objectification in lesbians. *Psychology of Women Quarterly, 32*, 181–187.

Haj-Yahia, M.M. (2000). Patterns of violence against engaged Arab women from Israel and some psychological implications. *Psychology of Women Quarterly, 24*, 209–219.

Halim, M.L., & Ruble, D. (2010). Gender identity and stereotyping un early and middle childhood. In J.C. Chrisler & D.R., McCreary (Eds.), *Handbook of gender research in psychology* (Vol. 1, pp. 495–526). New York: Springer.

Hall, C.C.I. (1995). Asian eyes: Body image and eating disorders of Asian and Asian American women. *Eating Disorders: The Journal of Treatment and Prevention, 3*, 8–19.

Hall, D.T. (1972). A model of coping with role conflict: The role behavior of college educated women. *Administrative Science Quarterly, 17*, 471–486.

Hall, J.A. et al. (2002). Assigned and felt status in relation to observer-coded and participant-reported smiling. *Journal of Nonverbal Behavior, 26*, 63–81.

Hall, J.A., & Carter, J.D. (1999). Gender-stereotype accuracy as an individual difference. *Journal of Personality and Social Psychology, 77*, 350–359.

Hall, J.A., & Mast, M.S. (2008). Are women always more interpersonally sensitive than men? Impact of goals and content domain. *Personality and Social Psychology Bulletin, 34*, 144–155.

Hall, R., & Rose, S. (1996). Friendships between African-American and White lesbians. In J. Weinstock & E. Rothblum (Eds.), *Lesbian friendships* (pp. 165–191). New York: New York University Press.

Halliwell, E. et al. (2011). Are contempoary media images which seem to display women as sexually empowered actually harmful to women? *Psychology of Women Quarterly, 35*, 38–45.

Halliwell, E. et al. (2011). Are contemporary media images which seem to display women as sexually empowered actually harmful to women? *Psychology of Women Quarterly, 35*, 38–45.

Halliwell, E., & Dittmar, H. (2003). A qualitative investigation of women's and men's body image concerns and their attitudes toward aging. *Sex Roles, 49*, 675–684.

Halpern, D.F. (1997). Sex differences in intelligence: Implications for education. *American Psychologist, 52*, 1091–1102.

Halpern, D.F. (2000). *Sex differences in cognitive abilities* (3rd ed.). Mahwah, NJ: Erlbaum.

Hamberger, L.K. et al. (1992). The prevalence of domestic violence in community practice and rate of physical inquiry. *Family Medicine, 24*, 283–287.

Hamby, S., & Jackson, A. (2010). Size does matter: The effects of gender on perceptions of dating violence. *Sex Roles, 63*, 324–331.

Hamilton, E.A. et al. (2007). Predictors of media effects on body dissatisfaction in European American women. *Sex Roles, 56*, 397–402.

Hamilton, J.A. (1996). Women and health policy: On the inclusion of females in clinical trials. In C.F. Sargent & C.B. Brettell (Eds.), *Gender and health: An international perspective* (pp. 292–325). Upper Saddle River, NJ: Prentice Hall.

Hamilton, J.A., & Jensvold, M. (1992). Personality, psychopathology, and depression in women. In L.S. Brown & M. Ballou (Eds.), *Personality and psychopathology: Feminist reappraisals* (pp. 116–143). New York: Guilford.

Hamilton, M.C. et al. (2006). Gender stereotyping and under-representation of female characters in 200 popular children's picture books: A twenty-first century update. *Sex Roles, 55*, 757–765.

Hampson, E., & Moffat, S.D. (2004). The psychobiology of gender: Cognitive effects of reproductive hormones in the adult nervous system. In A.H. Eagly, A.E. Beall, & R.J. Sternberg (Eds.), *The psychology of gender* (2nd ed.) (pp. 38–64). New York: Guilford.

Hampson, S.E. (1988). The dynamics of categorization and impression formation. In T.K. Srull & R.S. Wyer, Jr. (Eds.), *Advances in social cognition: Vol 1: A dual process model of impression formation* (pp. 77–82). Hillsdale, NJ: Erlbaum.

Hank, K. (2007). Parental gender preferences and reproductive behavior: A review of the recent literature. *Journal of Biosocial Science, 39*, 759–767.

Hanmer, J., & Saunders, S. (1984). *Well founded fear*. London: Hutchinson.

Hanna, W.J., & Rogovsky, E. (1991). Women with disabilities: Two handicaps plus. *Disability, Handicap and Society, 6*, 49–63.

Hannon, R. et al. (1996). College students' judgments regarding sexual aggression during a date. *Sex Roles, 35*, 765–780.

Hansen, F.J., & Osborne, D. (1995). Portrayal of women and elderly patients in psychotropic drug advertisements. *Women & Therapy, 16*(1), 129–141.

Hanson, K., & Gidycz, C.A. (1993). Evaluation of a sexual assault prevention program. *Journal of Consulting and Clinical Psychology, 61*, 1046–1052.

Hardie, E.A. (1997). Prevalence and predictors of cyclic and noncyclic affective change. *Psychology of Women Quarterly, 21*, 299–314.

Hardoy, I., & Schone, P. (2008). Subsidizing "stayers"? Effects of a Norwegian child care reform on marital stability. *Journal of Marriage and Family, 70*, 571–584.

Hardy, D.M., & Johnson, M.E. (1992). Influence of therapist gender and client gender, socioeconomic status and alcohol status on clinical judgments. *Journal of Alcohol and Drug Education, 37*, 94–102.

Hardy, M.A., & Hazelrigg, L.E. (1995). Gender, race/ethnicity, and poverty in later life. *Journal of Aging Studies, 9*, 43–63.

Hare-Mustin, R.T. (1983). An appraisal of the relationship between women and psychotherapy:

80 years after the case of Dora. *American Psychologist, 38,* 593–601.

Hare-Mustin, R.T., & Marecek, J. (1988). The meaning of difference: Gender theory, postmoderism, and psychology. *American Psychologist, 43,* 455–464.

Hargreaves, D.A., & Tiggemann, M. (2003). Female "thin ideal" media images and boys' attitudes toward girls. *Sex Roles, 49,* 539–544.

Harned, M.S. (2000). Harassed bodies: An examination of the relationships among women's experiences of sexual harassment, body image and eating disturbances. *Psychology of Women Quarterly, 24,* 336–348.

Harper, B., & Tiggemann, M. (2008). The effect of thin ideal media images on women's self-objectification, mood, and body image. *Sex Roles, 59,* 649–657.

Harrell, Z.A. et al. (2006). The role of trait self-objectification in smoking among college women. *Sex Roles, 54,* 735–743.

Harrell, Z.A.T., & Jackson, B. (2008). Thinking fat and feeling blue: Eating behaviors, ruminative coping, and depressive symptoms in college women. *Sex Roles, 58,* 658–665.

Harriger, J.A. et al. (2010). Body size stereotyping and internalization of the thin ideal in preschool girls. *Sex Roles, 63,* 609–620.

Harris, J.R. (1998). *The nurture assumption: Why children turn out the way they do.* New York: Free Press.

Harris, K.L. et al. (1999). The impact of women's studies courses on college students of the 1990s. *Sex Roles, 40,* 969–977.

Harris, M.B. (1995). Ethnicity, gender, and evaluators of aggression. *Aggressive Behavior, 21,* 343–357.

Harrison, A.C., & O'Neill, S.A. (2002). The development of children's gendered knowledge and preference in music. *Feminism & Psychology, 12,* 145–152.

Harrison, K. (2003). Televisions viewers' ideal body proportions: The case of the curvaceously thin woman. *Sex Roles, 48,* 255–264.

Harrison, K., & Fredrickson, B.L. (2003). Women's sport media, self-objectification, and mental health in Black and White adolescent females. *Journal of Communication, 53,* 216–232.

Harrison, L.A. et al. (2008). Effects of ingroup bias and gender role violations on acquaintance rape attributions. *Sex Roles, 59,* 713–725.

Harrison, L.A., & Esqueda, C.W. (2000). Effects of race and victim drinking on domestic violence attributions. *Sex Roles, 42,* 1043–1057.

Harrop, E.N., & Marlatt, G.A. (2010). The comorbidity of substance use disorders and eating disorders in women: Prevalence, etiology, and treatment. *Addictive Behaviors, 35,* 392–398.

Hartung, C.M., & Widiger, T.A. (1998). Gender differences in the diagnosis of mental disorders: Conclusions and controversies of the DSM-IV. *Psychological Bulletin, 123,* 260–278.

Haslam, N. (2006). Dehumanization: An integrative review. *Personality and Social Psychology Review, 10,* 252–264.

Haslett, B.B., & Lipman, S. (1997). Micro inequities: Up close and personal. In N.V. Benokraitis (Ed.), *Subtle sexism: Current practice and prospects for change* (pp. 34–53). Thousand Oaks, CA: Sage.

Hatfield, E. et al. (1988). Gender differences in what is desired in the sexual relationship. *Journal of Psychology and Human Sexuality, 1,* 39–52.

Hatoum, I.J., & Belle, D. (2004). Mags and abs: Media consumption and bodily concerns in men. *Sex Roles, 51,* 397–407.

Hauenstein, E.J., & Boyd, M.R. (1994). Depressive symptoms in young women of the Piedmont: Prevalence in rural women. *Women & Health, 21,* 105–123.

Hausenblas, H.A., & Downs, D.S. (2001). Comparison of body image between athletes and nonathletes: A meta-analytic review. *Journal of Applied Sport Psychology, 13,* 323–339.

Haver, B., & Dahlgren, L. (1995). Early treatment of women with alcohol addiction (EWA): A comprehensive evaluation and outcome study: I. Patterns of psychiatric comorbidity at intake. *Addiction, 90,* 101–109.

Hayden, J.M. et al. (2006). The transmission of birth stories from mother to daughter: Self-esteem and mother-daughter attachment. *Sex Roles, 55,* 373–383.

Hayes, J.A., & Mahalik, J.R. (2000). Gender role conflict ad psychological distress in male counseling center clients. *Psychology of Men and Masculinity, 1,* 116–125.

Hebl, M.R. et al. (2007). Hostile and benevolent reactions toward pregnant women: Complementary interpersonal punishments and rewards that maintain traditional roles. *Journal of Applied Psychology, 92,* 1499–1511.

Hebl, M.R., & Mannix, L.M. (2003). The weight of obesity in evaluating others: A mere proximity effect. *Personality and Social Psychology Bulletin, 29,* 28–38.

Hecht, M.A., & LaFrance, M. (1998). License or obligation to smile: The effect of power and sex on amount and type of smiling. *Personality and Social Psychology Bulletin, 24,* 1332–1342.

Heckert, T.M. et al. (2002). Gender differences in anticipated salary: Role of salary estimates for others, job characteristics, career paths, and job inputs. *Sex Roles, 47*, 139–151.

Heflick, N.A. et al. (2011). From women to objects: Appearance focus, target gender, and perceptions of warmth, morality and competence. *Journal of Experimental Social Psychology, 47*, 572–581.

Hegarty, P. (2006). Undoing androcentric explanations of gender differences: Explaining the effect to be predicted. *Sex Roles, 55*, 861–867.

Hegarty, P. et al. (2010). Graphing the order of the sexes: Constructing, recalling, interpreting, and putting the self in gender difference graphs. *Journal of Personality and Social Psychology, 98*, 375–391.

Hegarty, P., & Pratto, F. (2004). The differences that norms make: Empiricism, social constructionism, and the interpretation of group differences. *Sex Roles, 50*, 445–453.

Heidrich, S.M. (1993). The relationship between physical health and psychological well-being in elderly women: A developmental perspective. *Research in Nursing & Health, 16*, 123–130.

Heidrich, S.M., & Ryff, C.D. (1992). How elderly women cope: Concern and strategies. *Public Health Nursing, 9*, 200–208.

Heilman, M. E. et al. (2004). Penalties for success: Reactions to women who succeed at male gender-typed tasks. *Journal of Applied Psychology, 89*, 416–427.

Heilman, M.E., & Okimoto, T.G. (2007). Why are women penalized for success at male tasks? The implied communality deficit. *Journal of Applied Psychology, 92*, 81–92.

Heine-Suner, D. et al. (2005). Epigenetic differences arise during the lifetime of monozygotic twins. *Proceedings of the National Academy of Sciences of the United States of America, 102*(30), 10604–10609.

Heister, G. et al. (1989). Shift of functional cerebral asymmetry during the menstrual cycle. *Neuropsychologia, 27*, 871–880.

Helgeson, V.S. (1994a). Prototypes and dimensions of masculinity and femininity. *Sex Roles, 31*, 653–682.

Helgeson, V.S. (1994b). Relation of agency and communion to well-being: Evidence and potential explanations. *Psychological Bulletin, 116*, 412–428.

Helms, J.E. (Ed.). (1990). *Black and White racial identity: Theory, research, and practice*. New York: Greenwood.

Helms, J.E., & Cook, D.A. (1999). *Using race and culture in counseling and psychotherapy: Theory and practice*. Boston, MA: Allyn and Bacon.

Helms, R.L. et al. (2008). Body image issues in women with breast cancer. *Psychology, Health & Medicine, 13*, 313–325.

Helson, R. (1992). Women's difficult times and the rewriting of the life story. *Psychology of Women Quarterly, 16*, 331–347.

Helson, R. et al. (2002). Personality change ofer 40 years of adulthood: Hierarchical linear modeling analyses of two longitudinal samples. *Journal of Personality and Social Psychology, 83*, 752–766.

Helson, R., & Wink, P. (1992). Personality change in women from the early 40s to the early 50s. *Psychology and Aging, 7*, 46–55.

Helweg-Larsen, M. et al. (2004). To nod or not to nod: An observational study of nonverbal communication and status in female and male college students. *Psychology of Women Quarterly, 28*, 358–361.

Henderson-King, D. et al. (2001). Media images and women's self-evaluations: Social context and importance of attractiveness as moderators. *Personality and Social Psychology Bulletin, 27*, 1407–1416.

Henderson-King, D.H., & Stewart, A.J. (1997). Feminist consciousness: Perspectives on women's experiences. *Personality and Social Psychology Bulletin, 23*, 415–426.

Hendy, H.M. et al. (2001). Social cognitive predictors of body image in preschool children. *Sex Roles, 44*, 557–597.

Hengehold, L. (2000). Remapping the event: Institutional discourses and the trauma of rape. *Signs, 26*, 189–214.

Henley, N. M. et al. (1998). Developing a scale to measure the diversity of feminist attitudes. *Psychology of Women Quarterly, 22*, 317–348.

Henley, N.M. (1977). *Body politics: Power, sex, and nonverbal communication*. Englewood Cliffs, NJ: Prentice Hall.

Henley, N.M. (1995). Ethnicity and gender issues in language. In H. Landrine (Ed.), *Bringing cultural diversity to feminist psychology: Theory, research, and practice* (pp. 361–395). Washington, DC: American Psychological Association.

Henretta, J.C. et al. (1993). Gender differences in employment after spouse's retirement. *Research on Aging, 15*, 148–169.

Hequembourg, A.L., & Farrell, M.P. (1999). Lesbian motherhood: Negotiating marginal-mainstream identities. *Gender & Society, 13*, 540–557.

Herbert, J., & Stipek, D. (2005). The emergence of gender differences in children's perceptions of their academic competence. *Journal of Applied Developmental Psychology, 26*, 276–295.

Herbozo, S. et al. (2004). Beauty and thinness Messages in children's media: A content analysis. *Eating Disorders, 12*, 21–34.

Hercus, C. (1999). Identity, emotion, and feminist collective action. *Gender & Society, 13*, 34–55.

Herdt, G.H., & Davidson, J. (1988). The Sambra "Turnim-man": Sociocultural and clinical aspects of gender formation in male pseudohermaphrodites with 5–alpha-reductase deficiency in Papua New Guinea. *Archives of Sexual Behavior, 17*, 33–56.

Herman, J.L. (1992). *Trauma and recovery.* New York: Basic.

Herman, J.L. et al. (1989). Childhood trauma in borderline personality disorder. *American Journal of Psychiatry, 146*, 490–495.

Hermann, K.S., & Betz, N.E. (2004). Path models of the relationships of instrumentality and expressiveness to social self-efficacy, shyness, and depressive symptoms. *Sex Roles, 51*, 55–66.

Herrick, A.L. et al. (2011). Sex while intoxicated: A meta-analysis comparing heterosexual and sexual minority youth. *Journal of Adolescent Health, 48*, 306–309.

Herzog, D.B. et al. (1992). Body image satisfaction in homosexual and heterosexual women. *International Journal of Eating Disorders, 11*, 391–396.

Hesse-Biber, S. et al. (1999). A longitudinal study of eating disorders among college women: Factors that influence recovery. *Gender & Society, 13*, 385–408.

Hessler, R.M. et al. (1995). Gender, social networks and survival time: A 20–year study of the rural elderly. *Archives of Gerontology and Geriatrics, 21*, 291–306.

Hetsroni, A. (2000). Choosing a mate in television dating games: The influence of setting, culture, and gender. *Sex Roles, 42*, 83–106.

Hickman, S.E., & Muehlenhard, C.L. (1997). College women's fears and precautionary behaviors relating to acquaintance rape and stranger rape. *Psychology of Women Quarterly, 21*, 527–547.

Hill, C.A. (1999). Fusion and conflict in lesbian relationships? *Feminism & Psychology, 9*, 179–185.

Hill, M. (1987). Child-rearing attitudes of Black lesbian mothers. In Boston Lesbian Psychologies Collective (Eds.), *Lesbian psychologies* (pp. 215–225). Urbana, IL: University of Illinois Press.

Hill, M. et al. (1998). A feminist model for ethical decision making. *Women & Therapy, 21*, 101–121.

Hill, M., & Ballou, M. (1998). Making feminist therapy: A practice survey. *Women & Therapy, 21*, 1–16.

Hill, M.S., & Fischer, A.R. (2001). Does entitlement mediate the link between masculinity and rape-related variables? *Journal of Counseling Psychology, 48*, 39–50.

Hill, S.E., & Durante, K.M. (2011). Courtship, competition, and the pursuit of attractiveness: Mating goals facilitate health-related risk taking and strategies risk suppression in women. *Personality and Social Psychology Bulletin, 37*, 383–394.

Hinchliff, S.G. et al. (2010). Sex, menopause and social context: A qualitative study with heterosexual women. *Journal of Health Psychology, 15*, 724–733.

Hinck, S.S., & Thomas, R.W. (1999). Rape myth acceptance in college students: How far have we come? *Sex Roles, 40*, 815–832.

Hines, M. (2004a). Androgen, estrogen, and gender: Contributions of the early hormone environment to gender-related behavior. In A.H. Eagly, A.E. Beall, & R.J. Sternberg (Eds.), *The psychology of gender* (2nd ed.) (pp. 9–37). New York: Guilford.

Hines, M. (2004b). *Brain gender.* New York: Oxford.

Hines, M. (2010). Sex-related variation in human behavior and the brain. *Trends in Cognitive Sciences, 14*, 448–456.

Hiscock, M. et al. (2001). Is there a gender difference in human laterality? IV. An exhaustive survey from dual-task interference studies from six neuropsychology journals. *Journal of Clinical and Experimental Neuropsychology, 23*, 137–148.

Hitlan, R.T. et al. (2009). Antecedents of gender harassment: An analysis of person and situation factors. *Sex Roles, 61*, 794–807.

Ho, C.K. (1990). An analysis of domestic violence in Asian American communities: A multicultural approach to counseling. In L.S. Brown & M.P.P. Root (Eds.), *Diversity and complexity in feminist therapy* (pp. 129–150). New York: Harrington Park Press.

Hodson, G. et al. (2002). Processes in racial discrimination: Differential weighting of conflicting information. *Personality and Social Psychology Bulletin, 28*, 460–471.

Hoffman, C.D., & Moon, M. (2000). Mothers' and fathers' gender-role characteristics: The assignment of postdivorce child care and custody. *Sex Roles, 42*, 917–924.

Hoffmann, M.L. et al. (2004). An examination of gender differences in adolescent adjustment: The effect of competence on gender role differences in symptoms of psychopathology. *Sex Roles, 50*, 795–810.

Hoffman, L.W. (1989). Effects of maternal employment in the two-parent family. *American Psychologist, 44*, 283–292.

Hoffnung, M. (2006). What's in a name? Marital name choice revisited. *Sex Roles, 55*, 817–825.

Hogue, M. et al. (2010). Gender differences in pay expectations: The roles of job intention and self-view. *Psychology of Women Quarterly, 34*, 215–227.

Hohlstein, L.A. et al. (1998). An application of expectancy theory to eating disorders: Development and validation of measures of eating and dieting expectancies. *Psychological Assessment, 10*, 49–58.

Hogue, M., & Yoder, J.D. (2003). The role of status in producing depressed entitlement in women's and men's pay allocations. *Psychology of Women Quarterly, 27*, 330–337.

Hollander, J.A. (2001). Vulnerability and dangerousness: The construction of gender through conversation about violence. *Gender & Society, 15*, 83–109.

Holtzen, D.W., & Agresti, A.A. (1990). Parental responses to gay and lesbian children: Differences in homophobia, self-esteem, and sex-role stereotyping. *Journal of Social and Clinical Psychology, 9*, 390–399.

Hondagneu-Sotelo, P., & Avila, E. (1997). "I'm here, but I'm there": The meanings of Latina transnational motherhood. *Gender & Society, 11*, 548–571.

Horgan, T.G. et al. (2004). Gender differences in memory for the appearance of others. *Personality and Social Psychology Bulletin, 30*, 185–196.

Horner, M.S. (1970). Femininity and successful achievement: A basic inconsistency. In J.M. Bardwick, E. Douvan, M.S. Horner, & D. Gutman (Eds.), *Feminine personality and conflict* (pp. 45–74). Belmont, CA: Brooks/Cole.

Horvath, M., & Ryan, A.M. (2003). Antecedents and potential moderators of the relationship between attitudes and hiring discrimination on the basis of sexual orientation. *Sex Roles, 48*, 115–130.

Hotaling, G.T., & Sugarman, D.B. (1986). An analysis of risk markers in husband to wife violence: The current state of knowledge. *Violence and Victims, 1*, 101–124.

Howard, L.M. et al. (2010). Domestic violence and mental health. *International Review of Psychiatry, 22*, 525–534.

Hoyenga, K.B., & Hoyenga, K.T. (1993). *Gender-related differences: Origins and outcomes.* Boston, MA: Allyn & Bacon.

Hubbard, R. (1990). *The politics of women's biology.* New Brunswick, NJ: Rutgers.

Huerta, M. et al. (2006). Sex and power in the academy: Modeling sexual harassment in the lives of college women. *Personality and Social Psychology Bulletin, 32*, 616–628.

Huffman, M.L. (2004). Gender inequality across local wage hierarchies. *Work and Occupations, 31*, 323–344.

Huffman, S.B. et al. (2005). Menopause symptoms and attitudes of African American women: Closing the knowledge gap and expanding opportunities for counseling. *Journal of Counseling & Development, 83*, 48–56.

Hughes, F.M., & Seto, C.E. (2003). Gender stereotypes: Children's perceptions of future compensatory behavior following violations of gender roles. *Sex Roles, 49*, 685–591.

Hughes, I.A. (2004). Female development: All by default? *New England of Medicine, 351*, 748–750.

Hughes, T.L., & Wilsnack, S.C. (1994). Research on lesbians and alcohol: Gaps and implications. *Alcohol Health and Research World, 18*, 202–205.

Humphreys, T., & Herold, E. (2007). Sexual consent in heterosexual relationships: Development of a new measure. *Sex Roles, 57*, 305–315.

Hurt, M.M. et al. (2007). Feminism: What is it good for? Feminine norms and objectification as the link between feminist identity and clinically relevant outcomes. *Sex Roles, 57*, 355–363.

Hurtado, A., & Sinha, M. (2008). More than men: Latino feminist masculinities and intersectionality. *Sex Roles, 59*, 337–349.

Hutchison, I.W. (1999). Alcohol, fear, and woman abuse. *Sex Roles, 40*, 893–920.

Hutchison, I.W., & Hirschel, J.D. (1998). Abused women: Help-seeking strategies and police utilization. *Violence Against Women, 4*, 436–456.

Hyde, J.S. (1994). Should psychologists study gender differences? Yes, with some guidelines. *Feminism & Psychology, 4*, 507–512.

Hyde, J.S. (2005). The gender similarities hypothesis. *American Psychologist, 60*, 581–592.

Hyde, J.S. et al. (1991). Androgyny across the life span: A replication and longitudinal follow-up. *Developmental Psychology, 27*, 516–519.

Hyde, J.S., & Durik, A.M. (2000). Gender differences in erotic plasticity—evolutionary or sociocultural forces? Comment on Baumeister (2000). *Psychological Bulletin, 126*, 375–379.

Hyde, J.S., & Frost, L.A. (1993). Meta-analysis in the psychology of women. In F.L. Denmark & M.A. Paludi (Eds.), *Psychology of women: A handbook of issues and theories* (pp. 67–103). Westport, CT: Greenwood.

Hyde, J.S., & Grabe, S. (2008). Meta-analysis in the psychology of women. In F.L. Denmark & M.A.

Paludi (Eds.), *Psychology of women: A handbook of issues and theories* (pp. 142–173). Westport, CT: Praeger.

Hyde, J.S., & Linn, M.C. (1988). Gender differences in verbal ability: A meta-analysis. *Psychological Bulletin, 104*, 53–69.

Hyers, L.L. (2007). Resisting prejudice every day: Exploring women's assertive responses to anti-Black racism, anti-Semitism, heterosexism, and sexism. *Sex Roles, 56*, 1–12.

Hyman, S.E. (2010). The diagnosis of mental disorders: The problem of reification. *Annual Review of Clinical Psychology, 6*, 155–179.

Hynie, M. et al. (1997). Commitment, intimacy, and women's perceptions of premarital sex and contraceptive readiness. *Psychology of Women Quarterly, 21*, 447–464.

Hynie, M. et al. (2003). Perceptions of sexual intent: The impact of condom possession. *Psychology of Women Quarterly, 27*, 75–79.

Ickes, W. et al. (2000). Gender differences in empathic accuracy: Differential ability or differential motivation? *Personal Relationships, 7*, 95–109.

Idle, T. et al. (1993). Gender role socialization in toy play situations: Mothers and fathers with their sons and daughters. *Sex Roles, 28*, 679–691.

Imperato-McGinley, J. et al. (1979). Androgens and the evolution of male gender identity among male pseudohermaphrodites with a 5–alpha-reductase deficiency. *New England Journal of Medicine, 300*, 1236–1237.

Impett, E.A., & Peplau, L.A. (2002). Why some women consent to unwanted sex with a dating partner: Insights from attachment theory. *Psychology of Women Quarterly, 26*, 360–370.

Ingram, K.M. et al. (1996). The relationship of victimization experiences to psychological well-being among homeless women and low-income housed women. *Journal of Counseling Psychology, 43*, 218–227.

Inzlicht, M., & Ben-Zeev, T. (2000). A threatening intellectual environment: Why females are susceptible to experiencing problem-solving deficits in the presence of males. *Psychological Science, 11*, 365–371.

Irmen, L. (2006). Automatic activation and use of gender subgroups. *Sex Roles, 55*, 435–444.

Irving, L.M., & Berel, S.R. (2001). Comparison of media-literacy programs to strengthen college women's resistance to media images. *Psychology of Women Quarterly, 25*, 103–111.

ISNA. (2011). Intersex Society of North America. http://www.isna.org/

Ito, T. A., & Urland, R. (2003). Race and gender on the brain: Electrocortical measures of attention

to the race and gender of multiply categorizable individuals. *Journal of Personality and Social Psychology, 85*, 616–626.

IWPR. (Institute for Women's Policy Research). (2005, Sept.). *Memo to John Roberts: The gender wage gap is real*. Washington, DC. http://www.iwpr.org

IWPR (2010, Sept.) *The gender wage gap: 2009*. IWPR #C350 http://www.iwpr.org

IWPR. (2011a, April) *The gender wage gap: 2010*. IWPR #C350 http://www.iwpr.org

IWPR. (2011b, April) *The gender wage gap by occupation*. IWPR #C350a http://www.iwpr.org

Jack, D.C., & Dill, D. (1992). The Silencing the Self Scale: Schemas of intimacy associated with depression in women. *Psychology of Women Quarterly, 16*, 97–105

Jacklin, C.N., & McBride-Chang, C. (1991). The effects of feminist scholarship on developmental psychology. *Psychology of Women Quarterly, 15*, 549–556.

Jackson, D. (1992). *How to make the world a better place for women in five minutes a day*. New York: Hyperion.

Jackson, P.B. et al. (1995). Composition of the workplace and psychological well-being: The effects of tokenism on America's Black elite. *Social Forces, 74*, 543–557.

Jackson, S. (2001). Happily ever after: Young women's stories of abuse in heterosexual love relationships. *Feminism & Psychology, 11*, 305–321.

Jackson, T. et al. (2002). Gender differences in pain perception: The mediating role of self-efficacy beliefs. *Sex Roles, 47*, 561–568.

Jacobs, J. (2003). Detours on the road to equality: Women, work and higher education. *Contexts, 2*, 32–41.

Jacobs, J.A., & Lim, S.T. (1992). Trends in occupational and industrial sex segregation in 56 countries, 1960–1980. *Work and Occupations, 19*, 450–486.

Jacques-Tiura, A.J. et al. (2007). Why do some men misperceive women's sexual intentions more frequently than others do? An application of the confluence model. *Personality and Social Psychology Bulletin, 33*, 1467–1480.

Jaffe, D., & Straus, M.A. (1987). Sexual climate and reported rape: A state-level analysis. *Archives of Sexual Behavior, 16*, 107–124.

Jaffee, S., & Hyde, J.S. (2000). Gender differences in moral orientation: A meta-analysis. *Psychological Bulletin, 126*, 703–726.

James, J.B. (1997). What are the social issues involved in focusing on difference in the study of gender? *Journal of Social Issues, 53*(2), 213–232.

James, J.B. et al. (1995). Rethinking the gender identity crossover hypothesis: A test of a new model. *Sex Roles, 32*, 185–207.

Janoff-Bulman, R., & Frieze, I.H. (1983). A theoretical perspective for understanding reactions to victimization. *Journal of Social Issues, 39*(2), 1–17.

Jansz, J., & Martis, R.G. (2007). The Lara phenomenon: Powerful female characters in video games. *Sex Roles, 56*, 141–148.

Jeffcoate, W.J. et al. (1986). Correlation between anxiety and serum prolactin in humans. *Journal of Psychosomatic Research, 30*, 217–222.

Jeffreys, S. (2000). "Body art" and social status: Cutting tattooing, and piercing from a feminist perspective. *Feminism & Psychology, 10*, 409–429.

Jenen, J. et al. (2009). Implicit attitudes toward feminism. *Sex Roles, 60*, 14–20.

Jenkins, S.R. (1996). Self-definition in thought, action, and life path choices. *Personality and Social Psychology Bulletin, 22*, 99–111.

Johanson, J.C. (2008). Perceptions of femininity in leadership: Modern trend or classic component? *Sex Roles, 58*, 784–789.

Johnson, A.G. (2006). *Privilege, power, and difference* (2nd ed.). New York: McGraw Hill.

Johnson, B.E. et al. (1997). Rape myth acceptance and sociodemographic characteristics: A multidimensional analysis. *Sex Roles, 36*, 693–707.

Johnson, C.L., & Troll, L.E. (1994). Constraints and facilitators to friendships in late life. *Gerontologist, 34*, 79–87.

Johnson, D.J. et al. (2003). Studying the effects of early child care experiences on the development of children of color in the United States; Toward a more inclusive research agenda. *Child Development, 74*, 1227–1244.

Johnson, K.P., & Lennon, S.J. (Eds.) (1999). *Appearance and power.* New York: Berg.

Johnston, D.D., & Swanson, D.H. (2003). Invisible others: A content analysis of motherhood ideologies and myths in magazines. *Sex Roles, 49*, 21–33.

Johnston, D.D., & Swanson, D.H. (2004). Moms hating moms: The internalization of mother war rhetoric. *Sex Roles, 51*, 497–509.

Johnston, D.D., & Swanson, D.H. (2006). Constructing the "good mother": The experience of mothering ideologies by work status. *Sex Roles, 54*, 509–519.

Jones, D.C. (2001). Social comparison and body image: Attractiveness comparisons to models and peers among adolescent girls and boys. *Sex Roles, 45*, 645–664.

Jones, D.J. et al. (2004). Predictors of self-reported physical symptoms in low-income, inner-city African American women: The role of optimism, depressive symptoms, and chronic illness. *Psychology of Women Quarterly, 28*, 112–121.

Jordan-Young, R. (2010). *Brain storm: The flaws in the science of sex differences.* Cambridge, MA: Harvard.

Joseph, J. (1987). Warning. In S. Marts (Ed.), *When I am an old woman I shall wear purple.* Watsonville, CA: Papier-Mache.

Jost, J.T. (1997). An experimental replication of the depressed entitlement effect among women. *Psychology of Women Quarterly, 21*, 387–393.

Judd, C.M., & Park, B. (1988). Out-group homogeneity: Judgments of variability at the individual and group levels. *Journal of Personality and Social Psychology, 54*, 778–788.

Judge, T.A., & Cable, D.M. (2011). When it comes to pay, do the thin win? The effect of weight on pay for men and women. *Journal of Applied Psychology, 96*, 95–112.

Judge, T.A., & Livingston, B.A. (2008). Is the gap more than gender? A longitudinal analysis of gender, gender role orientation, and earnings. *Journal of Applied Psychology, 93*, 994–1012.

Judge, T.A., & Piccolo, R.F. (2004). Transformational and transactional leadership: A meta-analytic test of their relative validity. *Journal of Applied Psychology, 89*, 901–910.

Jussim, L. (1986). Self-fulfilling prophecies: A theoretical and integrative review. *Psychological Review, 93*, 429–445.

Kagan, L. et al. (2004). *Mind over menopause: The complete mind/body approach to coping with menopause.* New York Free Press.

Kahlor, L., & Morrison, D. (2007). Television viewing and rape myth acceptance among college women. *Sex Roles, 56*, 729–739.

Kahn, A.S. et al. (1994). Rape scripts and rape acknowledgment. *Psychology of Women Quarterly, 18*, 53–66.

Kahn, A.S. et al. (2003). Calling it rape: Differences in experiences of women who do or do not label their sexual assault as rape. *Psychology of Women Quarterly, 27*, 233–242.

Kahn, A.S., & Yoder, J.D. (1989). The psychology of women and conservatism: Rediscovering social change. *Psychology of Women Quarterly, 13*, 417–432.

Kahn, J.S. (2011). Feminist therapy for men: Challenging assumptions and moving forward. *Women & Therapy, 34*, 59–76.

Kahneman, D., & Frederick, S. (2002). Representativeness revisited: Attribute substitution in intuitive judgment. In T. Gilovich, D. Griffin, & D. Kahneman (Eds.), *Heuristics and biases: The psychology of intuitive judgment* (pp. 49–81). New York: Cambridge.

Kalichman, S.C. et al. (1996). Prevention of sexually transmitted HIV infection: A meta-analytic review of the behavioral outcome literature. *Annals of Behavioral Medicine, 18*, 6–15.

Kamerman, S.B., & Kahn, A.J. (1995). Innovations in toddler day care and family support services: An international overview. *Child Welfare, 74*, 1281–1300.

Kanin, E.J. (1985). Date rapists: Differential sexual socialization and relative deprivation. *Archives of Sexual Behavior, 14*, 219–231.

Kanter, R.M. (1977). *Men and women of the corporation*. New York: Basic.

Kanuha, V. (1994). Women of color in battering relationships. In L. Comas-Díaz & B. Greene (Eds.), *Women of color: Integrating ethnic and gender identities in psychotherapy* (pp. 428–454). New York: Guilford.

Karkazis, K. (2008). *Fixing sex: Intersex, medical authority, and lived experience*. Durham, NC: Duke.

Karraker, K.H. et al. (1995). Parents' gender-stereotyped perceptions of newborns: The eye of the beholder revisited. *Sex Roles, 33*, 687–701.

Karraker, K.H., & Coleman, P.K. (2005). The effects of child characteristics on parenting. In T. Luster & L. Okagaki (Eds.), *Parenting: An ecological perspective* (2nd ed.) (pp. 147–176). Mahwah, NJ: Erlbaum.

Kaschak, E. (1992). *Engendered lives: A new psychology of women's experience*. New York: Basic.

Kasinsky, R.G. (1998). Tailhook and the construction of sexual harassment in the media: "Rowdy Navy boys" and the women who made a difference. *Violence Against Women, 4*, 81–99.

Kaslow, F.W. et al. (1994). Long term marriages in Sweden: And some comparisons with similar couples in the United States. *Contemporary Family Therapy: An International Journal, 16*, 521–537.

Katerndahl, D.A., & Realini, J.P. (1993). Lifetime prevalence of panic states. *American Journal of Psychiatry, 150*, 246–249.

Katz, J. et al. (2002). Membership in a devalued social group and emotional well-being: Developing a model of personal self-esteem, collective self-esteem, and group socialization. *Sex Roles, 47*, 419–431.

Katz, J. et al. (2004). Effects of participation in a first women's studies course on collective self-esteem, gender-related attitudes, and emotional well-being. *Journal of Applied Social Psychology, 34*, 2179–2199.

Katz, J. et al. (2006). Leaving a sexually coercive dating partner: A prospective application of the investment model. *Psychology of Women Quarterly, 30*, 267–275.

Katz-Wise, S.L. et al. (2010). Gender-role attitudes and behaviors across the transition to parenthood. *Developmental Psychology, 46*, 18–28.

Keating, N., & Jeffrey, B. (1983). Work careers of ever married and never married women. *Gerontologist, 23*, 416–421.

Keddy, B. et al. (1993). Interrupted work histories: Retired women telling their stories. *Health Care for Women International, 14*, 437–446.

Keiller, S.W. (2010). Male narcissism and attitudes toward heterosexual women and men, lesbian women, and gay men: Hostility toward heterosexual women most of all. *Sex Roles, 63*, 530–541.

Keith, V.M. (1993). Gender, financial strain, and psychological distress among older adults. *Research on Aging, 15*, 123–147.

Keith, V.M. et al. (2010). Discriminatory experiences and depressive symptoms among African American women: Do skin tone and mastery matter? *Sex Roles, 62*, 48–59.

Kelly, J., & Bazzini, D.G. (2001). Gender, sexual experience, and the sexual double standard: Evaluations of female contraceptive behavior. *Sex Roles, 45*, 785–799.

Kelly, L. (1988). *Surviving sexual violence*. Minneapolis, MN: University of Minnesota Press.

Kelly, L., & Radford, J. (1996). "Nothing really happened": The invalidation of women's experiences of sexual violence. In M. Hester, L. Kelly, & J. Radford (Eds.), *Women, violence and male power* (pp. 19–33). Bristol, PA: Open University Press.

Kendler, K.S. et al. (1992a). A population-based twin study of major depression in women. *Archives of General Psychiatry, 49*, 257–266.

Kendler, K.S. et al. (1992b). Generalized anxiety disorder in women. *Archives of General Psychiatry, 49*, 267–272.

Kendler, K.S. et al. (1992c). The genetic epidemiology of phobias in women. *Archives of General Psychiatry, 49*, 273–281.

Kendler, K.S. et al. (1992d). A population-based twin study of alcoholism in women. *Journal of the American Medical Association, 268*, 1877–1882.

Kendler, K.S. et al. (2000). Sexual orientation in a U.S. national sample of twin and nontwin sibling pairs. *The American Journal of Psychiatry, 157,* 1843–1846.

Kendler, K.S. et al. (2011). The structure of genetic and environmental risk factors for syndromal and subsyndromal common DSM-IV axis I and all axis II disorders. *The American Journal of Psychiatry,168,* 29–39.

Kenrick, D.T. et al. (1996). Adolescents' age preferences for dating partners: Support for an evolutionary model of life-history strategies. *Child Development, 67,* 1499–1511.

Kenrick, D.T. et al. (2004). Sex roles as adaptation: An evolutionary perspective on gender differences and similarities. In A.H. Eagly, A.E. Beall, & R.J. Sternberg (Eds.), *The psychology of gender* (2nd ed.) (pp. 65–91). New York: Guilford.

Kerpelman, J.L., & Schvaneveldt, P.L. (1999). Young adults' anticipated identity importance of career, marital, and parental roles: Comparisons of men and women with different role balance orientations. *Sex Roles, 41,* 189–217.

Keshet, S. et al. (2006). Gender, status and the use of power strategies. *European Journal of Social Psychology, 36,* 105–117.

Kessler, R.C. et al. (2005). Prevalence, severity, and comorbidity of 12–Month DSM-IV disorders in the National Comorbidity Survey Replication. *Archives of General Psychiatry, 62,* 617–627.

Kessler, S.J. (1998). *Lessons from the intersexed.* New Brunswick, NJ: Rutgers University Press.

Khoo, P.N., & Senn, C.Y. (2004). Not wanted in the inbox: Evaluations of unsolicited and harassing e-mail. *Psychology of Women Quarterly, 28,* 204–214.

Kidder, L.H. et al. (1995). Recalling harassment: Reconstructing experience. *Journal of Social Issues, 51*(1), 53–67.

Kiefer, A. et al. (2006). How women's nonconscious association of sex with submission relates to their subjective sexual arousability and ability to reach organism. *Sex Roles, 55,* 83–94.

Kiefer, A., & Shih, M. (2006). Gender differences in persistence and attributions in stereotype relevant contexts. *Sex Roles, 54,* 859–868.

Kileen, L.A. et al. (2006). Envisioning oneself as a leader: Comparisons of women and men in Spain and the United States. *Psychology of Women Quarterly, 30,* 312–322.

Kilmartin, C.S. et al. (2008). A real time social norms intervention to reduce male sexism. *Sex Roles, 59,* 264–273.

Kim, J.L., & Ward, L.M. (2004). Pleasure reading: Associations between young women's sexual attitudes and their reading of contemporary women's magazines. *Psychology of Women Quarterly, 28,* 48–58.

Kimmel, J., & Amuedo-Dorantes, C. (2004). The effects of family leave on wages, employment and the family wage gap: Distributional implications. *Journal of Law and Policy, 15,* 115–142.

Kimmel, M.S., & Kaufman, M. (1997). Weekend warriors: The new men's movement. In M.R. Walsh (Ed.), *Women, men, and gender: Ongoing debates* (pp. 406–420). New Haven, CT: Yale.

Kimura, D., & Carson, M.W. (1995). Dermatoglyphic asymmetry: Relation to sex, handedness, and cognitive pattern. *Personality and Individual Differences, 19,* 471–478.

Kinsler, K., & Zalk, S.R. (1996). Teaching is a political act: Contextualizing gender and ethnic voices. In K.F. Wyche & F. Crosby (Eds.), *Women's ethnicities: Journeys through psychology* (pp. 27–48). Boulder, CO: Westview.

Kirk, K.M. et al. (2000). Measurement models for sexual orientation in a community twin sample. *Behavior Genetics, 30,* 345–356.

Kissling, E.A. (2002). On the rag on the screen: Menarche in film and television. *Sex Roles, 46,* 5–12.

Kite, M.E. (2001). Changing times, changing gender roles: Who do we want women and men to be? In R.K. Unger (Ed.), *Handbook of the psychology of women and gender* (pp. 215–227). New York: Wiley.

Kite, M.E. (2011). (Some) things are different now: An optimistic look at sexual prejudice. *Psychology of Women Quarterly, 35,* 517–522.

Kitzinger, C. (1990). Resisting the discipline. In E. Burmna (Ed.), *Feminists and psychological practice* (pp. 119–139). Newbury Park, CA: Sage.

Kitzinger, C. (1991). Feminism, psychology, and the paradox of power. *Feminism & Psychology, 1,* 111–129.

Kitzinger, C., & Wilkinson, S. (1995). Transitions from heterosexuality to lesbianism: The discursive production of lesbian identities. *Developmental Psychology, 31,* 95–104.

Klebanov, P.K., & Jemmott, J.B., III. (1992). Effects of expectations and bodily sensations on self-reports of premenstrual symptoms. *Psychology of Women Quarterly, 16,* 289–310.

Klebanov, P.K., & Ruble, D.N. (1994). Toward an understanding of women's experience of menstrual symptoms. In V.J. Adesso, D.M. Reddy, & R. Fleming (Eds.), *Psychological perspectives on women's health* (pp. 183–221). Washington, DC: Taylor & Francis.

Klein, K.J.K., & Hodges, S.D. (2001). Gender differences, motivation, and empathetic accuracy:

When it pays to understand. *Personality and Social Psychology Bulletin, 27*, 720–730.

Klein, M.H. et al. (1998). Maternity leave, role quality, work involvement, and mental health one year after delivery. *Psychology of Women Quarterly, 22*, 239–266.

Kleinspehn-Ammerlahn, A. et al. (2008). Self-perceptions of aging: Do subjective age and satisfaction with aging change during old age? *The Journals of Gerontology: Psychological Sciences, 63B*, 377–385.

Kline, S. (1993). *Out of the garden: Toys, TV, and children's culture in the age of marketing.* New York: Verso.

Kling, K.C. et al. (1999). Gender differences in self-esteem: A meta-analysis. *Psychological Bulletin, 125*, 470–500.

Klingenspor, B. (1994). Gender identity and bulimic eating behavior. *Sex Roles, 31*, 407–431.

Klingenspor, B. (2002). Gender-related self-discrepancies and bulimic eating behavior. *Sex Roles, 47*, 51–64.

Klinkenberg, D., & Rose, S. (1994). Dating scripts of gay men and lesbians. *Journal of Homosexuality, 26*, 23–35.

Klomsten, A.T. et al. (2004). Physical self-concept and sports: Do gender differences still exist? *Sex Roles, 50*, 119–127.

Klonis, S. et al. (1997). Feminism as a life raft. *Psychology of Women Quarterly, 21*, 333–345.

Klonoff, E.A. et al. (2000). Sexist discrimination may account for well-known gender differences in psychiatric symptoms. *Psychology of Women Quarterly, 24*, 93–99.

Klonoff, E.A., & Landrine, H. (1995). The schedule of sexist events: A measure of lifetime and recent sexist discrimination in women's lives. *Psychology of Women Quarterly, 19*, 439–472.

Knight, J.L., & Giuliano, T.A. (2001). He's a Laker; she's a "looker": The consequences of gender-stereotypical portrayals of male and female athletes by the print media. *Sex Roles, 45*, 217–229.

Knudson-Martin, C., & Mahoney, A.R. (2005). Moving beyond gender: Processes that create relationship equality. *Journal of Marital & Family Therapy, 31*, 235–246.

Knudson-Martin, C., & Mahoney, A.R. (2009). *Couples, gender, and power: Creating change in intimate relationships.* New York: Springer.

Kobrynowicz, D., & Branscombe, N.R. (1997). Who considers themselves victims of discrimination? Individual difference predictors of perceived gender discrimination in women and men. *Psychology of Women Quarterly, 21*, 347–363.

Koenig, A.M., & Eagly, A.H. (2005). Stereotype threat in men on a test of social sensitivity. *Sex Roles, 52*, 489–496.

Koenig, L.J., & Wasserman, E.L. (1995). Body image and dieting failure in college men and women: Examining links between depression and eating problems. *Sex Roles, 32*, 225–249.

Koff, E. et al. (1990). Conceptions and misconceptions of the menstrual cycle. *Women & Health, 16*, 119–136.

Kohlberg, L. (1981). *The philosophy of moral development: Essays on moral development* (Vols. I & II). San Francisco, CA: Harper & Row.

Kolb, B. (1989). Brain development, plasticity, and behavior. *American Psychologist, 44*, 1203–1212.

Kolivas, E.D., & Gross, A.M. (2007). Assessing sexual aggression: Addressing the gap between rape victimization and perpetration rates. *Aggression and Violent Behavior, 12*, 315–328.

Konrad, A.M. (2003). Family demands and job attribute preferences: A 4-year longitudinal study of women and men. *Sex Roles, 49*, 35–46.

Konrad, A.M. et al. (2000). Sex differences and similarities in job attribute preferences: A meta-analysis. *Psychological Bulletin, 126*, 593–641.

Korobov, N., & Thorne, A. (2009). The negotiation of compulsory romance in young women friends' stories about romantic heterosexual experiences. *Feminism & Psychology, 19*, 49–70.

Koropeckyj-Cox, T. et al. (2007). Through the lenses of gender, race, and class; Students' perceptions of childless/childfree individuals and couples. *Sex Roles, 56*, 415–428.

Kortenhaus, C.M., & Demarest, J. (1993). Gender role stereotypes in children's literature: An update. *Sex Roles, 28*, 219–232.

Koss, M.P. (1985). The hidden rape victim: Personality, attitudinal, and situational characteristics. *Psychology of Women Quarterly, 9*, 193–212.

Koss, M.P. (1990). The women's mental health research agenda: Violence against women. *American Psychologist, 45*, 374–380.

Koss, M.P. (1992). The underdetection of rape. *Journal of Social Issues, 48*(1), 63–75.

Koss, M.P. (1993). Rape: Scope, impact, interventions, and public policy responses. *American Psychologist, 48*, 1062–1069.

Koss, M.P. et al. (1987). The scope of rape: Incidence and prevalence of sexual aggression and victimization in a national sample of higher education students. *Journal of Consulting and Clinical Psychology, 55*, 162–170.

Koss, M.P. et al. (1988). Stranger, acquaintance, and date rape: Is there a difference in the victim's experience? *Psychology of Women Quarterly, 12,* 1–24.

Koss, M.P. et al. (1991). Criminal victimization among primary care medical patients: Prevalence, incidence, and physician usage. *Behavioral Sciences and the Law, 9,* 85–96.

Koss, M.P. et al. (1996). Traumatic memory characteristics: A cross-validated mediational model of response to rape among employed women. *Journal of Abnormal Psychology, 105,* 1–12.

Koss, M.P. et al. (2003). Depression and PTSD in survivors of male violence: Research and training initiatives to facilitate recovery. *Psychology of Women Quarterly, 27,* 130–142.

Koss, M.P., & Figueredo, A.J. (2004). Cognitive mediation of a cross-sectional model in longitudinal data. *Psychology of Women Quarterly, 28,* 273–286.

Koss, M.P., Goodman, L.A. et al. (1994). *No safe haven: Male violence against women at home, at work, and in the community.* Washington, DC: American Psychological Association.

Koss, M.P., & Heslet, L. (1992). Somatic consequences of violence against women. *Archives of Family Medicine, 1,* 53–59.

Kowalski, R.M., & Chapple, T. (2000). The social stigma of menstruation: Fact or fiction? *Psychology of Women Quarterly, 24,* 74–80.

Kozee, H.B. et al. (2007). Development and psychometric evaluation of the interpersonal sexual objectification scale. *Psychology of Women Quarterly, 31,* 176–189.

Kozee, H.B., & Tylka, T.L. (2006). A test of objectification theory in lesbian women. *Psychology of Women Quarterly, 30,* 348–357.

Kozol, W. (1995). Fracturing domesticity: Media, nationalism, and the question of feminist influence. *Signs, 20,* 646–667.

Krafka, C. et al. (1997). Women's reactions to sexually aggressive mass media depictions. *Violence Against Women, 3,* 149–181.

Krahé, B. et al. (2000). Ambiguous communication of sexual intentions as a risk marker of sexual aggressiveness. *Sex Roles, 42,* 313–337.

Krahé, B., & Krause, C. (2010). Presenting thin media models affects women's choices of diet or normal snacks. *Psychology of Women Quarterly, 34,* 349–355.

Krause, E.D. et al. (2000). A mediational model relating sociotropy, ambivalence over emotional expression and disordered eating. *Psychology of Women Quarterly, 24,* 328–335.

Kravetz, D., & Marecek, J. (1996). The personal is political: A feminist agenda for group

psychotherapy research. In B. DeChant (Ed.), *Women and group psychotherapy: Theory and practice* (pp. 351–369). New York: Guilford.

Kray, L.J. et al. (2001). Battle of the sexes: Gender stereotype confirmation and reactance in negotiations. *Journal of Personality and Social Psychology, 80,* 942–958.

Krefting, L.A. et al. (1978). The contribution of sex distribution, job content, and occupational classification to job sex-typing: Two studies. *Journal of Vocational Behavior, 13,* 181–191.

Kristiansen, C.M. et al. (1996). Recovered memories or child abuse: Fact, fantasy or fancy? *Women & Therapy, 19,* 47–59.

Kroska, A. (2004). Divisions of domestic work. *Journal of Marriage and the Family, 65,* 456–473.

Kubzansky, L.D. et al. (2009). A prospective study of posttraumatic stress disorder symptoms and coronary heart disease in women. *Health Psychology, 28,* 125–130.

Kuhn, T.S. (1970). *The structure of scientific revolutions* (2nd ed.). Chicago, IL: University of Chicago Press.

Kunstman, J.W., & Maner, J.K. (2011). Sexual overperception: Power, mating motives, and biases in social judgment. *Journal of Personality and Social Psychology, 100,* 282–294.

Kurdek, L.A. (1995). Developmental changes in relationship quality in gay and lesbian cohabiting couples. *Developmental Psychology, 31,* 86–94.

Kurdek, L.A. (2006). Differences between partners from heterosexual, gay, and lesbian cohabiting couples. *Journal of Marriage and Family, 68,* 509–528.

Kurdek, L.A. (2007). The allocation of household labor by partners in gay and lesbian couples. *Journal of Family Issues, 28,* 32–148.

Kurz, D. (1989). Social science perspectives on wife abuse: Current debates and future directions. *Gender & Society, 3,* 489–505.

Kurz, D. (1997). Physical assaults by male partners: A major social problem. In M.R. Walsh (Ed.), *Women, men, and gender: Ongoing debates* (pp. 222–231). New Haven, CT: Yale.

LaBrie, J.W. et al. (2008). Self-consciousness moderates the relationship between perceived norms and drinking in college students. *Addictive Behaviors, 33,* 1529–1539.

Lachance-Grzela, M., & Bouchard, G. (2010). Why do women do the lion's share of housework? A decade of research. *Sex Roles, 63,* 767–780.

Lackie, L., & deMan, A.F. (1997). Correlates of sexual aggression among male university students. *Sex Roles, 37,* 451–457.

Laennec, C., & Syrotinski, M. (2003). Insiders' perspectives on a feminist marriage. *Feminism & Psychology, 13*, 454–458.

Laflamme, D. et al. (2002). A comparison of fathers' and mothers' involvement in childcare and stimulation behaviors during free-play with their infants at 9 and 15 months. *Sex Roles, 47*, 507–518.

LaFrance, M. et al. (2004). Sex changes: A current perspective on the psychology of gender. In A.H. Eagly, A.E. Beall, & R.J. Sternberg (Eds)., *The psychology of gender* (2nd ed.) (pp. 328–344). New York: Guilford.

LaFromboise, T.D. et al. (1994). American Indian women. In L. Comas-Díaz & B. Greene (Eds.), *Women of color: Integrating ethnic and gender identities in psychotherapy* (pp. 30–71). New York: Guilford.

Lakoff, R. (1990). *Talking power: The politics of language.* New York: Basic.

Lamb, L.M. et al. (2009). Teaching children to confront peers' sexist remarks: Implications for theories of gender development and educational practice. *Sex Roles, 61*, 361–382.

Lamb, S., & Keon, S. (1995). Blaming the perpetrator: Language that distorts reality in newspaper articles on men battering women. *Psychology of Women Quarterly, 19*, 209–220.

Lambrew, J.M. (2001). *Diagnosing disparities in health insurance for women: A prescription for change* (Pub. No. 493). Washington, DC: The Commonwealth Fund. http://www.cmwf.org

Landrine, H. (1985). Race x class stereotypes of women. *Sex Roles, 13*, 65–75.

Landrine, H. (1988). Depression and stereotypes of women: Preliminary empirical analyses of the gender-role hypothesis. *Sex Roles, 19*, 527–541.

Landrine, H. (1989). The politics of personality disorder. *Psychology of Women Quarterly, 13*, 325–339.

Landrine, H. et al. (1992). Cultural diversity and methodology in feminist psychology: Critique, proposal, and empirical example. *Psychology of Women Quarterly, 16*, 145–163.

Landry, L.J., & Mercurio, A.E. (2009). Discrimination and women's mental health: The mediating role of control. *Sex Roles, 61*, 192–203.

Langhinrichsen-Rohling, J. (2010). Controversies involving gender and intimate partner violence in the United States. *Sex Roles, 62*, 179–193.

Larkin, J.E., & Pines, H.A. (2003). Gender and risk in public performance. *Sex Roles, 49*, 197–210.

LaRocca, M.A., & Kromrey, J.D. (1999). The perceptions of sexual harassment in higher education: Impact of gender and attractiveness. *Sex Roles, 40*, 921–940.

Larson, R.W., & Verma, S. (1999). How children and adolescents spend time across the world: Work, play, and developmental opportunities. *Psychological Bulletin, 125*, 701–736.

Latteier, C. (1998). *Breasts: The woman's perspective on an American obsession.* New York: Harrington Park Press.

Lauren, M.M., & Dozier, D.M. (2002). You look mahvelous: An examination of gender and appearance comments in the 1999–2000 prime-time season. *Sex Roles, 46*, 429–437.

Laurence, L., & Weinhouse B. (1994). *Outrageous practices: The alarming truth about how medicine mistreats women.* New York: Fawcett.

Lawrie, L., & Brown, R. (1992). Sex stereotypes, school subject preferences and career aspirations as a function of single/mixed-sex schooling and presence/absence of an opposite sex sibling. *British Journal of Educational Psychology, 62*, 132–138.

Lawton, C.A. et al. (1996). Individual- and gender-related differences in indoor wayfinding. *Environment & Behavior, 28*, 204–219.

Lawton, C.A. et al. (2003). The new meaning of Ms.: Single, but too old for Miss. *Psychology of Women Quarterly, 27*, 215–220.

Lea, S., & Auburn, T. (2001). The social construction of rape in the talk of a convicted rapist. *Feminism & Psychology, 11*, 11–33.

Lea, S.J. (2007). A discursive investigation into victim responsibility in rape. *Feminism & Psychology, 17*, 495–514.

Leaper, C. (2000). The social construction and socialization of gender during development. In P.H. Miller & E.K. Scholnick (Eds.), *Toward a feminist developmental psychology* (pp. 127–152). Florence, KY: Taylor & Francis/Routledge.

Leaper, C. et al. (1995). Mother-child communication sequences: Play activity, child gender, and marital status effects. *Merrill Palmer Quarterly, 41*, 307–327.

Leaper, C., & Ayres, M.M. (2007). A meta-analytic review of gender variations in adults' language use: Talkativeness, affiliative speech, and assertive speech. *Personality and Social Psychology Review, 11*, 328–363.

Lee, K.A., & Rittenhouse, C.A. (1991). Prevalence of perimenstrual symptoms in employed women. *Women & Health, 17*, 17–32.

Lee, K.A., & Rittenhouse, C.A. (1992). Health and perimenstrual symptoms: Health outcomes for employed women who experience perimenstrual symptoms. *Women & Health, 19*, 65–78.

Lee, S. (1995). Self-starvation in context: Towards a culturally sensitive understanding of anorexia nervosa. *Social Science and Medicine, 41,* 25–36.

Lee, T.L. et al. (2010a). Next gen ambivalent sexism: Converging correlates, causality in context, and converse causality: An introduction to the special issue. *Sex Roles, 62,* 395–404.

Lee, T.L. et al. (2010b). Ambivalent sexism in close relationships: (Hostile) power and (benevolent) romance shape relationship ideals. *Sex Roles, 62,* 583–601.

Lefley, H.P. et al. (1993). Cultural beliefs about rape and victims' response in three ethnic groups. *American Journal of Orthopsychiatry, 63,* 623–632.

Lehavot, K., & Simoni, J.M. (2011). The impact of minority stress on mental health and substance use among sexual minority women. *Journal of Consulting and Clinical Psychology, 79,* 159–170.

Leigh, B.C. (1989). Reasons for having and avoiding sex: Gender, sexual orientation, and relationship to sexual behavior. *Journal of Sex Research, 26,* 199–209.

Leigh, W.A. (1995). The health of African American women. In D.L. Adams (Ed.), *Health issues for women of color: A cultural diversity perspective* (pp. 112–132). Thousand Oaks, CA: Sage.

Lemieux, S.R., & Byers, E.S. (2008). The sexual well-being of women who have experienced child sexual abuse. *Psychology of Women Quarterly, 32,* 126–144.

Lemish, D., & Cohen, A.A. (2005). On the gendered nature of mobile phone culture in Israel. *Sex Roles, 52,* 511–521.

Lemons, M.A. (2003). Contextual and cognitive determinants of procedural justice perceptions in promotion barriers for women. *Sex Roles, 49,* 247–264.

Lent, R. W. et al. (1994). Toward a unifying social cognitive theory of career and academic interest, choice, and performance [Monograph]. *Journal of Vocational Behavior, 45,* 79–122.

Lenton, A.P. et al. (2007). We want the same thing: Projection in judgments of sexual intent. *Personality and Social Psychology Bulletin, 33,* 975–988.

Lenton, A.P., & Webber, L. (2006). Cross-sex friendships: Who has more? *Sex Roles, 54,* 809–820.

Leonard, D.K., & Jiang, J. (1995, April). *Gender bias in the college predictors of the SAT.* Paper presented at the annual meeting of the American Educational Research Association, San Francisco.

Leonardo, C., & Chrisler, J.C. (1992). Women and sexually transmitted diseases. *Women & Health, 18,* 1–15.

Lerman, H. (1986). From Freud to feminist personality theory: Getting here from there. *Psychology of Women Quarterly, 10,* 1–18.

Lerman, H. (1996). *Pigeonholing women's misery: A history and critical analysis of the psychodiagnosis of women in the twentieth century.* New York: Basic.

Lerner, G. (1992). Placing women in history: Definitions and challenges. In J.S. Bohan (Ed.), *Re-placing women in psychology: Readings toward a more inclusive history* (pp. 31–43). Dubuque, IA: Kendall/Hunt.

LeVay, S. (1991, August 30). A difference in hypothalamic structure between heterosexual and homosexual men. *Science, 253,* 1034–1037.

Leventhal, E.A. (1994). Gender and aging: Women and their aging. In V.J. Adesso, D.M. Reddy, & R. Fleming (Eds.), *Psychological perspectives on women's health* (pp. 11–35). Washington, DC: Taylor & Francis.

Levesque, M.J. et al. (2006). Toward an understanding of gender differences in inferring sexual interest. *Psychology of Women Quarterly, 30,* 150–158.

Levine, R. et al. (1995). Love and marriage in eleven cultures. *Journal of Cross-Cultural Psychology, 26,* 554–571.

Levine, S. (2000). *Father courage: What happens when men put family first.* New York: Harcourt.

Levine-MacCombie, J., & Koss, M.P. (1986). Acquaintance rape: Effective avoidance strategies. *Psychology of Women Quarterly, 10,* 311–320.

Levy, J. (1969). Possible basis for the evolution of lateral specialization of the human brain. *Nature, 224,* 614–615.

Lew, A. et al. (2007). Thin-ideal media and women's body dissatisfaction: Prevention using downward social comparisons on non-appearance dimensions. *Sex Roles, 57,* 543–556.

Lewin, T. (1994, Oct. 12). Men whose wives work earn less, studies show. *The New York Times,* pp. A1, A15.

Lewis, K.M. et al. (2011). Investigating motivations for women's skin bleaching in Tanzania. *Psychology of Women Quarterly, 35,* 29–37.

Liben, L.S. et al. (2002). Language at work: Children's gendered interpretations of occupational titles. *Child Development, 73,* 810–828.

Lichter, E.L., & McCloskey, L.A. (2004). The effects of childhood exposure to marital violence on adolescent gender-role beliefs and dating violence. *Psychology of Women Quarterly, 28,* 344–357.

Liem, J.H. et al. (1992). The need for power in women who were sexually abused as children: An exploratory study. *Psychology of Women Quarterly, 16*, 467–480.

Lienert, T. (1998). Women's self-starvation, cosmetic surgery and transsexualism. *Feminism & Psychology, 8*, 245–250.

Lightdale, J., & Prentice, D.A. (1994). Rethinking sex differences in aggression: Aggressive behavior in the absence of social roles. *Personality and Social Psychology Bulletin, 20*, 34–44.

Lindberg, S.M. et al. (2010). New trends in gender and mathematics performance: A meta-analysis. *Psychological Bulletin, 136*, 1123–1135.

Lindgren, K.P. et al. (2007). Sexual or friendly? Associations about women, men, and self. *Psychology of Women Quarterly, 31*, 190–201.

Lindner, K. (2004). Images of women in general interest and fashion magazine advertisements from 1955 to 2002. *Sex Roles, 51*, 409–421.

Lindsey, E.W., & Caldera, Y.M. (2006). Mother-father-child triadic interaction and mother-child dyadic interaction: Gender differences within and between contexts. *Sex Roles, 55*, 511–521.

Linn, M.C., & Petersen, A.C. (1985). Emergence and characterization of sex differences in spatial ability; A meta-analysis. *Child Development, 56*, 1479–1498.

Linz, D. (1989). Exposure to sexually explicit materials and attitudes toward rape: A comparison of study results. *Journal of Sex Research, 26*, 50–84.

Linz, D. et al. (1992). Sexual violence in the mass media: Legal solutions, warnings, and mitigation through education. *Journal of Social Issues, 48*(1), 145–172.

Lips, H., & Lawson, K. (2009). Work values, gender, and expectations about work commitment and pay: Laying the groundwork for the "motherhood penalty"? *Sex Roles, 61*, 667–676.

Lips, H.M. (1991). *Women, men, and power*. Mountain View, CA: Mayfield.

Lips, H.M. (2002). Female powerlessness: Still a case of "cultural preparedness"? In A.E. Hunter & C. Forden (Eds.), *Readings in the psychology of gender* (pp. 19–37). Boston, MA: Allyn and Bacon.

Lips, H.M. (2004). The gender gap in possible selves: Divergence of academic self-views among high school and university students. *Sex Roles, 50*, 357–371.

Lisak, D. (2000). Editorial. *Psychology of Men and Masculinity, 1*, 3.

Lisak, D. et al. (2010). False allegations of sexual assault: An analysis of ten years of reported cases. *Violence Against Women, 16*, 1318–1334.

Liss, M. et al. (2001). What makes a feminist? Predictors and correlates of feminist social identity in college women. *Psychology of Women Quarterly, 25*, 124–133.

Liss, M. et al. (2011). Empowering or oppressing? Development and exploration of the Enjoyment of Sexualization Scale. *Personality and Social Psychology Bulletin, 37*, 55–68.

Liss, M. et al. (2004). Predictors and correlates of collective action. *Sex Roles, 50*, 771–779.

Liss, M., & Erchull, M.J. (2010). Everyone feels empowered: Understanding feminist self-labeling. *Psychology of Women Quarterly, 34*, 85–96.

Littleton, H. et al. (2007). Rape scripts of low-income European American and Latina women. *Sex Roles, 56*, 509–516.

Littleton, H.L., & Axsom, D. (2003). Rape and seduction scripts for university students: Implications for rape attributions and unacknowledged rape. *Sex Roles, 49*, 465–475.

Littleton, H.L., & Breitkopf, C.R. (2006). Coping with the experience of rape. *Psychology of Women Quarterly, 30*, 106–116.

Livingston, J.A. et al. (2004). The role of sexual precedence in verbal sexual coercion. *Psychology of Women Quarterly, 28*, 287–297.

Locke, L.M., & Richman, C.L. (1999). Attitudes toward domestic violence: Race and gender issues. *Sex Roles, 40*, 227–247.

Lockwood, P. (2006). "Someone like me can be successful": Do college students need same-gender role models? *Psychology of Women Quarterly, 30*, 36–46.

Loden, M., & Rosener, J.B. (1991). *Workforce America: Managing employee diversity as a vital resource*. Homewood, IL: Business One Irwin.

Loevinger, J. (1976). *Ego development: Conceptions and theories*. San Francisco, CA: Jossey-Bass.

Loftus, E.F., & Ketcham, K. (1994). *The myth of repressed memory: False memories and allegations of abuse*. New York: St. Martins Press.

Logel, C. et al. (2009). Interacting with sexist men triggers social identity threat among female engineers. *Journal of Personality and Social Psychology, 96*, 1089–1103.

Logue, B.J. (1991). Women at risk: Predictors of financial stress for retired women workers. *Gerontologist, 31*, 657–665.

Lonsdale, S. (1992). *Women and disability*. New York: St. Martin's Press.

Lonsway, K.A. (1996). Preventing acquaintance rape through education: What do we know? *Psychology of Women Quarterly, 20*, 229–265.

Lonsway, K.A., & Fitzgerald, L.F. (1994). Rape myths: In review. *Psychology of Women Quarterly, 18,* 133–164.

Lopez, S. J., & Edwards, L. M. (2008). The interface of counseling psychology and positive psychology: Assessing and promoting strengths. In S. D. Brown & R. W. Lent (Eds.), *Handbook of counseling psychology* (4th ed.) (pp. 86–99). Hoboken, NJ: Wiley.

Lopez-Claros, A., & Zahidi, S. (2005). *Women's empowerment: Measuring the global gender gap.* Geneva, Switzerland: World Economic Forum. http://www.weforum.org/pdf/Global_ Competitiveness_Reports/Reports/gender_gap. pdf (Retrieved November 2005).

Lott, B. (1995). Distancing from women: Interpersonal sexist discrimination. In B. Lott & D. Maluso (Eds.), *The social psychology of interpersonal discrimination* (pp. 12–49). New York: Guilford.

Lott, B. (1997). The personal and social correlates of a gender difference ideology. *Journal of Social Issues, 53*(2), 279–298.

Lowe, R.H., & Wittig, M.A. (Eds.). (1989). Approaching pay equity through comparable worth. *Journal of Social Issues, 45*(4).

Lox, C.L. et al. (1998). Body image and affective experiences of subjectively underweight females: Implications for exercise behavior. *Journal of Applied Biobehavioral Research, 3,* 110–118.

Loya, B.N. et al. (2006). The role of social comparison and body consciousness in women's hostility toward women. *Sex Roles, 54,* 575–583.

Lubkin, I.M. (1995). *Chronic illness: Impact and interventions* (3rd ed.). Sudbury, MA: Jones & Bartlett.

Lucas-Thompson, R.G. et al. (2010). Maternal work early in the lives of children and its distal associations with achievement and behavior problems: A meta-analysis. *Psychological Bulletin, 136,* 915–942.

Lucero, K. et al. (1992). Frequency of eating problems among Asian and Caucasian college women. *Psychological Reports, 71,* 255–258.

Luecke, A.D. et al. (1995). Gender constancy and television viewing. *Developmental Psychology, 31,* 773–780.

Lykes, M.B., & Stewart, A.J. (1986). Evaluating the feminist challenge to research in personality and social psychology: 1963–1983. *Psychology of Women Quarterly, 10,* 393–412.

Lynam, D.R., & Widiger, T.A. (2007). Using a general model of personality to understand sex differences in the personality disorders. *Journal of Personality Disorders, 21,* 583–602.

Lynch, S.M., & Zellner, D.A. (1999). Figure preferences in two generations of men: The use of figure drawings illustrating differences in muscle mass. *Sex Roles, 40,* 833–843.

Lynn, R. (1994). Sex differences in intelligence and brain size: A paradox resolved. *Personality and Individual Differences, 17,* 257–271.

Lyon, D., & Greenberg, J. (1991). Evidence of codependency in women with an alcoholic parent: Helping out Mr. Wrong. *Journal of Personality and Social Psychology, 61,* 435–439.

Lyons, P. (2009). Prescription for harm: Diet industry influence, public health policy, and the "obesity epidemic." In E. Rothblum & S. Solovay (Eds.), *The fat studies reader* (pp. 75–87). New York: New York University Press.

Lytle, L.J. et al. (1997). Adolescent female identity development. *Sex Roles, 37,* 175–185.

Lyubomirsky, S. et al. (2001). What triggers abnormal eating in bulimic and nonbulimic women? The role of dissociative experiences, negative affect, and psychopathology. *Psychology of Women Quarterly, 25,* 223–232.

Maccoby, E.E. (1990). Gender and relationships: A developmental account. *American Psychologist, 45,* 513–520.

Maccoby, E.E. (1998). *Sex differences in behavior: The debate continues.* Cambridge, MA: Belknap Press of Harvard University Press.

Maccoby, E.E., & Jacklin, C.N. (1974). *The psychology of sex differences.* Stanford, CA: Stanford University Press.

MacFarlane, J. et al. (1992). Assessing for abuse during pregnancy: Severity and frequency of injuries associated with entry into prenatal care. *Journal of the American Medical Association, 267,* 3176–3178.

Mackey, R.A. et al. (2000). Psychological intimacy in the lasting relationships of heterosexual and same-gender couples. *Sex Roles, 43,* 201–227.

Madden, M.E. (1994). The variety of emotional reactions to miscarriage. *Women & Health, 21,* 85–104.

Madera, J.M. et al. (2009). Gender and letters of recommendation for academia: Agentic and communal differences. *Journal of Applied Psychology, 94,* 1591–1599.

Madriz, E.I. (1997). Images of criminals and victims: A study of women's fear and social control. *Gender & Society, 11,* 342–356.

Maeder, E.M. el al. (2007). Does a truck driver see what a nurse sees? The effects of occupation type on perceptions of sexual harassment. *Sex Roles, 56,* 801–810.

Mahaffy, K.A., & Ward, S.K. (2002). The gendering of adolescents' childbearing and educational plans: Reciprocal effects and the influence of social context. *Sex Roles, 46*, 403–417.

Mahalik, J.R., & Cournoyer, R.J. (2000). Identifying gender role conflict messages that distinguish mildly depressed from nondepressed men. *Psychology of Men and Masculinity, 1*, 109–115.

Mahalik, J.R. et al. (2005). Development of the Conformity to Feminine Norms Inventory. *Sex Roles, 52*, 417–434.

Maine, M. (2000). *Body wars: Making peace with women's bodies: An activist's guide.* Carlsbad, CA: Gurze Books.

Mainiero, L.A. et al. (2008). Retrospective analysis of gender differences in reaction to media coverage of crisis events: New insights on the justice and care orientations. *Sex Roles, 58*, 556–566.

Major, B. et al. (2009). Abortion and mental health: Evaluating the evidence. *American Psychologist, 64*, 863–890.

Mak, W.W. et al. (2007). Gender and ethnic diversity in NIMH-funded clinical trials: Review of a decade of published research. *Administration and Policy in Mental Health and Mental Health Services Research, 34*, 497–503.

Malcolmson, K.A., & Sinclair, L. (2007). The Ms. Stereotype revisited: Implicit and explicit facets. *Psychology of Women Quarterly, 31*, 305–310.

Malkin, A.R. et al. (1999). Women and weight: Gendered messages on magazine covers. *Sex Roles, 40*, 647–655.

Mannino, C.A., & Deutsch, F.M. (2007). Changing the division of household labor: A negotiated process between partners. *Sex Roles, 56*, 309–324.

Mansfield, P.K., & Koch, P.B. (1998). Qualities midlife women desire in their sexual relationships and their changing sexual response. *Psychology of Women Quarterly, 22*, 285–303.

Mansfield, P.K., & Voda, A.M. (1993). From Edith Bunker to the 6:00 news: How and what midlife women learn about menopause. *Women & Therapy, 14*, 89–104.

Maras, P., & Archer, L. (1997). "Tracy's in the home corner, Darren's playing Lego, or are they?": Gender issues and identity in education. *Feminism & Psychology, 7*, 264–274.

Marcus-Mendoza, S., & Wright, E. (2004). Decontextualizing female criminality: Treating abused women in prison in the United States. *Feminism & Psychology, 14*, 250–255.

Marecek, J. (1989). Introduction to special issue: Theory and method in feminist psychology. *Psychology of Women Quarterly, 13*, 367–378.

Marecek, J. (2001). Disorderly constructs: Feminist frameworks for clinical psychology. In R.K. Unger (Ed.), *Handbook of the psychology of women and gender* (pp. 303–316). New York: Wiley.

Marecek, J. et al. (2004). On the construction of gender, sex, and sexualities. In A.H. Eagly, A.E. Beall, & R.J. Sternberg (Eds.), *The psychology of gender* (pp. 192–216). New York: Guilford.

Marecek, J., & Hare-Mustin, R.T. (1991). A short history of the future: Feminism and clinical psychology. *Psychology of Women Quarterly, 15*, 521–536.

Marecek, J., & Kravetz, D. (1998a). Power and agency in feminist therapy. In I.B. Seu & M.C. Heenan (Eds.), *Feminism and psychotherapy: Reflections on contemporary theories and practices.* Thousand Oaks, CA: Sage.

Marecek, J., & Kravetz, D. (1998b). Putting politics into practice: Feminist therapy as feminist praxis. *Women & Therapy, 21*, 17–36.

Margolin, G. (1988). Interpersonal and intrapersonal factors associated with marital violence. In G.T. Hotaling, D. Finkelhor, J.T. Kirkpatrick, & M.A. Straus (Eds.), *Family abuse and its consequences: New directions for research* (pp. 203–217). Newbury Park, CA: Sage.

Marin, A.J., & Guadagno, R.E. (1999). Perceptions of sexual harassment victims as a function of labeling and reporting. *Sex Roles, 41*, 921–940.

Markey, C.N. et al. (2004). Understanding women's body satisfaction: The role of husbands. *Sex Roles, 51*, 209–216.

Markey, C.N., & Markey, P.M. (2009). Correlates of young women's interest in obtaining cosmetic surgery. *Sex Roles, 61*, 158–166.

Markman, A.B. (1999). *Knowledge representation.* Mahwah, NJ: Erlbaum.

Marks, J.L. et al. (2009). Family patterns of gender role attitudes. *Sex Roles, 61*, 221–234.

Marks, M.J., & Fraley, R.C. (2005). The sexual double standard: Fact or fiction? *Sex Roles, 52*, 175–186.

Marks, M.J., & Fraley, R.C. (2006). Confirmation bias and the sexual double standard. *Sex Roles, 54*, 19–26.

Markus, H. et al. (1982). Self-schemas and gender. *Journal of Personality and Social Psychology, 42*, 38–50.

Marler, J.H., & Moen, P. (2005). Alternative employment arrangements: A gender perspective. *Sex Roles, 52*, 337–349.

Marsh, M. (1995). Feminist psychopharmacology: An aspect of feminist psychiatry. *Women & Therapy, 16*(1), 73–84.

Marshall, T.C. (2010). Gender, peer relations, and intimate romantic relationships. In J.C. Chrisler

& D.R. McCreary (Eds.) *Handbook of gender research in psychology* (Vol. 2) (pp. 281–310). New York: Springer.

Marston, C., & King, E. (2006). Factors that shape young people's sexual behavior: A systematice review. *The Lancet, 368*, 1581–1586.

Marteau, T.M., & Senior, V. (1997). Illness representations after the human genome project: The perceived role of genes in causing illness. In K.J. Petrie & J.A. Weinman (Eds.), *Perceptions of illness and treatment: Current psychological research and implications* (pp. 241–266). Amsterdam: Harwood Academic Press.

Martell, R.F. et al. (1996). Male-female differences: A computer simulation. *American Psychologist, 51*, 157–158.

Martin, C.L., & Fabes, R.A. (2001). The stability and consequences of young children's same-sex peer interactions. *Developmental Psychology, 37*, 431–446.

Martin, C.L., & Halverson, C.F. (1983). The effects of sex-typing schemas on young children's memory. *Child Development, 61*, 1427–1439.

Martin, C.L., & Parker, S. (1995). Folk theories about sex and race differences. *Personality and Social Psychology Bulletin, 21*, 45–57.

Martin, K. (1998). Becoming a gendered body: Practices of preschools. *American Sociological Review, 63*, 494–511.

Martin, S.E. (1994). "Outsider within" the station house: The impact of race and gender on Black women police. *Social Problems, 41*, 383–400.

Martin, S.E., & Bachman, R. (1998). The contribution of alcohol to the likelihood of completion and severity of injury in rape incidents. *Violence Against Women, 4*, 694–712.

Martins, L.L., & Parsons, C.K. (2007). Effects of gender diversity management in perceptions of organizational attractiveness: The role of individual differences in attitudes and beliefs. *Journal of Applied Psychology, 92*, 865–875.

Martins, N. et al. (2009). A content analysis of female body imagery in video games. *Sex Roles, 61*, 824–836.

Martins, Y. et al. (2007). Those speedos become them: The role of self-objectification in gay and heterosexual men's body image. *Personality and Social Psychology Bulletin, 33*, 634–647.

Martire, L.M. et al. (1998). Emotional support and well-being of midlife women: Role-specific mastery as a mediational mechanism. *Psychology & Aging, 13*, 396–404.

Martire, L.M. et al. (2000). Centrality of women's multiple roles: Beneficial and detrimental consequences for psychological well-being. *Psychology & Aging, 15*, 148–156.

Martz, D.M. et al. (2009). Gender differences in fat talk among American adults: Results from the psychology of size survey. *Sex Roles, 61*, 34–41.

Masi, C.M. et al. (2007). Interventions to enhance breast cancer screening, diagnosis, and treatment among racial and ethnic minority women. *Medical Care Research and Review, 64*, 195S-242S.

Massa, L.J. et al. (2005). Individual differences in gender role beliefs influence spatial ability test performance. *Learning & Individual Differences, 15*, 99–111.

Masser, B.L. et al. (2006). Hostile sexism and rape proclivity amongst men. *Sex Roles, 54*, 565–574.

Masser, B.L. et al. (2010). Bad woman, bad victim? Disentangling the effects of victim stereotypicality, gender stereotypicality and benevolent sexism on acquaintance rape victim blame. *Sex Roles, 62*, 494–504.

Mast, M.S., & Hall, J.A. (2004). When is dominance related to smiling? Assigned dominance, dominance preferences, trait dominance, and gender as moderators. *Sex Roles, 50*, 387–399.

Mast, M.S., & Hall, J.A. (2006). Women's advantage at remembering others' appearance: A systematic look at the why and when of a gender difference. *Personality and Social Psychology Bulletin, 32*, 353–364.

Masten, W.G. et al. (1994). Depression and acculturation in Mexican-American women. *Psychological Reports, 75*, 1499–1503.

Masters, M.S., & Sanders, B. (1993). Is the gender difference in mental rotation disappearing? *Behavior Genetics, 23*, 337–341.

Masters, N. et al. (2006). How does it end? Women project the outcome of a sexual assault scenario. *Psychology of Women Quarterly, 30*, 291–302.

Masters, W.H., & Johnson, V.E. (1966). *Human sexual response*. Boston: Little Brown.

Matsui, T. et al. (1995). Work-family conflict and the stress-buffering effects of husband support and coping behavior among Japanese married working women. *Journal of Vocational Behavior, 47*, 178–192.

Matthews, K.A. et al. (1997). Women's Health Initiative: Why now? What is it? What's new? *American Psychologist, 52*, 101–116.

Mattis, J.S. (2002). Religion and spirituality in the meaning-making and coping experiences of African American women: A qualitative analysis. *Psychology of Women Quarterly, 26*, 309–321.

Maume, D.J. (1999). Glass ceiling and glass escalators: Occupational segregation and race and sex differences in managerial promotions. *Work and Occupations, 26*, 483–509.

Maurer, T.W., & Robinson, D.W. (2008). Effects of attire, alcohol, and gender on perceptions of date rape. *Sex Roles, 58*, 423–434.

Mauthner, N.S. (1998). "It's a woman's cry for help": A relational perspective on postnatal depression. *Feminism & Psychology, 8*, 325–355.

Mays, V., & Cochran, S.D. (1988). Issues in the perception of AIDS risk and risk reduction activities by Black and Hispanic/Latina women. *American Psychologist, 43*, 949–957.

Mays, V.M., & Cochran, S.D. (1993). Ethnic and gender differences in beliefs about sex partner questioning to reduce HIV risk. *Journal of Adolescent Research, 8*, 77–88.

Mazur, T. (2005). Gender dysphoria and gender change in androgen insensitivity or micropenis. *Archives of Sexual Behavior, 34*, 411–421.

McAninch, C.B. et al. (1996). Children's perception of gender-role-congruent and incongruent behavior in peers: Fisher-Price meets Price Waterhouse. *Sex Roles, 35*, 619–638.

McAuliffe, T.L. et al. (2007). Effects of question format and collection mode on the accuracy of retrospective surveys of health risk behavior: A comparison with daily sexual activity diaries. *Health Psychology, 26*, 60–67.

McCabe, M.P. et al. (2006). "Who thinks I need a perfect body?": Perceptions and internal dialogue among adolescents about their bodies. *Sex Roles, 55*, 409–419.

McCaughey, M. (1998). The fighting spirit: Women's self-defense training and the discourse of sexed embodiment. *Gender & Society, 12*, 277–300.

McCaw, J.M., & Senn, C.Y. (1998). Perception of cues in conflictual dating situations: A test of the miscommunication hypothesis. *Violence Against Women, 4*, 609–624.

McClearn, G.E., & Johansson, B. (1997). Substantial genetic influence on cognitive abilities in twins 80 or more years old. *Science, 276*, 1560–1564.

McClintock, M.K. (1971). Menstrual synchrony and suppression. *Nature, 229*, 244–245.

McClure, E.B. (2000). A meta-analytic review of sex differences in facial expression processing and their development in infants, children, and adolescents. *Psychological Bulletin, 126*, 424–453.

McCreary, D.R. (1990). Self-perceptions of life-span gender-role development. *International Journal of Aging and Human Development, 31*, 135–146.

McCreary, D.R. (1994). The male role and avoiding femininity. *Sex Roles, 31*, 517–531.

McDonald, P. et al. (2010). Outrage management in cases of sexual harassment as revealed in judicial decisions. *Psychology of Women Quarterly, 34*, 165–180.

McDonald, T.W. et al. (2004). The influence of social status on token women leaders' expectations about leading male-dominated groups. *Sex Roles, 50*, 401–409.

McEwan, S.L. et al. (2002). Ego-identity achievement and perception of risk in intimacy in survivors of stranger and acquaintance rape. *Sex Roles, 47*, 281–287.

McFarlane, J. et al. (1988). Mood fluctuations: Women versus men and menstrual versus other cycles. *Psychology of Women Quarterly, 12*, 201–223.

McFarlane, J. et al. (2000). Women filing assault charges on an intimate partner: Criminal justice outcome and future violence experienced. *Violence Against Women, 6*, 396–408.

McGlone, M.S. et al. (2006). Stereotype threat and the gender gap in political knowledge. *Psychology of Women Quarterly, 30*, 392–398.

McGrath, E. et al. (Eds.). (1990). *Women and depression: Risk factors and treatment issues*. Washington, DC: American Psychological Association.

McHugh, M.C. et al. (1993). Research on battered women and their assailants. In M. Paludi & F. Denmark (Eds.), *Handbook on the psychology of women* (pp. 513–552). New York: Greenwood Press.

McIntosh, P. (1995). White privilege and male privilege: A personal account of coming to see correspondences through work in Women's Studies. In M.L. Andersen & P.H. Collins, *Race, class, and gender: An anthology* (2nd ed.) (pp. 76–87). Belmont, CA: Wadsworth.

McIntyre, A., & Lykes, M.B. (1998). Who's the boss? Confronting Whiteness and power differences within a feminist mentoring relationship in participatory action research. *Feminism & Psychology, 8*, 427–444.

McKinley, N.M. (2004). Resisting body dissatisfaction: Fat women who endorse fat acceptance. *Body Image, 1*, 213–219.

McKinley, N.M., & Hyde, J.S. (1996). The Objectified Body Consciousness Scale: Development and validation. *Psychology of Women Quarterly, 20*, 181–215.

McMullin, D. et al. (2007). The impact of sexual victimization on personality: A longitudinal study of gendered attributes. Sex Roles, 56, 403–414.

McMullin, D., & White, J.W. (2006). Long-term effects of labeling a rape experience. *Psychology of Women Quarterly, 30*, 96–105.

Mecca, S.J., & Rubin, L.J. (1999). Definitional research on African American students and sexual harassment. *Psychology of Women Quarterly, 23,* 813–817.

Mednick, M.T. (1989). On the politics of psychological constructs: Stop the bandwagon, I want to get off. *American Psychologist, 44,* 1118–1123.

Meece, J.L., & Scantlebury, K. (2006). Gender and schooling: Progress and persistent barriers. In J. Worell & C. Goodheart (Eds.), *Handbook of girls' and women's psychological health: Gender and well-being across the lifespan* (pp. 283–291). New York: Oxford.

Mehta, C.M., & Strough, J. (2010). Gender segregation and gender-typing in adolescence. *Sex Roles, 63,* 251–263.

Melamed, T. (1995a). Career success: The moderating effect of gender. *Journal of Vocational Behavior, 47,* 35–60.

Melamed, T. (1995b). Barriers to women's career success: Human capital, career choices, structural determinants, or simply sex discrimination. *Applied Psychology: An International Review, 44,* 295–314.

Mellor, D. et al. (2010). Body image and self-esteem across age and gender: A short-term longitudinal study. *Sex Roles, 63,* 672–681.

Menacker, F., & Hamilton, B.E. (2010). *Recent trends in Cesarean delivery in the United States.* NCHS Data Brief, No. 35. Hyattsville, MD: National Center for Health Statistics.

Mendes-de-Leon, C.F. et al. (1994). Financial strain and symptoms of depression in a community sample of elderly men and women: A longitudinal study. *Journal of Aging and Health, 6,* 448–468.

Mensinger, J.L. et al. (2007). Perceived gender role prescriptions in schools, the superwoman ideal, and disordered eating among adolescent girls. *Sex Roles, 57,* 557–568.

Mercurio, A.E., & Landry, L.J. (2008). Self-objectification and well-being: The impact of self-objectification on women's overall sense of self-worth and life satisfaction. *Sex Roles, 58,* 458–466.

Merskin, D. (1999). Adolescence, advertising, and the ideology of menstruation. *Sex Roles, 40,* 941–957.

Merton, R.K. (1957). *Social theory and social structure.* New York: Free Press.

Messerschmidt, J.W. (2000). Becoming "real men": Adolescent masculinity challenges and sexual violence. *Men and Masculinities, 2,* 286–307.

Messman-Moore, T.L., & Brown, A.L. (2006). Risk perception, rape, and sexual revictimization: A prospective study of college women. *Psychology of Women Quarterly, 30,* 159–172.

Messner, M.A. (1997). *Politics of masculinities: Men in movements.* Thousand Oaks, CA: Sage.

Messner, M.A. (1998). The limits of "the male sex role": An analysis of the men's liberation and men's rights movements discourse. *Gender & Society, 12,* 255–276.

Messner, M.A. (2000). Barbie girls versus sea monsters: Children constructing gender. *Gender & Society, 14,* 765–784.

Meyer, S. et al. (1991). Gender and relationships: Beyond the peer group. *American Psychologist, 46,* 537.

Meyerowitz, B.E., & Hart, S. (1995). Women and cancer: Have assumptions about women limited our research agenda? In A.L. Stanton & S.J. Gallant (Eds.), *The psychology of women's health: Progress and challenges in research and application* (pp. 51–84). Washington, DC: American Psychological Association.

Michaelieu, Q. (1997). Female identity, gendered parenting and adolescent women's self-esteem. *Feminism & Psychology, 7,* 328–333.

Michaud, S.L., & Warner, R.M. (1997). Gender differences in self-reported response to troubles talk. *Sex Roles, 37,* 527–540.

Milewski, A.E., & Siqueland, E.R. (1975). Discrimination of color and pattern novelty in one-month human infants. *Journal of Experimental Child Psychology, 19,* 122–136.

Milgram, S. (1963). Behavioral study of obedience. *Journal of Abnormal and Social Psychology, 67,* 371–378.

Milkie, M.A. et al. (2002). Gendered division of childrearing: Ideals, realities, and the relationship to parental well-being. *Sex Roles, 47,* 21–38.

Millard, J.E., & Grant, P.R. (2006). The stereotypes of Black and White women in fashion magazine photographs: The pose of the model and the impression she creates. *Sex Roles, 54,* 959–673.

Millburn, M.A. et al. (2000). The effects of viewing R-rated movie scenes that objectify women on perceptions of date rape. *Sex Roles, 43,* 645–664.

Miller, B.A. et al. (1987). The role of childhood sexual abuse in the development of alcoholism in women. *Violence Victims, 2,* 157–172.

Miller, C.T., & Downey, K.T. (1999). A meta-analysis of heavyweight and self-esteem. *Personality and Social Psychology Review, 3,* 68–84.

Miller, D.T., & Turnbull, W. (1986). Expectancies and interpersonal processes. *Annual Review of Psychology, 37,* 233–256.

Miller, E.J. et al. (2000). The "skinny" on body size requests in personal ads. *Sex Roles, 43,* 129–141.

Miller, M.K., & Summers, A. (2007). Gender differences in video game characters' roles, appearances, and attire as portrayed in video game magazines. *Sex Roles, 57*, 733–742.

Miller, R.J. (2001). Gender differences in illusion response: The influence of spatial strategy and sex ratio. *Sex Roles, 44*, 209–225.

Minarik, M.L., & Ahrens, A.H. (1996). Relations of eating and symptoms of depression and anxiety to the dimensions of perfectionism among undergraduate women. *Cognitive Therapy and Research, 20*, 155–169.

Miner-Rubino, K. et al. (2009). More than numbers: Individual and contextual factors in how gender diversity affects women's well being. *Psychology of Women Quarterly, 33*, 463–474.

Miranda, V. (2011), Cooking, caring and Volunteering: Unpaid work around the world. *OECD Social, Employment and Migration Working Papers*, No. 116, OECD Publishing. http://dx.doi.org/10.1787/5kghrjm8s142–en

Mitchell, K.S., & Mazzeo, S.E. (2009). Evaluation of a structural model of objectification theory and eating disorder symptomatology among European American and African American undergraduate women. *Psychology of Women Quarterly, 33*, 384–395.

Mitchell, V., & Helson, R. (1990). Women's prime of life: Is it the 50s? *Psychology of Women Quarterly, 14*, 451–470.

Moen, P. et al. (2009). Learning from a natural experiment: Studying a corporate work-time policy initiative. In A.C. Crouter & A. Booth (Eds.), *Work-life policies* (pp. 97 – 132). Washington, DC: Urban Institute Press.

Mohr, J.J., & Daly, C.A. (2008). Sexual minority stress and changes in relationship quality in same-sex couples. *Journal of Social and Personal Relationships, 25*, 989–1007.

Mohr, J.J., & Fassinger, R.E. (2006). Sexual orientation identity and romantic relationship quality in same-sex couples. *Personality and Social Psychology Bulletin, 32*, 1085–1099.

Möller-Leimkühler, A.M. (2010). Higher comorbidity of depression and cardiovascular disease in women: A biopsychosocial perspective. *The World Journal of Biological Psychiatry, 11*, 922–933.

Monahan, J.L. et al. (1999). When women imbibe: Alcohol and the illusory control of HIV risk. *Psychology of Women Quarterly, 23*, 643–651.

Monro, F., & Huon, G. (2005). Media-portrayed idealized images, body shame, and appearance anxiety. *International Journal of Eating Disorders, 38*, 85–90.

Monson, R.A. (1997). State-ing sex and gender: Collecting information from mothers and fathers in paternity cases. *Gender & Society, 11*, 279–295.

Monsour, M. et al. (1994). Challenges confronting cross-sex friendships: "Much ado about nothing?" *Sex Roles, 31*, 55–77.

Montemurro, B. (2003). Not a laughing matter: Sexual harassment as "material" on workplace-based situation comedies. *Sex Roles, 48*, 433–445.

Montemurro, B., & McClure, B. (2005). Changing gender norms for alcohol consumption: Social drinking and lowered inhibitions at bachelorette parties. *Sex Roles, 52*, 279–288.

Mooney, K.M. & Lorenz, E. (1997). The effects of food and gender on interpersonal perceptions. *Sex Roles, 36*, 639–653.

Moos, R.H. (1968). The development of a Menstrual Distress Questionnaire. *Psychosomatic Medicine, 30*, 853–867.

Moos, R.H., & Moos, B.S. (1994). *A social climate scale: Family environment scale manual.* Palo Alto, CA: Consulting Psychologists Press.

Moradi, B. et al. (2000). Does "feminist" plus "therapist" equal "feminist therapist"? An empirical investigation of the link between self-labeling and behaviors. *Psychology of Women Quarterly, 24*, 285–296.

Moradi, B. et al. (in press). Disarming the threat to feminist identification: An application of person construct theory to measurement and intervention. *Psychology of Women Quarterly.*

Moradi, B. et al. (2005). Roles of sexual objectification experiences and internalization of standards of beauty in eating disorder symptomatology: A test and extension of objectification theory. *Journal of Counseling Psychology, 52*, 420–428.

Moradi, B., & Funderburk, J.R. (2006). Roles of perceived sexist events and perceived social support in the mental health of women seeking counseling. *Journal of Counseling Psychology, 53*, 464–473.

Moradi, B., & Huang, Y. (2008). Objectification theory and psychology of women: A decade of advances and future directions. *Psychology of Women Quarterly, 32*, 377–398.

Moradi, B., & Subich, L. M. (2002). Feminist identity development measures: Comparing the psychometrics of three instruments. *The Counseling Psychologist, 30*, 66–86.

Moraga, C. (1981). The welder. In C. Moraga & G. Anzaldúa (Eds.), *This bridge called my back: Writings by radical women of color* (pp. 219–220). New York: Kitchen Table: Women of Color Press.

Moran, P.B., & Eckenrode, J. (1991). Gender differences in the costs and benefits of peer relationships during adolescence. *Journal of Adolescent Research, 6*, 396–409.

Morawski, J.G. (1987). The troubled quest for masculinity, femininity, and androgyny. *Review of Personality and Social Psychology: Sex and Gender, 7,* 44–69.

Morgan, B.L. (1998). A three generational study of tomboy behavior. *Sex Roles, 39,* 787–800.

Morgan, E.M. et al. (2010). A longitudinal study of conversations with parents about sex and dating during college. *Developmental Psychology, 46,* 139–150.

Morman, M.T., & Floyd, K. (1998). "I love you, man": Overt expressions of affection in male-male interaction. *Sex Roles, 38,* 871–881.

Morokoff, P.J. et al. (1995). Women and AIDS. In A.L. Stanton & S.J. Gallant (Eds.), *The psychology of women's health: Progress and challenges in research and application* (pp. 117–169). Washington, DC: American Psychological Association.

Morris, C. (1997). Mental health matters: Toward a non-medicalized approach to psychotherapy with women. *Women & Therapy, 20,* 63–77.

Morrison, J. (1989). Childhood sexual histories of women with somatization disorder. *American Journal of Psychiatry, 146,* 239–241.

Morrison, R.L. (2009). Are women tending and befriending in the workplace? Gender differences in the relationship between workplace friendships and organizational outcomes. *Sex Roles, 60,* 1–13.

Morrison, T.G., & Sheahan, E.E. (2009). Gender-related discourses as mediators in the association between internalization of the thin-body ideal and indicants of body dissatisfaction and disordered eating. *Psychology of Women Quarterly, 33,* 374–383.

Morrongiello, B.A. et al. (2010). Understanding gender differences in children's risk taking and injury: A comparison of mothers' and fathers' reactions to sons and daughters misbehaving in ways that lead to injury. *Journal of Applied Developmental Psychology, 31,* 322–329.

Morrongiello, B.A., & Hogg, K. (2004). Mothers' reactions to children misbehaving in ways that can lead to injury: Implications for gender differences in children's risk taking and injuries. *Sex Roles, 50,* 103–118.

Morrow, S.L. et al. (1996). The application of a sociocognitive framework to the career development of lesbian women and gay men. *Journal of Vocational Behavior, 48,* 136–148.

Morrow, S.L., & Hawxhurst, D.M. (1998). Feminist therapy: Integrating political analysis in counseling and psychotherapy. *Women & Therapy, 21,* 37–50.

Morton, T.A. et al. (2009). Theorizing gender in the face of social change: Is there anything essential about essentialism? *Journal of Personality and Social Psychology, 96,* 653–664.

Mosher, C.E., & Danoff-Burg, S. (2004). Effects of gender and employment status on support provided to caregivers. *Sex Roles, 51,* 589–595.

Mosher, C.E., & Danoff-Burg, S. (2005). Agentic and communal personality traits: Relations to attitudes toward sex and sexual experiences. *Sex Roles, 52,* 121–129.

Moss-Racusin, C.A., & Rudman, L.A. (2010). Disruptions in women's self-promotion: The backlash avoidance model. *Psychology of Women Quarterly, 34,* 186–202.

Mowbray, C.T. (1995). Nonsexist therapy: Is it? *Women & Therapy, 16*(4), 9–30.

Moya, M. et al. (2007). It's for your own good: Benevolent sexism and women's reactions to protectively justified restrictions. *Personality and Social Psychology Bulletin, 33,* 1421–1434.

Moyer, R.S. (1997). Covering gender on memory's front page: Men's prominence and women's prospects. *Sex Roles, 37,* 595–618.

Muehlenhard, C.L. et al. (1992). Definitions of rape: Scientific and political implications. *Journal of Social Issues, 48*(1), 23–44.

Muehlenhard, C.L. et al. (1997). Rape statistics are not exaggerated. In M.R. Walsh (Ed.), *Women, men, and gender: Ongoing debates* (pp. 243–246). New Haven, CT: Yale.

Muehlenhard, C.L., & Linton, M.A. (1987). Date rape and sexual aggression in dating situations: Incidence and risk factors. *Journal of Counseling Psychology, 34,* 186–196.

Muehlenhard, C.L., & McCoy, M.L. (1991). Double standard/double bind: The sexual double standard and women's communication about sex. *Psychology of Women Quarterly, 15,* 447–461.

Muehlenhard, C.L., & Peterson, Z.D. (2011). Distinguishing between *sex* ang *gender*: History, current conceptualizations, and implications. *Sex Roles.* doi: 10.1007/s11199–011–9932–5

Muehlenhard, C.L., & Rodgers, C.S. (1998). Token resistance to sex: New perspectives on an old stereotype. *Psychology of Women Quarterly, 22,* 443–463.

Muehlenhard, C.L., & Schrag, J. (1991). Nonviolent sexual coercion. In A. Parrot & L. Bechhofer (Eds.), *Acquaintance rape: The hidden crime* (pp. 115–128). New York: Wiley.

Muehlenkamp, J.J. et al. (2005). Self-objectification, risk taking, and self-harm in college women. *Psychology of Women Quarterly, 29,* 24–32.

Muehlenkamp, J.J., & Saris-Baglama, R.N. (2002). Self-objectification and its psychological outcomes for college women. *Psychology of Women Quarterly, 26*, 371–379.

Muise, A., & Desmarais, S. (2010). Women's perceptions and use of anti-aging products. *Sex Roles, 63*, 126–137.

Mukerjee, M. (1995). Sexual and other abuse may alter a brain region. *Scientific American, 273*, 14–20.

Murnen, S.K. et al. (2002). If "boys will be boys," then girls will be victims? A meta-analytic review of the research that relates masculine ideology to sexual aggression. *Sex Roles, 46*, 359–375.

Murnen, S.K. et al. (2003). Thin, sexy women and strong, muscular men: Grade-school children's responses to objectified images of women and men. *Sex Roles, 49*, 427–437.

Murnen, S.K., & Kohlman, M.H. (2007). Athletic participation, fraternity membership, and sexual aggression among college men: A meta-analytic review. *Sex Roles, 57*, 145–157.

Murnen, S.K., & Smolak, L. (2009). Are feminist women protected from body image problems? A meta-analytic review of relevant research. *Sex Roles, 60*, 186–197.

Murnen, S.K., & Byrne, D. (1991). Hyperfemininity: Measurement and initial validation of the construct. *Journal of Sex Research, 28*, 479–489.

Murphy, D.G.M. et al. (1996). Sex differences in human brain morphometry and metabolism: An in vivo quantitative magnetic resonance imaging and position emission tomography study on the effect of aging. *Archives of General Psychiatry, 53*, 585–594.

Murstein, B.I., & Adler, E.R.(1995). Gender differences in power and self-disclosure in dating and married couples. *Personal Relationships, 2*, 199–209.

Mustanski, B.S., & Bailey, J.M. (2003). A therapists guide to the genetics of human sexual orientation. *Sexual and Relationship Therapy, 18*(4), 429–436.

Muth, J.L., & Cash, T.F. (1997). Body-image attitudes: What difference does gender make? *Journal of Applied Social Psychology, 27*, 1438–1452.

Myers, T.A., & Crowther, J.H. (2008). Is self-objectification related to interoceptive awareness? An examination of potential mediating pathways to disordered eating attitudes. *Psychology of Women Quarterly, 32*, 172–180.

Nash, H.C., & Chrisler, J.C. (1997). Is a little (psychiatric) knowledge a dangerous thing? The impact of premenstrual dysphoric disorder on perceptions of premenstrual women. *Psychology of Women Quarterly, 21*, 315–322.

National Victims Center. (1992). *Rape in America: A report to the nation.* Arlington, VA: Author.

NCIPC (National Center for Injury Prevention and Control). (2005). *Intimate partner violence: Fact sheet.* Centers for Disease Control and Prevention. http://www.cdc.gov/ncipc/factsheets/ipvfacts.htm (Retrieved November 2005).

NCVC. (2005). Sexual assault statistics. http://www.ncvc.org/ncvc/main.aspx?db Name=Documen tViewer&DocumentID=32291#97. (Retrieved November 2005).

Neff, L.A., & Karney, B.R. (2005). Gender differences in social support: A question of skill or responsiveness? *Journal of Personality and Social Psychology, 88*, 79–90.

Neighbors, L. et al. (2008). Weighing weight: Trends in body weight evaluation among young adults, 1990 and 2005. *Sex Roles, 59*, 68–80.

Neill, C.M., & Kahn, A.S. (1999). The role of personal spirituality and religious social activity on the life satisfaction of older widowed women. *Sex Roles, 40*, 310–329.

Nelson, A. (2000). The pink dragon is female: Halloween costumes and gender markers. *Psychology of Women Quarterly, 24*, 137–144.

Nelson, A. (2005). Children's toy collections in Sweden – A less gender-typed country? *Sex Roles, 52*, 93–102.

Nelson, C.G. et al. (2007). Organizational responses for preventing and stopping sexual harassment: Effective deterrents or continued endurance. *Sex Roles, 56*, 811–822.

Nelson, D.L. et al. (1990). Politics, lack of career progress, and work-home conflict: Stress and strain for working women. *Sex Roles, 23*, 169–185.

Nelson, M. (1991). Empowerment of incest survivors: Speaking out. *Families in Society, 72*, 618–624.

Nelson, R.L., & Bridges, W.P. (1999). *Legalizing gender inequality. Courts, markets, and unequal pay for women in America.* New York: Cambridge.

Nelson, T.E. et al. (1996). Irrepressible stereotypes. *Journal of Experimental Social Psychology, 32*, 13–38.

New View. (2011). *New view campaign.* http://www.newviewcampaign.org (Retrieved September 2011).

Newheiser, A. et al. (2010). Others as objects: How women and men perceive the consequences of self-objectification. *Sex Roles, 63*, 657–671.

Newman, A.L., & Peterson, C. (1996). Anger of women incest survivors. *Sex Roles, 34*, 463–474.

Nicholson, P. (1995). The menstrual cycle, science and femininity: Assumptions underlying menstrual cycle research. *Social Science Medicine, 41*, 779–784.

Niemela, P., & Lento, R. (1993). The significance of the 50th birthday for women's individuation. *Women & Therapy, 14*, 117–127.

Noland, V.J. et al. (2004). Connotative interpretations of sexuality-related terms. *Sex Roles, 51*, 523–534.

Nolen-Hoeksema, S., & Hilt, L.M. (2009). Gender differences in depression. In I.H. Gotlib & C.L. Hammen (Eds.), *Handbook of depression* (pp. 386–404). New York: Guilford.

Nolen-Hoeksema, S., & Jackson, B. (2001). Mediators of the gender difference in rumination. *Psychology of Women Quarterly, 25*, 37–47.

Nolen-Hoeksema, S., & Keita, G.P. (2003). Women and depression: Introduction. *Psychology of Women Quarterly, 27*, 89–90.

Noll, S.M., & Fredrickson, B.L. (1998). A mediational model linking self-objectification, body shame, and disordered eating. *Psychology of Women Quarterly, 22*, 623–636.

Norris, J. et al. (1999). When a date changes from fun to dangerous: Factors affecting women's ability to distinguish. *Violence Against Women, 5*, 230–250.

Norton, M.I. et al. (2004). Casuistry and social category bias. *Journal of Personality and Social Psychology, 87*, 817–831.

Novak, M., & Thacker, C. (1991). Satisfaction and strain among middle-aged women who return to school: Replication and extension of findings in a Canadian context. *Educational Gerontology, 17*, 323–342.

Nowatzki, J., & Morry, M. M. (2009). Women's intentions regarding, and acceptance of, self-sexualizing behavior. *Psychology of Women Quarterly, 33*, 95–107.

National Science Foundation. (2009). *Doctorate recipients from U.S. universities: Summary report 2007–2008.* http://www.nsf.gov/statistics/nsf10309/pdf/nsf10309.pdf

Nurmi, J.E. (1991). How do adolescents see their future? A review of the development of future orientation and planning. *Developmental Review, 11*, 1–59.

Nussbaum, M.C. (1999). *Sex and social justice.* Oxford England: Oxford University Press.

Nye, W.P. (1993). Amazing grace: Religion and identity among elderly Black individuals. *International Journal of Aging and Human Development, 36*, 103–114.

O'Byrne, R. et al. (2006). "You couldn't say 'no,' could you? Young men's understandings of sexual refusal. *Feminism & Psychology, 16*, 133–154.

O'Brien, K.E. et al. (2010). A meta-analytic investigation of gender differences in mentoring. *Journal of Management, 36*, 537–554.

Ochman, J.M. (1996). The effects of nongender-role stereotyped, same-sex role models in storybooks on the self-esteem of children in grade three. *Sex Roles, 35*, 711–735.

O'Connell, A.N. (1989). Psychology of women students' self-concepts, attitudes, and assertiveness: A decade of research. *Teaching of Psychology, 16*, 178–181.

O'Connell, A.N., & Russo, N.F. (Eds.). (1990). *Women in psychology: A bio-bibliographic sourcebook.* New York: Greenwood.

O'Connell, A.N., & Russo, N.F. (Eds.). (1991). Women's heritage in psychology: Origins, development, and future directions [Special Issue]. *Psychology of Women Quarterly, 15*(4).

Offer, D., & Schonert-Reichl, K.A. (1992). Debunking the myths of adolescence: Findings from recent research. *Journal of the American Academy of Child and Adolescent Psychiatry, 31*, 1003–1014.

Offman, A., & Matheson, K. (2004). The sexual self-perceptions of young women experiencing abuse in dating relationships. *Sex Roles, 51*, 551–560.

Ogletree, S.M., & Drake, R. (2007). College students' video game participation and perceptions: Gender differences and implications. *Sex Roles, 56*, 537–542.

Ogletree, S.M. et al. (2004). Pokemon: Exploring the role of gender. *Sex Roles, 50*, 851–859.

Ohse, D.M., & Stockdale, M.S. (2008). Age comparisons in workplace sexual harassment perceptions. *Sex Roles, 59*, 240–253.

Ojerholm, A.J., & Rothblum, E.D. (1999). The relationships of body image, feminism and sexual orientation in college women. *Feminism & Psychology, 9*, 431–448.

Okamoto, D., & England, P. (1999). Is there a supply side to occupational segregation? *Sociological Perspectives, 42*, 557–582.

Older Women's League. (2005). *The state of older women.* http://www.owl-national.org/owlreports/index.html. (Retrieved October 2005).

Olenick, N.L., & Chalmers, D.K. (1991). Gender-specific drinking styles in alcoholics and nonalcoholics. *Journal of Studies on Alcohol, 52*, 325–330.

Oliver, M.B., & Green, S. (2001). Development of gender differences in children's responses to animated entertainment. *Sex Roles, 45*, 67–88.

Oliver, M.B., & Hyde, J.S. (1993). Gender differences in sexuality: A meta-analysis. *Psychological Bulletin, 114*, 29–51.

Oliver, W. (2000). Preventing domestic violence in the African American community: The rationale for popular culture interventions. *Violence Against Women, 6*, 533–549.

Olkin, R. (1999). The personal, professional and political when clients have disabilities. *Women & Therapy, 22,* 87–103.

O'Meara, J.D. (1989). Cross-sex friendship: Four basic challenges of an ignored relationship. *Sex Roles, 21,* 525–543.

Ondersma, S.J. et al. (2001). Sex with children is abuse: Comment on Rind, Tromovitch, and Bauserman (1998). *Psychological Bulletin, 127,* 707–714.

Oppliger, P.A. (2007). Effects of gender stereotyping on socialization. In R.W. Preiss et al. (Eds.), *Mass media effects research: Advances through meta-analysis.* Mahwah, NJ: Erlbaum.

Orbach, S. (2010). *Bodies.* London, England: Profile Books.

Orchowski, L.M. et al. (2008). Evaluation of a sexual assault risk reduction and self-defense program: A prospective analysis of a revised protocol. *Psychology of Women Quarterly, 32,* 204–218.

Ormerod, A.J. et al. (2008). Critical climate: Relations among sexual harassment, climate, and outcomes for high school girls and boys. *Psychology of Women Quarterly, 32,* 113–125.

Ortner, T.M., & Sieverding, M. (2008). Where are the gender differences? Male priming boosts spatial skills in women. *Sex Roles, 59,* 274–281.

Osman, S.L. (2007). The continuation of perpetrator behaviors that influence perceptions of sexual harassment. *Sex Roles, 56,* 63–69.

Osmond, M.W. et al. (1993). The multiple jeopardy of race, class, and gender for AIDS risk among women. *Gender & Society, 7,* 99–120.

Oswald, D.L., & Lindstedt, K. (2006). The content and function of gender stereotypes: An exploratory investigation. *Sex Roles, 54,* 447–458.

Ouimette, P.C. et al. (2000). Consistency of reports of rape behavior among nonincarcerated men. *Psychology of Men and Masculinity, 1,* 133–139.

Outtz, J.H. (1996). *Are Mommies dropping out of the labor force?* Washington, DC: Institute for Women's Policy Research.

Overstreet, N.M. et al. (2010). Beyond thinness: The influence of a curvaceous body ideal on body dissatisfaction in Black and White women. *Sex Roles, 63,* 91–103.

Oxley, T. (1998). Menstrual management: An exploratory study. *Feminism & Psychology, 8,* 185–191.

Oyserman, D., & Lee, S.W.S. (2008). Does culture influence what and how we think? Effects of priming individualism and collectivism. *Psychological Bulletin, 134,* 311–342.

Ozer, E.M. (1995). The impact of childcare responsibility and self-efficacy on the psychological health of professional working mothers. *Psychology of Women Quarterly, 19,* 315–335.

Padavic, I., & Reskin, B. (2002). *Women and men at work* (2nd ed.). Thousand Oaks, CA: Pine Forge.

Palmerton, P.R., & Judas, J. (1994, July). *Selling violence: Television commercials targeted to children.* Paper presented at the annual meeting of the International Communication Association, Sydney, New South Wales, Australia.

Paludi, M.A. (1992). *The psychology of women.* Dubuque, IA: Brown & Benchmark.

Papadatou-Pastou, M. et al (2008). Sex differences in left-handedness: A meta-analysis of 144 studies. *Psychological Bulletin, 134,* 677–699.

Parasuraman, S. et al. (1996). Work and family variables, entrepreneurial career success and psychological well-being. *Journal of Vocational Behavior, 48,* 275–300.

Parent, M.C., & Moradi, B. (2010). Confirmatory factor analysis of the Conformity to Feminine Norms Inventory and the development of an abbreviated version: The CFNI-45. *Psychology of Women Quarterly, 34,* 97–109.

Parent, M.C., & Moradi, B. (2011). An abbreviated tool for assessing conformity to masculine norms: Psychometric properties of the Conformity to Masculine Norms Inventory-46. *Psychology of Men and Masculinity, 12,* 339–353.

Park, S. et al. (2007). Do third-person perceptions of media influence contribute to pluralistic ignorance on the norm of ideal female thinness. *Sex Roles, 57,* 569–578.

Parker, G., & Brotchie, H. (2010). Gender differences in depression. *International Review of Psychiatry, 22,* 429–436.

Parks, J.B., & Robertson, M.A. (2000). Development and validation of an instrument to measure attitudes toward sexist/nonsexist language. *Sex Roles, 42,* 415–438.

Parks, K.A. et al. (2008). Women's social behavior when meeting new men: The influence of alcohol and childhood sexual abuse. *Psychology of Women Quarterly, 32,* 145–158.

Parks-Stamm, E.J. et al. (2008). Motivated to penalize: Women's strategic rejection of successful women. *Personality and Social Psychology Bulletin, 34,* 237–247.

Parlee, M.B. (1993). Psychology of menstruation and premenstrual syndrome. In F.L. Denmark & M.A. Paludi (Eds.), *Psychology of women: A Handbook of issues and theories* (pp. 325–377). Westport, CT: Greenwood Press.

Parrot, A., and Bechhofer, L. (Eds.) (1991). *Acquaintance rape: The hidden crime.* New York: Wiley.

Parsons, E.M., & Betz, N.E. (2001). The relationship of participation in sports and physical activity to body objectification, instrumentality, and locus of control among young women. *Psychology of Women Quarterly, 25*, 209–222.

Parvin, R., & Biaggio, M.K. (1991). Paradoxes in the practice of feminist therapy. *Women & Therapy, 11*(2), 3–12.

Patel, K.A. & Gray, J.J. (2001). Judgment accuracy in body preferences among African Americans. *Sex Roles, 44*, 227–235.

Patrick, J.H. et al. (2001). Gender, emotional support, and well-being among the rural elderly. *Sex Roles, 45*, 15–29.

Paul, E. (1993). The women's movement and the movement of women. *Social Policy, 23*(4), 44–50.

Pearson, J. (2006). Personal control, self-efficacy in sexual negotiation, and contraceptive risk among adolescents: The role of gender. *Sex Roles, 54,* 615–625.

Pearson, J. et al. (2009). Gendered fields: Sports and advanced course taking in high school. *Sex Roles, 61*, 519–535.

Pedersen, S., & Seidman, E. (2004). Team sports achievement and self-esteem development among urban adolescent girls. *Psychology of Women Quarterly, 28*, 412–422.

Pedriana, N. (2004). Help wanted NOW: Legal resources, the women's movement, and the battle over sex-segregated job advertisements. *Social Problems, 51*(2), 182–201.

Penha-Lopes, V. (2006). "To cook, sew, to be a man:" The socialization for competence and Black men's involvement in housework. *Sex Roles, 54*, 261–274.

Penning, M.J., & Strain, L.A. (1994). Gender differences in disability, assistance, and subjective well-being in later life. *Journals of Gerontology, 49*, S202–S208.

Peplau, L.A. et al. (1998). A critique of Bem's "exotic becomes erotic" theory of sexual orientation. *Psychological Review, 105*, 387–394.

Peplau, L.A., & Conrad, E. (1989). Beyond nonsexist research: The perils of feminist methods in psychology. *Psychology of Women Quarterly, 13*, 379–400.

Peplau, L.A., & Fingerhut, A. (2004). The paradox of the lesbian worker. *Journal of Social Issues, 60*(4), 719–735.

Pereda, N. et al. (2009). The prevalence of child sexual abuse in community and student samples: A meta-analysis. *Clinical Psychology Review, 29*, 328–338.

Perkins, K. (1993). Working class women and retirement. *Journal of Gerontological Social Work, 20*, 129–146.

Perry, E.L. et al. (1998). Propensity to sexually harass: An exploration of gender differences. *Sex Roles, 38*, 443–460.

Petersen, A.C. (1988). Adolescent development. *Annual Review of Psychology, 39*, 583–607.

Petersen, J.L. & Hyde, J.S. (2010). A meta-analytic review of research on gender differences in sexuality, 1993–2007. *Psychological Bulletin, 136*, 21–38.

Petersen, S., & Benishek, L.A. (2001). Special construction of illness: Addressing the impact of cancer on women in therapy. *Women & Therapy, 23*, 75–100.

Petersen, T., & Morgan, L.A. (1995). Separate and unequal: Occupation-establishment sex segregation and the gender wage gap. *American Journal of Sociology, 101*, 329–365.

Petersen, T., & Saporta, I. (2004). The opportunity structure for discrimination. *American Journal of Sociology, 109*, 852–901.

Peterson, R.D. et al. (2008). Empowerment and powerlessness: A closer look at the relationship between feminism, body image and eating disturbance. *Sex Roles, 58*, 639–648.

Peterson, Z.D., & Muehlenhard, C.L. (2004). Was it rape? The function of women's rape myth acceptance and definitions of sex in labeling their own experiences. *Sex Roles, 51*, 129–144.

Petrie, T.A. et al. (2002). Factorial and construct validity of the Body Parts Satisfaction Scale-Revised: An examination of minority and nonminority women. *Psychology of Women Quarterly, 26*, 213–221.

Petrie, T.A. et al. (2010). Biopsychosocial and physical correlates of middle school boys' and girls' body satisfaction. *Sex Roles, 63*, 631–644.

Pettigrew, T.F. (1998). Intergroup contact theory. *Annual Review of Psychology, 49*, 65–85.

Petty, R.E. et al. (2008) *Attitudes: Insights from the new implicit measures.* New York: Psychology Press.

Pezdek, K. (1995, November). *What types of false childhood memories are not likely to be suggestively implanted?* Paper presented at the annual meeting of the Psychonomic Society, Los Angeles, CA.

Pezdek, K. (1996, November). *False memories are more likely to be planted if they are familiar.* Paper presented at the annual meeting of the Psychonomic Society, Chicago, IL.

Pharr, S. (1988). The common elements of oppression. In S. Pharr, *Homophobia: A weapon of sexism* (pp. 53–64). Inverness, CA: Chardon Press.

Phelan, J.E. et al. (2008). Competent yet out in the cold: Shifting criteria for hiring reflect backlash toward agentic women. *Psychology of Women Quarterly, 32*, 406–413.

Phelan, J.E. et al. (2010). The danger in sexism: The links among fear of crime, benevolent sexism, and well-being. *Sex Roles, 62*, 35–47.

Phillips, L. (1998). *The girls report: What we know and need to know about growing up female.* New York: The National Council for Research on Women. http://www.ncrw.org (Retrieved November 2001).

Philpot, C.L. et al. (1997). *Bridging separate gender worlds: Why men and women clash and how therapists can bring them together.* Washington, DC: American Psychological Association.

Pike, J.J., & Jennings, N.A. (2005). The effects of commercials on children's perceptions of gender appropriate toy use. *Sex Roles, 52*, 83–91.

Pingitore, R. et al. (1994). Bias against overweight job applicants in a simulated employment interview. *Journal of Applied Psychology, 79*, 909–917.

Pino, N., & Meier, R.F. (1999). Gender differences in rape reporting. *Sex Roles, 40*, 979–990.

Pinquart, M., & Sorensen, S. (2001). Gender differences in self-concept and psychological well-being in old age: A meta-analysis. *Journals of Gerontology, 56B*(4), 195–213.

Pinzler, I.K., & Ellis, D. (1989). Wage discrimination and comparable worth: A legal perspective. *Journal of Social Issues, 45*(4), 51–65.

Pinzone-Glover, H.A. et al. (1998). An acquaintance rape prevention program: Effects on attitudes toward women, rape-related attitudes, and perceptions of rape scenarios. *Psychology of Women Quarterly, 22*, 605–621.

Pipher, M.B. (1994). *Reviving Ophelia: Saving the selves of adolescent girls.* New York: Putnam.

Piran, N. (2001). Re-inhabiting the body from the inside out: Girls transform their school environment. In D. Tolman & M. Brydon-Miller (Eds.), *From subjects to subjectivities: A handbook of interpretive and participatory methods* (pp. 218–238). New York: New York University Press.

Pliner, P. et al. (1990). Gender differences in concern with body weight and physical appearance over the life span. *Personality and Social Psychology Bulletin, 16*, 263–273.

Plous, S., & Neptune, D. (1997). Racial and gender biases in magazine advertising: A content-analytic study. *Psychology of Women Quarterly, 21*, 627–644.

Pollard, J.W. (1994). Treatment for perpetrators of rape and other violence. In A. Berkowitz (Ed.), *Men and rape: Theory, research, and prevention programs in higher education* (pp. 51–66). San Francisco, CA: Jossey-Bass.

Polusny, M., & Follette, V. (1996). Remembering childhood sexual abuse: A national survey of psychologists' clinical practices, beliefs, and personal experiences. *Professional Psychology: Research and Practice, 27*, 41–52.

Poole, M.E., & Langan-Fox, J. (1992). Conflict in women's decision-making about multiple roles. *Australian Journal of Marriage and Family, 13*, 2–18.

Pope, K.S. (1996). Memory, abuse, and science: Questioning claims about the false memory syndrome epidemic. *American Psychologist, 51*, 957–974.

Pope, K.S., & Brown, L.S. (1996). *Recovered memories of abuse: Assessment, therapy, forensics.* Washington, DC: American Psychological Association.

Popp, D. et al. (2003). Gender, race, and speech style stereotypes. *Sex Roles, 48*, 317–325.

Poran, M.A. (2002). Denying diversity: Perceptions of beauty and social comparison processes among Latina, Black, and White women. *Sex Roles, 47*, 65–81.

Poran, M.A. (2006). The politics of protection: Body image, social pressures, and the misrepresentation of young Black women. *Sex Roles, 55*, 739–755.

Porter, D.M. (2001). Gender differences in managers' conceptions and perceptions of commitment to the organization. *Sex Roles, 45*, 375–398.

Porter, N. (1995). Supervision of psychotherapists: Integrating anti-racist, feminist, and multicultural perspectives. In H. Landrine (Ed.), *Bringing cultural diversity to feminist psychology: Theory, research, and practice* (pp. 163–175). Washington, DC: American Psychological Association.

Posavac, H. D. et al. (2001). Reducing the impact of media images on women at risk for body image disturbance: Three targeted interventions. *Journal of Social and Clinical Psychology, 20*, 324–340.

Poulin, F., & Pedersen, S. (2007). Developmental changes in gender composition of friendship networks in adolescent girls and boys. *Developmental Psychology, 43*, 1484–1496.

Pratto, F. et al. (1997). The gender gap in occupational role attainment: A social dominance approach. *Journal of Personality and Social Psychology, 72*, 37–53.

Pratto, F., & Walker, A. (2004). The bases of gendered power. In A.H. Eagly, A.E. Beall, & R.J. Sternberg

(Eds.), *The psychology of gender* (2nd ed) (pp. 242–268). New York: Guilford.

Preisser, A.B. (1999). Domestic violence in South Asian communities in America: Advocacy and intervention. *Violence Against Women, 5*, 684–699.

Prentice, D.A., & Carranza, E. (2002). What women and men should be, shouldn't be, are allowed to be, and don't have to be: The contents of prescriptive gender stereotypes. *Psychology of Women Quarterly, 26*, 269–281.

Prentky, R.A., & Knight, R.A. (1991). Identifying critical dimensions for discriminating among rapists. *Journal of Consulting and Clinical Psychology, 59*, 643–661.

Press, J.E., & Townsley, E. (1998). Wives' and husbands' housework reporting: Gender, class and social desirability. *Gender & Society, 12*, 188–218.

Prilleltensky, I., & Gonick, L. (1996). Politics changes, oppression remains: On the psychology and politics of oppression. *Political Psychology, 17*, 127–148.

Prilleltensky, I., & Prilleltensky, O. (2003). Synergies for wellness and liberation in counseling psychology. *The Counseling Psychologist, 31*, 273–281.Prilleltensky, O. (1996). Women with disabilities and feminist therapy. *Women & Therapy, 18*, 87–97.

Prokos, A.H. et al. (2009). Nonstandard work arrangements among women and men scientists and engineers. *Sex Roles, 61*, 653–666.

Ptacek, J. (1988). Why do men batter their wives? In K. Yllö & M. Bograd (Eds.), *Feminist perspectives on wife abuse* (pp. 133–157). Newbury Park, CA: Sage.

Pulerwitz, J. et al. (2000). Measuring sexual relationship power in HIV/STD research. *Sex Roles, 42*, 637–660.

Pulerwitz, J. et al. (2002). Relationship power, condom use and HIV risk among women in the USA. *AIDS Care, 14*, 789–800.

Pulerwitz, J., & Dworkin, S. L. (2006). Give-and-take in safer sex negotiations: The fluidity of gender-based power relations. *Sexuality Research & Social Policy: A Journal of the NSRC, 3*, 40–51.

Pumariega, A.J. et al. (1994). Eating attitudes in African-American women: The *Essence* Eating Disorders Survey. *Eating Disorders: The Journal of Treatment and Prevention, 2*, 5–16.

Quam, J.K., & Whitford, G.S. (1992). Adaptation and age-related expectations of older gay and lesbian adults. *The Gerontologist, 32*, 367–374.

Quina, K. et al. (2000). Sexual communication in relationships: When words speak louder than actions. *Sex Roles, 42*, 523–549.

Quina, K., & Carlson, N.L. (1989). *Rape, incest, and sexual harassment: A guide for helping survivors.* New York: Praeger.

Quinn, D.M. et al. (2006a). Body on my mind: The lingering effects of state self-objectification. *Sex Roles, 55*, 869–874.

Quinn, D.M. et al. (2006b). The disruptive effect of self-objectification on performance. *Psychology of Women Quarterly, 30*, 59–64.

Quinones, B. et al. (1999). Beliefs and attitudes about sexual aggression: Do parents and daughters share the same belief system? *Psychology of Women Quarterly, 23*, 559–572.

Raag, T. (1999). Influences of social expectations of gender, gender stereotypes, and situational constraints on children's toy choices. *Sex Roles, 41*, 809–831.

Raag, T., & Rackliff, C.L. (1998). Preschoolers' awareness of social expectations of gender: Relationships to toy choices. *Sex Roles, 38*, 685–700.

Ragins, B.R. (1991). Gender effects in subordinate evaluations of leaders: Real or artifact? *Journal of Organizational Behavior, 12*, 259–268.

Raley, S., & Bianchi, S. (2006). Sons, daughters, and family processes: Does gender of children matter? *Annual Review of Sociology, 32*, 401–421.

Ramirez de Arellano, A.B. (1996). Latino women: Health status and access to health care. In M.M. Falik & K.S. Collins (Eds.), *Women's health: The Commonwealth Fund survey* (pp. 123–144). Baltimore, MD: Johns Hopkins University Press.

Ramist, L., & Arbeiter, S. (1986). *Profiles, college-bound seniors, 1985.* New York: College Entrance Examination Board.

Randall, M., & Haskell, L. (1995). Sexual violence in women's lives: Findings from the Women's Safety Project, a community-based survey. *Violence Against Women, 1*, 6–31.

Randle, N. (1992, July 5). Their time at bat. *Chicago Tribune Magazine*, pp. 11–15.

Rankin, E.D. (1993). Stresses and rewards experienced by employed mothers. *Health Care for Women International, 14*, 527–537.

Rankin, L.E., & Eagly, A.H. (2008). Is his heroism hailed and hers hidden? Women, men, and the social construction of heroism. *Psychology of Women Quarterly, 32*, 414–422.

Rathore, S.S. et al. (2000). The effects of patient sex and race on medical students' ratings of quality of life. *American Journal of Medicine, 108*, 561–566.

Raver, J.L., & Kishii, L.H. (2010). Once, twice, or three times as harmful? Ethnic harassment, gender harassment, and generalized workplace harassment. *Journal of Applied Psychology, 95,* 236–254.

Reading, A.E. (1994). Pain. In V.J. Adesso, D.M. Reddy, & R. Fleming (Eds.), *Psychological perspectives on women's health* (pp. 223–246). Washington, DC: Taylor & Francis.

Reardon, P., & Prescott, S. (1977). Sex as reported in a recent sample of psychological research. *Psychology of Women Quarterly, 2,* 157–161.

Rebecca, M. et al. (1976). A model of sex-role transcendence. *Journal of Social Issues, 32*(3), 197–206.

Rebensdorf, A. (2001, June 12). Sarafem: The pimping of Prozac for PMS. AlterNet. http://www.alternet.org/story/11004 (Retrieved November 2005).

Rederstorff, J.C. et al. (2007). The moderating roles of race and gender-role attitudes in the relationship between sexual harassment and psychological well-being. *Psychology of Women Quarterly, 31,* 50–61.

Reeves, M.J. et al. (2008). Sex differences in stroke: Epidemiology, clinical presentation, medical care, and outcomes. *The Lancet Neurology, 7,* 915–926.

Reevy, G.M., & Maslach, C. (2001). Use of social support: Gender and personality differences. *Sex Roles, 44,* 437–459.

Reid, A. (2004). Gender and sources of subjective well-being. *Sex Roles, 51,* 617–629.

Reid, P., & Finchilescu, G. (1995). The disempowering effects of media violence against women on college women. *Psychology of Women Quarterly, 19,* 397–411.

Reid, P.T. et al. (1995). Socialization of girls: Issues of ethnicity in gender development. In H. Landrine (Ed.), *Bringing cultural diversity to feminist psychology: Theory, research, and practice* (pp. 93–111). Washington, DC: American Psychological Association.

Reid, P.T. et al. (2008). Girls to women: Developmenal theory, research, and issues. In F.L. Denmark & M.A. Paludi (Eds.), *Psychology of women: A handbook of issues and theories* (2nd ed.) (pp. 237–270). Westport, CT: Praefer.

Reid, P.T., & Bing, V.M. (2000). Sexual roles of girls and women: An ethnocultural lifespan perspective. In C.B. Travis & J.W. White (Eds.), *Sexuality, society, and feminism* (pp. 141–166). Washington, DC: American Psychological Association.

Reis, H.T. (1998). Gender differences in intimacy and related behaviors: Context and process. In D.J. Canary & K. Dindia (Eds.), *Sex differences and similarities: Critical essays and empirical investigations of sex and gender in interaction* (pp. 203–231). Mahwah, NJ: Erlbaum.

Reis, H.T. et al. (1985). Sex differences in the intimacy of social interaction: Further examination of potential explanations. *Journal of Personality and Social Psychology, 48,* 1204–1217.

Reitz, R.R. (1999). Batterers' experiences of being violent: A phenomenological study. *Psychology of Women Quarterly, 23,* 143–165.

Reitzes, D.C., & Multran, E.J. (1994). Multiple roles and identities: Factors influencing self-esteem among middle-aged working men and women. *Social Psychology Quarterly, 57,* 313–325.

Remen, A.L. et al. (2002). Gender differences in the construct validity of the Silencing the Self Scale. *Psychology of Women Quarterly, 26,* 151–159.

Remennick, L.I. (1999). Women of the "sandwich" generation and multiple roles: The case of Russian immigrants of the 1990s in Israel. *Sex Roles, 40,* 347–378.

Renk, K. et al. (2003). Mothers, fathers, gender role, and time parents spend with their children. *Sex Roles, 48,* 305–315.

Renzetti, C.M. (1997). Violence in lesbian and gay relationships. In L. O'Toole & J.R. Schiffman (Eds.), *Gender violence: Interdisciplinary perspectives* (pp. 285–293). New York: New York University Press.

Resick, P.A., & Markaway, B.K. (1991). Clinical treatment of adult female victims of sexual assault. In C.R. Hollin & K. Howells (Eds.), *Clinical approaches to sex offenders and their victims* (pp. 261–284). New York: Wiley.

Reskin, B.F. (1988). Bringing the men back in: Sex differentiation and the devaluation of women's work. *Gender & Society, 2,* 58–81.

Reskin, B.F. et al. (1999). The determinants and consequences of workplace sex and race composition. *Annual Review of Sociology, 25,* 335–361.

Reskin, B.F., & Roos, P.A. (1990). *Job queues, gender queues: Explaining women's inroads into male occupations.* Philadelphia, PA: Temple.

Rhodes, F. et al. (1990). Risk behaviors and perceptions of AIDS among street injection drug users. *Journal of Drug Education, 20,* 271–288.

Rhodes, R., & Johnson, A. (1997). A feminist approach to treating alcohol and drug-addicted African-American women. *Women & Therapy, 20,* 23–37.

Ricciardelli, L.A. et al. (2004). Sociocultural influences on body image concerns and body change strategies among indigenous and non-indigenous Australian adolescent girls and boys. *Sex Roles, 51,* 731–741.

Richardson, D.S., & Hammock, G.S. (2007). Social context of human aggression: Are we playing too much attention to gender? *Aggression and Violent Behavior, 12,* 417–426.

Richman, E.L., & Shaffer, D.R. (2000). "If you let me play sports": How might sport participation influence the self-esteem of adolescent females? *Psychology of Women Quarterly, 24,* 189–199.

Rickabaugh, C.A. (1995). College students' stereotypes of gender and political activism. *Basic and Applied Social Psychology, 16,* 319–331.

Rickard, K.M. (1989). The relationship of self-monitored dating behaviors to level of feminist identity on the feminist identity scale. *Sex Roles, 20,* 213–226.

Rickard, K.M. (1990). The effect of feminist identity level on gender prejudice toward artists' illustrations. *Journal of Research in Personality, 24,* 145–162.

Ridgeway, C.L. (1991). The social construction of status value: Gender and other nominal characteristics. *Social Forces, 70,* 367–386.

Ridgeway, C.L., & Smith-Lovin, L. (1999). The gender system and interaction. *Annual Review of Sociology, 25,* 191–216.

Ridgeway, C.L., & Correll, J. (2004). Motherhood as a status characteristic. *Journal of Social Issues, 60*(4), 683–700.

Riger, S. (2000a). *Transforming psychology: Gender in theory and practice.* New York: Oxford University Press.

Riger, S. (2000b). From snapshots to videotape: New directions in research on gender differences. In S. Riger, *Transforming psychology: Gender in theory and practice* (pp. 39–51). New York: Oxford.

Riger, S. (2000c). What's wrong with empowerment. In S. Riger, *Transforming psychology: Gender in theory and practice* (pp. 97–106). New York: Oxford.

Riger, S., & Gordon, M.T. (1981). The fear of rape: A study in social control. *Journal of Social Issues, 37*(4), 71–92.

Riggs, J.M. (1997). Mandates for mothers and fathers: Perceptions of breadwinners and caregivers. *Sex Roles, 37,* 565–580.

Riggs, J.M. (2005). Impressions of mothers and fathers on the periphery of child care. *Psychology of Women Quarterly, 29,* 58–62.

Rind, B. et al. (1998). A meta-analytic examination of assumed properties of child sexual abuse using college samples. *Psychological Bulletin, 124,* 22–53.

Rindfuss, R.R. et al. (1987). Disorder in the life course: How common and does it matter? *American Sociological Review, 52,* 785–801.

Risman, B.J. (1987). Intimate relationships from a microstructural perspective: Men who mother. *Gender & Society, 1,* 6–32.

Ritter, B.A., & Yoder, J.D. (2004). Gender differences in leader emergence persist even for dominant women: An updated confirmation of role congruity theory. *Psychology of Women Quarterly, 28,* 187–193.

Rix, S.E. (Ed.). (1988). *The American woman 1988–89.* New York: Norton.

Roberts, T. (2004). Female trouble: The Menstrual Self-Evaluation Scale and women's self-objectification. *Psychology of Women Quarterly, 28,* 22–26.

Roberts, T. et al. (2002). "Feminine protection": The effects of menstruation on attitudes towards women. *Psychology of Women Quarterly, 26,* 131–139.

Roberts, T., & Gettman, J.Y. (2004). Mere exposure: Gender differences in the negative effects of priming a state of self-objectification. *Sex Roles, 51,* 17–27.

Robertson, J., & Fitzgerald, L.F. (1990). The (mis) treatment of men: Effects of client gender role and life-style on diagnosis and attribution of pathology. *Journal of Counseling Psychology, 37,* 3–9.

Robins, R.W. et al. (2000). Two personalities, one relationship: Both partners' personality traits shape the quality of their relationship. *Journal of Personality and Social Psychology, 79,* 251–259.

Robinson, C.H., & Betz, N.E. (2008). A psychometric evaluation of Super's Work Values Inventory—Revised. *Journal of Career Assessment, 16,* 456–473.

Robinson, D.T. et al. (2004). Sorority and fraternity membership and religious behaviors: Relation to gender attitudes. *Sex Roles, 50,* 871–877.

Robinson, J.P. (1988). Who's doing the housework? *American Demographics, 10,* 24–28, 63.

Robnett, R.D., & Susskind, J.E. (2010). Who cares about being gentle? The impact of social identity and the gender of one's friends on children's display of same-gender favoritism. *Sex Roles, 63,* 820–832.

Rodgers, R.F. et al. (2009). Gender differences in parental influences on adolescent body dissatisfaction and disordered eating. *Sex Roles, 61,* 837–849.

Rodin, J., & Ickovics, J.R. (1990). Women's health: Review and research agenda as we approach the 21st century. *American Psychologist, 45,* 1018–1034.

Roesler, T.A., & McKenzie, N. (1994). Effects of childhood trauma on psychological functioning in adults sexually abused as children. *Journal of Nervous and Mental Disease, 182*, 145–150.

Roiphe, K. (1993). *The morning after: Sex, fear, and feminism on campus.* Boston, MA: Little, Brown.

Roman, L.G. (1993). White is a color! White defensiveness, postmodernism, and anti-racist pedagogy. In C. McCarthy & W. Crichlow (Eds.), *Race identity and representation in education* (pp. 71–88). New York: Routledge.

Roos, P.A., & Reskin, B.F. (1992). Occupational desegregation in the 1970s: Integration and economic equity? *Sociological Perspectives, 35*, 69–91.

Root, M.P.P. (1990). Disordered eating in women of color. *Sex Roles, 22*, 525–536.

Root, M.P.P. (1991). Persistent, disordered eating as a gender-specific, post-traumatic stress response to sexual assault. *Psychotherapy, 28*, 96–102.

Root, M.P.P. (1992). Reconstructing the impact of trauma on personality. In L.S. Brown & M. Ballou (Eds.), *Personality and psychopathology: Feminist reappraisals* (pp. 229–265). New York: Guilford.

Root, M.P.P. (1996). *The multiracial experience: Racial borders as the new frontier.* Thousand Oaks, CA: Sage.

Rose, S. (1995). Women's friendships. In J.C. Chrisler & A.H. Hemstreet (Eds.), *Variations on a theme: Diversity and the psychology of women* (pp. 79–105). Albany, NY: SUNY Press.

Rose, S. (1996). Who to let in: Women's cross-race friendships. In J.C. Chrisler, C. Golden, & P.D. Rozee (Eds.), *Lectures on the psychology of women* (pp. 211–226). New York: McGraw-Hill.

Rose, S. (2000). Heterosexism and the study of women's romantic and friend relationships. *Journal of Social Issues, 56*(2), 315–328.

Rosen, K.H., & Bezold, A. (1996). Dating violence prevention: A didactic support group for young women. *Journal of Counseling Development, 74*, 521–525.

Rosen, L.N., & Martin, L. (1998). Predictors of tolerance of sexual harassment among male U.S. Army soldiers. *Violence Against Women, 4*, 491–504.

Rosenberg, M.J., & Rosenthal, S.M. (1987). Reproductive mortality in the United States: Recent trends and methodologic considerations. *American Journal of Public Health, 77*, 833–836.

Rosenbluth, S.C., & Steil, J.M. (1995). Predictors of intimacy for women in heterosexual and homosexual couples. *Journal of Social and Personal Relationships, 12*, 163–175.

Rosenfield, S. (1997). Labeling mental illness: The effects of received services and perceived stigma on life satisfaction. *American Sociological Review, 62*, 660–672.

Rosenthal, R. (1991). Meta-analysis: A review. *Psychosomatic Medicine, 53*, 247–271.

Rosette, A.S., & Tost, L.P. (2010). Agentic women and communal leadership: How role prescriptions confer advantage to top women leaders. *Journal of Applied Psychology, 95*, 221–235.

Rosewater, L.B. (1988). Feminist therapies with women. In M.A. Dutton-Douglas & L.E.A. Walker (Eds.), *Feminist psychotherapies: Integration of therapeutic and feminist systems* (pp. 137–155). Norwood, NJ: Ablex.

Rosewater, L.B. (1990). Diversifying feminist theory and practice: Broadening the concept of victimization. In L.S. Brown & M.P.P. Root (Eds.), *Diversity and complexity in feminist therapy* (pp. 299–311). New York: Harrington Park Press.

Rosnow, R.L., & Rosenthal, R. (1989). Statistical procedures and the justification of knowledge in psychological science. *American Psychologist, 44*, 1276–1284.

Rospenda, K.M. et al. (2009). Prevalence and mental health correlates of harassment and discrimination in the workplace: Results from a national study. *Journal of Interpersonal Violence, 24*, 819–843.

Ross, L. (1977). The intuitive psychologist and his shortcomings: Distortions in the attribution process. In L. Berkowitz (Ed.), *Advances in experimental social psychology*, Vol. 10 (pp. 174–221). New York: Academic Press.

Ross, L., & Nisbett, R.E. (2011). *The person and the situation: Perspectives of social psychology.* New York: McGraw-Hill.

Rostosky, S.S., & Travis, C.B. (1996). Menopausal research and the dominance of the biomedical model 1984–1994. *Psychology of Women Quarterly, 20*, 285–312.

Rostosky, S.S., & Travis, C.B. (2000). Menopause and sexuality: Ageism and sexism unite. In C.B. Travis & J.W. White (Eds.), *Sexuality, society, and feminism* (pp. 181–209). Washington, DC: American Psychological Association.

Rothblum, E.D. (1990). Depression among lesbians: An invisible and unresearched phenomenon. *Journal of Gay and Lesbian Psychotherapy, 1*, 67–87.

Rothblum, E.D. (1994). Transforming lesbian sexuality. *Psychology of Women Quarterly, 18*, 627–641.

Rothman, E.F. et al. (2011). The prevalence of sexual assault against people who identify as gay, lesbian, or bisexual in the United States: A systematic review. *Trauma, Violence, & Abuse, 12*, 55–66.

Rotundo, M. et al. (2001). A meta-analytic review of gender differences in perceptions of sexual harassment. *Journal of Applied Psychology, 86,* 914–922.

Rouner, D. et al. (2003). Adolescent evaluation of gender role and sexual imagery in television advertisements. *Journal of Broadcasting & Electronic Media, 47,* 435–454.

Roy, R.E. et al. (2007). Effects of stereotypes about feminists on feminist self-identification. *Psychology of Women Quarterly, 31, 146–156.*

Rozee, P.D. (1996). Freedom from fear of rape: The missing link in women's freedom. In J.C. Chrisler, C. Golden, & P.D. Rozee (Eds.)., *Lectures on the psychology of women* (pp. 309–322). New York: McGraw-Hill.

Rozin, P. et al. (2003). Food and life, pleasure and worry, among American college students: Gender differences and regional similarities. *Journal of Personality and Social Psychology, 85,* 132–141.

Rubenzahl, S.A., & Corcoran, K.J. (1998). The prevalence and characteristics of male perpetrators of acquaintance rape: New research methodology reveals new findings. *Violence Against Women, 4,* 713–725.

Rubin, L.J. et al. (1997). Sexual harassment of students by professional psychology educators: A national survey. *Sex Roles, 37,* 753–771.

Rubin, L.R. et al. (2004). Exploring feminist women's body consciousness. *Psychology of Women Quarterly, 28,* 27–37.

Rubin, L.R., & Tannenbaum, M. (2011). "Does that make me a woman?": Breast cancer, mastectomy, and breast reconstruction decisions among sexual minority women. *Psychology of Women Quarterly, 35,* 401–414.

Rubinstein, S., & Caballero, B. (2000). Is Miss America an undernourished role model? *Journal of the American Medical Association, 283,* 1569.

Ruble, D.N. et al. (2006). Gender development. In N. Eisenberg et al. (Eds.), *Handbook of child psychology: Vol. 3. Social, emotional, and personality development* (6th ed., pp. 858–932). New York: Wiley.

Rudd, N.A., & Lennon, S.J. (1999). Social power and appearance management among women. In K.P. Johnson & S.J. Lennon (Eds.), *Appearance and power* (pp. 153–172). New York: Berg.

Rudman, L.A. (1998). Self-promotion as a risk factor for women: The costs and benefits of counterstereotypical impression management. *Journal of Personality and Social Psychology, 74,* 629–645.

Rudman, L.A., & Borgida, E. (1995). The afterglow of construct accessibility: The behavioral consequences of priming men to view women as sexual objects. *Journal of Experimental Social Psychology, 31,* 493–517.

Rudman, L.A., & Fairchild, K. (2007). The F word: Is feminism incompatible with beauty and romance? *Psychology of Women Quarterly, 31,* 125–136.

Rudman, L.A., & Glick, P. (2008). *The social psychology of gender: How power and intimacy share gender relations.* New York: Guilford.

Rudman, L.A., & Heppen, J.B. (2003). Implicit romantic fantasies and women's interest in personal power: A glass slipper effect? *Personality and Social Psychology Bulletin, 29,* 1357–1370.

Rudman, L.A., & Phelan, J.E. (2007). The interpersonal power of feminism: Is feminism good for romantic relationships? *Sex Roles, 57,* 787–799.

Rudolfsdottir, A.G., & Jolliffe, R. (2008). "I don't think people really talk about it that much": Young women discuss feminism. *Feminism & Psychology, 18,* 268–274.

Russell, B.L., & Trigg, K.Y. (2004). Tolerance of sexual harassment: An examination of gender differences, ambivalent sexism, social dominance, and gender roles. *Sex Roles, 50,* 565–573.

Russell, G.M., & Bohan, J.S. (1999). Hearing voices: The uses of research and the politics of change. *Psychology of Women Quarterly, 23,* 403–418.

Russell, P.L., & Davis, C. (2007). Twenty-five years of empirical research on treatment following sexual assault. *Best Practices in Mental Health: An International Journal, 3,* 21–37.

Russo, N.F., & Denious, J.E. (1998). Why is abortion such a controversial issue in the United States? In L.J. Beckman & S.M. Havey (Eds.), *The new civil war: The psychology, culture, and politics of abortion* (pp. 25–59). Washington, DC: American Psychological Association.

Russo, N.F., & Denmark, F.L. (1987). Contributions of women to psychology. *Annual Review of Psychology, 38,* 279–298.

Russo, N.F., & Pirlott, A. (2006). Gender-based violence: Concepts, methods, and findings. In F.L. Denmark et al. (Eds.), Violence and exploitation against women and girls (pp. 178–205). Boston, MA: Blackwell.

Russo, N.F., & Vaz, K. (2001). Overview: Roles, fertility and the motherhood mandate. *Psychology of Women Quarterly, 25,* 7–15.

Rust, J. et al. (2000). The role of brothers and sisters in the gender development of preschool children. *Journal of Experimental Child Psychology, 77,* 292–303.

Rust, P.C. (1993). "Coming out" in the age of social constructionism: Sexual identity formation among lesbian and bisexual women. *Gender & Society, 7*, 50–77.

Rust, P.C.R. (2000). Bisexuality: A contemporary paradox for women. *Journal of Social Issues, 56*(2), 205–221.

Rutherford, A. et al. (2010). Responsible opposition, disruptive voices: Science, social change, and the history of feminist psychology, *Psychology of Women Quarterly, 34*, 460–473.

Rutte, C.G. et al. (1994). Organization of information and the detection of gender discrimination. *Psychological Science, 5*, 226–231.

Ruuskanen, J.M., & Ruoppila, I. (1994). Physical activity and psychological well-being among people aged 65–84 years. *Journal of Gerontology, 49*, 292–296.

Ryan, B. (1992). *Feminism and the women's movement: Dynamics of change in social movement, ideology and activism.* New York: Routledge.

Ryan, K.M., & Kanjorski, J. (1998). The enjoyment of sexist humor, rape attitudes, and relationship aggression in college students. *Sex Roles, 38*, 743–756.

Ryan, M.K. et al. (2004). Who cares? The effect of gender and context on the self and moral reasoning. *Psychology of Women Quarterly, 28*, 246–255.

Ryan, M.K. et al. (2010). Politics and the glass cliff: Evidence that women are preferentially selected to contest hard-to-win seats. *Psychology of Women Quarterly, 34*, 56–64.

Ryan, W. (1972). *Blaming the victim.* New York: Vintage.

Ryff, C. D. (1989). Happiness is everything, or is it? Explorations on the meaning of psychological well-being. *Journal of Personality and Social Psychology, 57*, 1069–1081.

Sabik, N.J. et al., (2010). Are all minority women equally buffered from negative body image: Intra-ethnic moderators of the buffering hypothesis. *Psychology of Women Quarterly, 34*, 139–151.

Sabik, N.J., & Tylka, T.L. (2006). Do feminist identity styles moderate the relation between perceived sexist events and disordered eating? *Psychology of Women Quarterly, 30*, 77–84.

Sadker, M., & Sadker, D. (1994). *Failing at fairness: How America's schools cheat girls.* New York: Macmillan.

Safir, M.P. et al. (2005). When gender differences surpass cultural differences in personal satisfaction with body shape in Israeli college students. *Sex Roles, 52*, 369–378.

Saguy, T. et al. (2010). Interacting like a body: Objectification can lead women to narrow their presence in social interactions. *Psychological Science, 2*, 178–182.

Salk, R.H., & Engeln-Maddox, R. (2011). "If you're fat, then I'm humongous!": Frequency, content, and impact of fat talk among college women. *Psychology of Women Quarterly, 35*, 18–28.

Saltzberg, E.A., & Chrisler, J.C. (1995). Beauty is the beast: Psychological effects of the pursuit of the perfect female body. In J. Freeman (Ed.), *Women: A feminist perspective* (5th ed., pp. 306–315). Mountain View, CA: Mayfield.

Salvaggio, A.N. et al. (2009). Ambivalent sexism and applicant evaluations: Effects on ambiguous applicants. *Sex Roles, 61*, 621–633.

Salvatore, J., & Marecek, J. (2010). Gender in the gym: Evaluation concerns as barriers to women's weight lifting. *Sex Roles, 63*, 556–567.

Samuel, D.B., & Widiger, T.A. (2009). Comparative gender biases in models of personality disorder. *Personality and Mental Health, 3*, 12–25.

Sanchez, D.T. et al. (2006). Sexual submissiveness in women: Costs for sexual autonomy and arousal. *Personality and Social Psychology Bulletin, 32*, 512–524.

Sanchez, D.T., & Broccoli, T.L. (2008). The romance of self-objectification: Does priming romantic relationships induce states of self-objectification among women. *Sex Roles, 59*, 545–554.

Sanchez, D.T., & Crocker, J. (2005). How investment in gender ideals affects well-being: The role of external contingencies of self-worth. *Psychology of Women Quarterly, 29*, 63–77.

Sanchez, D.T., & Kwang, T. (2007). When the relationship becomes her: Revisiting women's body concerns from a relationship contingency perspective. *Psychology of Women Quarterly, 31*, 401–414.

Sanchez, L., & Thomson, E. (1997). Becoming mothers and fathers: Parenthood, gender, and the division of labor. *Gender & Society, 11*, 747–772.

Sanday, P.R. (1981a). *Female power and male dominance: On the origins of sexual inequality.* New York: Cambridge.

Sanday, P.R. (1981b). The socio-cultural context of rape: A cross-cultural study. *Journal of Social Issues, 37*(4), 5–27.

Sandnabba, N.K., & Ahlberg, C. (1999). Parents' attitudes and expectations about children's cross-gender behavior. *Sex Roles, 40*, 249–263.

Sandoz, C.J. (1995). Gender issues in recovery from alcoholism. *Alcoholism Treatment Quarterly, 12*, 61–69.

Sang, B.E. (1993). Existential issues of midlife lesbians. In L.D. Garnets & D.C. Kimmel (Eds.), *Psychological perspectives on lesbian and gay male experiences* (pp. 500–516). New York: Columbia University Press.

Santor, D.A. et al. (1994). Nonparametric item analyses of the Beck Depression Inventory: Evaluating gender item bias and response option weights. *Psychological Assessment, 6*, 255–270.

Saraga, E., & MacLeod, M. (1997). False memory syndrome: Theory of defence against reality? *Feminism & Psychology, 7*, 46–51.

Sargent, P. (2005). The gendering of men in early childhood education. *Sex Roles, 52*, 251–259.

Sassler, S. (2000). Learning to be an "American lady"? Ethnic variation in daughters' pursuits in the early 1900s. *Gender & Society, 14*, 184–209.

Sassler, S. (2010). Partnering across the life course: Sex, relationships, and mate selection. *Journal of Marriage and the Family, 72*, 557–575.

Sattel, J.W. (1976). Men, inexpressiveness, and power. In L. Richardson & V. Taylor (Eds.), *Feminist frontiers: Rethinking sex, gender, and society* (pp. 242–246). New York: Random House.

Saunders, K.A., & Senn, C.Y. (2009). Should I confront him? Men's reactions to hypothetical confrontations of peer sexual harassment. *Sex Roles, 61*, 399–415.

Saunders, K.J., & Kashubeck-West, S. (2006). The relationships among feminist identity development, gender-role orientation, and psychological well-being in women. *Psychology of Women Quarterly, 30*, 199–211.

Sayer, L.C., & Fine, L. (2011). Racial-ethnic differences in U.S. married women's and men's housework. *Social Indicators Research, 10*, 259–265.

Sayers, J. (1982). *Biological politics: Feminist and anti-feminist perspectives.* New York: Tavistock.

Scali, R.M. et al. (2000). Gender differences in spatial task performance as a function of speed or accuracy orientation. *Sex Roles, 43*, 359–376.

Scarr, S., & Eisenberg, M. (1993). Child care research: Issues, perspectives, and results. *Annual Review of Psychology, 44*, 613–644.

Schafran, L.H. (1995, August 26). Rape is still underreported. *The New York Times*, p. 15.

Schaie, K.W. (1988). Ageism in psychological research. *American Psychologist, 43*, 179–183.

Schewe, P., & O'Donohue, W. (1993). Rape prevention: Methodological problems and new directions. *Clinical Psychology Review, 13*, 667–682.

Schick, V.R. et al. (2008). Safer, better sex through feminism: The role of feminist ideology in women's sexual well-being. *Psychology of Women Quarterly, 32*, 225–232.

Schick, V.R. et al. (2010). Genital appearance dissatisfaction: Implications for women's genital image self-consciousness, sexual esteem, sexual satisfaction, and sexual risk. *Psychology of Women Quarterly, 34*, 394–404.

Schiebinger, L.L. (1992). The gendered brain: Some historical perspectives. In A. Harrington (Ed.), *So human a brain: Knowledge and values in the neurosciences* (pp. 110–120). Boston, MA: Birkhauser.

Schmader, T. et al. (2004). The costs of accepting gender differences: The role of stereotype endorsement in women's experience in the math domain. *Sex Roles, 50*, 835–850.

Schmitt, D.P. et al. (2008). Why can't a man be more like a woman? Sex differences in Big Five personality traits across 55 cultures. *Journal of Personality and Social Psychology, 94*, 168–182.

Schmitz, S. (1999). Gender differences in acquisition of environmental knowledge related to wayfinding behavior, spatial anxiety and self-estimated environmental competencies. *Sex Roles, 41*, 71–93.

Schneer, J.A., & Reitman, F. (1993). Effects of alternate family structures on managerial career paths. *Academy of Management Journal, 36*, 830–843.

Schneider, B.E., & Gould, M. (1987). Female sexuality: Looking back into the future. In B.B. Hess & M.M. Ferree (Eds.), *Analyzing gender: A handbook of social science research* (pp. 120–153). Thousand Oaks, CA: Sage.

Schneider, D.J. (2004). *The psychology of stereotyping.* New York: Guilford.

Schneidewind-Skibbe, A. et al. (2008). The frequency of sexual intercourse reported by women: A review of community-based studies and factors limiting their conclusions. *Journal of Sexual Medicine, 5*, 301–335.

Schooler, D. et al. (2004). Who's that girl: Television's role in the body image development of young White and Black women. *Psychology of Women Quarterly, 28*, 38–47.

Schuller, R.A., & Hastings, P.A. (2002). Complainant sexual history evidence: Its impact on mock juror's decisions. *Psychology of Women Quarterly, 26*, 252–261.

Schwartz, F.N. (1989, Jan.-Feb.). Management women and the new facts of life. *Harvard Business Review, 89*, 65–75.

Schwartz, M.D., & Leggett, M.S. (1999). Bad dates or emotional trauma? The aftermath of campus sexual assault. *Violence Against Women, 5*, 251–271.

Scott, K. (2004). African American-White girls' friendships. *Feminism & Psychology, 14*, 383–388.

Scott, S.E. (1997). Feminists and false memories: A case of postmodern amnesia. *Feminism & Psychology, 7,* 33–38.

Scott-Sheldon, L.A. et al. (2010). Sexual risk reduction interventions for patients attending sexually transmitted disease clinics in the United States: A meta-analytic review. *Annals of Behavioral Medicine, 40,* 191–204.

Scully, D., & Bart, P. (2003). A funny thing happened on the way to the orifice: Women in gynecology textbooks. Reprinted in *Feminism & Psychology, 13*(1), 11–16.

Sczesny, S. et al. (2004). Gender stereotypes and the attribution of leadership traits: A cross-cultural comparison. *Sex Roles, 51,* 631–645.

Seal, D.W. et al. (2008). Urban heterosexual couple's sexual scripts for three shared sexual experiences. *Sex Roles, 58,* 626–638.

Sechrist, G.B., & Delmar, C. (2009). When do men and women make attributions to gender discriminations? The role of discrimination source. *Sex Roles, 61,* 607–620.

Seedat, S. et al. (2009). Cross-national associations between gender and mental disorders in the World Health Organization World Mental Health Surveys. *Archives of General Psychiatry, 66,* 785–795.

Seem, S.R., & Clark, M.D. (2006). Healthy women, healthy men, and healthy adults: An evaluation of gender role stereotypes in the 21st century. *Sex Roles, 55,* 247–258.

Segura, D.A., & Pierce, J.L. (1993). Chicana/o family structure and gender personality: Chodorow, familism, and psychoanalytic sociology revisited. *Signs, 19,* 62–91.

Sekaquaptewa, D., & Thompson, M. (2003). Solo status, stereotype threat, and performance expectancies: Their effects on women's performance. *Journal of Experimental Social Psychology, 39,* 68–74.

Sellers, J.G. et al. (2007). Is silence more golden for women than men? Observers derogate effusive women and their quiet partners. *Sex Roles, 57,* 477–482.

Senn, C.Y. et al. (2011). Emancipatory sexuality education and sexual assault resistance: Does the former enhance the latter? *Psychology of Women Quarterly, 35,* 72–91.

Serbin, L.A. et al. (1993). The development of sex typing in middle childhood. *Monographs for the Society for Research in Child Development, 58*(2, Serial No. 232).

Serewicz, M.C.M., & Gale, E. (2008). First-date scripts: gender roles, context, and relationship. *Sex Roles, 58,* 149–164.

Settles, I.H. et al. (2006). The climate for women in academic science: The good, the bad, and the changeable. *Psychology of Women Quarterly, 30,* 47–58.

Settles, I.H. et al. (2008). Through the lens of race: Black and White women's perceptions of womanhood. *Psychology of Women Quarterly, 32,* 454–468.

Severy, L.J. et al. (1993). Menstrual experiences and beliefs: A multicountry study of relationships with fertility and fertility-regulating methods. *Women & Health, 20,* 1–20.

Shackelford, T.K. et al. (2005). Universal dimensions of human mate preferences. *Personality and Invidiual Differences, 39,* 447–458.

Shanok, A.F., & Miller, L. (2007). Stepping up to motherhood among inner-city teens. *Psychology of Women Quarterly, 31,* 252–261.

Shapiro, B.A. (1995). The dismissal of female clients' reports of medication side effects: A first hand account. *Women & Therapy, 16*(1), 113–127.

Shapiro, J., & Kroeger, L. (1991). Is life just a romantic novel? The relationship between attitudes about intimate relationships and the popular media. *American Journal of Family Therapy, 19,* 226–236.

Sharps, M.J. et al. (1994). Spatial cognitions and gender: Instructional and stimulus influences on mental image rotation performance. *Psychology of Women Quarterly, 18,* 413–426.

Shaw, S.N. (2002). Shifting conversations on girls' and women's self-injury: An analysis of the clinical literature in historical context. *Feminism & Psychology, 12,* 191–219.

Shea, G.F. (1994). *Mentoring: Helping employees reach their full potential.* New York: American Management Association.

Sheets, V.L., & Lugar, R. (2005). Friendship and gender in Russia and the United States. *Sex Roles, 52,* 131–140.

Sheffer, C.E. et al. (2002). Sex differences in the presentation of chronic low back pain. *Psychology of Women Quarterly, 28,* 329–340.

Sheffield, C.J. (1989). Sexual terrorism. In J. Freeman (Ed.), *Women: A feminist perspective* (4th ed.) (pp. 3–19). Mountain View, CA: Mayfield.

Sheldon, J.P. (2004). Gender stereotypes in educational software for young children. *Sex Roles, 51,* 433–444.

Shelton, J.N., & Chavous, T.M. (1999). Black and White college women's perceptions of sexual harassment. *Sex Roles, 40,* 593–615.

Shelton, J.N., & Stewart, R.E. (2004). Confronting perpetrators of prejudice: The inhibitory effects of social costs. *Psychology of Women Quarterly, 28,* 215–223.

Shepherd, M. et al. (2011). I'll get that for you: The relationship between benevolent sexism and body self-perceptions. *Sex Roles, 64,* 1–8.

Sherif, C.W. (1979). Bias in psychology. In J.A. Sherman & E.T. Beck (Eds.), *The prism of sex* (pp. 93–133). Madison, WI: University of Wisconsin Press.

Sherif, C.W. (1982). Needed concepts in the study of gender identity. *Psychology of Women Quarterly, 6,* 375–395.

Shih, M. et al. (1999). Stereotype susceptibility: Identity salience and shifts in quantitative performance. *Psychological Science, 10,* 80–83.

Shin, K.R. (1994). Psychosocial predictors of depressive symptoms in Korean-American women in New York City. *Women & Health, 21,* 73–82.

Shinn, L.K., & O'Brien, M. (2008). Parent-child conversational styles in middle childhood: Gender and social class differences. *Sex Roles, 59,* 61–67.

Shore, G. (1999). Soldiering on: An exploration into women's perceptions and experiences of menopause. *Feminism & Psychology, 9,* 168–178.

Short, L.M. et al. (2000). Survivors' identification of protective factors and early warning signs for intimate partner violence. *Violence Against Women, 6,* 272–285.

Shouse, S.H., & Nilsson, J. (2011). Self-silencing, emotional awareness, and eating behaviors in college women. *Psychology of Women Quarterly, 35,* 451–457.

Shumaker, S.A., & Smith, T.R. (1995). Women and coronary heart disease: A psychological perspective. In A.L. Stanton & S.J. Gallant (Eds.), *The psychology of women's health: Progress and challenges in research and application* (pp. 25–49). Washington, DC: American Psychological Association.

Shye, D. et al. (1995). Gender differences in the relationship between social network support and mortality: A longitudinal study of an elderly cohort. *Social Science and Medicine, 41,* 935–947.

Sibley, C.G. et al. (2007a). Antecedents of men's hostile and benevolent sexism: The dual roles of social dominance orientation and right-wing authoritarianism. *Personality and Social Psychology Bulletin, 33,* 160–172.

Sibley, C.G. et al. (2007b). When women become more hostilely sexist toward their gender: The system-justifying effect of benevolent sexism. *Sex Roles, 56,* 743–754.

Sibley, C.G., & Perry, R. (2010). An opposing process model of benevolent sexism. *Sex Roles, 62,* 438–452.

Siebler, F. et al. (2008). A refined computer harassment paradigm: Validation and tests of hypotheses about target characteristics. *Psychology of Women Quarterly, 32,* 22–35.

Sigal, J. et al. (2003). Effects of type of coping response, setting, and social context on reactions to sexual harassment. *Sex Roles, 48,* 157–166.

Sigal, J. et al. (2005). Cross-cultural reactions to academic sexual harassment: Effects of individualistic vs. collectivist culture and gender of the participants. *Sex Roles, 52,* 201–215.

Sigmon, S.T. et al. (2000). Menstrual reactivity: The role of gender-specificity, anxiety sensitivity, and somatic concerns in self-reported menstrual distress. *Sex Roles, 43,* 143–161.

Sigmon, S.T. et al. (2007). Are we there yet? A review of gender comparisons in three behavioral journals through the 20th century. *Behavior Therapy, 38,* 333–339.

Signorielli, N., & Bacue, A. (1999). Recognition and respect: A content analysis of prime-time television characters across three decades. *Sex Roles, 40,* 527–544.

Silvan-Ferrero, M.P., & Lopez, A.B. (2007). Benevolent sexism toward men and women: Justification of the traditional system and conventional gender roles in Spain. *Sex Roles, 57,* 607–614.

Silverschanz, P. et al. (2008). Slurs, snubs, and queer jokes: Incidence and impact of heterosexual harassment in academia. *Sex Roles, 58,* 179–191.

Silverstein, L.B. (1991). Transforming the debate about child care and maternal employment. *American Psychologist, 46,* 1025–1032.

Silverstein, M., & Waite, L.J. (1993). Are Blacks more likely than Whites to receive and provide social support in middle and old age? Yes, no, and maybe so. *Journals of Gerontology, 48,* S212–S222.

Simoni, J.M. et al. (2000). Safer sex among HIV+ women: The role of relationships. *Sex Roles, 42,* 691–708.

Simonson, K., & Subich, L.M. (1999). Rape perceptions as a function of gender-role traditionality and victim perpetrator association. *Sex Roles, 40,* 617–634.

Sinacore, A.L. et al. (2002). A qualitative analysis of the experiences of feminist psychology educators: The classroom. *Feminism & Psychology, 12,* 339–362.

Sinclair, H.C., & Bourne, L.E. (1998). Cycle of blame or just world: Effects of legal verdicts on gender patterns in rape-myth acceptance and victim empathy. *Psychology of Women Quarterly, 22,* 575–588.

Singleton, R.A., & Vacca, J. (2007). Interpersonal competition in friendships. *Sex Roles, 56,* 617–627.

Skedsvold, P.R., & Mann, T.L. (Eds.). (1996). Linking research, policy and implementation in affirmative action programs. *Journal of Social Issues, 52*(4).

Sklover, B. (1997). Women and sports: The 25th anniversary of Title IX. *AAUW Outlook, 90,* 12–17.

Skomorovsky, A. et al. (2006). The buffering role of social support perceptions in relation to eating disturbances among women in abusive dating relationships. *Sex Roles, 54,* 627–638.

Skrypnek, B.J., & Snyder, M. (1982). On the self-perpetuating nature of stereotypes about women and men. *Journal of Experimental Social Psychology, 18,* 277–291.

Slater, A., & Tiggemann, M. (2002). A test of objectification theory in adolescent girls. *Sex Roles, 46,* 343–349.

Slater, A., & Tiggemann, M. (2010). Body image and disordered eating in adolescent girls and boys: A test of objectification theory. *Sex Roles, 63,* 42–49.

Slavkin, M., & Stright, A.D. (2000). Gender role differences in college students from one- and two-parent families. *Sex Roles, 42,* 23–37.

Slevec, J., & Tiggemann, M. (2010). Attitudes toward cosmetic surgery in middle-aged women: Body image, aging anxiety, and the media. *Psychology of Women Quarterly, 34,* 65–74.

Slevec, J.H., & Tiggemann, M. (2011). Media exposure, body dissatisfaction, and disordered eating in middle-aged women: A test of the sociocultural model of disordered eating. *Psychology of Women Quarterly, 35,* 617–627.

Small, D.A. et al. (2007). Who goes to the bargaining table? The influence of gender and framing on the initiation of negotiation. *Journal of Personality and Social Psychology, 93,* 600–613.

Smith, C.A. (1999). I enjoy being a girl: Collective self-esteem, feminism and attitudes toward women. *Sex Roles, 40,* 281–293.

Smith, D.R. et al. (2001). Favoritism, bias, and error in performance ratings of scientists and engineers: The effects of power, status, and numbers. *Sex Roles, 45,* 337–358.

Smith, G. et al. (2008). Sexual double standards and sexually transmitted illnesses: Social rejection and stigmatization of women. *Sex Roles, 58,* 391–401.

Smith, J.L., & White, P.H. (2002). An examination of implicitly activated, explicitly activated, and nullified stereotypes on mathematical performance: It's not just a woman's issue. *Sex Roles, 47,* 179–191.

Smith, K. (2002). *Who's minding the kids? Child care arrangements: Spring 1997.* Current Population Reports (pp. 70–86). U.S. Census Bureau Washington, DC: U.S. Government Printing Office.

Smith, M. (1997). Psychology's undervaluation of single motherhood. *Feminism & Psychology, 7,* 529–532.

Smith, P.H. et al. (1999). Beyond the measurement trap: A reconstructed conceptualization and measurement of woman battering. *Psychology of Women Quarterly, 23,* 177–193.

Smith, S.J. et al. (2009). The effects of contact on sexual prejudice: A meta-analysis. *Sex Roles, 61,* 178–191.

Smolak, L., & Munstertieger, B.F. (2002). The relationship of gender and voice to depression and eating disorders. *Psychology of Women Quarterly, 26,* 234–241.

Smucker, M.K. et al. (2003). An investigation of job satisfaction and female sports journalists. *Sex Roles, 49,* 401–407.

Snyder, R., & Hasbrouck, L. (1996). Feminist identity, gender traits, and symptoms of disturbed eating among college women. *Psychology of Women Quarterly, 20,* 593–598.

Sokol, J. et al. (2010). Marketing pharmaceutical drugs to women in magazines: A content analysis. *American Journal of Health Behavior, 34,* 402–411.

Sokoloff, N.J. (1988). Evaluating gains and losses by Black and White women and men in the professions, 1960–1980. *Social Problems, 35,* 36–53.

Sommer, I.E.C. et al. (2004). Do women really have more bilateral language representation than men? A meta-analysis of functional imaging studies. *Brain, 127,* 1845–1852.

Sommers-Flanagan, R. et al. (1993). What's happening on music television? A gender role content analysis. *Sex Roles, 28,* 745–753.

Sonnert, G., & Holton, G. (1996). Career patterns of women and men in the sciences. *American Scientist, 84,* 63–71.

Sorenson, S.B., & Siegel, J.M. (1992). Gender, ethnicity, and sexual assault: Findings from a Los Angeles study. *Journal of Social Issues, 48*(1), 93–104.

Sorenson, S.B., & White, J.W. (1992). Adult sexual assault: Overview of research. *Journal of Social Issues, 48*(1), 1–8.

Souchon, N. et al. (2009). Referees' decision making about transgressions: The influence of player gender at the highest national levels. *Psychology of Women Quarterly, 33,* 445–452.

Sparks, E.E. (1996). Overcoming stereotypes of mothers in the African American context. In K.F. Wyche & F.J. Crosby (Eds.), *Women's ethnicities: Journeys through psychology* (pp. 67–86). Boulder, CO: Westview.

Spence, J.T. (2011). Off with old, one with the new. *Psychology of Women Quarterly, 35*, 504–509.

Spence, J.T., & Buckner, C.E. (2000). Instrumental and expressive traits, trait stereotypes, and sexist attitudes. *Psychology of Women Quarterly, 24*, 44–62.

Spence, J.T., & Hahn, E.D. (1997). The Attitudes Toward Women Scale and attitude change in college students. *Psychology of Women Quarterly, 21*, 17–34.

Spence, J.T., & Helmreich, R.L. (1972). The Attitudes Toward Women Scale: An objective instrument to measure attitudes toward the rights and roles of women in contemporary society. *Catalog of Selected Documents in Psychology, 2*, 66. (Ms No. 153).

Spence, J.T., & Helmreich, R.L. (1978). *Masculinity and femininity: Their psychological dimensions, correlates, and antecedents.* Austin, TX: University of Texas Press.

Spence, J.T., Helmreich, R.L. (1980). Masculine instrumentality and feminine expressiveness: Their relationships with sex-role attitudes and behaviors. *Psychology of Women Quarterly, 5*, 147–163.

Spender, D. (1984). In R. Rowland (Ed.), *Women who do and women who don't join the women's movement.* London: Routledge & Kegan Paul.

Sperberg, E.D., & Stabb, S.D. (1998). Depression in women as related to anger and mutuality in relationships. *Psychology of Women Quarterly, 22*, 223–238.

Spitzer, B.L. et al. (1999). Gender differences in population versus media body sizes: A comparison over four decades. *Sex Roles, 40*, 545–565.

Sprecher, S. et al. (1998). Beliefs about the outcomes of extramarital sexual relationships as a function of the gender of the "cheating spouse." *Sex Roles, 38*, 301–311.

Sprecher, S. et al. (2007). Expectations for mood enhancement as a result of helping: The effects of gender and compassionate love. *Sex Roles, 56*, 543–549.

Sprecher, S., & Felmlee, D. (1997). The balance of power in romantic heterosexual couples over time from "his" and "her" perspectives. *Sex Roles, 37*, 361–379.

Srull, T. K., & Wyer, S. (1979). The role of category accessibility in the interpretation of information about persons: Some determinants and implications. *Journal of Personality and Social Psychology, 37*, 1660–1672.

Stahly, G.B., & Lie, G. (1995). Women and violence: A comparison of lesbian and heterosexual battering relationships. In J.C. Chrisler & A.H. Hemstreet (Eds.), *Variations on a theme: Diversity and the psychology of women* (pp. 51–78). Albany, NY: State University of New York Press.

Stake, J.E. (2007). Predictors of change in feminist activism through women's and gender studies. *Sex Roles, 57*, 43–54.

Stake, J.E. et al. (1994). The women's studies experience: Impetus for feminist activism. *Psychology of Women Quarterly, 18*, 17–24.

Stake, J.E., & Gerner, M.A. (1987). The women's studies experience: Personal and professional gains for women and men. *Psychology of Women Quarterly, 11*, 277–283.

Stake, J.E., & Hoffmann, F.L. (2000). Putting feminist pedagogy to the test: The experience of women's studies from student and teacher perspectives. *Psychology of Women Quarterly, 24*, 30–38.

Stake, J.E., & Rose, S. (1994). The long-term impact of women's studies on students' personal lives and political activism. *Psychology of Women Quarterly, 18*, 403–412.

Stankiewicz, J.M., & Rosselli, F. (2008). Women as sex objects and victims in print advertisements. *Sex Roles, 58*, 579–589.

Stanko, E. (1985). *Intimate intrusions.* London: Routledge & Kegan Paul.

Stanton, A.L. (1995). Psychology of women's health: Barriers and pathways to knowledge. In A.L. Stanton & S.J. Gallant (Eds.), *The psychology of women's health: Progress and challenges in research and application* (pp. 3–21). Washington, DC: American Psychological Association.

Stanton, A.L., & Danoff-Burg, S. (1995). Selected issues in women's reproductive health: Psychological perspectives. In A.L. Stanton & S.J. Gallant (Eds.), *The psychology of women's health: Progress and challenges in research and application* (pp. 261–305). Washington, DC: American Psychological Association.

Stark, E., & Flitcraft, A. (1996). *Women at risk: Domestic violence and women's health.* Thousand Oaks, CA: Sage.

Stark-Wroblewski, K. et al. (2005). Acculturation, internalization of Western appearance norms, and eating pathology among Japanese and Chinese international student women. *Psychology of Women Quarterly, 29*, 38–46.

Statistical Abstracts of the United States. (2011). U.S. Census Bureau. http://www.census.gov/compendia/statab/ (Retrieved October 2011).

Statistics Canada. (2005). *Canada e-book: The people: The labour force.* www.statcan.ca (Retrieved November 2005).

Statistics Canada (2011). http://www.statcan.ca

Stato, J. (1993). Montreal gynocide. In P.B. Bart & E.G. Moran (Eds.), *Violence against women: The bloody footprints* (pp. 132–133). Newbury Park, CA: Sage.

Staub, E. (1989). *The roots of evil: The origins of genocide and other group violence.* Cambridge: Cambridge University Press.

Steele, C.M. (1997). A threat in the air: How stereotypes shape intellectual identity and performance. *American Psychologist, 52*, 613–629.

Steele, J. et al. (2002). Learning in a man's world: Examining the perceptions of undergraduate women in male-dominated academic areas. *Psychology of Women Quarterly, 26*, 46–50.

Stein, M.D. et al. (2000). Delays in seeking HIV care due to competing caregiver responsibilities. *American Journal of Public Health, 90*, 1138–1140.

Steinberg, R. (1987). Radical challenges in a liberal world: The mixed success of comparable worth. *Gender & Society, 1*, 466–475.

Steinem, G. (1978, October). If men could menstruate--. *Ms, 7*, 110.

Steinem, G. (1983). Far from the opposite shore. In *Outrageous acts and everyday rebellions* (pp. 341–362). New York: Holt.

Stern, M., & Karraker, K.H. (1989). Sex stereotyping of infants: A review of gender labeling studies. *Sex Roles, 20*, 501–522.

Stevens, D.P. et al. (2006). Family work performance and satisfaction: Gender ideology, relative resources and emotion work. *Marriage and Family Review, 40*, 47–74.

Stewart, A.J., & Maddren, K. (1997). Police officers' judgments of blame in family violence: The impact of gender and alcohol. *Sex Roles, 37*, 921–933.

Stewart, A.J., & Newton, N.J. (2010). Gender, adult development, and aging. In J.C. Chrisler & D.R. McCreary (Eds.), *Handbook of gender research in psychology* (Vol. 1, pp. 559–580). New York: Springer.

Stewart, A.J., & Vanderwater, E.A. (1999). "If I had it to do over again...": Midlife review, midcourse corrections, and women's well-being in midlife. *Journal of Personality and Social Psychology, 76*, 270–283.

Stickney, L.T., & Konrad, A.M. (2007). Gender-role attitudes and earnings: A multinational study of married women and men. *Sex Roles, 57*, 801–811.

Stockdale, M.S. (1998). The direct and moderating influences of sexual harassment pervasiveness, coping strategies, and gender on work-related outcomes. *Psychology of Women Quarterly, 22*, 521–535.

Stone, S.D. (1993). Getting the message out: Feminists, the press and violence against women. *Canadian Review of Sociology and Anthropology, 30*, 377–400.

Stone, S.D. (1995). The myth of bodily perfection. *Disability and Society, 10*, 413–424.

Stoner, S.A. et al. (2007). Effects of alcohol intoxication and victimization history on women's sexual assault resistance intentions: The role of secondary cognitive appraisals. *Psychology of Women Quarterly, 31*, 344–356.

Storey, A.E. et al. (2000). Hormonal correlates of paternal responsiveness in new and expectant fathers. *Evolution and Human Behavior, 21*, 79–95.

Stovall-McClough, K., & Cloitre, M. (2006). Unresolved attachment, PTSD, and dissociation in women with childhood abuse histories. *Journal of Consulting and Clinical Psychology, 74*, 219–228.

Strahan, E.J. et al. (2008). Victoria's dirty secret: How sociocultural norms influence adolescent girls and women. *Personality and Social Psychology Bulletin, 34*, 288–301.

Straus, M.A. (1997). Physical assaults by women partners: A major social problem. In M.R. Walsh (Ed.), *Women, men, and gender: Ongoing debates* (pp. 210–221). New Haven, CT: Yale.

Straus, M.A. et al. (1980). *Behind closed doors: Violence in the American family.* Garden City, NY: Anchor Press.

Street, A.E. et al. (2007). Gender differences in experiences of sexual harassment: Data from a male-dominated environment. *Journal of Consulting and Clinical Psychology, 75*, 464–474.

Strelan, P.M. et al. (2003). Self-objectification and esteem in young women: The mediating role of reasons for exercise. *Sex Roles, 48*, 89–95.

Strelan, P.M., & Hargreaves, D. (2005). Women who objectify other women: The vicious cycle of objectification? *Sex Roles, 52*, 707–712.

Strickland, B.R. (1988). Sex-related differences in health and illness. *Psychology of Women Quarterly, 12*, 381–399.

Stroh, L.K. et al. (1992). All the right stuff: A comparison of female and male managers' career progression. *Journal of Applied Psychology, 77*, 251–260.

Stroh, L.K. et al. (1996). Family structure, glass ceiling, and traditional explanations for the differential rate of turnover of female and male managers. *Journal of Vocational Behavior, 49,* 99–118.

Strough, J. et al. (2007). From adolescence to later adulthood: Femininity, masculinity, and androgyny in six age groups. *Sex Roles, 57,* 385–396.

Strough, J., & Diriwaechter, R. (2000). Dyad gender differences in preadolescents' creative stories. *Sex Roles, 43,* 43–60.

Strube, M.J. (1988). The decision to leave an abusive relationship: Empirical evidence and theoretical issues. *Psychological Bulletin, 104,* 236–250.

Strube, M.J., & Barbour, L.S. (1984). Factors related to the decision to leave an abusive relationship. *Journal of Marriage and the Family, 46,* 837–844.

Struthers, N.J. (1995). Differences in mentoring: A function of gender or organizational rank? *Journal of Social Behavior and Personality, 10,* 265–272.

Stuhlmacher, A.F. et al. (2007). Gender differences in virtual negotiation: Theory and research. *Sex Roles, 57,* 329–339.

Su, R., Rounds, J., & Armstrong, P.I. (2009). Men and things, women and people: A meta-analysis of sex differences in interests. *Psychological Bulletin, 135,* 859–884.

Sudderth, L.K. (1998). "It'll come right back at me": The interactional context of discussing rape with others. *Violence Against Women, 4,* 572–594.

Sue, D.W. et al. (2007). Racial microaggressions in everyday life: Implications for clinical practice. *American Psychologist, 62,* 271–286.

Sue, D.W., & Sue, D. (2003). *Counseling the culturally diverse: Theory and practice* (4th ed.). New York: Wiley.

Suitor, J.J., & Reavis, R. (1995). Football, fast cars, and cheerleading: Adolescent gender norms, 1978–1989. *Adolescence, 30,* 265–272.

Sullins, C.D. (1998). Suspected repressed childhood sexual abuse: Gender effects on diagnosis and treatment. *Psychology of Women Quarterly, 22,* 403–418.

Sullivan, E.G. (1996). Lupus: The silent killer. In C.F. Collins (Ed.), *African-American women's health and social issues* (pp. 25–35). Westport, CT: Auburn House.

Susskind, J.E. (2003). Children's perception of gender-based illusory correlations: Enhancing preexisting relationships between gender and behavior. *Sex Roles, 48,* 483–494.

Susskind, J.E., & Hodges, C. (2007). Decoupling children's gender-based in-group positivity from out-group negativity. *Sex Roles, 56,* 707–716.

Sutfin, E.L. et al. (2008). How lesbian and heterosexual parents convey attitudes about gender to their children: The role of gendered environments. *Sex Roles, 58,* 501–513.

Swami, V., & Tovee, M.J. (2006). The influence of body mass index on the physical attractiveness preferences of feminist and nonfeminist heterosexual women and lesbians. *Psychology of Women Quarterly, 30,* 252–257.

Swan, K. (1995, April). *Saturday morning cartoons and children's perceptions of social reality.* Paper presented at the annual meeting of the American Educational Research Association, San Francisco, CA.

Swim, J.K. (1994). Perceived versus meta-analytic effect sizes: An assessment of the accuracy of gender stereotypes. *Journal of Personality and Social Psychology, 66,* 21–36.

Swim, J.K. et al. (1989). Joan McKay versus John McKay: Do gender stereotypes bias evaluations? *Psychological Bulletin, 105,* 409–429.

Swim, J.K. et al. (1995). Sexism and racism: Old-fashioned and modern prejudices. *Journal of Personality and Social Psychology, 68,* 199–214.

Swim, J.K. et al. (2004). Understanding subtle sexism: Detection and use of sexist language. *Sex Roles, 51,* 117–128.

Szymanski, D.M. (2003). The Feminist Supervision Scale: A rational/theoretical approach. *Psychology of Women Quarterly, 27,* 221–232.

Szymanski, D.M. (2004). Relations among dimensions of feminism and internalized heterosexism in lesbians and bisexual women. *Sex Roles, 51,* 145–159.

Szymanksi, D.M. et al. (2009). Internalized misogyny as a moderator of the link between sexist events and women's psychological distress. *Sex Roles, 61,* 101–109.

Szymanski, D.M., & Henning, S.L. (2007). The role of self-objectification in women's depression: A test of objectification theory. *Sex Roles, 56,* 45–53.

Szymanski, D.M., & Owens, G.P. (2008). Do coping styles moderate or mediate the relationship between internalized heterosexism and sexual minority women's psychological distress? *Psychology of Women Quarterly, 32,* 95–104.

Szymanski, D.M., & Stewart, D.N. (2010). Racism and sexism as correlates of African American women's psychological distress. *Sex Roles, 63,* 226–238.

Taft, C.T. et al. (2009). Intimate partner violence against African American women: An examination of the socio-cultural context. *Aggression and Violent Behavior, 14,* 50–58.

Takiff, H.A. et al. (2001). What's in a name? The status implications of students' terms of address for male and female professors. *Psychology of Women Quarterly, 25*, 134–144.

Talaga, J.A., & Beehr, T.A. (1995). Are there gender differences in predicting retirement decisions? *Journal of Applied Psychology, 80*, 16–28.

Tangri, S.S., & Jenkins, S.R. (1997). Why expecting conflict is good. *Sex Roles, 36*, 725–746.

Tannen, D. (1990). *You just don't understand: Women and men in conversations.* New York: Ballantine.

Tantleff-Dunn, S. (2001). Breast and chest size: Ideals and stereotypes through the 1990s. *Sex Roles, 45*, 231–242.

Tavris, C. (1992). *The mismeasure of woman.* New York: Simon & Schuster.

Taylor, C.R. et al. (1995). Portrayals of African, Hispanic, and Asian Americans in magazine advertising. *American Behavioral Scientist, 38*, 608–621.

Taylor, R., & Langdon, R. (2006). Understanding gender differences in schizophrenia: A review of the literature. *Current Psychiatry Reviews, 2*, 255–265.

Taylor, S.E., & Fiske, S.T. (1975). Point of view and perceptions of causality. *Journal of Personality and Social Psychology, 32*, 439–445.

Taylor, V., & Whittier, N. (1997). The new feminist movement. In L. Richardson, V. Taylor, & N. Wittier (Eds.), *Feminist Frontiers IV* (pp. 544–561). New York: McGraw Hill.

Taylor, V., & Whittier, N. (1998). Special issue: Gender and social movements, Part 1. *Gender & Society, 12*(6).

Taylor, V., & Whittier, N. (1999). Special issue: Gender and social movements, Part 2. *Gender & Society, 13*(1).

Teets, J.M. (1995). Childhood sexual trauma of chemically dependent women. *Journal of Psychoactive Drugs, 27*, 231–238.

Teig, S., & Susskind, J.E. (2008). Truck driver or nurse? The impact of gender roles and occupational status on children's occupational preferences. *Sex Roles, 58*, 848–863.

Tenbrunsel, A.E. et al. (1995). Dynamic and static work-family relationships. *Organizational Behavior and Human Decision Processes, 63*, 233–246.

Tepper, C.A., & Cassidy, K.W. (1999). Gender differences in emotional language in children's picture books. *Sex Roles, 40*, 265–280.

Tests, M., & Livingston, J.A. (1999). Qualitative analysis of women's experiences of sexual aggression: Focus on the role of alcohol. *Psychology of Women Quarterly, 23*, 573–589.

Teti, M. et al. (2010). "Pain on top of pain, hurtness on top of hurtness": Social discrimination, psychological well-being, and sexual risk among women living with HIV/AIDS. *International Journal of Sexual Health, 22*, 205–218.

Tetlock, P. (1992). The impact of accountability on judgment and choice: Toward a social contingency model. In M.P. Zanna (Ed.), *Advances in Experimental Social Psychology* (Vol. 25, pp. 331–376). New York: Academic Press.

Thomas, G., & Fletcher, G.J.O. (2003). Mind-reading accuracy in intimate relationships: Assessing the roles of the relationship, the target, and the judge. *Journal of Personality and Social Psychology, 85*, 1079–1094.

Thomas, G.M., & Maio, G.R. (2008). Man, I feel like a woman: When and how gender-role motivation helps mind-reading. *Journal of Personality and Social Psychology, 95*, 1165–1179.

Thomas, J.K., & French, K.E. (1985). Gender differences across age in motor performance: A meta-analysis. *Psychological Bulletin, 98*, 260–282.

Thomas, S. (1995). Planning the prevention of alcohol and other drug-related problems among women. *Drug and Alcohol Review, 14*, 7–15.

Thomas, V. (1994). Using feminist and social structural analysis to focus on the health of poor women. *Women & Health, 22*, 1–15.

Thompson, B.W. (1992). "A way outa no way": Eating problems among African-American, Latina, and White women. *Gender & Society, 6*, 546–561.

Thompson, B.W. (1995). *A hunger so wide and deep.* Minneapolis, MN: University of Minnesota Press.

Thompson, E.M., & Morgan, E.M. (2008). "Mostly straight" young women: Variations in sexual behavior and identity development. *Developmental Psychology, 44*, 15–21.

Thompson, M.P., & Norris, F.H. (1992). Crime, social status, and alienation. *American Journal of Community Psychology, 1*, 97–119.

Thompson, S.H. et al. (1997). Ideal body size beliefs and weight concerns of fourth-grade children. *International Journal of Eating Disorders, 21*, 279–284.

Thompson, T.L., & Zerbinos, E. (1997). Television cartoons: Do children notice it's a boy's world? *Sex Roles, 37*, 415–432.

Thornhill, R., & Palmer, C.T. (2000). *A natural history of rape: Biological bases of sexual coercion.* Cambridge, MA: MIT Press.

Thorp, S.R. et al. (2004). Postpartum partner support, demand-withdraw communication, and maternal stress. *Psychology of Women Quarterly, 28*, 362–369.

Thurer, S.L. (1994). *The myths of motherhood: How culture reinvents the good mother.* Boston: Houghton Mifflin.

Tichenor, V.J. (2005). *Earning more and getting less: Why successful wives can't buy equality.* Piscataway: Rutgers University Press.

Tiedje, L.B. (2004). Processes of change in work/home incompatibilities: Employed mothers 1986–1999. *Journal of Social Issues, 60*(4), 787–800.

Tiefer, L. (1991). A brief history of the Association for Women in Psychology: 1969–1991. *Psychology of Women Quarterly, 15,* 635–649.

Tiefer, L. (1994). *Sex is not a natural act and other essays.* Boulder, CO: Westview.

Tiefer, L. (2000). The social construction and social effects of sex research: The sexological model of sexuality. In C.B. Travis & J.W. White (Eds.), *Sexuality, society, and feminism* (pp. 79–107). Washington, DC: American Psychological Association.

Tiegs, T.J. et al. (2007). My place or yours? An inductive approach to sexuality and gender role conformity. *Sex Roles, 56,* 449–456.

Tiggemann, M. (2006). The role of media exposure in adolescent girls' body dissatisfaction and the drive for thinness: Prospective results. *Journal of Social and Clinical Psychology, 25,* 523–541.

Tiggemann, M., & Boundy, M. (2008). Effect of environment and appearance compliment on college women's self-objectification, mood, body shame, and cognitive performance. *Psychology of Women Quarterly, 32,* 399–405.

Tiggemann, M., & Hodgson, S. (2008). The hairlessness norm extended: Reasons for and predictors of women's body hair removal at different body sites. *Sex Roles, 59,* 889–897.

Tiggemann, M., & Miller, J. (2010). The internet and adolescent girls' weight satisfaction and drive for thinness. *Sex Roles, 63,* 79–90.

Tiggemann, M., & Slater, A. (2001). Person x situation interactions in body dissatisfaction. *International Journal of Eating Disorders, 29,* 65–70.

Tiggemann, M., & Williams, E. (2012). The role of self-objectification in disordered eating, depressed mood, and sexual functioning among women: A comprehensive test of objectification theory. *Psychology of Women Quarterly, 36,* 66–75.

Tiggemann, M., & Williamson, S. (2000). The effect of exercise on body satisfaction and self-esteem as a function of gender and age. *Sex Roles, 43,* 119–127.

Todosijevic, J. et al. (2005). Relationship satisfaction, affectivity, and gay-specific stressors in same-sex couples joined in civil unions. *Psychology of Women Quarterly, 29,* 158–166.

Toerien, M. et al. (2005). Body hair removal: The "mundane" production of normative femininity. *Sex Roles, 52,* 399–406.

Tolin, D.F., & Foa, E.B. (2006). Sex differences in trauma and posttraumatic stress disorder: A quantitative review of 25 years of research. *Psychological Bulletin, 132,* 959–992.

Toller, P.W. et al. (2004). Gender role identity and attitudes toward feminism. *Sex Roles, 51,* 85–90.

Tolman, D.L. et al. (2006). Looking good, sounding good: Femininity ideology and adolescent girls' mental health. *Psychology of Women Quarterly, 30,* 85–95.

Tolman, D.L., & Brown, L.M. (2001). Adolescent girls' voices: Resonating resistance in body and soul. In R.K. Unger (Ed.), *Handbook of the psychology of women and gender* (pp. 133–155). New York: Wiley.

Tom-Orme, L. (1995). Native American women's health concerns: Toward restoration of harmony. In D.L. Adams (Ed.), *Health issues for women of color: A cultural diversity perspective* (pp. 27–41). Thousand Oaks, CA: Sage.

Toneatto, A. et al. (1992). Gender issues in the treatment of abusers of alcohol, nicotine, and other drugs. *Journal of Substance Abuse, 4,* 209–218.

Tougas, F. et al. (1995). Neosexism: Plus ca change, plus c'est pareil. *Personality and Social Psychology Bulletin, 21,* 842–849.

Towns, A., & Adams, P. (2000). "If I really loved him enough, he would be okay": Women's accounts of male partner violence. *Violence Against Women, 6,* 558–585.

Townsend, T.G. (2002). The impact of self-components on attitudes toward sex among African American preadolescent girls: The moderating role of menarche. *Sex Roles, 47,* 11–20.

Traustadottir, R. (1991). Mothers who care: Gender, disability, and family life. *Journal of Family Issues, 12,* 211–228.

Travis, C.B. (1988a). *Women and health psychology: Biomedical issues.* Hillsdale, NJ: Lawrence Erlbaum.

Travis, C.B. (1988b). *Women and health psychology: Mental health issues.* Hillsdale, NJ: Lawrence Erlbaum.

Travis, C.B. (1993). Women and health. In F.L. Denmark & M.A. Paludi (Eds.), *Psychology of women: A Handbook of issues and theories* (pp. 283–323). Westport, CT: Greenwood Press.

Travis, C.B. (2005). 2004 Carolyn Sherif Award Address: Heart disease and gender inequity. *Psychology of Women Quarterly, 29,* 15–23.

Travis, C.B. et al. (1995). Health care policy and practice for women's health. In A.L. Stanton &

S.J. Gallant (Eds.), *The psychology of women's health: Progress and challenges in research and application* (pp. 531–565). Washington, DC: American Psychological Association.

Travis, C.B. et al. (2009). Tracking the gender pay gap: A case study. *Psychology of Women Quarterly, 33,* 410–418.

Travis, C.B., & Compton, J.D. (2001). Feminism and health in the Decade of Behavior. *Psychology of Women Quarterly, 25,* 312–323.

Tripp, M.M., & Petrie, T.A. (2001). Sexual abuse and eating disorders: A test of a conceptual model. *Sex Roles, 44,* 17–32.

Trope, Y., & Thompson, E.P. (1997). Looking for truth in all the wrong places? Asymmetric search of individuating information about stereotyped group members. *Journal of Personality and Social Psychology, 73,* 229–241.

Trudeau, K.J. et al. (2003). Agency and communion in people with rheumatoid arthritis. *Sex Roles, 49,* 303–311.

Truman, D.M. et al. (1996). Dimensions of masculinity: Relations to date rape supportive attitudes and sexual aggression in dating situations. *Journal of Counseling and Development, 74,* 555–562.

Truman, J.L. (2011, Sept.). *Criminal victimization, 2010.* National Crime Victimization Survey, U.S. Department of Justice. http://bjs.ojp.usdoj.gov/content/pub/pdf/cv10.pdf

Tuleya, L.G. (Ed.). (2007). *Thesaurus of psychological index terms* (11th ed.). Washington, DC: American Psychological Association.

Tulloch, M.I., & Tulloch, J.C. (1992). Attitudes to domestic violence: School students' responses to a television drama. *Australian Journal of Marriage and Family, 13,* 62–69.

Turchik, J.A. et al. (2009). Prediction of sexual assault experiences in college women based on rape scripts. *Journal of Consulting and Clinical Psychology, 77,* 361–366.

Turgeon, L. et al. (1998). Clinical features in panic disorder with agoraphobia: A comparison of men and women. *Journal of Anxiety Disorders, 12,* 539–553.

Turkheimer, E., , & Halpern, D. F. (2009). Sex differences in variability for cognitive measures: Do the ends justify the genes? (Commentary on Johnson et al., 2009). *Perspectives on Psychological Science, 4,* 612–614.

Turner, B.F., & Turner, C.B. (1991). Bem Sex-Role Inventory stereotypes for men and women varying in age and race among National Register psychologists. *Psychological Reports, 69,* 931–944.

Turner, H.A. (1994). Gender and social support: Taking the bad with the good? *Sex Roles, 30,* 521–541.

Turner, P.J., & Gervai, J. (1995). A multidimensional study of gender typing in preschool children and their parents: Personality, attitudes, preferences, behavior, and cultural differences. *Developmental Psychology, 31,* 759–779.

Twenge, J.M. (1997). Changes in masculine and feminine traits over time: A meta-analysis. *Sex Roles, 36,* 305–325.

Twenge, J.M., & Campbell, W.K. (2002). Self-esteem and socioeconomic status: A meta-analytic review. *Personality and Social Psychology Review, 6,* 59–71.

Tylka, T.L., & Hill, M.S. (2004). Objectification theory as it relates to disordered eating among college women. *Sex Roles, 51,* 719–730.

U.S. Bureau of Labor Statistics. (2010, June). *Highlights of women's earnings in 2009.* Report 1025. U.S. Department of Labor, Report 1025.

U.S. Bureau of Labor Statistics. (2011, Apr. 8). College enrollment and work activity of 2010 high school graduates. USDL-11–0462. http://www.bls.gov/cps

U.S. Census Bureau. (2011a). *Statistical Abstracts of the United States: 2011* Section 12: Labor Force, Employment, & Earnings. http://www.census.gov

U.S. Census Bureau. (2011b). *Statistical Abstract of the United States: 2011.* Table 228: Mean Earnings by Highest Degree Earned, 2008. http://www.census.gov

U.S. Congress Joint Economic Committee. (2010, Aug.). *Women and the economy 2010: 25 years of progress but challenges remain.* http://jec.senate.gov

U.S. Department of Labor. (1991). *A report on the glass ceiling initiative* (#91–656–P). Washington, DC: Government Printing Office.

U.S. Department of Labor. (2002). *Facts on Executive Order 11246 – Affirmative Action.* http://www.dol.gov/esa/regs/compliance/ofccp/aa.htm (Retrieved November 2005).

U.S. Department of Labor (2011). *Wage and Hour Division's 2000 Survey.* http://www.dol.gov/whd/fmla/chapter3.htm (Retrieved July 2011)

Uggen, C., & Blackstone, A. (2004). Sexual harassment as a gendered expression of power. *American Sociological Review, 69,* 64–92.

Uhlmann, E.L., & Cohen, G.L. (2007). Constructed criteria: Redefining merit to justify discrimination. *Psychological Science, 16,* 474–480.

Ullman, S.E. (2000). Psychometric characacteristics of the Social Reactions Questionnaire: A measure of reactions to sexual assault victims. *Psychology of Women Quarterly, 24,* 257–271.

Ullman, S.E. (2010). *Talking about sexual assault: Society's response to survivors.* Washington, DC: American Psychological Association.

Ullman, S.E. et al. (1999). Alcohol and sexual aggression in a national sample of college men. *Psychology of Women Quarterly, 23,* 673–689.

Ullman, S.E. et al. (2007). Structural models of the relations of assault severity, social support, avoidance coping, self-blame, and PTSD among sexual assault survivors. *Psychology of Women Quarterly, 31,* 23–37.

Ullman, S.E., & Brecklin, L.R. (2003). Sexual assault history and health-related outcomes in a national sample of women. *Psychology of Women Quarterly, 27,* 46–57.

Ullman, S.E., & Knight, R.A. (1991). A multivariate model for predicting rape and physical injury outcomes during sexual assaults. *Journal of Consulting and Clinical Psychology, 59,* 724–731.

Ullman, S.E., & Knight, R.A. (1993). The efficacy of women's resistance strategies in rape situations. *Psychology of Women Quarterly, 17,* 23–38.

Ulrich, M., & Weatherall, A. (2000). Motherhood and infertility: Viewing motherhood through the lens of infertility. *Feminism & Psychology, 10,* 323–336.

Unger, R.K. (1979). Toward a redefinition of sex and gender. *American Psychologist, 34,* 1085–1094.

Unger, R.K. (1983). Through the looking glass: No wonderland yet! (The reciprocal relationship between methodology and models of reality). *Psychology of Women Quarterly, 8,* 9–32.

Unger, R.K. (1986). Looking toward the future by looking at the past: Social activism and social history. *Journal of Social Issues, 42*(1), 215–227.

Unger, R.K. et al. (2010). Feminism and women leaders in SPSSI: Social networks, ideology, and generational change. *Psychology of Women Quarterly, 34,* 474–485.

United Nations. (1995). *The world's women 1995: Trends and statistics.* New York: United Nations Publications.

United Nations. (1999). *1999 World survey of the role of women in development: Globalization, women, and work.* New York: United Nations Publications. ISBN 92–1–130200–5.

United Nations. (2000). *The world's women 2000: Trends and statistics.* New York: United Nations Publications. ISBN 92–1–161428–7.

United Nations. (2010). *The world's women 2010: Trends and statistics.* New York: United Nations Publications. ISBN 978–92–1–161539–5

United Nations Population Fund. (2000). *The state of world population 2000: Lives together, worlds apart: Men and women in a time of change.* New York. http://www.unfpa.org

Unknown. (1997). "The rape" of Mr. Smith. In M. Crawford & R. Unger (Eds.), *In our own words: Readings on the psychology of women and gender* (pp. 129–130). New York: McGraw-Hill.

Up and out: Americans get heavier. (2004, Oct. 28). *The New York Times,* p. A14.

Urbaniak, G.C., & Kilmann, P.R. (2006). Niceness and dating success: A further test of the nice guy stereotype. *Sex Roles, 55,* 209–224.

Ussher, J. (1990). Choosing psychology or not throwing the baby out with the bathwater. In E. Burman (Ed.), *Feminists and psychological practice* (pp. 47–61). Newbury Park, CA: Sage.

Ussher, J.M., & Perz, J. (2010). Gender differences in self-silencing and psychological distress in informal cancer carers. *Psychology of Women Quarterly, 34,* 228–242.

Uttal, L. (1996). Custodial care, surrogate care, and coordinated care: Employed mothers and the meaning of child care. *Gender & Society, 10,* 291–311.

Valentine, S.R. (2001). Men and women supervisors' job responsibility, job satisfaction, and employee mentoring. *Sex Roles, 45,* 179–197.

Van Anders, S.M. (2004). Why the academic pipeline leaks: Fewer men than women perceive barriers to becoming professors. *Sex Roles, 51,* 511–521.

van der Velde, M.E.G. et al. (2003). Gender differences in the influence of professional tenure on work attitudes. *Sex Roles, 49,* 153–162.

van der Waerden et al. (2011). Psychosocial preventive interventions to reduce depressive symptoms in low-SES women at risk: A meta-analysis. *Journal of Affective Disorders, 128,* 10–23.

van Wel, R. et al. (2002). Changes in parental bond and the well-being of adolescents and young adults. *Adolescence, 37,* 317–334.

Vandell, D.L. (2000). Parents, peer groups, and other socializing influences. *Developmental Psychology, 36,* 699–710.

Vandell, K., & Dempsey, S.B. (1991). *Stalled agenda: Gender equity and the training of educators.* Washington, DC: American Association of University Women.

Vandello, J.A. et al. (2008). Precarious manhood. *Journal of Personality and Social Psychology, 95,* 1325–1339.

Vandenheuvel, A. (1997). Women's roles after first birth: Variable or stable? *Gender & Society, 11,* 357–368.

Vasquez, M.J.T. (1994). Latinas. In L. Comas-Díaz & B. Greene (Eds.), *Women of color: Integrating ethnic and gender identities in psychotherapy* (pp. 114–138). New York: Guilford.

Vega, W.A. (1990). Hispanic families in the 1980s: A decade of research. *Journal of Marriage and the Family, 52*, 1015–1024.

Veniegas, R.C., & Peplau, L.A. (1997). Power and quality of same-sex friendships. *Psychology of Women Quarterly, 21*, 279–297.

Viki, G.T. et al. (2003). The "true" romantic: Benevolent sexism and paternalistic chivalry. *Sex Roles, 49*, 533–537.

Viki, G.T., & Abrams, D. (2002). But she was unfaithful: Benevolent sexism and reactions to rape victims who violate traditional gender role expectations. *Sex Roles, 47*, 289–293.

Voda, A.M. (1997). *Menopause, men and you: The sound of women pausing*. Binghamton, NY: Harrington Park Press.

Vogel, D.L. et al. (2003). Confirming gender stereotypes: A social role perspective. *Sex Roles, 48*, 519–528.

Vogeltanz, N.D., & Wilsnack, S.C. (1997). Alcohol problems in women: Risk factors, consequences, and treatment strategies. In S. Gallant et al. (Eds.), *Health care for women: Psychological, social and behavioral influences* (pp. 75–96). Washington, DC: American Psychological Association.

Volkom, M.V. (2003). The relationships between childhood tomboyism, siblings' activities, and adult gender roles. *Sex Roles, 49*, 609–618.

Voyer, D. (1996). On the magnitude of laterality effects and sex differences in functional lateralities. *Laterality, 1*, 51–83.

Voyer, D. et al. (1995). Magnitude of sex differences in spatial abilities: A meta-analysis and consideration of critical variables. *Psychological Bulletin, 117*, 250–270.

Wade, J.C., & Brittan-Powell, C. (2001). Men's attitudes toward race and gender equity: The importance of masculinity ideology, gender-related traits, and reference group identity dependence. *Psychology of Men and Masculinity, 2*, 42–50.

Wade, M.L., & Brewer, M.B. (2006). The structure of female subgroups: An exploration of ambivalent stereotypes. *Sex Roles, 54*, 753–765.

Wade, T.J., & DiMaria, C. (2003). Weight halo effect: Individual differences in perceived life success as a function of women's race and weight. *Sex Roles, 48*, 461–465.

Wagner, H.L., & Smith, J. (1991). Facial expression in the presence of friends and strangers. *Journal of Nonverbal Behavior, 15*, 201–214.

Wakelin, A., & Long, K.M. (2003). Effects of victim gender and sexuality on attributions of blame to rape victims. *Sex Roles, 49*, 477–487.

Walker, K. (1994). Men, women, and friendship: What they say, what they do. *Gender & Society, 8*, 246–265.

Walker, L.E.A. (1979). *The battered woman*. New York: Harper & Row.

Walker, L.E.A. (1986, August). *Diagnosis and politics: Abuse disorders*. Paper presented at the meeting of the American Psychological Association, Washington, DC.

Walker, L.E.A. (1989). *Terrifying love: Why battered women kill and how society responds*. New York: Harper.

Walker, L.E.A. (1994). *Abused women and survivor therapy: A practical guide for the psychotherapist*. Washington, DC: American Psychological Association.

Walsh, M. et al. (1999). Influence of item content and stereotype situation on gender differences in mathematical problem solving. *Sex Roles, 41*, 219–240.

Wang, F. et al. (2011). Leisure-time physical activity and marital status in relation to depression between men and women: A prospective study. *Health Psychology, 30*, 204–211.

Want, S.C. (2009). Meta-analytic moderators of experimental exposure to media portrayals of women on female appearance satisfaction: Social comparisons as automatic processes. *Body Image, 6*, 257–269.

Ward, C.A. (1995). *Attitudes toward rape: Feminist and social psychological perspectives*. Thousand Oaks, CA: Sage.

Ward, L.M. et al. (2005). Contributions of music video exposure to Black adolescents' gender and sexual schema. *Journal of Adolescent Research, 20*, 143–166.

Ward, R.E. (2004). Are doors being opened for the "ladies" of college sports? A covariance analysis. *Sex Roles, 51*, 697–708.

Warner Chilcot. (2005). http://www.warnerchilcott.com/ products/sarafem.php (Retrieved November 2005).

Warner, R.L., & Steel, B.S. (1999). Child rearing as a mechanism for social change: The relationship of child gender to parents' commitment to gender equity. *Gender & Society, 13*, 503–517.

Warshaw, R. (1994). *I never called it rape*. New York: Harper Perennial.

Watson, C.M. et al. (2002). Career aspirations of adolescent girls: Effects of achievement level, grade, and single-sex school environment. *Sex Roles, 46*, 323–335.

Way, N. (1998). *Everyday courage: The lives and stories of urban teenagers*. New York: New York University Press.

Wayne, J.H. (2000). Disentangling the power bases of sexual harassment: Comparing gender, age, and position power. *Journal of Vocational Behavior, 57*, 301–325.

Wayne, J.H., & Cordeiro, B.L. (2003). Who is a good organizational citizen? Social perception of male and female employees who use family leave. *Sex Roles, 49*, 233–246.

Weaver, A.D., & Byers, E.S. (2006). The relationships among body image, body mass index, exercise, and sexual functioning in heterosexual women. *Psychology of Women Quarterly, 30*, 333–339.

Weaver, J.J., & Ussher, J. (1997). How motherhood changes life: A discourse analytic study with mothers of young children. *Journal of Reproductive and Infant Psychology, 15*, 51–68.

Weaver, J.R. et al. (2010). The proof is in the punch: Gender differences in perceptions of action and aggression as components of manhood. *Sex Roles, 62*, 241–251.

Webb, W. (1992). Treatment issues and cognitive behavior techniques with battered women. *Journal of Family Violence, 7*, 205–217.

Webel, A.R. (2010). Testing a peer-based symptom management intervention for women living with HIV/AIDS. *AIDS Care, 22*, 1029–1040.

Weer, C.H. et al. (2006). The role of maternal employment, role-altering strategies, and gender in college students' expectations of work-family conflict. *Sex Roles, 55*, 535–544.

Weidner, G. (1994). Coronary risk in women. In V.J. Adesso et al. (Eds.), *Psychological perspectives on women's health* (pp. 57–81). Washington, DC: Taylor & Francis.

Weinberger, N., & Stein, K. (2008). Early competitive game playing in same- and mixed-gender peer groups. *Merrill-Palmer Quarterly: Journal of Developmental Psychology, 54*, 499–514.

Weiner, K.M. (1998). Tools for change: Methods of incorporating political/social action into the therapy session. *Women & Therapy, 21*, 113–123.

Weiner, K.M. (1999). Morality and responsibility: Necessary components of feminist therapy. *Women & Therapy, 22*, 105–115.

Weinshenker, M.N. (2006). Adolescents' expectations about mothers' employment: Life course patterns and parental influence. *Sex Roles, 54*, 845–857.

Weinstein, N. (1993). Psychology constructs the female, or the fantasy live of the male psychologist. *Feminism & Psychology, 3*, 195–210.

Weisbuch, M. et al. (1999). How masculine ought I be? Men's masculinity and aggression. *Sex Roles, 40*, 583–592.

Weller, A., & Weller, L. (1992). Menstrual synchrony in female couples. *Psychoneuroendocrinology, 17*, 171–177.

Wellesley Centers for Women (1998, July). *The wife rape information page.* http://www.wellesley.edu/WCW/projects/mrape.html (Retrieved November 2005).

Wenger, A.A., & Bornstein, B.H. (2006). The effects of victim's substance use and relationship closeness on mock jurors' judgments in an acquaintance rape case. *Sex Roles, 54*, 547–555.

Wertheim, E.H. et al. (1999). Relationships among adolescent girls' eating behaviors and their parents' weight-related attitudes and behaviors. *Sex Roles, 41*, 169–187.

Wesselmann, E.D., & Kelly, J.R. (2010). Cat-calls and culpability: Investigating the frequency and functions of stranger harassment. *Sex Roles, 63*, 451–462.

West, C., & Fenstermaker, S. (1995). Doing difference. *Gender & Society, 9*, 8–37.

West, C., & Zimmerman, D.H. (1987). Doing gender. *Gender & Society, 1*, 125–151.

Westen, D. (1998). The scientific legacy of Sigmund Freud: Toward a psychodynamically informed psychological science. *Psychological Bulletin, 124*, 333–371.

Westman, M., & Etzion, D. (1990). The career success/personal failure phenomenon as perceived in others: Comparing vignettes of male and female managers. *Journal of Vocational Behavior, 37*, 209–224.

Whisenant, W.A. (2003). How women have fared as interscholastic athletic administrators since the passage of Title IX. *Sex Roles, 49*, 179–184.

Whisenant, W.A. et al. (2002). Success and gender: Determining the rate of advancement for intercollegiate athletic directors. *Sex Roles, 47*, 484–491.

Whitaker, D.J. et al. (2008). Risk factors for the perpetration of child sexual abuse: A review and meta-analysis. *Child Abuse & Neglect, 32*, 529–548.

Whitbourne, S.K., & Powers, C.B. (1994). Older women's constructs of their lives: A quantitative and qualitative exploration. *International Journal of Aging and Human Development, 38*, 293–306.

Whitbourne, S.K., & Skultety, K.M. (2006). Aging and identity: How women face later life transitions. J. Worell & C.D. Goodheart (Eds.), *Handbook of girls' and women's psychological health: Gender and well-being across the lifespan* (pp. 370–378). New York: Oxford.

White, J.B., & Gardner, W.L. (2009). Think women, think warm: Stereotype content activation in women with a salient gender identity, using a modified Stroop task. *Sex Roles, 60,* 247–260.

White, J.H. (1992). Women and eating disorders, Part I: Significance and sociocultural risk factors. *Health Care for Women International, 13,* 351–362.

White, J.W., & Kowalski, R.M. (1994). Deconstructing the myth of the nonaggressive woman: A feminist analysis. *Psychology of Women Quarterly, 18,* 487–508.

White, J.W. et al. (2000). Social construction of sexuality: Unpacking hidden meanings. In C.B. Travis & J.W. White (Eds.), *Sexuality, society, and feminism* (pp. 11–34). Washington, DC: American Psychological Association.

White, J.W. et al. (2001). A developmental examination of violence against girls and women. In R.K. Unger (Ed.), *Handbook of the psychology of women and gender* (pp. 343–357). New York: Wiley.

White, J.W., & Kowalski, R.M. (1994). Deconstructing the myth of the nonaggressive woman: A feminist analysis. *Psychology of Women Quarterly, 18,* 487–508.

White, J.W., & Kowalski, R.M. (1998). Violence against women: An integrative perspective. In R.G. Geen & E. Donnerstein (Eds.), *Perspectives on human aggression.* New York: Academic Press.

White, M.J., & White, G.B. (2006). Implicit and explicit occupational gender stereotypes. *Sex Roles, 55,* 259–266.

Whitehead, B.D., & Popenoe, D. (2001). *Who wants to marry a soul mate?* Piscataway, NJ: Rutgers University's National Marriage Project. http://marriage.rutgers.edu

Whitehead, G.I., & Smith, S.H. (2002). When illnesses or accidents befall others: The role of gender in defensive distancing. *Sex Roles, 46,* 393–401.

Whitley, B.E. (1997). Gender differences in computer-related attitudes and behavior: A meta-analysis. *Computers in Human Behavior, 13,* 1–22.

Whitley, B.E., Jr., & Kite, M. E. (2010). *The psychology of prejudice and discrimination* (2nd ed.). Belmont, CA: Wadsworth.

Whorley, M.R., & Addis, M.E. (2006). Ten years of psychological research on men and masculinity in the United States: Dominant methodological trends. *Sex Roles, 55,* 649–658.

Widom, C.S. (1989). Does violence beget violence? A critical examination of the literature. *Psychological Bulletin, 106,* 3–28.

Wiener, R.L., & Hurt, L.E. (2000). How do people evaluate social sexual conduct at work: A psychological model. *Journal of Applied Psychology, 85,* 75–85.

Wilcox, S., & Stefanick, M.L. (1999). Knowledge and perceived risk of major diseases in middle-aged and older women. *Health Psychology, 18,* 346–353.

Wilke, D. (1994). Women and alcoholism: How a male-as-norm bias affects research, assessment, and treatment. *Health and Social Work, 19,* 29–35.

Wilkinson, S. (1990). Women organizing within psychology. In E. Burman (Ed.), *Feminists and psychological practice* (pp. 140–151). London: Sage.

Wilkinson, S. (2001). Theoretical perspectives on women and gender. In R.K. Unger (Ed.), *Handbook of the psychology of women and gender* (pp. 17–28). New York: Wiley.

Wilkinson, S., & Kitzinger, C. (1994). Towards a feminist approach to breast cancer. In S. Wilkinson & C. Kitzinger (Eds.), *Women and health: Feminist perspectives* (pp. 124–140). London: Taylor & Francis.

Wilkinson, W.W. (2008). Threatening the patriarchy: Testing an explanatory paradigm of anti-lesbian attitudes. *Sex Roles, 59,* 512–520.

Williams, C.L. (1992). The glass escalator: Hidden advantages for men in the "female" professions. *Social Problems, 39,* 253–267.

Williams, J. (2001). *Unbending gender: Why work and family conflict and what to do about it.* Oxford, UK: Oxford University Press.

Williams, J. C., & Cooper, C. (2004). The public policy of motherhood. *Journal of Social Issues, 60*(4), 849–865.

Williams, J.E., & Best, D.L. (1982). *Measuring sex stereotypes: A thirty-nation study.* Beverly Hills: Sage.

Williams, J.E., & Best, D.L. (1990). *Measuring sex stereotypes: A multination study.* Newbury Park, CA: Sage.

Williams, K., & Umberson, D. (1999). Medical technology and childbirth: Experiences of expectant mothers and fathers. *Sex Roles, 41,* 147–168.

Williams, L.K. et al. (2006). A comparison of the sources and nature of body image messages perceived by indigenous Fijian and European Australian adolescent girls. *Sex Roles, 55,* 555–566.

Williams, M.J. et al. (2010). The masculinity of money: Automatic stereotypes predict gender differences in estimated salaries. *Psychology of Women Quarterly, 34,* 7–20.

Willness, C.R. et al. (2007). A meta-analysis of the antecedents and consequences of workplace sexual harassment. *Personnel Psychology, 60,* 127–162.

Wilmoth, G.H. (1992). Abortion, public health policy, and informed consent legislation. *Journal of Social Issues, 48*(3), 1–17.

Wilsnack, S.C. et al. (1991). Predicting onset and chronicity of women's problem drinking: A 5–year longitudinal analysis. *American Journal of Public Health, 81*, 305–318.

Wilsnack, S.C. et al. (1994). How women drink: Epidemiology of women's drinking and problem drinking. *Alcohol Health and Research World, 18,* 173–181.

Wine, J. (1985). Models of human functioning: A feminist perspective. *International Journal of Women's Studies, 8,* 183–192.

Wisconsin Coalition Against Sexual Assault. (1989). *Encouraging communities to respond to incest survivors and their needs.* Madison, WI.

Wittig, M.A., & Lowe, R.H. (1989). Comparable worth theory and policy. *Journal of Social Issues, 45*(4), 1–21.

Woll, S. (2002). *Everyday thinking: Memory, reasoning, and judgment in the real world.* Mahwah, NJ: Erlbaum.

Womack, M.E. et al. (1999). Helping mothers in incestuous families: An empathic approach. *Women & Therapy, 22,* 17–34.

Wood, E. et al. (2002). The impact of parenting experience on gender stereotyped toy play of children. *Sex Roles, 47,* 39–49.

Woodhill, B.M., & Samuels, C.A. (2003). Positive and negative androgyny and their relationship with psychological health and well-being. *Sex Roles, 48,* 555–565.

Woods, N.F. (1995). Women and their health. In C.I. Fogel & N.F. Woods (Eds.), *Women's health care: A comprehensive handbook* (pp. 1–22). Thousand Oaks, CA: Sage.

Woods, N.F. et al. (1994). Depressed mood and self-esteem in young Asian, Black, and White women in America. *Health Care for Women International, 15,* 243–262.

Wooten, L.P. (2001). What makes women-friendly public accounting firms tick? The diffusion of human resource management knowledge through institutional and resource pressures. *Sex Roles, 45,* 277–297.

Worell, J. (1988). Women's satisfaction in close relationships. *Clinical Psychology Review, 8,* 477–498.

Worell, J. (1996). Feminist identity in a gendered world. In J.C. Chrisler et al. (Eds.), *Lectures on the psychology of women* (pp. 358–370). New York: McGraw-Hill.

Worell, J. (2001). Feminist interventions: Accountability beyond symptom reduction. *Psychology of Women Quarterly, 25,* 335–343.

Worell, J. et al. (1999). Educating about women and gender: Cognitive, personal and professional outcomes. *Psychology of Women Quarterly, 23,* 797–811.

Worell, J., & Johnson, D. (2001). Therapy with women: Feminist frameworks. In R.K. Unger (Ed.), *Handbook of the psychology of women and gender* (pp. 317–329). New York: Wiley.

Worell, J., & Remer, P. (2003). *Feminist perspectives in therapy: Empowering diverse women* (2nd ed.). Hoboken, NJ: Wiley.

World Health Organization, (2011). *In brief: Fact Sheet, February 2011.* http://www.guttmacher.org/pubs/fb_IAW.html (Retrieved October 2011).

Wright, C.V., & Fitzgerald, L.F. (2007). Angry and afraid: Women's appraisal of sexual harassment during litigation. *Psychology of Women Quarterly, 31,* 73–84.

Wright, D. (1992). Impediments to safer heterosexual sex: A review of research with young people. *AIDS Care, 4,* 11–23.

Wright, J. et al. (2006). Being fit and looking healthy: Young women's and men's constructions of health and fitness. *Sex Roles, 54,* 707–716.

Wright, P.H. (1982). Men's friendships, women's friendships and the alleged inferiority of the latter. *Sex Roles, 8,* 1–20.

Wrong, D.H. (1979). *Power: Its forms, bases and uses.* New York: Harper Colophon Books.

Wrosch, C., & Heckhausen, J. (2005). Being on-time or off-time: Developmental deadlines for regulating one's own development. In A. Perret-Clermont (Ed.), *Thinking time: A multidisciplinary perspective on time* (pp. 110–123). Asland, OH: Hogrefe & Huber.

Wyatt, G.E. (1989, August). *The terrorism of racism.* Paper presented at the meeting of the American Psychological Association, New Orleans, LA.

Wyatt, G.E. (1992). Differential effects of women's child sexual abuse and subsequent sexual revictimization. *Journal of Consulting and Clinical Psychology, 60,* 167–173.

Wyatt, G.E., & Riederle, M.H. (1994). Reconceptualizing issues that affect women's sexual decision-making and sexual functioning. *Psychology of Women Quarterly, 18,* 611–625.

Wyche, K.F. (1993). Psychology and African-American women: Findings from applied research. *Applied and Preventive Psychology, 2,* 115–121.

Wyche, K.F., & Rice, J.K. (1997). Feminist therapy: From dialogue to tenets. In J. Worell & N.G. Johnson (Eds.), *Shaping the future of feminist psychology: Education, research, and practice* (pp. 57–72). Washington, DC: American Psychological Association.

Yagil, D. et al. (2006). Is that a "No"? The interpretation of responses to unwanted sexual attention. *Sex Roles, 54*, 251–260.

Yakushko, O. (2007). Do feminist women feel better about their lives? Examining patterns of feminist identity development and women's subjective well-being. *Sex Roles, 57*, 223–234.

Yamamiya, Y. et al. (2005). Women's exposure to thin-and-beautiful media images: Body image effects of media-ideal internalization and impact-reduction interventions. *Body Image, 2*, 74–80.

Yamamiya, Y. et al. (2006). Sexual experiences among college women: The differential effects of general versus contextual body images on sexuality. *Sex Roles, 55*, 421–427.

Yang, Y. et al. (2009). Participation of women in clinical trials for new drugs approved by the Food and Drug Administration in 2000–2002. *Journal of Women's Health, 18*, 303–310.

Yanowitz, K.L., & Weathers, K.J. (2004). Do boys and girls act differently in the classroom? A content analysis of student characters in educational psychology textbooks. *Sex Roles, 51*, 101–107.

Yao, H.H.C. (2005). The pathway to femaleness: Current knowledge on embryonic development of the ovary. *Molecular and Cellular Endocrinology, 230*, 87–93.

Yllö, K., & Bograd, M. (Eds.). (1988). *Feminist perspectives on wife abuse.* Newbury Park, CA: Sage.

Yoder, J.D. (2001). Making leadership work more effectively for women. *Journal of Social Issues, 57*(4), 815–828.

Yoder, J.D. (2002). 2001 Division 35 presidential address: Context matters: Understanding tokenism processes and their impact on women's work. *Psychology of Women Quarterly, 26*, 1–8.

Yoder, J.D. (2010). Does "making a difference" still make a difference?: A textbook author's reflections. *Sex Roles, 62*, 173–178.

Yoder, J.D. et al. (1998). Empowering token women leaders: The importance of organizationally legitimated credibility. *Psychology of Women Quarterly, 22*, 209–222.

Yoder, J.D. et al. (2007a). Changes in students' explanations for gender differences after taking a Psychology of Women class: More constructionist and less essentialist. *Psychology of Women Quarterly, 31*, 415–425.

Yoder, J.D. et al. (2007b). What good is a feminist identity? Women's feminist identification and role expectations for intimate and sexual relationships. *Sex Roles, 57*, 365–372.

Yoder, J.D. et al. (2008). Are television commercials still achievement scripts for women? *Psychology of Women Quarterly, 32*, 303–311.

Yoder, J.D. et al. (2011). When declaring "I am a feminist" matters: Labeling is linked to activism. *Sex Roles, 64*, 9–18.

Yoder, J.D. et al. (in press). How are feminist beliefs linked with optimal psychological functioning? *The Counseling Psychologist.*

Yoder, J.D., & Aniakudo, P. (1996). When pranks become harassment: The case of African American women firefighters. *Sex Roles, 35*, 253–270.

Yoder, J.D., & Aniakudo, P. (1997). "Outsider within" the firehouse: Subordination and difference in the social interactions of African American women firefighters. *Gender & Society, 11*, 324–341.

Yoder, J.D., & Berendsen, L.L. (2001). "Outsider within" the firehouse: African American and White women firefighters. *Psychology of Women Quarterly, 25*, 27–36.

Yoder, J.D., & Kahn, A.S. (1992). Toward a feminist understanding of women and power. *Psychology of Women Quarterly, 16*, 381–388.

Yoder, J.D., & Kahn, A.S. (1993). Working toward an inclusive psychology of women. *American Psychologist, 48*, 846–850.

Yoder, J.D., & Kahn, A.S. (2003). Making gender comparisons more meaningful: A call for more attention to social context. *Psychology of Women Quarterly, 27*, 281–290.

Yost, M., & McCarthy, L. (2012). Girls gone wild? Heterosexual women's same-sex encounters at college rarties. *Psychology of Women Quarterly, 36*, 7–24.

Young, A.M. et al. (2007). Adolescents' sexual inferences about girls who consume alcohol. *Psychology of Women Quarterly, 31*, 229–240.

Young, D.J., & Fraser, B.J. (1992, April). *Sex differences in science achievement: A multilevel analysis.* Paper presented at the annual meeting of the American Research Association, San Francisco, CA.

Young, I.M. (1992). Five faces of oppression. In T.E. Wartenberg (Ed.), *Rethinking power* (pp. 174–195). Albany, NY: State University of New York Press.

Zambrana, R.E., & Ellis, B.K. (1995). Contemporary research issues in Hispanic/Latino women's health. In D.L. Adams (Ed.), *Health issues for women of color: A cultural diversity perspective* (pp. 42–70). Thousand Oaks, CA: Sage.

Zebrowitz, L.A. et al. (1991). The impact of job applicants' facial maturity, gender, and academic achievement on hiring recommendations. *Journal of Applied Social Psychology, 21*, 525–548.

Zepplin, H. et al. (1987). Is age becoming irrelevant? An exploratory study of perceived age norms. *International Journal of Aging and Human Development, 24*, 241–256.

Zhou, L. et al. (2004). American and Chinese college students' predictions of people's occupations, housework responsibilities, and hobbies as a function of cultural and gender influences. *Sex Roles, 50*, 547–563.

Zimbardo, P.G. (1972). *The Stanford prison experiment.* Slide show produced by Philip G. Zimbardo, Inc.

Zosuls, K.M. et al. (2009). The acquisition of gender labels in infancy: Implications for gender-typed play. *Developmental Psychology, 45*, 688–701.

Zoucha-Jensen, J.M., & Coyne, A. (1993). The effects of resistance strategies on rape. *American Journal of Public Health, 83*, 1633–1634.

Zucker, A.N. (2004). Disavowing social identities: What it means when women say "I'm not a feminist but…" *Psychology of Women Quarterly, 28*, 423–435.

Zucker, A.N. et al. (2001). Smoking in college women: The role of thinness pressures, media exposure, and critical consciousness. *Psychology of Women Quarterly, 25*, 233–241.

Zucker, A.N., & Landry, L.J. (2007). Embodied discrimination: The relation of sexism and distress to women's drinking and smoking behaviors. *Sex Roles, 56*, 193–203.

Zucker, A.N., & Stewart, A.J. (2007). Growing up and growing older: Feminism as a context for women's lives. *Psychology of Women Quarterly, 31*, 137–145.

Zucker, K.J. et al. (1995). Children's appraisals of sex-typed behavior in their peers. *Sex Roles, 33*, 703–725.

Zurbriggen, E.L., & Morgan, E.M. (2006). Who wants to marry a millionaire? Reality dating television programs, attitudes toward sex, and sexual behaviors. *Sex Roles, 54*, 1–17.

Index